THE
SOVIET
PROPAGANDA
MACHINE

T·H·E
SOVIET
PROPAGANDA
MACHINE

MARTIN EBON

McGRAW-HILL BOOK COMPANY

New York   St. Louis   San Francisco   Hamburg   Mexico   Toronto

1 2 3 4 5 6 7 8 9 D O C D O C 8 7

ISBN 0-07-018862-9

LIBRARY OF CONGRESS CATALOGING-IN-PUBLICATION DATA

Ebon, Martin.
    The Soviet propaganda machine.
    Bibliography: p.
    Includes index.
    1. Propaganda, Communist—Soviet Union.   2. Mass
media—Soviet Union.   3. Public opinion—Soviet Union.
4. Soviet Union—Foreign relations.   I. Title.
HX311.5.E26 1986   327.1′4′0947   86-21303
ISBN 0-07-018862-9

BOOK DESIGN BY PATRICE FODERO

Contents

Introduction

Western analysts of Soviet affairs run the risk of yielding to public and official tendencies toward overstating and overrating changes within the Soviet Union. This applies to the significance of personnel changes in Kremlin leadership and to economic, military, and cultural developments, as well as to more esoteric matters, such as demographic shifts and generational conflicts. Certainly in the area of Soviet propaganda, its principles, techniques, success and failure, there is a temptation to come to sweeping conclusions, to utter grand generalities.

But propaganda is yet another creation of that complex mixture of Russian history, psychocultural characteristics, and modern methods that keeps puzzling the West with its contradictions, its attractions and repulsions. This book is no exception. To weigh all contradictions, to strike a perfect balance, is quite impossible—if only because various elements keep changing and shifting. The generational change, symbolized by the emergence of Mikhail Gorbachev as general secretary of the Communist Party of the Soviet Union, brought a new team to the fore: men who know the techniques of modern communications, of public relations and media exploitation, of psychological factors in opinion making, and of appealing to different geographic, ethnic, cultural, and economic groupings. And yet the new technicians face traditional handicaps within their own society, their personal upbringing, and when they encounter alien environments on a rapidly changing world scene.

This book focuses on Soviet propaganda and deals with topics on its periphery only briefly. Even so, nearly every chapter could be expanded into a book in itself. Some topics had to be ignored, although they were pressing for inclusion. There is interaction between the Soviet Union's domestic and foreign propaganda, and a great deal can be said about Kremlin efforts to influence and control opinion at home. Certain topics had to be treated all too briefly, such as the use of sports, ballet, film, and other cultural channels. The use of "fraternal cities," tours by special-interest groups, the exchange of delegations, appeals to businesspeople— all these are part of a propaganda effort that interlocks with diplomacy, trade and economic relations. Western blunders, of which there are many, provide ammunition for Soviet propaganda campaigns. These had to be ignored, including Washington's covert supply of arms to Iran in 1986.

The West's propaganda efforts are mentioned only in passing, although they are major and well-established. These include the various activities of the U.S. Information Agency (USIA), such as the Voice of America broadcasts. Also backed by the U.S. government are the services of Radio Liberty, which broadcasts in the languages of the U.S.S.R., and Radio Free Europe, which broadcasts in the major languages of Eastern Europe. The multilanguage radio transmissions of the British Broadcasting Corporation (BBC) and of West Germany's Deutsche Welle are well known in the U.S.S.R. and throughout the world. Other channels used by the USIA include libraries abroad; these have equivalents in facilities offered by the British Council and West Germany's "Goethe Houses."

The struggle for that elusive element, "world opinion," is constant and complex. This book deals only with one aspect of it, and is limited by the author's own interests and capacities. Of course, many individuals and some institutions have been helpful. Among these were the Research Libraries of Radio Liberty in Munich and New York, the Hoover Institution Archives at Stanford University, and, last but not least, the New York Public Library. Herbert Romerstein, of the U.S. Information Agency in Washington, D.C., provided much helpful assistance. As a concession to the mood of our time, it should be said that no governmental or private institution, nor any foundation, provided financial support for the preparation of this book.

As is the ritual for introductory notes: The author alone is responsible for any shortcomings in this work. And finally, as I approach my seventieth year, I firmly intend not to engage in any such demanding research-cum-writing project again; may another generation undertake such tasks, with my blessings!

M. E.

PART · 1

AGITPROP IN ACTION

CHAPTER · 1

From Lenin to Gorbachev

Soviet propaganda maintains, quite simply, that the United States is an "imperialist" power, seeks world domination, and is arming for a nuclear war that would destroy civilization. By contrast, Moscow maintains, the Soviet Union leads the globe's "progressive" forces toward "peace." This dual theme, in variations without number, is constantly repeated in official Soviet statements, newspaper articles, radio and TV commentaries, in cartoons, photographs, art, films, books, periodicals, at press conferences, scientific conventions, theatrical performances, poetry readings, travel and educational programs, by the indoctrination of professional agitators and secret agents—throughout the vast machinery of Soviet opinion making, at home and abroad.

Mikhail Gorbachev—General Secretary of the Soviet Communist Party and the nation's outstanding leader—said on the occasion of the fortieth anniversary of the end of World War II (May 8, 1985): "American imperialism is at the forward edge of the war menace to mankind." He attributed U.S. policies to "the aggressive strivings of the ruling elite of that country" engaged in "stepping up the arms race, especially the nuclear arms race, and in the dangerous plans for the militarization of space." By contrast, he said, the Soviet Union stood "for a world without wars, for a world without weapons." In its broad official policy statement, designed to be valid until the end of the twentieth century, the Soviet Communist Party made these points:

"The citadel of international reaction is U.S. imperialism. It is from here, above all, that the threat of war emanates. Laying claim to world domination, it arbitrarily declares whole continents to be zones of its 'vital

3

interests.' The policy pursued by the United States of *diktat,* of imposing unequal relations on other states, of supporting repressive unpopular re- gimes, and of discrimination against countries that are inconvenient to the United States, sows disorganization in interstate economic and political relations and hampers their normal development.''

This statement was contained in the draft program for the 27th Congress of the Communist Party of the Soviet Union, adopted in February 1986 and published in *Pravda,* the party's national daily newspaper, on October 26, 1985. As such, it bore the imprint of centrally approved policy, as well as a propaganda directive, valid for decades to come.

Americans find it difficult to believe that anyone, anywhere, might view them as villains, and not only day-in and day-out, but hour after hour, in a constant barrage of words and images that circle the globe. Soviet citizens are subject to a subliminal impact of these messages which leaves a residue, an accumulation of subconscious beliefs, deposited in their minds since early childhood. The term "American" has thus become so tainted, in many parts of the world, that its very sound creates a reflexive emotion of fear and hate. It is not only Soviet children, organized as Young Pioneers, who learn early to loathe "the American imperialists"; little boys and girls, innocent as cherubs, sing lustily in faraway Nicaragua, "Here or there, the Yankees will die!" Is it any wonder, then, that Americans are the primary targets of bombs, guns, hijackings and kidnappings? The Soviets' dual propaganda message has penetrated the world, lightly in some countries, profoundly in others; and it continues its impact, grinding away, driven by a machinery that moves unceasingly.

On the one hand, the Soviet propaganda machine fills airwaves, printed pages, and images on the screen with hatred and fear of the United States. On the other hand, it reassures and upbraids the American public, playing the counterpoint of hope-and-fear toward its Number One Antagonist. Another propaganda barrage is directed at Western Europe, designed to alienate nation after nation from the United States. And in Third World countries, the largest target audience, the image of "American imperial- ism" as grasping, exploiting, as the root cause of all miseries and frustra- tions, as a dealer in death, is imprinted deeply.

How is this done? In hundreds of ways; in thousands of ways.

There is hardly an event, a speech, a meeting, from which Soviet prop- aganda might not extract an image or a phrase that implements one of its themes. Here are a few pieces of the propaganda mosaic:

- On a Sunday morning, two of the three major U.S. television net- works feature interviews with aggressive but smooth English- speaking Soviet propagandists, including Moscow Radio's top commentator, Vladimir Posner, and Georgi Arbatov, director of the

Soviet Union's Institute for the Study of the U.S.A. and Canada.

- The *Washington Post* carries a full-page advertisement, placed by the Soviet embassy, which puts forward the Soviet position on arms control.

- Tass, the Soviet news agency, reports the death of 13-year-old Samantha Smith, the girl from Maine who visited the Soviet Union in 1983, in so intricate a manner that rumors are rife in Moscow, apparently circulated by the KGB, the Soviet secret service, that Samantha's death was engineered by the U.S. Central Intelligence Agency.

- Radio Moscow broadcasts in 81 languages for a total of 2,175 hours per week. In English alone, Radio Moscow World Service transmits 24 hours a day.

- *Time,* the weekly U.S. news magazine, devotes the better part of one issue (September 9, 1985) to an interview with Soviet leader Mikhail Gorbachev. The interview, translated and published in *Pravda* (September 2, 1985), results in worldwide publicity. Subsequently, the three major U.S. television networks also seek to arrange interviews with the Soviet leader.

- Using the Soviet journalist Viktor Louis as an intermediary, the KGB repeatedly disseminates news concerning the health and status of Soviet physicist Andrei Sakharov. Louis also places still photographs and films of Sakharov with the West German newspaper, *Bild,* which are then given worldwide circulation.

- Within the Soviet Union, major propaganda tasks are in the hands of Tass, the news agency, and of *Pravda,* the Communist Party daily, which has a circulation of some 11 million copies and is printed at a network of plants throughout the U.S.S.R. Tass reaches around the globe in Russian, English, German, French, Spanish, and Arabic.

- Russia's Novosti service supplements Tass with feature articles, a full-fledged book publishing program (Progress Publishers) in many languages, and films and television programs. The agency provides research and contacts for foreign media.

- The far-flung activities of the Committee for State Security (KGB) extend into the branches of the Soviet propaganda machine. Estimates suggest that more than one-third of all Soviet correspondents abroad, including those of Tass and *Pravda,* are at least part-time KGB agents. *Disinformation,* the circulation of false or distorted information, is a KGB specialty, as is the organization of seemingly spontaneous demonstrations that invite dramatic media coverage.

- Major channels of Soviet propaganda abroad are the Union of Soviet Societies for Friendship and Cultural Relations with Foreign Countries, the World Peace Council, the World Federation of Trade Unions, the Women's International Democratic Federation, the World Federation of Democratic Youth, the Christian Peace Conference, together with a variety of related, supplementary, and regional organizations.

Of course, the preceding paragraphs give only a minute indication of the complexity, flexibility, and extent of Soviet propaganda operations; a comprehensive account of all such activities would fill several volumes and embrace an analysis of the historical and psychological elements that create the specific pattern of Soviet self-image-making. With Muscovy at the center, the empire of the czars expanded, in ever-widening circles, conquering the national and ethnic groups which today form the Union of Soviet Socialist Republics. To justify such territorial expansion, at home and abroad, has always been a formidable task.

Russian efforts at influencing opinion, substituting positive images for less attractive realities, predate the Bolshevik Revolution of 1917 by centuries. Prof. Ronald Hingley, in *The Russian Mind,* speaks of "the wide gulf between appearance and reality" in official propaganda and political myth that was "an abiding feature of Muscovite imperial and post-imperial Russia." Attempts at bridging this gulf can be found throughout Russian history. Best known, and themselves half-myth and half-reality, were the legendary "Potemkin villages," attributed to the eighteenth-century prince, Gregori A. Potemkin, a favorite of Catherine the Great. The empress had added the Crimea to her domain, largely because of Potemkin's successful conquests. She yearned to see the new territories firsthand.

As historical legend has it, Catherine traveled down the Dnieper River, early in 1787, while Potemkin moved groups of pseudo-inhabitants along the riverbanks, from village to village, in order to convince the empress of the region's prosperity and of its citizens' enthusiastic loyalty. Historians have some doubts about the record concerning this feat. A gossipy German historian, with friends in the Russian capital, is the often-quoted source for Potemkin's successful effort at propagandizing Catherine. Writing in the Hamburg monthly magazine *Minerva* (May 1798), Georg Adolf Wilhelm von Helbig planted the seeds from which the jungle of Potemkiniana has since grown:

"One was under the impression of seeing villages in the distance, but these were only houses and church steeples painted on boards. Villages close to the river, just built, seemed to be inhabited. But villagers had been forced to come from as far as forty miles away. They had to leave their houses each evening and rush to other villages, which they then inhabited for a few hours, as long as the Empress was passing by."

One biographer, George Soloveytchik, author of *Potemkin: A Picture of Catherine's Russia,* found ample "evidence" that the "vile accusations" of Potemkin's detractors were "not true." Still, he observed, "there is no doubt that, with his gift of showmanship," Potemkin "managed to endow everything appertaining to this Crimean journey with special pomp and splendour." Whatever means he used, Potemkin had a single target for his propagandistic tour de force, Catherine the Great, and his methods were eminently successful.

Official efforts at opinion making were formalized when Czar Nicholas I (1825–1855) established the "Third Section" of the Imperial Chancery, the court's secret police. According to Prof. Sidney Monas, in *The Third Section,* one of its functions was "the formation of a favorable public opinion, both in Russia and abroad." The unit expected good publicity from a visit, in 1839, by a prominent French author-traveler, the Marquis Astolphe de Custine. Although he was given V.I.P. treatment, Custine's book, *La Russie en 1839,* was a grave disappointment to the Third Section. Published four years after the visit, the book contained stinging criticisms of the Russian court and society.

The Third Section tried to enlist "counterauthors," as it were. Among these, the immensely popular Honoré de Balzac was promptly accused by critics of having been offered a sumptuous Russian bribe in the form of an estate, complete with serfs, in return for a denunciation of Custine. One Ivan Tolstoy, who lived in Paris, wrote two anti-Custine books, one under his own name, another under a pseudonym. Tolstoy, nominally attached to the Russian embassy as an education specialist, was on the Third Section's payroll. According to Monas, his job was to refute "attacks on Russia that appeared in the French press and to report to the Third Section on the course of French politics." The two Tolstoy books did nothing to reduce Custine's prestige as France's leading authority on Russia.

In the twentieth century, before and after the Bolshevik Revolution of 1917, Russian propaganda was pioneered by Vladimir Ilyich Ulianov-Lenin (1870–1924), whose revolutionary tactics combined agitation and propaganda (later fused into the term "Agitprop"). In one of his early works, *What Is to be Done?,* he urged his followers to approach the population "as theoreticians, propagandists, agitators and organizers." Initially, Lenin defined "propaganda" as an approach to opinion-making circles, while "agitation" applied to persuasion of the masses. Lenin practiced both, in his speeches as well as in his voluminous writings. After the revolution he used newspapers, telegraphic news transmission, and radio to carry his propagandist messages. Other terms, such as "indoctrination" and "ideological education," were later used alternatively.

Since Lenin's days, Soviet propaganda has fluctuated to meet the challenges of modern communication, of sophisticated public relations and advertising techniques, and of opportunities offered by television. Still, not until Mikhail Gorbachev took office did a Kremlin leader fully exploit the opportunities presented by open press conferences and TV talk shows; traditionalism, doctrinaire fears, and bureaucratic rigidity had stood in the way. Even a few months before the Reagan-Gorbachev summit meeting at Geneva in 1985, *Washington Post* correspondent Dusko Doder was able to say, with conviction and accuracy, that, among Moscow officials, "nobody speaks impromptu." He told Joseph Finder, who quoted him in "Reporting in Moscow," an article in the *Washington Journalism Review* (June 1985), that in Soviet society "the written word is all-important." He added: "Speeches are read from prepared texts. When you read a paper here, the language is repetitive and carefully chosen." But soon afterward Gorbachev answered questions from French television interviewers in an unrehearsed interchange, and he concluded the Geneva summit, on November 21, with a 45-minute press conference. Lenin and his corevolutionary, Leon Trotsky, could have done the same; but the high risks of "deviation" from the policies of Joseph Stalin induced a supercaution that became ingrained and ritualized during successive Soviet regimes.

The methods and trappings of Western communication media have provided Soviet propagandists with fresh means of advancing their cause, but the basic characteristics and themes have remained unchanged. As Frederick C. Barghoorn noted in *Soviet Foreign Propaganda,* "the phraseology of political messianism" has permeated Soviet propaganda from the start and "the vision of the glorious society of the future, free of coercion and exploitation, which is allegedly being built in the Soviet Union, has normally played a conspicuous role in Soviet propaganda."

While Soviet propaganda has dropped terms such as "world revolution" from its routine vocabulary, substituting less inflammatory words ("peace," "democracy," "socialism," etc.), it has retained what Prof. Barghoorn called the "utopian" aspects of its appeal. The program adopted by the Soviet Communist Party's 27th Congress pledged the party to "uphold the revolutionary ideals and Marxist-Leninist fundamentals of the world communist movement, creatively develop the theory of scientific socialism, consistently fight against dogmatism and revisionism, all influences of bourgeois ideology on the working class movement." In addition, the program committed Soviet communism to "do its utmost for cohesion and cooperation among fraternal parties, international solidarity of the Communists, for upping the contribution of the communist movement to the cause of preventing world war."

Since the days of Lenin, terms like "cohesion" and "cooperation," in contexts such as these, have asserted the unquestioned leadership role of the Soviets over "fraternal" Communist parties, and over the countries they control. This doctrine, also called *proletarian internationalism,* found its most dramatic expressions in Hungary, Czechoslovakia, Poland, and Afghanistan. The program also pledged the party to "pursue a consistent policy of unity of action in the international working class movement, of all working people in the struggle for their common interests, for lasting peace and security of peoples, for national independence, democracy and socialism." This sentence may be seen as an open-ended commitment to support, encourage, inspire, or create movements wherever the Soviet state and its Communist Party see an opportunity to gain influence, beyond Ethiopia, South Yemen, Angola, Cuba, and Nicaragua, toward other political-military footholds.

Barghoorn said that "utopian-ritualistic aspects of Soviet propaganda" remain important. He added: "Like the sacred tenets of any belief system, these aspects bolster the sense of righteousness of those who profess to believe in them. They also serve to rationalize the policies of the communist leadership." Indeed, the neo-religious aspects of Soviet communism are striking. Its propaganda expresses an aggressive missionary spirit. The Latin word *propaganda* has, in fact, an ecclesiastical origin: The long-established *Sacra Congregatio de Propaganda Fide* (Sacred Congregation for Propagation of the Faith) functions as the Vatican's missionary arm. While the term itself and utilization of propaganda retain negative connotations in the West, the role of the propagandist-agitator is seen as essentially positive in Soviet society.

The continuous problem of Soviet propaganda has been that of an angler who is trying to land an obstreperous fish: He must let go, now and then, be flexible, but remain unswerving in his long-range aim, to haul in the fish. Personality changes, internal power struggles, economic and military problems, shifts on the world scene—these and other factors have prompted numerous tactical adjustments in Soviet propaganda over the years. Still, strategic aims have remained constant. And what, precisely and bluntly, have been and are these aims?

In Lenin's day, following the Bolshevik Revolution (now retroactively renamed the "Great October Socialist Revolution"), Bolshevik leaders really anticipated an early "world revolution." After Russia, they assumed, Germany would succumb to Bolshevism, and so would the rest of Europe, with its colonial territories, particularly in Asia.

The organizational tool for worldwide Agitprop operations, as Lenin envisaged them, was the Communist International (Comintern), established in March 1919. In a series of talks, held during May and June 1920, Lenin dealt with the topic "Agitation and Propaganda of the Communist

International." Applying techniques that had led to the success of the Bolshevik Revolution in Russia, he advocated worldwide propagandistic utilization of the "consciousness, will, passions and imagination" of "dozens of millions who have been whipped into action by the fiercest of class struggle." Linking revolutionary propaganda to "the main tasks faced by contemporary communism in Western Europe and America," Lenin asked that "the interests of the revolution (propagandistic, agitational, organizational)" be "gauged realistically," responding to local conditions.

Soviet propaganda has passed through several clearly defined periods of tactical adjustments. Postrevolutionary euphoria was dampened during the Bolsheviks' battles against holdovers from the czarist regime, attempts at Allied intervention, and the Bolshevik regime's subjugation of such nationalities as the Georgians and Kazakhs, which had hoped for independence after the fall of the monarchy. The call for immediate "world revolution," which attracted some followers abroad and alienated others, was muted when Lenin was faced with domestic difficulties, notably a severe grain shortage, and decided to introduce the New Economic Policy (NEP) in 1921. This created situations whereby Moscow sought economic and diplomatic cooperation by "capitalist" foreign governments, while sending agitators and funds abroad to undermine these self-same governments through its Comintern apparatus. Lenin's commissar for foreign affairs, Georgi V. Chicherin, tried to maintain the fiction that the Soviet government could not be held responsible for the machinations of Comintern agents.

For a few years after Lenin's death in 1924, Kremlin cultural policies seemed relatively benign, and this translated into cordial relations with well-wishers abroad. It was during this period that one of Lenin's young followers, the German Willi Münzenberg, developed front organizations and cultural conduits which enlisted the services of well-meaning supporters for seemingly uncontroversial charitable and politico-cultural aims; it is a tactic that has remained remarkably successful, even today.

When Stalin introduced the first Five Year Plan in 1928, and generally tightened his one-man rule, the propaganda machinery changed gears to support "socialism in one country," which made it quite clearly an adjunct to Soviet policies. Stalin's ruthlessness was largely ignored abroad. Worldwide depression encouraged the illusion that the Soviet system was managing to function well, while free economies were in crisis. The 1930s became a decade of impressive Soviet propaganda successes among Western intellectuals.

The 1930s were full of contradictions. On the one hand, Soviet propaganda projected the image of the U.S.S.R. as a bulwark against Nazi Germany's political and territorial expansion. On the other hand, Moscow was the scene of macabre trials of Old Bolsheviks whom Stalin was in the process of eliminating. In Spain, Russia supported the Loyalists, but Stalin's agents were killing off "Trotskyists" within Republican ranks. Nazi Germany and Fascist Italy were backing the military takeover by Generalissimo Francisco Franco. The Moscow trials not only led to the execution of such long-time associates of Lenin and Stalin as Gregori Y. Zinoviev, Lev B. Kamenev, and Nikolai I. Bukharin but virtually eliminated a generation of military leaders, headed by Marshal Mikhail N. Tukhachevsky.

Nothing strained the Soviet propaganda machine more than the Nazi-Soviet Pact (August 23, 1939), which utterly reversed the image of Russia as a focus of principled anti-Nazi resistance. Communist propaganda denounced Western opposition to Germany's advances as part of an "imperialist war" and sought to undermine the Allied war effort. The dilemma was resolved, overnight, when Adolf Hitler's armies invaded the Soviet Union, despite the "nonaggression" pact between Berlin and Moscow, on June 22, 1941.

After the Japanese attack on Pearl Harbor, the following December 7, the United States entered the war on the Allied side. The lines of battle, as well as those of emotional alignments, became clear-cut. At this point, and throughout World War II, Stalin's outrages were forgotten; the primary Allied task was, after all, the defeat of Nazi Germany. Wartime partnership between the U.S.S.R. and the Western countries created the hope, among leaders such as U.S. President Franklin D. Roosevelt, that the Soviet Union would continue to be a cooperative partner in worldwide reconstruction. But Stalin's armies imposed Communist rule on countries of Eastern Europe, set up a regime in Northern Iran, and took firm control even in Czechoslovakia, which had been viewed as a neutral bridge between Eastern and Western interests.

Stalin dissolved the Communist International in 1943 and broke with the Yugoslav Communist government of Marshal Josip (Broz) Tito. Moscow created the Information Bureau of Communist and Workers' Parties (Cominform), at least partly to suppress "Titoist" heresies in other Communist-governed countries. The late 1940s and early 1950s stood under the shadow of Stalin's increasing paranoia. His death, on March 3, 1953, opened a period that enabled Soviet propagandists to use the slogan of "peaceful coexistence" with new verve and notable success.

The ebullient Nikita S. Khrushchev, the Kremlin's leading personality from 1954 to 1964, exploded a series of ideological rockets when, in 1956, he used the 20th Congress of the Soviet Communist Party to denounce Stalin and his secret service chief, Lavrenti P. Beria, citing a careful selection of their misdeeds. Khrushchev's apparent candor and frequent travels were, on the whole, a much-needed asset for the Soviet propaganda machine. But Khrushchev was abruptly removed from Kremlin leadership, in 1964, by a Politburo group that looked to the Communist Party's chief ideologist and propaganda guardian, Mikhail A. Suslov, for guidance.

During the Khrushchev years, the Soviet Union had, in 1956, crushed a move toward greater independence and liberalism in Hungary. Under the leadership of Leonid I. Brezhnev, which lasted until 1982, Russian tanks put an end to a similar movement in Czechoslovakia in 1968. The Soviet Union sent massive air and ground forces into Afghanistan in 1979, seeking to replace one Communist-controlled government with another, more closely allied with Moscow. These moves disrupted ongoing diplomatic and propaganda campaigns centered on détente between the U.S.S.R. and the Western nations, notably the United States.

One consistent theme has permeated Soviet propaganda from the end of World War II to the present: that of a peace-loving Soviet Union, facing a war-minded, "imperialist" United States bent on arming itself and threatening world peace. The war ended with the surrender of Japan, following the atom-bombing of Hiroshima and Nagasaki in 1945. The United States, at that time, had "The Bomb," whereas Russia did not. However, the United States and its European allies quickly demobilized their armies, once Nazi Germany was defeated; the Soviet army, however, remained largely intact and undertook not only the occupation of eastern Germany but also the task of imposing Communist rule on Poland, Romania, Hungary, Czechoslovakia, Yugoslavia, and Bulgaria.

Almost immediately, Soviet propaganda switched from what had been a muted, half-hearted support of the Allied cause to attacks on the Western powers. By turning its propaganda on targets in the Near and Far East, and in Africa, the U.S.S.R. sought to strengthen its role in what later became known as the Third World. This included China, where Mao Zedong's armies gained full control in 1949. The Soviet Union utilized the services of captured German scientists, as well as its espionage apparatus, to hasten the development of its own nuclear arsenal. This campaign was accelerated after the Cuban Missile Crisis, in 1962, which dramatized U.S. nuclear superiority and forced the Kremlin to withdraw the missiles it had placed on Cuban soil.

Soviet propaganda campaigns against U.S. weaponry were directed against specific projects, depending on whatever current development the United States was considering. When the U.S.S.R. was still engaged in developing its own nuclear arsenal, the slogan "Ban the Bomb!" resounded throughout Soviet-supported movements favoring "peace and disarmament." Vladimir Bukovski, who left the Soviet Union in 1976 and settled in Cambridge, England, dealt with this topic in "The Peace Movement and the Soviet Union," an article in *Commentary* (May 1982). He noted that Russia's earlier "passion for peace was resurrected shortly after the war was over, while the Soviet Union was swallowing a dozen countries in Central Europe and threatening to engulf the rest of the continent." He recalled "the marches, the rallies and petitions of the 1950s" and observed,

"It is hardly a secret now that the whole campaign was organized, conducted, and financed from Moscow, through the so-called Peace Fund and
the Soviet-dominated World Peace Council."

Since Lenin's day, such terms as "the people," "the working class,"
"the proletariat," and "progressive forces" have served as a facade vocabulary for Soviet policies. It is extraordinarily difficult to present appropriate definitions for terms in the Communist propaganda terminology
without sounding either cynical or crude. And yet, as George Orwell taught
the world in his enlightening satire, *1984,* "newspeak" is a way of turning
meanings upside-down and inside-out. Bukovski, in an effort at clarification, quoted Lenin as stating, "As an ultimate objective, peace simply
means Communist world control"; he added, "Once they recognized the
power of 'peace' as a weapon, the Communists have never let go of it."
Bukovski then went into detail:

"We must at the same time bear in mind that wars are the 'inevitable
consequence of the clash of imperialist interests under capitalism,' and
therefore they will continue to be inevitable as long as capitalism exists.
The only way to save humanity from the evil of wars, then, is to 'liberate'
it from the 'chains of capitalism.' Accordingly, there is a very precise
distinction to be made between 'just wars' and 'unjust wars.' 'Just wars'
are those fought 'in the interest of the proletariat.' It is perfectly simple
and perfectly clear: just wars are absolutely justifiable because they lead
to the creation of a world in which there will be no wars, forevermore.
Proletarians are all brothers, are they not? So, once the world is rid of
capitalists, imperialists, and various other class enemies, why should those
who are left fight one another?"

Bukovski recalled that the peace slogans advanced by Soviet front organizations in the 1950s were "enthusiastically taken up by millions, some
of them Communists, some loyal fellow-travelers, a number of them
muddleheaded intellectuals, or hypocrites seeking popularity, or clerics
hungry for publicity—not to mention professional campaigners, incorri-
gible fools, youths eager to rebel against anything, and outright Soviet
agents."

While, later on, much of the peace movement was spontaneous and
genuine, it did follow a path opened by Soviet-sponsored groups. Targets
succeeded one another; they included the B-1 bomber, the cruise missile,
the MX missile, and the neutron bomb. The campaign reached a temporary
crescendo in 1982, when Kremlin propaganda tried to discourage the placing of U.S. intermediate missiles in Western Europe, to match Soviet SS-
20 missiles stationed in the East. When this drive did not succeed, and a
"nuclear freeze" movement also lost momentum, Soviet propaganda concentrated on the so-called Star Wars program, the Strategic Defense Initiative (SDI), designed as an antimissile weapon. Under the new leadership

of Mikhail Gorbachev, the Soviet Union applied a tried-and-true propaganda strategy, but used more flexible tactics than those employed by Gorbachev's predecessors.

Basically, the Soviet Union recognizes three distinct target areas for its propaganda campaigns. The outer rim, as it were, is represented by the Third World nations of Asia, Africa, and Latin America, many of them former colonial territories that won their independence after World War II. A second target consists of the nations of Western Europe, particularly those united in the North Atlantic Treaty Organization (NATO) and linked with the United States by a military alliance; here, Soviet propaganda tactics are largely designed to create a split between the NATO powers and the United States. Finally, the United States itself is a target for Soviet propaganda: its open society, its competitive media—often enjoying an adversary relation to the government—and its fair-play traditions provide a ready forum to Soviet tactical approaches.

Abroad, the Soviet propaganda machine can utilize the media, front organizations, prominent personalities, the United Nations and its agencies, special-interest groups, and competing ethnic forces. At the center of that machine stand Tass, Novosti (the technically independent press, photo, film, and television service), *Pravda* and other Soviet newspapers and periodicals, as well as various agencies of the Soviet government and of the Communist Party. The Soviet propaganda apparatus is directed by the Central Committee of the Soviet Communist Party, specifically its International Department. The Soviet Council of Ministers, through press briefings by the Ministry of Foreign Affairs, maintains direct contact with international media. Soviet diplomats establish their own information channels abroad. The KGB supplements overt propaganda with covert, or "black," propaganda, including forgeries, fraudulent news, and disinformation operations.

Although Soviet society emphasizes collective, rather than individual, activity, key personalities have emerged in the propaganda field. Historically, the country's leading personalities—from Lenin and Stalin to Brezhnev and Gorbachev—symbolize the public image of the U.S.S.R. Successive leaders have projected differing images abroad, including the pipe-smoking, benign "Uncle Joe" Stalin, the boorish but lovable peasant visage of Khrushchev, the hedonistic bonhomie of Brezhnev, the ascetic disciplinarian Andropov, the wan nonentity of Chernenko, and the aggressive modernity of Gorbachev.

Despite the Soviet Union's efforts to de-emphasize human elements in leadership personalities and Kremlin power struggles, the worldwide impact of successive leaders has been strong. In the United States, in particular, each change in leadership has created waves of hope for a more liberal, accommodating, and cooperative Soviet stance. Over and over again, these hopes have been dashed; while appearances and tactics changed, substance and strategies did not. Specifically, in its attacks on U.S. "imperialism," West German "revanchism," Israeli "racism," Japanese "militarism," and Pakistan's role as "a bridgehead for terrorism" in Afghanistan, Soviet propaganda has been relentless. Some campaigns have come and gone, notably that against Mao Zedong's China, which Mao countered with attacks on the "new czars" in the Kremlin.

Domestically, the Soviet newspaper network has long been supplemented by extensive radio propaganda. Today, television news programs, commentaries, documentaries, and entertainment shows add visual aspects to the same internal propaganda themes as the older media. Television has become a major channel for domestic propaganda in the U.S.S.R. Abroad, Radio Moscow has for decades played a powerful role in disseminating news, commentaries, and features in a variety of languages, beamed at every corner of the world, 24 hours a day. The technically "unofficial" service of Radio Peace and Progress supplements Radio Moscow with aggressive broadcasts, designed to exploit regional conflicts and grievances.

This machinery operates with remarkable precision, considering its size, complexity, and varied targets. Still, conflicts at the top, involving personalities, policies, or both, are clearly unavoidable. Often, these reflect changes within the upper Kremlin hierarchy. After Gorbachev took office, the head of the Communist Party's domestic propaganda section, Boris I. Stukalin, was demoted to ambassador to Hungary. The director of international propaganda, Leonid M. Zamyatin, known for his often abrasive manner, became ambassador to the United Kingdom. Tactical disputes are chronic within front organizations; doctrinaire officials dislike working with half-committed fellow travelers, while others regard cooperation with such men and women as essential to an organization's influence.

The Soviet propaganda bureaucracy differs from any counterparts in the West by the consistency of its growth and aims, by the lifetime careers that officials devote to this highly specialized field, and by enormous investments in funds and manpower. Among its expenses, the U.S.S.R. spends substantial sums on broadcasting jamming sounds. Allowing for the inevitable frictions and inefficiencies that come with the overlapping of functions, Soviet propaganda services have developed a high degree of cooperation with such agencies as the KGB, the Foreign Ministry, and sections of the U.S.S.R. Academy of Sciences, such as its Institute for the U.S.A. and Canada, and similar institutes that deal with Asia, Africa, and Latin America.

The propaganda services of the Soviet Union maintain constant cooperation with parallel services in other Communist-governed countries, where press services, newspapers, and other media often either closely resemble their Soviet counterparts or lean heavily on material originating in the U.S.S.R. One example of such liaison is the monthly news magazine *Prisma,* published in English, Spanish, and Portuguese, distributed in 46 countries, edited in Havana, and printed in Czechoslovakia. In one way or another, this example can be duplicated dozens of times, at various levels of publishing, broadcasting, and other forms of propaganda dissemination.

From Lenin to Gorbachev, the Soviet propaganda machine has developed into a formidable, highly professional undertaking. Its impact, while incalculable, is worldwide, profound, and consistent.

CHAPTER · 2

Myth, Ritual, and Official Amnesia

Soviet communism, being atheistic, had to create an antireligion of its own. To fill the void of faith, it substituted legend for historic reality, embellishing some events and suppressing others. The new doctrine created demons and heretics, while elevating Lenin toward divinity. Out of the chaos of prerevolutionary Russia, Soviet propaganda suggests, Lenin created a New World. Lenin worship in the U.S.S.R. has reached such excesses that it provokes satire, and a Kremlin version of "Genesis" might begin as follows:

"In the beginning Lenin created the heavens and the earth. Now the earth was a formless void, there was bourgeois darkness everywhere, and Lenin's spirit hovered in faraway Zurich. Lenin said, 'Let there be Revolution,' and there was Revolution. Lenin saw the Light of Revolution, and found it good, and he divided it from the darkness of feudalism, and he cried out, 'Let there be Peace, Land, and Bread, and All Power to the Bolsheviks.' And, lo, there was the October Revolution, and if Mankind did not live happily ever after, it was largely the fault of the American imperialists."

After about seven decades of Soviet history and persistent, relentless propaganda, the people of the Soviet Union must see the figure of Lenin as that of a Divine Creator and view prerevolutionary Russia as a vast blur and the Great October Socialist Revolution as an act of cataclysmic purification and rebirth. Not only within the Soviet Union has myth outrun historic fact; in the West, too, the age of docudrama has by now substituted simplistic legend for the complexities of history.

On November 7, 1985, the sixty-eighth anniversary of the Bolshevik

17

Revolution, viewers of New York's television station WNET (Channel 13) and of other Public Broadcasting Service stations could see a show with the title "Ten Days That Shook the World." It was a well-edited amalgam of newsreel film, still photographs, and "reenactments," purporting to be a visual history of the Bolshevik Revolution. The voice of Orson Welles provided a commentary, as well as semipoetic excerpts from the book *Ten Days That Shook the World,* by the American writer John Reed. Well-known British actors spoke other quotations, including, of course, words of Lenin.

The film, advertised variously as "a documentary" and as "dramatic reconstructions of events," came to its climax with a storming of the Winter Palace in Petrograd, with wave after irresistible wave of Bolshevik Red Guards crashing through a wrought-iron gate, rushing up stairways and along corridors, while the music of a full orchestra reached a gripping crescendo. All through the film, Lenin could be seen as he addressed crowds, apparently urging them on to complete the revolution.

But that was not the way it happened. One clue to the odd distortions of history that this TV show presented came at the end, when the credits showed that it had been jointly produced by Britain's Granada Television and Novosti, the Soviet feature service. Although the program bore the title of Reed's book, it was not directly linked to it. Nor was it clear where "dramatic reconstructions" took over from newsreel footage. Quite possibly, segments of it had been taken from a fictionalized version of the revolution, the motion picture *October,* directed by Serge Eisenstein; in fact, Eisenstein's one-time assistant, Grigori Aleandrov, production head of Moscow Film Studios (Mosfilm), was listed as coproducer of the TV show.

When the film was first presented by Granada TV, a press release described it as a documentary and as "the most complete and accurate film account of the Revolution that the world is likely to see." Yet, in historical fact, the Winter Palace was never actually taken by storm, but infiltrated through its numerous side entrances, after most of the soldiers guarding it had slipped away. And, of course, Lenin was not in the center of Petrograd when Bolshevik units occupied such key points as the post office and the railroad station; after Trotsky's units had taken over these strategic positions, facing little resistance, Lenin arrived at Bolshevik headquarters, having taken a streetcar. While the siege of the Winter Palace dragged on, the two men were lying on the floor in their office, trying to get some rest.

There are ample historic records to document the Bolshevik Revolution accurately. Still, the Granada-Novosti film did show Trotsky for a few seconds, and much of the newsreel footage was fascinating. All in all, television viewers were treated to a moving, highly dramatic, expertly edited and narrated film, which served to perpetuate central myths on the origins of the Soviet state.

Shortly after this rerun of the Granada-Novosti film (it had been shown several times previously), *Good Morning America* on ABC television used the occasion of the Reagan-Gorbachev meeting at Geneva in November 1985 for another glimpse at Soviet history. The show's cohost, David Hartman, reading from a script, said that "centuries of civil strife and periodic rebellions by peasants" had ended "in November 1917, when a man by the name of Vladimir Ilyich Ulianov, Lenin to us, led the revolution that overthrew the Czars and began what we know as the Soviet Union."

But, once again, that was not the way it happened. The rule of Czar Nicholas II (1868–1918) ended with his resignation in March 1917, while Lenin was in Switzerland. The Bolsheviks were a minority within a loose coalition, led by Alexander Kerensky—and it was the Kerensky government, while trying to establish a parliamentary government, that was overthrown by the Bolsheviks in the October-November revolution. The ABC researcher-writer who prepared the script for Mr. Hartman had fallen victim to Soviet myth making, which aggrandizes one group of historical figures (in this case, Lenin) while erasing others (in this case, Kerensky).

How far this sort of thing can go is illustrated by the case of Beria, Stalin's last chief of secret police. After Stalin's death early in 1953, Beria's peers felt their lives endangered by the police chief's powers and ambitions. Just how they managed to separate him from his bodyguards will probably never be known; he was arrested in July, tried by a secret tribunal, and shot on December 23, 1953. The next step was to eliminate him from historical memory, including the *Great Soviet Encyclopedia.* Subscribers to the encyclopedia were instructed to tear out the pages that contained Beria's biography and to substitute an expanded entry on the Bering Straits, which was included in the notification. It would be difficult to imagine a more striking illustration of Soviet methodology in creating an "unperson."

Myth making and amnesia induction wash over modern Soviet history in successive waves. John Reed's *Ten Days That Shook the World* was Lenin's favorite book, and he hoped that it would be published "in millions of copies and translated into all languages." Ironically, Russians today can't obtain the original book, because it speaks highly of such "unpersons" as Trotsky and of Old Bolsheviks whom Stalin had executed, notably Zinoviev and Kamenev. British historian A. J. P. Taylor, in an introduction to one edition of the Reed book, cautioned readers against taking it literally. Reed, he said, "heightened the drama" of events, and "this drama sometimes took over from realities." Even some Bolshevik revolutionaries, Taylor wrote, "often based their recollections more on Reed's book than on their memories."

Soviet histories picture the October Revolution as a huge edifice, standing virtually alone in a desert of events. But it followed historic developments that can be traced, beyond the mid-nineteenth century, to concessions by several czars, to internal opposition movements that ranged from the abortive plot of young officers, the "Decembrists," in January 1826, to serious uprisings in 1905, and to an influx of Western European thought that included not only Marxism but concepts of parliamentary rule and cultural freedom.

Reed's personal myth as a poet-revolutionary was ensured when he died of typhoid in Moscow in 1920 and was buried in the Kremlin wall. During the 1980s, Hollywood rediscovered Reed, together with his companion, Louise Bryant. The result was a motion picture with the half-ironic title *Reds* that was part erotic fantasy, part docudrama, and part pageant. Lewis Feuer, in an analysis of *Reds* for the Toronto *Sun,* said Reed's "obsession with revolution" had made him "a symbol for so many intellectuals—that mixture of the will to revolt, self-destructiveness, adventurousness, longing for ideological creed, contempt toward established institutions, faith in a transcending social leap, the desire to identify with wielders of power, claiming to be the locomotive engineers of history."

Lenin, of course, had become just such a prime wielder of power. While he did not plan his own sanctification, he set the stage for it. Nina Tumarkin, in *Lenin Lives!,* recalled that "political imperatives" demanded "dramatic images and symbols to legitimize the Bolshevik regime." She added: "Published agitation about Lenin began to spread his idealized image across Russia. That image was varied during the years he ruled Russia and provided the basis for the myth his later cult was to celebrate. Early Soviet agitation gave rise to a demonology and hagiography of Soviet Russia. It was within this fantastic creation that the myth of Lenin gradually emerged. The party built on that myth and contributed to it in the effort to strengthen the acknowledged authority of the new political order."

Immediately following the Bolshevik Revolution, the period of "war communism" demanded enormous sacrifices from the Russian population. If the Russians had hoped that Bolshevik economics would make life easier, they were mistaken. Yet Lenin was able to sustain the original enthusiasm with his own messianic rhetoric, supported by highly effective Agitprop techniques. Tumarkin notes that public support was "largely due to the vast agitation-propaganda work carried out in myriad forms by members of the party and their supporters during the civil war years." It was in the context of "this agitation," she said, "that the cult of Lenin began to emerge." Postrevolutionary propaganda drew sharp lines between good and evil. Tumarkin noted that "agitation was adapted to the new conditions" and wrote:

"The spoken word was supplemented by the entire range of available spectacles and modes of communication. Festivals, street theater, film, radio, posters, paintings, poems, songs, bric-a-brac, hastily erected busts and statues, emblems, badges, flags, banners, monuments, and printed flyers carried simple messages comprehensible even to the illiterate. Capitalists, imperialists, Nicholas II, landlords, priests, illiteracy, the Entente, all were evil; they were the enemy. Workers, poor peasants, and Communists were the champions of good and the friends of the people."

The party's Central Committee established its Agitprop Department in the fall of 1920. Within the government, known as the Council of People's Commissars, Anatoli V. Lunacharski became commissar of education. This position gave Lunacharski ample opportunity to utilize his long-standing contacts with writers, artists, and theater people. A well-traveled linguist, Lunacharski combined eager support for Lenin and the Bolshevik cause with ideas of relatively unrestricted expression. By 1929, these ideas, which included the preservation of art and architecture from czarist times, collided with Stalin's policies, and Lunacharski was removed from his post. Under Lenin, the Commissariat established a department for political education (*Glavpolitprosvet*). The symbol of the hammer and sickle was chosen to represent the roles of workers and peasants. Annual festivities, centering around the first of May and the anniversary of the October Revolution, were instituted.

While Lenin imported Western ideas, as it were, notably the teachings of Karl Marx, his Agitprop themes were designed to create a deep resonance with the Russian population. James H. Billington, in *The Icon and the Axe,* wrote, "Lenin benefited from the Russian predilection for theories of history that promise universal redemption but attach special importance to Russian leadership." Historically, he noted, "The belief that Russia was destined to provide ideological regeneration for the decaying West had been propagandized by conservative as well as radical theorists." Billington also pointed to "the indigenous traditions of Russian radical thought" in viewing "the people" as a source of moral sanction. Opponents of the Bolshevik regime were denounced as "enemies of the people," ministries were named "people's commissariats," and "summary executions soon came to be glorified as 'people's justice.' " Outside the Soviet state, "people's democracies" appeared.

Among early Agitprop inventions were agit-trains and agit-ships, movable centers of propaganda that could criss-cross the countryside. Tumarkin recalls that the first such "Lenin Train" left Moscow in mid-August 1918, bearing on its roof the slogan "Workers of the World, Unite" and "entirely covered with frescoes depicting heroic workers and soldiers." This was "the first of several trains that went to the front laden with books, brochures, newspapers, posters, films, and projectors—and trained agitators."

Messianic, missionary, and other neo-religious themes permeated post-revolutionary propaganda, and have done so ever since. Tumarkin noted that the influence of religious images was "strikingly evident in the posters and leaflets of that period." Some posters consciously or unconsciously resembled icons, and good-versus-evil images bore close resemblance to the traditional image of St. George slaying the dragon. "Winged horses figured prominently in civil war posters," Tumarkin said, "and their riders are invariably men holding sacred texts or killing beasts." She added:

"The presence of religious images in Soviet agitation has several possible explanations, each of which is likely to be necessary but not sufficient for a comprehensive understanding of the phenomenon. Some agitators and graphic artists were doubtlessly moved by a genuine iconoclasm and meant their creations to be deliberate and cutting parodies of icons. For others, in contrast, the revolution had inspired deep feelings of religious veneration, which they expressed through the only symbols that could adequately convey them. Indeed, the very power of symbols lies in their ability instantly to communicate emotions and attitude. Still other artists and agitators may have been intentionally attempting to create works that would effectively move peasant viewers and readers who were reared on saints' lives and the Bible, calculating that religious symbols were likely to resonate in the peasant soul and transfer deep-seated feelings of reverence for holy images to equally profound stirrings of devotion to the Communist Party."

This propagandistic campaign, in all its manifold expressions, was designed to establish a double facade, at home and abroad, behind which the horrors and deprivation of the civil war could remain unnoticed, or at least be diminished. Abroad, the image of Soviet Russia as a socialist utopia was disseminated by the Comintern; at home, the concept of a Leninist salvation was advanced with missionary fervor. As Tumarkin put it, "The trauma of revolution and civil war had intensified the most basic emotions, tearing the fabric of civilized life with promises of ancient hopes realized and primal vengeances satisfied, and brought into high relief the fantastic expectations of the oppressed."

That a chaotic and starving Soviet Russia could dream, plot, and agitate for world revolution was, of itself, a triumph of Lenin's single-minded vision. At first, the Comintern was no more than an assembly of oddly assorted individuals, bombastically identified as "representatives" of whole nations and continents; later, Comintern meetings were actually attended by delegates from all over the world. It was Lenin's unswerving feeling of certainty, his truly missionary fervor, that provided the Soviet state and the Communist International with their remarkably widespread and loyal followings. Lenin's personality succeeded in mobilizing a wide range of human hopes, frustrations, fears, drives, loves, and hates—funneling all this into a movement which, ultimately, had only one goal: to extend Soviet power in all directions.

The tendency to make the "world revolution" a Russian-controlled undertaking, a weapon of Soviet expansionism, did not emerge immediately or clearly. Lenin himself, with his many years of life in Western Europe, often expressed aversion to "Great Russian chauvinism." Trotsky, who was fluent in French and German and knew English well, regarded the revolutionary days in Petrograd merely as the opening scenes of a worldwide drama. Trotsky, whose Red Army encountered the regime's domestic antagonists in the North, South, East, and West, shared the prevailing optimism of the Bolshevik leadership that "world revolution" was, so to speak, just around the corner.

In retrospect, it looks very much as if the masters of Agitprop came to believe their own propaganda. They tended to ignore disagreeable realities, were intoxicated by their own successes, and had become prisoners of their own often-repeated slogans. But the Russian economy did not respond to the measures of "Marxism-Leninism," and Western Europe, Germany in particular, did not follow the Russian example. It took several years for these facts to penetrate the self-created wall of propaganda. Meanwhile, funds and agitators made their—largely illegal—way into the "capitalist" countries, perceived by the Bolshevik leadership as ripe for revolution.

Romantic rebellion was a strong undercurrent during the First and Second Congresses of the Communist International. The First Congress (March 2 to 6, 1919) had originally been planned for Amsterdam or Berlin, although it eventually took place in Moscow. The dominant language of the congress was German, which most of the participants spoke and understood. Delegates, who had traveled to Russia, in many cases by illegal routes and with false papers, were carried along by an atmosphere of euphoria. Even then, visitors were shielded from the hardships of the Russian masses, kept busy with sightseeing and endless rounds of discussions and meetings. The congress began as a secret meeting, but on March 5, at 9 p.m., the Communist International (Comintern) became a public entity. Zinoviev became president of the Comintern; Angelica Balabanoff, a Russian-born Italian Socialist, was named secretary. Very soon, however, disillusioned with Russian domination of the Comintern and financial manipulations, she resigned the position.

The Comintern's Second Congress (July 19 to August 7, 1920) took place at a time when the Russian economy was still in a state of near-chaos. Soviet leaders took comfort in reports of revolutionary movements abroad. While foreign delegates looked to Russia for support, the Russians hoped that drastic revolutionary developments elsewhere would serve to justify their policies. According to official statistics, 217 delegates, representing 37 countries, participated in the Second Congress.

The meeting stood under the shadow of the Red Army's advance into Poland. Again, caught up in their own propaganda, Lenin and others assumed that Warsaw, Poland's capital, would fall to the Bolsheviks. For three weeks, meetings opened with an examination of a giant wall map of the Russo-Polish border, red flags indicating the positions of Bolshevik army units. Lenin, assuming that Poland would fall and Russian armies would move toward Germany's East Prussia province, asked German Communist delegates whether East Prussia's peasants would join the Bolsheviks. He, too, had become self-propagandized; the Germans had to remind him that the population of East Prussia was totally unsympathetic toward the Russian Bolsheviks. Lenin replied, "You should be aware that the Central Committee certainly does not share your views." In any event, the Russian advance collapsed soon afterward.

Contrasts between the optimistic atmosphere at the Congress and Russia's day-to-day realities prompted the Belgian delegate Viktor Serge to observe: "The one thing the foreign delegates did not discover was the living, real Moscow, with its starvation rations, its arrests, its dirty prison stories, its black market. Instead, delegates were taken to museums, to immaculate pre-school centers, which gave the representatives of world communism the frequent impression that they were on vacation or traveling as tourists in the land of the world revolution." All of it recalled the Potemkin villages, and foreshadowed thousands of future guided tours of the U.S.S.R.

Among 21 "conditions" adopted by the Second Comintern Congress, were calls for agitation and propaganda within labor unions and among the peasantry and for campaigns among the socialist parties. In colonial countries, particularly in the Far East, Communist parties were urged to collaborate with nationalist movements and leaders. The status of the Comintern was clearly defined: "The Communist International must represent, and be in fact, a unified Communist Party of the whole world. Parties active within each country, are simply individual sections."

When the delegates met again, a year later, for the Third Comintern Congress (June 22 to July 12, 1921), reality had begun to penetrate the barriers of auto-propaganda. Among the 605 delegates from 48 countries were men and women who had become aware that the Comintern's funds and agents had made little impact in the world and that the Soviet state experienced food shortages and other economic problems. At the same time, the air of international camaraderie that had characterized earlier meetings was giving way to increasingly heavy-handed Russian control. On the world scene, the Soviet state sought diplomatic recognition and trade with the "capitalist" countries, while propagandizing and plotting the overthrow of the very governments with which it was negotiating.

In his history of the early Comintern years, *Völker hört die Signale*,

Wolfgang Leonhard wrote that delegates became aware of starvation in the Volga region, a widespread typhus epidemic, and a breakdown in Moscow's water supply and sewage system. Essential foods were in short supply, and the city's streetcar system had broken down. Lenin had instituted the New Economic Policy (NEP) a few months earlier, letting a few whiffs of capitalism enter the socialist atmosphere. Despite the depressing conditions, the Hungarian delegate Sandor Rado recalled, "Whoever I had to do with, they all were full of enthusiasm, filled with a belief in the future." Leonhard recorded that other delegates shared this "mood which anticipated the world revolution with messianic expectations." As before, the congress administration treated delegates to theater performances, concerts, outings, and military parades. Lenin and Trotsky made it their business to meet with delegates in small groups, practicing a form of hands-on public relations that has, more recently, become known as "stroking."

Trotsky's discussion was "The Economic World Crisis and the New Tasks of the Communist International," while Lenin's speech was "On the Tactics of the Russian Communist Party." Lenin applied his new economic policies to the international scene, and even cautioned, "We are not alone in the world." Delegates noticed Lenin's fatigue and his frequent headaches; his new caution seemed to go hand in hand with physical and emotional exhaustion. He was remarkably tolerant, even sad, when the disillusioned Angelica Balabanoff asked to be relieved of her post with the Comintern.

The following year brought renewed Comintern activities throughout the world, including the United States and the Far East. Worldwide propaganda campaigns served to disguise the internal crisis of the Comintern, as well as Lenin's fatal illness. His condition overshadowed the Fourth Congress (November 5 to December 5, 1922); 404 delegates from 58 countries took part. While new delegates were struck by Moscow's threadbare appearance, more experienced visitors found that Lenin's New Economic Policy had begun to take effect and life was slowly gaining in vitality. The fifth anniversary of the Bolshevik Revolution was celebrated with huge public demonstrations. Red Square was filled with thousands of Muscovites, and the ritual of commemoration heightened the spirits of the Comintern delegates.

Trotsky outdid himself with a speech that analyzed the prospects of revolutionary developments in France. He first spoke in French for an hour and a half, and then repeated his talk in German and Russian. Intellectually impressive as his four-and-a-half hours of oratory was, several tired delegates saw it as an exercise in self-indulgence. Trotsky's vigor stood in contrast to Lenin's fading strength. Lenin had suffered a stroke in May and did not resume work until October. His speech to the congress was careful, slow, clearly lacking in spirit and strength. A second stroke, on

December 23, paralyzed Lenin's right arm and leg. He dictated a series of
memoranda, including one that warned the Communist Party leadership
against Stalin's character and manner. After a third stroke, in March 1923,
Lenin was taken to the town of Gorki. He died on January 21, 1924.

With Lenin's death, the whole appearance of the Soviet state and the
Communist International underwent a decisive change. But the propaganda machinery Lenin had created took on a life of its own. By sheer
momentum, it managed to embellish the facade of the Soviet state, to
impress much of the world with an image of humane and economic progress. Creation of the Lenin cult strengthened this image, at home and
abroad, enveloping it with an air of propagandistic incense. Lenin had
always demanded propagandistic professionalism. He was very angry when
he saw that the proceedings of the Comintern's First Congress fell short
of his standards; he wrote:

"Upon perusal of the brochure *The Third International,* published by
the State Publishing House, Moscow, Price 8 Rubles, 99 pages, I must
express severe disapproval concerning such a publication and demand that
all members of the State Publishing House read this letter of mine, and
develop precise procedures which guarantee that nothing as scandalous as
this will ever be repeated. The brochure is repelling. The whole thing is
one big mess. No Table of Contents. Some kind of idiot or slob, apparently
illiterate or drunk, has taken all the material, articles and speeches, and
had them printed up, every which way. There is no Introduction, no guide-
line, not even the full text of the Resolutions, no separation of the Resolutions from speeches, articles, or notes; nothing of the sort! Just an utter
disgrace! A great historic event has been disgraced by such a brochure.

"I demand: 1. Corrections through glued-in inserts, 2. Imprisonment
of those responsible, so they can correct all copies by re-gluing them, one
by one."

From then on, the output of the Agitprop Department improved mark-
edly. On the other hand, Soviet propaganda long retained a Lenin-type
tendency toward long speeches, abstract argumentation, and old-fashioned
typography mixed with grandiose illustrations. Following Lenin's death,
Stalin moved slowly and relentlessly to the pinnacle of Kremlin power,
eliminating all possible rivals. This was reflected in public images. As Nina
Tumarkin noted: "The cult of Lenin did not survive the tenth anniversary
of his death. By 1934, the idealized Lenin was relegated to the supporting
role of Sacred Ancestor as the cult of Stalin took center stage in Soviet
political ritual. For the next two decades Lenin remained an object of
organized reverence, but only within the context of the extravagant veneration of his 'worthy continuer.' " Official paintings showed Lenin in
earnest conversation with Stalin. The anniversary of Lenin's death, January
21, continued to be observed. According to Tumarkin, "It suited the man-

agers of the Stalin cult that individual items glorifying Lenin should pay obeisance to the founder of Bolshevism, and should find their way into museums, while Stalin should pose with Lenin (or figure alone) in the widely distributed cult artifacts.''

Once Stalin was gone, Khrushchev denounced the Stalinist "cult of the individual" in his 1956 speech, saying that it was "impermissible and foreign to the spirit of Marxism-Leninism to elevate one person, to transform him into a superman possessing supernatural characteristics, akin to those of a god." There it was, a denunciation of the divinity of Stalin; but Khrushchev reintroduced the divinity of Lenin when, on January 11, 1955, he decreed that Lenin's birthday should be celebrated, rather than the day of his death. "With this act," Tumarkin says, "he inaugurated the slick and cloying cult of Lenin still in evidence today."

While Stalin's image faded from the Soviet scene, Lenin's reemerged everywhere. Tumarkin commented: "In scope this cult fulfilled the dreams of the *Glavpolitprosvet* propagandists of 1924. They had envisioned an ongoing celebration of Lenin that would imprint his name, face, life story, and doctrine on every heart and mind—at least on ceremonial occasions."

The Lenin image has come to represent continuity within Soviet society, particularly during times of rapid changes in the top leadership, as when Brezhnev was succeeded by Andropov, Chernenko took Andropov's place, and Gorbachev took over after Chernenko's death. Much as a monarch represents ceremonial continuity, the Lenin cult provides an image of stability. And while ritual references to Lenin, and quotations from his writings, have become less frequent in speeches and public documents, the term "Leninist" provides a reassuring stamp of legitimacy. Notably, at the end of speeches, where Western orators might invoke the Divinity, Soviet leaders refer to Lenin. Thus, Gorbachev, in his report to the party's Central Committee, as quoted in *Pravda* (October 16, 1985), concluded, "The policy of the Leninist Party, its wisdom and conscience, correctly express what is realized by the people, its thoughts, aspirations and hopes. And we are convinced that the great cause of communism, to which the Party has devoted itself, is invincible."

Clearly, the pragmatic Mikhail Gorbachev knew the lasting value of ritual terminology.

CHAPTER · 3

Pravda, Then and Now

Among the world's leading newspapers, Moscow's *Pravda* (Truth) is unique. Nowhere is a daily paper as authoritative, as clearly the voice of a nation's highest policy-making levels, as is *Pravda*. It is not the official organ of the Soviet government, but of the Central Committee of the Communist Party. This in itself illustrates the paper's unique position: in the U.S.S.R., the government is secondary to the party, and not the other way around.

Every day, all over the Soviet Union, some 11 million copies of *Pravda* are distributed, and it is estimated they are read by some 50 million people. *Pravda*'s large pages, six or eight daily, are filled with texts, news items, commentaries, letters, and various features that are selected and written with the utmost care. Lacking advertising, the relatively few pages are filled with a great deal of material each day, and this reading matter is chosen, researched, drafted, written, and rewritten by a large staff of professional journalists.

Together, *Pravda* and the Tass news agency represent the two most formidable elements in the Soviet propaganda machine. Often, *Pravda* commentaries are distributed by Tass, and much that appears in the Moscow paper is reprinted in regional newspapers throughout the country. The way *Pravda* makes up its pages, the manner in which it gives prominence to, or downplays, news items, acts as guidance for publications elsewhere. *Pravda* is must reading, because what it prints can affect the daily life, careers, and social and economic well-being of millions, from top bureaucrats down to common soldiers. Compared with other leading newspapers, even the traditional Western European *Le Monde*, *Neue Zürcher Zeitung*, *Corriere della Sera* (and formerly *The Times* of London), *Pravda* looks dull; but it can be fascinating and informative for the nuances of its news items and commentaries, its obscure items, and the manner in which it says, or does not say, any number of things.

For all its glistening modern machinery and up-to-date journalistic technology, *Pravda* continues to fulfill the role that Lenin laid down for the Soviet press, to act as "a collective propagandist, collective agitator, and collective organizer." More than any other publication, *Pravda* is the ever-alert watchdog of Soviet society, its guide and guardian, its Agitprop educator. "Press day," celebrated annually in the Soviet Union, is the anniversary of *Pravda*'s first issue, May 12, 1912.

The paper was born of a marriage of agitational tactic and financial opportunity. Early in 1912, Lenin called a group of handpicked party members to a conference in Prague. Those in attendance rubber-stamped Lenin's plans and resolutions, which included a call to armed uprisings among workers and a series of radical demands. Later that year, in order to get close to St. Petersburg, Lenin left his residence at 4 Rue Marie-Rose in Paris and moved with his wife to Cracow, a Polish city within the Austrian Empire. Mail to the Russian capital was faster from Cracow than from Paris, and he could send his articles to the revolutionary press relatively quickly. To reach a large public every day, Lenin's Bolshevik faction needed a daily paper, and it was fortuitous that a financial "angel" had appeared earlier. As Bertram D. Wolfe noted in *Three Who Made a Revolution,* young Viktor Tikhomirov, heir to a Kazan millionaire's fortune, "one fine day dropped in" on Lenin and offered him 100,000 rubles "for the purpose of founding a legal Bolshevik daily."

Not only did Tikhomirov become *Pravda*'s business manager, administering his father's money; he also introduced another Kazan youth, Vyacheslaff Scriabin, to Lenin. This young revolutionary, a nephew of the composer Alexander Scriabin, later adopted the name Molotov and served for many years as foreign minister and head of state during the Stalin era. He became a member of the original *Pravda* board of editors. Among the St. Petersburg group around *Pravda* were two of Lenin's emissaries from the Prague conference, Kamenev and Roman Malinovsky —both, for very different reasons, striking figures in Bolshevik history.

But all did not go well between Lenin, in his Cracow isolation, and the *Pravda* editors. Soviet propaganda seeks to present Lenin's early days as a period of his unquestioned leadership. Historically, quarrels before and following the Bolshevik Revolution were constant, usually because Lenin called for extreme actions and demanded total loyalty. In the case of *Pravda,* a paper by the same name had been published by Leon Trotsky in Vienna, and even in those days, personality clashes were often violent. Trotsky's *Pravda* was a bimonthly, written mainly by him and his editor, Adolf A. Joffe, later Russia's ambassador to Germany. A major part of the disagreement was Lenin's insistence on denouncing as "liquidators" those revolutionaries who no longer felt a need to undertake illegal operations. In effect, Lenin raged against all who preferred parliamentary procedures and other legal political activities to the illegal, underground methods that Lenin had inherited from Russia's clandestine conspirators.

The Soviet historian Roy Medvedev quotes Stalin in his book *Let History Judge* as writing, "Our Party is not a religious sect, it cannot be divided into groups on the basis of philosophical tendencies." It is interesting that Stalin, with his seminary education, should choose this theological comparison. According to Medvedev, Stalin "sneered at Lenin's agitation against these deviations," did not understand "the essence of the decisions that the Prague Conference adopted on the liquidationists," and "sharply deviated" in editing *Pravda.*

Certainly, Lenin, sitting in Cracow, was dissatisfied with *Pravda*'s relatively conciliatory editorials at that time. Harrison Salisbury, in *Black Night, White Snow,* noted that Lenin's first articles appeared only in the second and third issues of *Pravda,* in early May of 1912. The editors frequently rejected Lenin's articles or toned them down, insisting that "their workers audience had no interest in the arrow polemics which so absorbed Lenin." By contrast, Stalin advocated what his biographer, Isaac Deutscher, labeled "sweet reasonableness." He maintained that "a strong and full-blooded movement is unthinkable without controversy." In a choice of phrase that can only be called prophetically macabre, Stalin said, "Full conformity of views can be achieved only at a cemetery." He wanted *Pravda* to achieve "peace and friendly collaboration inside the movement."

Lenin's wife said in a letter that her husband had often been furious with the *Pravda* editors when they cut "all his polemics with the Liquidators." On January 12, 1913, Lenin wrote that the editors had sent him a "stupid and impudent" letter and that their attitude toward him was "monstrous." The *Pravda* controversy mirrored tactical disagreements. Lenin wanted to break with rival factions during elections to the Duma and sought to carry the break into the parliament itself.

Lenin managed to sidetrack Stalin from the *Pravda* editorship by asking him to come and visit in Cracow, and to take a trip to Vienna. He commissioned Stalin to write a lengthy paper on the question of nationalities. As a Georgian by birth, he had firsthand knowledge of the role of minorities within the Russian state, and research in Vienna enabled him to gather data on other nationality problems. Back at the *Pravda* office, Stalin reflected Lenin's views more nearly when he attacked Trotsky's concept of collaboration with the Mensheviks as a "childish plan for merging the unmergeable" and as favoring the "liquidators."

By then, Lenin had maneuvered Jacob Sverdlov, who later became president of the Soviet Republic, into the position of *Pravda*'s managing editor, thereby removing Stalin from editorial decision making. However, neither Sverdlov nor Stalin survived the intrigues of the mysterious Malinovsky. Together with still another member of *Pravda*'s editorial board, Miron Chernomazov, Malinovsky supplied the secret police with information on Bolshevik activities and even actively implemented secret police policies. Although Lenin used cover names for his fellow conspirators and secret writing techniques for his communications, the secret police knew the details of his instructions. Malinovsky first told the police where Sverdlov was to be found; then he tipped them off that Stalin was attending a fund-raising concert for *Pravda*. Both men were arrested, imprisoned, and exiled.

To fill the *Pravda* editorial position, twice vacated by arrests, Lenin sent Kamenev from Cracow to St. Petersburg. Lenin's wife described their trepidations, as they took Kamenev to the train, wondering how long he would last in the editorial job. Wolfe noted that Kamenev managed to stay on, despite Malinovsky's betrayals, because he fell into the category of "literary political" offender, covered by an amnesty in celebration of the Romanov dynasty's 300th anniversary. Wolfe wrote: "So, instead of turning Kamenev in, Malinovsky provided him with excellent copy by fiery denunciations of his Menshevik fellow-Deputies. The new line found a willing supporter in the new editor-in-chief of *Pravda*, Miron Chernomazov, another police agent."

Lenin was delighted with the paper's newly aggressive editorial stance. Where he had earlier been annoyed with its editors, he now had nothing but praise. In October 1913 he wrote that everyone was so "satisfied with the newspaper and its editor," presumably Kamenev, that there had not been "a single word of criticism." By then, *Pravda* was engaged in editorial warfare against every revolutionary faction, "liquidators" included, except Lenin's loyal Bolsheviks. And, as Wolfe crisply observed, "the police, too, were satisfied" with these disruptive tactics.

Meanwhile the two ex-editors, Sverdlov and Stalin, were even forced to share one room in their exile village, Kureika. The room was part of a house belonging to a village family, including several unruly children. Although Sverdlov's letters to his family were couched in diplomatic terms, he apparently found his fellow editor's habits disconcertingly casual. At one point he wrote that "the Georgian Djugashvili" was "too much of an individualist," whose habits clashed with his own efforts to maintain "at least some appearance of order." This Odd Couple broke up when Sverdlov was transferred, while Stalin remained behind.

Malinovsky's machinations kept Stalin in exile until the overthrow of the czarist regime in 1917. But, throughout 1913 and the first half of 1914, *Pravda* continued publishing, if only under various guises. When it was banned under one name, it went right on appearing, with only slight changes in its masthead, renaming itself *Northern Pravda, Workers' Pravda,* or some other variation, while retaining its characteristic typographical image. By July 21, 1914, however, *Pravda* and other opposition papers were shut down for good.

While Stalin was in Siberian exile and Lenin in Zurich, Russia experienced the turmoil and deprivation of World War I. The ill-prepared army suffered grievously. The home front was reeling from shortages of daily necessities, notably food. All the accumulated bitterness of peasants, workers, and soldiers was slowly but surely channeled into revolutionary sentiment. For the time being, these sentiments were amorphous, largely negative, directed against the czarist regime, but not yet in favor of any specific political path.

During the war, the capital city's name was changed from the Germanic St. Petersburg to Petrograd. In this city, early in 1917, history was moving along, step by step. A series of strikes for higher wages, unrest among troops, and a general defiance of czarist authority permeated the city during February and March. As in 1905, so-called Soviets, councils of workers' deputies, battled with the Duma for governmental power. The Petrograd Soviet emerged as a powerful element. Czar Nicholas telegraphed General Sergei S. Khabalov: "I command you to end the disorders tomorrow, in the capital, which are impermissible at a time of difficult war with Germany and Austria."

But the Petrograd troops began to mutiny and to join the milling crowds, which broke into arsenals, armed themselves, freed prisoners, seized government offices, lynched policemen, and burned down the police headquarters building. The czarina, from Tsarskoye Selo, telegraphed the czar at army headquarters in Mogilev: "Concessions essential. Uprising continues. Many troops have gone over to the Revolution." The czar continued to hope and to hesitate. Telephone and telegraph connections were disrupted. Whatever loyal troops remained were running out of supplies. The regime had, for all practical purposes, ceased to exist.

Personal accounts from this period indicate that revolutionary chaos created fear all around, even among the revolutionaries, the troops, members of the Duma, and opposition leaders. The Duma set up a Provisional Committee, the closest thing to an interim government, from which Alexander F. Kerensky emerged as the most prominent figure. Kerensky hoped that a parliamentary republic could replace the czarist regime, while holding the line against chaos.

The czar, cut off from the czarina and their children, shuttled back and forth in his train; he finally signed his resignation at Pskov at 3 p.m., March 2, 1917, yielding power to Prince George Lvov. The czarina first heard of her husband's resignation when Grand Duke Pavel brought her a copy of *Izvestia* with news of the abdication. "I don't believe it," she said. "It is all lies. The newspaper invented it. I believe in God and the Army. They haven't deserted us yet."

Six days later, Stalin and two fellow Bolsheviks, Kamenev and Matvei K. Muranov, were on their way back to the capital. They telegraphed Lenin in Zurich, "Fraternal greetings. Leaving today for Petrograd." They arrived on March 12. Three days later, Stalin and Kamenev took editorial control of *Pravda,* which had been run by Scriabin-Molotov during the preceding ten days.

Maxim Gorki, the world-renowned Russian author, had often provided Lenin with funds during his exile years. At one point, Lenin traveled to Gorki's home in Capri, Italy, to convince him of the correctness of his tactics and to obtain financial support. Now, Gorki put up 3,000 rubles to finance *Pravda*'s second incarnation. The paper printed 100,000 copies, about double its previous circulation.

Under Molotov's initial postrevolutionary editorship, the paper reflected Lenin's radicalism. Once Stalin and Kamenev took over, *Pravda* began to sound more conciliatory; it was all a bit reminiscent of 1912, when Lenin was angered by the editors' caution. Salisbury wrote: "The early Molotov issues did have Lenin's imprint—uncompromising, antagonistic to the Provisional Government and the Duma men, lukewarm if not hostile to the Soviet, where the Mensheviks and Socialist Revolutionaries dominated, opposed to the policy of continuing the war to a victorious conclusion."

Deutscher, in *Stalin: A Political Biography,* has suggested that Stalin was steering a middle course during this period and that his *Pravda* articles reflected these tactics. He noted that, barely a week after his return from Siberia, "a note of acute disquiet over the prospects of the revolution crept into one of Stalin's articles." Deutscher said that Stalin had "grasped with clarity the latent conflict between the Soviets and the Provisional Government" and had actually written that the army stood "between revolution and counter-revolution." During this period, moderate Bolsheviks wanted to give Prince Lvov a chance to restore stability. Stalin commented on the regime's supposed goals: "The readers of *Pravda* know that those war aims are imperialist: the conquest of Constantinople, the acquisition of Armenia, the dismemberment of Austria and Turkey, the acquisition of northern Persia."

Medvedev has concluded that Stalin virtually sabotaged Lenin's policies during this period, publishing material "that did not reflect Lenin's line on the basic problems of revolution but actually contradicted that line." Lenin, on the eve of his departure from Zurich, wrote a series of articles, called "Letters from Afar." These, Medvedev asserted, the *Pravda* editors either did not print or mangled. Three were not printed, and "the one they did publish appeared in distorted or abridged form." While Stalin and Kamenev were on the scene, Lenin's comments on events in Petrograd reflected his remoteness, in time and space, from the fast-moving events in the Russian capital.

Medvedev, who has been writing his unique analyses within the Soviet Union, could manage to be critical of Stalin but not possibly of the officially sanctified Lenin. If one reads the "Letters from Afar," unpublished in *Pravda* but resurrected in Lenin's *Collected Works*, it becomes clear that the author had been thrown into a frenzy by events in Petrograd. On the one hand, he was frustrated while still in exile; on the other hand, he expressed a visionary extremism that justified Stalin's and his fellow editors' decision to keep Lenin's outpourings out of the paper.

As Robert Payne commented in *The Life and Death of Lenin,* "being a conspirator," Lenin "imagined conspiracies everywhere." In one of his "Letters," Lenin spoke of "a conspiracy by the Anglo-French imperialists" to encourage non-Bolshevik leaders "to seize power in order to prolong the imperialist war, and to conduct the war even more ferociously and stubbornly, and slaughter new millions of Russian workers and peasants," and to "exchange one monarch for another."

The new Petrograd leaders, in power only about a week, were half-drowning in a sea of chaos. Lenin imagined, or pretended to imagine, that the armed workers of Petrograd would establish a rule of "absolute order and comradely discipline, practiced with enthusiasm." As so often before, Lenin wrote with a vague flourish about the kind of regime that would result from the revolution. In his exuberance, he saw the regime as supplying a bottle of wholesome milk to each child, converting czarist palaces into homes for the destitute, and providing food supplies to meet all needs. As to how such administrative accomplishments were to be achieved, Lenin merely said that "the workers and the entire population" would do it all "a hundred times better than any theoretician could propose." Still, he denied that he was advocating rulerless anarchy, writing that "we need the state" and outlining plans for an armed militia.

Payne says that "these extraordinary" letters were "written in a state of exhaustion," calling on the one hand for "complete freedom" for everyone, while promising a "magnificent organization of the proletariat." The *Pravda* editors, dealing with almost hourly changes in the delicate military-political balance of power in Petrograd, could hardly be blamed for trying to save Lenin from his own exuberance by putting three out of four of his "Letters from Afar" into their files. Later on, Lenin must have agreed with them; the articles were published only after his death.

Lenin also quarreled, before, during and after the Bolshevik Revolution, with his long-time supporter, Maxim Gorki. Soviet propaganda has done much to put a retrospective gloss on Gorki's attitude toward the

Bolshevik leaders and their policies. True, Lenin admired Gorki's novels and short stories, widely read in Western Europe, and he sought to coopt him into his movement as the living symbol of "proletarian" literature. Gorki's early life had been spent with down-and-outers on the fringes of Russian society. His writings presented the lives of unfortunates—hobos, drunkards, outlaws—with empathy and in moving detail; but his protagonists could hardly be classified as members of Karl Marx's working elite, the industrial proletariat. Nevertheless, Lenin and Gorki got on well, part of the time, and the author not only used much of his earnings to finance *Pravda,* other publications, and Bolshevik activities but also raised money from well-to-do acquaintances.

Still, Gorki was straight-laced in his political morals; appalled by Lenin's suppression of all opposition, he said so quite openly in letters and in his own periodical, *Novaya Zhizn* (which, eventually, Lenin banned). Born Maximovich Peshkov, he adopted the name "Gorki," which stands for "The Bitter," as a *nom de lettres.* Somewhat heavy-handed, Lenin used his fourth "Letter from Afar" to say that Gorki's views had given him "a bitter feeling" and represented "prejudices which are extremely prevalent among the petty bourgeoisie." Gorki's desire to avoid needless clashes within Russian society struck Lenin as "the same as approaching the proprietor of a house of ill-fame with a sermon on virtue." He anticipated the founding of the Communist International and the worldwide range of agitation and propaganda in this fourth letter when he said: "The Russian proletariat will be the vanguard of the international proletarian revolution." He wrote this letter in Zurich on March 25, 1917, and sent it off to *Pravda.* When Lenin himself arrived in Petrograd's Finland Station, the first words he spoke to Kamenev were, "What is this you have been writing in *Pravda?* We have read a few issues and have cursed you roundly."

Lenin, Deutscher wrote, was surprised and shocked by the "political idyll" he encountered; he had expected a reflection of his own revolutionary images, punctuated by harsh conflict and violence. He asserted that *Pravda*'s "demand of the Government of the capitalists that it renounce annexations was nonsense." He accused the editors of operating in "a fog of deception."

According to Deutscher, Lenin's "argument and invective drove Stalin into protective silence." Stalin's earlier shilly-shallying, according to Deutscher, "had reflected his own embarrassment; and it was now a relief to be freed from it. Nor was Lenin bent on making those who led the party in his absence lose face once they had given up the fight. Stalin remained the editor of *Pravda;* and Lenin helped him adjust himself. Barely ten days after Lenin came out with his [April] Theses, Stalin hastened to demonstrate, in *Pravda,* his solidarity with Lenin." In a signed editorial, "Land for the Peasants," Stalin publicly reversed himself and called on the peasants to take over the land, "without waiting for any permission" from ministers "who put spokes in the wheels of revolution."

These were the days when *Pravda* at last lived up to Lenin's concept of the press as the instrument of agitation and propaganda, as battering ram against the government's efforts to replace the czarist regime with a parliamentary administration. No matter what Kerensky tried to do, *Pravda* found it a betrayal, part of an imperialist plot, evidence of bourgeois thinking, or a counterrevolutionary undertaking. The quarrel over Lenin's "April Theses" was short but bitter. As published in *Pravda,* the theses were signed only with Lenin's name, not by his party or associates. Here is Payne's summary:

"1. No concessions to be made to revolutionary defensism. The proletariat may give its consent to a revolutionary war only on condition that all power is transferred to the proletariat and the poor peasantry and the war is not undertaken for the sake of conquest. Fraternization.

"2. The present situation in Russia represents the transition from the bourgeois revolution to the revolution of the proletariat and the poor peasants. This transition is characterized by the maximum of legality. Russia being the freest of all the belligerent countries in the world. Vast masses of the proletariat have only recently been awakened to political life, and the Bolsheviks are therefore in an advantageous position to adapt themselves to the changing circumstances.

"3. The Provisional Government to be unmasked and exposed for the falsity of its promises, especially those relating to the renunciation of annexations.

"4. Recognition of the fact that within the Soviets of Workers' Deputies the Bolsheviks are in a minority. The work of the party therefore must consist of patient, systematic and persistent criticism.

"5. Not a parliamentary republic, but a Soviet of Workers' and Peasants' Deputies 'throughout the land from top to bottom.' Abolition of the police, army and bureaucracy. The universal army of the people to be substituted for the standing army. All officers to receive salaries which do not exceed the average wage of a competent worker.

"6. Nationalization of all lands in private possession. Creation of model agricultural settlements.

"7.   Immediate merger of all banks into a single general national bank controlled by the Soviet of Workers' Deputies.

"8.   Not the introduction of socialism as an immediate task. The Soviet of Workers' Deputies to control social production and the distribution of goods.

"9.   Party tasks: Immediate calling of a party convention; the party program to be changed to include the demand for a 'Commune' state modeled on the Paris Commune. Change name.

"10.   Restoration of the International. Taking the initiative in the creation of a revolutionary International to fight against the social-chauvinism and the 'center.' "

Kamenev's critique of these sweeping, high-handed and rather casual ten commandments, published in *Pravda* the very next day, found many an echo among Bolsheviks and Mensheviks, some of them Lenin's long-time associates. At a subsequent party meeting, Lenin defended his position fiercely, and by sheer force of personality began to widen the circle of supporters. Yet his autocratic tactics alarmed some of the most thoughtful among the revolutionaries. Viktor Cherno, writing in *Delo Naroda,* provided this penetrating portrait of Lenin, as projected at that time:

"Lenin is a man of great capacities, but the abnormal conditions of underground life have dwarfed and stunted them most horribly. Lenin can now say of himself, 'I know not where I am going, but I am going there with determination.' Lenin is certainly devoted to the revolution, but with him this devotion is embodied in his own person: 'I am the State!' To him, there is no difference between personal policy and the interests of the party, the interests of socialism. Lenin is an extraordinary intellect, but it is one-sided. He is absolutely honest, but a man with a one-track mind. For that reason, his moral sense has been dulled. Lenin's socialism is a blunt socialism; he uses a big axe where a scalpel is needed."

The honeymoon of Lenin's arrival in Petrograd was followed by weeks of disillusion and questioning. The Provisional Government, with Kerensky at its head, faced the manifold problem that grew from the downfall of the czar: disrupted communications, food shortages, disciplinary break-downs in the armed forces, strikes and demonstrations that led to violence, looting and other forms of anarchy, as well as a growing sense of aimlessness among the general population.

Lenin's public appearances fell off. He sought to counter attacks against him, while keeping up his violent criticism of the Kerensky government. His writings for *Pravda* were numerous, often brief, always furiously aggressive. At one point he published as many as five short articles in *Pravda* per day, breaking his own earlier record, when he wrote some 300 articles during the paper's first two years of existence. From March to October 25,

1917, he contributed 207 articles in *Pravda*. The *Great Soviet Encyclopedia* states that the paper's circulation rose to 85,000 or 90,000, and defines *Pravda*'s role during this period as follows: "The newspaper promoted the strategy and tactics of the Bolshevik Party and performed a vital ideological and educational function. It consistently exposed the essentially anti-popular policies of the bourgeois Provisional Government, unmasked the opportunism of the Mensheviks and Socialist Revolutionaries and mobilized the masses for the socialist revolution."

The months of May, June, and July were marked by an uneasy balance of power between the Provisional Government, the Petrograd Soviet, and the various units of the army and navy stationed in and around the city. More and more arms drifted into the hands of civilians of various political colorations. Lenin's policies were under fire as pro-German, and the increasing number of assassinations, murders, and lynchings created a justified uneasiness in Lenin's circle. He had good reason to fear for his life.

On July 16, the pro-Bolshevik First Machine Gun Regiment put on a show of force that looked like a coup attempt. The soldiers massed before the Tauride Palace, where the parliament was in session, and shouted, "Down with the Provisional Government! All power to the Soviets!" Trucks filled with Red Guards and soldiers criss-crossed the city. The following day, 20,000 sailors from Kronstadt landed on the northern bank of the Neva River and marched to the Kshesinskaya Palace. There, Lenin greeted them with a speech that called for "firmness, steadfastness and vigilance."

The episode was both menacing and curiously ineffective. Kerensky recaptured the Kshesinskaya Palace from the Bolsheviks without a shot being fired. Captured documents showed that the Bolsheviks had planned an uprising for three months, but had not followed through on their plans. On July 18, Lenin told Trotsky, "Now they will shoot us down, one by one. This is the right time for them." On the night of July 17, Lenin was working in the *Pravda* office. Less than an hour after he left, military cadets invaded the place, broke up the furniture, overturned the files, smashed the type and disabled the presses.

From then until October, the paper returned to its earlier camouflage technique, appearing under different names, such as *Listok "Pravdy"* (Leaflet of Pravda), *Rabochi i Soldat* (Worker and Soldier), *Proletari* (Proletarian), *Rabochi* (Worker) and *Rabochi Put* (Workers' Way). After the unsuccessful July uprising, rumors spread that the police had found documents which proved that Lenin had, in fact, been a German agent. After first considering to face these accusations publicly, Lenin decided to hide, and Zinoviev went along with him.

Lenin cut off his beard and went into a peripatetic form of underground exile. Equipped with false identity papers and a wig, he first moved from one apartment to another, then into the countryside close to the Finnish border, and finally into the city of Helsingfors (Helsinki). At times seriously cut off from communications with Petrograd, he passed from periods of frustration to serenity, and back again. The Kerensky regime faced a German offensive that succeeded in capturing the Latvian capital, Riga. At home, Kerensky had to deal with the intrigues and military ambitions of General Lavr G. Kornilov. The armed forces and the civilian population alternately passed through periods of passionate involvement, lethargy, cynicism, and disillusionment. Rumors were rife. At one point, Lenin was convinced that England and Germany would make a separate peace, and then throw themselves on Russia to crush the revolutionary movement. He accused Kerensky of wasting Russian lives in fighting the Germans, but also of giving in to Germany.

Throughout all these changes in events and perceptions, Lenin pressed ever harder for an early Bolshevik move to take total power. Every real or imagined event was fuel for the fire of his determination to provoke the Bolshevik leadership into immediate armed action. Workers supportive of the Bolsheviks had, in fact, been given guns, but they were still outnumbered by opposing forces. Lenin called for the use of propaganda and agitation to neutralize all opposition and manipulate a small but tightly led armed force to take over the city. The papers that acted as surrogates for *Pravda* kept up their propagandistic fire against Kerensky. When news of Kornilov's military plans reached Lenin, he urged that the Bolsheviks use this development to strengthen their forces, but avoid aiding Kerensky in the process. He wrote that these events "can lead us to power, but we must speak of this as little as possible in our propaganda." Since Lenin's "April Theses," Bolshevik propaganda had pounded away at the simple, and simplistic, slogan, "Peace! Land! Bread!" The Bolshevik Central Committee had, in effect, forbidden Lenin to return to Petrograd prematurely. It felt that he was in serious danger, and it was obviously alarmed by his manic insistence on an immediate uprising. Salisbury described his state of mind:

"From now on the day would hardly pass when Lenin would not urge, plead, beg, threaten, and demand from his colleagues that they act, act immediately, act decisively, take power. There was no wavering. The July days were behind him. The June days were of the past. The braggadocio of April was forgotten. Day after day Lenin's words pounded at the skull of the Party. The tension levels rose and rose. There had been examples before, often enough, when Lenin had whipped himself into a frenzy. But nothing like this. He had total conviction that he was right and that the moment was now. Immediately. This very day. This hour. This minute."

Lenin smuggled himself back into Petrograd, to the surprise and chagrin of the Central Committee, during the second half of September. On October 10, the committee met, with Lenin present and several members still in their underground disguises. Zinoviev and Kamenev urged caution: "Before history, before the international proletariat, before the Russian Revolution and the Russian working class, we have no right to stake the whole future on the card of an armed uprising." But Lenin carried the day. Of the twelve committee members, ten, including Stalin, voted for insurrection.

Zinoviev and Kamenev were so strongly opposed to Lenin's insurrection plans, which did lack precision and cohesion, that they actually published their views in Gorki's paper, *Novaya Zhizn,* following a further Central Committee meeting on October 16. Lenin was, of course, furious and attacked both men in the *Pravda* surrogate, calling them "traitors to the revolution" and asking that they be expelled from the party. Stalin, as editor of *Rabochi Put,* accompanied Lenin's attack with an editorial that advocated continued interparty unity. This, in turn, angered Lenin, and at the next committee meeting both Stalin and Kamenev offered to resign.

Meanwhile, the armed workers of the Military Revolutionary Committee were strengthening their positions in and around the city. Trotsky began to emerge as the most prominent commander. The Kerensky government, installed at the czar's old Winter Palace, could not fail to be aware that the Bolsheviks were agitating for its violent overthrow. While the government sat at the Winter Palace, Trotsky's command post was at the Smolny, a sprawling three-story building that had previously served as a school for daughters of the nobility.

When the Kerensky government finally decided to suppress the Bolsheviks, one of its actions was to cut telephone lines to the Smolny. Around 5:30 on the morning of October 24, soldiers carrying a warrant signed by the commander of the Petrograd area arrived at the plant where the day's issue of *Rabochi Put* was being readied. They smashed the plates, destroyed some 6,000 copies of the paper, seized documents and manuscripts, and sealed the premises. They did not disable the typesetting and printing machinery and posted only a symbolic guard at the building.

As an action to forestall a Bolshevik coup, all this was quite ineffective. The Smolny stayed in touch with its outposts by messengers (phone service was soon restored), and the paper's staff sent word to Trotsky that troops had closed down the printing plant. As Robert Payne narrates the events in his Lenin biography, this is what happened:

"These were the first acts in the revolutionary war which was not to end until the whole of Russia came under the domination of the Bolsheviks.

"When Trotsky woke up on the morning of November 6, he was confronted with the news that the Bolsheviks had lost their newspaper and their telephones. A motorcycle courier service was immediately organized to maintain contact with the factories and the regiments which favored the

Bolsheviks. The problem of the printing press was solved by a young woman who had escaped from the building. She told how the guards had sealed the doors with sealing wax.

" 'Why don't we break the seals?' she asked.

" 'Why not?' Trotsky replied, and for years to come he would muse ironically on how the Russian Revolution began with the breaking of a few inches of official sealing wax at the suggestion of a young woman whose name he could never remember."

Trotsky's armed workers outnumbered the soldiers who were guarding the printing plant, apparently rather half-heartedly. Within a few days, *Pravda* was rolling off its presses under its original name. By then, the momentous hours of the Bolshevik Revolution were history.

As noted earlier, the events of the revolution have themselves become propagandistic legend. Seizure of the printing plant could be presented as evidence of the Kerensky government's "counterrevolutionary conspiracy." Trotsky sent a regimental unit and several engineers to guard the plant, and his Military Revolutionary Committee issued a decree commanding that the printing plant be kept functioning.

This was the first of a series of decrees issued by the revolutionaries, acting in governmental fashion. Having "freed" the *Pravda* plant, the Bolsheviks simply moved from one target in Petrograd to another. The second decree, drafted by Trotsky and sent to all units of the city's garrison, stated: "The enemy of the people took the offensive during the night. The Military Revolutionary Committee is leading the resistance to the assault of the conspirators." The Smolny building was turned into a guarded fortress. From a corner room of its third floor, orders went out to factories, regiments, and battleships. Revolutionary units occupied such key spots as the post office, telephone and telegraph bureaus, and other public utilities.

The Bolsheviks, by momentum and default, undercut the Kerensky administration. The ministers, meeting at the Winter Palace, were in limbo. Kerensky's orders were countermanded by the Military Revolutionary Committee. The government had, throughout the preceding weeks and days, lost contact and authority; into this vacuum, the Bolsheviks moved— at first with puzzled hesitation, and then with increasing certainty. Among their tactical achievements was the capture of key bridges leading into the central city. Lenin joined the revolution by streetcar, traveling from his hiding place in an apartment in the Vyborg district to the Smolny headquarters. There, the guards would not let him in! He had an invalid pass, but the zealous guards finally gave way.

In Room 100, Lenin took off the bandage that hid half his face and rid himself of the wig that had served to disguise him. He had never before been to the Smolny headquarters. Trotsky had to bring him up to date on the day's happenings. Somehow, it had all been too bloodless for the man whose *Pravda* articles and fiery speeches had anticipated a violent revolution, after the French model. Nikolai Sukhanov, a member of the Petrograd Soviet and a historian of the revolution, wrote, "Everything happened with fabulous ease."

Yet the "Storming of the Winter Palace," as a propagandistic image of Soviet history, has taken on a mythic reality all its own. In numerous paintings, histories, films, and television dramas, this event has become the central symbol of the Bolshevik Revolution. The Winter Palace was the last target of the revolution. Trotsky had managed to talk the troops at the Peter and Paul Fortress into joining the revolution, and only the palace was actually guarded.

Alexander Kerensky, who had borrowed a car from the American legation, was driven through the streets of Petrograd, and hoped to make contact with troops at the front. Except for two minor ministers who had been arrested in the streets, the members of the Provisional Government stayed in the Winter Palace, hoping that troops would arrive to free them. Throughout the day, revolutionary units encircled the palace. Its defenders, some 2,000 at the outset, were military cadets, cossacks from the Ural mountains, and a so-called Women's Batallion of 170 members. Arrayed against them were units from army and navy forces, together with Red Guards, numbering tens of thousands. The cruiser *Aurora,* allied with the Bolsheviks, had its guns trained on the palace, and the Peter and Paul Fortress could reach it by cannon.

Yet the surrender of the Winter Palace turned into a long, drawn-out, desultory undertaking. Most of the palace was taken up by a hospital unit that housed war-wounded. The ministers of the Provisional Government occupied only a few rooms. With its hundreds of entrances on all sides, the vast building could not be effectively guarded against intruders, nor could troops be prevented from filtering out. As the siege went on, defenders melted away; some left openly, such as mounted cossacks, many more went singly and in small groups, through side exits. There were a few skirmishes, and missiles damaged odd bits of the building's vast exterior. More and more revolutionaries simply made their way through entrances, stairways, and corridors of the palace, finally overwhelming the remaining troops by sheer number.

While Lenin and Trotsky waited impatiently at the Smolny, infiltrators entered the palace in large numbers after midnight. It was 2:10 in the morning when one of the three commanders of the siege, Vladimir A. Antonov-Ovseyenko, entered the dining room in which the ministers were sitting. The ministers were arrested and taken to the Peter and Paul Fortress; most of them, were, of course, anticzarist revolutionaries themselves.

Six people had been killed during the 12-hour siege, all in isolated encounters. The ministers handed over their handguns, signed a protocol, and were led out of the building. The legendary "Red October," the heroic Bolshevik Revolution that was popularized in such works as John Reed's *Ten Days That Shook the World,* had drifted into history.

In the words of the *Great Soviet Encyclopedia,* it was *Pravda*'s task, "after the victory of the Great October Socialist Revolution," to publish "the most important resolutions of the Communist Party and the Soviet government, as well as articles and reports by Lenin setting forth the tasks involved in building the world's first socialist state." From November 7, 1917, to mid-January 1928 the paper published 345 of Lenin's articles. The revolution was merely the beginning of the civil war that eventually enabled the Bolsheviks to control all of what became the U.S.S.R. The encyclopedia reported that during this internal conflict, from 1918 to 1920, *Pravda*'s main task was to "mobilize the masses to resist the united forces of domestic and international counterrevolution."

Domestically, the Bolsheviks not only suppressed the remaining czarist loyalists but they also wiped out such fellow revolutionaries as the Mensheviks and Social Revolutionaries. Jesse D. Clarkson, in *A History of Russia,* wrote, "In a fairy tale, one could at this point record that the fair maiden of the Revolution having been rescued from the evil sorcerer Kerensky by the bold knight Lenin, everyone lived happily ever after." Actually, he noted, "To most socialists and liberals," the "successful Bolshevik coup simply spelled disaster," because the Bolsheviks set about retaining power at any price, eliminating not only open antagonists but yesterday's friends and allies as well.

Lenin himself, and Stalin after him, used *Pravda* as his major forum. After the revolution, the paper at first continued to reflect controversy within the Bolshevik leadership, but it eventually became just the daily expression of the Soviet leadership's dogma. As definitions of "Marxism-Leninism" varied with the changing fates of the leaders themselves, the paper served as the basic record of fluctuating ideological virtues and sins. Terms such as "leftist deviations," "rightist deviation," and soon "Trotskyism" often turned the pages of *Pravda* into a jungle of theoretical verbiage that both disguised and revealed the fierce struggles behind the scenes.

Throughout the 1920s and early 1930s, *Pravda* sought to make the incredible plausible: Stalin's accusations and maneuvers against Trotsky, Zinoviev, Kamenev, and Bukharin, against thousands and eventually millions who, in one way or another, were alleged to have committed heretic sabotage. The Bolshevik Revolution was followed by "war communism," by severe economic dislocations, partly alleviated when Lenin instituted the New Economic Policy (NEP). The Soviet encyclopedia said that *Pravda* urged "the masses" to "counteract the economic dislocation and to work for the reconstruction of industry and agriculture." In its bland terminology, the encyclopedia covered much of the Stalin era with this sentence: "At all stages of the development of Soviet society, *Pravda* was an instrument of the party in its struggle to carry out its strategic, tactical, and organizational tasks, to maintain the purity of Marxist-Leninist doctrine, to put into practice the economic development plans, and to raise the workers' material and cultural level." The encyclopedia added:

"During the prewar five-year plans (1929–40) *Pravda* did a great deal of organizational work in developing socialist emulation, promoting shock-work methods and the Stakhanovite movement, and fostering a communist attitude toward labor among workers." The *Stakhanovite movement* was modeled after the alleged achievement of one Alexei G. Stakhanov, who worked in the Donbas coal mines from 1927 to 1935 and was credited with developing a speed-up system that exceeded official production quotas. *Pravda* established editorial "field offices" in such industrial centers as the Stalingrad Tractor Works, the Gorki Automotive Plant and the Dnieper Hydroelectric Power Plant.

Stalin's ruthless collectivization of agriculture, which led to the uprooting and death of millions of farmers, was noted in the encyclopedia when it stated that *Pravda* made "a most important contribution to the strengthening of *kolkhozes* [collective farms], machine and tractor stations, and *sovkhozes* [state farms]." According to this account, "The paper disseminated the great principles of Soviet democracy, urging the working people to participate in the governing of the country."

The periods of the purges of the Old Bolsheviks, the changes in Comintern policies to a "united front," the Stalin-Hitler Pact, and other pre-World War II developments were covered by the encyclopedia in these terms:

"*Pravda* played a significant part in carrying out the cultural revolution in the USSR, systematically discussing questions relating to the development of public education, literature, and art, and publishing the best work by Soviet writers. Among prominent Soviet scientists and scholars who contributed to *Pravda* were I. V. Michurin [biologist and horticulturist], N. I. Vavilov [plant geneticist], O. Iu. Schmidt [mathematician, astronomer, and geophysicist], D. N. Prianishnikov [natural scientist], and I. M. Gubkin [petroleum and mining geologist]." The encyclopedia also mentioned prominent writers whose work appeared in *Pravda* and stated: "While focusing primarily on problems of economic development, *Pravda* also called for the strengthening of the defense capabilities of the USSR. It educated the Soviet people in patriotism, proletarian internationalism, and political vigilance, exposed fascism, and campaigned against the imperialist warmongers." The encyclopedia further stated:

"During the Great Patriotic War (1941–45), *Pravda* was the fiery agitator and organizer of the nationwide struggle against the fascist aggressors. Through *Pravda* the party Central Committee addressed the people and the army, confronting them with the most urgent tasks relating to the war. The newspaper made the masses aware of the Leninist idea of defending the socialist fatherland and disseminated the current slogans of the party. It published speeches and articles of party, government, and military leaders."

These were, of course, the years when *Pravda* and all other Soviet media continually published Stalin's words, his picture, and numerous Stalin quotations in the articles and speeches of others. The encyclopedia listed Stalin's name among five editorial board members in 1917, but his name does not appear among those "party activists" who "spoke through the pages of *Pravda*" during World War II. Leaders of foreign Communist parties whose articles appeared in *Pravda* did appear in the encyclopedia account, including Georgi Dimitrov (Bulgaria), Kurt Gottwald (Czechoslovakia), Dolores Ibarruri (Spain), Wilhelm Pieck (Germany), Palmiro Togliatti (Italy), Maurice Thorez (France), and Walter Ulbricht (Germany). None of the U.S. Communist Party leaders—Earl Browder, William Z. Foster, etc.—were mentioned.

According to the encyclopedia, *Pravda*, during the war, "published communiqués issued by the Soviet Information Bureau, information about domestic and international events, and articles about the heroism of Soviet soldiers and guerrillas, the heroic feats of labor by workers and collective farmers, and the patriotic acts of Soviet citizens. It also published documents revealing the brutality of the Hitlerites. The paper's circulation increased by 150 per cent." The summary contained no reference to the general Allied war effort in Western Europe, the Far East, and North Africa; actually, *Pravda* published an absolute minimum of reports on them.

After the war, Soviet internal and external propaganda quickly turned toward hostility against the West generally and the United States in particular. These were also the years of Stalin's break with Tito of Yugoslavia, and the purges of alleged "Titoists" among the Communist leaders of Eastern Europe. According to the encyclopedia, "After the victory of the Soviet Union in the Great Patriotic War, *Pravda* gave extensive coverage to the Soviet people's efforts to restore and further develop the national economy. The newspaper devoted considerable space to questions concerning the establishment of the world socialist system, the national liberation movement, and the peace policy of the USSR." Among "famous fighters for peace" whose writings were published in *Pravda* during this period, the encyclopedia mentioned Frédéric Joliot-Curie, J. D. Bernal, Anna Seghers, Paul Robeson, and Pablo Neruda. The paper's coverage of worldwide propaganda efforts, such as the World Peace Council's manifold activities, is a continuation of this tradition.

Beyond doubt, the tasks of *Pravda*'s editors have been and remain uniquely delicate. Other Soviet publications may imitate and echo *Pravda*, but the paper itself cannot escape primary responsibility for always hitting precisely the right key in the ever-changing orchestration of "Marxist-Leninist doctrine." To fill its six or eight pages daily, the staff relies on a mechanism by which news items and commentaries pass through a series of sieves that make the editorial process as close to truly collective as possible. When it comes to doctrinal purity in editing, collective function spreads responsibility. Thus, for purposes of political self-preservation, *Pravda* writers, at least in theory, welcome the tedious process by which their work passes through numerous hands for scrutiny and revision. This is essential when new policies are instituted or old policies revised. *Pravda* takes the lead in campaigns that range from attacks on U.S. policies in the Near East to drives against drunkenness or the feeding of bread to livestock. In all cases, writers must avoid going beyond officially sanctioned limitations.

Despite the emphasis on collective journalism, *Pravda* has always had prominent chief editors, going back to the Stalin-Molotov days of 1912. Among its better-known editors were Mikhail Suslov, who served on the paper in 1949 and 1950, and Mikhail V. Zimyanin, a veteran Agitprop professional, who was the paper's chief editor for over a decade, from 1965 to 1976. Zimyanin handed the job over to Viktor G. Afanasyev, a man whose background was in education before he became, successively, the editor of two of the most prestigious Soviet periodicals. Afanasyev emerged as a versatile member of the Moscow propaganda establishment; he has given interviews to European and American journalists and participated in a conference on East-West military problems in Edinburgh, Scotland, in September 1983.

Afanasyev was born on November 18, 1922, in Aktanysh, in the Tatar autonomous region. His family background is unknown. Official biographies state that he graduated from the N. G. Chernyshevsky State Pedagogical Institute at Chita in 1950, gained his doctorate in philosophy in 1964, and became a professor in 1965. Afanasyev joined the Communist Party in 1943, while serving in the Soviet army. After the war, he was a teacher at the Chelyabinsk Pedagogical Institute, from 1953 to 1954, and then the institute's deputy director until 1959. He concluded his stay in Chelyabinsk with two years, until 1960, as head of the institute's philosophy department.

These years in the study and teaching of philosophy, certainly based on Marxist ideology and its application, as well as his administrative tasks, prepared Afanasyev for his next position: head of the Chair of Scientific Communism at the Academy of Social Sciences of the Central Committee in Moscow; he stayed on this job from 1960 until about 1968, and spent the next two years as deputy to the editor-in-chief of *Pravda.* The editor at that point was Zimyanin, and Afanasyev served specifically as his deputy for "theoretical questions," which must have included the discussion and solution of editorial-ideological problems.

At the same time, from 1968 on, Afanasyev served on the editorial board of the prestigious periodical *Voprosy Filosofii* (Problems of Philosophy), a journal that often devotes itself to topics concerning the application of Marxist-Leninist concepts to concrete contemporary matters. In 1970, Afanasyev moved up further on the administrative ladder of *Pravda:* For the next four years he served as Zimyanin's first deputy editor. In 1972, he became a corresponding member of the U.S.S.R. Academy of Sciences. His *Pravda* career was interrupted in 1974, when he was appointed chief editor of *Kommunist,* the party's central theoretical journal.

The year Afanasyev replaced Zimyanin as *Pravda's* editor-in-chief, he also became a full member of the party's Central Committee. Zimyanin moved into the Central Committee position of secretary, with special responsibilities in the field of propaganda. Afanasyev has also been active in two international front organizations: In 1976 he became vice president of the International Organization of Journalists, and in 1977 he became the chairman of the U.S.S.R. Committee of the World Congress of Peace-loving Forces and vice president of its International Forum. He has traveled in Europe, Latin America, and the Far East. During the Soviet Communist Party's 25th Congress, in 1976, he served as spokesman to the foreign press.

Afanasyev is one of the professional ideologists and propagandists whose credentials go back to the Stalin-Khrushchev years. He is eight years younger than his predecessor and sometime mentor, Zimyanin. Back in 1976, Afanasyev's appointment as editor of *Kommunist* ran into an unexplained snag; nine months passed before it was confirmed, and analysts abroad interpreted the delay to a disagreement among senior officials. The realignments that have taken place since Brezhnev's death would seem to have removed such obstacles. Afanasyev's performance as *Pravda* editor has clearly been satisfactory to decision-making Central Committee and Politburo members.

Viktor Afanasyev oversees a large staff that includes 22 departments, as well as the *Pravda* press bureau, which prepares material for local papers. In addition to well over 100 full-time correspondents, at home and abroad, the paper uses the services of hundreds of nonstaff contributors. As the central organ in Soviet journalism, *Pravda* publishes a sort of journalistic house organ, *The Worker or Peasant Correspondent,* as well as the periodical for professional journalists, *Zhurnalist;* this periodical is issued jointly with the Union of Journalists of the U.S.S.R.

At the V. I. Lenin Printing House, the *Pravda* plant, a number of other papers and periodicals are printed and issued by the Pravda Publishing House. These include the youth daily *Komsomolskaya Pravda,* with a circulation of close to 10 million, *Sovietskaya Rossiya,* close to 3 million, and magazines devoted to industrial, economic, and cultural affairs, as well as the periodicals *Kommunist* and *Agitator.*

Pravda is tradition-conscious; as part of the Lenin legend, the paper's masthead reproduces daily V. I. Lenin's head in the form of the two Orders of Lenin that were awarded to the paper in 1945 and 1962, as well as the Order of the October Revolution, awarded in 1972. Above the word "Pravda," is the old slogan, "Workers of the World, Unite!" Underneath its name, the paper is identified as the Organ of the Central Committee of the Soviet Communist Party. Each page is 23 × 16½ inches in size (slightly larger than the *New York Times*) and eight columns wide. Special features, such as front-page editorials, are set to a width of two columns and in bold type.

In its own way, *Pravda* is a journal of record in that it carries full texts of party and government documents, complete with all signatures. Typefaces for headlines differ, which provides a certain amount of variety. Photographs are used sparingly, and are rarely larger than two columns in width. In the absence of advertisements, and with relatively few illustrations, a typical issue provides some 40 columns of reading matter. Of this material, the majority consists of longer articles, often between 2,000 and 4,000 words in length. News dispatches, usually taken from Tass, are grouped together. Television programs and other entertainment listings take up about one-third of the last page.

Pravda is printed in 42 cities throughout the U.S.S.R. The pages are transmitted either by facsimile over telecommunication lines or as matrixes that are mailed to individual cities. In the tradition of the propaganda poster, newspaper pages are often on display at public places. True to its original purpose, to quote the Soviet encyclopedia once more, *Pravda* is concerned with "inculcating in Soviet citizens a conscious and creative attitude toward labor and a responsible attitude toward society," while it deals with "every aspect of the present-day world revolutionary process and systematically examines questions relating to the international communist and workers' movement and the national liberation struggle of various peoples."

The Gorbachev drive for greater candor and efficiency put great pressure on *Pravda* as the flagship of Soviet media. The paper actually criticized the major television news program, *Vremya* for stodginess, but found it difficult to disengage from its own wordy, pompous prose. In June 1986, Afanasyev attended the fortieth anniversary of the founding of the International Organization of Journalists in Prague. He gave an interview to the local Communist Party organ, *Rude Pravo* (June 14). He acknowledged that *Pravda* and Soviet papers generally used to avoid criticizing certain "forbidden zones." Among these taboo areas were the Moscow district administration and "the work agencies of the Ministry of Interior." Afanasyev said that such "protected" areas no longer existed, "beginning with the lowest grade, all the way up to a minister or ranking party personnel."

The *Pravda* editor noted that in the past the paper had tried to be critical but that "criticism must really be consistently constructive nowadays. In the past we also tried to write like that, but we often did not succeed in bringing a problem to a conclusion. Those criticized frequently did not even bother to answer." He added that provincial papers were often "still not in step with the central information media." Falling back on standard abstract verbiage, Afanasyev said that they "have not accepted as their own the principles of the concept of the acceleration of our society's development." Sparkling prose, be it in writing or conversation, was still not *Pravda*'s strong point.

CHAPTER · 4

Lenin's Young Pied Piper

Willi Münzenberg was a legend in his lifetime and, to political historians, in the evolution of modern propaganda. He can be credited with inventing and developing the concept of the "front organization," the introduction of outwardly independent newspapers, mass-circulation magazines, motion picture companies, book publishing firms, and a myriad of associations and publications that serve dramatic causes of opportunity. Münzenberg originated interlocking and camouflaged movements that effectively hid their Moscow backing. Like an elusive financial empire that piles corporations on corporations and shifts funds across borders and oceans, his enterprises often appeared and disappeared before they could be tracked down and identified.

In another time and place, Willi Münzenberg might have become a highly successful entrepreneur in publishing and the entertainment industry. A psychobiographer might find ample material in Willi's early life to explain his aversion to the social and economic establishment in which he grew up. He was born on August 14, 1889, in the German town of Erfurt and lived in a village nearby. His mother died when he was five years old. His father, a moody and restless man, ran a village inn. Willi did the odd jobs and picked up a good deal of the talk and attitude among men who frequented the place. He half-admired and half-loathed his father, whose only diversion was hunting. The man drank heavily. At times he beat or threatened the boy. When he was 11 years old, Willi ran away from home, "to become a soldier" and join the Boers during the Boer War in South Africa. His father, for once, smiled approvingly when the spunky kid was returned by the police. About two years later, in another drunken state, the father tried to clean one of his guns and shot himself fatally. Thus, at the age of thirteen, Willi Münzenberg was an orphan and moved in with an older sister. A year later he went to work for a barber in the town of Gotha, to serve as an apprentice.

This was the beginning of Willi's social rebellion. To be an apprentice in fields such as the hotel and restaurant trade, in bakeries, and in barbershops meant unlimited service; there were no days off. His apprenticeship ended when, in a fight with a fellow employee, Willi suffered a concussion. He accompanied his sister to Erfurt, where he found a job as an unskilled assistant in a shoe factory. As he recalled later, like other youngsters, he thought of little but food and card playing.

But young Willi was intellectually restless. One of the older workers, a veteran Social Democrat, suggested he join a group—fatefully named "Education Group Propaganda"—that met regularly above a restaurant. The moving spirit within this discussion group was a toolmaker, Georg Schumann. The new company stimulated young Münzenberg's wide-ranging curiosity. He quickly familiarized himself with a cross-section of reference works, novels, poetry, and, of course, socialist literature. Babette Gross wrote in *Willi Münzenberg,* biography of her long-time friend: "It undoubtedly reflects one of Münzenberg's decisive characteristics that he was not satisfied to sit, by himself, at this richly-endowed table. Others had to share it with him." The propagandist-educator was born, and with him the promoter and organizer. Before long, Willi ran the little group, multiplied its membership, and established contact with like-minded organizations.

It is well to keep in mind that the Communist International (Comintern, or Third International) grew out of the affiliation of the various pre-World War I Socialist parties that formed the so-called Second International. In Germany, the Social Democratic Party—which was recreated after the collapse of the Hitler regime in 1945—today enjoys worldwide recognition, largely because of two prominent leaders, former Chancellors Willi Brandt and Helmut Schmidt. The German Social Democrats were instrumental, during the second half of the nineteenth century, in advancing social legislation that laid the groundwork for unemployment compensation, social security legislation, and health insurance in many of the world's countries.

Prior to World War I, the Social Democrats represented a wide spectrum of political temperament, ranging from relative conservative and nationalistic elements to radical, antimilitarist and near-anarchistic factions. The young socialists, to whom Münzenberg originally belonged, were generally viewed by their more conservative elders as noisy, irresponsible upstarts. In September 1908, Münzenberg traveled to Berlin to participate in a youth congress. Back in Erfurt he took part in a meeting on election law reform, where he advocated the vote for 20-year-olds. He was then 17. Willi became too revolutionary for his employers when he circulated a manifesto supporting a general strike in Sweden. He was fired and, at a time of much unemployment, could not find another job in Erfurt.

For a short time, Willi Münzenberg became a hobo. He made his way from town to town, from village to village, always in search of a way to earn a little money. The adventure was brief and a failure. Hungry and ill, he returned to Erfurt, where he worked for the Social Democrats for a few months. But in the early summer of 1910 he was on the road once more, this time all the way to Switzerland. In Zurich he was welcomed by the local socialist youth group, but could not find a job. Eventually, in Berne, he was hired to serve at a bar; childhood skills came in handy. His new Zurich friends soon wrote that they had found him a job at a pharmacy. With some reluctance—he had been dreaming of emigrating to the United States!—Willi returned to Zurich. The city was then a center of international revolutionary activity, a clearinghouse for agitation and propaganda which, in several other countries, was illegal.

The same skill and drive that had propelled Willi in his first "Propaganda" group made him a powerhouse in Zurich. He quickly reorganized and enlarged the socialist youth organization, became its paid secretary, and, quite soon, secretary of the socialist Youth International. When war broke out, in 1914, the Second International experienced a severe shock: Instead of holding on to international solidarity and antimilitarism, the various Socialist parties reverted to strictly national sentiments and supported the war effort of their countries. From Switzerland, Babette Gross wrote: "The new international youth secretariat immediately began its hectic activity. . . . The socialist youth movements in the warring countries, which stood in opposition to their parties' leadership, were bombarded with a mass of material, with manifestos, leaflets, periodicals, particularly the *Youth International,* which had its first issue, dated September 1915. There was hardly a means it did not use in order to smuggle this illegal material into Germany, France or Italy. It was hidden in marmalade containers, cigar boxes and food packages. In addition, a busy courier service maintained effective liaison."

In Zurich, during this period, Münzenberg met men who later became prominent in the leadership of the Soviet state. One of them was Leon Trotsky, whom he met in Berne in the spring of 1915. Trotsky impressed him with his forceful, somewhat condescending manner. By contrast, Polish-born journalist Karl Radek, who had been active in Germany until the war, showed himself as witty and engaging. And then, of course, there was Vladimir I. Lenin himself! He made no secret of his contempt for the leadership of the Second International, but could be stubborn as well as diplomatic, firm but cordial.

As head of the newly created Youth International, and thus a prominent and promising member of the young generation, Willi saw Lenin and his wife fairly frequently. They had a small apartment in the Spiegelgasse, next to a sausage factory. The three of them ate in the kitchen. Gross wrote: "Lenin examined the temperamental go-getter with unfailing patience and tried to turn the emotional young rebel into a consciously-acting Marxist revolutionary. No doubt, Lenin put his best foot forward in dealing with Münzenberg and the young socialists, whom he tried to win over to his side. But even those who were captured by his magic did not miss the fact that, behind his quiet Socratic manner there lay something else: a ruthless, ice-cold manipulator of men." Lenin was giving Münzenberg a lesson in one-on-one propaganda, as he practiced quiet persuasion across the kitchen table.

On September 5, 1915, a group of antiwar socialists from several European countries met at Zimmerwald, not far from Berne, the Swiss capital. Most of them attended on their own, because the major Socialist parties supported their countries' war efforts, and antiwar activities were often regarded as treason.

The Zimmerwald meeting resolved that the war would not "liberate oppressed nations and serve democracy" and that "the real struggle for freedom" was the fight "for socialism." Lenin had demanded a more aggressive wording, which would have called for "civil war, not civil peace," but the majority of delegates voted against him. Only a small group, the "Zimmerwald Left," supported him and his call for the establishment of a new, separate Third International. Münzenberg, together with other members of the youth organization, supported Lenin's group. They met weekly, camouflaged as a bowling society—bowling balls at the ready, for use whenever the police might show up. Lenin participated in several of these meetings.

Münzenberg participated in a follow-up meeting at Kienthal, on April 24, 1916, where Lenin gained a few more supporters and raged against the "pacifist illusion." David Shub, in his biography *Lenin*, wrote: "Isolated from events in Russia, deserted by many of his early followers, struggling to pay his modest living expenses, Lenin at the end of 1916 was hitting the bottom rung of his ladder. Never did his words seem to attract fewer followers. Many looked on him as a crackpot." Willi Münzenberg was one of the few who stuck by Lenin, and who could deliver the relatively strong support of the Youth International.

Everything changed when, in March 1917, revolution broke out in Russia and Czar Nicholas II resigned. Lenin, still in Zurich, quickly realized that he had to rush home, or events would get away from him. This led to one of the oddest and most controversial events of twentieth-century history: Lenin's transport, by train, on April 9, 1917, through Germany, while that country was still at war with Russia. Clearly, the Germans assumed that Lenin would play a significant part in Russia's further dis-

solution and either contribute to German victory or help end the war in
the East, freeing Germany to throw its total military weight against the
Western powers.

Münzenberg remained in Switzerland, but as a German national, after
all, he was accused of being a spy there. The Swiss had banned his magazine, *Youth International,* but he was able to issue another pro-Bolshevik
publication, using the pen name "E. Arnold." As Lenin maneuvered his
way to power in Russia, crushing opposition and rival revolutionaries alike,
he clearly expected Germany to follow the Russian example and become
the next Soviet state. Münzenberg echoed Lenin's hard-hitting revolutionary rhetoric, alienating Swiss public opinion. Following public unrest, the
authorities decided to intern the foreign agitator. On the eve of his scheduled imprisonment, Willi's friends gathered at a Zurich restaurant, Ris-
torante Cooperativa, where they celebrated his forthcoming internment
with roast goose and Italian wines. Once in the prison at Witzwil, young
Münzenberg apparently charmed his warden, and when he was transferred
to interrogation facilities at the regional prison in Meilen, on Lake Zurich,
he had a cell overlooking the lake. The state attorney, Brunner, summoned
Willi every afternoon, by boat across the lake. The interviews, in a cordial
atmosphere, were often accompanied by coffee and cake. Brunner made
the following appraisal of Münzenberg:

"What lifts him above the mass of like-minded people, are his many-
fold, including literary, gifts; constant efforts to fill the gaps in his education, and to help others at the same time; an unrestrained urge to activity;
tremendous work capacity; and a drive, powering his ruthless and shrewd
pursuit of his goals, that one might not assume to find in someone who
remains as soft and youthful in appearance as he does. In addition, he
commands a great, popular power as a speaker, the skill of gauging the
mood of his audience, cordiality in social contact, and, above all, a rare
talent for organization and agitation. One also needs to acknowledge the
selfless nature of his actions in the interest of the youth movement, as he
conceives it. Typical for Münzenberg is the mixture of a gifted youth
educator, a convinced fighter for the improvement of young workers' conditions, and of a revolutionary who feels that he is destined to greater
deeds."

The state attorney concluded that Willi and his cohorts bore a moral
responsibility for the unrest that had occurred in August 1917, but he
counseled against charges that might not be provable. The case against
Münzenberg was dropped on December 28, 1918. Shortly afterward the
German Republic was established, the Kaiser fled to Holland, and it looked
as if Lenin's prophecy for Germany would come true. The Swiss did not
want to harbour any more German revolutionaries and decided to expel
young Willi. Two gendarmes took him to the border. He wrote later that

he ran across the frontier on November 10, 1918: "Suddenly, I found myself, up to my neck, in a water-filled ditch. With great difficulty, I managed to scramble out of it. All of a sudden, I faced a German soldier, gun at the ready, who yelled at me: 'Stay where you are. You are under arrest!' I was back in Germany!" Willi Münzenberg had left his homeland as a restless youngster; he returned as an Agitprop professional.

CHAPTER · 5

Münzenberg's Magic Touch

After the Bolshevik Revolution, Münzenberg's fate was uneven. When two young Scandinavian socialists visited Lenin in Moscow in November 1918, Lenin's first questions concerned Münzenberg. Was he still in a Swiss jail, the new Russian leader wanted to know, or had he managed to go to Germany and help prepare for revolution there? Willi had, indeed, begun work in Germany, and at a fever pitch: writing, organizing, holding meetings, traveling, making speeches. Twice he was felled by illness and overwork. Together with others, he was imprisoned for five months, charged with seeking to overthrow the government; but the charges were dropped. The Communist Party, bringing together an assortment of opposition socialists, established itself as *Kommunistische Partei Deutschlands* (KPD), but remained illegal for some time.

For five years Münzenberg followed party lines, but in June 1921, the Third Comintern Congress moved the headquarters of Youth International from Berlin to Moscow, and Münzenberg was replaced by a Russian. He found himself on the sidelines, moping in a Moscow hotel room. Babette Gross recalled that, after dealing with the Bolsheviks, he had come to know their methods well enough, but in his heart of hearts he regarded the whole affair as "treason and human failure among friends." He developed a "nervous stomach," which remained chronic for the rest of his life; Russian food did not agree with him, and he began to loath the ever-present caviar.

Frustrated and restless, Willi kept nagging for something to do. But the Comintern bureaucrats had little use for someone as aggressive and independent-minded as young Münzenberg. Finally, Lenin rescued him.

He well understood Willi's special gifts, and he was also keenly aware of a major task; the alleviation of Russia's serious food shortage and general economic chaos. To help stem the famine, the Soviet leaders had, with reluctant gratitude, accepted the aid of the American Relief Administration, directed by future U.S. President Herbert Hoover. Various smaller aid organizations, some of them prompted by ideological sympathy for the "Soviet experiment," had also sprung up. Lenin summoned Münzenberg and offered him the task of pulling together these and other organizations.

Willi accepted with alacrity. The umbrella organization that was thus born eventually became known by its German initials, IAH (*Internationale Arbeiter-Hilfe*, or International Workers' Aid); it evolved into the model for all later front organizations, and was itself often used as a cover for a variety of Agitprop and espionage activities. Münzenberg's success with Workers' Aid caused a good deal of envy among the leadership of the German Communist Party and within the Comintern bureaucracy. Lenin's backing gave Münzenberg a relatively free hand; still, the power struggle within the Kremlin, well under way even while Lenin was still alive (he suffered his first stroke in 1922), indirectly affected all Münzenberg was able to do.

For the time being, however, he moved from success to success. His Workers' Aid was able to mobilize people and money among humanitarians of varied political hues. It was a gigantic fund-raising operation that utilized many of the methods that have, since then, become widely accepted. Münzenberg pioneered the use of prominent personalities, artists, and writers in mass meetings and appeals. Particularly impressive was a poster based on a moving drawing by Käthe Kollwitz, whose work continues to be acclaimed, showing a wide-eyed, starving child reaching for a huge, empty bowl, captioned simply, "Hunger."

With illustrated leaflets and appeals directed at such varied professional groups as musicians and automobile workers, and above all with still photographs and motion pictures, Workers' Aid blanketed the world. From the United States, in one operation alone, labor leader Sidney Hillman forwarded a contribution of $250,000. Within the Soviet state, food was being distributed in accordance with strict politico-economic criteria. Workers' Aid itself sponsored factories, fishing operations, food distribution, and means of transportation. Waste and favoritism were in evidence, but were ignored and overshadowed by the emotion-laden rhetoric of Münzenberg's antifamine propaganda. Feeding starving children was the perfect theme, and it helped to further the image of the Soviet state as a nation that not only was in need of humanitarian aid but was itself humanitarian in theory and practice. And who could resist, on so-called "Flower Days," when children roamed the streets in North European cities, selling flowers in return for gifts to Workers' Aid?

One by-product of this campaign was the publication of a weekly il-lustrated magazine, largely devoted to Soviet photographs, that eventually had the name *Arbeiter Illustrierte Zeitung* (AIZ), equivalent to "Workers' Illustrated." Photos and texts naturally dramatized and glamourized Soviet achievements, alternating at first with heartrending pictures of famine-stricken children and of aides providing food, clothing, and medical care. Crass emotionalism was the mood of the day, in any event, following the horrors of World War I, and the cliché-ridden one-sidedness of this new mass magazine was generally taken for granted. The weekly eventually achieved a circulation of 420,000.

The Russian famine had, in fact, been caused by a variety of factors, ranging from wartime dislocations and interruptions of food supplies to ravages caused by the Bolshevik Revolution, White Russian attempts to crush it, and the chaos caused by reorganization of the country's agriculture and distribution system, in accordance with doctrinaire socialist concepts. Suffering was, however, all too real. Statistics were unreliable or non-existent; the number of dead from starvation was eventually given as 2 million, but this could have been no more than a top-level guess. Mün-zenberg apparently had the greatest difficulties in obtaining reliable infor-mation from his Russian counterparts, and he seems to have been at odds with the Moscow headquarters of International Workers' Aid a good deal of the time. Corruption, mismanagement, and nonaccountability lay hidden behind the tall waves of the antifamine propaganda campaign.

Mr. Hoover's American Relief Administration provided the equivalent of $63 million in food, clothing, and medications, of which $20 million had been voted by the U.S. Congress. Various charitable organizations con-tributed another $10 million in aid. By comparison, the $5 million provided by the Münzenberg operation was small; but his Workers' Aid did, so to speak, jump from a standing position, while Hoover's operation was able to function on the basis of extensive wartime experience. Soviet propa-ganda tended to downgrade aid provided by "the bourgeoisie" and to dramatize aid of "the international proletariat." Propaganda benefits de-rived from the Workers' Aid campaigns were incalculable.

By 1922, adjuncts to Workers' Aid began to take commercial shape. Münzenberg founded a corporation in Berlin, the Construction, Industry & Commerce Corp., which began activity by acting as a Russian agent for German film producers. In August of that year, he established another company, designed to market Soviet bonds, at an interest rate of 5 percent, repayable on January 1, 1933. The Soviet bond drive was mainly directed at labor unions, pension funds, workers' health insurance companies, and individual employees. The bonds were actually honored, a decade later, by a Soviet office in Berlin that functioned well into the Hitler period and had extraterritorial status.

Workers' Aid was able to function where the Comintern was under suspicion, and where Communist parties were therefore suspect or illegal. In the United States, Attorney General A. Mitchell Palmer personified the country's concern about the legal as well as the illegal activities of various groups. Anarchists who, even before the Bolshevik Revolution, had become a center of public concern, were once again in the limelight after the war. The Comintern's aggressive optimism, which pictured a world revolution practically around the corner, prompted it to send agents abroad who financed and directed propaganda aimed at the overthrow of "bourgeois" governments. In the United States, the Bureau of Investigation (later, the Federal Bureau of Investigation) sought to keep these various groups and personalities under surveillance.

But the center of the Comintern's attention then was still Germany. Münzenberg's widening operations had the behind-the-scenes cooperation of the Soviet ambassador, Nikolai N. Krestinsky, although the Soviet Commissariat of Foreign Affairs tried to maintain the fiction that it had no contact with, and certainly no control over, the machinations of the Comintern, then the special province of Gregori E. Zinoviev. A decisive development was the Treaty of Rapallo, which Russia and Germany signed in April 1922. According to Gross, "This was the wave that helped Münzenberg to swim forward," and "through his ability as organizer, his talent as a propagandist, he advanced the Soviet cause among middle-class Germans."

According to a pamphlet prepared by the German labor union federation, published in 1925 and apparently based on authentic data, Münzenberg explained his principles to a preparatory committee for a comprehensive international conference in Berlin. He said that he expected representatives of Fridtjof Nansen's international refugee organizations, of the Quakers, and of various national Red Cross chapters to participate. He also expected some 80 representatives of industry, engineers, entrepreneurs, scientists, artists, writers, journalists, "people associated with the club 'Friends of the New Russia,' as well as delegates from various unions, and two representatives of the Italian Socialist Party who previously had spoken out against Soviet Russia." According to this source, Münzenberg added, candidly:

"As you can see, we will have a colorful mixture at our little get-together. Only previously approved speakers are to be permitted to address the meeting, and all political debates should be avoided. The whole thing should wind up with a resolution that expresses willingness to participate in Russia's reconstruction. Businessmen should return from the conference, ready to provide agitation and propaganda for Soviet Russia. And we must do everything possible to complete the conference within one day, or it is likely to blow up."

The meeting took place according to plan, and Münzenberg is supposed to have said, afterward, that future activity should include the establishment of "political propaganda, parliamentary intervention, the attraction of bourgeois circles, formation of many committees, child welfare, a motion picture division, and commercial enterprises. . . ." Apparently referring to the so-called "Palmer raids" in the United States, he said, "Recent events in America illustrate that we are subject to police action, and so we must defend ourselves as skillfully as possible against the charge of being a purely Communist organization." He added: "We must gather outside names, and associate with other groups, in order to hamper persecution." He advocated the establishment of "Clubs of Innocents," to enlist academicians, artists, and others, "and to say to everyone that Russia will give up everything, is ready to humble itself, will do all that is imaginable, just so world peace is maintained."

The use of the Workers' Aid organization as camouflage and refuge for the Communist movement had thus been well prepared, and just in time, too. The year 1923 tested the young German Republic severely. In addition to inflation of gigantic proportions, the country was wracked by a series of severe outbreaks of violence, of which quite a few could be traced directly to the Comintern's machinations. As a result, on November 23 the Communist Party and all its subsidiary organizations were banned. But not the International Workers' Aid!

In fact, the IWA arranged an international congress in Berlin on December 1. It now practiced "aid in reverse," a shrewd piece of propagandistic prestidigitation: It set up food centers for the unemployed in 246 towns; there were 58 centers in Berlin itself. Earlier, the organization had shipped Ukrainian wheat into North German harbors. Communists and Social Democrats served as soup kitchen volunteers. For the time being, Münzenberg said, the "revolutionary period" in Germany had come to an end, although some Communist leaders hankered for a Soviet Germany and even ridiculed the Workers' Aid operation as Münzenberg's "Red Salvation Army."

By far the toughest analysis of the Münzenberg operation came from an Austrian socialist leader, Friedrich Adler, who had been an early firsthand observer of the IWA. On May 6, 1924, he circulated a memorandum from the London Secretariat of the Second International, which cited the organization's executive session in Luxembourg as having revealed Workers' Aid as "a Communist institution, disguised as a 'united front' and designed to function politically for the Communists." The IWA, it stated, served as Moscow's "diplomatic instrument" and practiced calculated confusion; Workers' Aid "collects funds under the guise of welfare activities, enlists unsuspecting help, particularly among the bourgeoisie," in order to advance Moscow's plans for world revolution. The memorandum disclosed that the agency's 5 executive members and 21 members of its board were all Communists, and that the whole organization "has been founded specifically to service Communist Party aims." Individual Socialist and Labor parties differed in their view of Workers' Aid.

As it happened, the organization was able to gain influence, largely because Münzenberg skillfully juggled its links to the Soviet Communist Party, the Comintern, and the Soviet labor union, while keeping a safe distance from the often explosive controversies within the German Communist Party. The fight for Lenin's succession, which had begun before his death on January 21, 1924, complicated every aspect of the worldwide Communist movement. Gross wrote that Münzenberg returned from Lenin's funeral and a Comintern meeting "depressed and downhearted." Joseph Stalin, Leon Trotsky, Gregori Zinoviev, and Leon Kamenev were at the center of the historic stage in the Kremlin. Stalin was playing the others off against each other, and would eventually eliminate them all.

There has been a tendency, on the part of Münzenberg's friends and biographers, to view him as a victim of Kremlin betrayal. Still, during the years that followed Lenin's death, Willi Münzenberg was part of a decoy operation that drew attention away from the suffering that Lenin and Lenin's heirs were inflicting on the people living in the Union of Soviet Socialist Republics. Münzenberg was participant, as well as victim; he was eminently successful in drawing attention away from the essence of Soviet society. One by one, his own old friends were being eliminated, demoted, exiled, killed; for the time being, Willi Münzenberg was spared, and he prospered.

In Berlin, a sharp-tongued town, they even called him "the Red Millionaire." That was wrong, of course. He did not own millions, but he did collect, administer, invest, disburse, and control millions in the world's major currencies. And while he remained a simple fellow in his tastes and pleasures, he blithely ignored his fellow Communists' ostentatiously "proletarian" life style. Münzenberg had no fixed office hours, and he clearly enjoyed Berlin's lively tempo, its theaters, movie houses, and pleasant surrounding countryside.

Münzenberg's central office was located in a well-worn mansion, on the city's main boulevard, the tree-lined Unter den Linden. The premises had earlier been used by the Russian embassy, but Moscow had managed to repossess the old czarist embassy, and Willi's crowd inherited one floor of sprawling, crowded offices. No matter how reluctant the German Communists were to endorse Willi's way of doing things, the IWA offices were a favorite stopover point for a colorful succession of visiting Comintern emissaries and other more or less secretive agents.

Like most official Communist organs, the Berlin *Rote Fahne* (Red Flag) was both predictable and boring. In any event, Münzenberg felt that he needed a paper that could speak in less doctrinaire terms to a wide audience. It happened that a noisy, left-leaning evening paper, *Welt am Abend* (Evening World) had fallen on lean days. By 1926, its circulation was a mere 5,000, and the owners were looking for someone to take the money-losing property off their hands. After some political and financial maneuvering, Münzenberg bought the paper and quickly brought his promotional talents to bear. He used the distribution machinery that already existed for the illustrated weekly, but soon developed a network that fitted the capital city of 4 million worldly wise inhabitants and the needs of a daily schedule.

The Communist Party, at that time, was going through one of its low-keyed phases. This permitted Münzenberg to mix Communists and non-Communists among the staff of editors and reporters. The paper downplayed party politics and gave plenty of space to scandal and entertainment. It successfully maintained itself against its long-established conservative rival, *Nachtausgabe* (Night Edition), published by the monarchist Hugenberg publishing house. Although the party insisted that the paper's chief editor be a trusted member, this did not at first hamper its appeal. When Moscow introduced a policy that called for continuous attacks on the Social Democrats as "social fascists," editors felt that the growing Nazi menace was a much weightier threat. At times, this came down to what front-page headline to pick, and Münzenberg was then called upon to make the final, risky decision.

Willi's touch could be found in some of the promotional events that *Welt am Abend* sponsored and that made the paper a popular element on the lively Berlin scene. It arranged matinee performances at variety theaters, some spiced with sharp political humor, but much of it sheer entertainment. It sponsored huge public dances in the outdoor Luna Park. And when the Workers' Aid arranged its annual "International Solidarity Day" on each June 14, beginning in 1929, huge crowds, with marching bands and banners, crowded suburban beer gardens. The Depression had come, but Berliners still liked a good time, regardless of political coloration.

With the evening paper booming, the Communist Party and the *Welt am Abend* managers decided to branch out and publish a morning paper. This would be in direct competition to the faltering party organ, *Rote Fahne*. Early in 1931, *Berlin am Morgen* (Berlin at Dawn) was launched. Despite the Depression, the paper broke even within 18 months. The editorial formula was eminently journalistic: inside stories, exposés, scandal in high places; it was meaty stuff, and the sauce was an easy pink, rather than a bright red. Not everything the publishing firm touched was a success. It tried its hand at a satiric journal, with many cartoons. But there the hand of politics proved too heavy. Published under the name *Eulenspiegel* (literally, Owl's Mirror), it continues to be published in East

Germany today, and is a poor imitation of Moscow's widely read *Krokodil*.

Münzenberg had bought a book publishing firm, Der Neue Deutsche Verlag, which had at first limited itself to publishing party-line literature for a mass audience. But it also issued a special-audience periodical, *Der Arbeiterphotograph* (Worker's Photography), organ of a society of amateur photographers. In a way, it was a companion to the highly professional illustrated weekly, and could thus be run as an inexpensive sideline. Another successful project, launched amid the Depression, was an illustrated magazine for women, *Weg der Frau* (Woman's Way), which reached a circulation of 100,000 and buried its political line amidst fashion, recipes, sport, and child care.

As just about everything was being politicized, from sports groups to architecture, it was no surprise that the Münzenberg firm entered the cigarette business. Manufacturers had begun using pictures of prominent sports figures and film stars as promotion items in their cigarette packages. The Nazi Party was pushing a cigarette called "The Drummer," with photos of party leaders. The Münzenberg publishing firm collaborated with a cigarette manufacturer who put out a brand called "Solidarity," featuring pictures of prominent workers and unionists. The company issued cigarettes under the names "Red Mixture" and "Collective."

Next, movies! The emotional impact of photographs, and their propagandistic and commercial potential, had been dramatized by the success of Münzenberg's illustrated weekly. The even greater strength of the motion picture was all too clear. Workers' Aid had acted as the licensee for German film exports to Russia as far back as 1922. Now that sound had been added to motion pictures, it seemed to Willi Münzenberg that Communist propaganda was limping behind other social forces. He wanted the Russians to produce films that could make their way in the world market and carry their political message at the same time.

Münzenberg was apparently instrumental in the establishment of a joint film production studio in Moscow, Meshrabpom-Russ, designed to provide a steady output of entertainment and propaganda. Babette Gross wrote that the history of this enterprise showed "to what degree the Soviet regime strengthened its control, so that any avant garde artist collectives were eventually disbanded." One success was *Mother,* based on a novel by Maxim Gorki; another, *The End of St. Petersburg,* celebrated the tenth anniversary of the Bolshevik Revolution; and *Thunder over Asia* was a political attack on colonialism.

It is not entirely clear how strong Münzenberg's role in furthering Soviet motion-picture production was. Clearly, he encouraged its more subtle propagandistic aspects and he provided marketing skills and facilities. The Russians had both a reservoir of acting and directing talent, not to mention a tradition in drama and fiction that could feed directly into film production.

Münzenberg was instrumental in creating a joint German-Russian production unit, and he absorbed a film distribution firm, Prometheus, that had belonged to the Communist Party and had been used to produce a propaganda film, *Nameless Heroes*. Prometheus had not been a financial success, but struck it rich with Sergei Eisenstein's much-discussed classic, *Battleship Potemkin,* which depicted a sailors' mutiny in striking cinematic terms. It is a film which continues to be shown in universities as part of the study of communications (together, ironically, with Leni Riefenstahl's Nazi propaganda film, *Triumph of Will*).

Münzenberg had great difficulties getting the Potemkin film past German censorship, as it could be interpreted as advocating revolution. The film was screened before successive boards, approved, censored, banned, and reapproved. Eventually, it became both a critical and popular success. Much of the film's success had to do with the way it was captioned and edited for the German viewing audience, but Eisenstein's talent for creating the visually striking was clearly decisive; like many others, his career was truncated during the Stalin years.

Münzenberg, of course, used the Potemkin controversy to organize protest meetings that were attended by the *crème de la crème* of the Berlin art and entertainment society, which was only too ready to join in this particular "united front" expression of cultural freedom. Although Prometheus was highly active in those years, it kept running out of money, and the other Münzenberg enterprises had to pick up the tab. The Russians took a dim view of having funds, which were due them from Soviet-produced films, diverted into German productions, but on the whole, the motion-picture branch of this propaganda network was least subject to the whims and strictures of Moscow.

While Soviet propaganda drives are often designed to show the Soviet Union in a favorable light, one standard Agitprop tactic has always been to draw attention away from the U.S.S.R. and to spotlight, and possibly exacerbate, problems elsewhere. Since World War II, Soviet propaganda has been mainly directed against the United States. But before the Second World War, a major target was Great Britain, which the Kremlin leaders perceived as their main antagonist.

Comintern efforts to introduce a powerful revolutionary movement had been unsuccessful in Britain, although Russia was able to attract influential leftwingers within the Labour Party and a segment of Britain's cultural elite. Soviet efforts to prolong the British general strike of 1924, by providing funds and aiding agitation, had failed. The electoral success of the Conservative Party was, in part, ensured by the publication of a possibly forged letter, allegedly written by Zinoviev on September 15, 1924, urging the British Communist Party to prepare for revolution and establish military "cells." Concluding that it was tactically unwise to direct agitation

and propaganda at British home targets, the Comintern decided to concentrate on the much more vulnerable periphery, the outlying territories
of the British Empire.

Colonialism and its excesses had, of course, been under attack from
many quarters. For idealistic-humanitarian reasons, substantial anticolonial
sentiments existed even within the countries that controlled overseas possessions, including not only Britain but notably France and the Netherlands. In the colonies, leaders of prominence had arisen whose eloquence
and popular appeal had given them worldwide prestige. Münzenberg had
used humanitarian appeals in earlier propaganda drives, and the project
of a super-congress on the theme of anticolonialism seemed like a natural
extension of previous campaigns. At Comintern headquarters, the ideological question was: Are these anticolonial leaders our socialist allies, or
are they mere "bourgeois nationalists"? To Münzenberg, this was a secondary consideration; the main point of an anticolonialist appeal, as im-
perceptibly backed by the Communists as possible—while benefiting the
Soviet Union indirectly—was to weaken the colonial powers, in particular
Great Britain.

Comintern guidelines had emphasized, all along, that the time had come
to mobilize "sympathetic mass organizations" geared toward a "peace
movement, directed against war" and "against the colonial atrocities and
oppression of the nations of the Orient." The guidelines called for a veritable "solar system of organizations and smaller committees circling around
the Communist Party and responding to the party's actual influence (although not its mechanical leadership)." The image of the Communist Party
as a sun, with front organizations circling it like planets and stars, provided
an astronomically romantic, but nevertheless quite accurate, and certainly
vivid, metaphor.

Münzenberg revived a moribund League Against Imperialism. He fa-
vored the organization of a conference on colonies in an article in *Inprekorr
(Internationale Pressekorrespondenz)*, a Comintern publication, published
August 5, 1926. The Second International, together with like-minded socialist labor union leaders, had to agree to an anticolonial drive in principle.
When Münzenberg suggested Brussels as a site for a conference, he was
told that such a meeting had to avoid criticism of conditions in the Belgian
Congo; he accepted, and the government provided conference facilities in
the medieval Palais Egmont.

The next hurdle were the vested interests within the Comintern, where
Münzenberg found resistance to the participation of "bourgeois nationalists." But when it turned out that the fiery Jawaharlal Nehru and his
distinguished-lawyer father, Motilal Nehru, leader of India's Congress Party,
were willing to attend the conference, internal Comintern opposition faded.
Henri Barbusse, the French writer, was named to act as president of the

conference. For years, Barbusse served as a malleable and prestigious front man to conferences, manifestos, and appeals initiated by Münzenberg. As a distinguished man of letters, winner of the Prix Goncourt in 1917 for his brutally realistic antiwar work, *Le Feu,* Barbusse was an ever-useful part of Münzenberg's stable of reliable collaborators. In outward appearance, too, Barbusse conveyed an air of dignity and responsibility. Born in 1874, he died in 1935 and never witnessed the ultimate degree of Stalin's purges. As a member of the French Communist Party he was subject to its discipline, but the party needed him more than he needed it, and any disagreements were usually well-hidden from the outside world.

It would be an exaggeration to say that the evolution of an Afro-Asian bloc in the United Nations, often voting in coalition with the Communist-governed countries, is an extension of the Brussels Congress that Willi Münzenberg masterminded. But it is certainly true that among the 174 delegates from 37 countries were several who later emerged as leaders of strong nationalist and anticolonial movements. They and their successors came to power following World War II, and the term "American imperialism" retained some of the connotations of Communist-anticolonialist solidarity that were dramatized at Brussels. There were 104 representatives from colonies at the congress, or at least from countries that could be labeled as suffering from "imperialist oppression." It provided a rare opportunity for representatives from China, India, and Indonesia and from Africa and Latin America to meet and gain strength from mutual support.

A newly powerful League Against Imperialism emerged from Brussels, and the Comintern could conclude that its money had been well spent. In fact, Münzenberg was able to return a wad of leftover dollars to Ossip Piatnitzki, the Comintern paymaster, who remarked dryly that the project had turned out to be cheaper than he had anticipated. The anticolonial drive was a long-range investment for the Kremlin. The League Against Imperialism illustrated how a propaganda theme and campaign can help to give impetus to political and military activities, and that it can function to support significant elements in shifting world power. Beyond doubt, the colonial era was coming to an end. Germany had lost its colonies as a result of the First World War, and the process of decolonization was hastened by such aspects of World War II as Japan's ouster of British, Dutch, and French influence in southern Asia. Within the British Labour Party, anticolonialism had become an established credo. Consequently, the Brussels conference, and all that followed it—innumerable meetings, publications, manifestos—caught and deepened an emerging and ultimately prevailing mood.

If anything is needed to illustrate historic links, it is the appearance of General Augusto Sandino from Nicaragua at the Second Congress of the League Against Imperialism in Frankfurt, Germany, on July 21, 1929.

Sandino, after whom the governing Sandinista movement was named in the 1980s, brought a blood-stained flag to the congress. The United States had intervened in Nicaragua's civil war. In 1933, a newly elected government signed a peace agreement with Sandino. A year later, upon leaving the presidential palace in Managua, Gen. Sandino was assassinated, quite possibly on orders of the war minister, Gen. Anastasio Somoza, whose family governed Nicaragua ruthlessly and like a private fief—until a revolution overthrew the Somozas, and the anti-Somoza coalition was absorbed in Leninist fashion by the pro-Moscow Sandinistas.

The Frankfurt Congress revealed a sharpening of the Comintern's policy, which once again included attacks on Socialist parties as "social fascists" and a sharp attack on the British Labour Party's policies in India. The Soviet delegation was clearly in command at Frankfurt. The Brussels ambiance of conciliatory camaraderie was absent. British delegates had by then withdrawn from participation, except James Maxton, who functioned as the league's secretary. Münzenberg could not have been happy with the new trend, and the damage was not repaired until 1935, when Moscow, finally alarmed by Hitler's ambitions, returned to the tried-and-true "united front" formula. Meanwhile, in 1931, a plenary meeting of the League Against Imperialism, held in Germany, went so far as to denounce Nehru as "a traitor in the matter of liberation of the Indian people from the British imperialist yoke." This was Stalinist language, uttered by men who used extremist talk to ensure that they, themselves, would not be denounced as some kind of counterrevolutionaries. Still, while Europe's Communist movement was in ferment and the theme of collaboration was discredited, economic depression in the United States opened the doors to what one-time Tass editor Eugene Lyons called the *Red Decade*. He recorded this impact in a book, titled after the phrase, that became a classic for the period.

Münzenberg found himself more and more in a position of seeking to defend, with committees and statements, Stalin's excesses. These included not only his successive attacks and trials of former Old Bolsheviks and their alleged followers in the Soviet Communist Party and the Soviet army but also the disastrous results of forced collectivization. The various front organizations and their publications were forced to echo the theme of an alleged war danger to the U.S.S.R. A series of groups categorized as "Friends of Soviet Russia" was mobilized, a periodical with the title *The Threatening War* was produced, and a conference on this theme was organized in the German city of Essen in 1930. The "imperialists" who were said to be plotting an attack on the Soviet Union were presumably spearheaded by Great Britain and France, but the charge remained vague. In retrospect, much of this policy, in diplomacy and propaganda, may be attributed to Stalin's mounting paranoia, which internally sought to crush

all possible real or imaginary antagonists and externally felt itself threatened by encirclement by powers that were determined to crush his regime.

In 1931, Münzenberg celebrated the tenth anniversary of Workers' Aid,
with the participation of hundreds of delegates. Among reports presented
to this meeting were statements by an assortment of writers that included
not only such stalwarts as Henri Barbusse and Anna Louise Strong but
also Eugene Lyons and Louis Fischer, who later could be counted among
the severest and best-informed critics of the Stalin regime. Another notable
string in Münzenberg's bow was a workers' book club, the Universum
Library for Everyone, which had gathered a membership of 40,000 by
1931, as well as a periodical, *Das Magazin für Alle* (Everybody's Magazine).

But the Communists and Social Democrats were rapidly losing ground
to the Nazis. It should be remembered that the Hitler movement's original
aims were a form of socialism with a national orientation. Its basic 25 point
program, largely ignored once Hitler came to power, contained several
demands for the nationalization of industry and commerce. The full name
of the Nazi Party, *National-Sozialistische Deutsche Arbeiter-Partei* (NSDAP),
translates into National Socialist German Workers' Party. Many of the
techniques eventually perfected by Dr. Joseph Goebbels, who became
minister of public enlightenment and propaganda, were imitations or ad-
aptations of methods used by Communists and Socialists. For the next few
years, Münzenberg became Goebbels's most active and effective antagonist.

CHAPTER · 6

Beyond the Reichstag Fire

While Moscow continued to call for attacks on Social Democrats as "betrayers of the Class Struggle" and Münzenberg was limited to a mammoth "peace movement" conference in Amsterdam, the Nazi threat within Germany turned into reality. Elections to the German parliament, or *Reichstag,* on July 31, 1932, gave the Nazi Party over 37 percent of the vote; the party's parliamentary delegation increased from 107 to 230. The Social Democrats received more than 24 percent of the vote, and the Communists more than 14 percent. On January 30, 1933, Adolf Hitler became German chancellor.

To gain ultimate psychological advantage, the Nazis needed a dramatic event that lent itself to total propagandistic exploitation. Such an event occurred on February 27, less than a month after their takeover, when fire destroyed the impressive Reichstag building, symbol of parliamentary democracy, at the center of Berlin. The new regime blamed the fire on a Communist plot to overthrow the government. Wholesale arrests were made. Communist and Social Democratic organizations and publications were shut down. The general reign of terror ensured the Nazi leaders' total control over the country's population; following a succession of aggressive moves abroad, this ultimately led to World War II.

The Communist Party, for all its experience with illegal and underground activities, was ill-prepared for this crushing blow. Only a relatively small number of key personalities escaped the Nazi net. The offices of the Münzenberg enterprises were seized by the police the day after the fire. Willi Münzenberg and Babette Gross managed to cross the border into France by a ruse. The next few years amounted to a propagandistic rearguard action, hampered by Moscow's continued anti-Western policies that pictured Britain and France as an overriding "imperialist" threat, placed the Nazi regime in a lower-priority category, and waited until the Seventh Congress of the Comintern in 1935 to establish a "united front" policy.

Münzenberg established new propaganda headquarters in Paris, where he had excellent governmental contacts. He could remain active, as long as he did not technically interfere in French domestic affairs. His Agitprop machinery employed a number of able and well-known organizers and writers, including Arthur Koestler, who later wrote the searing anti-Sta-linist novel, *Darkness at Noon.* Using his tried-and-true methods, Münzenberg created committees, published leaflets, books and periodicals, and even smuggled disguised anti-Nazi literature into Germany. In *Koestler: A Biography,* Iain Hamilton has written of Koestler's work for the World Committee for the Relief of the Victims of German Fascism, describing it as "a brilliantly successful example of a Communist-controlled 'front,' " skillfully "camouflaged as a philanthropic organization" with branches throughout Europe and North America. Koestler recalled that he shared seats on the executive committee with "highly respectable people, from English duchesses to American columnists and French savants, who had never heard the name of Münzenberg and thought that the Comintern was a bogey invented by Dr. Goebbels."

In a foreword to Gross's biography of Münzenberg, Koestler recalled his first meeting with the master propagandist in the fall of 1933. It lasted all of five minutes, and Koestler found himself, that very afternoon, "a low-level participant in the gigantic propaganda battle between Berlin and Moscow," with both sides trying to prove to the world that their opponent had set fire to the Reichstag building. Koestler described Münzenberg's casual but efficient way of delegating work, notably to his tall, reticent Man Friday, Hans Schulz. As Koestler remembered it, Münzenberg dictated mere suggestions: "Write to Feuchtwanger [the novelist Lion Feucht-wanger]. Tell him, article gratefully received, etcetera. Tell him, we need a leaflet from him; about sixteen pages, we shall smuggle ten-thousand copies into Germany; he should talk about cultural heritage, the Goethe tradition and all that. Leave the rest to him. Hugs and kisses. Next, Hans, buy a book on meteorology. Study the Highs and Lows, and all that, how the wind travels across the Rhine, how large a size leaflet a balloon can carry, where the balloons are likely to come down, and all that. Next, Hans, get in touch with a few balloon manufacturers, tell 'em it's for export to Venezuela, request cost estimates for ten thousand balloons, wholesale. Next, Hans . . ."

To counter Nazi propaganda claims that the Communists had set fire to the Reichstag, Münzenberg produced the first *Brown Book,* a work that put the blame on the Nazis themselves. The book, hard-hitting but largely based on informed conjecture, was published in French, English, and all other major languages, including German. The German edition consisted of two camouflaged volumes, packaged as paperbacks, concealed under a drama-classic cover.

Münzenberg also had the task of creating world opinion in favor of Georgi Dimitrov, the Bulgarian Comintern man who had been arrested in Berlin and was to be tried as part of the Reichstag conspiracy. The Nazi trial was scheduled for September 21, 1933, with Dimitrov among the team of accused. As it happened, the Bulgarian had been castigated previously as too "conciliatory, with rightist tendencies," but he was fiercely defended by the Comintern leadership and made a strong impression during the trial. It was Münzenberg's idea to arrange a countertrial in Great Britain that would provide a forum to defend the Dimitrov group and hear the evidence implicating the Nazi leadership itself, notably Hermann Göring. To achieve a major impact, he went out of his way to enlist the cooperation of prominent international jurists, including the U.S. civil liberties figure Arthur Garfield Hays and, from Britain, Sir Stafford Cripps, who later served as chancellor of the exchequer.

The London countertrial was timed for the period from September 4 to 19, the very eve of the Leipzig trial. As a result, the London verdict was publicized, worldwide, before the Nazi tribunal had even met. The London trial, officially the International Judicial Investigations Committee on the Reichstag Fire, was conducted in an atmosphere of judicial restraint, notably on the part of Cripps. The proceedings were in the hands of D. N. Pritt, king's counsellor and later Labor member of parliament. Pritt became prominent in several front organizations and was a frequent honored guest of the German Democratic Republic (East Germany). When Pritt, on the eve of the Leipzig trial, stated the conclusions of the countertrial, he noted that the participants had found Dimitrov and his group innocent of the charges and that, while the Communists had nothing to gain from the Reichstag fire, the Nazi regime had gained overriding advantages from the conflagration. The Leipzig trial, which concluded on December 23, 1933, found Marinus Van der Lubbe, a mentally retarded Dutch national, guilty of having set fire to the Reichstag building. He was sentenced to death. Dimitrov and several associates were acquitted because of lack of evidence. Moscow conferred Soviet citizenship on them and applied for their repatriation; they arrived in the U.S.S.R. the following February.

Continuing the themes of the Amsterdam Peace Congress, the Committee Against War and Fascism met in Paris on June 5, 1933. Because his presence in France was predicated on noninterference in French internal affairs, Münzenberg took no direct part in the Paris meeting, but its Communist orientation was underlined by the presence of a strong Russian delegation. Once the Paris meeting was concluded, Münzenberg went to Moscow, where he sought to tighten his contacts with the Comintern administration. His role in relation to the Soviet branch of Workers' Aid was complex; although located in Moscow, it was theoretically under Münzenberg's direction, and he had to deal with its internal problems. The Nazi takeover in Germany had robbed the organization of much of its prestige inside the U.S.S.R. leadership, and the Soviet secret service (then GPU, now KGB) mistrusted all foreigners and fought their special status.

Back in Paris, Münzenberg turned increasingly to long-range propaganda aims and methods. He had absorbed a small book publishing firm, Editions du Carrefour, which published mainly German-language exile literature, but also promoted French and English translations. One of its popular items was an exposé of Nazi operations abroad, entitled *The Brown Network;* another documented the secret development of the German air force. Among the authors published by Editions du Carrefour were Louis Aragon, Arthur Koestler, Bert Brecht, Lion Feuchtwanger, and André Malraux. In 1937, Willi Münzenberg published his own analysis of the tactics used by Goebbels's Propaganda Ministry, with the title *Propaganda as Weapon.* As before, he published camouflaged leaflets and pamphlets to be smuggled into Germany, some of them hidden in shipments of fashion magazines.

All this was facilitated by Moscow's change in tactics, aimed at a "united front," which became noticeable in 1934 and was made official policy at the Comintern's Seventh Congress in 1935, under the direction of Georgi Dimitrov. In France, the tactic led to a merger in the labor movement and to a working relationship between the Communist and Socialist parties. The Nazi regime released Dimitrov from prison in February 1934. Stalin personally congratulated him. But later that year, an event oddly similar to the Reichstag fire occurred in Leningrad: The local Communist Party secretary, Sergei Kirov, was assassinated, and Stalin used this event to justify a murderous and long-lasting purge, just as the Nazis had used the fire as an excuse to crush all opposition to their rule.

The Seventh Comintern Congress took place against the background of Stalin's ever more tyrannical rule. Babette Gross, who accompanied Münzenberg to the congress in Moscow, observed: "The final hour of the International Workers' Aid had come. The paranoia, with Stalin's constant emphasis on alleged war dangers and related espionage risks, had become rampant xenophobia. The IWA representation, mainly staffed by foreigners, among them quite a few German exiles, was regarded by the GPU as a disturbing foreign body." The organization was disbanded, its facilities absorbed by the rival Red Aid organization. Ultimately, Stalin's paranoia led to the extermination of scores of prominent foreign Communists, including veterans of the Spanish Civil War and many who had fled Germany for seemingly safe refuge in the Soviet Union, Hitler's professed arch enemy.

Speaking for the Soviet Communist Party and the Comintern, Dmitri Manuilsky said, "Long live the loyal, much-tested fellow-fighter of the great Stalin, the helmsman of the Comintern, Comrade Dimitrov!" Münzenberg returned to Paris with Dimitrov's instructions to encourage cooperation with socialists and "bourgeois" exiles. A formal effort to achieve such a working coalition was made at the Hotel Lutetia in Paris on February 6, 1936. Among the 118 participants were several prominent German writers, including Heinrich and Klaus Mann, Lion Feuchtwanger, and Emil Ludwig, as well as leading politicians. From then on, Heinrich Mann, brother of Thomas Mann and best known as author of the novel that was the basis for the motion picture *The Blue Angel,* became a reliable regular in Münzenberg's stable. The emerging group was sufficiently heterogeneous in composition to be perceived as a legitimate and representative forum of anti-Nazi personalities. Heinrich Mann became one of the editors of a bilingual press service, *German Information,* which was discreetly subsidized by Münzenberg. He also created a refugee committee that interceded in individual cases and acted as liaison with French authorities. Similar committees were formed overseas, including Mexico and Argentina.

Perhaps the most distinctive pattern for all later "peace movement" congresses was established at a meeting in Brussels on September 7 and 8, 1936. The framework for it was a new initiative by the Soviet labor unions, rather than the Comintern. Under the secretaryship of Louis Dolivet, later the editor of *Free World* magazine in New York, a *Rassemblement Universel pour la Paix* (RUP), or simply World Peace Movement, was established. It formulated an "Open Letter to All Friends of Peace," published on June 1, 1936, and signed by Norman Angell, André Malraux, John Dos Passos, Sherwood Anderson, Paul Langevin, and Francis Jourdain. Dos Passos, of course, later turned strongly against Communist and related movements. The "Open Letter" formed the basis for the actual congress, which assembled 5,500 delegates, representing a relatively wide spectrum of opinions and affiliations. The congress called for support of the League of Nations, collective security, and "indivisible peace."

At the same time, the Moscow purges of Münzenberg's long-time contacts and associates were proceeding. As chief of the secret police, Lavrenti Beria acted on Stalin's instructions. In other fields, such as cultural policy, Andrei Zhdanov was the major figure. To Münzenberg, Zhdanov was a man devoid of sufficient knowledge or judgment to gauge foreign reaction to events in the U.S.S.R. When Münzenberg visited Moscow once again, in October 1936, two of Lenin's and Stalin's former comrades, Zinoviev and Kamenev, had been executed and a host of less prominent Comintern functionaries had been arrested.

Perhaps luckily for Münzenberg, Manuilsky and Dimitrov were not in Moscow when he arrived. The senior Comintern official at that moment was the Italian Palmiro Togliatti (pseudonym: Ercoli), who later provoked Kremlin ire by advocating a "poly-centric" policy that would permit national Communist parties a degree of independence, thus foreshadowing the uneven path of "Eurocommunism." It was Togliatti's task to tell Münzenberg that he had, in effect, been fired as director of the many-sided Paris operation; that his position would be taken by Bohumil Smeral, a former Czechoslovak socialist who became an agent in the Near East and Asia; and that he, Münzenberg, was to join the staff of the Agitprop Department of the Comintern.

Münzenberg had fallen from Stalin's grace, such as it was. More threatening than the reassignment from Paris to Moscow was the fact that he was being interrogated by the International Control Commission, the Comintern's version of Stalin's internal party control apparatus, designed to track down potential heretics, deviationists, and renegades. These were some of the labels being used to eliminate men and women who, for whatever reason, had aroused the suspicion of Stalin and his secret police. In Willi Münzenberg's case, he had to defend himself against "lacking revolutionary alertness." Specifically, he was being questioned about the employment, in his Paris office, of a secretary, Liane Klein, whose father was alleged to be a spy for the Spanish regime of Generalissimo Francisco Franco. Whether or not the accusations against her father were correct, Münzenberg maintained that Klein, who had been a shorthand-typist with the League Against Imperialism in Berlin, and who later settled in Paris, had never had access to confidential material and by then had joined her father in Mallorca.

But the Control Commission continued to question Münzenberg on this issue, and it began to dawn on him that, with his many international contacts, it would be all too easy to create a net of suspicions, innuendos, and circumstantial evidence that might ultimately trap him. Others had been exiled or executed for less. He then managed to escape from Russia, as he had from Nazi Germany three years earlier.

Back in Paris, Münzenberg turned over his organizations' records, lists, receipts, funds, and premises to Smeral. He went to live at a sanatorium, taking time off for medical treatment for a "mild heart neurosis," but possibly a nervous breakdown. Meanwhile, the second show trial was taking place in Moscow, with former comrades accusing themselves of the most outlandish conspiracies against Stalin's regime. The International Control Commission sent a representative to Paris, where Münzenberg's long-time right-hand man, Hans Schulz, was interrogated, because he had allegedly uttered some critical remarks during a get-together in Moscow several years before.

Although Münzenberg had become sufficiently disillusioned with Moscow generally and its belated "united front" policy, in particular, to make snide remarks about it in private conversations, he went through the motions of conducting the first (and last) Conference of the German Popular Front, at a hall on Paris' Rue Cadet on April 10, 1937. However, well aware that the Soviet secret police had him listed as a "renegade," Münzenberg did not participate in the organizing committee that emerged from the meeting.

Among those present were two men whose role was of more than passing interest. Both later came to the United States. One of them, Hermann Budzislawski, became an assistant and idea man to the widely read columnist Dorothy Thompson, wife of novelist Sinclair Lewis. The other, Alfred Kantorowicz, became active on the New York emigré scene, worked for the Columbia Broadcasting System, emerged as a literary figure in postwar East Germany, and, finally, became disillusioned with communism and made his way to West Germany, where he died. Both men were career Communists. It is fair to say that they served as cultural agents, abroad, of the Communist International.

Münzenberg did an odd, but characteristic thing: He founded a new weekly, *Die Zukunft* (The Future). He stated in the magazine's November 1939 issue that the Comintern had begun to sabotage the "united front" slogan of its 1935 congress as early as 1936 and that all "Popular Front" activities were merely designed to trap ever-new individuals and groups under Communist Party control. Babette Gross recalled that she used to accompany Münzenberg frequently to Heinrich Mann's homes, one a house in Briancon, an Alpine town at the foot of Mont Cenis, the other an apartment in Nice, where Mann lived with his second wife, Nelly, surrounded by canaries. "This friendly relationship," Gross wrote, "lasted until the Communists finally got fed up with Heinrich Mann's intimate relations with the renegade Münzenberg. Wilhelm Pieck [who became a leader in postwar East Germany] went to Nice and urged Mann to cut his ties with Münzenberg." By that time Heinrich Mann had become so enmeshed with the Communists that he could not resist their pressure; he wrote his old friend Willi that he had decided to "let events unfold."

It is significant that, in his book *Propaganda as Weapon,* mainly an analysis of Nazi techniques, Dimitrov was quoted three times and Stalin only once, although Münzenberg called him "the great leader of the Soviet Union and architect of the world's first socialist state." The Communist press criticized the book as exaggerating the importance of Nazi propaganda and downgrading the effect of Communist propaganda. Nevertheless, as Walter Krivitsky wrote in *In Stalin's Secret Service,* Dimitrov continued to write to Münzenberg, urging him to come to Moscow, where important tasks awaited him. Others had yielded to such assurances and temptations, but Willi Münzenberg did not. Krivitsky, incidentally, fled to the United States, where he wrote a highly revelatory autobiography. He correctly forecast Stalin's alliance with Hitler. Krivitsky died in a Washington hotel, as mysteriously as, ultimately, did Münzenberg.

In March 1939, Willi Münzenberg announced his resignation from the German Communist Party. Writing in *Die Zukunft*, he cited difference in views concerning several "political and tactical problems," including those of the "Popular Front" and of "propaganda methods, and basic concepts of internal party democracy, and in the viewpoints concerning the relation of the party to individual members." He ended with a declaration of loyalty toward the Communist movement's traditions, notably his own early adherence to the principles of Lenin. He told a later biographer, Kurt Kersten, late in 1938, "By now I am nearly the last of the survivors of the Zimmerwald Left, which met, back then, in Kienthal." As one of the last of the Old Bolsheviks, most of whom were killed off by Stalin, Münzenberg seems to have mixed nostalgia with well-justified apprehension. His break with the German Communists was, of course, a break with the Communist International. He knew that his life was now in danger.

Together with like-minded people, including Koestler, Münzenberg sought to establish a "Popular Front" type of organization that excluded the Communists. By that time, Hitler had made his triumphal entry into Austria, and the country had been annexed to Germany.

In the spring of 1940, Hitler's armies struck down Denmark and Norway, then Holland, Belgium, and Luxembourg. The Nazi armies moved toward France, bypassed the fortified but ineffective Maginot Line, and quickly made their way to Paris. German nationals were being interned by the French authorities, regardless of political affiliations or anti-Nazi record. Babette Gross managed to flee to Portugal and then to Mexico. Münzenberg was arrested, spent three days in internment in Paris, and was then sent southward as part of a group of about 100 internees.

Münzenberg's group was placed in a camp at Chambaran, southeast of Lyon. But when news of the advancing German army reached the inmates, they appealed to the commander to let them march southward. When this was finally permitted, on June 20, the inmates broke into the camp files and obtained their identity cards; without them, they would have been nonpersons and their hoped-for escape would have been even more difficult. Münzenberg, with the aid of a Michelin map, plotted an escape into Switzerland.

On October 22, 1940, a press report, date-lined Saint Marcellin, stated: "Two mountain hunters have found the body of a man at the foot of an oak tree in the forest of Caugnet. His death appears to have occurred several months ago. The unknown person apparently hanged himself, as part of a rope was still fastened around his neck. The gendarmerie at Saint Marcellin investigated this case and established that the body is that of a certain Willi Münzenberg, 51 years old, a writer born in Erfurt."

The death of Willi Münzenberg—its time, its place, and the circumstances—ensured that his life would become legend. He had been a Pied Piper who had listened to his own tune, and walked into oblivion.

CHAPTER · 7

All in the Name of Peace

In the name of peace, Soviet propaganda has launched campaign after campaign, at home and abroad. The theme has permeated Soviet public events to such a degree that even the East European bicycle competition, held from May 9 to 11, 1985, was labeled the "Peace Cycle Race." Literally hundreds of other happenings—from huge international congresses to children's competitions in local schools—were arranged under a peace banner.

To be for peace, in terms of Soviet propaganda efforts, has always meant to be against something, usually an undertaking, a project, or a policy of the United States, often merely identified as "the imperialists" (which could include the NATO countries or other nations). These relentless campaigns, appealing to man's best instincts and worst fears, have for decades been spearheaded by the World Peace Congress (WPC), one of the oldest and certainly the most active and best financed of the Soviet-sponsored front organizations.

Writing about what is usually called, more or less vaguely, "the peace movement" is fraught with danger. The World Peace Congress and its regional branches are so intertwined with other action groups that one is forever running the risk of spreading guilt by association. Everyone is, or should be, in favor of peace, and most of us want to do something concrete to fight the dangers of war, halt aggression, prevent massacres and genocide, or simply stop basic violations of human rights, whether those of a group or of an individual. As a result, the world is full of groupings that have nothing in common with Soviet totalitarianism, but often sound like one of the Soviet-organized groups or have names that are easily confused with yet another WPC offspring.

Trying to sort out Soviet propaganda drives, under the mantle of a "peace movement," and separating them from grassroots efforts in favor of peace, disarmament, or similarly desirable aims, often touches delicate nerves. One example of this dilemma can be found in Switzerland's 1983 crackdown on the Soviet news and feature service Novosti. (See also Chapter 16, "Novosti Comes of Age.") The Swiss public prosecutor and the police found evidence which showed that Soviet press service personnel helped to organize demonstrations under the "peace" label. As a result, Novosti's office in the Swiss capital, Berne, was closed and the agency's chief deported.

This may sound quite simple, but it wasn't simple at all. Acting on the request of the federal attorney, Rudolf Friedrich, made on the basis of police investigations, the Swiss parliament *(Bundesrat)* decided on April 29, 1983, to close Novosti's Berne bureau and to order the agency's office chief, Alexei Dumov, to leave the country. This move, which attracted international attention, was almost overshadowed within Switzerland by the fact that the secret internal report on Novosti's activities appeared mysteriously in the mail of a number of opinion makers. This "indiscretion," as it was called, created a furor. Who, it was asked, had wanted to give the document such publicity, either to strengthen its effect or to lessen it?

Copies of the document showed that they had been made from an original that contained a paper flaw on page 20. This original had been assigned to the Finance Department. Still, a year later, on March 27, 1984, the state attorney's office announced that inquiries into the "indiscretion" had been concluded, but that evidence had been insufficient to take legal action against any violation of official secrets.

Meanwhile, the arguments about the charges against Novosti and its two Swiss staff members, Martin Schwander and Philippe Spillmann, raged in the parliament as well as on the political scene generally. As Swiss citizens, Schwander and Spillmann had been in their rights to participate in the planning and execution of various demonstrations; but Novosti, their employer, had, in the view of the federal attorney's office, intruded into Swiss domestic affairs and operated "essentially as an agitation and subversion center." Novosti, according to this view, had manipulated the Swiss peace movement.

The controversial report, compiled under the title "Official Report of the Federal Attorney's Office Concerning Activities of the Soviet Press Agency NOVOSTI," stated that the agency had been active in the preparation of "demonstrations, actions and rallies." It cited a 1980 series of anti-U.S. demonstrations in various Swiss cities, initiated by the Cuban embassy but "directly controlled and coordinated" by Novosti's Berne office. Similarly, on May 17, 1980, Spillmann was the "responsible leader" of a "solidarity rally" concerning El Salvador. A demonstration in Berne was characterized as follows:

"Some 50 demonstrators who assembled outside the U.S. Embassy in Berne on January 20, 1981, in an allegedly spontaneous action, among other things presented a petition, 'USA—Hands Off Cuba,' signed by 575 Swiss parliamentarians, journalists, etc. The Federal Police had been aware of the demonstration as early as January 14, 1981. This was the day on which Cuban Embassy officials inquired at APN [Novosti] concerning the assembly point and the time of the demonstration(!). The Cuban ambassador later testified as to the propagandistic success of this action."

With regard to another El Salvador demonstration (April 3, 1982), the report stated that the Novosti men had "directed disinformation in such a way that a quite impressive anti-USA manifestation resulted." The report also accused Novosti of using "false news reports and disinformation maneuvers" to influence Swiss media concerning events in Lebanon, during June and July 1982. When President Reagan visited Bonn on June 10, 1982, Novosti provided "orientation and advice" to Swiss participants in anti-U.S. demonstrations in the West German capital. Novosti's staff member Schwander acted as "responsible demonstration leader" and the agency itself as a clearinghouse in the case of demonstrations against the military governments of Chile and Turkey on September 11, 1982.

On June 23, 1982, there were demonstrations inside the Swiss parliament. Banners were displayed from the gallery and leaflets scattered, demanding asylum for Salvadoran exiles in Honduras. The report stated: "The case in question illustrates with total clarity that the Soviet and Swiss APN people did not hesitate to bring their actions all the way into the confederate Parliament. The foreign organization even went so far as to have its actions directly controlled and observed by its own employees." According to the report, Spillmann was present during the demonstration, sitting in the gallery's front row; he left when the incident was concluded. According to the report, "That the Soviets attributed great propagandistic importance to the actions inside the Parliament building could be seen from the fact that APN undertook to inform Radio Moscow, Tass, ADN [East German news service] and *Neues Deutschland* [organ of the East German party] of this undertaking."

The federal attorney's report cited incidents of Novosti involvement in other activities, including a "Swiss Appeal for Peace," which collected 120,000 signatures and passed the appeal to the Department on Foreign Affairs. Visits by Soviet "peace delegations" to Switzerland were also cited. One U.S.S.R. delegation included Vladimir Lomeiko, then chief of the West European section of Novosti's Moscow headquarters.

The report stated: "It is not surprising that the Soviet Union is taking advantage of the opportunity to influence, and possibly to direct, the current peace movement in Western Europe, giving it its own meaning." It added: "In doing so, it uses the condition that the wish for peace exists on the broadest possible basis, and it knows extremely well, by means of 'active measures,' how to expose western governments and parliaments to the manipulative pressures of the street and of the media, in order to advance its own strategic concept of peace. Current efforts in the East are generally designed to undermine the defensive energies of the West, to disparage the American presence in Western Europe and to create an optimum negotiation position for the continuing disarmament discussions."

Referring specifically to conditions in Switzerland, the report contained these comments:

"Many well-meaning citizens, throughout Europe and within Switzerland, desire peace. This demand is legitimate. What causes concern in this connection are not the citizens who support the peace movement, but the individuals and organizations that stand behind it, and which seek to present a threat to peace exclusively as a fault of the West and who, by means of skillful propaganda activity in the service of the East, seek to achieve a weakening of the defensive readiness of the West. The demonstrations organized by them permit no doubt about their ideological direction."

The report continued: "Many peace-loving citizens, notably in ecclesiastical circles, are unable to see through this game." It elaborated: "They provide—not only in our country—their names and their prestige to a cause which, if they knew all the conditions, they would never support. It is precisely this which characterizes the danger and deceit of eastern propaganda activity in the form of 'active measures'—what is actually Moscow's will is presented to those in positions of responsibility in governments and parliaments in western nations, including Switzerland, as having autonomously developed domestically and representing tendencies designed to influence decisions, which, in the long run, they are able to achieve. Such intervention in the development of political decision-making of other nations results in injury to the elementary principles of national sovereignty."

By employing Schwander and Spillmann, Novosti has violated what has frequently been a principle in the overseas operations of Soviet agencies: Do not hire known local Communists; rely on qualified Soviet nationals, or employ either uncommitted technicians or sympathizers who are not actually members of Communist parties. The Swiss Communist Party, known as the Workers' Party (*Partei der Arbeit,* or PdA), has a long history within the world Communist movement; it was in Zurich, after all, that Lenin made his final plans for the Bolshevik Revolution.

Martin Schwander had worked for Novosti since 1977, first in the agency's Geneva office (established in 1965), but active in Berne ever since that bureau was opened. He served as deputy director, as well as a working journalist. At the time of the federal attorney's report, he was a member

of the Communist Party's Central Committee, president of the party's
Berne action, president of the Society Switzerland-Cuba, a member of the
Society Switzerland-GDR (German Democratic Republic), a member of
the Society Switzerland-Palestine, a member of the World Peace Council,
and a member of the Peace Movement. His colleague, Philippe Spillmann,
was also a member of the (Communist) Workers' Party, a member of the
board of the Society Switzerland-U.S.S.R., president of the Society Switzerland-GDR, and a member of the Peace Movement. Both had refused
service in the Swiss army and had been dismissed from the armed services.
Spillmann had been on the Novosti staff since 1979.

The political fallout from the report, partly directed against federal
Attorney Rudolf Friedrich, culminated in a parliamentary debate on June
20 and 21, 1983. Some members felt that the report on Novosti went too
far in questioning the judgment of individuals, such as church-affiliated
supporters of peace demonstrations; others saw a lack of distinction between active followers of Soviet-controlled organizations and those who,
in one way or another, had engaged in knowing or unknowing cooperation
with such organizations. Among those who spoke in favor of the report
were parliamentarians who accused the parliament and government of lack
of courage in facing up to large-scale Soviet operations, ranging from
excessively large embassy staffs to propagandistic and intelligence-gathering activities. The discussion could not, of course, define the line that
separated such Soviet-controlled bodies as the World Peace Council and
its local arm, the Swiss Peace Movement (*Schweizerische Friedens-Bewe-
gung,* or SFB), from independent movements, but it succeeded in pointing
up the worldwide dilemma.

This dilemma is always with us when dealing with Moscow-directed
front organizations. In 1982, when there was considerable publicity for the
cause of freezing the nuclear arsenals of the U.S. and the U.S.S.R., President Reagan said twice that the nuclear-freeze movement was manipulated
from outside. This implied that advocates of a freeze on the production of
nuclear weapons were influenced from the Soviet Union. The President
said on October 4 in Columbus, Ohio, that the movement was manipulated
by people who "want the weakening of America," and on November 11
in Washington that "the Soviet Union saw an advantage in a peace movement built around the idea of a nuclear freeze, since they are out ahead."
Soviet leader Mikhail Gorbachev repeated the suggestion of a mutual nuclear freeze on Easter Sunday, 1985, and on August 18, 1986; the issue,
and the responses to it, had remained the same. But to what extent did
Moscow manipulate the peace movement related to it? And what role,
specifically, did the World Peace Council play in this intricate but crucial
game of psychological warfare?

Like all Moscow-controlled front organizations, the World Peace Council's basic function grew out of the "united front" tactics adopted by the Communist International in the 1920s and 1930s. The multiplicity of front organizations testifies to the variety and changing nature of their targets. They are all, in a sense, the spiritual grandchildren of Willi Münzenberg. As we noted earlier, "united front" tactics were designed to enlist the support of anyone and any group that could be enticed to form an alliance, no matter how temporary, with Moscow or its local parties, for "limited aims." These aims could be quite sweeping, such as "Against War and Fascism!" or as specific as "Join the Tenant Council: We Want Heat, Not Frozen Babies!"

As anyone knows who has ever been involved in a committee, be it to establish a playground or clean up a waste dump, the day-to-day work is always done by a small group of people: They attend all meetings, stay late and vote, prepare handbills, and ring doorbells. In crucial movements of the "united front" kind, Communists or those supported by them are often prominent members of such a diligent and dynamic core; in Communist Party parlance, they are the "cell" that implements party policies and gets things done. There is another almost universal pattern: Often, the head of an organization is a prominent personality, and on his or her side is a far less public figure who is quite often a cell member.

This is how the World Peace Council came into being. The Information Bureau of the Communist and Workers' Parties (Cominform), which was the successor to the Communist International (Comintern), at a meeting in November 1949 heard a report, "Defense of Peace and the Fight against the Warmongers," delivered by the Kremlin's chief ideologist, Mikhail Suslov. Richard H. Shultz and Roy Godson, in their book *Dezinformatsia: Active Measures in Soviet Strategy* (1984), recall that "the initiation of this 'peace' effort coincided with the first Soviet atomic test," and while the U.S.S.R. thus "embarked on a campaign to promote the disarmament of the West," it began the "buildup of its own nuclear forces that continues today." Suslov said: "For the first time in history, an organized peace front has arisen, which has made its aim to save mankind from another world war, to isolate the warmonger clique and to ensure peaceful cooperation among nations."

Despite what Suslov said, this was not really the first time the world Communist movement had sought to build an alliance around a "peace" slogan, but earlier efforts had become mired in wrangling from within and without the Comintern. Then, as now, Moscow did not trust any universally pacifist sentiment, because it might demand as much disarmament from the Soviet Union as from the United States, NATO, and other countries. It was the same back in the 1920s and early 1930s, when the Münzenberg technique became so successful that it threatened to take on a momentum of its own.

One of the front organizations that sprung up in central Europe was the League Against Imperialism, which held a congress in Berlin in May 1931. A prominent participant was Jawaharlal Nehru, who later, together with other non-Communists, resigned over the issue of Moscow domination. Earlier, in 1928, the Sixth Comintern Congress had begun to celebrate August 1, the anniversary of the outbreak of World War I in 1914. Two years later, in 1930, the Comintern journal, *Communist International,* devoted a double issue, Nos. 19 and 20, to the peace theme. The issue contained an article, signed "Alfred," with the title "Against Indifference on the Question of the War Danger." The author using this pseudonym was Palmiro Togliatti, the Italian Communist Party leader and Comintern executive.

Later that year, on December 11, a Committee for the Defense of the Soviet Union against Imperialist Warmongers was created; it issued a manifesto bearing the signatures, among others, of Maxim Gorki, the American author Upton Sinclair, the prominent French pro-Communist writer Henri Barbusse, and, of course, Münzenberg. The Central Committee of the Comintern resolved in March 1931 that the international proletariat should protect the Soviet Union through "the preservation of peace among nations." When Japan invaded Manchuria, the U.S.S.R. feared that its own borders might be penetrated, and it welcomed worldwide revulsion against Tokyo's aggression on Chinese soil. None of this fitted the slogan of a danger from an "imperialist war," considering that the United States and the countries of Western Europe which opposed Japan's military adventure were all "imperialist" in the Soviet vocabulary.

On March 30 and 31, 1932, the Western European Bureau of the Comintern, meeting in Berlin, began a campaign designed to "win over new masses by party slogans." In *Twilight of the Comintern: 1930–1935* (1982), the British historian E. H. Carr observed, "The notion of a world-wide campaign against war, into which broad strata of the Left in western countries, both workers and intellectuals, could be drawn, on the model of the joint campaign against imperialism, was probably the brain-child of Münzenberg." But all was not well for Münzenberg and such a broad peace campaign. Togliatti had his hands slapped when he advocated a "struggle for peace" while Moscow feared that pacifist sentiments might weaken Western European resistance to Japan and to a Germany that was becoming increasingly Nazified.

While the Münzenberg group was preparing a peace congress to take place in Geneva, Togliatti (as "Alfred") wrote an article titled "On the Inopportune Application of the Peace Slogan," which appeared in the Comintern journal (No. 13, 1932); in it, he reversed his earlier position and criticized some French and German Communist spokesmen. A pacifist group, the International Antimilitarist Commission, was angered by changes that turned a general antiwar congress into a meeting solely in defense of the Soviet Union and China. The Swiss government, keen to maintain a neutral position, withdrew permission for the congress to take place in Geneva. It was shifted to Amsterdam, where it met on August 27, 1932. The Dutch government did not permit the Soviet delegates, Gorki and Nikolai Shvernik, later a high Kremlin official, to enter the Netherlands. But Barbusse gave the opening address, and Münzenberg guided the crowd of 2,196 "delegates" toward a manifesto that organized a "world committee against imperialist war." An array of international supporters signed the document. An antiwar demonstration was held in Paris, where the Soviet delegates had a chance to make the speeches they had been prevented from delivering in Amsterdam.

Carr observed that "reaction in Moscow to the congress was oddly mixed," as Comintern officers were "ever wary of the danger of an infiltration of pacifism into communist doctrine." Still, he added, the peace movement had been "too successful to be ignored." Efforts were under way to shunt Münzenberg aside, but following Hitler's takeover he managed to arrange a peace congress at the Salle Peyel, in Paris, on April 16 and 17, 1933. Similar meetings and organizations attracted public attention and, as Carr said, "Münzenberg's skilled and practiced hand was visible in the organization of these events; and the funds necessary to mount them certainly came from Moscow."

Not until the Seventh Congress of the Comintern in 1935 did the kind of "united front" which these efforts represented have Moscow's full endorsement. The policy was again disrupted when the Nazi-Soviet Pact burst onto world history in 1939. The Communist Party line all over the world flip-flopped and forced eager, as well as reluctant, followers to label the Allied war effort nothing but part of an "imperialist war." Once Hitler attacked his ally, Stalin, in mid-1941, the "united front" was immediately resuscitated. The joint war effort was goaded toward an early Second Front in Western Europe, to take the Nazi pressure off the Soviet Union. Stalin did not permit any postwar "pacifist" sentiments to take root among the war-weary people of the U.S.S.R. Hardly had the devastated regions of the Soviet western territories recovered, when the Kremlin felt threatened all over again.

By this time, following the Yalta agreement of 1945, the map of Eastern Europe had changed radically. Borders had shifted, sovereignties had changed, and, above all, Communist leaders had come from Moscow to Poland, East Germany, Romania, Hungary, Czechoslovakia, and Yugoslavia to install Soviet-oriented regimes. In Greece, first British and then U.S. support aided the Greek government in winning a civil war that was supported by Moscow through Yugoslavia, Albania, and Bulgaria. Tito's defection added another level to Stalin's edifice of fears and hatreds.

Thus, when Suslov told the Cominform meeting in 1949 that a peace movement had been organized "for the first time," he ignored all the Münzenberg-type efforts and Moscow's worry about pacifist infections. He pinpointed the target of the new undertaking clearly enough, however, when he added that the "peace movement arose as a protest movement of the Masses against the Marshall Plan and the aggressive Western union and the North Atlantic alliance." He paid tribute to "the World Peace Congress in Paris and Prague," which had "represented" 600 million "organizers for peace."

It was at the Prague Congress, in April 1949, that the World Peace Council was organized. The WPC has been in continuous existence ever since, and it has withstood the changing tides of Soviet policies and the occasionally heavy winds created by Moscow leadership changes. Beyond this, the organization has a remarkable record of maintaining an image of well-meaning dedication and of maintaining contacts with opinion makers in many countries of the world. While Americans are naturally concerned about the impact that a Soviet-controlled body such as the World Peace Council may have achieved in the United States, the WPC's main targets really lie elsewhere. As much Soviet propaganda is directed to the so-called Third World, so is the WPC geared toward opinion makers, news media, and the public in the Near and Far East, Africa, and Latin America.

WPC is personified, to many of its adherents, by the skillful leadership of Romesh Chandra, a prominent member of the Indian Communist Party and a WPC activist since its early years. In a report issued by the Permanent Select Committee on Intelligence of the U.S. House of Representatives, "CIA Report on Soviet Propaganda Operations," based on a hearing of April 20, 1978, Chandra is described as "clever, ambitious and vain" and as a man who, for many years, has been known in India as "the Indian with the Russian contacts." Only a year after the World Peace Council was set up, when Romesh Chandra was 30 years old, he was prominent as a behind-the-scenes emissary from Moscow to the Indian Communists. He has been credited with convincing the Communist Party that it was better to refrain from criticizing Prime Minister Nehru so that he would be more likely to remain neutral in East-West disputes. On a reverse mission, in 1963, Chandra is believed to have pleaded India's case in Moscow at the time of a border dispute between China and India. The CIA report, cited before the congressional committee, stated that "those familiar with the workings of the WPC" regard Chandra's frequent trips to Moscow as a means of keeping him "posted on the party line."

The CIA report noted that, in 1977, Chandra was advanced from the position of the WPC's secretary general to that of president, and added: "The honor was well deserved from the Soviet point of view because Chandra, possibly the best-known of all front officials, had faithfully fol-

lowed the Moscow line throughout his quarter century in the front movement. Year after year, Chandra has praised Soviet peace initiatives and
condemned Western 'imperialists.' The WPC, Chandra said in Moscow in
1975, 'positively reacts to all Soviet initiatives in international affairs.' Two
years earlier, at a 1973 Moscow peace conference, Chandra asserted that
those peace organizations which took an anti-Soviet stance 'ceased to be
genuine peace organizations.' Chandra has never strayed—even during
such periods of stress as the Warsaw Pact invasion of Czechoslovakia in
1968. He stood up for Moscow even though there were widespread protests
from leaders of some other front groups who were subsequently ousted
from office."

To put not too fine a point on it: Romesh Chandra is the quintessential
Communist organization bureaucrat, well suited by ethnic background as
an international common denominator—cutting a statesmanlike and even
debonair figure, and coming from a nonaligned, developing, former colonial nation—who is just as much at home in Helsinki as in New Delhi,
in Nairobi as in Vienna. After he became a member of the WPC executive
committee and one of its secretaries in 1953, he was instrumental in setting
up another Soviet-sponsored front, the Afro-Asian People's Solidarity Organization (AAPSO). The Soviet Union had not been permitted to take
part in the founding conference of the nonaligned nations, the grouping
formed under the leadership of Prime Minister Nehru, President Gamal
Abdel Nasser of Egypt, and President Tito of Yugoslavia. It was presumably Tito's fresh memory of Moscow's efforts at interfering in Yugoslavia's
affairs that prompted the policy of excluding the Soviet Union. Since the
deaths of these three original leaders, the nonaligned movement has been
courted by the U.S.S.R. and at times, as when Fidel Castro chaired its
proceedings, has acted almost as if it were following a front organization
pattern.

While Romesh Chandra functioned as WPC president, the presence of
a Soviet functionary on the council's secretariat always served as insurance
that the organization, sprawling as it is, did not stray from Moscow's narrow
policy path. Above all, any hint that the WPC or one of its affiliates might
apply to the U.S.S.R. the same critical standards that it uses toward the
United States, NATO, Japan, and elsewhere is quickly erased. The fiction
that the WPC is a spontaneously organized, independent body is only thinly
maintained. After all, Chandra's writings appear in the central ideological
journal of the worldwide Communist movement, *World Marxist Review;*
in one article, "Postponing or Eliminating the Threat of War" (January
1981), he wrote: "The activities of the World Peace Council have acquired
a new content: 700 million signatures were collected to the WPC's new
Stockholm Appeal to Halt the Arms Race and handed over to UN Sec-
retary-General Kurt Waldheim on the occasion of the Special Session of

the UN General Assembly on Disarmament in May 1978. In Europe, the struggle to curb the arms race has become a mass demonstration against the deployment of new US missiles; in North and Latin America, in Asia and Africa it has developed into mass action against the arms build-up, against the military bases and stepped up tensions in the Indian Ocean, the Persian Gulf, and the Caribbean."

Arkadi Shevchenko, the Soviet diplomat who served as undersecretary general of the United Nations under Secretary General Kurt Waldheim, said in *Breaking With Moscow* that "ceaseless requests from Moscow to assist the Soviet-controlled World Peace Council" were "particularly annoying" during his functions within the UN Secretariat. He wrote that the WPC "swarmed with KGB officers" and added: "Every year I was expected to help organize Chandra's speeches to UN bodies, arrange his meeting with UN officials, distribute Council propaganda and persuade Waldheim to send Secretariat representatives to attend various Council-sponsored conferences. Moscow wanted to boost the Council's prestige by creating high visibility via UN recognition of the Council's 'great role in the world movement for peace.' I never developed a skin thick enough not to cringe inwardly with embarrassment when I approached Waldheim's deputies with my next recommendation for UN participation in another World Peace Council activity."

Shultz and Godson have stated that the WPC has "played a significant role in Soviet efforts to influence political developments in the West over the past thirty years," functioning as an instrument to reinforce Moscow's "overt propaganda campaigns." They noted that the Soviet Union has maintained control over the WPC and other front organizations by manipulating the presidency, the Secretariat, and the President Committee of the Council through "individuals sympathetic—if not completely loyal—to the CPSU." Schultz and Godson added: "The overwhelming majority of persons in these WPC executive bodies are officials or nationals from the following types of countries and international organizations: the USSR and the East European bloc countries; Communist countries which are outside the Eastern bloc but loyal to Moscow; Soviet-backed guerrilla movements; non-ruling Communist parties in developed and developing countries that are linked to the CPSU International Department; and other Soviet-controlled international front organizations."

Control of front organizations is in the hands of the International Department (ID) of the party's Central Committee. The department, headed from 1955 to 1986 by Boris Ponomarev, inherited the files and some of the personnel of the defunct Communist International (Comintern). Ponomarev served as deputy director of the Comintern's successor agency, the Communist Information Bureau (Cominform) in 1947 and 1948. His duties in that position overlapped with those of first deputy director of the committee's International Department, a post he held from 1948 to 1955. The department oversees a multitude of activities, and the labyrinthine network of front organizations requires a large administrative section of its own. This function is performed by the ID's International Social Organization Sector. While front organizations of a minor nature come and go, the major bodies have been in existence for decades, interlocking with one another and with Communist and non-Communist organizations of various types.

Colonel Wallace Spaulding, now retired from the U.S. Air Force, has monitored Communist front organizations for many years. In "Communist Fronts in 1984," a review of front organization activities that appeared in *Problems of Communism* (March–April 1985), he listed the following ten major organizations, the year of their founding, and the locations of their headquarters:

World Peace Council, 1949, Helsinki

World Federation of Trade Unions, 1945, Prague

Women's International Democratic Federation, 1945, East Berlin

World Federation of Democratic Youth, 1945, Budapest

Afro-Asian Peoples' Solidarity Organization, 1953, Cairo

World Federation of Scientific Workers, 1946, London

International Organization of Journalists, 1946, Prague

Christian Peace Conference, 1958, Prague

International Organization of Democratic Lawyers, 1946, Brussels

A few glimpses into the interlocking mazes of these organizations and their subsidiaries will indicate the range of their activities. The World Peace Council, from its headquarters in Helsinki, maintains contact with 135 affiliates and publishes the periodicals *New Perspectives* and *Peace Courier*. It has permanent representatives at the United Nations offices in New York and Geneva and at the United Nations Educational and Scientific Organization (UNESCO) in Paris. Among the WPC regional organizations are the International Committee for European Security and Cooperation (Brussels), the International Campaign Committee for a Just Peace in the Middle East, the International Committee of Solidarity with the Arab People and Their Central Cause—Palestine (Tripoli), the International Committee on Southern Africa, and the Movement for the Peace and Sovereignty of the Peoples (Havana).

WPC executive committees and secretariats contain representatives from countries where the WPC is particularly active. Of these, three are from India and the U.S.S.R.; two each are from Cuba, Australia, Poland, the

United Kingdom, Egypt, Zimbabwe, Panama, Bulgaria, Iraq, the United States, and East Germany; one representative each comes from Malagasy, Vietnam, Syria, Guinea, France, Ethiopia, Portugal, Angola, Lebanon, Italy, Argentina, Finland, Jordan, Hungary, Czechoslovakia, Chile, Madagascar and Mali; and one representative each is assigned to Palestine and to the African National Congress.

Identification of Moscow-controlled front organizations becomes difficult when a front creates fronts of its own. In the case of the World Peace Council there are at least 11 major "fronts of a front." These are:

International Institute for Peace, Vienna

International Liaison Forum of Peace Forces, Helsinki

Committee on the Non-aligned Movement

International Committee for Solidarity with Cyprus

International Commission on Human Rights

Commission on Mass Media and Information

Commission on Scientific Research for Peace

Commission on Ending the Arms Race and Disarmament

Commission on Development and the New International Order

International Federation of Resistance Fighters

International Committee for Solidarity with the Palestinian People

Other committees, commissions, etc., are formed as occasions arise. Every major front organization has an affiliate within the Soviet Union, and funding is apparently funneled through these bodies as well as through other channels. In the case of the World Peace Council, the Soviet Committee for the Defense of Peace and the Soviet Peace Fund are, so to speak, the "mother lode" among financial sources. On the one hand, Soviet publications at times reveal that money collected within the U.S.S.R. is used by peace movement activists abroad; on the other hand, funds flow into front groups through a variety of hidden channels that are only rarely publicized.

The Novosti publication *Sputnik* (February 1982) replied to an Indian reader's inquiry as to what the Soviet Peace Fund (SPF) was actually doing. The editors replied that Soviet citizens, acting on "their own initiative," had started to "send money and other voluntary contributions" to various addresses after World War II and that the SPF was created to "receive such funds." They added that the fund "gives financial support to organizations, movements and people struggling for the consolidation of peace, the development of friendship and cooperation among peoples, the banning of all types of nuclear weapons and other means of mass annihilation, and the achievement of universal and total disarmament." The fund, they wrote, "allocates funds for the organization of international congresses, symposiums, festivals and exhibitions." The reply stated that the Soviet Peace Fund had nearly 75 million "voluntary contributors" and receives box office receipts from "specially organized concerts, stage productions, exhibitions and sports events."

While the Soviet Peace Fund may well be a source of funds for the World Peace Council and its affiliates, it clearly provides only a segment of the total sum expended by the Soviet Union for WPC-type organizations per annum. The Soviet Committee in Defense of Peace (SCDP), the WPC "affiliate" within the Soviet Union, is another source of public financial support. When Yuri Zhukov, chairman of the committee, spoke on Soviet television on May 22, 1980, he gave the number of citizens contributing to peace funds as 80 million, 5 million more than the *Sputnik* figure, and identified the committee as a nongovernmental, or "public," body. Zhukov said that "donations" to the committee were being made through *Gosbank,* the state banking institution. Often, such funds are collected in factories and on farms that contribute a day's wages to the peace movement; in effect, this is an imposed "donation," centrally administered and locally enforced. Various Soviet institutions, including the Moscow Patriarchate of the Orthodox Church, contribute to the peace funds on a regular basis or as the result of special drives and events.

Overlapping between other propaganda efforts and the peace movement, familiar from the Swiss case against Novosti, emerged in Denmark in 1982. According to the Danish Ministry of Justice, the Copenhagen journalist Arne Herlov Petersen had acted as an agent for the second secretary of the Soviet embassy, Vladimir Merkulov, who was expelled from Denmark for engaging in activities inconsistent with his diplomatic status. In less formal terms, Merkulov had functioned as a KGB officer who employed the services of Petersen. The journalist, recruited by one of Merkulov's predecessors, had been active for several years.

While the Petersen case is discussed in greater detail elsewhere in this book, it is of interest here because he acted not only as an agent for routine propaganda tasks, including disinformation, but also as a conduit of funds to peace committees. According to the Danish Ministry of Justice, Petersen used a variety of means for "influencing the opinion of the Danish public." The ministry stated: "A single, but illustrative, case in point is the promise made by the Soviet Embassy in the summer of 1981 to partially finance the expenditure incurred in connection with the publication of a number of advertisements in which a number of Danish artists expressed support of an initiative to establish a Nordic nuclear-free zone. The collection of signatures was organized by Arne Herlov Petersen, who said in several telephone conversations that the Soviet Embassy was involved. The Soviet Embassy was also informed of the course of the collection campaign on several occasions."

Cases such as the Novosti interference in domestic Swiss affairs and Petersen's role as a contact between the Soviet embassy and the Danish nuclear-ban campaign are rare, at least as far as public knowledge is concerned, because the men who control the World Peace Council and its numerous affiliates and collaborating organizations are, on the whole, careful to avoid compromising associations. Keeping within a traditional and standard procedure, the Soviet embassy in Denmark asked Petersen to refrain from joining the Communist Party and, as the Justice Ministry put it, warned him that "if he did so, the Embassy would break its connection with him."

A comprehensive account of the activities of the various Soviet-controlled front organizations, even just within a single year, would fill a large volume. Suffice it to say that the WPC operation alone virtually penetrates the nooks and crannies of its target areas. Far from Red Square, an item in the Sunday *Star-Ledger,* Newark, New Jersey (June 2, 1985), carried the headline "Myths erased for Jerseyans on trip to Soviet." The story began, "Mention the Soviet Union and it might conjure up thoughts of breadlines, oppression and a nation of warmongers. But those conceptions were shattered by 78 Americans who found ample supplies, no unemployment and a populace terrified of nuclear war." The report stated that participants in a two-week tour, organized by "the International Peace Congress," said they had been "overwhelmed by the friendliness of the Soviet people." Bread, of course, has been in ample supply in the Soviet Union for decades, "oppression" is not found by peace tourists on a two-week trip, and whether such a group can be certain that the 270-million "populace" of the U.S.S.R. is "terrified of nuclear war" or merely echoes and reacts to its government's unrelenting scare campaign is a matter of polite conjecture. The New Jersey group did come to a fairly routine conclusion, however: "Despite the hospitality they experienced in Russia," the report noted, "the representatives all conceded they prefer living in the United States."

It is against the background of such historic and sociological innocence as that of the New Jersey peace tourists, and their "instant enlightenment," that the effectiveness of the Soviet-controlled front organizations must be measured. When President Reagan, in 1982, suggested that the nuclear-freeze movement was being manipulated from abroad, whereby he clearly meant the Soviet Union, the accuracy of his charge was publicly questioned. The issue had been dramatized by the large turnout for a rally that took place in New York's Central Park on June 12 of that year, with more than 500,000 people crowding the park. To what degree, if any, did the rally reflect Soviet-inspired "manipulation"? Leslie Cagan, one of the rally's coordinators, said, "The assertion that the American people are being manipulated by 'foreign agents' only serves to divert our energies away from the real issues: the clear and present dangers presented by our nuclear arsenals."

The overall tenor of the rally, sober and nonviolent as it was, reflected criticism of U.S. policies rather than an evenhanded critique of Soviet, as well as United States, nuclear armaments. Subtle factors of mass psychology are involved in this tendency, going back to the antiestablishment demonstrations of the 1960s, and a public habit of regarding it as useless or ill-mannered to criticize the Soviet Union, while it is socially acceptable to engage in sharp self-criticism.

But organizational factors may also have been involved. If one studies the tradition of "united front" coalitions, the presence of even a small number of Moscow-oriented participants at planning levels may, at the very least, provide a veto over the selections of slogans, speakers, and texts of resolutions. The Federal Bureau of Investigation, in a report published March 25, 1983, noted that "Soviet-controlled organizations participated at the highest levels of the June 12 Committee and exerted pressure" in positive and negative directions. Earlier, the FBI's assistant director of intelligence, Edward J. O'Malley, had said that Soviet front groups had been "actively involved in the planning and implementation of the June 12 demonstration in New York."

The organizations in question were the World Peace Council; its national affiliate, the United States Peace Council; and the Communist Party of the United States. Everyone could undoubtedly agree that the United States should hasten disarmament, but the presence of WPC and like-minded representatives made agreement on any critique of the Soviet Union impossible. No banners saying, "Moscow, Take Your SS-20s Out of Europe!" or "Kremlin Nukes Are Just as Deadly!" were visible on that sunny day in New York's Central Park.

The FBI report stated: "Based on information available to us, we do not believe the Soviets have achieved a dominant role in the U.S. peace and nuclear freeze movement, or that they directly control or manipulate the movement." It added: "It is extremely difficult to determine the extent to which various peace organizations and coalitions are being influenced or manipulated by the Soviet Union." The report noted, however, that the U.S.S.R. seeks to "play on the sentiments of the Western peace movements" and tries to "create the impression that the Soviet Union is more interested than the United States in serious arms control and disarmament negotiations."

The FBI, in this instance, could be said to have phrased its conclusion with scholarly detachment.

CHAPTER · 8

Targets, Tactics, and Troubles

When the Reverend Billy Graham preached at the Leningrad House of Prayer, some 2,000 Baptists filled the hall. As he was leaving, several young men unfurled banners protesting the imprisonment of 200 Soviet Baptists who had been arrested for proselytizing. The crowd was much smaller at Moscow's Church of the Resurrection, a few days later. Approaches to the church were sprinkled with KGB agents who made sure that nothing untoward happened. In all, Graham's trip, in September 1984, enabled him to give more than 50 sermons, lectures, and speeches.

Soviet propaganda depicted the visit as a contribution to its ongoing "peace" campaign. Interviewed in the Viru Hotel in Tallinn, Estonia, Graham was asked this leading question: "During the 1982 World Conference, 'Religious Workers for Saving the Sacred Gift of Life from Nuclear Catastrophe,' you spoke of the increasing danger of nuclear war. Today you repeat that message. Many people throughout the world share your opinion. But there is the so-called 'silent majority.' Many people in the Third World believe that the issue is of no concern to them. How can they be involved in the just struggle for peace?"

Graham's answer, or at least the part printed in the Soivet press, was: "Many of them are struggling to survive from day to day, because they live in poverty. I do find that in many of those countries they are not overly concerned about a war that may destroy them, as they are [more concerned] about living and getting enough to eat that day."

The 1982 tour had exposed Graham to the charge that he permitted himself to be manipulated by Soviet peace movement propagandists who were exploiting delegations of clergy members by playing on their naiveté or vanities. After his 1984 tour, Graham told *U.S. News:* "I'm asked: Was I being used by Soviet officials? I have to reply, 'Possibly.' But it is a risk that I thought was worth taking for the sake of preaching the Gospel and, secondly, for the cause of world peace. To that extent, I was using them, and if lots of KGB agents were in those churches, that's all to the good because they are among the ones I want to reach."

Serge Schmeman, writing in the *New York Times* (September 17, 1985), commented: "The conflicting images of believers weeping and taping the words of the American evangelist, of K.G.B. agents lurking on the periphery, and of press accounts of Mr. Graham campaigning for peace, seemed to encapsule the contradictions inherent in his Soviet crusade. Two years earlier, when Mr. Graham came to Moscow for a church-sponsored anti-nuclear conference and to preach in the capital, he came under criticism in the United States for seeming naive about the plight of believers in the atheist state. He returned, this time, convinced that the impact of his words would outweigh whatever the strictures on his visit and the use the state tried to make of it."

Opening the Soviet-sponsored peace movement to the likes of Billy Graham troubled some Moscow officials. This had led to disagreement within the World Peace Council itself. The most startling public result was the demotion of Yuri Zhukov, for years the key Soviet official linking the Kremlin with this most influential of front organizations. At the height of his influence, Zhukov, a long-time staff member of *Pravda* and a candidate member of the Central Committee of the Soviet Communist Party, served simultaneously as chairman of the Soviet Committee for the Defense of Peace (SCDP) and as a vice president of the World Peace Council. Yet, following the World Assembly for Peace and Life, which took place in Prague from June 21 to 26, 1983, Zhukov was dropped from the roster of WPC vice presidents. This removed him from a "position behind the throne," that of chief Soviet adviser and guide to WPC President Romesh Chandra.

Who, after that, became the top Soviet personality in the peace movement and therefore in the front organization machinery generally? And what, exactly, had caused Zhukov's removal? As the Communist Party's Central Committee runs the front organization network through the International Department's International Social Organization's Sector, two men stand out: Vitali Shaposhnikov, the department's deputy chief and a member of the WPC Presidential Committee, and Yevgeni Primakov, a WPC vice president, who serves as first deputy chairman of the Soviet Peace Committee and holds the post of director of the Oriental Institute of the Academy of Science. Although Yuri Zhukov disappeared from the World Peace Council roster of vice presidents, Primakov remained as a transmitter of Soviet policies and general watchdog.

Zhukov lost a fight with the ghost of Willi Münzenberg; he had opposed the policy that opened the peace movement to all comers—including the likes of Graham—regardless of ideological impurity or lack of devotion to Kremlin atheistic policies. Zhukov tried to crack down on heretics within the European peace movement in 1982. He even sent a letter to several hundred non-Communist peace groups, denouncing those who were blaming not only NATO but also the Warsaw Pact for the arms race and world tensions. Zhukov first singled out the Bertrand Russell Foundation. The following year, he cracked down on the Working Group for a Nuclear-Free Europe, with headquarters in West Berlin, which had organized a Berlin disarmament conference in May 1983. He accused the group of not concentrating on NATO and of distracting the "peace-loving public from the main source of the deadly threat posed against the people of Europe—the plans for stationing a new generation of nuclear missiles in Europe."

The director of the Russell Foundation, Kenneth Coates, wrote Zhukov that he was doing "a disservice" to the World Peace Council with his "crude attempts to present us as mere *agents provocateurs* under the influence of Western powers." Zhukov was also criticized in the Yugoslav daily *Delo* (March 3, 1983), which castigated the letter as "crude interference in the internal affairs" of other countries and as an indirect attack on the spontaneous, unofficial peace movements then surfacing in East Germany and even in the Soviet Union. Zhukov had denounced Western peace groups for supporting "unofficial" East European peace activists. He failed to acknowledge that the tiny Committee to Establish Trust between the USSR and the USA had been crushed by Soviet authorities and cut off from contact with foreign correspondents; its key members were imprisoned.

Zhukov may have written this harsh round-robin letter without approval from the then director of the International Department, Boris Ponomarev, or of his influential deputy, Vadim Zagladin. Both men published articles that advocated continuing cooperation with anyone willing to join the World Peace Council or other front organizations in denouncing U.S. and NATO defense projects. Overall, this Münzenberg-type "united front" policy stood the Soviet Union in good stead, broadened Kremlin influence beyond the narrow limits of Soviet ideological followers, and permitted the recruitment, or entrapment, of "bourgeois" pacifists and other idealists.

By casting the peace net wide, the Central Committee men took calculated risks. Inevitably, the Soviet Union's own nuclear and conventional armamentarium had to attract attention. And the fears engendered by the propaganda campaign within the U.S.S.R. prompted the occasional sprouting of a home-grown mini-peace movement. In May 1983, a group of British women brought a bona fide Soviet peace activist into a Soviet Peace Committee meeting, headed by Oleg Kharkahardin. Two British delegates, Ann Pettitt and Karmen Cutler, were accompanied by an American, Jean McCollister, a Rhodes scholar from Seattle. The Soviet citizen who joined them, Olga Medvedkova, had been among the founders of an "unofficial" peace group in June 1982. Her group was harassed by Soviet authorities, and the British peace activists wanted to express their solidarity with a person who, after all, was pursuing aims ultimately identical with theirs. Cutler reported that, when the Russian woman was introduced, the "reaction was incredible." Medvedkova tried to explain her group's aims, but was interrupted. The Soviet delegate denounced the visitors for their "provocation" and "unfriendly act" and demanded to know whether this was "the way you do things in Britain." Pettitt explained that this was exactly the way things were done at home. Medvedkova quietly withdrew, and thus ended the encounter.

In East Germany, where memories of Nazi warfare have been kept alive, some young people have moved toward pacifism and religiously oriented opposition to war-related activities. The number of men who refuse armed service is relatively high; they are enlisted in civilian capacities. At the same time, churches have experienced a welling-up of pacifism, including preferences for hymns extolling peace. Such trends risk a momentum of their own. The Communist leadership in East Germany has sought to channel such sentiments, whose spontaneity it views with misgiving and distrust, into government-controlled peace activities.

The U.S. State Department, in a research study titled "Soviet Active Measures: The World Peace Council" (April 1985), noted that the WPC "lost substantial credibility among non-Communist European peace groups," because of its "unqualified support for controversial Soviet foreign policies and refusal to criticize any Soviet action." The study noted that, "in an effort to overcome the credibility gap and promote a unified anti-U.S peace platform in Europe," the World Peace Council and the Soviet Peace Committee attended the third European Nuclear Disarmament (END) convention in Perugia, Italy, from July 17 to 21, 1984. A year earlier, when Zhukov was still a WPC vice president, the council had boycotted an END convention, then in West Berlin, because of its "anti-Soviet character."

Two Soviet representatives came to the Perugia meeting, and it must surely have been one of their most difficult assignments. About 1,500 delegates attended the Perugia convention, some as individuals, others representing non-Communist antinuclear groups. The meeting opened with a row of seats left empty, decorated with flowers, set aside for "absent friends." This was a tribute to "unofficial" peace activists from Eastern European countries and the Soviet Union, who had been refused permission to travel; 59 Eastern activists, who had applied for visas, were turned down by their governments. A tragicomic matter of Soviet verbiage was involved. On the one hand, such groups as the Soviet Peace Committee claimed that they were "unofficial," not governmental, agencies; on the other hand, spontaneously organized peace groups in the U.S.S.R. and

Eastern Europe were denounced by them as "unofficial." Gregori Lokshin, a secretary of the Soviet Peace Committee, angered convention participants when he claimed that imprisoned Soviet peace activists had not been punished for advocating mutual disarmament, but because they were guilty of "hooliganism." He said of one Soviet peace assembly, known as the "Trust Group," that it was "supported by President Reagan." When challenged by a British delegate, Lokshin shouted, "I know better. I live in the Soviet Union, not in the United Kingdom."

The second Soviet representative, Yevgeni Sylin, identified as deputy chairman of the Council for European Security and Cooperation, a WPC affiliate, encountered sharp questioning during a press conference attended by more convention participants than reporters. He was asked why the Soviet Peace Committee had never questioned the Soviet placing of nuclear missiles in Czechoslovakia and East Germany. He replied that there were no differences of opinion between the Soviet government and its people. He prompted derisive laughter when he explained: "Public opinion and official opinion are the same in our society. They are always the same. We have ways of establishing this link."

Zhukov, who remained active as chairman of the Soviet Peace Committee, might well have regarded his original position as justified by the Perugia debacle. Shortly after the END convention (August 6, 1984), the Soviet Peace Committee arranged one of its "peace shifts" in the Russian Federation, the Ukraine, and the Central Asian republics. Zhukov told Tass, "People will work in their spare time and remit the earnings to the Peace Fund." He recalled the atom-bombing of Hiroshima and Nagasaki by the United States, 39 years earlier, saying that history would "never forgive the American military its heinous crime" and that "the Soviet people reiterate their solidarity with the struggle of the progressive Japanese people for a comprehensive ban on nuclear weapons, against the policy of remilitarizing their country and attempts at dragging it into U.S. military adventures, and for a peace-loving and neutral Japan."

Moscow media refrained from commenting on the Perugia convention until the Communist Party's theoretical journal, *Kommunist,* published its August issue (No. 12, 1984). The journal charged that "irresponsible" and "clamorous Trotskyists and leftist-anarchists" had tried to use the meeting to create a "Cold War confrontation." *Kommunist* denounced the END's concept of equal East-West responsibility for nuclear arms as a "perfidious essence." It concluded, nevertheless, by calling for "dialogue, persuasion and patient explanation," even when the positions of others are "inconsistent or wrong." The journal urged Western peace activists not to aim at an "equal distance," but to direct their "main blow" at the "source and cause of the nuclear threat." In other words, despite the Perugia confrontation, the ghost of Münzenberg was not to be denied.

Actually, several Soviet propaganda campaigns suffered mini-Perugias and maxi-Perugias, which shook various front organizations, during more than a third of the century. The World Peace Council was originally formed in 1949 as the World Committee of Partisans for Peace, but adopted its briefer, all-encompassing name a year later. For a year, it had its headquarters in Paris. It suffered its first defeat when the French government, noting the council's "fifth column nature," refused to accommodate it. Next, the WPC made its home in Prague; then, moving cautiously west again, it settled in Vienna from 1954 to 1957. But the Austrian government, conscious of the country's delicately balanced diplomatic status, refused further hospitality. Still, the WPC retained a foothold in Vienna, keeping its International Institute for Peace, identified as a "research" body, at the council's old address. The World Peace Council finally established permanent headquarters in Helsinki. Other propaganda bodies, such as some of Novosti's international publishing activities, also operate from the Finnish capital.

Northern European centers, Helsinki and Stockholm prominent among them, have served as springboards of numerous propaganda drives. The first major campaign, featuring the "Ban the Bomb!" slogan, was launched as the "Stockholm Peace Pledge" in March 1950 with the following appeal: "We demand the absolute banning of the atom weapon, arm of terror and mass exterminator of populations. . . . We consider that any government which would be first to use the atom weapon against any country would be committing a crime against humanity and should be dealt with as a war criminal. . . . We call on all men of good will throughout the world to sign this appeal." The World Peace Council, at its Second Congress in November 1950, claimed that 500 million people had signed the "Stockholm Peace Pledge." Linking the appeal to Stockholm, capital of traditionally neutral and liberal Sweden, gave the pledge an air of humanitarian objectivity. As Shultz and Godson note, the campaign "was directed against the United States and NATO" and lasted for two decades, as long as "the United States held a nuclear advantage." They added that "once the WPC peace and disarmament campaign was under way, other Soviet international fronts followed the lead of this group and organized similar efforts."

When North Korea attacked South Korea in mid-1950, prompting the dispatch of UN forces, the World Peace Council again selected the United States as its target. This lasted until 1953 and culminated in the charge that U.S. troops were practicing germ warfare against North Korean troops. The then-president of the WPC, the prominent French scientist and Communist Party member Frédéric Joliot-Curie, sent telegrams to U.S. officials, denouncing the alleged "germ warfare."

From the end of the Korean War until Nikita Khrushchev's secret speech in 1965 revealing Stalin's excesses, and the subsequent Soviet military crackdown on Czechoslovakia, the WPC and its subfronts concentrated on such overall themes as disarmament and efforts to drive a wedge between the NATO powers and the United States. For one of these years a helpful report and analysis exists in *Target: The World; Communist Propaganda Activities in 1955,* edited by Evron M. Kirkpatrick (1956). The names and initials of the various front organizations, their slogans, the themes of their conferences, the number of signatures allegedly collected, the texts of their resolutions, and the travels of their spokesmen and participants are all quite numbing.

Following the example of the earlier Stockholm and Warsaw Appeals, the WPC began the year 1955 with a "Vienna Appeal," designed to spread ban-the-bomb pledges and the collection of still more signatures. The WPC meeting in the Austrian capital, in January, was attended by representatives of the World Federation of Trade Unions (WFTU), the Women's Democratic International Federation (WDIF), the World Federation of Democratic Youth (WFDY), and the International Federation of Resistance Fighters.

The following month, a Conference for the Peaceful Solution of the German Problem was held in Warsaw (it had originally been scheduled for Paris, but the French government refused visas for several delegates from Communist-governed countries). It was followed in April by the Asian Conference for Relaxation of International Tensions in New Delhi, which created an Asian Solidarity Committee and passed a 13-point resolution.

The main WPC event of 1955 was the World Assembly for Peace in Helsinki (June 22 to 29). It had originally been planned for April, but shifts in the Soviet Union's position on the disarmament question seemed to have caused a postponement. According to WPC accounts, the meeting was attended by 1,841 persons from 68 countries. It ended with a "Helsinki Appeal" that contained such demands as a united front of "peace movements and big political organizations of Christian and socialist tendencies," German reunification outside the NATO framework, and an end to a "policy of strength, military blocs and the arms race." The meeting switched from earlier demands for the destruction of atomic weapons to calls for a gradual "abolition of nuclear weapons," to be achieved "by agreed stages." By then, the Soviet Union had developed its own atomic weapons, and it no longer favored across-the-board "destruction" of such devices.

With the "Vienna Appeal" as their springboard, various front organizations saw a tempting theme in the "day of protest" against atomic weapons that had been planned by Japanese organizations. Pressure from WPC-controlled groups and delegates for admission to the planned three-day commemoration in Hiroshima, beginning August 6, was so massive that the government could not control it. Hiroshima city authorities eventually disowned the "International Rally against Atomic and Hydrogen Weapons"; the meeting was so effectively infiltrated, or overrun, that it passed a "Manifesto" against "the forces planning atomic war."

The World Peace Council still had to complete its shift, away from the call for destruction of atomic stockpiles, demanded in the "Vienna Appeal," and in line with the new Soviet policy of protecting its own atomic interests, while pushing its propaganda-cum-diplomacy campaign against U.S. atomic strength. The WPC's executive bureau met twice toward the end of 1950, first in Vienna in October and then in Helsinki in December. In Vienna, Emmanuel d'Astier de la Vigerie, acting as deputy for the absent council President Joliot-Curie, said the "Vienna Appeal" should cease to be "the central theme" of the peace movement, but be linked with the whole disarmament question, although "its fundamental demand" remained "of value." The Vienna session ended on the noncontroversial note of planning to honor such "representatives of science, literature and the arts" as Benjamin Franklin, Wolfgang Amadeus Mozart, Heinrich Heine, Bernard Shaw, Pierre Curie, Henrik Ibsen, the Hindu dramatist Kalidas, Toyo Oda, and Fyodor Dostoyevski.

The WPC's December meeting in Helsinki dropped all references to the destruction of atomic stockpiles, demanded a "world campaign for disarmament," and attacked "advocates of the Cold War" in the United States and Great Britain. An embarrassing note was struck by a Canadian participant, the Reverend D. C. Candy, who questioned whether the World Peace Council was not, after all, under Communist control. A number of speakers sought to answer this fairly obvious question in the negative.

The record of other major front organizations during the fairly routine year of 1955 documents the accuracy of the French truism, *plus ça change, plus c'est la même chose;* over some three decades, a great deal of Soviet-controlled front activity has remained the same. The World Federation of Democratic Youth held its Fifth International Festival of Youth and Students in Warsaw from July 31 to August 15, 1955, a smaller version of the Youth Festival in Moscow in 1985. The World Federation of Trade Unions declared March 10, 1955, as "International Fighting Day against the Paris Agreement," a rather innocuous and long-forgotten document which the WFTU denounced as advancing "remilitarization of Western Germany." This target closely resembled the campaign against German "revanchism" undertaken by the front groups three decades later. The WFTU, in the best "united front" spirit of the Vienna meeting, called for cooperation with such organizations as the International Federation of Christian Trade Unions, "for the improvement of relations and cooperation between trade unions of different trends."

Also along "united front" lines, the International Union of Students (IUS) spoke of cooperation during its annual council meeting in Sofia,

Bulgaria. The meeting followed the Warsaw festival by ten days. IUS President Jiri Pelikan called for "even greater efforts to achieve cooperation and unity on a national and international scale." (In later years, Pelikan divorced himself from the IUS and all Soviet-controlled front organizations, citing their undemocratic procedures and strict adherence to Soviet policies.)

The Women's International Democratic Federation in 1955 concentrated on celebrating International Women's Day on March 8. It prepared to hold a World Congress of Mothers, first scheduled for Paris, then for Copenhagen, and finally held in Lausanne, Switzerland, from July 7 to 10. More than 1,200 delegates from 66 countries were said to have attended. Their resolution called for "large-scale general disarmament." Evron Kirkpatrick commented: "The activities of other Communist international-front groups in general repeated the pattern set by the World Peace Council. Their principal efforts during 1955 therefore centered on prohibition of atomic weapons, disarmament, opposition to German disarmament, and utilizing the 'Geneva spirit' in an effort to form united fronts with legitimate groups in their various spheres of influence." The "Geneva spirit" of 1955 found its equivalent in the slogans of "peaceful coexistence" and "détente." In fact, even in 1955, the International Association of Democratic Lawyers held a Conference of Asian Democratic Lawyers in Calcutta, in January, that prepared for a Rome meeting that failed to receive Italian government approval, but developed into a Vienna meeting which called for concentration of "problems of peaceful coexistence, examined from the point of view of international public rights."

The International Organization of Journalists (IOJ) met in Sofia in October. As Khrushchev was making his peace with Yugoslavia, the IOJ revoked an earlier decision to expel a Yugoslav journalist. The World Congress of Doctors, which did not make a lasting impact, sought to gain attention with an International Medical Conference on Radioactivity in Japan. Its findings led to the conclusion that "explosions of atomic and hydrogen bombs should not be allowed to be repeated and that the use of atomic energy should be limited to peaceful and constructive purposes."

The World Federation of Teachers' Unions prepared for a world conference, celebrated International Teachers Day on October 1, and called for "improved contacts" with teachers in "capitalist countries." The World Federation of Scientific Workers concentrated on "scientific aspects" of a ban on atomic weapons and on informing the public on "questions of vital importance." Joliot-Curie, president of the WPC, was reelected president of the scientific federation as well.

After this year of wide-ranging but undramatic activity, 1956 came like a thunderbolt, followed by lightning, torrential rains, and much damage!

First, Khrushchev's speech threw the international Communist movement into chaos; next, the self-deluded optimism of the Hungarian Communist Party and regime, which interpreted Khrushchev's revelations as the beginning of serious liberalization, led to the suppression of Hungarian aspirations by Soviet tanks. As the front organizations always contained a mixture of unrealistic hopefuls, the Hungarian events caused much unrest and defection within the World Peace Council and lesser front groups. However, Moscow managed to bottle up such dissents within each organization; published versions of proceedings, as well as the ultimate texts of the inevitable resolutions, manifestos, and proclamations adhered strictly to the Soviet line.

Over the years, successive crises within the front movements occurred whenever the Soviet Union made one of its blatant moves, such as the invasion of Czechoslovakia in 1968 and of Afghanistan in 1979. The unrest in Poland, which led to a ban on the Solidarity labor union, also presented a recurring problem to the leadership of the World Peace Council and lesser front groups. Sheer persistence and repetition, together with control of finances, access to meetings, and "packing" of committees and executive bodies, enabled the Soviet Communist Party's International Department to continue long-range control, despite some serious defections.

Suppression of dissent in East Germany, Poland, Hungary, and Czechoslovakia occurred during periods when the power struggle in the Kremlin created splits within Soviet leadership, as well as within the Communist parties and the sprawling front organizations. Once Khrushchev was removed, in 1964, Soviet leadership settled down to a long stretch of single-minded policies that included the 1968 invasion of Czechoslovakia and establishment of the so-called "Brezhnev Doctrine" (named for party leader Leonid Brezhnev): the concept that the Soviet Union had the right and duty to use force in putting down any serious ideological and administrative deviation in one of the "fraternal" Communist-governed countries. The concept was incorporated into policies advocated by the various front organizations, although they usually refrained from actually defining positive policies, in contrast to negative attacks on the alleged wrongdoings of the United States and its "imperialist" allies.

U.S. involvement in the Vietnam War, which prompted widespread opposition even within the United States itself, was a boost to the World Peace Council and its satellite organizations. Once again, the Swedish capital was chosen as the springboard for a long-range and far-flung propaganda campaign. The WPC organized the Stockholm Conference on Vietnam, which became an annual event from 1967 to 1972. Using the Vietnam issue as a wedge, the WPC sought to weaken the U.S. position in Europe by linking the war with local issues. Romesh Chandra told the Budapest assembly of the World Peace Council, which met from May 13 to 16, that the Vietnam War should be juxtaposed with "the problems of European security, of the ending of aggressive imperialist pacts and bases."

The Stockholm meeting, in turn, organized the World Conference on Vietnam, Laos, and Cambodia (November 1970). Once the Vietnam War was over, Shultz and Godson noted, "The fronts again shifted their main focus to NATO. Beginning in the mid-1970s, WPC activities concentrated first on the neutron weapon, and then on the modernization of NATO's nuclear forces." It should not be forgotten that, while the WPC and other front organizations engaged in such "unofficial" propaganda activities, the Soviet Union's diplomatic and other official facilities were concentrating on identical tactical targets. The fronts also took aim, on and off, at other targets, notably Germany and other NATO countries, and at Japan. When Chinese and Vietnamese troops clashed early in 1979, the World Peace Council organized the International Conference in Vietnam (Hanoi, 1980), which denounced the Peking action and celebrated the ninetieth anniversary of Ho Chi Minh's birth.

The neutron bomb, described as capable of being directed against personnel rather than buildings and other facilities, was a ready-made target for the WPC-directed peace movement. The bomb was under consideration, with a good deal of misgivings and domestic opposition, during the administration of U.S. President Jimmy Carter. In the face of strong opposition, some of it orchestrated by the WPC, Carter dropped the project. During the campaign, Chandra himself contributed to the WPC's output. In his introduction to the council's pamphlet *Neutron Bombs No!* he wrote: "The world-wide campaign launched by the World Peace Council in August 1977 for the prohibition of the neutron bomb is the most powerful mass movement in recent times against weapons of mass destruction and for the ending of the arms race. The call of the World Peace Council has been supported actively by numerous international and national organizations representing literally tens of millions of people in all countries." In the face of strong opposition, at home and abroad, with support from the WPC, President Carter dropped the project in April 1978.

Taking its cues from the 1980 U.S. presidential election campaign, the front organizations followed the official Moscow line of depicting the incoming Reagan administration as aggressive, war-minded, and intent on creating U.S. arms superiority over the U.S.S.R. During the Carter years, there had been three major peace congresses: the World Congress of Peace Forces, held in Moscow from October 25 to 31, 1973; the World Assembly of Builders of Peace, held in Warsaw from May 6 to 11, 1977; and the World Parliament of Peoples for Peace, held in Sofia from September 23 to 27, 1980. The Moscow Congress was opened by Chandra, who greeted

3,200 delegates from 144 countries. Brezhnev pledged support "from the CPSU, the Soviet Government and all the Soviet people." The congress passed a series of resolutions, including one on collective security in Asia that caused protests from Japanese and Australian delegates. The final communiqué was not signed by the World Federation of United Nations Organizations, nor by the World Veterans Association, which considered it "one-sided."

The Warsaw Congress, attended by 1,500 delegates from 125 countries, also received a Brezhnev pledge of Soviet support. It denounced "imperialism" and "neocolonialism" and passed resolutions ranging from criticism of religious discrimination to support of Soviet proposals for "complete and general disarmament." The Sofia Congress was attended by 2,260 delegates from 137 countries. It, too, received a message of support from Brezhnev. Bulgarian President Todo Zhivkov gave an opening address critical of the United States and NATO. WPC President Chandra praised "victories" won by the peoples of Angola, Mozambique, Guinea-Bissau, Ethiopia, and Nicaragua.

. The Sofia Congress took place less than a year after the Soviet invasion of Afghanistan, and the country's Moscow-supported leader, Babrak Karmal, sent a message to the congress. The congress was also distinguished by the presence of Boris Ponomarev, who denounced U.S. efforts to "foist" new nuclear weapons on Western Europe, and assured the meeting that "the Soviet Union threatens nobody, not the United States, nor China, nor Japan, nor Western Europe." The meeting unanimously adopted the World Peace Parliament Charter, and Chandra said at a concluding press conference that "the peace policy of the Soviet Union is a thing for which all peoples are striving."

In 1986, the World Peace Council utilized the United Nations as a conduit for its statements, within the framework of the International Year of Peace, proclaimed by the UN General Assembly. On May 16, Western European Communist parties ended a strategic meeting in Vienna, which *Pravda* (May 17) defined as dealing with "problems of Communists' cooperation with new public movements in the industrially developed capitalist countries." The meeting was sponsored jointly by the Communist Party of Austria and the magazine *Problems of Peace and Socialism (World Marxist Review)*, the theoretical journal of the world Communist movement. The Vienna meeting followed a session of the World Peace Council in Sofia, Bulgaria, late in April. Chandra was once again named council president. The post of general secretary, which had been vacant, was filled by Johannes Pakaslahti of Finland. Yuri Zhukov appeared restored to prominence. As head of the Soviet delegation and chairman of the Soviet Peace Committee, he gave the key address at the meeting, calling for

"thorough and self-critical discussions about the future work of the movement, with regard to the more intricate international situation." Zhukov
acted as chairman of the Soviet committee to administer the International
Year of Peace, including a congress to be held in Copenhagen from October
15 to 19. He told the British Communist paper *Morning Star* (February
24) that, if U.S. President Reagan had backed Soviet "peace initiatives,
we wouldn't have been afraid of being labeled pro-American."

PART · 2

OVERT AND COVERT

CHAPTER · 9

New York–Paris–Moscow

The image has become familiar: the U.S. television anchorman sits in New York; the Soviet spokesman, by satellite, speaks from Moscow. While Soviet propaganda is directed at multiple targets all over the world, New York has become its top target—if only as a transmission point to all of the United States and much of the rest of the Western world. When Mikhail Gorbachev wanted to take his message directly to the American public, and a worldwide audience generally, before meeting with President Reagan in 1985, it was *Time* magazine, edited in New York, that proved a highly effective vehicle. The U.S. television networks, with their vast audiences, have increasingly been used to channel Moscow's version of events abroad. And it is from its offices at New York's Columbia University that the W. Averell Harriman Institute for Advanced Study of the Soviet Union monitors Russia's domestic television transmissions.

After the Bolshevik Revolution, Lenin fully expected a worldwide Marxist revolution, beginning with Germany. Characteristically, the common language used at the offices and meetings of the Communist International was German, rather than Russian. When Willi Münzenberg operated his front organizations, fund-raising campaigns, and publications, the center of activity was Berlin. After the Hitler takeover, the operation was moved to Paris. While British intellectuals who were attracted to the Soviet Union before World War II became active fellow travelers and even joined Moscow's espionage apparatus, London remained a secondary target for Soviet propaganda activities. Amsterdam, Stockholm, and Geneva served as conference centers, but purely as a matter of passing convenience and to provide a neutral meeting ground. Today, Vienna and Helsinki serve similar purposes.

When Münzenberg's front organizations were looking for causes, funds, and the names of prominent supporters in the United States, they centered their attention on New York. During World War II, Mexico City served as a temporary haven for Communist intellectuals, some of whom settled in East Germany after the war. For a time, an active group of Communists and sympathizers functioned in Hollywood, including screenwriters, actors, and motion-picture executives. As the U.S. Communist Party and its sympathizers lost support, following World War II, and the Communist International ceased to exist, Moscow-directed propaganda began to flow through other channels. Still, the U.S. Communist Party continued to publish its daily paper (formerly the *Daily Worker,* later the *Daily World*), its theoretical monthly, *Political Affairs,* and special publications aimed largely at labor and minorities. From its headquarters building, called *Unity Center,* in Manhattan, the party continues propaganda functions through mass meetings, briefings of party members, and classes and conferences at its People's School for Marxist Studies; its Unity Bookstore provides a wide range of books, pamphlets, and periodicals. Russian-language literature and English-language material, published in the U.S.S.R., were available for decades at the Four Continent Book Corporation on Fifth Avenue in New York, but the corporation was succeeded in 1983 by Victor Kamkin, Inc., with headquarters in Rockville, Maryland. Other U.S. outlets are Imported Publications, Inc., in Chicago, and the Znanie Book Store in San Francisco.

At the time of the Bolshevik Revolution, the key pro-Bolshevik publication was the magazine *The Masses,* succeeded by *The New Masses.* The magazine turned into a proving ground for a generation of writers and cartoonists, many of whom achieved considerable success later on, and quite a few of whom broke sharply with Soviet doctrine at various points of their careers. These included Max Eastman, an editor of *The Masses* as far back as 1912, who sided with Trotsky and became his biographer, wrote widely, and elegantly, and concluded his career as an editor of *Reader's Digest.*

The Communist movement and its satellite organizations and publications acted as conveyor belts in the lives of men and women who, in many cases, had a youthful flirtation with the promises of the Soviet state. A reverse path was taken by one U.S. author, Theodore Dreiser, whose novels gave him prominence during the first two decades of the century; of these, *An American Tragedy* (1925) was the most widely acclaimed. Münzenberg's drive to enlist prominent intellectuals was then in full swing. On October 11, 1927, F. G. Biedenkapp, secretary of International Workers' Aid, approached Dreiser on Münzenberg's behalf. He told him he represented something like "Russia's Red Cross" and uttered an irresistible compliment: "The Soviets believe you to be the outstanding literary intelligence in America." With that, he invited Dreiser to visit the Soviet Union.

The result was a book, *Dreiser Looks at Russia,* filled with a mixture of naive admiration, petty irritations, ideological passages, and a great deal of sheer ego display. This was, after all, the period of Stalin's consolidation of power, great economic difficulty, and increasing cultural control. Dreiser rebelled against much he saw, but felt constrained to explain it away, to himself as much as to his readers. For example: "This dictatorship is a weapon for a particular end—the bringing of that classless, brother-loving society in which no dictatorship will be needed." Dreiser's data were so carelessly assembled that even his tolerant biographer, W. A. Swanberg, wrote in *Dreiser* that, "in his search for ultimate truths," he "was often shaky in mere facts and figures." As a traveler, Dreiser went no further east than Baku but claimed he had been as far as Samarkand, possibly for the simple reason that he liked the exotic sound of the city's name.

In many of his observations, whether in praise or criticism, Dreiser sounded like the quintessential rube, the true provincial, shocked by Russian untidiness and cultural underdevelopment. "And yet," he wrote apologetically, there is "not a city, not a village or hamlet in all Russia today that is not feeling the thrill of the new intellectual and social life emanating from the leaders and theorists in Moscow." It is like aiming at a sitting duck to note that Dreiser had not been in every city, village, and hamlet, could not know the "thrill" of the Russian masses, and had all-too-lofty ideas of Stalin and his men.

What truly annoyed Dreiser was the ever-present propaganda. He devoted 15 pages to "the endless outpour and downpour" of it, on schoolchildren, soldiers, workers, peasants, mothers, fathers, and everyone in between. "Really," he exclaimed, "I never saw its equal anywhere—almost a nightmare of propaganda." One poster he encountered everywhere was done in "flaming red," which showed "a massed group of young and valiant Communist workers, guns in hand, bayonets fixed, standing as a red wall against an approaching storm of capitalistic ills, pictured in this instance as a mass of black water overhung by tumultuous and sinister clouds, in their turn composed of greedy and sensuous and selfish faces and eyes and hands." It was, he added, "quite vivid."

For all his tendency to be forgiving and apologetic, Dreiser "took a particular interest in the Communists' repeated declaration that in Russia there was absolute freedom of the press to think and say what it chose— criticize the Communist rule if it chose." But, he discovered, there was no "news or criticism or opinion of any kind that was not safely held within the lines of *Isvestia* or *Pravda* and always with the intellectual slant directed by the central group in Moscow." He noted that provincial papers imitated the Moscow papers, "with not a trace of deviation."

Dreiser also found displeasing "this business of propagandizing as well as censoring, or censoring as well as propagandizing" theaters, motion pictures, and the opera. The great actor-director Konstantin Stanislavsky told Dreiser he would have liked to put on his two plays, *The Hand of the Potter* and *An American Tragedy,* but "the Communist censor would have none of it." On the other hand, Dreiser discovered that a production of *The Robbers,* by the German poet-dramatist Friedrich von Schiller, had been "edited and furnished with a prologue and an epilogue in order to make it teach independence to the rising youth of Russia." This doctrinal revision struck Dreiser as "annoying and pestiferous." A Leningrad showing of *Uncle Tom's Cabin* had been altered, "with little Eva left out and Simon Legree shot by a young negro introduced into the play especially for this purpose," to dramatize "opposition to tyranny."

Dreiser viewed Soviet propaganda as heavily militaristic, anticipating a war with the "capitalist" nations as "inescapable." He ended his trip with mixed feelings, and confessed that, after Moscow, the capitals of Western Europe were a refreshing change. Still, by 1932, his ideological emotions had evolved to a point where he asked Earl Browder, then head of the U.S. Communist Party, to let him become a full-fledged member. Dreiser expected the party to welcome him with enthusiasm; instead, Browder turned him down, as sweetly as possible. He could not very well have done otherwise. For a party member, Dreiser was much too volatile, egocentric, and eccentric; but as a nonparty fellow traveler, he was continually useful.

During the 1940s, Dreiser looked back with nostalgia on his visit to the Soviet Union. When Browder was dismissed from the Communist Party's leadership and replaced by William Z. Foster, Dreiser once again applied for party membership. A letter, dated July 20, 1945, and drafted for his signature, cited Dreiser's reasons for wanting to join the party. *The New Masses* announced this membership (August 7) under the heading, "Dreiser Joins the Vanguard." He died later that year, on December 28.

Other fellow travelers followed a reverse route, from enthusiasm to disillusionment. With some, this journey was undertaken quietly; others made their changes of heart and mind publicly and dramatically known. Such traumatic events as the killings of Trotsky, the Nazi-Soviet Pact, the invasions of Hungary and Czechoslovakia, Khrushchev's revelations, and the invasion of Afghanistan were landmarks along the way. As many prominent fellow travelers were highly individualistic personalities, their roles varied. Changing interests and life paths influenced decisions. In France, the veteran supporter of front organizations, Henri Barbusse, died before he had to face a historic event that might have led to disillusion. The

French novelist Romain Rolland, a veteran Münzenberg supporter, kept his doubts private; he died in France during World War II.

A vivid case of public disillusionment, among French intellectuals, was that of André Gide, roughly a contemporary of Dreiser. As a prominent French novelist and essayist well into the 1930s, Gide was viewed by the Communists with mixed emotions until excerpts were published from his diaries in *La Nouvelle Revue Française* (July 1932) that revealed his wish "to live long enough to see the plans of Russia succeed." Subsequent diary installments expanded on these sentiments. Herbert R. Lottman wrote in his politico-literary history *The Left Bank,* "With this declaration of love for the Soviet Union, Gide was to be drawn into history. Soon after the first sensational pages of his journal appeared in print, he was asked to endorse a World Congress Against War which Henri Barbusse and Romain Rolland were promoting." This meeting, mentioned in an earlier chapter, took place in March 1933. There, Gide stated, in a manner reminiscent of Dreiser, that even if the Soviet Union restricted freedom, this was done "to make it possible, at long last, to establish a new society."

These years, just before World War II, roughly between 1935 and 1939, were the highpoint of the Popular Front period. Moscow had adopted its "united front" tactic. The Nazi menace enabled Soviet policy makers to enlist wide support behind slogans of "anti-Fascism," while intellectuals in Europe and the United States were eager to gain a reputation as political activists. French writers were being wooed by their Soviet equivalent, the versatile, talented Ilya Ehrenburg, who was perhaps culturally more at home in Paris than in Moscow. To the world of literature generally, Maxim Gorki remained the foremost representative of Russia's proletarian novelists.

Among France's prominent left-wing authors, André Malraux then outranked even Barbusse and Rolland. All of them were eager to have Gide join the pro-Moscow bandwagon, and he was promptly swept along by the tidal wave of this politico-intellectual propaganda drive. In January 1934, Gide accompanied Malraux to Berlin. They left a note with Propaganda Minister Joseph Goebbels, urging that Georgi Dimitrov, accused of planning the Reichstag fire, be released from prison; a few weeks later, Dimitrov was freed. True to the Münzenberg method, Gide was now on the propagandistic conveyor belt, busily addressing meetings and signing proclamations that implemented "united front" policies.

As Lottman recalled, "It was the decade of pilgrimages to the Soviet Union. Gide had been planning such a journey for years." Now he was being urged to make just such a pilgrimage himself. The Soviet public, he was told, had come to vastly appreciate his writings. Ehrenburg told him that he had a duty to dramatize, in person, the Franco-Soviet alliance. Louis Aragon, the French Communist Party's untiring literary stalwart, was the Paris contact who notified Moscow that Gide was, indeed, about to depart for the Marxist utopia: He left from Le Bourget airport on June 16, 1936.

André Gide, a man of determined good will, arrived on Soviet soil ready to overlook shortcomings, even injustices, as long as he could be sure that Moscow's long-range aims were pure and grand. Gorki died shortly after his arrival in Moscow, and Gide eulogized Gorki in a memorial meeting on Red Square. The rest of his trip had a Potemkin-like flair. Some 100,000 postcards featuring Gide's face had been distributed. Students assembled for a Gide exhibition at their university. But banners in his honor, on display at successive railway stops, actually accompanied Gide in a forward railroad car; they were put in place, complete with cheering crowds, before he was permitted to alight from the train. Gide was not fooled.

On one occasion, when Gide drafted a thank-you telegram to Stalin, his guide-interpreters refused to pass it along until he had added several sycophantic terms. This happened in Gori, Soviet Georgia, Stalin's birthplace. Gide recalled later that he had written something like this: "Passing through Gori, in the course of our wonderful journey, I feel the need to send you my most cordial . . ." His translator bridled at the use of a plain "you" in addressing the great Stalin, saying that it sounded "positively shocking." Gide was told that some added phrase such as "leader of the workers" or "master of the peoples" was necessary. Naively, Gide protested that Stalin was surely above such primitive flattery. But he was bluntly told that some such term had to be added, or there would be no telegram. His speeches were also "touched up," with adjectives such as "glorious" added when he mentioned the Soviet Union. In reverse, he was told that he could not call a monarch, any monarch, "great," and so that word was excised.

There was a great deal more of this sort of thing. Still, Gide completed his tour quietly, acting more or less according to the plans that had been set out for him. But he took notes on his observations, and started to write a critical account of his Soviet visit as soon as he returned to France. The book, *Retour de l'URSS,* went to the printer on October 21, its text carefully kept secret. Yet Ehrenburg somehow managed to read all of it before the presses started to turn. He quietly cautioned Gide to delay the book long enough to avoid hurting the Republican cause in the Spanish Civil War. Other pressures were less diplomatic.

The fateful book was published on November 5, and from then on Gide was ostracized by much of the French literary establishment. Where he had been lionized before, he now met cold indifference. Lottman wrote: "Gide became a pre-Orwellian unperson. His name disappeared from Communist-controlled publications, from the boards of their organizations.

Polemicists were enlisted to denounce him on the floor at meetings of the House of Culture, in the columns of Party organs and fellow-traveling periodicals." *Pravda* in Moscow and *L'Humanité,* the French Communist Party organ in Paris, joined in denouncing the man they had hailed a few months earlier. One friend, Jean Guéhenno, noted, "The human warmth with which he had felt surrounded for several years, this affection which was perhaps on order, but nevertheless this affection which had borne him for a time, he felt that—again on order—it was being withdrawn." They were letting Gide "marinate," and this was a tactical mistake.

Gide had actually pulled his punches when he wrote *Retour de l'URSS.* Several of his most acerbic observations had been left out of the book. Being the detailed note taker he was, Gide had retained a number of tidbits. These, together with reflections made following publication of the earlier book, were then published under the title *Retouches à mon Retour de l'URSS.* The little book dotted the i's and crossed the t's. In it, Gide confessed that he had read Leon Trotsky's writings, and those of the Belgian-born Soviet emigré Viktor Serge, only after he published his earlier work. Like much of the rest of the pro-Communist litterateurs, he had been swept up by Soviet propaganda and fallen victim to his own ignorance. This was the last straw. Ehrenburg lashed out at Gide, calling him "wicked" and a "crybaby."

The whole pro-Moscow phalanx trained its guns on Gide, including a multitalented German novelist, Lion Feuchtwanger. Just how ubiquitous Feuchtwanger was, and is, emerged in 1984: Both East and West Germany celebrated the one-hundredth anniversary of his birth on July 7, 1884, with new editions of his works, public celebrations, and television dramas based on his works. Under the title, "An Esthete in the Soviet Union," published in the German-language periodical *Das Wort* in Moscow (February 1937), Feuchtwanger said Gide had merely left "the ivory tower of the esthete," and gone to the Soviet Union "because he was bored and needed some exercise." Gide looked on the U.S.S.R. "with an all-too-keen eye," Feuchtwanger said, "noting thousands of small imperfections, lack of taste and comfort, but failed to see the great, imposing blueprint of the whole." Feuchtwanger, later less enthusiastic about the Soviet Union, acknowledged that, in several Soviet areas, "greater tolerance would be desirable." He noted that Gide had denounced the "pagan worship" of Stalin, but attributed this phenomenon to a "naive, natural, human expression of agreement with socialism and with the regime." Unlike other sometime enthusiasts of Soviet policies, Feuchtwanger did not settle in East Germany; he died in Pacific Palisades, California, on December 21, 1958.

The Nazi-Soviet Pact, the German attack on the Soviet Union, and the World War II alliance created changes in the political and cultural climate. Once the embarrassment of the "nonaggression" pact between Hitler and

Stalin was erased, the "united front" was reborn. The switchover was accomplished with as much grace as possible. Resentment of Nazi aggression and Japanese expansionism was strong enough, during the war years, to overshadow misgivings about Stalin's ultimate aims.

The astonishing acceptance of Moscow's version of Stalinist actions in two major events, forced collectivization and the show trials, can be traced to psychological as well as information factors. To begin with, there was an emotional habit not to speak ill of the Soviet "experiment," as it had been the target of so much wishful thinking during the 1920s and into the 1930s; then, there was a successful effort by the Kremlin propaganda machine to discourage adverse reports and favor correspondents who reported events inside the Soviet Union in accordance with official wishes.

Foreign correspondents who wished to retain access to news sources in the Soviet capital could get along by being "selective" in their coverage. One of these was *New York Times* correspondent Walter Duranty, whose dispatches did little to inform the world of the true nature of the Stalinist regime. One *New York Times* man, John Chamberlain, who was a book reviewer at the time, recalled in his autobiography, *A Life with the Printed Word,* how disenchantment with Duranty's cynicism triggered his own disillusionment with Communists and their fellow travelers.

Chamberlain was about to review the book *Escape from the Soviets,* by Tatiana Tchernavina, who described the hardships she suffered in order to make her way to the West. "If it had been a few months earlier," Chamberlain wrote, "I probably would have put the book to one side on the specious theory that the Russian Revolution, while admittedly imperfect, needed time to work itself out without being hectored by dissenters." He added: "But I heard something from the *Times*'s own Moscow correspondent, Walter Duranty, that was really disquieting. To a group in the *Times* elevator Duranty had almost casually mentioned that three million people had died in Russia in what amounted to a man-made famine. Duranty, who had floated the theory that revolutions were beyond moral judgment ('You can't make an omelette without breaking eggs'), did not condemn Stalin for the bloody elimination of the kulaks who had deprived the Russian countryside of necessary sustaining expertise. He simply let the three-million figure go at that."

What struck Chamberlain was "the double iniquity of Duranty's performance": He was not only "heartless about the famine, he had betrayed his calling as a journalist by failing to report it." Duranty downplayed news that would reflect unfavorably on the Stalin regime, because he felt, probably correctly, that the Soviet government would not renew his correspondent's visa if he acted otherwise. He argued, to himself and others, that trimming his journalistic sails to the Soviet winds was the lesser of two evils—the other evil being the loss of his Moscow post, and possibly the *New York Times*'s loss of its bureau in the Soviet capital altogether.

The ultimate death toll, following Stalin's forced collectivization, was higher than the 3 million figure Duranty mentioned in the elevator. No one, of course, actually counted the dead or was able to compile accurate statistics; but the figure may, in the end, have come to some 10 million. In his dispatches to the *New York Times,* Duranty adroitly masked the devastating facts with such terms as "serious food shortages" and "widespread mortality due to malnutrition." In one such dispatch, Duranty said: "In short, conditions are definitely bad in certain sections—Ukraine, North Caucasus, and Lower Volga. The rest of the country is on short rations but nothing worse. These conditions are bad, but there is no famine."

Eugene Lyons was particularly incensed by the gap between Duranty's private accounts of famine conditions and the reassuring dispatches he sent to New York; much of it was a juggling of words: denials of "famine" but admission of something as technical-sounding as "partial crop failures." Of course, people don't die of starvation, as such; death may be caused by pneumonia or heart failure brought about by the body's failing immunology system, due to malnutrition. The Soviet rulers were, for the most part, successful in preventing foreign correspondents from visiting famine areas and in discouraging them from reporting the eyewitness accounts of others.

In his book *Assignment in Utopia,* Lyons reported that he and his wife were having dinner with Anne O'Hare McCormick, a *New York Times* roving correspondent. Duranty, returning from a two-week tour of the previously forbidden Ukraine and North Caucasus regions in mid-1933, joined them to give "his fresh impressions in brutally frank terms and they added up to a picture of ghastly horror." Lyons wrote that Duranty's estimates of the dead from famine "were the most startling I had as yet heard from any one."

When McCormick exclaimed, "But, Walter, you don't mean that literally?" Duranty answered: "Hell I don't. . . . I'm being conservative." In his book, Lyons quoted no figure, but in a memorandum he wrote in December 1937 to Malcolm Muggeridge, who reported to the *Manchester Guardian,* he said: "His estimate, I say, was the largest I had yet heard. In the book I didn't mention the figure he used, but it was 7 million! Having passed on that figure to us in private conversation, he went home and wrote his famous dispatches pooh-poohing the famine."

Being cautious as well as skillful, Walter Duranty built a reputation for reliability and evenhandedness. Born in England, he worked for the *New York Times* from 1913 to 1934 and remained on a retainer basis until 1945. Marco Carynnyk, writing in *Commentary* (November 1983) under the heading "The Famine the 'Times' Couldn't Find," called Duranty "one of the best-known journalists in the world" and "certainly the most famous correspondent to be stationed in Moscow." Duranty's autobiographical work, *I Write As I Please,* was a best-seller and, according to Carynnyk, "influenced both public attitudes and government policies." In 1932 he received the Pulitzer Prize for his "dispassionate, interpretative reporting of the news from Russia."

One can't just let the Duranty case go by without looking for an explanation that goes beyond journalistic opportunism, beyond making a pact with the devil named Kremlin propaganda tactics. Duranty's writings, in retrospect, convey an air of the elegant and the contemptuous. At one point, talking about Kremlin-induced suffering, Duranty is supposed to have said, "After all, they're only Russians!" His books and dispatches do, in fact, convey a disdain for the peasants who, with primitive stubbornness, resisted Stalin's collectivization. In one report, Duranty stated, "A large number of peasants thought they could change the Communist party's collectivization policy by refusing to cooperate." He explained Stalin's extermination of peasants by saying, "The Bolshevist leaders are just as indifferent to the casualties that may be involved in their drive toward socialization as any general during the war who ordered a costly attack, to show his superiors that he and his division possessed the proper soldierly spirit." In fact, he added, "The Bolshevists are more indifferent because they are animated by fanatical convictions."

Over the years, Duranty's detachment appeared to have turned to callous indifference. As senior foreign correspondent, he had access to the top Soviet leadership. Stalin granted him one of his rare personal interviews. Maxim Litvinov, commissar for foreign affairs from 1930 to 1939, treated Duranty as a peer. Indeed, as the *New York Times* correspondent in Moscow, he may have contributed to the decision of President Roosevelt to establish diplomatic relations with the U.S.S.R. in 1933. Duranty covered the Moscow show trials, the accusations of "Trotskyism" and of Old Bolsheviks' conspiracies and espionage, with the same bland acceptance of the Stalinist version of events. He was, of course, not the only one who managed to be beguiled by Kremlin pressures and flatteries. World public opinion seemed, on the whole, incapable of penetrating the macabre facade of the trials.

World opinion later recoiled from another event, as incongruous as it was horrible: the death of some 15,000 Polish reservists, some of whose bodies were found in a mass grave in the Katyn Forest, near the city of Smolensk. Polish and Western historians tend to attribute the death of these Polish reserve officers to the Stalin regime, which regarded them as hostile "class enemies." The conditions that prevailed at the time need to be recalled: Hitler and Stalin had signed their "nonaggression" pact, and the armies of both states invaded Poland, Nazi Germany from the west and the U.S.S.R. from the east. The officers, mobilized in early September

1939, when Germany first invaded Poland, were rounded up by invading Russians later that month. Until the spring of 1940, these men, held in three camps in western Russia, were able to send letters to their families. By May, the letters stopped coming. Stalin's mind-set, which even regarded Soviet prisoners of war as mere traitors, could easily write off these Polish officers as antagonists, a nuisance at best, a danger at worst. At any rate, the bodies of 4,321 Polish officers were later found in the Katyn Forest mass grave.

One of Duranty's successors, *New York Times* Moscow correspondent Harrison Salisbury, recounted Soviet efforts at a public relations coup at Katyn in his book *A Journey for Our Time*. He recalled that bodies of the Polish officers had been found, each with a pistol bullet in his head, by advancing German armies on April 13, 1943. The Germans were quick to blame the Russians. Salisbury wrote: "Forensic specialists, academicians of various countries, an international commission of inquiry, foreign journalists, were hurried to the scene, graves were opened, bodies exhumed, autopsies performed, letters and newspaper clippings presented, to suggest that the men had been killed in April and May of 1940—that is, when still in custody of the Russians."

After the Russians recaptured Smolensk in September 1943, Salisbury wrote, "they were about to explode their own propaganda bomb" and invited Western correspondents stationed in Moscow as "part of the stage setting." Salisbury added: "I am deeply grateful to the Soviet press department for arranging this expedition. It was (and remains) a vivid lesson in Soviet methodology. There was the embarrassing extravagance of the train, outfitted with snowy linen, perfumed soap, down quilts, white-jacketed waiters, luxury fit for the Czar. In fact, it may have been one of the Czar's special trains. To sit in the dining car, tables laden with bottles, crystal and silver, plates heaped with *zakuski* [appetizers], and looking through lace curtains at wooden freight trains where wounded Red Army men, heads in bloody bandages, arms in splints, legs amputated, gazed from the next track, shivering around pot-bellied stoves, was almost too much."

Salisbury recalled that U.S. Ambassador W. Averell Harriman had welcomed the Russian project of taking the correspondents to the Katyn Forest. He had grown irritated with the Polish government in exile, in London, which had accepted as valid the claim that the Polish officers had been massacred by the Russians. The ambassador's daughter, Kathy, accompanied the correspondents on their trip, as did an embassy attaché. Reporters on the special train found themselves in a mahogany-paneled dining car, complete with "quantities of caviar, champagne, butter, white bread, smoked salmon, cake, beef Stroganov, cutlets Kiev." Salisbury remembered, "We all wanted to believe that the Germans had done Katyn."

He wrote: "Whatever their idiosyncrasies, the Russians were our allies. We hated the Nazis. Atrocities were what the Nazis were all about. What more natural than to kill the Polish officers, blame it on the Russians and sow trouble?"

However, Salisbury noted, "The Russian expedition got off on the wrong foot and never changed." The inquiry was held by the Commission to Investigate the German Atrocities at Katyn Forest, which, by its very name, made the results a foregone conclusion. From Smolensk, the correspondents were driven to the forest on a new road. Red Army soldiers were busy with shovels and trench-building equipment. Doctors and nurses engaged in autopsies on the bodies, stacked neatly in rows.

Salisbury found the evidence of the commission of inquiry to be "poor" and its presentation "worse." The witnesses, he concluded, were prisoners who, after the inquiry, would presumably go back to prison, "potent incentives for them to tell the story as their captors wanted them to tell it." The correspondents had expected the Russians to present an airtight case, with convincing evidence, based on meticulous examination. His reports on the trip amounted to the Scotch verdict of "guilt not proven," but Soviet censors "killed all skeptical remarks and deleted references to the caviar."

Mixing corpses with caviar, a clumsy public relations ploy at best, marks a low point in Soviet propaganda. If the Soviet or Polish governments wanted to prove German guilt convincingly, Salisbury wrote, "the sober bookkeeping evidence, the orders, the statistics, the whole dreary business, would long since have turned up, no matter how cleverly it had been hidden," but few Poles remain "who do not believe it was Stalin's secret police who committed the crime."

Warsaw's war cemetery, early in 1985, displayed a stark new monument, recalling the deaths of the Katyn Forest victims and attributing them to "Hitlerite fascism." There had been no ceremony, no public unveiling of the monument, and no announcement of its completion. On April 8, as 30 memorial candles flickered beneath the monument, someone had scratched the legend "N.K.V.D—1940" into the earth beside it. The initials were those of the Soviet secret police, today's KGB.

CHAPTER · 10

Mosaic of Mixed Motives

You cannot judge a huge mosaic from a few of its pieces, and the variety of "fellow-traveling" activities defies presentation within a single theme or general analysis. Even before Willi Münzenberg practiced his propagandistic magic, Lenin's ideas attracted the well-meaning and idealistic—indeed, much of the early support the Bolsheviks enjoyed was born of the nineteenth-century belief in the perfectability of humankind. The road Theodore Dreiser and André Gide traveled, in opposite directions, has been traversed by men and women for reasons ranging from the most selfless devotion to the crassest of egotism, with endless admixtures of other motives. Starting with the earliest admirers of the Soviet "experiment," through the heyday of pro-Soviet sentiments during the 1930s and World War II, the cold war period of the 1950s, the emotional upheavals of the 1960s, and down into our own day, the Soviet state has attracted or repulsed thousands of prominent personalities in the arts, literature, the sciences, and other opinion-making roles. At times, they were manipulated by Soviet propaganda; at other times, they have clearly acted on their own. Among them have been the sophisticated, the ignorant, the idealistic, the opportunistic.

The 1950s are a period to which the mosaic metaphor peculiarly applies; totally new images may be constructed from selected pieces, bearing little resemblance to original events and personalities. One such revisionist image appeared on the New York stage on January 16, 1986: the one-woman play *Lillian,* by William Luce, in which the actress Zoe Caldwell played the role of playwright Lillian Hellman. Frank Rich, in the *New York Times* (January 17, 1986), said Caldwell's performance "only rarely ascends from a first-rate impersonation to a compelling characterization," because "too many pieces are missing from the story to allow the role to add up."

The pieces of this mosaic had earlier been scrambled by Hellman herself. In four volumes of memoirs, she provided a version of a personal history that was, at the very least, highly selective. The congressional hearings and the McCarthy period of the early 1950s played havoc with the careers of public personalities who had, rightly or wrongly, been linked with Communist or pro-Communist activities. The motion-picture industry established a blacklist of actors and writers, who found it virtually impossible to find work for several years. Their actual or alleged pro-Communist activities varied greatly, ranging from the passive signing of resolutions to active membership in Communist cells in unions and other groups.

The Hellman case stands out because, as a dramatist-historian of the era, she found a resonance for her views among a new wave of antiestablishment sentiment that had developed during the Vietnam War. Double distillation of history, resulting in Luce's play, served to compound Hellman's own myth making.

Hellman enjoyed two periods of prominence: first, as a dramatist, mainly with her plays *The Children's Hour* (1934), which dealt with two teachers accused of a lesbian relationship, and *The Little Foxes* (1939), an indictment of immoral greed within a southern family. Hellman later wrote a good deal about her long-standing affair with the mystery writer Dashiell Hammett, a member of the U.S. Communist Party.

Hellman's testimony before the House Committee on Un-American Activities became the centerpiece of her book *Scoundrel Time* (1976), which received a good deal of attention at a time of disillusionment, following the Watergate conspiracy that led to the resignation of President Richard M. Nixon. Hellman consistently referred to herself and Hammett as "radicals." She certainly understood that Stalinist rule brought a series of disasters to the Soviet Union. In her main autobiography, *An Unfinished Woman* (1969), she referred to "the hurricane of the 1937–1938 purges" and added that "great honor must and will be paid those who did protest the criminal purges." But she dealt with "the sins of Stalin Communism" in a mere aside in *Scoundrel Time,* putting herself at center stage, saying that "there were plenty of sins and plenty that for a long time I mistakenly denied." However, her reading of the historical record was quirky. Her main antagonists were not the proponents of Soviet totalitarianism, but anti-Communists.

Alfred Kazin, the literary historian, in his article "The Legend of Lillian Hellman," which appeared in *Esquire* (August 1977), noted that she "convinced the generation that has grown up since the Fifties" that she was "virtually alone in refusing to name past or present Communist party members" to the congressional committee. Being a playwright, Hellman displayed a natural sense of the dramatic. Before appearing at the 1952 hearing, she bought a new hat and a chic Balmain dress. She wrote a memorable line for herself: "I cannot and will not cut my conscience to fit this year's fashions." According to Kazin, Hellman had been "dramatizing herself ever since she stopped writing plays."

Hellman died June 29, 1984, at the age of 79. Her libel suit against novelist Mary McCarthy, the Educational Television Corporation, and the interviewer Dick Cavett died with her. Hellman had sued them for damages of $1.75 million, because McCarthy had accused the playwright of being "a dishonest writer." In much of her writing, Hellman had expressed disdain for money and money making. Certainly one reason for Soviet acceptance of her play *The Little Foxes* was its depiction of financial manipulation and greed within bourgeois society. Once, in Moscow, she bewildered a woman cashier who was handing over her royalties by refusing to count the money, suggesting that she didn't care much about it.

After her death, Hellman's estate was valued at $3.5 million. Her will established the Dashiell Hammett Fund, designed to support "the promotion and advancement of political, social and economic equality, civil rights and civil liberties." The fund's trustees, Hellman specified, were to be "guided by the political, social and economic beliefs"—which, of course, were radical—"of the late Dashiell Hammett, who was a believer in the doctrines of Karl Marx."

Alexander Grechant, writing in *Moscow News* (July 7, 1985), appraised Lillian Hellman on the eightieth anniversary of her birth. He noted that her works had been published in the Soviet Union five times, with a print run of 54,000 copies, and that her plays had been performed in Soviet theaters since the early 1940s. He recalled that, in 1967, she attended the Fourth Congress of Soviet Writers in Moscow. Grechant failed to mention that she had died.

Among essays that evaluated Hellman's role at the time she published her memoirs, Sidney Hook's "Lillian Hellman's Scoundrel Time" in *Encounter* (February 1977) was the most comprehensive. Hook wrote that she "seems to have duped a generation of critics devoid of historical memory and critical common sense." He analyzed her account of Henry Wallace, Roosevelt's vice president and later a presidential candidate for the Communist-supported Progressive Party. Hook noted that Hellman presented "a jeering caricature" of Wallace as "a kind of eccentric hick and skinflint at a time when the worst thing about him was his political innocence." Hellman, he wrote, accused Wallace of lying when he turned against the Communists and denounced them for their "force, deceit and intrigues" in the Progressive Party; she said that she had told him earlier of Communist influence in the party.

According to Hook, Hellman's "most valuable contribution to the Com-

munist cause was her activity on behalf of their front organizations." She
was a keynote speaker at the Cultural and Scientific Conference for World
Peace at the Waldorf-Astoria Hotel in New York (March 25–26, 1949),
which was preceded by the World Congress of Intellectuals for Peace at
Wroclaw-Breslau, Poland (August 25–28, 1948) and followed by the World
Peace Conference in Paris (April 20–23, 1949). The Waldorf conference,
a landmark of front organization activity, offered a gala production in the
Münzenberg tradition. In content and tenor it followed Soviet policies
unmistakably. Hook recalled that Hellman "valiantly defended the Conference against its critics—whose chief point of protest was the refusal of
the Conference to speak up for the dissenting or nonconformist intellectuals
who were being martyred in Communist countries." This was the period,
prior to Stalin's death, that was characterized by purges all through Eastern
Europe. Hook lists the cornerstones of Stalinist and post-Stalinist actions,
each one an occasion for soul-searching and often alienation of fellow
travelers all over the world. He wrote:

"The record of what Lillian Hellman has written—and not written—
makes it clear that she did not know about the political crimes of Stalin
during the Purges and Moscow Frame-Up Trials during the '30s; the deportation of the peasants and the resulting famine in the Ukraine; the Nazi-
Soviet Pact; the invasion of Poland and the destruction of the Baltic States;
the Soviet attack on Finland; the surrender of German Jewish Communists,
who had fled in 1933, by Stalin to Hitler in 1940; the liquidation of the
anti-Fascist Jewish leaders, Alter and Ehrlich, by Stalin as 'spies for Hitler';
the Katyn massacre of the Polish officers; the mass executions and depor-
tations of returning Russian prisoners-of-war after World War II; the overthrow of the democratic Czechoslovak government in 1948; the Berlin
blockade; the Communist invasion of South Korea; the suppression of the
German workers' revolt in East Berlin and East Germany in 1953."

Hook then cited events during the post-Stalin years, particularly following Khrushchev's crucial speech in 1956. "After all," Hook recalled,
"Miss Hellman visited the Soviet Union in 1937, 1944, 1966, and 1967.
But not a single word of criticism of what she saw or heard or of disavowal
of her past tributes to the Soviet Union appeared." Of the Communists,
he noted, "she writes with sadness and pity; of the liberal anti-Communists
she writes with virulent hatred."

Rich noted in his *New York Times* review of *Lillian* that the play admits
to Hellman's faults, but that "her flaws are never as grave as those of her
antagonists, and her anger is always in the cause of right." This "roseate"
version of Lillian Hellman, the reviewer commented, would give her partisans an "opportunity to worship at the shrine," while her detractors "will
probably be reduced to apoplexy."

The Broadway stage, in this instance, was using the methods of television's *docudrama,* a hybrid of fact and fiction that puts historic events at the mercy of scriptwriters with a penchant for yielding to "dramatic needs," quick action, and easily defined heros and villains.

People in public life have entered and left the Communist movement and its auxiliaries by the thousands, and for the most part quietly. Publicity usually centers on writers, because their testimony is more voluble than that of scientists or artists. Among the landmarks on the road of disillusionment stands Arthur Koestler's novel *Darkness at Noon,* which explored the mind of an Old Bolshevik who is manipulated into a fraudulent confession of anti-Soviet conspiracy, just because he remains ultimately loyal to The Cause. Koestler also was one of the contributors to the symposium *The God That Failed;* others included the Italian novelist-essayist Ignazio Silone, André Gide, and Stephen Spender. On the same theme of fraudulent divinity, the American novelist Howard Fast explored his own exit from the Communist Party. He had been a Communist sympathizer from youth, joined the party in 1943, and broke with it after Khrushchev's speech. In *The Naked God,* he described what it was like to be a creative writer, trying to toe the precarious party line. Fast, an extraordinarily prolific writer, is probably best known for his novel *Spartacus,* which became a motion picture starring Kirk Douglas. The case of *Spartacus* vividly illustrated his troubles with the party leadership.

As Fast recalled it, his early years were filled with "work, poverty and hunger," but he soon discovered the world of books and came to the Communists by way of the John Reed Club. He stayed with them until the Stalin-Hitler Pact, when "my wife and I broke with our Communist friends in a bitter climax of growing resentment." The fight against Hitler was uppermost in his mind: "I lived, as so many of my generation lived, that fascism might perish." Early in World War II he was passionately pro-British, while the Communists were busily denouncing the "imperialist war," and he looked upon his Communist friends "with contempt and anger." He added: "Yet four years later I joined the Communist Party—not because I ever changed my judgment on their part, not because I could ever forgive it or pardon it, which my friends in the Party knew—but because when I, in my whole body and being, became a part of that terrible moment in history which we call World War II, I came to accept the proposition that the truest and most consistent fighters in the anti-Fascist struggle were the Communists."

During the war, Fast served as a correspondent with a special signal corps unit in the China-India-Burma theater. In 1945 he became a member of the World Peace Council, and from 1950 to 1955 he was an American Labor Party candidate for the U.S. Congress. All the while, he was writing fiction, facing what he called "the method whereby the Communist Party *must* destroy the independence, the skill and the talent of the artist who becomes part of it." As a member of the board of the Joint Anti-Fascist Refugee Committee, Fast was called before the House Committee on Un-American Activities. He refused to provide the organization's records, was found guilty of contempt of Congress, and went to prison for three months in 1950. Then he spent a year and a half writing *Spartacus*.

Clearly, as a Communist, the theme of a Roman slave who leads a successful rebellion appealed to Fast. He felt sure that the novel would find a good reception among party members and the Communist leadership. When the book was rejected by seven publishers, Fast decided to publish it himself. Other self-published books had been failures, but *Spartacus* was successful and was picked up by a commercial publisher a year later. The Communist Party's "cultural commissar" decided, however, that the novel violated the party line. Fast observed:

"My own stupidity was inexhaustible; my own inability to learn was beyond correction. For two years and more I had labored to produce a book that would be an epic of the oppressed, a paean to liberty and the high conscience of mankind. I had labored under the notion that I was furthering and giving more complete expression to the values that had guided my life. But the lashing tongue of the commissar informed me otherwise."

What was wrong with *Spartacus?* It was filled with "brutalism" and "sadism," contained psychoanalytic terms such as "inner struggle," and generally violated Marxist-Leninist principles on human relations. Fast wrote: "The commercial book publishers of the United States had hustled me out of their offices because I was a Communist; the Communist Party had established its discipline because I was a writer. I sat down that night and wept, because it was the end." In the book, Fast had added fictional elements to the story of Spartacus, the Roman slave and gladiator who led a revolt which, Fast said, "almost overthrew Rome itself." Spartacus's wife Varinia was taken captive by a Teutonic tribe. In his novel, Fast "took the liberty of creating a psychological situation where, to the two most important Roman characters in the book, she became the mysterious symbol of what their lives most lacked, purity and integrity." Thus, in Fast's book, Crassus, an aristocratic general, "found his victory hollow unless he could possess Varinia through her own consent," while another Roman, Gracchus, "low-born, but brilliant and ruthless," yearns that Varinia "explain to him the enigma of his own life—Spartacus."

Whatever the mixture of symbolism and realism that Fast, as a story-teller, wished to achieve in developing this plot, including "the strange and complex virtue of Gracchus," the Communist "commissars" of literature found him guilty of exalting Gracchus, a "capitalist beast," while degrading Varinia, a "Communist woman, a woman of the oppressed toilers." The

Daily Worker (February 17, 1952) accused Fast of creating "a reverse for the class theme," showing the "destructive influence of Freudian mystifications concerning the erotic as against the social basis of character."

All this took place at a time when Soviet writers and Communist literature everywhere felt the whip of Stalinist critiques. Fast recalled, "In all my years in the Communist Party I never received a paragraph worth being called honest and thoughtful criticism, only the type of mumbo-jumbo printed above, alternating with equally ridiculous and thoughtless praise which shamed me by describing me as the 'greatest' this and the 'greatest' that." Fast said that later books lacked the "spark of life and the flame of passion" that he had given *Spartacus,* but they found favor among Communist Party watchdogs, who found them free from "the dread thing called 'error.' "

Once he had left the Communist Party, Fast began a new career as a novelist for a mass audience, notably with a trilogy, *The Immigrants, The Second Generation,* and *The Establishment.* Whatever residue of class warfare remained in his writings, it had been sublimated into the narratives of All-American epics.

Fast cannot be fairly compared to Hellman, nor Dreiser to Gide—nor can any two men or women, within or on the fringes of the Communist movement, be truly found to resemble each other. National characteristics and settings add to this variety. In France, where fellow traveling had, at one time, become respectable to the point of being commonplace, disillusionment with Soviet policies later decimated the ranks of Communist sympathizers. In the 1980s, it seemed as if only one steadfast figure had remained behind, the poet-novelist Louis Aragon.

One popular couple, the actress Simone Signoret and her husband, the singer-actor Yves Montand, had for years signed Münzenberg-type resolutions and graced rallies amid red banners—until they visited Hungary, where Montand gave several performances, and were deeply shocked by the killing of Prime Minister Imre Nagy, following the popular uprising that was crushed by Soviet troops. Signoret described their disillusionment in her autobiography, *Nostalgia Isn't What It Used to Be,* and Montand made a series of television appearances presenting his political views. Simone Signoret died on September 30, 1985.

While others might move from illusion to disillusion, Jean-Paul Sartre, the philosopher-essayist who gained worldwide prominence as the "godfather of existentialism," followed a political path that first led from illusion to disillusion, then back to illusion, next to disillusion, and so forth, over and over, for much of his life. This love-hate relationship between Sartre and the Soviet Union was further complicated by changes within the Paris intellectual scene, shifts in the French Communist Party, and Sartre's personal life. For example, Sartre's exasperation over Soviet cultural policies prompted him to write in *What Is Literature?* that "the politics of Stalinist Communism in France are incompatible with honest practice of the literary craft." Written in 1947, this work was translated into English in 1950; that year, he attacked Stalin's labor camps in his main literary outlet, the magazine *Les Temps Modernes.*

David Caute said in *The Fellow-Traveler*: "Only two years later Sartre committed himself without reservation to the cause of Soviet communism." Caute stated: "His conversion, which was sudden and virtually unheralded, took both communists and non-communists by surprise." Sartre had acted in response to arrests, following an anti-NATO demonstration. Caute also found Sartre had become "increasingly convinced that the Moscow-inspired Peace Movement had to be accepted at face value." Still, there were further disillusionments, reconciliations, and all the rest of by-then-familiar Sartre-isms.

In the end, Sartre seemed to have baffled himself about as much as he baffled others. He told his long-time companion Simone de Beauvoir that he often felt compelled to "think against himself." De Beauvoir, in *Adieux: A Farewell to Sartre,* quoted him on his ambivalent relations with the Communists. He knew quite well that they simply exploited his prominence and his emotional attachment to radical causes. Although he saw himself as a man of principle, Sartre reacted more strongly against the Soviet invasion of Czechoslovakia than of Hungary, if only because two of his plays were being staged in Prague at the time of the invasion. He told de Beauvoir, "the intervention in Czechoslovakia seemed to me particularly revolting because it clearly showed the attitude of the USSR toward the socialist countries." Actually, Russia's policy of directly intervening whenever and wherever a "fraternal" regime seemed to elude Moscow's grip had become standard Soviet doctrine.

Despite his feelings of revulsion, Sartre attended various Communist front events, mainly so-called peace congresses. At that time, he recalled, "The Communist party's attitude toward me had changed and so had mine toward it; we had become allies." Simone de Beauvoir asked whether he had regarded the Communists as "something like a stage in the direction of socialism." Sartre agreed: "Yes, I did. I did not think our aims were the same, but going along with them was easy enough." He was again on good terms with them, de Beauvoir recalled, when Sartre visited the Soviet Union in 1954. But he cautioned: "Yes, but what I saw in the USSR did not fill me with enthusiasm. Of course, they showed me what could be shown, and I had great reservations." He was rediscovering what hundreds of others, including Gide, had discovered during preceding decades, and he then misled his readers in an astonishingly unethical way. De Beauvoir reminded Sartre, "Yet, you wrote a very laudatory piece in *Libération.*" Sartre explained, "It was Cau who wrote it."

In other words, here was a writer of world renown who permitted a crucial article, summarizing his impressions of the Soviet Union, to be ghost-written by a partisan associate. De Beauvoir, looking for an excuse, said, "It must be admitted that you were exhausted." Sartre added: "I gave him a certain number of leading points and then I went off for a holiday with you." They had their vacation. Next, they attended yet another Soviet-sponsored peace congress, this one in Helsinki. Sartre and de Beauvoir revisited the USSR twice in 1962, and then again in 1963, 1964, and 1965.

De Beauvoir tried to unravel Sartre's relations with the Communists. "But on the whole, the way the Communists made use of you," she said, "without your being able to have a really human, personal, friendly, trustful relation with them; didn't you find that disagreeable?" Sartre replied, "Yes, it was extremely disagreeable."

Still, when all was said and done, Sartre did not seem to comprehend that the Communists he met, and some of whom he liked, were simply carrying out instructions. They were either courting him, upbraiding him, seeking him out, or avoiding him—depending upon prevailing Moscow tactics and Sartre's usefulness in implementing these tactics. Sartre confessed himself puzzled that Communists he knew appeared to wear "masks over their faces," that "they smiled, they talked, they replied to the questions I asked them, but in fact it was not they who were replying." He noted that, as individuals, they "vanished and became characters whose principles one knows" and who gave answers that *Humanité,* the Communist newspaper, "would have given in the name of these principles." He failed to add that *Humanité* echoed *Pravda.*

Sartre's on-again, off-again relations with the French Communists were reflected in his book *The Communists and Peace,* a collection of essays written in the 1950s and published during the following decade, when the French Left represented an amalgam that included anarchists, various shades of student activism, and self-styled Maoists. Violent encounters between members of these groups, notably students, and the police attracted international attention; Sartre's personal appearance at some of these demonstrations provided him with the image of a Sage on the Barricades.

In *The Communists and Peace,* designed to clarify his ideological position, Sartre engaged in arguments such as these: "The working class, such as I conceived it, probably united by the Communist Party, could, in its revolutionary movements, apprehend concrete totalities, that is to say, syntheses of the concrete and the universal: this strike, this claim. For I see it, in itself, like a concrete universal: unique since it was made with these particular men, in these particular circumstances—universal since it embraces an entire collection."

Sartre, whose worldwide reputation as an original philosopher grew out of his espousal of existentialism, advanced his thesis on collaboration with the Communists in terms that were close to incoherent. He wrote: "In order to darken the workers' consciousness, our industrialists have chosen to dim themselves; they hope the atrophy of production will be lived internally by the proletariat in the form of generalized anemia. Thanks to their practices, in fact, there is both too little and too much of the French proletariat. For an economy which would propose to fulfill all the needs of the nation by mass production, the proletariat is not large enough." He spoke out in favor of "permanent agitation," designed to overcome what he regarded as the workers' basic lack of initiative: "The inertia of the masses, on the other hand, is such that movement comes to them from outside; inertia therefore implies its counterpart, agitation, the goal of which is to maintain by a perpetual process of fermentation a rudiment of collective life that is perpetually threatened by death. Without agitation, the great popular movements would be more hesitant, they would take longer to come into being and they could be put down more easily."

This elitist concept was expanded by Sartre when he wrote that "never do the masses mandate" and that though they may "indicate the goal to be attained, it is up to the militant to find the shortest path." The Communist Party, as the avant garde of the working class—by its self-definition—allocated to itself this role of "the militant"; as Sartre added, "The militant takes the responsibility for the permanent conflict which sets the revolutionary movement, the tasks of which are infinite, over against the revolutionary *élan*, which postulates the ends all at once in order to call for their immediate realization."

Such musings, which in earlier decades would have aroused Lenin's ideological ire, were certain to create mixed feelings within the leadership of the French Communist Party; to them, Sartre was a useful stalking horse, now and then, a cosigner of protests and manifestos, but clearly lacking in ideological discipline.

François Fejtö dealt with the Sartre enigma in a brief article, "Sartre, the Illustrious Innocent," in *Encounter* (April 1985), which concluded, "He became the very prototype of the intellectual masochist, predisposed toward fellow-traveling." But why did Sartre permit himself to be manipulated by the Communists, over and over again? Fejtö observed that, after a number of false starts, "the Communists finally caught on to the advantages they could derive from this illustrious innocent, *ce naif au grand prestige*." When Sartre, after his return from Moscow in 1954, wrote that there was "total freedom to criticize in the USSR," he did so because Ilya Ehrenburg had said so. But Ehrenburg, a Soviet writer of sophistication and cynical insight, confided later to a French acquaintance, Emmanuel d'Astier de la Vigerie, that he had to talk such blatant nonsense, because he was under constant KGB surveillance. Ehrenburg said, "I honestly thought that Sartre was smart enough to understand my play-acting and that he wouldn't believe me."

All of which prompts a variation on an American colloquialism, the question, "If you're so famous, why ain't you smart?" Some answers suggest themselves and they are, characteristically, highly personal; they cannot be applied, easily, to other fellow travelers. Aside from the simple human vanities, the applause, the invitations, the Communist-orchestrated public adulation, Sartre had a lifelong desire to be a man of action, or to share the stage with men of action, or to live within an illusion of action. He also seemed to long for youth. He delighted in association with youth and reveled in youthful rebellion. His naiveté may have had partly biological causes: addiction to drugs, as well as nutritional self-neglect that worsened his diabetes and hastened his blindness. His confusions seemed like naiveté, and his naiveté wore the mantle of political activism.

At times, Sartre appeared to be the political-emotional prisoner of one or another young disciple. It was a weakness that played havoc with the judgment of another prominent philosopher, Britain's Bertrand Russell. His role in Soviet "peace" campaigns came very late in life, in contrast to much early insight into the harshness of Bolshevik rule and Stalinist repression. Russell had been aware of, and fascinated by, Lenin's ascension. In 1920, his dream of visiting Soviet Russia was about to come true. Even before his departure he wrote a pro-Soviet article that appeared in the New York *Liberator* under the headline "Bertrand Russell Goes Bolshevik." According to his biographer, Ronald W. Clark, "His enthusiasm for the great new experiment was at white heat." Alas, as Clark notes in *The Life of Bertrand Russell,* he returned from Russia "almost completely disillusioned." Throughout his long life, Russell see-sawed in his attitude toward the Soviet Union and its policies. He tended to comment on issues of the day in provocative terms; he was a relentless attention-getter and activist, and much of what he did and said in later life fitted quite well into the aims of Soviet propaganda or followed the pattern of its tactics.

Clark wrote that Russell visited Russia "in a mood of almost unqualified optimism," which was shared by most of the delegation members. The anarchist Emma Goldman noted that most of them "fell for the show and became the more pliable the longer they stayed," whereas Russell "from the very first refused to be chaperoned." He met Lenin, Trotsky, and Kamenev and conscientiously talked to fellow philosophers, and there was a boat trip down the Volga. But once he returned to the ambiance of Sweden, Russell wrote that he had found "Bolshevism is a close tyrannical bureaucracy, with a spy system more elaborate and terrible than the Tsar's."

In later life, Russell became the stormy petrel of antinuclear demonstrations, at a time when the Soviet Union favored that type of drive. Russell supported unilateral abandonment of nuclear testing. Together with Albert Einstein, he advanced what became known as the "Russell-Einstein Manifesto," yet he also said that "if you are not going to get from the other side a *quid pro quo* which is really of equal military importance," he did not want to see "thermo-nuclear weapons abolished." The manifesto, entitled "Man's Peril," led to the so-called Pugwash Conferences. Throughout the 1950s, Russell was intensely active in a manner that, as Clark put it, "made him a key figure of the nuclear-disarmament movement" and the Council of Nuclear Disarmament which he headed "fought a constant battle against the accusation that it was being used, even if unknowingly, to further Communist aims."

The Communists did all they could to benefit from Russell's activities. Here, after all, was a Nobel Prize Winner, a Fellow of the Royal Society, a man whose name was known the world over. In consequence, his name turned up as a sponsor of the Stockholm Peace Congress in 1958, clearly an enterprise stage-managed by the Soviet-controlled World Peace Council. Russell wrote the congress's organizers, withdrawing his sponsorship and castigating the council as "more pro-Communist than I can agree with." He noted that the council was always ready to denounce the West but unwilling to "condemn actions by Communist States."

Still later, under the influence of a hard-driving, self-assertive assistant, Russell helped to create the International War Crimes Tribunal, echoing Münzenberg's countertrial on the Reichstag fire in 1933. Russell had created the Bertrand Russell Peace Foundation, designed to use the Tribunal as a forum on which to "try" those who had committed atrocities during the Vietnam War. But the impartial collection of evidence and the selection of distinguished international jurors were negated when, at the very outset, the organizers called for a trial of "the war criminals," who were identified as U.S. President Lyndon Johnson, Secretary of State Dean Rusk, Secretary of Defense Robert S. McNamara, "and their fellow-criminals." Clark observed: "Worse was to come. For it was soon obvious that Russell had abandoned any belief that the Tribunal should concern itself with the alleged crimes of both sides." Instead, only "alleged American and South Vietnamese atrocities would be investigated but not those of the North Vietnamese or the Vietcong."

The Bertrand Russell Peace Foundation, discredited by this one-sided approach, was unable to place the tribunal in Switzerland or France. It was first convened in Sweden, then in Denmark. The Americans were roundly denounced and judged guilty, but, as Clark wrote, the verdict was "accepted only by dedicated members of the Left," and it seemed that "the verdict would have been the same whatever the evidence." Russell had lost control over the Foundation that bore his name; he died two years later, on February 2, 1970, at the age of 97.

Early in 1985, *Moscow News* (January 6) recalled the "Russell-Einstein

Manifesto" and linked it to "the birth of the Pugwash movement of the scientists of the world, in which Soviet scientists take an active part." The occasion was a press conference given by five Soviet scientists, recalling the Pugwash "Declaration on the Dangers of Nuclear War," which was "proclaimed in 1982 and signed by 111 Nobel Prize winners." The names of Russell, Einstein, and Frédéric Joliot-Curie were little more than symbolic, in 1985, and the "Pugwash" label must have been obscure to the press conference participants. The movement took its name from an estate in Nova Scotia (Canada) owned by the Cleveland industrialist Cyrus S. Eaton, the setting of the original East-West conference that Eaton had sponsored.

Nikita Khrushchev, during his first visit to the United States, toured Eaton's 800-acre Acadia farm, southeast of Cleveland. After Khrushchev's ouster, Eaton visited the Kremlin's new rulers and told the Associated Press (December 27, 1964) that the Soviet Union was ready to relax international tensions and wanted more trade with the United States. Eaton paraphrased what, coming from businessmen interested in Soviet trade, was a fairly standard theme. "I think the place to start is in commerce and trade," he said. "It's the best, because you're not concerned with the economic, political and religious views of those buying your product. The only thing that matters is profit and competitive advantage."

By 1985, the term "Pugwash" had been annexed to the Soviet propaganda machine. *Pravda* reported from London (December 11, 1985) that "an international symposium of the Pugwash Movement" had ended with a statement that "resolutely condemns the U.S. plans for the preparation of 'Star Wars.' " The meeting had dealt with the topic "War or Peace in Space." Shortly afterward, Tass reported from Moscow (December 23) that Pugwash scientists had sent a message to President Reagan, "expressing their profound concern about the escalating nuclear arms race and the mortal danger threatening mankind."

Efforts to recapture the spirit of fellow traveling have encountered diminishing returns. The Polish government sponsored the Congress of Intellectuals for the Peaceful Future of the World, which took place in Wroclaw (Breslau) early in 1986. Remembering the star-studded forum of the Wroclaw peace conference, 37 years earlier, the organizers had hoped to enlist participants of similar prominence and luster. However, although the World Congress of Intellectuals, which took place in 1948, benefited from the postwar atmosphere of the anti-Nazi alliance, even its well-wishers had their doubts or experienced disillusion. True, Pablo Picasso presented his celebrated painting of the Peace Dove to the conference. But Albert Einstein's message to the meeting, which warned against the growth of government power, was not publicized in Poland until the Solidarity movement published it in 1980. Julian Huxley, the British geneticist who served as general secretary of UNESCO, felt that scientific inquiry was being hampered by Soviet dogmatism.

Still, the 1948 conference was endorsed by Sartre. Joliot-Curie attended, as did writers like Jorge Amado of Brazil, Martin Andersen Nexo of Denmark, and Paul Eluard, Roger Vaillard, and Vercors of France. Ehrenburg came from the Soviet Union. By contrast, invitations to the 1986 conference remained largely unanswered. The organizers had sent invitations to prominent people in the United States, among them writer Erskine Caldwell, actor Paul Newman, scientist I. I. Rabi, playwright Arthur Miller, former Defense Secretary Robert S. McNamara, author Isaac Bashevis Singer, astronomer Carl Sagan, actor-director Woody Allen, conductor Leonard Bernstein, actress Meryl Streep, and financier David Rockefeller. They did not accept. Neither did British authors Iris Murdoch and Graham Greene, actor-director Peter Ustinov, or former Prime Minister Sir Harold Wilson. Other turndowns came from Marcel Marceau, the mime, and Charles Aznavour, the singer, of France, former U.N. Secretary General Kurt Waldheim of Austria, musician Ravi Shankar of India, authors Alberto Moravia and Umberto Eco of Italy, Akira Kurosawa of Japan, and Gabriel García Márquez of Colombia.

Bogdan Suchodolski, chief organizer of the congress and chairman of Poland's National Council of Culture, made these comments: "We must realize that there are fewer and fewer people of science and culture whose work and moral stance would authorize them to speak on the issues of supreme importance in the world. Where is there a painter today, comparable to Picasso, a philosopher who could be likened to Sartre or Bertrand Russell?" But no one could be sure that either Russell or Sartre, were they alive, would be ready to trim their "moral stance" to fit into post-Solidarity Poland.

CHAPTER · 11

The Battle for UNESCO

On September 14, 1984, Tass teletypes transmitting the Soviet news agency's English-language service carried a commentary from Moscow headlined, "UNESCO: Washington Continues Blackmail." The commentator, Tass news analyst Oleg Shirokov, had this to say:

"U.S. Assistant Secretary of State Gregory Newell, speaking yesterday in one of the committees of the House of Representatives of the U.S. Congress, said that the Washington Administration has not changed its stand with regard to quitting UNESCO, the United Nations specialized Educational, Scientific and Cultural organization. In this way an official representative of the administration confirmed again that the United States is not going to abandon the policy of blackmail with regard to that international organization. It threatens to quit UNESCO by the end of 1984, unless it alters its conduct in the spirit suiting Washington.

"In what way has UNESCO done the present U.S. Administration wrong? That organization, don't you see, deals too much, in Washington's opinion, with 'political matters' that are not in its competence: condemns the Israeli and South African racist regimes that are conducting a discriminatory policy, specifically in the sphere of education and culture. The United States would like UNESCO's rostrum to be barred to those who believe and declare that education, science and culture cannot be developed successfully in conditions when priority is given to the preparation for war. Washington demands that UNESCO also give up its efforts toward creating a new international economic and information order, should keep mum when witnessing attempts to impose an alien way of life on peoples of emergent developing countries and to deprive them of cultural identity.

"The United States mass media has long been conducting an unbridled campaign against UNESCO. Press organs of a number of other Western countries that take their cue from Washington joined in this campaign. Conducting the policy of blackmail against UNESCO, Washington tries to involve in it its most zealous supporters and is not averse to making a recourse to arm-twisting to achieve this. Threats to UNESCO now also come from Britain, which declared that it is considering the question of its stay in that international organization. Threats in a more veiled form come from the FRG [Federal Republic of Germany; West Germany], the Netherlands and some other Western countries.

" 'UNESCO has been created, not in order to serve the interest of one state or some group of states. If it acted in this way, it would lose its international character.' UNESCO's Director General Amadou-Mahtar M'Bow said this in an interview to the Parisian journal *Politique Etrangère*. He also stressed that those who now deplore what they call UNESCO's 'politicization' apparently do so for the reason that viewpoints different from their own are expressed in that organization.

"They, in Washington, would like that only calls suiting the United States should be made from UNESCO's international rostrum. UNESCO, by the way, is not the first United Nations specialized institution which Washington would like to press down. The overweened Washington leaders even tried to take in hand the United Nations Organization itself by threatening to expell it from the U.S. territory. All this attests to the ineradicable striving of the Washington administration to usurp the right to decide unilaterally the destinies of the whole world."

The Moscow commentary was prompted by the intention of the United States, expressed late in 1983, to leave the United Nations Educational, Cultural and Scientific Organization (UNESCO), with headquarters in Paris, unless the organization's Secretariat specifically, and UNESCO generally, undertook a series of reforms. The U.S. Department of State announced on December 29, 1983, that the U.S. would, effective on December 31, withdraw from the organization. This decision, it said, was based on the conclusion that UNESCO has "extraneously politicized virtually every subject it deals with; has exhibited a hostility toward the basic institutions of a free society, especially a free market and a free press; and has demonstrated unrestrained budgetary expansion."

The U.S. announcement acknowledged, in effect, that the Soviet Union had succeeded, with great tactical skill and tenacity, in turning UNESCO into an international body whose rhetoric, personnel selection, publications, and programs closely resembled those of a Soviet-manipulated front organization. Over the years, Soviet bloc countries and the majority of Third World member countries had transformed the organization into a forum whose stance was reminiscent of the World Peace Council, the Afro-

Asian Solidarity Organization, or the Women's International Democratic Federation. Viewed within the history of such front organizations, the Soviet Union can be seen as applying techniques, developed earlier by Willi Münzenberg, to intergovernmental organizations during the second half of the twentieth century.

The United States decided to act in the case of UNESCO, whose Secretariat had been largely reshaped by the personal and political interests of M'Bow, because the agency had gone farther and faster toward a front organization pattern than any other United Nations agency. A report titled "Soviet Presence in the U.N. Secretariat," issued by the U.S. Senate Select Committee on Intelligence (May 1985), noted, "Moscow has effectively and consistently exploited UNESCO programs in education, science, and communications." It added: "UNESCO is tailor-made for Soviet initiatives designed to influence media content, particularly in the Third World, to establish contact with influential persons in UNESCO-interested fields, and to gain specific technical information. The Soviets have developed contacts with Secretariat officials responsible for publication and broadcasting and have targeted UNESCO information services as a vehicle for disseminating Soviet propaganda."

UNESCO did not become a choice outpost of the Soviet propaganda machine overnight. While the United States and other major powers dealt with it in fits and starts, keeping the organization on the periphery of their interests, the Soviet Union placed increasingly qualified officials into its UNESCO delegation and saw to it that seasoned, well-trained Soviet nationals were appointed to key posts within the organization. One of M'Bow's top deputies, Assistant Director General Sioma Tanguiane, was identified by the congressional report as "the senior Soviet in the Secretariat" and as "a tough bureaucrat in his third tour in UNESCO." The report noted that Tanguiane had "great influence over the employment process in the Education Sector" and "approves lists of individuals invited by UNESCO to represent nongovernmental organizations at all UNESCO meetings."

Tanguiane's background combined studies in education and languages with Marxist ideology. He graduated from the State Institute for Foreign Languages in Moscow, which trains personnel for diplomatic, KGB, and other assignments abroad. After teaching duties at home, Tanguiane joined the UNESCO staff in 1956. Until 1962 his position was that of a program specialist in education. After an interval of three years, on other assignments, Tanguiane returned to UNESCO in 1965 as division chief, and in 1967 advanced to the post of director in the Education Division. Following yet another outside assignment, he rejoined the organization in 1975, this time as assistant director-general for education. Tanguiane is the author of studies and articles on educational problems in the U.S.S.R., France, and Algeria.

It goes virtually without saying that UNESCO, because of its politico-cultural role and geographic location, has also been used as a center of Soviet intelligence operations. This point was documented in 1983, when France expelled 47 Soviet nationals on espionage charges, at a time when the KGB had sharply increased the number of its targets in Western Europe. Among those expelled, twelve were UNESCO staff members, of whom three held top positions in the Secretariat. The Soviet Union strongly supported M'Bow, a Senegal national, for his position as the agency's director-general. While he collected a tax-free salary in excess of $180,000 per annum and enjoyed the use of a rent-free penthouse apartment atop the UNESCO building in Paris, Soviet nationals were forced to return a fixed percentage of their UNESCO salaries to the comptroller of the Soviet embassy.

In this and other major respects, UNESCO is typical of United Nations organizations generally. According to the congressional report, the U.S.S.R. "received about $20 million per year in salary kickbacks from Soviet employees in the United Nations and its specialized agencies," which thus became "a major subsidy for Soviet diplomatic and intelligence efforts." The report specified:

"An identical kickback system is at work throughout the United Nations. Each position in the UN Secretariat is assigned a rank and pay grade equivalent to that in the Soviet Mission, which is roughly comparable to an individual's diplomatic status. No matter his rank or grade, each Soviet employee is required to turn over his entire UN salary to a finance clerk in the Soviet Mission. The clerk then pays the Soviet Secretariat employee the standard hard currency salary paid to mission personnel of the same rank, plus 10 percent. If the Soviet resides outside the Soviet compound, he also receives an apartment allotment. The payment usually does not meet the actual rental expenses. The hard currency contribution Soviets make to the UN pension fund is turned over to the Soviet Mission when they leave the UN Secretariat."

While it was originally intended that members of UN secretariats, including that of UNESCO, were to have the status of international civil servants, the Soviet Union has consistently enforced the concept that its nationals were essentially responsible to their government, rather than to their UN superiors. Their status was defined as follows: "Members of the Secretariat shall subscribe to the following oath or declaration: I solemnly swear (undertake, affirm, promise) to exercise in all loyalty, discretion and conscience the functions entrusted to me as an international civil servant of the United Nations, to discharge these functions and regulate my conduct with the interests of the United Nations only in view, and not to seek or accept any instructions in regard to the performance of my duties from any Government or other authority external to the Organization."

While UNESCO serves as a compact example of Soviet efforts to use a UN agency as a propaganda conduit, the UN apparatus as a whole is increasingly being used in the same manner. The congressional report noted, "Soviet employees use the United Nations to support Soviet propaganda activities worldwide," and added: "Soviet Secretariat officials received instructions directly from Moscow on propaganda placements for coverage in the Soviet media and to arrange for the UN Secretary General to make favorable reference to statements of Soviet leaders or announcements of the Central Committee. Documents supporting Soviet interest are entered into UN records and later presented as a UN document in Soviet propaganda placements."

The report also noted that the United Nations has been hooked into the propaganda network that links the Soviet-controlled front organizations. The report stated, "Key Soviet personnel have been placed in UN offices responsible for UN relations with nongovernmental organizations and Soviet front groups" so that organizations such as the World Peace Council participated in UN activities. "Soviet interest in these groups stems from their ability to influence UN debate," the report stated, as well as "the domestic political process in their own countries."

The number of Soviet nationals employed by UNESCO, at the time the congressional report was compiled in 1984, was the third-largest among 16 agencies. With offices in New York, Vienna, and Nairobi, the United Nations itself employed 469 Soviet nationals, the International Atomic Energy Agency in Vienna had 69, and UNESCO employed 59. Perhaps the main reason UNESCO has become so controversial, and why its stance so closely resembles that of the by-now-traditional front organizations, is the idealism that motivated its creation and the amorphous manner in which its tenets could be interpreted, utilized, or exploited.

The idealistic sentiment that permeated the Allied nations in their struggle against Nazi Germany and Japanese militarism during World War II encouraged the hope that widespread education, cultural advancement, and scientific progress would ensure worldwide peace. The preamble to UNESCO's founding charter stated, "Since wars begin in the minds of men, it is in the minds of men that the defense of peace must be constructed." The charter committed the new agency to advancing "the unrestricted pursuit of objective truth and the free exchange of ideas and knowledge." One former assistant director-general, the British scholar Dr. Richard Hoggart, said in his study of UNESCO, *An Idea and Its Servants,* that the original image of the agency as a supernational unit in search of truth embodied "the two fine fictions on which UNESCO is founded."

The hope and optimism that surrounded the birth of the United Nations in San Francisco in 1945, and of its specialized agencies, was largely shared by the victorious Allied powers; this seemingly included the Soviet Union.

True, Joseph Stalin wrested odd concessions from his allies, foremost among them U.S. President Franklin D. Roosevelt, in setting up the United Nations. These included an arrangement whereby the Ukraine and Byelorussia, both integral parts of the Soviet Union, were admitted to the United Nations as separate delegations, thus tripling the voting power of the U.S.S.R. from the very moment of the UN's creation.

While the fictions of an independent Ukraine and Byelorussia have long been accepted by diplomats and the largely unknowing public, the issue was once raised—out of the mouths of babes, as it were—during a UNESCO sideshow. At the Palace of Nations in Geneva, a youth forum, sponsored by the National Swiss Commission for UNESCO, held its annual meeting in 1978. Acting the part of UN delegations, the youngsters, from various parts of Switzerland and French border regions, used as their topic "The Charter of the United Nations and the Human Rights Declaration." One boy, acting the part of a delegate from the United Arab Emirates, proposed that the two UN seats occupied by the Ukraine and Byelorussia be removed; he argued that the Soviet Union, as a prominent violator of human and civil rights, should not have three votes, two of them obviously extraneous. The make-believe United Nations adopted his motion.

As the congressional report recounts the event, this youthful bit of play-acting came to the ears of Soviet Ambassador Zoya Mironova, who promptly woke the director of the Palace of Nations the following morning and demanded that he ban the youngsters from the building. When the boys and girls arrived, at 9 a.m., they found the doors locked. The report stated: "The decision has been made by the official in charge of conference services, Vladimir Lobachev, a Soviet, without consulting the director of the Palace. The young people had lost. They left the Palace and never returned to disturb the peace and quiet of the diplomats." Subsequent meetings of the youth group were held at Geneva's city-owned International Conference Center.

The Soviet Union has been able to apply Münzenberg tactics to UNESCO in a series of moves, consolidating its position as its expertise of operating on the international scene increased. During the immediate postwar period, when Stalin's purges rocked Eastern Europe, the U.S.S.R. and its satellites ignored UNESCO. The fear of intellectual cross-fertilization that prompted Stalin to dissolve the Comintern also prompted his suspicion of UN-related activities. Hoggart described the second phase of Soviet involvement, beginning in the late 1950s, after Stalin's death, when UNESCO first became a forum for East-West conflicts. In the 1960s, according to Hoggart, a third phase started with the addition of newly independent countries of Africa and Asia, and with emphasis on UNESCO as a base for knowledge by advancing literacy. This led to a campaign against illiteracy and the allocation of funds to protect such artistic treasures as the Temple of Abu Simbel in Egypt and Borobudur in Indonesia.

Hoggart viewed the fourth phase of UNESCO operations, its "near-total politicalization," as starting when the agency's Third World majority, joined by the Soviet bloc, began to harass Israel. This phase coincided with the election of M'Bow to the agency's directorship. Several policies and activities, notable for their pro-Soviet and anti-Western aims, coincided with a period of financial extravagance on the part of the Secretariat.

Among specific target areas, widest publicity was gained by the project known as the New World Information and Communication Order (NWICO), which included wider use of new communications technology among developing countries, extended governmental control over the journalistic profession and the flow of information, or both. Another controversial target area was a drive within UNESCO to redirect attention to human rights and their violations. The agency's charter, like that of the United Nations itself, contains a specific commitment to uphold human rights; but successive efforts within UNESCO tended to substitute a concept of "peoples' rights" and to define it along lines advanced by the Soviet delegation. One American participant, Leonard Sussman, executive director of Freedom House, noted in "UNESCO: Up Against the U.S. Ultimatum" (*Freedom at Issue,* July–August 1984): "Human rights became a cold-war issue in 1982 when the Extraordinary General Conference of UNESCO for the first time approved programs for 1984–1989 that would discuss 'peoples' rights' along with human rights." Sussman added:

"The term 'peoples' rights' aroused American suspicion and opposition. It was quickly assumed that a new hidden agenda was being unveiled—that peoples' rights would be interpreted to mean collectivist or states rights in the pattern of communist definition of the supreme authority of governments over the rights of citizens; indeed, of the rights of the group over the rights of the individual. All this could readily be perceived in the breadth of the term and in the absence of any of the supporting papers."

Yet Mr. Sussman, a vice chair of the U.S. National Commission for UNESCO, maintained that the United States failed to take sufficient advantages of discussions concerning the communications debate, that Western press coverage of the proposal had overstated its risks, and that the United States might well find advantages in participating actively in the "peoples' rights" debates. He said, "Not a single resolution, not a single statement of a top official of UNESCO ever called for licensing, governmental codes for journalists, monitoring of journalistic output, or censorship." In Sussman's view, UNESCO's role in pushing for the New World Information and Communication Order had been oversimplified by press accounts that dealt with it as a single-issue matter, the endangering of a free flow of information. He offered these specifics:

"By any current definition of news, UNESCO's communications debates last year [1983] were newsworthy. Of forty-nine communications resolutions introduced, thirty-three (including those of the U.S. and its friends) were not objectionable to free-press advocates. Of the remaining sixteen, the worst—introduced by the Soviet Union and the German Democratic Republic—were withdrawn without ever reaching the floor. On the positive side, the first time in a decade, the general conference approved programs to study the 'watchdog' role of the press, examine governmental censorship, and self-censorship. Most important, UNESCO decided to treat the New World Information and Communications Order as an 'evolving process,' not a series of imposed regulations. Each of these programs represents a gain for free-press supporters and a loss for authoritarians of the left and the right."

Sussman, who participated in several key UNESCO meetings, advocated a dispassionate view of UNESCO proceedings. Surveying press and other media coverage, he found that they did not distinguish between "expansion of communications facilities, and the improvement of the quality of the flow, on the one hand; and the desire of some control over the *content* of the flow for authoritarian purposes" on the other. He noted that UNESCO had not made clear that "it was not seeking to support a single, normative system of news and information flow." Too often, Sussman wrote, "it appeared that a universal standard for journalism was sought" and the agency's Secretariat, "at middle levels," appeared to push for the creation of "a normative system of journalism." As a result of all this, he clearly felt, UNESCO had become a punching bag for much of the Western press.

On the delicate matter of the "peoples' rights" issue, Sussman also advocated a less judgmental approach by Western observers. Originally, the communications program had been introduced by Third World delegates; it was only later that the Soviet Union, sensing opportunities for developing a "united front" with other nations, began to advance resolutions that implemented its own concepts of what news and comment should be. The "peoples' rights" issue had been initiated by African countries, and Sussman noted that a debate on this topic "could open a process of definition, and further description of the term." He asked: "Should Americans regard the debate as threatening? Should we respond to the human rights debate in the same self-defeating ways we reacted to the communications debates at UNESCO?" Sussman concluded:

"Properly understood, peoples' rights can be seen as an integral part of the democratic tradition. We should not let the implication become accepted that, because democracy begins with a consideration of the rights of individuals, it does not recognize, as essential to their expression, collective institutions that secure these rights in a community or among communities composed of many individuals with necessarily conflicting rights."

Writing in *Business Week* (March 4, 1985), Sussman suggested the United States return to UNESCO and work at redressing the agency's ills by, first of all, exploring "missed opportunities." He wrote: "Now the political point has been made, and it may have a salutary impact. It is in the national interest of the U.S. to return to a reformed UNESCO with clearly defined objectives, effective supervision, and the determination to stay the course. The absence of diplomacy invites others to fill the political vacuum and clinch the sales."

Another U.S. delegate to the UNESCO conference on education, held in Paris in April 1983, took a harsher view of the U.S. chances inside the agency. Chester E. Finn, Jr., professor of education and public policy at Vanderbilt University, found that, at UNESCO, the United States "subsidizes the erosion of intellectual freedom, the degradation of democratic values, the redefinition of human rights, and the manipulation of education into an instrument of political indoctrination by those who wish us ill." Like Sussman, Finn called for sustained U.S. attention to UNESCO's operations, instead of dealing with it by fits and starts.

In a detailed article, "How to Lose the War of Ideas," in *Commentary* (August 1983), Finn described his experiences and impressions at UNESCO, noting that what was once "a fundamentally beneficent undertaking, even a noble one," had largely been turned into "an instrument of destruction that is wielded to chip away at the idea of freedom and the practice of democracy." Finn noted that the Soviet Union takes the agency "very seriously indeed, recognizing it as an important theater in the world of ideas and in the competition for Third World favor."

Finn found that the U.S.S.R. assigns "senior people with great skill at ideological combat" to the agency, who "do their home work with awesome meticulousness." He added: "They accumulate gains from one event to the next, turning a phrase adopted at one conference into a full policy statement at the next and into a new UNESCO program (and budget item) at the session after. UNESCO, for them, is serious enough to warrant including in long-term foreign policy planning. They have a UNESCO strategy, and in recent years it has been notably successful."

That strategy, essentially the Münzenberg technique, has been perfected through decades of such operations as the World Peace Council, including "fronts of fronts" that are hardly recognizable as puppets on very long Soviet strings. According to Finn, "the Western democracies have no such strategy," so "their resistance to Soviet gains is fitful and ambivalent." Finn found that Western nations send some representatives who are "able statesmen," while others "are weary careerists with no appetite for any kind of combat, and still others are idealistic academics who regard UNESCO as an extended sherry hour in the international common room." Finn's analysis of the UNESCO operation included the observation that the U.S.S.R. and its associates "have figured out how to manipulate the language of liberalism, to exploit the cultural neuroses of the Western democracies, and to take advantage of the West's moral commitment to evenhanded-ness."

Finn's observations on this point can be applied to a variety of other targets of Soviet propaganda. He noted that the days of crude diatribes, of references to "running dogs of imperialism," are gone. Instead, "ter-rorist bands are called liberation movements," and there is "an array of brutal despotisms that style themselves 'democratic republics.' " Beyond this, Finn said, UNESCO uses "a linguistic code of its own." Specifically: "In this code, 'peace' is understood to refer to a condition that the Soviet Union favors and that the United States opposes. The 'arms race' is actually not a race at all, for only the Western democracies are running in it, and it is well known that their purpose is not to safeguard their own security but to squander resources that would otherwise be transferred to the Third World as part of the 'new international economic order.' 'Interference in the internal affairs of states' is what the United States engages in when it calls attention to human rights violations in the Soviet Union, not what Moscow is doing in Afghanistan or Cuba in Central America. 'Nazism and neo-Nazism' are widespread contemporary Western ideologies that pose imminent threats to peace, human rights, and international understand-ing." Finn concluded that the concept of "human rights" was being trans-formed into "peoples' rights" in order to change "individual rights into group interests," which "makes the state their source and arbiter, rather than itself the creature of citizens whose rights are antecedent and in-alienable."

Finn's encounter with UNESCO prompted him to conclude: "It little avails us to send a capable ambassador to Paris if UNESCO is to be regarded as a remote policy enclave, if its decision-making sessions are treated as isolated episodes, and if the tactics employed in what is essentially a battle of ideas are the products of a bureaucracy that instinctively opts for compromise, invisibility, and damage control." He also said: "Within the intellectual communities, UNESCO is, for obvious reasons, rarely crit-icized from the Left. Although it is frequently attacked from the Right, the attackers usually take for granted that the United States should with-draw entirely from all UN activities; as a result, they are not obliged to pay serious attention to what actually happens in Paris and tend therefore to depict UNESCO as if it were a primitive society or alien planet with little relevance or consequence for the United States."

The Soviet Union's tactics at UNESCO and at similar targets are to attack in successive waves and at several fronts. Attacks on the Associated Press, United Press International, and the Reuters and Agence France Presse, picturing them as monopolistic enterprises in the hands of "imperialists" or "neocolonialists," can be followed by campaigns against other worldwide enterprises, already labeled negatively as "multinationals," ranging from magazines with international editions, such as *Reader's Digest* and *Time,* to automobile manufacturers and the products of IBM. The syndication of U.S. television series has already been labeled "cultural imperialism"; while it is debatable whether some American TV shows help or harm the nation's image abroad, they are part of the free flow of ideas.

The experiences of delegates, such as Sussman and Finn, have been supplemented by Owen Harries, Australia's ambassador to UNESCO in 1982–1983, who has narrated his impressions in several publications. His most traumatic experience was, clearly, the agency's World Conference on Cultural Policies, which took place in Mexico City in the summer of 1982. The meeting showed a cost overrun that may well be unique in bureaucratic history. Budgeted at $54,800, the conference actually cost nearly $600,000. Interpreting services alone came to $103,000, double the estimated cost of the whole conference. The catch-all category of "hospitality" consumed $60,000.

The cultural policies conference had originally been scheduled for Paris, with 400 participants. Naturally, everything, including travel costs, increased substantially when the meeting was shifted to Mexico and 700 people participated. When Director-General M'Bow added an extra day to the conference, an additional sum of $40,000 was needed just to handle some 200 draft resolutions submitted just before the closing date. These details were recorded in a report issued by the U.S. General Accounting Office (GAO), "Improvements Needed in UNESCO's Management, Personnel, Financial and Budgeting Practices" (November 30, 1984). Ambassador Harries described the meeting as resembling "a Mad Hatter tea party of propaganda and palaver, with conference procedure routinely flouted or else manipulated for political purposes, with key documents untranslated or undistributed." Harries said in the *Reader's Digest* that he found "the chaos in Mexico City an accurate reflection of the vast pretenses, incredible inefficiency and vicious anti-Western ideology that now pervade UNESCO."

Ambassador Harries' vivid language stood in contrast to the style in which the U.S. General Accounting Office described the agency's functions. Its report, a model of bureaucratic self-control and understatement, cited "observations on certain management areas it believes need attention." The GAO did not deal with political tactics used by the Soviet-led coalition, abetted by the M'Bow-controlled Secretariat, but it did note managerial manipulations that enabled these tactics to succeed.

The GAO observed that the director-general "makes most of the substantive and many routine decisions concerning operations," including appointments of the deputy director-general, the assistant directors-general, and the division directors. M'Bow also approves "all requests for funds from member states," as well as the "extensions of all employee contracts," which run from 400 to 600 each year, and "determines which employees will receive long-term contracts," of which 164 were written in 1984. He also "grants promotions," which totaled 359 in 1983. As the selection, appointment, and promotion of personnel amounts to control of UNESCO's staff, Director-General M'Bow could favor those who went along with his policies and exclude men and women who disagreed with him. His staff control was aided by the director of personnel, Serge Vieux, his wife's cousin. Some of those interviewed by the GAO said, "Officials do not try to make decisions because they perceive that the Director-General wants to retain all decision-making authority."

The GAO reported that the Secretariat had become more and more self-reliant and decisive in running UNESCO's affairs, because the agency's "governing bodies" had let their authorities slip away. While external auditors had made "repeated recommendations to the Secretariat in successive years," the "Executive Board has not followed up to help ensure an adequate response by the Secretariat." According to outside observers of the agency's day-to-day operations, "The General conference has become too dependent upon the Secretariat, which influences its agenda and drafts many of its resolutions." Putting matters as clearly as diplomatic-bureaucratic vernacular would permit, the GAO reported: "The Executive Board is viewed as accepting the program and budget provided by the Secretariat without obtaining information necessary for effective oversight and as not playing an adequate role in overseeing the execution of the program."

Over the years, UNESCO vastly increased its headquarters staff, and this has made for striking changes in the ratio between the Paris office and the number of agency representatives in the field. By 1984, 2,428 of its 3,380 employees were stationed in the French capital. The GAO report showed that, a year earlier, the agency also employed an additional 2,362 supplemental staff members, categorized as "consultants and supernumeraries." As a result, the GAO observed, "UNESCO, in essence, has a dual personnel system."

The GAO report did not go into details as to how education and travel grants, funding of regional projects, or contributions to government projects were selected, how allocations were decided, or how disbursements were controlled. It did mention unusual aspects of these activities, some of them certainly subject to personal and political influence, but it did not name names or cite specific figures. The GAO did report that, according to UNESCO's Secretariat, travel money spent from 1981 through 1983 totaled $29.4 million. Travel to conferences and meetings, including travel by members of its Executive Board, came to $11 million. Travel by consultants totaled $4.9 million, and travel simply categorized as "for other official purposes" amounted to $4.4 million.

UNESCO is not egalitarian in defining "travel and subsistence entitlements" for its officials. Only its director-general commanded "first class accommodations on all flights." M'Bow likes traveling, being received with the honors due an official whose agency distributes funds abroad, and devotes about half of each year to such visits. As an international civil servant who has risen to his position from that of a schoolmaster at home, he also appreciates honorary doctorates and decorations. As of early 1985, he had accumulated 40 honorary doctorates and 34 governmental decorations, among them honorary degrees from Moscow State University, the State University of the Mongolian Peoples Republic, Tashkent University, located in the capital of Soviet Uzbekistan, and Kliment Okhridski University, located in Sofia, Bulgaria.

Amadou-Mahtar M'Bow was born on March 2, 1921, at Dakar, Senegal. He received his advanced education in Paris, first at an electrical engineering school (Ecole d'ingénies électriciens Breguet) and then at the Arts Faculty of the University of Paris. His teaching career began with a post at Rosso College in Mauritania. From 1953 to 1957 he directed Senegal's Department of Basic Education and, in 1957 and 1958, served in Senegal's preindependence cabinet as minister of education and culture. From 1958 to 1964, M'Bow taught at the Lycée Faidherbe in Saint Louis, Senegal. For the next two years, he taught at a teachers' training institute in Dakar.

With the independent government of Senegal established, M'Bow served as minister of education (1966–1968) and as minister for youth and cultural affairs and concurrently as a member of the National Assembly (1968–1970). From 1970 to 1974 he held the position of UNESCO's assistant director-general for education, and on November 17, 1974, he was appointed the agency's director-general.

Andrei Grachov, a Soviet writer who frequently deals with UNESCO matters, reported in the *Moscow News* (September 25, 1983) that Director-General M'Bow endorsed the communications project while visiting Tashkent, saying, "Now that the world is living through very hard times, the activities of the International Program for the Development of Communications seem to be especially important. Unanimous recognition of the IPDC objectives and tasks by all participants in the current session can contribute to better international relations." The occasion was the Tashkent session of the IPDC Intergovernmental Council, held in the capital of Uzbekistan from September 5 to 12, 1983. Over 120 delegates from 47 countries participated.

Grachov quoted one delegate as saying that "the information services of the Third World" had to depend on an "international Mafia," the worldwide news services that control "the flow of information from the industrialized capitalist countries." He added: "The one-way traffic in the area of information has been described by the participants in the session as information colonialism. Representatives of Nicaragua, Mozambique and several other countries accused the US mass media of open ideological aggression." Grachov, in an article written jointly with Igor Danilin, said that, as part of "neocolonialist policies," the West was engaged in "aggression" that was "primarily directed against progressive regimes in the newly-free countries." He also wrote:

"In a situation such as this, the desire of the developing countries to put the aggressive activities of Western information monopolies under international control is quite understandable. On the other hand, a special international 'mechanism' was required to mobilize the resources needed to assist the developing countries in extending their mass information infrastructures."

The article quoted M'Bow as anticipating an increase in UNESCO's budget share on communications projects for 1984–1985 by 11 percent, placing "communication in the service of people." It noted that "representatives of many developing countries criticized major Western powers, primarily the USA, for supporting the IPDC in word only, while withholding material support," while "the USSR supports the IPDC actively." The article cited Sharaf Rashidov, first secretary of the Central Committee of the Communist Party of Uzbekistan, as telling the conference: "Equal news exchange among nations is only possible on condition that information sovereignty is guaranteed for all countries, both large and small."

The project that linked UNESCO most directly with such front organizations as the World Peace Council and the "peace movement" generally was a series of "peace and disarmament" initiatives for which $750,000 was budgeted. By contrast, the agency voted only $32,000 for a program designed to educate refugees who were faced with difficult postmigration adjustments. The very term "peace and disarmament" is identical with terminology used in the Soviet-controlled front organizations. It is thus part of the "language of liberalism," which, as Finn had observed, was transformed by the UNESCO Secretariat into an internal code.

Assistant Director-General Tanguiane's special area of responsibility within UNESCO has been education, a major segment of the agency's administrative categories. One-fifth of the yearly budget is earmarked for education, and conferences frequently deal with such topics as "democratization of education" and other problems concerning youth. The 1984–1985 budget for education was $86.5 million, and its projects included literacy training, childhood and adult education, technical cooperation, environmental education, elimination of racism and apartheid, human rights education, and peace studies. The education program employed 311 people at the Paris headquarters and 262 in the field.

What the State Department had called UNESCO's "unrestrained budgetary expansion" remained a point of disagreement, essentially unresolved, as the agency prepared for its General Conference at Sofia, Bulgaria, in October 1985. For seven weeks, during the early summer, the agency's Executive Board struggled with program and budget revisions that resulted in a still-controversial compromise. The United States and several other major powers had objected to UNESCO's budget of $374.4 million for a two-year period, a substantial increase at a time when other UN agencies were holding the line on expenditures. With the United States absent, the board faced a choice between across-the-board reductions and the cutting back of projects that were heavily "politicized."

The board ended its sessions with a victory for the Soviet-led coalition, which favored proposed savings of $97 million, directed equally against UNESCO's uncontroversial projects and its controversial ones. There were cutbacks in "peace and disarmament" projects and in the New World Information and Communication Order, but $2.3 million remained to "identify future world problems." An almost routine Soviet–Third World denunciation of Israel, castigating archaeological explorations in Jerusalem and alleging suppression of education and cultural rights of Arabs in the West Bank area, was passed.

M'Bow had sought to replace funds lacking from the agency's budget, because of U.S. withdrawal, by using money set aside to act as a buffer against inflation and currency fluctuation. Great Britain and other countries objected to this financial manipulation, observing that it violated UNESCO's budgetary rules and was, therefore, illegal. The matter was among the topics discussed, later in the year, at UNESCO's Twenty-third General Conference in Sofia, Bulgaria, which lasted from October 8 to November 9, 1985. Among the topics explored were "Peace, International Understanding, Human Rights and the Peoples' Rights" and "UNESCO's Role in Shaping World Public Opinion With a View to Fostering and Promoting a New Mentality in the Nuclear Age in Order to Remove the Threat of a Thermonuclear Catastrophe."

The head of the Soviet delegation, Victor Stukalin, told Tass (October 6, 1985) that the U.S.S.R. regarded the agency as "an important instrument of peace" and expressed the hope that "some countries" would renounce "their claims to a privileged position in this organization." Stukalin, a deputy foreign minister, was appointed Soviet ambassador to Greece soon after the conference ended. The Ukrainian delegate, G. Tsvetkov, accused the British delegation of showing "a negative approach to the agency's programs in defense of peace" and called for the convocation of a world conference, "Scientists for Safeguarding Life on Earth." (In 1984, UNESCO had bestowed its Prize for Peace Education, the sum of $60,000, on International Physicians for the Prevention of Nuclear War; this was a year before the Nobel Peace Prize was awarded to the group, creating a worldwide controversy. The UNESCO award was presented to Dr. Bernard Lown on October 30, 1984.)

The Sofia session began with efforts by the Soviet Union, Algeria, India, and Cameroon to have UNESCO dismiss all 130 American nationals who were on its staff, following the U.S. withdrawal from the agency. This demand, as well as pressure that the United States close its observer mission, were ultimately rejected. The conference also voted down M'Bow's suggestion that the United States be prosecuted before the World Court for not paying its share of UNESCO's budget. The meeting, attended by 2,000 delegates from 152 countries, failed to respond to pressure from Great Britain and other countries to reallocate funds in such a way that practical programs designed to strengthen poorer nations would receive proportionally more money than the controversial New World Information and Communication Order and "peace and disarmament" programs.

UNESCO's budget for 1986–1987 contained the ambitious and amorphous category "Education for Peace and Respect for Human Rights and the Rights of Peoples." Allocation of funds fell into such categories as "Maintenance of Peace and International Understanding," "Reflection on the Factors Contributing to Peace," "Research into the Causes and Consequences of the Arms Race and the Creation of Conditions Conducive to Disarmament," and, as one of the subprograms, "Implementation of the 1974 Recommendations and Follow-up to the Intergovernmental Conference on Education for International Understanding, Co-Operation and Peace and Education Relation to Human Rights and Fundamental Freedoms, Favorable to the Strengthening of Security and Disarmament." Among the "modalities of action," the plan foresaw conferences and meetings, studies and research, training (including fellowships), technical and advisory services, "other," and indirect apportioned program costs.

Advanced knowledge of accountancy, sophisticated political analysis, and expertise in decoding UNESCO's specialized bureaucratese were required to comprehend the impact of this plan, which took up pages 487 to 514 of the agency's *Draft Programme and Budget*.

Looking back on UNESCO's performance during the year, Great Britain decided to withdraw from the organization as of December 31, 1985. The British government felt that its effort at achieving reform within UNESCO had been unsuccessful. Timothy Raison, minister for overseas development, told Parliament on December 5 that Britain had been on the forefront for UNESCO reform and that "there have been reforms." But, he asked, "Have we really achieved the objectives?" and added, "Our answer has to be 'No.' " Britain had been one of the key founders of the agency, which was established in London in 1945. Raison recalled those origins when he said: "It is sad that an organization which began with such high hopes, and to which this country had contributed so much in the past, should have gone so wrong. But we have to deal with what the organization has become."

Soviet tactics for control of the agency were illustrated during the Twenty-fourth Coordinating Conference of the Socialist Countries' UNESCO Affairs Commission, held in Minsk. *Izvestia* reported (July 6, 1986) on the closing resolutions passed the day before. Delegations incuded all the Eastern European countries, separate representatives for Byelorussia and the Ukraine (in accordance with general United Nations membership), as well as Cuba, Laos, Kampuchea, Afghanistan, South Yemen, Mozambique, and Ethiopia. For the "forthcoming two-year period and the subsequent six years, UNESCO's activity" was resolved to be centered on "safeguarding peace and curbing the arms race and helping to narrow the gap between developed and developing countries"—lofty generalities that could provide the framework for any and all Soviet bloc policies.

UNESCO had become what it was, because Münzenberg tactics had been applied to it with consistency, skill, and patience, while the West limited itself to haphazard forays of damage control. It was an uneven contest.

CHAPTER · 12

Eager Agents of Influence

Anna Louise Strong was born in the United States and died in China; Wilfred Peter Burchett was born in Australia and died in Bulgaria. Both crisscrossed the world, were highly effective propagandists of communism, and alternated between the Soviet Union and the Communist-governed countries of Asia. Yet they differed greatly in character and methods. While Strong contributed to Communist causes, using her income from popular writings, Burchett solicited subsidies from the Communist regimes on whose activities he reported. Throughout her life, Anna Louise Strong remained amateurishly naive about the nature of Communist state machineries; Wilfred Burchett skillfully maneuvered his way between Moscow, Peking, and Hanoi.

Strong, a minister's daughter, was at heart a missionary, devout in her adherence to political dogma and pro-underdog by sheer reflex; Burchett, who also had a clergyman as a parent, operated in a shadow world where propaganda and espionage overlap. Anna Louise Strong's father, a Congregational minister, taught her that "neither money nor fame nor human opinion are to be counted against being 'right in one's soul.' " Appropriately, her cobiographers, Tracy B. Strong and his wife Helene Keyssar, called their book *Right in Her Soul*. Their compassionate narrative noted that Strong occasionally expressed doubts and irritations, although these hardly ever found their way into print. Steeped in Christian tradition, Strong could not avoid being troubled in her soul; yet, outwardly and defiantly, she was a dedicated Marxist. Where her ancestors had gone out to convert the heathens, Strong preached the gospel according to Marx, Lenin, Stalin, and Mao to Americans. She was a missionary in reverse.

Born on November 24, 1885, Anna Louise Strong was essentially a nineteenth-century woman, heir to the liberal conviction that humankind is perfectible. Where reality did not fit her hopes or illusions, she opted for self-delusion, wishful thinking, and a more or less reluctant hypocrisy. Her life was a continuous search for affection, identity, and service. Her religio-humanitarian socialism had prompted Anna Louise Strong to sympathize with Bolshevism from the very beginning. In 1917, she was one of the first foreign correspondents to meet the Soviet leaders. She was particularly taken with Leon Trotsky's verve and commanding air of certainty. In later years, when Stalin exiled Trotsky and purged the Old Bolsheviks, Strong retreated into a mixture of personal bewilderment and public adherence to Stalin's policies.

At first, Strong had high hopes for her own role in Soviet society. She wanted to be an active participant, rather than a writing outsider. Strong plunged into a succession of projects, ranging from a Russian-American club to a children's colony, that did not yield to her Yankee enthusiasm. Russian xenophobia and bureaucratic hurdles finally convinced her to go back to the typewriter. Her magazine articles, which included profiles of Lenin, Trotsky, and Stalin, were the forerunners of several successful books, beginning with *The First Time in History,* with a preface by Trotsky, that appeared the year Lenin died.

After a quick sojourn in the United States, early in 1925, Strong made her first trip to China. Her enthusiasm was rekindled. She spoke of Peking as a city with which she had quickly "fallen in love." In China, she encountered Michael Borodin, then the Comintern's number one emissary, whom she had met previously in Chicago and Moscow. He was Moscow's liaison to the National Government, the *Kuomintang.*

Her infatuation with China was interrupted by a return to the United States, a visit to Mexico, a stopover in Europe, and another stay in Moscow. Her father, puzzled by her travels, talks, and writings, asked her in a letter, "Please tell me if you are a communist?" She answered, in staccato style, "*Not a party member.* Will not deny much sympathy with Communist ideas, even agreement often. What *is* a communist? ALS."

Back in China, she spent much time in Hankow, where Borodin tried to implement baffling, often quite unrealistic Comintern instructions. On June 1, 1927, Stalin ordered Borodin to proceed with land confiscation and to form a new army of peasants and workers. By then, the Nationalists were closing in on the Communists, and Borodin decided to return to Moscow. Strong joined the Borodin party, traveling through China's northwestern provinces and the Gobi desert by car, the rest of the way by train. Her biographers state: "Through the long evenings of talk and the difficult days of passage, Borodin grew increasingly close. She was the best audience for his discourses on opera, theater, movies and literature, and with her he could begin to sort through the complexities of the last few years that had ended with this strange excursion." In her subsequent book, *China's Millions,* Strong expressed peripheral doubts about Communist policies; but, as her biographers note, "Beyond these passages she held her tongue in print and in public. There might be a role for her in Moscow; there was none in China."

The Moscow scene was strenuous. Borodin was caught in Stalin's meat-grinder, although only slowly. He was forced to utter "criticism and self-criticism," then given the position of deputy director of the Paper and Lumber Trust of the U.S.S.R. This was the period of one of Stalin's most ruthless undertakings, the forced collectivization of agriculture, which led to destruction of the kulaks, Russia's supposedly reactionary farmers, to chaos and starvation in the countryside, and to the death of millions. Strong wrote a whole book about the Soviets' alleged successes in grain production and distribution, their supposed defeat of hunger; called *The Soviets Conquer Wheat,* it was well received in the United States, then in the midst of an economic depression that had badly hurt agriculture. In 1935 she indirectly disavowed her earlier appraisal of Soviet grain policies. With apparent reluctance, she wrote, "I had thought that splendid harvest of 1930 had conquered wheat," whereas "in the early winter of 1932" disquieting news had come from the southern regions. "Slowly, as the spring of 1933 deepened into summer," she wrote, "the tension in the country grew" and foreign correspondents in Moscow actually "cried famine."

By 1936, in her book *This Soviet World,* Strong argued that Stalin acted in a benevolently forgiving manner: "Saboteurs reform and win posts of honor; kulaks come back from exile to factories and farms; children have an equal start now, regardless of father." In the same book she claimed: "Step by step, the Soviet Union fights forward towards that complete democracy which has never existed anywhere on earth." By then, the mass deaths of the kulaks were a historical statistic. Stalin's purges were well under way. Strong confessed: "I tell not the 'whole truth,' for the truth is never whole."

Surely, there are limits to self-deception, and Strong could not, at that point, have felt "right in her soul." In *I Change Worlds,* she spoke up for Borodin, with whom she continued to work closely in those days, and claimed that "they" were "not telling what I called the whole story" to Borodin. She observed, "Every Communist to whom you mention the hunger glares at you as if you talked treason"; when she confronted Borodin with the question, "How many people are dying?" he turned on her and shouted, "What makes it your business!"

At last, Strong found a niche in which she could use her writing skills to make a contribution to Soviet society. Together with Borodin, she was authorized to publish an English-language paper, the *Moscow Daily News,* mainly for the benefit of Americans working in the U.S.S.R. But she simply could not grasp Soviet rules and rigidities of internal propaganda and censorship, nor the rude realities of Stalin's role and rule. From the start, she ran into tragicomic problems. When she wanted to publish a satirical article on the trouble of finding an apartment in Moscow, the censor called it a "slander to the Soviet Union." Miss Strong tried to explain nuances of the American sense of humor, but although she argued fiercely, the article was cut.

She only worked for three weeks on the new paper—enthusiastically, of course—and then left for a lecture tour in the United States. At this point, all contact with Moscow stopped. Her articles were not printed; her cables went unanswered. When she returned to Moscow, there was no one to meet her at the train. At the paper, the editorial staff had been replaced by what she called "highly paid typists and translators who were busy turning dull Russian into bad English." She couldn't even get her own desk back.

To make matters worse, and in the best tradition of bureaucratic rivalry, a second English-language paper, *Worker's News,* had made its appearance; it even attacked Strong's paper as "too bourgeois." Strong threatened to resign and "go to China." During this period she worked closely with Joel Shubin. He had been a Foreign Office press officer and was then editing the *Peasant Gazette,* a periodical Strong liked. Shubin, a widower with a teenage daughter, moved into an apartment with Strong, and, in the manner of others in their circle, they considered themselves married.

All this happened in 1931 and 1932. She was between books and between countries, between her family and her new husband, between illusions and realities, between her own image of what a Soviet newspaper in English should be and what the Agitprop bureaucrats wanted to see in print. And then she met Stalin!

The *Moscow Daily News* continued to have difficulties. Once, when Strong summarized an exceptionally long Stalin speech, her superior ordered the full text printed in the English-language paper, together with a picture of Stalin. He argued, "Who is to say what the gist of the great Stalin's speech is?" Strong countered, "But we look just like *Pravda*." She really did not comprehend Stalin's all-encompassing role. Instead, she fumed, threatening to expose Soviet journalism in the United States. An "especially sensitive" official, probably Borodin, urged her to write to Stalin personally. The result was an interview with Stalin in the presence of two other top officials. After a brief discussion of technicalities, Stalin let it be known that he favored just one English-language paper, with Borodin as "responsible editor." Strong, together with two others, would serve as assistant editors.

Of this meeting, Strong wrote: "It gave me a method. Other hours in my life marked by great emotion—when I have adored great men—have all died out. I cannot recapture their feeling. But that half hour grows with years. Even today I can feel the atmosphere of that meeting—its sympathetic but unemotional analysis, seeking fundamental lines and acting to set them right." She even told Shubin: "I'd like to take orders from those men anywhere in the world. I feel they wouldn't give an order until I knew myself it was the thing to do."

After another visit to the United States, Strong returned to Moscow in 1934. She started on her autobiography but was quickly stalemated by difficulties in dealing with the subject of Trotsky. Borodin patiently explained that Trotsky was no longer important. The biographer noted that "her fluid and efficient prose" was "barely masking her attempt to convince herself and the American Communist Party that she was now worthy of membership." But she simply did not understand the Soviet system, even in her own chosen field, writing and propaganda. Submitting drafts of articles and book chapters to Glavlit, the literary censorship bureau, continued to frustrate her. She asked: "Isn't propaganda merely a question of deceiving our friends without deceiving our enemies?" To which Borodin replied: "Not so. Our enemies suspect, but they do not know."

After *I Change Worlds* was published in the United States in 1935, Strong had lunch with Eleanor Roosevelt, wife of President Franklin D. Roosevelt. This led to a relationship, mainly an exchange of letters, that lasted for a decade. Still, the Communist Party did not want her to become a full-fledged member. Its general secretary at the time, Earl Browder, said she would be more useful outside the party, as a "non-party Bolshevik." She continued to make regular financial "contributions" to the party, but did not receive a membership card.

The *Moscow Daily News* was caught in a morass of "ideological" pseudo news and articles, and even Strong's gift for dramatizing individual experiences began to fail her. There was much worse to come. The notorious Moscow trials began, and Strong heard prominent leaders condemn themselves as traitors. Soon, 98 out of the 139 members of the Communist Party's Central Committee were judged guilty of treason and shot.

Strong virtually fled to Spain, where the Civil War could be said to separate heroes and villains clearly and cleanly—but, of course, the long arm of Stalin's secret police reached into the ranks of the Spaniards, just as it did into the top membership of Communist parties abroad. Strong wrote a book about her impressions, *Yanks in Spain,* but confusion inside the U.S. Communist Party prevented it from being issued in the United States; it later appeared in Russia. Back in Moscow, she finally sensed, but either did not fully comprehend or failed to admit to herself, the extent of Stalin's purges. All around her, former friends and heroes were being executed or exiled or simply disappeared.

Once again, Strong chose escape to China. Edgar Snow had published *Red Star Over China* in 1937, providing an account of Communist activities during the preceding decade. Strong envied Snow this scoop. Similarly, the travels and writings of Agnes Smedley, who had spent several months with the Communist Eighth Route Army, made Strong jealous. Back in Moscow once more, the repressive atmosphere prompted her to shorten her stay. Strong traveled through central Europe, and then to California. When Joel Shubin was made codirector of the Soviet Pavilion at the New York World's Fair, 1939–1940, she tried hard to have Eleanor Roosevelt go and meet him. She spent the second weekend in August with Mrs. Roosevelt at her home in Hyde Park, New York. Strong was thrown into confusion by the announcement of the Nazi-Soviet Pact. She nevertheless tried to follow the party line, even in her letters to Mrs. Roosevelt, who decided that the pact "just lets Germany do its will." Mrs. Roosevelt did not go to the Soviet Pavilion, but invited Shubin and Strong to her New York apartment.

The Soviet Pavilion was abruptly closed on December 2, 1939. Shubin was called back to Moscow. To return to the Soviet Union herself, Strong traveled to Germany. In Berlin, as France surrendered, she saw "at first hand how the victors control the writing of history." She went to Lithuania, managed to travel to Moscow with the Lithuanian delegation to the Supreme Soviet, and even accompanied the Lithuanians to a lunch with Soviet deputies. The Soviet Press Department, which had been delaying a promised press pass, forbade Strong to attend the sessions with the Lithuanian delegates.

Shubin suggested she had better go back to the United States. Once again, she chose China as her refuge from the realities of Moscow. Chungking, at that point, was a center of Nationalist government activity, although Chou En-lai also lived quietly in the city. He invited her for several late-evening interviews. Her biographers state: "Chou had clearly outlined her task to her. She was to attempt to reach not just the Western left but Chiang's American backers, hoping to persuade them to withdraw their support when they learned that Chiang was using American aid to fight a civil war rather than a war against Japan." While she did not succeed in meeting U.S. Treasury Secretary Henry Morgenthau through Mrs. Roosevelt, she advised John Paton Davies in the State Department and Harry Dexter White in the Treasury Department. And while she was unable to write two planned articles for the *New York Times,* through the North American Newspaper Alliance, the foreign editor of the New York *Herald-Tribune,* Joseph Barnes, used her material, together with other information.

When Nazi Germany attacked the Soviet Union, Strong's pro-Soviet bias made her writing and lectures newly popular. Her book *The Soviets*

Expected It was widely read, her lecture schedule crowded. After many vain efforts to receive word on Shubin, she was advised in August that he had died five months earlier of a "lingering lung disease," actually pneumonia, in a Ural mountain town. She collaborated on a documentary on the Dnieper Dam, wrote a novel about two young Russians, *Wild River,* and compiled a secondary school textbook, *People of the U.S.S.R.*

Her biographers wrote: "There was probably not a new thought in the book; a sad parody of her earlier work, it signed the practical end of Anna Louise's writing about the U.S.S.R." Under wartime conditions, she made her way to the Soviet Union by way of Alaska. She wanted to go to the front, but the Russians were in no mood to have foreign correspondents mingle with their troops. The pro-Soviet Polish group, however, took her along to the east bank of the Vistula, facing Warsaw. When she returned to Moscow, the Russians were even more hostile, unwilling to publish the story about "the heroic Poles" or to give her material about the Soviet Union.

Strong was surprised, on a visit to Yugoslavia in the summer of 1945, that the Yugoslavs fiercely disliked the Russians. Back in Moscow, she encountered new anxieties, following the U.S. atom-bombing of Hiroshima. She completed a book, *I Saw the New Poland.* The manuscript was shipped to the United States by diplomatic pouch, with the help of Harry Hopkins, President Roosevelt's close adviser. Her U.S. lecture tours ran into opposition, as Moscow was busily engaged in setting up puppet regimes all over Eastern Europe; still, Strong insisted the Russians "care nothing for having other countries copy their government."

Again, she sought emotional refuge in China. Although she traveled with credentials from the pro-Communist Federated Press, she made her headquarters at the American Board of Missions in what was then called Peiping (Peking). Few of the missionaries had returned to China. Her credentials, by way of family tradition, were good; after all, she was both the daughter and aunt of Congregational ministers. She visited Peiping's Union Church for Sunday services, where she was able to sing all the hymns from memory.

But the highlight of her trip—very likely the highlight of her life—was her visit to Yenan in 1946–1947. In the decades that have passed, the Yenan period of the Chinese Communist movement has taken on the patina of legend. In the caves of Yenan, the Communists had entrenched themselves. There, their eventual conquest of China was planned. Strong's simple, clean personal cave was hollowed into the loess of the mountainside.

The Yenan leaders had clearly decided to use Strong as a messenger to the outside world: to the U.S. government and public and to sympathizers of the Chinese Communist cause everywhere. Stalin regarded Mao as an upstart, an ideological deviant, a heretical rival. Moscow's attitude was reflected inside the U.S. Communist Party, which underwent a Moscow-directed shake-up in leadership and policies, much to the discomfort of its top people. Strong, full of pro-Yenan enthusiasm, did not grasp its significance to her own position.

Arriving in Moscow, Strong expected top-level attention for her Yenan observations, but she was given a cold shoulder. The Chinese, Soviet observers maintained, had failed in their military efforts and were now forced to move about the countryside. In her book manuscript *Dawn Over China,* Strong outlined Mao's tactic of eventually encircling the cities. While her book was about to appear in India, the Moscow state publishing house was reluctant to accept it. Even Borodin's intervention did not help. Nor did Strong's success of getting her book published in Czechoslovakia, Poland, Hungary, Yugoslavia, and East Germany; such undertakings, in Moscow's eyes, made her something of a Chinese agent.

Talks with Chinese representatives in Moscow covered plans ranging from her editing of Mao's works in English translation to the establishment of shortwave radio contact between the Chinese Communists and sympathizers in the United States. Back in the United States, Strong lectured widely on her Yenan impressions and became active in the presidential election campaign, in support of Henry Wallace. A coalition, including the Communists, had formed the Progressive Party, with Wallace as its candidate. While Strong hoped to act as some sort of foreign policy adviser, the new party's leadership was anxious to play down Communist backing. The Communists themselves shied away from the flamboyant woman and her enthusiastic oratory.

When she was ready, once again, to return to China, by way of the U.S.S.R., the Soviet consulate would only give her a visa that would get her as far as Moscow. Once in the Soviet capital, Strong began to haunt the Press Department of the Foreign Office, asking for a transit visa to Manchuria; by then the border area was under Chinese Communist control, and Stalin had to count on Mao's ultimate victory. Soviet officialdom was hostile to Strong's travel plan. They were downplaying the Chinese Communist advances, and had no intention of facilitating the work of a pro-Mao publicist. But Strong was relentless, headstrong, and increasingly vocal about the failings of Soviet bureaucracy. Her all too frank remarks were endangering friends and acquaintances.

The Soviet secret police had undoubtedly received accounts of Strong's conversations, interrogated her visitors, and even transcribed exchanges recorded by their listening devices. The last straw was Strong's visit to a Chinese representative, Liu Ning-yi, at the National Hotel. He assured her that all necessary travel arrangements would be made. Strong called the Foreign Office the following morning, February 13, 1949, and told them that "the Chinese comrade" would help her obtain a Soviet visa.

That night, about 10:30, there was a knock at her door. Two uniformed men, carrying sidearms, ordered her to come with them, as she was "under arrest." Strong was taken to secret police headquarters, the notorious Lubyanka, given a medical examination, had her clothes searched, and was interrogated by a "commissar" who had no knowledge of her devoted propaganda work for the Soviet cause. Instead, he interpreted her many trips to the U.S.S.R., her travels within the country, her interviews and data gathering as cumulative evidence of "spying activities." He was clearly upset that Soviet officialdom had permitted this inquisitive foreigner to come and go for more than 30 years. She was told that she would be expelled across the Soviet frontier. Her choice was to be sent to Poland.

On the morning of the sixth day of Strong's stay at the Lubyanka she was given her belongings, passport, and cash. A small plane took her to an open field, and she was taken by jeep to a bridge that crossed the Soviet-Polish border. From there, the train took her to Warsaw, where she had reservations at the Hotel Bristol. Still incapable of accepting the fact that she had become *persona non grata* in the Communist world, Strong visited friends at the Polish news agency Telepress, who got rid of her as quickly as possible. From Warsaw she went to Paris, then by air to New York.

News that Strong, an advocate of the Soviet cause all her life, had been charged as a spy and imprisoned in Moscow reached the United States ahead of her. In interviews she maintained that, like everywhere else, police in the U.S.S.R. could make mistakes and that she did not want her case to contribute to the cold war. The Associated Press quoted her as saying that "war hysteria in the American Press" had caused her expulsion.

To Strong, the years that followed were a period of confusion and hesitation. She was unable to draw clear-cut conclusions from Stalin's purges of Communist leaders in Eastern Europe, men she had known and liked. She confessed herself puzzled by events following Stalin's death in 1953, including the secret trial and execution of Lavrenti Beria, Stalin's secret police chief. On March 4, 1955, six years after her expulsion from Moscow, the Soviet news agency Tass carried this report:

"In February 1949 the American journalist A. L. Strong, who was at that time in the U.S.S.R., was arrested by the organs of the State Security of the U.S.S.R. on a suspicion of espionage and sabotage against the Soviet Union and deported from the U.S.S.R. As a result of an investigation conducted by the procurator's office of the U.S.S.R. it has been established that the former leader of the Ministry of State Security, Beria, presented the above charges against Miss Strong without grounds. In view of this, she is now exonerated from these charges."

Strong welcomed the new Soviet procedures for clearing those who had been treated unjustly and noted that these methods "work pretty well."

Unless, she added, "the people are already dead." Among the many who shared this fate was her old friend Borodin, who had been sent to a prison camp and death. As part of the policies initiated by Khruschev, Soviet Ambassador Georgi Zarubin invited her for lunch and asked her to visit the Soviet Union once again.

When, the following year, she heard of Khrushchev's secret speech at the Soviet Communist Party Congress, with its revelations about Stalin and Beria, Strong told the head of the California Communist Party: "We knew all these things twenty-five years ago, and I kept silent for the cause of socialism. What am I supposed to say?" In the midst of her distress she found solace, of all things, in a Stalin phrase, "The logic of events is stronger than the logic of intentions," and she used it as the epigraph for her book *The Stalin Era*. She tried not to give way to the anti-Stalin revulsions that had come to characterize much of world opinion at that point, aided by Khrushchev's partial candor. Strong said that Stalin's "collective thinking" made him different from the "despots of history, despite many despotic acts."

The State Department refused her a passport, citing her associations and activities. But a Supreme Court decision in June 1958, favoring the painter Rockwell Kent, reversed any practice of denying passports because of a holder's "belief or association." Strong promptly left for the Stockholm Peace Conference, intending to go on to China. But she was persuaded to make a lengthy stopover in Moscow. At the seedy Hotel Metropol, and in dealing with Soviet bureaucracy, her first reactions were annoyance and irritations. But when she was wildly applauded, telling a meeting that she came as an emissary of "those Americans, and there are many, who do not agree with Mr. [John Foster] Dulles' foreign policy," she felt appreciated once more and right at home. The Soviet Writers' Union became a considerate host and even paid for a month's stay at a rest home outside Moscow.

Despite all this hospitality, Moscow made Strong uneasy; together with her companion, Emily Pierson, she left for Peking on September 20, 1958. She was then 73 years old. Shortly after Strong's arrival in the Chinese capital, Premier Chou En-lai gave a reception for her, where she met other Americans who had settled in Communist China and were working for the new regime in various capacities, including broadcasting and publishing. Among the officials was Minister of Propaganda Lu Ting-yi, who reported that her book *The Stalin Era* had "sold" 110,000 copies in the Chinese translation. The regime treated Strong as its guest, paying for room, board, and transportation.

Strong's last years coincided with the disastrous and chaotic early period of the Cultural Revolution, the unleashing of young "Red Guards" on traditions, the educational system, and older Chinese leadership. Her eightieth birthday was supervised by Mao, but rifts between him and other party veterans were obvious. After that, Strong's Chinese and American friends were increasingly pulled into the whirlpool of events, with humiliations, arrests, and imprisonments. All this puzzled and irritated her. Even her labored apologias for the Cultural Revolution were not circulated. Her writing became stilted and anemic.

Strong died on March 28, 1970. Her ashes were interred at the Revolutionary Martyrs Cemetery, outside Peking. The gravestone reads: "Progressive American Writer and Friend of the Chinese People." She was spared the worst excesses of the Cultural Revolution.

Unlike Strong, whose naive willfulness landed her in the Lubyanka prison, Wilfred Burchett (1911–1983), who was born in Australia, knew how to trim his sails. In his book *Passport: An Autobiography,* Burchett wrote that, in his early years, he observed much poverty and illness, particularly while working as a farm laborer. He wanted to travel and had an interest in languages. During the Depression, in 1936, Burchett went to England.

After a brief period as a travel agent with Thomas Cook & Sons, he obtained a position in which he could use his limited knowledge of Russian. According to the Australian correspondent Denis Warner (*The Reporter,* June 1, 1967), Burchett established contact with Ivan Maisky, the Soviet ambassador in Great Britain, "who selected him to open the London office of *Intourist,*" the agency which handles tourism in the U.S.S.R. In his article "Who Is Wilfred Burchett?" Warner wrote that it was "his interest in languages and left-wing politics" that led Burchett to the Linguists' Club and his contact with Maisky. At the club, he also met his first wife, Erna Hamer, a Jewish refugee from Nazi Germany. Because of restrictions in tourist exchanges between Britain and the Soviet Union, the Intourist office closed. Burchett went to work for the Palestine-Orient Lloyd, a travel agency whose activities took him to Germany and gave him a firsthand view of Nazi rule. Shortly before World War II, Burchett returned to Australia where he worked for the government's Department of Information, monitoring foreign broadcasts.

Burchett's first major journalistic target was the overthrow of the pro-Nazi, Vichy-controlled government of French New Caledonia, a thousand miles off the east coast of Australia. He obtained assignments from the *Daily Express,* London, and reported Far Eastern warfare and political developments for the paper from China and Burma throughout the war. He was accredited to the U.S. Army, as it fought its way from island to island and eventually occupied Japan.

While other correspondents clustered around General Douglas MacArthur's headquarters, Burchett took a train to Hiroshima. He was thus the first Western correspondent to give an eyewitness report on the devastation caused by the atom bomb. This scoop strengthened his reputation as an aggressive, professional reporter. He wrote for the *Daily Express,* covering a good part of postwar Europe. The testimony of one Soviet defector, Yuri Krotkov, throws light on Burchett's dual position as a Western correspondent and an active Soviet partisan. Krotkov, using the pseudonym "George Karlin," testified before the Committee on the Judiciary of the U.S. Senate (November 3 and 10, 1969) where he described several encounters with Burchett in East Germany.

After the war, Krotkov was in Berlin, ostensibly as a "correspondent," but actually serving with the Soviet Information Bureau to guide and influence foreign reporters. His testimony suggested that Burchett regarded him as a link to the Soviet intelligence services and tried to "sell" himself as able to serve them in various capacities. Krotkov said that, in 1947, he met with an influential intelligence official, one Bespalov, who suggested that he make the acquaintance of three correspondents for British newspapers, one of them Burchett. Krotkov had known Bespalov earlier as a Tass reporter.

Burchett introduced himself to Krotkov as the "second correspondent" of the *Daily Express* in Berlin. Together with two others, he wanted to visit the town of Peenemünde, launching point of Germany's devastating V2 rockets. Another correspondent was Denis Warner, then representing the *Manchester Guardian.* The group spent several days in Peenemünde. Krotkov recalled: "The procedure for foreign correspondents, at that time, to visit the Soviet Zone was very complicated, and it was necessary to have a personal permission from the assistant to the commander. Later I have done it for many foreigners. But what I want to say is this: the reality of Peenemünde was different than [what] we showed these foreign correspondents, and there was a particular place which was prepared to show them."

During this period, Krotkov played the role of fellow reporter, in order to make any propaganda story convincing. He said he was eager to "find any buyer and to look who will buy me, and that was my duty." He was surprised, therefore, when Burchett sought him out and said: "I want you to know that one top official from Admiralty, from London, came to see me and talk to me, and he asked me everything about Peenemünde." This remark interested Soviet intelligence, as it indicated British military interest in the rocket-launching installations. Krotkov wondered why Burchett had volunteered this tidbit of information and concluded: "He did it only because he wanted to tell the Soviet side more than necessary. At that time I thought, probably that's not a buyer, that's a man who wants to sell himself. He was looking for a buyer, too. That was his first hint."

Eight years later, Burchett and Krotkov met in Moscow. Burchett had, by then, established contacts in China, notably with Chou En-lai, and in

Vietnam, even with Ho Chi Minh. He had also been in North Korea during the Korean War of 1951–1952, where his role was highly controversial. Krotkov had heard in Moscow that Burchett "was a real and very good" newspaperman, so he was pleased when "in 1956 the telephone in my flat rang and when I took the receiver it was Burchett's voice." He had just arrived in Moscow and was staying at the Hotel Savoy (later renamed the Hotel Berlin), where the *New York Times* and the Reuters news agency also had offices.

Krotkov promptly called his "KGB boss," a man named Krasilnikov, told him Burchett was in town, and asked whether it was all right to meet with him. The KGB officer called back later and told Krotkov, "Go and talk to him and probably you will know what he wants, why he called, where he is going, and so on." Krotkov continued:

"I went to see him. He was on his way from Hanoi to Bulgaria, to Sofia. Because he was married; it was his second marriage, the Bulgarian girl. He wanted to go to Sofia, then to Warsaw, then to Berlin. That was his idea. Yes, it was the beginning of 1956, because I remember when he came back he told me about some unsettled situation in Poland, particularly Posnan. And in that time when I visited him and we went to a restaurant, he openly told me that he is a member of the Australian Communist Party, but for the benefit of the party, he is on the illegal underground position, and that—he showed me his document, that was a rather strange paper, which was issued in Hanoi, by the North Vietnamese Government—but he told me that he hadn't an Australian passport. He told me that the Australian authority had refused to give him the passport."

Burchett's role as a journeyman propagandist, roaming the Far East from Korea to Vietnam, has remained complex and opaque. His book *Forty Years on the Cutting Edge of History* (1981) carried an introduction by Harrison Salisbury, former *New York Times* editor and correspondent, who wrote: "Burchett's conventional journalistic companions have found him a well-informed, useful source and warm and decent friend. They almost always could check out a report or a rumor with Burchett, regardless of whether it fitted Communist ideology or party propaganda. On most occasions they got a straightforward answer, one which was trustworthy and which stood the test of time. In written reportage, it might be a different story. Burchett was an advocate, and he wrote in support of the cause to which he adhered at a given moment."

Stephen J. Morris, in his article "A Scandalous Journalistic Career," published in *Commentary* (November 1981), noted that Burchett returned briefly to Australia in 1951, where he lectured for the Australian Peace Council. He went to China as a correspondent for the French Communist daily *L'Humanité* and *Ce Soir,* no longer reporting for the *Daily Express* or for the *Times,* London, as he had done earlier. He published a book,

China's Feet Unbound, which was fiercely critical of the United States and referred to "American germ warfare launched against China's neighbor."

Morris considered that "last clause" as "significant," because "it previewed Burchett's next major public act—dissemination of the story that the United States was using germ warfare against North Korea." After a visit to prisoner-of-war camps, Burchett wrote: "This camp looks like a holiday resort in Switzerland. The atmosphere is also nearer that of a luxury resort than a POW camp." But, Morris recalled, returned Allied prisoners later gave vastly different accounts and even "maintained that Burchett had collaborated with the Chinese Communists in interrogation procedures."

From 1953 to 1956, Burchett moved back and forth between China, North Vietnam, Laos, and Cambodia. "In these countries, as previously in Korea," Morris wrote, "he reported on the supposed strength and popularity of the Communist forces." The Vietnamese supplied him with a travel document—the one he showed Krotkov in Moscow—that took the place of his withdrawn Australian passport.

After Nikita Khrushchev's eye-opening speech to the 20th Congress of the Soviet Communist Party in 1956, rumblings of independent thought could be heard in Eastern Europe. Burchett visited Hungary and Poland, and Morris noted that he was "most disturbed by the growth of liberal and nationalist ideals among some of the anti-Stalinist party leaders and intellectuals who took him into their confidence." Krotkov remembered that Burchett had talked to some people in Eastern Europe, and "when he came back to Moscow he told me there is a very, very dangerous situation now in Poland." Krotkov said, "He came and he told me, and he knew that I would report it, that the situation now basically and generally in Poland is very deteriorated, and there is some—he worried that there could be some revolution against the Soviet puppets, against the Communist regime, and he told me that he talked to some intellectuals and that their 'brains' are not good enough, that they are thinking too free, and that they want to change [the] situation which was at that time."

Krotkov obviously felt that this unsolicited appraisal of the Polish situation was another Burchett attempt to ingratiate himself with the KGB, to give an example of his manifold usefulness, actual and potential. "Well, I guess it was very valuable information," Krotkov added, "for the KGB as much as for the Central Committee, for the Kremlin's leaders, for Khrushchev at that time, I might say. And again, Wilfred gave this information to show that he could be useful in that way, too, not only in the direct KGB channels."

Krotkov also said Burchett had mentioned having had an affair with a fellow correspondent, Marguerite Higgins of the New York *Herald-Tribune.* As Higgins had meanwhile married an American general, Burchett hinted that these contacts might be exploited to extract military intelligence from Higgins or her husband.

Krotkov actually called Burchett a "KGB agent" when he admitted that he did not know how the whole matter was resolved: "I don't know, unfortunately, whether later, when Burchett became KGB's agent, they made any attempt to use the situation which I described above." In current parlance, Burchett's role at various times might best be described as an "agent of influence," a contact able to exert influence in directions desired by Soviet propaganda and overall policies. At one point, when Krotkov was asked whether Burchett "recognized you as KGB," he answered, "Well, probably not exactly, but you know, he could."

Krotkov was not a KGB staff member. As John Barron described his role in *KGB* (1974), he was a dramatist and screenwriter by profession whose whole life "had been intertwined with the KGB." His major coup was the arrangement of a series of assignations for Maurice Dejean, a French ambassador in Moscow, which led to the ambassador's entrapment, with a hope for future blackmail. Similar plans, although not executed, were made for an Indian diplomat who had met Burchett several times and who used the Australian to send regards to Krotkov from China.

During his stopover in Moscow, Burchett told Krotkov that he hoped to come to an arrangement with the Soviet authorities, similar to those he had enjoyed in Hanoi and Peking. This would have included living quarters, reimbursement for maintenance, travel expenses, and other perquisites. Burchett said Khrushchev's 1956 speech had made Moscow a world center of news, and he felt that his presence in the Soviet capital could be most valuable. At that time, he was planning to travel to several Eastern European capitals, and he suggested that his fares be paid.

Krotkov recalled that he forwarded this request to his KGB superiors: "I reported to the KGB, and the first reaction was good, and they wanted to give him that money and then they said, well, there was no money, and he went to Sofia, to Warsaw, and to Berlin without it. But he was such a man who, from the first moment, said, 'I must be paid, I need money.' " On another occasion, when one KGB officer had agreed to make a payment to Burchett, but his successor appeared to renege, Burchett suggested they get in touch with representatives of the Australian Communist Party, then visiting Moscow, to confirm his status, and this move eased his relations with the KGB.

The ouster of Khrushchev in 1964 and increased fighting in Vietnam prompted Burchett to transfer his attention once again to Hanoi. From there, the indefatigable Burchett wrote for a great variety of Western papers, ranging from the prestigious *Le Monde,* Paris, to the left-wing U.S. *National Guardian,* later the *Guardian* (which had also printed the writings of Strong). From his privileged position as a skilled reporter stationed "on the other side," Burchett was able to provide a journalistic counterpoint which "even-handed" coverage of events demanded. Morris wrote: "The articles tended to deal with the alleged effects of American bombing on North Vietnam. Stories of civilian suffering were combined with tales of the indomitable Vietnamese will to resist 'imperialist aggression.' Burchett also provided advance notice of changes in Hanoi's position on the issue of negotiations." For a time, the Associated Press distributed Burchett's dispatches.

When the *New York Times* published its obituary on Burchett (he died on September 27, 1983, in Sofia), it touched on the delicate matter of how he was categorized when his dispatches were printed. The paper explained: "When Western newspapers published articles by Mr. Burchett they sometimes identified him as a 'leftist newsman,' or a journalist 'with close connections with Communists.' But often there was no political identification." The *Times* summarized his activities this way:

"Beginning in the early 1950s, Mr. Burchett developed close relationships with the Communist leaders in Vietnam, Cambodia and China and wrote scores of articles that portrayed their governments in a favorable light. He also screened requests for visits to some of the countries by Western journalists and often conducted the journalists on tours after they arrived."

Burchett's second wife, a former Bulgarian culture ministry official, Vessa Ossikovska, shared much of his travels. In 1968 they settled in Paris, but returned to her native Bulgaria in 1982. His Australian passport had been restored in 1972. By sheer journalistic skill and a quality of apparent momentary sincerity, Burchett was able to link facts and ideologies that others found unbridgeable. Small wonder Stephen Morris's final appraisal was tinged with exasperation: "What is most remarkable about Burchett is not his record, but how he has managed to retain credibility and respectability in the eyes of so many Western intellectuals"; he added: "And in all this he is presented to readers not as what he is, a Communist propagandist, but as what he is not, an independent, radical humanist, or, simply, an 'Australian journalist.'"

Even after his death, Burchett's role continued to cause controversy at home. Writing in *Australian Society* (August 1984) Dr. Gavan McCormack, a historian at La Trobe University, Melbourne, took the position that Burchett had been "a journalist inspired by an uncommon moral passion." A year later, Dr. Robert Manne's article "The Fortunes of Wilfred Burchett" appeared in the monthly *Quadrant* (August 1985). The article, covering 19 pages and citing 136 references, utilized Burchett's correspondence files, as well as records of the Australian Security Intelligence Organization

(ASIO), released earlier that year under a 30-year secrecy rule. In one letter to his father, Burchett explained his financial position in Peking as follows:

"I don't have to worry about finances here. I am treated on the same basis as a local writer, although you need not spread this news outside our own circle. In other words I am relieved of financial cares and given facilities to see what I want to see, travel where I want to travel, interview who I want to interview. Luxury needs are not catered for but basic needs are. Most government employees live on that basis. What I need, for example, comes to me, from food and writing paper and typewriter ribbons. I sign for it and it's a book entry somewhere. That's how all artists and writers operate here and I am treated as an honoured foreign guest writer."

Manne commented that he did not wish to imply that Burchett had decided to "work for the Chinese Communist Party for monetary gain," but made his decision for ideological reasons. He quoted from another letter to Burchett's father, which stated: "I would do anything at all for their people and their government." He was, then, certainly not just another foreign correspondent, but in his own eyes an active propagandist, or, in modern Moscow parlance, an agent of influence.

CHAPTER · 13

"Tass Is Authorized to State . . ."

In the summer of 1984, Soviet television presented a ten-part spy series, complete with Russian hero and American villain, that bore the title *"Tass Is Authorized to State . . ."* The series implemented several themes of internal propaganda, while its title reflected the commanding role which Tass, the official news agency, plays inside and outside the Soviet Union. Twenty-four hours a day, Tass acts as the mouthpiece of the Soviet government: It collects and disseminates carefully selected news items; it prepares commentaries on world affairs, answers statements by other governments, and publicizes a wide variety of accusations, directed mainly against "the imperialists" and their leading force, the United States.

The television series, based on a novel by Yulian Semyonov, attracted a large viewing audience within the U.S.S.R. during prime evening time. It dramatized warnings against dealing with foreigners generally and Americans in particular. The series showed the CIA blowing up a Soviet freighter off the coast of Nagonia (a fictitious African country), a Russian spying for the Americans who killed himself when caught, and a CIA agent poisoning his chief. Whereas in past decades, the work of the KGB had not been publicized, Soviet domestic propaganda now pictures the agency dramatically as the nation's "shield and sword." The television series depicted the American agents as masking their spy activities behind seemingly innocent errands.

In the series, the KGB intercepts radio instructions from the U.S. embassy in Moscow to a local agent. He is then trapped at night by the Soviet agents, using infrared scopes, under a railroad bridge. The U.S.

embassy building on the capital city's Tchikovsky Street is even included in the film, complete with a U.S. flag and rooftop antennas.

In the final encounter between the handsome KGB agent and the whining American, the trapped spy is seen crying, "Let me go. I am an American diplomat. This is unlawful. I am an American diplomat. I am an American diplomat." In a warning comment, a voice-over states: "Gold coins, poison ampules, and microfilm are not the only proof of American subversion in this country."

The warning against associating with Americans—any one of whom, presumably, might be that kind of spy—was further dramatized in peripheral vignettes. In one scene, the wife of an alcoholic husband who is under suspicion of working with Americans protests, "Oh no, we keep away from them. We have been carefully educated. They are even more dangerous than vodka!"

The phrase "Tass is authorized to state" lent an ominous sound to the title when it came to the show's ending. As *New York Times* correspondent Seth Mydans reported (August 11, 1984), it is "the threat of revelations by the official Soviet press agency that finally brings a stuttering American ambassador to his knees in the story's final scene, where, confronted with the evidence, he pleads with Soviet officials not to publicize the spy affair." In return, the U.S. ambassador "promises contritely to call off American subversion" in the fictional pro-Soviet African country, vaguely resembling Ethiopia.

The spy story was based on at least one espionage case reported by Tass: the capture of Martha D. Peterson, a vice consul at the U.S. embassy in Moscow, who was expelled from the Soviet Union, allegedly trapped at the railroad bridge in central Moscow with a collection of espionage paraphernalia.

The initials *TASS* stand for *Telegrafnoye Agentstvo Sovyetskoyo Soyouza;* its full name translates as Telegraph Agency of the Soviet Union of the Council of Ministers of the U.S.S.R., which puts it squarely under central governmental authority. According to the *Great Soviet Encyclopedia* (1976), Tass, as the "central news organ of the USSR" collects "official and other national news, international news and photographic reports, which it disseminates to organs of the Soviet press, television and radio stations, other organizations in the Soviet Union, and subscribing organizations abroad."

On the surface, Tass operates in the manner of the world's major news services, such as the Associated Press, Reuters, United Press International, and Agence France Presse. Their initials, AP, UPI, and AFP, appear in newspapers all over the world; their dispatches form the basis of television and radio news. Like the other press services, Tass has a busy headquarters and offices all over the world that collect and disseminate millions of words daily. The difference is in content, as dictated by aim and function.

Tass does not aim to be "objective" in terms of what Soviet ideologists call "bourgeois." It has the specific function of searching for news and selecting, arranging, and distributing it to further the aims of the Soviet Union, as these aims are seen and defined by its leadership at a given time. At the time of the Bolshevik Revolution, on November 6, 1917, revolutionary sailors occupied the offices of the Petrograd Telegraph Agency, and Vladimir I. Lenin transformed this press service into the central information organ of the Council of People's Commissars. On September 9, 1918, the government press service and the telegraph agency were combined into the Russian Telegraph Agency (Rosta); all competitive services were closed down.

Lenin advocated that information is agitation by means of interpreted facts, and this principle has remained in force ever since. Until 1922, Rosta executed Lenin's directives by disseminating news, decrees, agitation, and propaganda material of various types. Lenin, whose career and successes had been largely due to the printed word, took a keen interest in technological advances in press wireless and radio transmissions. From 1922 on, Rosta functioned exclusively as a news service. In 1925 it was restricted to the Russian republics and superseded by Tass, which developed an ambivalent relation to the various news services of the Soviet republics: On the one hand, regional cultural and linguistic identities were being encouraged as political concessions; on the other hand, Tass represented central authority, like other political, cultural, and economic agencies within the country.

In its entry "Telegraph Agencies of the Union Republics," the *Great Soviet Encyclopedia* refers to the "news agencies belonging to the integrated state news system of the USSR and under the authority of the Union republic councils of ministers," as well as Tass. The entry says that the "Union-republic telegraph agencies enjoy the right of state committees of the Union-republic councils of ministers." The encyclopedia adds:

"The telegraph agencies of the Union republics disseminate in the republics national and foreign news and photographic reports received from Tass, gather news and photographic reports about the life in their republics for the republic press, television and radio, and transmit news of national and foreign interest to Tass for dissemination in the USSR and abroad. They transmit reports in Russian and reports translated into the languages of the Union republics, and they have networks of their own offices and correspondents to gather news in the republics."

The encyclopedia specifies that "the Tass system" includes telegraph agencies serving the republics of the Ukraine, Byelorussia, Uzbekistan,

Kazakhstan, Georgia, Azerbaijan, Lithuania, Latvia, Kirgizia, Tadzhik-istan, Armenia, Turkmenistan, and Estonia. It goes without saying that, for example, Armenpress, Tass's service in Soviet Armenia, does not gather material about Armenian-Americans directly, nor does it disseminate material to the Armenian-language papers in the United States; if any such material crosses frontiers, it is cleared through the Tass offices in Moscow and New York.

The emphasis that Tass gives news items, the length of dispatches and commentaries, clearly indicates the prominence such items will be given in the regional press. Often, the dispatches themselves indicate their importance. Alternatively, the headlines, layout, and illustrations of each daily issue of *Pravda* invite imitations by regional papers in the languages of the different republics. Nevertheless, there is a good deal of regional news, and there are regional commentaries to be found in the provincial and union papers. In addition to the material Tass provides, provincial papers carry items on such delicate topics as local corruption, labor indiscipline, or alcoholism that are not reported nationally by Tass. Possibly for this reason, Moscow readers—including foreign correspondents—have found it nearly impossible to subscribe to or otherwise obtain most out-of-town newspapers.

While Lenin's emphasis on the use of news and commentaries for purposes of propaganda served to heighten Tass's importance after 1925, it took more than a decade for the press service to achieve technological maturity. At first, even teletype machines were lacking in Soviet newspaper offices outside Moscow, and Tass had to rely heavily on Western press services for world news. The agency's Moscow editors were largely restricted to the selection and rewriting of news items, emphasizing troubles in the world at large while glorifying Soviet achievements. During the Moscow trials of Joseph Stalin's actual or imagined rivals in the 1930s, Tass pumped millions of words on the trials' official version into the Soviet press and into available channels abroad.

During World War II, foundation for Tass's later growth was laid, at least partly, with the creation of two major institutions: the Press Bureau of the People's Commissariat for Foreign Affairs and the Sovinformburo. Staff members of both offices later became prominent in the upper echelons of the Soviet propaganda machine. Foreign correspondents in Moscow during the war were frequently at loggerheads with the spokesman of the foreign office, Nikolai G. Palgunov. After the war, Palgunov was instrumental in modernizing Tass, when he served as its director general from 1953 to 1960.

During his service with the press agency, Palgunov redefined the role of Tass, saying that its task was "not to disseminate information as such, which by its content and nature is like a mere photographic process."

Rather, he wrote, the agency should distribute information "based on Marxist-Leninist theory, which provides an analysis of events." He said, "The strength of press lies in the fact that it is directed by the Communist Party at all times and in everything," and added: "Information must not simply illuminate this or that fact or event, though there might be reason for such illumination; it must also pursue a definite end. Information must serve and help the solution of the fundamental tasks which face our Soviet society and our Soviet communism. Information must be didactic and instructive."

Tass editors continually face the task of processing news in accordance with such propagandistic principles. Monotony is unavoidable when each news item must be weighed as to whether or not it will favor the Soviet Union, place the United States in a poor light, reflect glory in one direction or disdain in another. Tass has been a target for criticism within the Soviet leadership itself. As a near monopoly on major news and comment and as the main ingredient even of such central papers as *Pravda* and *Izvestia*, Tass presents a wide target.

As far back as 1946, *Kultura e Zhizn,* organ of the Propaganda Administration of the Soviet Communist Party's Central Committee, criticized Tass for its "unsatisfactory domestic and foreign news reports." It singled out the agency's coverage of the 1945 Paris Peace Conference and said, "From Tass reports it was difficult to comprehend just what exactly took place." In an article designed to explain Tass's functions and problems, D. Goryunov stated in *Za Rubezhom* (November 1965): "We are sometimes accused of being late in providing the information of Tass, by comparison with western agencies, and there is obviously an element of truth in this." He added, "There is still much for us to do, both in the sphere of providing technical equipment and in the development of communications." He said that there was "one distinguishing peculiarity in our information," in that "Tass does not pass on unchecked information." What he could not state, and what complicates the tasks of Tass editors, is the need for them to check, in all too many instances, with officials in the various ministries and in other government and Communist Party agencies or with the KGB. Often, they surely decide that it is better to wait than to commit a political or ideological error. In two flagrant instances of propaganda failures, the misleading reports on Yuri Andropov's health prior to his death and the shooting down of the Korean airliner in 1983, Tass simply acted as a conduit for high-level fumbling, confusion, and indecision.

During the reign of Nikita Khrushchev, when some people thought it was all right to be rather outspoken, Khrushchev's son-in-law Aleksei Adzhubei, then editor of *Izvestia,* wrote in 1964 that "Tass information is extremely dry" and "sometimes foreigners write about us far more vividly than we write about ourselves." Radio transmissions from abroad, notably the Russian-language services of Radio Liberty, the BBC, and the Voice of America, have become true competitors to Soviet news services. As a result, even *Pravda* has criticized Tass and the Soviet domestic radio network for the slowness and obscurity of their news coverage. As quoted by the Associated Press in a Moscow dispatch (December 13, 1982), the paper urged Tass to assist radio stations by providing more up-to-date news. The paper noted that all kinds of "radio voices" were coming into the country and needed to be answered quickly and effectively. Economic news that spoke of quotas being "fulfilled," "overfulfilled," or "put into action" were giving "no impression of the scope of success achieved."

Despite the complexity of its tasks and its rapid growth, Tass has consistently gained in prestige at home and abroad. Its central position as the tireless voice of Soviet leadership was officially acknowledged when, by a decree from the U.S.S.R. Council of Ministers, Tass was on January 10, 1972, placed directly under the council itself and thus given the status of a state committee of the U.S.S.R. Council of Ministers. In a legal sense, its status within the structure of the Soviet state now parallels that of such agencies as the KGB or, to site a lesser example, the Soviet Broadcasting and Television Committee, which achieved state committee status in 1970.

In late 1977, Tass moved into new quarters at 10–12 Tverskoy Boulevard in Moscow. Facing the boulevard, in a high rise with large windows and prominent ground-floor displays, are the agency's main offices. They overflow into two older buildings, in back of the new one. As Moscow Radio reported at the time, the Tass building did not represent merely additional space, as its old headquarters had been outgrown, but incorporated such technical facilities as computer teletypes and satellite links.

At that time, Tass said that its services were being used by more than 3,600 Soviet newspapers, as well as by radio and television. Among subscribers in foreign countries were 300 newspapers, as well as radio and television companies in some 80 nations. Tass maintained reporters and offices in more than 100 countries, transmitting a volume equal to 10,000 typewritten pages during each 24-hour period.

In order to hasten modernization, Tass ordered a computer system from the U.S. Sperry-Univac Corporation in 1978. However, the administration of President Jimmy Carter blocked the sale of these and similar computers to the Soviet agency, as they were regarded as having potential military use. The following January, the British firm of International Computers Limited (ICL) signed a computer contract with Tass. That March, a French company, Sedeteg, arranged with a Soviet state agency, Electronorgtekhnik, for delivery of a supplementary computer system.

The Tass-computer theme was heard once again in November 1983, when the Tass computer in Moscow erroneously transmitted a strictly internal report to Western embassies and news offices. This Russian-language report dealt with a sophisticated computer memory under development for the U.S. armed forces. By using "photon memory," the computer was to facilitate the rapid gathering and processing of air reconnaissance and similar intelligence for the use of military commanders.

A dispatch from Moscow by *Los Angeles Times* correspondent Robert Gillette (November 18, 1983) said that the Tass report, on its English-language news service, was "clearly not intended for publication" and "totally out of character with ordinary Tass articles." The Tass account, apparently based on an article in a U.S. technical periodical, "added to already considerable evidence that the news agency's activities in the United States and other foreign countries range beyond the gathering of news." Gillette noted that, in addition to its news service, Tass prepares a classified daily news report for limited use by government and Communist Party officials. Known as "White Tass," access to this bound 100-page insiders' report is restricted to well-connected persons and its use is regarded as prestigious. Tass also publishes, or did publish in the past, a daily digest of foreign press comment, controversial news dispatches, and exclusive information, transmitted by its correspondents, printed on pink paper, and known as "Red Tass." A second summary, on green paper, was made available to lower-level officials.

The complexity of Tass is illustrated by the fact that the agency uses virtually every means of modern communication in transmitting material at home and abroad, much of it over its own facilities. These include radiotelegraph, wireless transmission on a variety of wavelengths, telephone lines, radioteletype (RTTY), cable teletype, computer teletype, and satellite transmission and reception.

Tass competes with government messages for transmission facilities, but its texts of decrees and speeches have the same priorities as central government documents. In order to transmit material to distant points, Tass utilizes relay stations abroad, including facilities in Cuba. The agency works closely with *Prensa Latina*, the Spanish-language news service centered in Havana and serving Latin America. *Moscow News* reported (June 17, 1984) that *Prensa Latina*, under the direction of Gustavo Robreno, maintains correspondents in nearly 40 countries and "maintains good businesslike relations with Tass and APN [Novosti]." Although *Prensa Latina* has far more leeway than the ethnic press services in the Soviet republics, it may be regarded as the Latin American Tass. *Moscow News* stated that this Spanish-language service transmits some 8,000 news items every day, prepares commentaries, issues bulletins on a variety of topics, and publishes magazines, including the periodical *Cuba*, in Russian, for distribution in the Soviet Union and among Soviet residents and visitors in Cuba.

At its Moscow headquarters, where Tass has approximately 2,000 employees, its editorial section is subdivided into departments. The Foreign News Department, known by its Russian initials as INOTASS, receives foreign correspondents' reports, in Russian as well as other languages. It translates and otherwise processes these reports in various geographical sections. Regional editors are selected for their special linguistic, political, economic, and cultural knowledge of the regions from which the material originates. A section of INOTASS receives foreign newspapers and magazines; these are scanned for news items and background information, clipped, and filed in the agency's archives.

Another unit, which prepares "News for Abroad," known as RIDZ, is part of INOTASS and works in reverse to the section that processes incoming material. RIDZ is staffed with translators who convert Russian texts into English, German, French, and Spanish—the main languages, in addition to Russian, in which Tass transmits material abroad. This section acts as a conduit for Tass's foreign and domestic news departments. One of its functions has been local reporting from central government offices and within the city of Moscow, with attention to news angles of special interest to selected foreign audiences.

Among the numerous functions of Tass is the transmission of selected texts and excerpts from leading Moscow dailies to the provincial press. These include the lead editorial from *Pravda,* the Communist Party daily, which is given the widest dissemination. It also includes editorials from the Communist Youth newspaper *Komsomolskaya Pravda,* which is sent to youth organs, and the lead article from the military newspaper *Krasnaya Zvezda,* which goes to all military journals. Summaries and excerpts from the dailies *Izvestia,* the government paper, and *Trud,* the organ of the trade union organization, are also distributed by the Tass network.

This does not exhaust the varied list of Tass activities, both overt and covert. The agency also maintains an extensive photographic archive and a large, modern domestic and international photo service, Fotokhronika Tass. The technical, professional, and artistic quality of Tass pictures is high. The agency is able to supply photographs from many parts of the Soviet Union. It covers current events and cultural and industrial-agricultural enterprises, and supplies black-and-white and color photographs that rival those of commercial photographic services and publications.

In its photo service, as in its news transmission, Tass has a myriad of exchange agreements with major and minor news agencies, notably the Associated Press. Because it is able to provide its services, at times, for minimal payments—or none at all—Tass has been able to sign up a large number of clients in Third World countries. It is in Africa and parts of Asia, as well as in Latin America (through *Prensa Latina* and separately), that Tass has perhaps its strongest impact. On October 2, 1984, for example, Tass reported that it had signed a new and more comprehensive cooperation agreement with ANGOP, the Angolan news agency. The agreement, signed by Tass director Sergei Losev and his Angolan counterpart, Sotto Mayor, specified that the two services would exchange photographic material and that Angolan reporters and editors would go to Moscow for training in the Tass office.

The Angolan example illustrates the close politico-military and Agitprop links between the two countries. Together with Ethiopia, Angola had become the Soviet Union's most active ally on the continent, acting as a conveyor to other African countries. Tass maintains training facilities for its own editorial and reporting staff, regularly indoctrinates young Soviet and foreign journalists at its headquarters, and seeks to maintain high ideological and professional standards.

The times when Tass staffers could succeed on the basis of Communist Party standing and Marxist ideological reliability alone are past. Although family connections and party membership remain valuable career assets, as they do throughout much of Soviet society, Tass seeks continually to upgrade the quality of its staff, expand coverage, and reduce transmission time of news events. From the beginning, upper-level Tass executives came from high posts within the Communist Party, government service, and propaganda establishment.

During its formative period, Tass employed foreign journalists as its correspondents, if only because the right combination between linguistic and professional skills was not then available among Soviet personnel.

Tass's predecessor agency, Rosta, had been organized by Lenin as an agitation and propaganda machine in relatively primitive terms. Lenin's versatile, internationally versed colleague Karl Radek recruited Jacob Doletzki as the agency's first director. When Karl Bickel, then president of United Press, visited Russia in 1922, he found Doletzki's staff operating in the somewhat incongruous setting of the palatial Moscow residence of a former Czarist official, Prince Lvov. They had only one or two telephones and did not use them much. The staff, which wrote its topical revolutionary commentaries "in a high degree of remoteness," was spread through a labyrinth of offices. Bickel's observations retain a good deal of contemporary validity, as when he wrote:

"In Russia reporters of the American type were nonexistent; if they had existed they'd have been instantly arrested in both the old or new government. If the various governments had anything to report—such as a battle or disturbance or any change in internal domestic policy or in banking or in tax policy, the department sent over their copy and unless they sent it over nothing was ever printed. To print without this formal governmental permission was just out of a Russian mind—it was, at that time, largely beyond their general comprehension."

At Bickel's suggestion, Doletzki set up a newsroom in the old Lvov residence. Head of its foreign news desk was Constantine Oumansky. According to Theodore E. Kruglak, in *The Two Faces of Tass* (its news agency facade and its role as an intelligence and propaganda arm of the Soviet state), Oumanski was a Tass man "marked for success in the American newspaper tradition—the copy boy who became editor. When he joined Rosta at age seventeen while working his way through Moscow University, young Oumanski must have stood out among the collection of holdover Mensheviks and doctrinaire Communists Doletzki inherited from his predecessor. Within a year after Doletzki's arrival, Oumanski was foreign news editor, presiding over Bickel's American-styled newsroom. In two years he was assigned the job of reorganizing the Rome bureau and then became the head of the agency's most important office—Paris."

Eugene Lyons, who came to the United States from Russia as a boy, and who originally regarded the Soviet Union as the virtual road to a socialist paradise, served as one of the Tass correspondents in New York. In his autobiography, *Assignment in Utopia,* he described the enthusiasm that then pervaded the Tass staff. Lyons knew Tass from the inside during its early years; he worked from offices in the old New York *World* building, which then also served as headquarters of United Press. When UP was looking for a Moscow correspondent who knew Russian, Lyons took the job with enthusiasm—but was soon treated by his former colleagues in Moscow as yet another bourgeois correspondent, to be held at arm's length and regarded as a likely antagonist and potential spy.

Lyons witnessed how the purges undertaken by Stalin affected the Tass operation. Among those accused of making common cause with Stalin's rival, Leon Trotsky, was Radek—and, by association, the baffled, frightened, luckless Tass director Doletzki. The more or less professional staff Tass had begun to employ was eliminated, replaced by men who could be relied on to adhere, unquestioning, to Stalin's wishes. Kruglak wrote, "Whatever happened to Doletzki is shrouded in the Stalinist fog"; he cited speculation among former acquaintances that ranged from successful and unsuccessful suicide attempts to Doletzki's deportation to a prison camp or quick execution. Kruglak noted: "A query to Tass in Moscow remained unanswered."

Yet Doletzki's name was mentioned in a long and laudatory article on the press service that appeared in the illustrated Soviet monthly *Ogonyok* (February 1975). The article described a historic exhibit of Tass, with photographs dating back to the early days of Rosta and including a picture showing Doletzki at a reception given by Lenin's wife, Nadezhda K. Krupskaya. The article commented that "the employees of Tass are very proud of the fact that history of Tass is so closely linked with V. I. Lenin," but it did not—of course!—mention the man's fate at the hands of Lenin's successor.

The magazine article also noted that, during its early years, "the agency cooperated with S. M. Kirov." In the history of the Soviet Union, the name of Sergei M. Kirov has explosive connotations; he was assassinated in Leningrad in 1934, and this event, like a match that sets off a conflagration, began the years of Stalin's purges of the Soviet government, Communist Party, and armed forces.

At Tass, the Stalin regime replaced Doletzki with Joseph Khavinson, of whom Kruglak said that his "sole credential appeared to be his violent espousal of the Stalin line." He added: "Tass was temporarily downgraded during the Khavinson regime. It continued to maintain its relations with the international news agencies, but other organizations took over some of its former functions. The Soviet Information Bureau, of minor importance before the purges, assumed the distribution of official handouts. The Foreign Office Press Bureau took on a number of new duties, among them closer control over news going abroad, and, with the outbreak of World War II, it became the chief point of contact with the foreign correspondents in Moscow. To head this division, the Foreign Office recalled Nikolai Palgunov, the former editor of the *Northern Worker,* who had joined Tass in 1929."

Palgunov had been Tass correspondent in Paris, and while he was not too popular with the hard-pressed Western correspondents in Moscow, his experiences and contacts were helpful when, in 1943, he replaced Khavinson as director of Tass. This changeover, in the midst of the war, prepared the ground for Tass's role in Eastern Europe, which was beginning to come under Red Army control, as Nazi Germany suffered a series of decisive defeats.

The Tass teleprinters in Moscow, originally bought from United Press, were sent to offices in the various republics. New equipment was installed, either captured from the Germans or brought from the United States. But Palgunov could not truly modernize Tass as long as Stalin was in power. Kruglak wrote that the dictator's "megalomania prevented Tass from exercising its true function—its reports were written with the Kremlin in view and in the constant fear that The Man might find something personally distasteful in the daily Tass book delivered to him." Therefore, Palgunov had to wait until the Khrushchev takeover, and its temporary "thaw," before Tass could even attempt to imitate the major news services and utilize the talent at its disposal to serve Soviet propaganda aims on a properly professional level. Kruglak said of Palgunov: "Following Stalin's death, he was able to lay the groundwork for the editorial developments now taking place under his successors."

The role of Tass within the Soviet network of government agencies, newspapers, and general international activities has been reflected in the careers of the men who successively headed the agency. When Palgunov retired in 1960, the post of Tass director was assigned to Dmitri F. Goryunov, who had previously been editor of *Komsomolskaya Pravda,* the Communist Youth daily, and deputy director of *Pravda,* the central party paper. He served in this post for seven years, much of the time during the regime of the ebullient Khrushchev; Goryunov was able to continue the modernization, technically and journalistically, that had begun under Palgunov.

The next director of Tass was Sergei G. Lapin, who had served as ambassador to China from 1965 to 1967, but had actually alternated between posts in diplomacy and communications. Born in 1912, and thus a member of what may be called the second generation of the Soviet elite, Lapin attended the Leningrad Historical-Linguistic Institute until 1932. He then worked as a journalist on various publications in the Leningrad area for about eight years. Next, he attended the Communist Party High School, operated by the party's Central Committee, and graduated in 1942. After two years of administrative work in the committee, Lapin joined the Committee of Radio Installations and Broadcasting in 1944, first as chief editor of political broadcasting and then as deputy chairman of the committee from April 1945 to 1953.

Lapin's diplomatic career began in 1954. He served as ambassador to Austria from 1956 to 1960 and as foreign minister of the Russian Republic for another two years. His next post was that of deputy foreign minister of the U.S.S.R., followed by his appointment to Peking. The China assignment coincided with the serious rift between the Khrushchev regime and the Chinese government under Mao Zedong. Lapin left his Peking post several months before his appointment to the Tass directorship. The news agency thus gained the services of a man of varied domestic and international experience.

In 1970, Lapin moved on to the post of general director of the State Committee for Radio Broadcasting and Television, an agency that was gaining increasing importance. He was replaced by Leonid M. Zamyatin, whose career and personality will be described in a later chapter. Certainly, the Zamyatin appointment—and the directorship, which lasted for eight years—helped strengthen Tass's position still further, emphasizing the agency's role on the international scene. But when Zamyatin moved on, early in 1978, to head the Department of International Information of the Communist Party's Central Committee, a period of indecision began. Christian Duevel, Soviet affairs analyst of Radio Liberty in Munich at that time, commented that the transfer of Zamyatin was followed by "prolonged wrangling about candidates for the job," with the result that the position was left unfilled for almost five months. During this interim period, the man whom Zamyatin had appointed as one of his deputies, Sergei A. Losev, acted as temporary director.

Eventually, according to *Pravda* (July 14, 1978), Vladimir P. Khatuntsev was made Tass director. Duevel noted at the time: "If the successor
of Zamyatin was to be chosen from within Tass, rather than from the
Central Committee apparatus or the USSR Foreign Ministry (the two most
likely sources of candidates), it would appear that the initial decision has
already been made in favor of Losev, as being best suited for the post of
general director, though his final appointment might have been delayed.
It must, therefore, be regarded as most unusual that Khatuntsev, one of
the ordinary deputies to the general director of Tass, has now been promoted over the head of the First Deputy General Director Losev."

The Duevel analysis proved to be quite prophetic when, on April 19,
1979, Khatuntsev died at age 69, after only nine months in office. A month
later, on May 5, Tass reported that Losev had, at last, been confirmed as
the general director of Tass. While he had been associated with the agency
for nearly three decades, Losev could look back to a wide range of other
experiences, notably in the international field. Born in 1927, Losev attended the State Institute of International Relations of the Foreign Ministry
in Moscow. After graduation, he joined Tass in 1950 at its headquarters,
where he worked for the most part in various sections of INOTASS. In
1955, Losev became chief correspondent in the Near East and from 1960
to 1963 directed its editorial offices for African countries.

Losev spent six years in the United States, from 1963 to 1969, while
acting as chief correspondent for Tass in the United States and as director
of its New York office. Upon returning to Moscow headquarters, Losev
joined the agency's Main Editorial Office for Foreign Information as chief
deputy editor. Three years later he was appointed a member of the collegium, the central editorial board of Tass, and became the board's chairman. The next two appointments came in 1973, when Losev was made
deputy general director of Tass, and in 1978, when he was made first deputy
general director under Zamyatin.

Losev's appointment as general director of Tass, while in his fifties,
illustrated generational shifts within the Soviet information and propaganda
apparatus. He was a child during Stalin's purges, was in his early teens
during World War II, and made his career, at least partly, during the
ferment of the Khrushchev years. At the Tass foreign desk in New York
and in his continuous perusal of Western dispatches, newspapers, and
periodicals, Losev certainly became fully aware of the complex task the
agency had to perform, including services for radio and television and
competition with the state's broadcasting networks.

According to the *Ogonyok* magazine article, cited earlier, "Whatever
happens on this planet, we know about it, without delay, from Tass." The
article commented, "Whether it is the opening of a new and mighty industrial plant in Siberia, the public appearance of a government official,

a government change in England or a coal mine explosion in Pennsylvania, we know about it." Needless to say, changes in Soviet government are less quickly reported than those in England, and mine explosions in the Urals are, usually, not reported at all. The article contrasted the emphasis which Tass places on reports of Soviet achievements with those of the "western information agencies, the newspapers of the bourgeoisie," which "in their depraved manner pursue sensation, rumors, scandalous divorce proceedings, the bedroom secrets of movie stars"; in other words, everything that is politically piquant and trivial is used by the bourgeois press.

The editors of the Associated Press, United Press, Reuters, and Agence France Presse, and the readers of the *New York Times,* the *Times* of London, *Le Monde* of Paris, *Neue Zürcher Zeitung* of Switzerland, *La Prensa* of Buenos Aires, *Kathimerini* of Athens, *Asahi Shimbun* of Tokyo, and dozens of others are unlikely to recognize this image of their "bourgeois" subject matter. On the other hand, sensation-hungry tabloids and mass audiences do abound, giving Western readers a choice between the sublime and the ridiculous, the responsible and the reckless, and all manner of shadings in between.

At Tass there are no different shades, although its younger brother Novosti tries to add variety to the sameness of the fare provided by the "official" news agency by offering "unofficial" material; but more about that later. According to the Moscow magazine article, Tass "works at the very front line of the ideological war" and its reporters "regard it as their obligation to provide prompt and effective rebuffs to the fictitious reports of the western press, to its slanders."

In December 1985, Losev contributed an article to the Moscow journal *International Affairs,* which reflected his role as Tass director as well as that of a member of the Foreign Affairs Commission of the U.S.S.R. Supreme Soviet. He noted that Tass by then supplied 300 to 320 items of domestic and international news to 4,000 Soviet newspapers and radio and television stations. Losev said that the agency offered its services in eight languages and that its subscribers included 600 foreign news agencies, information ministries, editorial boards of newspapers, magazines, television and radio companies, and diplomatic and trade missions from 115 countries. The article came out strongly in support of the New International Information and Communication Order, supported by the Soviet bloc in UNESCO, and said that the U.S. government was seeking to establish "tough censorship, cut off channels of objective information and to gain an influence over its dissemination." Losev also wrote: "Slanderous campaigns which present the state of affairs in some countries or their policies in a distorted light are inadmissible."

CHAPTER · 14

The World According to Tass

Although it enjoys the label of "Tass, the Soviet news agency," the Tass service does not compete with the news collection and dissemination of the worldwide Western news agencies. Tass is frankly and clearly a propaganda arm of the Soviet government, using the techniques and facilities of twentieth-century news dissemination in order to implement Moscow's day-to-day propaganda directives.

Even a random look at the daily Tass output, as it comes over high-speed printers into the editorial rooms of English-language papers and news agencies in the United States, illustrates the manner in which Soviet editors select, angle, and comment on the day's news. On two unexceptional days in 1985—May 2 and 6—the Tass service provided what may be taken as an average supply of items. Early in the day, May 2, still in time for some morning papers in North America, particularly in the Western parts of the United States and Canada, Tass carried a dispatch from Bonn, the West German capital, which stated: "Yielding to demands of residents of Heilbronn, the Communal Council of that West German City decided to name one of the squares in the city center 'peace square.' " It quoted a local politician as saying that the name "expressed the striving of the people of Heilbronn for peace and disarmament and their protest against the siting of new first-strike nuclear missiles in West Germany." The dispatch added:

"A nuclear missile is known to have caught fire and exploded January 11 at Waldheide U.S. Military base, not far from Heilbronn. Three American servicemen were killed and 16 others seriously injured in the accident, which could have had disastrous proportions and effect. The Communal

Council of Heilbronn urged the West German government to remove U.S. nuclear missiles from the country's territory." The Tass item was transmitted at 2:38 a.m., eastern daylight time, and provided a fair example of news selection and backgrounding.

Tass then transmitted an early morning wrap-up by two of its correspondents in Bonn, Vladimir Serov and Sergei Sosmouski, concerning what they called "an annual meeting of leaders of the seven major capitalist nations," the United States, West Germany, Great Britain, France, Italy, Japan, and Canada, which was about to open that day in the West German capital. The Tass correspondents anticipated that, "under the flag of the community of 'Western ideals and values,' Washington intends to use the Bonn summit meeting, above all, for thrusting its militarist, adventuresome course on its partners, for drawing them deeper into the policy of confrontation with Socialist countries and curtailing mutually advantageous trade and economic cooperation with them for working up international tensions." The commentary ran to about 500 words.

Tass then transmitted, under the heading "There Are Real Chances," a report on a press conference given in Moscow by Marshal Vasili Petrov, first deputy minister of defense. Held at the Press Center of the Soviet Foreign Ministry, the press conference was one of many events commemorating the fortieth anniversary of the end of World War II, or, as the Tass dispatch said, "the world-wide historical significance of the Soviet people's victory in the Great Patriotic War."

Petrov quoted Mikhail Gorbachev, general secretary of the Soviet Communist Party, as saying that there were "opportunities for an improvement of Soviet-U.S. relations," which "should be put on the plane of concrete policy and practical decisions." The press conference, according to the unsigned Tass story, was attended by "Soviet and foreign journalists."

Tass then summarized a *Pravda* commentator, Gennadi Zafesov, who said that U.S. President Reagan had "decided to teach the Italians how they should use their voting rights." He said that Reagan, in answering questions from an Italian correspondent, had told Italians they should prevent a Communist-led government from coming to power, as otherwise they ran the risk of "losing" all their rights. Zafesov said the U.S. President must have "forgotten" about "elementary norms of inter-state relations, which provide for non-intervention in the internal affairs of other countries."

Sergei Kulik, a Tass political news analyst, referred to Reagan's "pathological hatred" of the Sandinistas, a term that was picked up by Western correspondents in their own dispatches from Moscow. Kulik wrote: "Having suffered a serious defeat on Capitol Hill, where the House of Representatives refused to meet the demand of the Administration on more financial aid to anti-Nicaraguan terrorist bands, Ronald Reagan decided

Loafing on the job is a frequent target of cartoons appearing in the Moscow satirical magazine *Krokodil*. The caption quotes the construction worker leaning on the fence as telling his resting, and presumably drunk, colleague: "Get yourself transferred to us, Vasya; we pay more." Cartoons of this type have been a feature in *Krokodil* for many years, predating Gorbachev's drive for more responsibility among workers.

Above: Backward technology has been a target of criticism for decades. This cartoon, captioned "Automated Workshop," appeared in *Krokodil* on February 10, 1965. **Right:** Even during the regime of Nikita Khrushchev, connivance among officials was the theme of domestic propaganda drives and of this cartoon in *Krokodil* (May 10, 1963). The store manager on the left and the controller on the right have obviously struck a bargain. The caption reads: "They have agreed on a draw."

Willi Münzenberg (1889–1940), German protégé of Lenin, developed the tactic of using front organizations and prominent fellow travelers to advance Soviet interest.

Richard Sorge, Soviet spy in Japan during World War II, has become a legendary figure in the U.S.S.R. This Moscow monument pictures him, complete with trench coat, walking through a wall.

Georgi Arbatov, director of the United States of America and Canada Institute, Moscow, is the Kremlin's most prominent "Americanist" and a highly visible public figure abroad.

This pamphlet, featuring the seal of the U.S. Department of Defense, purported to document U.S. nuclear targets in Western Europe. Based on authentic material, the texts were altered to fan European distrust of U.S. intentions. The pamphlet was circulated in more than 20 countries.

TOP SECRET DOCUMENTS ON US FORCES HEADQUARTERS IN EUROPE

HOLOCAUST
AGAIN FOR EUROPE

NATO SECRET

SUPREME HEADQUARTERS ALLIED POWERS EUROPE
GRAND QUARTIER GENERAL DES PUISSANCES ALLIEES EN EUROPE
BELGIUM

26 June 1979

His Excellency Joseph M.A.H. Luns
The Secretary General
North Atlantic Treaty Organization
Brussels/Zaventem Autoroute
B-1110 Brussels, Belgium

Dear Joseph,

Thank you for your letter of June 25 setting out certain results of our joint work which have had, I believe, a direct and lasting effect on the formulation and realization of the allied defense program. For my part, I highly appreciate your cooperation and hope that you are equally satisfied.

On leaving the post of Supreme Allied Commander in Europe, I feel it my duty to stress once again certain aspects of allied strategy which demand our further attention and effort.

As you know, one of our presuppositions in nuclear planning is that, under certain circumstances likely to develop in Europe, we may be forced to make first use of nuclear weapons. This obviously requires that the allied nuclear deterrent should be strengthened and its links with major U.S. strategic systems tightened. Moreover, it is vital to speed up and finalize current projects for the limited use of U.S. nuclear forces in Europe and for other military measures at our disposal for a possible emergency. This strategy will be more realistic and effective if a decision on the modernization of allied tactical nuclear forces is taken.

With your help, a great deal of progress has been made recently toward strengthening the Alliance. Yet, in my view, planning for the deployment and use of modernized nuclear forces in Europe can be adequately accomplished only if full understanding and cooperation are achieved. It is therefore necessary to prepare, systematically and persistently, a basis for making a success of the NATO Council meeting in December, bearing in mind primarily the crisis inside the Alliance over neutron weapons deployment. Every effort should be made to counter any hesitation or vacillation among the allied nations during decision-making meetings.

When General Alexander M. Haig left his position as NATO commander, this forged letter, dated June 26, 1979, was circulated within NATO countries. The letter, addressed to NATO Secretary General Joseph Luns and conspiratorial in tone, was designed to heighten European opposition to an intermediate-range nuclear force (INF).

Five-kopek stamp, issued in the U.S.S.R. in memory of Samantha Smith.

Samantha Smith wearing the Russian national costume presented to her by Moscow Young Pioneers.

The somewhat convoluted style of Soviet cartoonist Vsevolod Asenyev is familiar to readers of the weekly *Moscow News,* which is published in Russian, French, English, Spanish, and Arabic. This drawing shows a heavily armed figure, symbolizing the United States, with the caption, "I've decided to go down in history. This is bound to be its last page." It appeared on October 20, 1985.

Anti-U.S. propaganda within the Soviet Union has remained unchanged for years. The cartoon pictures a "typical" American—smoking the inevitable "capitalist" cigar—who says, "As you can see, gentlemen, we keep the door open for talks." This cartoon appeared in *Krokodil* and was reprinted in other Soviet publications in February 1982.

This *Pravda* cartoon (October 25, 1985) shows the Italian lira, the German deutsche mark, and the British pound on the verge of drowning, while the U.S. dollar and the weight of armaments pull them down. Shortly afterward, these and other currencies strengthened, while the U.S. dollar weakened substantially.

Тянет на дно.   Рисунок Ю. Черепанова.

The offhand treatment that some Soviet shops give their customers is satirized in this *Krokodil* cartoon. The young man who has taken his garment to the tailor shop asks, "My coat is torn. Do you have any suggestions?" He is told, "Yes, get married!"

Contempt for customers in Soviet restaurants and shops is widespread. Waiters often ignore guests for long periods of time. In this *Krokodil* cartoon, the waitress asks, "What did you order? Was it breakfast, lunch, or dinner?"

SOVIET LIFE

November 1982 • $1.25

Perhaps the most professionally produced Soviet periodical abroad is *Soviet Life,*
a monthly issued by the U.S.S.R. embassy in Washington and containing material
provided by the Novosti press agency. By reciprocal arrangement, the U.S. In-
formation Agency distributes the illustrated journal *Amerika* in the Soviet Union.
Soviet Life, which in quality of production exceeds magazines published in the
U.S.S.R. itself, emphasizes such aspects of Soviet life as the arts, literature, science,
sports, and colorful regional customs. The illustrated monthly is also published in
Arabic, Bengali, Chinese, Finnish, German, Hindi, Hungarian, Italian, Japanese,
Korean, Mongolian, Portuguese, Romanian, Russian, Serbo-Croatian, Spanish,
Urdu, and Vietnamese.

A captionless satire of inefficiency in the construction industry is this cartoon from *Krokodil* (August 1985).

This *Ogonyok* cartoon castigates two domestic practices that are long-range re-education targets: alcoholism and vandalizing the environment.

to vent his pathological hatred for the Sandinista revolution in a different field. He imposed an embargo on trade and air travel between the U.S. and Nicaragua and made plans for a series of other measures which, in his opinion, must cause damage to that nation."

The Kulik news analysis, which came in seven "takes," or separately transmitted segments, on the Tass teleprinters, totaled close to 650 words and incorporated several domestic U.S. criticisms of the embargo against Nicaragua. It was followed by a Washington dispatch that dealt with possible additional sanctions against Nicaragua: A Moscow interview with E. Malte, vice president of the Union of Workers in the Field of Education of Quebec Province, Canada, that had appeared in the newspaper *Trud,* noted that Malte had been "a guest of the May Day Holiday." From Tokyo, Tass reported that the Okinawa branch of the Socialist Party of Japan had called for the dismantling of all U.S. military installations on that island. From London, Tass picked up additional critiques of the Nicaragua embargo, and from New York it quoted Archbishop John J. O'Connor as urging President Reagan not to visit the West German cemetery at Bitburg, where members of the Waffen SS unit were buried, together with other war dead.

Tass, at 6:13 a.m., carried a Moscow report, quoting the newspaper *Sovetskaya Rossiya,* that the U.S. military had plans to turn Allied territories into radioactive "deserts" in order to create "an effective barrier" against advancing Communist troops. Citing a "Project Zebra," the paper stated that plans existed to set off 141 nuclear devices in the eastern part of West Germany's Hessen region.

This was followed by a New York report, written by Tass correspondent Arkadi Sidoruk, quoting additional opposition to the Nicaragua embargo; a Washington dispatch on a vote by a subcommittee of the House Armed Services Committee, approving production of an additional 21 MX missiles; a San Francisco quote from Alejandro Martinez, Nicaragua's foreign minister, denouncing the embargo; a dispatch from Baghdad, quoting an Iraqi military spokesman as claiming that the country's air force had hit "a major naval target" near the Iranian island of Kharg; and a Nicosia (Cyprus) monitoring of the Iranian news agency, IRNA, reporting "intensive artillery duels" with Iraq.

Canadian reaction to the embargo was reported by Artem Melikyan, Tass correspondent in Ottawa, suggesting that Canada would not follow the example of U.S. sanctions. The agency quoted another *Trud* interview with a labor leader who had attended Moscow May Day celebrations, William Perry, president of the New York branch of the International Union of Longshoremen of the U.S. East Coast. Perry was quoted as saying that "a majority of Americans" favored "peace and cooperation," although "transnational corporations in pursuit of superprofit keep developing ever-new lethal weapon systems." At 10:01 a.m., Tass reported from Moscow that the Soviet national soccer team was leading 4–0 after the first half of its World Cup qualifying match against Switzerland. One minute later, Tass stated that Erich Honecker, the East German party leader, would visit the U.S.S.R. in a few days. By 10:56, Tass was able to announce that the Soviet soccer team had defeated Switzerland; the score at the end of the match was still 4–0.

From Tokyo, the agency reported that "the Japanese press" was interpreting a meeting between Prime Minister Yasuhiro Nakasone and German Chancellor Helmut Kohl as a step toward Japan's "direct participation" in President Reagan's "notorious 'Star Wars' programme." (Tass, which sends its English-language service to many parts of the world, often uses British rather than American spelling, such as "programme" rather than "program"; otherwise, like the British news service Reuters, it follows what might be called a common-denominator Anglo-Saxon style and technique in its English-language service.)

At 12:58 p.m., Tass transmitted what was, in effect, a commentary by its Washington correspondent Mikhail Beglov, which is reproduced here in full:

"While seeking to gain military superiority over the Soviet Union, the Reagan administration displays an openly obstructionist attitude to the Soviet-American talks in Geneva. This has been confirmed again by Paul Nitze, arms control talks adviser to the President and the Secretary of State, who made known Washington's official assessment of the First Round of the Geneva talks at the National Press Club Wednesday [May 1].

"Nitze grossly distorted the essence of the Soviet stance in a bid to 'prove' that it is the Soviet Union, not the United States, which blocks progress at Geneva. He made clear that success in working out an agreement is possible only on American terms. The adviser reaffirmed the Administration's apparent unwillingness to consider in earnest the arms restriction proposals and initiatives advanced by the Soviet Union, reiterating the arguments, refuted more than once, that a freeze of the nuclear potentials of both sides will allegedly consolidate 'Soviet military superiority.' Meanwhile, even Pentagon papers acknowledge a rough nuclear parity between the USSR and the United States.

"That the Administration lacks a serious approach to the talks was demonstrated once again by Nitze's negative reaction to the Soviet Union's unilateral suspension till November this year of the deployment of its medium-range missiles in Europe and its proposal for introducing a moratorium throughout the period of the talks on the development, including research, testing and deployment of space-based strike systems.

"Nitze failed to make a single new, concrete proposal in these fields, confirming that the United States has nothing to offer in response to the

Soviet constructive initiatives. The adviser merely reaffirmed the discredited 'ideas' advanced by the Washington Administration in the past, which are intended at securing American superiority in certain categories of armaments. He also said that the United States would like to take outside the framework of the Geneva talks the issue of non-militarization of Outer Space, stressing the Administration's intention to continue work on President Reagan's 'Strategic Defense Initiative.'

"Nitze's speech convincingly proved that the Reagan Administration is more interested in building up armaments, rather than in reaching arms control accords with the Soviet Union."

In Stockholm, Tass correspondent Nikolai Vukolov interviewed Eva Palme, chairperson of the Union of Sweden-U.S.S.R. Societies, who had been awarded the International Lenin Peace Prize. Her remarks paraphrased several basic Soviet policy themes, ranging from a demand for a "nuclear-free zone in Northern Europe" to an endorsement of the Soviet Union's resistance to "the forces of reaction and imperialism that incite another war."

From Belgrade, Tass quoted Nicaragua's President Daniel Ortega, on a tour of Eastern European countries, as rejecting the claim of the "Washington propaganda media" that his government was a "threat to peace in the region," charging instead that it was "the United States which poses a threat to peace and security."

Under the heading "Soviet Squad Enhances Chances," Tass carried an analysis of the Soviet-Swiss soccer game that had resulted in victory for the U.S.S.R. team. This, Tass noted, increased the Soviet team's chance "to qualify for the World Cup final tournament." It gave the lineups of the Soviet and Swiss teams and the names of the three Belgian judges.

The Bonn dispatch was followed by a brief item from New York, citing White House chief of staff Donald Regan as stating on ABC television that the United States planned to press its partners at the Bonn summit "into making drastic trade concessions." From San Francisco, Tass correspondent Yuri Algunov reported that a Los Angeles magistrate had ordered the "Croatian Himmler,"Andrija Artukovic, to be deported to his native Yugoslavia. The Tass report stated that Judge Volney Brown had yielded to "pressure from the international public," after Artukovic had "enjoyed the patronage of influential American politicians who helped him evade responsibility for the crimes he had committed."

While this summary of the Tass output of May 2, 1985, shows that the agency does not so much cover world news as select items that implement specific policy and propaganda aims, it fails to indicate the service's capacity for picking up, cross-reporting, and originating material when a special propaganda opportunity arises. This was the case, a few days later, when President Reagan visited the German cemetery at Bitburg, which had among its buried war dead 49 members of the Waffen SS, a unit that had gained notoriety toward the end of World War II. In the United States, Jewish groups and veterans organizations were at the forefront of protesters against the visit. For several days, Soviet reaction to these developments was hesitant; but then, and largely ignoring the particularly bitter memories of Jews who had suffered under SS guards in concentration camps, spokesmen in the U.S.S.R. incorporated the controversy into their commentaries.

The following pages present a summary of Tass's English-language output for May 6, 1985. Again, this is significant not only for what it contains but for what it ignores—innumerable events and developments inside the U.S.S.R. and the United States, as well as worldwide, that do not, somehow, aid in making strong propagandistic points, but which actually make up the daily news budget of the major news agencies.

One of the early items in the Tass news file for May 6 was a Tokyo item reporting on pickets outside the Labor Ministry. The agency said that the All-Japan Council of Building and Time-Workers' Union had "launched [a] massive nation-wide campaign" for employment, adding that "the number of jobless in Japan is more than 1.7 million." Next, from San Francisco, the agency reported on a conference in Colorado Springs that had "sounded a vigorous call for a ban on all types of space weapons."

Under the heading "To the Joy of the Revanchists," Tass carried excerpts from a *Pravda* commentary by Yuri Zhukov, the paper's political analyst. The commentary denounced the results of the Bonn summit meeting as well as President Reagan's talks during the week, which "emphasized in every way that ostensibly both the Hitlerite butchers and their victims were equally 'victims of the Holocaust.' " Zhukov also said that the West German "revanchists" had "not disarmed themselves" and were welcoming the new support.

Tass reported from Moscow that the city of Smolensk had been awarded the honorary title of "Hero City," by a decree of the Presidium of the Supreme Soviet, in recognition of the courage and fortitude of its defenders and "for the mass heroism of the working people in the struggle against the Nazi invaders during the years of the Great Patriotic War."

From London, the agency relayed the information that demonstrations had taken place in Israel, with protesters outside the U.S. embassy in Tel Aviv denouncing President Reagan's visit to the Bitburg cemetery. From Amman, Tass quoted the Jordanian Preparatory Committee for Celebrations of the 40th Anniversary of the Victory over Fascism as calling upon "all people of goodwill" to "struggle for peace, against imperialism's dangerous militaristic designs." Having previously recorded the same honor for Smolensk, Tass reported that the northern port city of Murmansk had also been awarded the title of "Hero City." The announcement acknowledged that the port had received wartime shipments "supplied by the Allied countries in the struggle against Fascist Germany."

Tass reported from Beirut that six persons were killed and more than thirty wounded in armed clashes in the city, and that, in the Israeli-occupied portion of southern Lebanon, "patriots fired from grenade-launchers at interventionists' combat positions." Vladimir Svelov reported from Berlin, presumably East Berlin, that the city of Barth, on the Baltic coast, had celebrated its "liberation by the Soviet Army from Fascist yoke," while "war veterans from the USSR and USA participated in a mass meeting." In a dispatch from Tokyo, Tass cited British Prime Minister Margaret Thatcher as having told Japanese Prime Minister Nakasone that Japan had "insufficiently opened" its market to foreign goods. The report commented, "In London they feel great irritation over Tokyo's unwillingness to open its home market."

All these dispatches had been carried on Tass's English-language service before 9 a.m. on May 6. But a heavy schedule was still ahead, with more detailed dispatches and commentaries. Next was a feature, "Soviet Economy during the War," which, under a Moscow dateline, contained an interview with Lev Volodarski, head of the Central Statistical Board of the U.S.S.R. He concluded that, during World War II, in "a clash of economies, the Socialist economy of the USSR proved its superiority."

Eldar Abdullayev, correspondent in La Paz, contributed an interview with Bolivia's Foreign Minister Edgar Camacho. He paid tribute to the Soviet Union's role in World War II and noted that the Bolivian government "wholly and entirely supports the nonaligned movement which stands for détente, for peaceful coexistence, for prevention of nuclear threat, for disarmament and immediate termination of the arms race, so that the means thus released be channeled for the good of the peoples, for social advancement."

From Tokyo, the agency cited the Women's Council of New Japan as finding that microelectronics, robots, and automatic machinery had intensified the "exploitation" of women workers. From London, correspondent Nikolai Pakhomov reported that the government refused to make public information about Nazi criminals Klaus Barbie and Josef Mengele. The correspondent cited "the London-based anti-fascist magazine *Searchlight*" as its source.

In another anniversary story, a dispatch from Riga spoke of a meeting in the small Latvian town of Ezere, where veterans of World War II celebrated their victory. From (East) Berlin, the agency reported on a meeting between Honecker and Pyotr Demichev, an alternate member of the Soviet Politburo. Honecker said that millions "would never forget that the Soviet Union made the decisive contribution to the defeat of criminal

Fascism," and he praised "the memories of 20 million Soviet people who died fighting Fascism."

From Karditsa, Greece, Tass correspondent Anatoli Tkachyuk reported that a "mammoth rally" had celebrated the support which Soviet airplanes had brought to Greek resistance fighters during the war. From Bonn, the agency cited the press bulletin of a group of Social Democrats who demanded that state aid to any organization of former SS men be halted. In Moscow, the All-Union Council of Evangelical Christian-Baptists issued an appeal on the war's anniversary. The dispatch cited similar statements by other religious denominations.

Under the heading "Who Are They Playing Up To?" Tass quoted Vikenti Matveyev, writing in *Izvestia,* that Washington's pressure on the "capitalist seven" at the Bonn summit conference had failed, with France showing the greatest degree of opposition to U.S. policies. Concerning the meeting's closing declaration, the Moscow columnist said that it failed to show conciliation, but "followed in the footsteps of politicians thinking in terms of confrontation."

Around noon, Tass carried an original news analysis by Valentin Vasilets, from Moscow, which used the sixty-fifth anniversary of the case of Sacco and Vanzetti to suggest that their execution had established a precedent in U.S. practice, whereby "democratically-minded citizens are victimized for their convictions, while their cases are presented as criminal ones." Vasilets cited several contemporary cases as indicating that "reprisals for political convictions are now rife in the U.S.A."

The day's third Tass news analysis, from Alexei Grigoryev, was transmitted shortly after 2 p.m. and dealt with President Reagan's visit to Hambach, West Germany, a traditional center of German freedom efforts. Grigoryev said that this historic setting "emphasized the political hypocrisy of Reagan, who is distorting historic facts and moral truths." The 500-word commentary ended by stating that the visit was part of the "propaganda show business whose trend is set by the President himself."

From New Delhi, the Tass correspondent quoted a message from India's Prime Minister Rajiv Gandhi to the Friends of the Soviet Union, hailing the victory anniversary and welcoming "the many initiatives taken by the Soviet Union towards détente." Tass quoted U.N. Secretary General Javier Perez de Cuellar as condemning the "referendum" among the Turkish community of Cyprus on the question of a so-called constitution for the "Republic of Northern Cyprus." The United Nations does not recognize any other state on the island except the Republic of Cyprus, and the Tass dispatch stayed firmly within that framework.

The UN secretary general was also being quoted in a Vienna dispatch by Tass man Alexander Semyonou, addressing a seminar preparatory to the organization of the International Year of Peace in 1986. Of all the Tass dispatches on the English-language service during the day, this was perhaps the most objective, in terms of simply conveying the gist of an event. It also quoted Austria's minister of science and research, speaking generally on needs for cooperation and disarmament. While the event fitted into the general "peace" emphasis of the Tass output, and general Soviet media directives, the Semyonou dispatch lacked the clichés glorifying the U.S.S.R. and demonizing the United States.

The final Tass commentary of the day, written in Moscow by Lev Aksyonou, carried the headline " 'Freedom,' Third Reich Style" and took its theme from an article by West German deputy Herbert Hupka that had appeared in the magazine *Silesia*. The territory of Silesia was incorporated into Poland, and Hupka heads the Association of Fellow German Countrymen from Silesia. According to Aksyonov, Hupka accused the Soviet Union of using the fortieth anniversary of the war's end to "distract attention" from the "oppression to which it subjects people" and from the "deprivation of millions of their human rights." The Tass commentator accused Hupka of "spreading malicious slander against the Soviet Union and trying to cast aspersions on the historic feat of arms of the Soviet people," thereby making common cause with those who wish to "re-carve the political map of Europe and the whole world."

At the same time, Tass transmitted a Moscow statement originating from the International Committee for European Security and Cooperation, which said that Europeans must fight "energetically against the attempts at revision of political and territorial realities." The committee spoke out against "deployment of new medium-range nuclear missiles that was started against the will of peoples."

From Geneva, Tass carried a brief report on the thirty-seventh session of the UN International Law Commission, dealing with international conventions on such matters as responsibility of states, legal immunities of states and their property, status of diplomatic messengers, a code of crimes against peace and mankind's security, and other issues. From Prague, the agency covered the fortieth anniversary meeting of the International Organization of Journalists (IOJ), one of the Soviet-supported front organizations specifically designed to influence professionals. It passed a resolution "against revanchism and Fascism," which called for exposure of "malicious attacks against the Yalta and Potsdam agreements."

Tass reported from Leningrad that Soviet and American war veterans who had met on the Elbe River in 1945 "exchanged friendly handshakes in Leningrad" after a tour that also took them to Kiev and Volgograd (the former Stalingrad, scene of a decisive defeat of the German army in World War II). Among other points of interest, the American veterans visited Leningrad schools that featured instructions in English.

In Prague, Tass reported, Czechoslovak Communist Party leader Gustav Husak received Nicaragua's President Ortega. The dispatch concluded: "Daniel Ortega highly stressed solidarity, political and economic assistance that Czechoslovakia gives to the Nicaraguan people in its revolutionary struggle, in the defense of the gains of the Sandinist Revolution."

From Moscow, the service provided a roundup of the Soviet National Soccer Championship. During the tenth round of the competition, eight matches were held, with the Dynamo Club of Kiev (Ukraine) retaining its first position, followed by Dynamo of Tbilisi (Georgia).

According to a Tass dispatch from Paris, the French Ministry of External Relations criticized the U.S. decision to introduce a trade embargo against Nicaragua. The agency quoted a ministry spokesman as saying that trade sanctions would hinder efforts of the Contadora group of countries to normalize the situation in Central America.

The next morning, as the Tass printer came to life, it typed out the following message:

"Attention Tass Subscribers

"Tass news service is to include today, May 7, the following news stories:

Havana. On 25th anniversary of Soviet-Cuban Relations.

San Francisco. Nazi War Criminals in the USA.

Managua-New York. Nicaragua's request for U.N. Security Council to call a meeting to discuss the Situation in Central America.

Madrid. Continuation of Ronald Reagan's European Tour."

With that, at 5:16 a.m., a new day of "the world according to Tass" had begun!

A survey of the day's output shows that, compared with the two days summarized above, Tass presented "the mixture as before"—and, presumably, 365 days a year. Again, there was a profusion of opinion, most of it critical of the U.S. government, and an absence of what Western newspaper editors would regard as "hard news." One exception was a report from Pyongyang, North Korea, stating that Hu Yaoban, general secretary of the Chinese Communist Party, had made an "unofficial visit," conferring with his North Korean counterpart, Kim Il Sung. Tass also transmitted a tabulation of the relative standing of all 19 teams in the U.S.S.R. Soccer Championship. The agency further reported that Nicaraguan President Ortega had left Prague; East German cyclist Lutz Hesslich had broken his own world record in the 200-meter heat, flying start, on the cycling track at Tbilisi in 10.322 seconds; Greece protested the NATO maneuvers "Distant Hammer-85" in the Aegean Sea; in Gorki, on the Volga River, the keel of the first ship of a new generation of dry-cargo vessels, the *Zhiguli,* had been laid down; and, in Moscow, a sculpture celebrating the espionage feats of Richard Sorge had been unveiled.

This final item was intriguing, as Sorge is one of the few Soviet spies whose existence and achievements have ever been publicly acknowledged. He had been posthumously awarded what Tass called "the lofty title of Hero of the Soviet Union," and "a sculptural composition" was placed on a Moscow street named after him. Tass recalled Sorge's achievements as follows:

"Richard Sorge, an ardent patriot and internationalist, devoted all his life to the defense of his Motherland. Being a staunch Communist, he served the Motherland devotedly. Sorge named in advance the exact date of the Hitler invasion of the USSR territory, informed the Soviet command that the Far Eastern borders were not threatened with an attack by Japan. Being a correspondent of the [German] newspaper *Frankfurter Zeitung* in Tokyo, he was getting top secret information, and it seemed that no obstacles were insurmountable to him. Therefore, it is symbolic that the authors of the monument portrayed Sorge as a man passing through a wall, a man to whom nothing was impossible."

What Sorge did not succeed in doing, however, was to convince Stalin of the accuracy and importance of the German invasion plans he forwarded to Moscow. Gordon W. Prange, in his book *Target Tokyo: The Story of the Sorge Spy Ring* (1984), recalled that not only Sorge's intelligence but the predictions of Soviet military attachés, as well as those of U.S. and British sources, "bounced off the Kremlin walls without making a dent," because "Stalin knew best." Sorge's reports were filed away as "doubtful and misleading information," possibly reflecting a "capitalist trick to drive a wedge between Moscow and Berlin." So much for a historical footnote to a Tass report from Moscow, on May 7, 1985, at 10:34 EDT.

CHAPTER · 15

Secret Tasks of Tass

The line between the gathering of information for publication and the collection of secret data for intelligence purposes can be a thin one, a twilight zone in which some Tass representatives function. Tass reporters often have access to sources that cannot be approached, with equal ease or legitimacy, by diplomats or other Soviet representatives. We have already seen that much of what Tass sends back to Moscow never gets into public print but is circulated, as classified information, among high officials and policymakers. In addition, the giant vacuum cleaner that is the KGB undoubtedly makes use of Tass personnel to gather information or recruit agents.

Former Tass employees and other Soviet emigrés have estimated that as many as 50 percent of Tass staffers abroad are KGB agents who use the press service's credentials as a convenient cover and entrée. Such estimates must vary, because the term "agent" covers a variety of functions, from those of a full-time KGB agent who only pretends to work for Tass to those of a hardworking correspondent who writes an occasional background memorandum, personality profile, or analysis that goes directly or indirectly to the KGB or the GRU, the intelligence branch of the Soviet armed forces.

Over time, Tass correspondents have changed their image. Edward Crankshaw, an experienced analyst of the Soviet scene, once wrote in the New York *Herald-Tribune* (December 7–8, 1957) that Soviet leaders find it impossible to regard a foreign correspondent as "anything other than a paid spy," because "the man from Tass is precisely that." He noted that most of what a Tass correspondent sends to Moscow "does not appear in the newspapers at all: it is collected, analyzed and evaluated as more or less secret intelligence—political, economic, military, etc. What does get into print or on the air is selected for its propaganda value." Crankshaw wrote that, very often, a chief correspondent for Tass is not a journalist but "a permanent member of the police: always he may be called to assist the secret police." He will, however, the writer added, have on his staff men and women who are capable journalistic technicians.

It may well be that, during the reorganization of the KGB under Yuri Andropov, who was the secret service chief from 1967 to 1982 and served as top leader until his death the following year, Tass representatives were used more selectively for intelligence purposes than before. Scattered exposures of correspondents created a patchwork pattern of spy activities under Tass cover. In Belgium, on April 19, 1967, Tass correspondent Anatol Ogorodnikov was arrested in Brussels and expelled. The Foreign Ministry said the correspondent had been asked to leave for "state security reasons." In neighboring Holland, Tass correspondent Vadim Leonov was identified as a KGB agent in 1981 and expelled for his aid to the Dutch "peace movement." At one point, while intoxicated, Leonov was heard to claim, "If Moscow decides that 50,000 demonstrators must take to the streets in the Netherlands, then they take to the streets. Do you know how you can get 50,000 demonstrators at a certain place within a week? A message through my channels is sufficient."

Nevertheless, the number of Tass people exposed as linked to the KGB or GRU has been relatively small in recent years, compared to earlier decades. In the 1950s, Lieutenant Colonel Yuri Rastvorov, who had served in Tokyo as a Soviet GRU agent under the cover of embassy second secretary, said that about 85 to 90 percent of all Tass personnel abroad were intelligence agents. Ismail Ege, another military intelligence agent, defected and in 1956 gave the U.S. Senate's Internal Security Subcommittee a similar estimate of the use of Tass personnel for Soviet intelligence. Ege, whose real name was Ismail G. Akhmedov, was Tass bureau chief in Berlin while actually employed by the GRU. Later, Ege served as press attaché in the Soviet embassy in Turkey. He told the committee that Tass representatives in the United States were used "more extensively" for intelligence purposes and found their task relatively easy, because Americans simply "could not comprehend" that people with journalistic credentials could be espionage agents.

According to Rastvorov, the Tass office in postwar Japan acted as an intelligence channel, with successive correspondents: Constantine Smolivov, also known as Sonini; Yakov Kisilev; and Evgeni Egorov. Basing its findings on the testimony of defector Vladimir Petrov in Australia, a report of the Royal Commission on Espionage (August 22, 1955) stated that from 1949 to 1953 three successive Tass representatives had been intelligence agents.

When 47 Soviet officials were expelled by the French government in 1983—at a time of an expulsion move in Britain and one in Spain—Tass people were among the persons described by the Interior Ministry as "agents of the secret services of the Soviet Union." Among the families sent back to the Soviet Union were those of Oleg Shirokov, the Paris bureau chief of Tass, and Vladimir Kulikovskikh, a Tass reporter. Even before he entered France, the government's counterintelligence agency, the Direction de la Surveillance du Territoire (DST) had identified Shirokov as a KGB representative; he had earlier served in Laos and Cambodia, as well as at other posts. Ironically, it was the Tass agency which disseminated protests against the French action, signed by Soviet scientists, writers, and artists.

The ambivalent role Tass plays at times exposes it to surprising reactions. In Paris, in June 1983, Communist Party leader Georges Marchais disputed the Tass version of his statement on the status of missiles in Eastern and Western Europe. Tass had reported that Marchais had assigned responsibility for endangering peace solely on "the intentions of American imperialism of placing new medium-range rockets in Europe." Marchais insisted that he had emphasized the need for "balanced disarmament," and Tass was obliged to correct its report accordingly. The agency had obviously failed to make allowances for the delicate position of the French Communist Party as a member of the governing alliance with the Socialist Party, and had assumed that the usually complacent Marchais would simply echo the routine Moscow propaganda phrases.

In 1982, the independent Nicaraguan newspaper *La Prensa* sued Tass for libel, because the agency had accused the paper of plotting terrorist attacks on the government. United Press International reported (February 9) from Managua that the paper, which had been closed half a dozen times by the pro-Moscow Sandinista regime during the preceding year, had filed a suit in the Nicaraguan capital's Third District Court. The paper's lawyer, Salomon Calvo Arrieta, charged Tass and its Managua bureau chief, Vladimir Shejovtsov, with disseminating the accusation that *La Prensa* was engaged in a "terrorist and counter-revolutionary plot" against the government. The Tass dispatch was distributed on January 9, and four days later a riotous rally took place outside the paper's office. *La Prensa* charged that only Tass had implicated the paper in the plot and that while the paper "may be anti-Soviet and anti-Communist," it was "never terrorist." Shejovtsov attributed the disputed aspect of its dispatch to a "technical editing error," but *La Prensa* demanded a full retraction, although it did not call for payment of damages. The paper was closed down on June 26, 1986.

Damages were awarded by a court in Lebanon (April 7, 1973) against

Tass and its Beirut bureau chief, Raymond Saade. The agency was found guilty of libel when two years earlier, it had disseminated charges by the former British intelligence officer and Soviet spy, Harold ("Kim") Philby, who had accused leading Lebanese politicians and journalists of being paid foreign agents. The court asked that Tass pay 1,000 Lebanese pounds penalty and 40,000 pounds restitution, to be divided among four claimants. The case affirmed the official position of Tass as an agency of the Soviet government, as the court had been requested by the Russian embassy to grant Saade diplomatic immunity and cancel the legal proceedings.

The delicate relationship between the Soviet Union and the Iranian regime of Ayatollah Khomeini affected the status of the Tass bureau in Teheran. Western news agencies had found it increasingly difficult, often impossible, to maintain normally functioning offices in the Iranian capital, but Tass had steadfastly remained after the Khomeini takeover. For the most part, Soviet media refrained from criticizing the regime and occasionally disseminated Iran's anti-Western statements. However, following a demonstration outside the Soviet embassy in Teheran on December 27, 1982, Tass reported that Iranian authorities had failed to curb the actions of Afghan refugees. This dispatch prompted the Iranian Ministry of Islamic Guidance to cancel the residence permit of the Tass bureau chief, which prompted the agency to close the office entirely.

In the United States—where, as former Tass man Ege had claimed, people did not "comprehend" the agency's full role—there has been little embarrassment on either side. By some subtle choreography, Tass and U.S. officialdom manage to get along with each other. Occasionally, delicate situations call for special solutions. In curious contradiction, correspondents for the Voice of America, the U.S. government's overseas broadcasting service, had been banned from the press galleries of the U.S. Congress, while Tass and other foreign services were able to send their accredited representatives. The congressional correspondent of Tass was Boris Ivanov, and his presence in the press gallery aroused the interest of Senator John P. East, a Republican from North Carolina. In a letter to Senator Charles McC. Mathias Jr., Republican from Maryland, Senator East wrote: "An employee of the Soviet news agency Tass, and an accredited member of the Senate press gallery, Boris Ivanov, is in fact an officer or agent of the Soviet intelligence service, the KGB."

Having thus alerted the chairman of the Senate's Rules and Administration Committee, East added that he did not regard it as "appropriate for a Soviet spy to enjoy the privileges of the members of the free press." Further: "Nor do I believe that it is appropriate for an arm of the Soviet propaganda machine such as Tass to have representatives in the press gallery of the Senate, especially since the Voice of America itself has never been granted such privileges on the grounds that it is a government news agency." As quoted by *Washington Post* columnist Jack Anderson (March 27, 1984), East's letter concluded: "Tass is also a government news agency, yet it has full press credentials in the Senate, even though some of its employees, and Ivanov in particular, have long been known to be intelligence officers under cover."

East's plea that the Voice of America (VOA) be permitted to place a correspondent in the Senate's gallery won additional support from 50 other senators. This prompted Mathias to hold a hearing on the matter. A major handicap was the fear of other press representatives that once VOA had a person in the Senate, other government agencies might also send observers, men or women who were not actually working reporters. The Senate nevertheless eventually decided to give the Voice of America access to its gallery.

Boris Ivanov was, indeed, known as an experienced KGB agent prior to his Tass assignment, which included the observation and recording of Senate sessions and congressional hearings. According to a prominent Soviet defector, Yuri I. Nosenko, Ivanov had been the KGB resident in New York City in the early 1960s. This made him a key figure in the intelligence agency's main information-gathering center, which includes UN headquarters. Shortly after East's intervention, Ivanov left Washington in the fall of 1983 and presumably returned to the Soviet Union. Anderson quoted a Soviet embassy spokesman as saying that the senator's accusation of KGB affiliation had not caused Ivanov "any embarrassment at all." He added: "Boris left for good because he had completed successfully his duty here."

The Washington office of Tass, in the National Press Building, is a busy place, but not half as hectic as its New York headquarters in the Associated Press Building of Rockefeller Center. (The agency maintains a second bureau in New York, in the building occupied by the UN Secretariat.)

One Tass reporter, Yuri Romantsov, in a rare interview given to *New York Times* reporter Edward A. Gargan in 1981, described his own work as relatively routine and even humdrum. In 1979, he had been assigned to reporting in New York City for two years (his second assignment in New York). He said, "When I first came here, everything was new, but when I came back in 1979, it wasn't true." He added: "I don't really have any fresh impressions." Gargan noted that after some thought, Romantsov conceded, "There aren't any cities like New York in the Soviet Union, or for that matter in the United States."

Romantsov made this uncontroversial observation against the background of the Tass office, and, as Gargan observed, "with his shirt sleeves rolled up past his elbows, Mr. Romantsov looks pretty much like any harried journalist as he pounds away on his aging typewriter. The clatter of wire-service teletypes and the stack of unsorted newspaper clippings around him hardly distinguish the New York bureau of Tass from offices of other news organizations." Romantsov said that he was less interested in covering the colorful New York scene than in dealing with international issues. "Our primary interest," he said, "is in American foreign policy. We report what the American press thinks about what [the then U.S. Secretary of State Alexander] Haig or [Secretary of Defense Caspar] Weinberger says. Recently we did a story on how U.S official circles and the press are writing on the elections in Greece. Whenever something here happens we consider of interest to Soviet readers or our international readers, we cover it."

Romantsov said that New Yorkers tend to be guarded when they realize that a Soviet reporter wants to interview them, but that in the smaller communities people tend to be surprised and then comparatively open when approached by a Russian interviewer. Tass correspondents, like other Soviet reporters, are restricted in their travels. If they plan to travel more than 25 miles outside their residences in New York, Washington, or San Francisco, they have to notify the Department of State. Tass reporters are banned from visiting upstate New York, much of the South, and parts of northern and southern California, just as many sections of the Soviet Union are out of bounds to foreign correspondents. Such reciprocity applies to the number of correspondents, as well: The number of Russian correspondents permitted in the United States is the same as the number of American reporters permitted to stay in the Soviet Union.

In 1976, Tass opened an office in San Francisco, with Aleksei Morozov as bureau chief. This followed an increase in staff on the part of the Soviet consulate in San Francisco, indicating the Soviet Union's keen interest in the technological developments in the so-called Silicon Valley, south of the city, known worldwide for its advancements in computer research. The area also became known as a hotbed of industrial espionage; cynics ascribed the expansion of the Russian consulate and Tass's new role to a very active Soviet curiosity in the area's technological aspects. In an interview with Brad Knickerbocker of the *Christian Science Monitor* (December 9, 1976), Morozov said that what he saw as a major part of his task was "to form public opinion" in the Soviet Union toward "the ideal of communism." To do this, he said, "we must show the people how they can participate in the building of communism and by what political means." Reporting and analyzing the news from the U.S. West Coast, in a suitably selective manner, was apparently the Tass correspondent's specific assignment.

Just how the effort at public education and political guidance is seen at Tass headquarters in Moscow was explained to a Swiss correspondent on the scene, Andreas Oplatka of the *Neue Zürcher Zeitung* (May 11, 1984). The Swiss reporter had been invited to visit the modern Tass headquarters building, and he requested that, beyond observing offices and word processors, he be allowed to ask about the "principles that guide Tass in its work." As a result, and for an hour and a half, Oplatka had a chance to question two "highly placed representatives" of the agency (whose names he did not give and who presumably chose to remain anonymous).

Over coffee and cake, the three men talked about Tass's unique position and function. Oplatka noted, "There was insufficient time to discuss or even mention all the dubious methods used by Tass." The conversation began with a discussion of just how influential Tass actually is and why even Soviet papers that send reporters to press conferences in Moscow then publish only the Tass version, which they are not permitted to rewrite or shorten. The Tass spokesmen attributed this phenomenon to laziness on the part of reporters who were simply unwilling to sit down at the typewriter. Another interpretation might be that Soviet papers find it safer to "go with Tass" than to risk potentially dangerous political criticism.

The Swiss correspondent asked why, on occasion, Tass is remarkably slow, as when it needed half a day before reporting a press conference by U.S. President Ronald Reagan. He was told that, on such occasions, Tass is expected to supply an official viewpoint rather than simply to report on the event, and this required time for careful consideration and consultation. Consultation with whom? Well, "for example, with the government." On the one hand, then, Tass is pictured as an independent agency; on the other, it prides itself on acting as the voice of the Soviet Union. But do Tass dispatches always represent an official viewpoint? That, the spokesmen said, was tantamount to a frequent exaggeration by foreign correspondents, who placed Tass on an equal level with the Kremlin, "something that would be too flattering to us."

A more specific point: Tass reported, triumphantly, that in March 1984 the United Nations Commission on Human Rights had refused to adopt a U.S.-proposed resolution on human rights violations in Poland; two days later, however, Tass failed to record that the same commission had viewed the withdrawal of foreign troops from Afghanistan as a condition for the restoration of human rights in that country. The Swiss correspondent reported that his "hosts" said they wished to "place the conversation on a higher level" by noting that Western media failed to mention the most important Soviet peace initiatives while filling front pages with unimportant dispatches. To which the correspondent replied with a supplementary question: Did they feel that reporting on the UN commission's decision to ignore the Poland resolution had served peace while reporting on the Afghanistan resolution would have promoted conflict? And was it Tass's conception that it had to ignore the Afghanistan resolution because it did not fit Soviet foreign policy?

This led to a series of quite long-winded replies and explanations and to the admission that Soviet journalists had to utilize an "ability to differentiate" between suitable and unsuitable events. The Tass representatives saw the Afghanistan issue as part of an American effort to "encircle" the U.S.S.R. and create a mood similar to that of "a fortress under siege." Did this mean that Soviet citizens, during times of international stress, should be protected from unpleasant news? That wasn't the issue, the Tass spokesmen said. As Soviet citizens had "a thousand possibilities to know the western version," Tass and the Soviet Union refused to take on the function of Western radio stations. (Not mentioned, apparently, was the Soviet effort to insulate listeners in the Soviet Union from foreign transmissions in Russian and other languages by using its own transmitters to jam broadcasts from the West.)

The key questions, eventually, were these: What is Tass doing, then, at this point? Is it engaged in reporting what is going on in the world, day in and day out, while providing a variety of opinions; or is its activity in the main of a political and propagandistic nature?

While the Tass spokesmen said they preferred the first concept of journalistic activity, they could not deny the existence of the second concept in their task. Yes, Tass was an "engaged news agency," because this was necessary for survival in the midst of psychological warfare. Western media, they said, do not give an objective picture of the U.S.S.R. But why, they were asked, would the Soviet press not even report words by the U.S. President that were declarations of his love of peace? But were these "really important?" they answered. The Swiss reporter posed the counteranswer: Who was to decide, in such a case, what was "really important?" Who was to decide what was important and what was unimportant, and thus control the flow of news to a nation of 270 million people?

Oplatka's dispatch concluded:

"And thus one arrived at the final point of the discussion, at the basic difference. The hosts counterattack by asking, how dare western journalists blacken the image of the Soviet Union as an enemy country where there is nothing but prisons and dissidents and that schemes, single-mindedly, the conquest of the West? Certainly, one can admit that most of the commentaries and reports of western media are critical of the Soviet system. But we are not afraid to present our public with the other side, such as publishing the speeches of Soviet leaders in great detail. No one 'at the top' decides what the average citizen should know or think, but this decision lies with each individual. The Tass editors, for their part, deny that the Soviet viewpoint is always correctly conveyed in the West, but they do not contradict the observation that their own information activities have an educational nature. The question that remains unanswered, however, is by what right a minority may treat a population of adults as children who have to be politically schooled."

How this daily menu of news selection and commentaries is compiled was outlined in the *Ogonyok* article, cited earlier. The editorial collegium meets at 10:30 a.m. in the boardroom at Tass headquarters in Moscow. A large wall map shows the world, and flags are stuck in places where Tass has assigned its correspondents: There are 73 blue flags marking various cities in the Soviet Union and more than 100 appropriately red flags "spread all over the map, reaching the most remote corners of the world."

Tass's editor in chief begins the planning meeting with a listing of news priorities: a large blast furnace has begun operations in Krivoy Rog, cotton production in Tadjikhistan has reached new records, at the Baltic Sea a lighthouse now gets its energy from nuclear power, Moscow enjoys an art festival called "Russian Winter," archaeologists have discovered origins of the ancient city of Varkhsha, Tass man Boris Grishchenko reports on progress in a tunnel being dug through the mountains at Nort-Muysk, etc.

Spread throughout the room, under the map with the blue and red pins, sit the Tass editors and local reporters, some of them recent graduates of the Institute of Foreign Affairs, the schools of foreign languages, the academies of sciences that specialize in various branches of technology, or the universities' departments of journalism. The cream of these graduates go out into the world to feed information back into the radio teletypes at Tass headquarters on Tverskoi Boulevard, supplying the five-language world service, the general domestic service, and the exclusive "White Tass" and "Red Tass" services.

Abroad, the new breed of Tass reporters mingle with correspondents from the Western press agencies and reporters from the major newspapers at public events and interviews. In Washington, on October 17, 1984, White House correspondents questioned press secretary Larry Speakes on the significance of an interview Soviet leader Konstantin U. Chernenko had given in Moscow. Speakes read a detailed statement that outlined the official U.S. position on the points Chernenko had mentioned. But the Tass reporter, the then 37-year-old Aleksandr A. Shalnev, spoke up when the questioning was finished and, in his slightly accented but fluent English, demanded that Speakes give a simple yes or no answer as to whether the U.S. administration "rejected" the main points of the Soviet leader's proposal.

Speakes, well aware that here was a Soviet government representative as well as a somewhat aggressive Tass reporter, flushed slightly and said, "I would leave that to the judgment of you and the Soviets, which are one and the same in your case."

CHAPTER · 16

Novosti Comes of Age

Soviet television viewers were told on October 28, 1984, that the U.S.S.R. Supreme Soviet's Presidium had awarded the Order of the Red Banner of Labor to the Novosti Press Agency "for services in publicizing the domestic and foreign policies of the Communist Party of the Soviet Union and of the Soviet state, and for keeping world opinion informed about the achievements of the Soviet people." It was equivalent to bestowing the Congressional Medal of Honor on an American news feature service. The Red Banner Order was particularly noteworthy, as Novosti's status is unusual in that—technically, at least—it is not an "official" Soviet agency.

Yet bestowing a high honor on the Novosti press service, a relative newcomer to the international propaganda field, would seem to be well justified. Throughout its quarter-century existence, the agency has been successful on various levels and in a great variety of activities. Basically, Novosti backstops the officially "official" Tass news agency with news features, articles, photographs, films, and television material. Beyond that, the agency has grown into a highly professional conveyor of anything and everything that is audiovisual and tells the Soviet story. For a fee, often a very large fee, Novosti arranges interviews, escorts visiting reporters and television producers, arranges trips, cuts red tape, and generally acts as the knowledgeable middleman between Western media, Soviet sources, and at times elusive news-feature targets.

But it would not be an agency of the Soviet Union, official or unofficial, if Novosti did not occasionally find itself in distinctly awkward situations. One such event, described further in an earlier chapter, took place in Switzerland in 1983 and led to the deportation of the local Novosti chief,

Aleksei Dumov, from Berne, the Swiss capital. Expelled with him was Leonid Ovchinnikov, first secretary at the Soviet embassy, who functioned as press attaché and was identified as the KGB officer responsible for Novosti's operations on Swiss soil.

What prompted the usually low-keyed and always neutral Swiss to oust two Soviet officials, one of whom, on the record, was merely the local bureau chief of a press agency? According to the Federal Prosecutor Rudolf Friedrich, Novosti's main office and some of its Swiss staff members had been guilty of "grave interferences in internal Swiss affairs." Specifically, the agency's staff was accused of having "exerted an influence on segments of the Swiss peace movement." Two Novosti staff members, the journalists Martin Schwander and Philip Spillmann, were members of the Swiss Communist Party, the Party of Labor. While the chronology of their actions in encouraging demonstrations has been in dispute, there appears little doubt that they succeeded in deflecting any possible criticism of the Soviet Union and in concentrating attacks on U.S. policies. The government's 25-page memorandum noted that "the slogans for the demonstration units of the Party of Labor were, for the most part selected and supplied" by the Novosti journalists. These included "Stop the Cowboy" and "No to the Neutron Bomb." Schwander admitted: "The Central Secretariat of the Labor Party in Geneva called me at the Novosti office concerning the slogans for the various party units." The news agency also coordinated such things as meeting places, signs, and parking facilities. The government noted: "According to the findings of the Federal Police, the APN [Novosti] office played a substantial role in the organization and proceedings of these demonstrations, although this could not be observed from the outside."

Novosti bureau chief Dumov's credentials had been specific: The Swiss authorities had accepted him as a "journalist and correspondent" of the press service, "to the exclusion of all other activities." The federal prosecutor told the Swiss weekly *Weltwoche* (May 25, 1983): "Novosti had been assigned the function of a normal press agency, which means that it was to obtain and supply information for the media. But it was never understood that the agency would be a base from which it could interfere in the domestic political opinion-making of Switzerland."

The government memorandum had been secret, but it was apparently photocopied by staff members of the Finance Ministry and thus circulated, within two weeks of its presentation, among interested parties inside and outside the government. Friederich told interviewers that it had seemed the better part of diplomacy to keep the names of certain foreign officials from becoming public knowledge, including that of Marta Jimenez Martinez, Cuba's ambassador, who had played a relatively minor role in encouraging Swiss youngsters, some of whom formed a "Che Guevara" youth group. While Novosti bureau chief Dumov was still in the country when the Swiss government's ouster order was issued, his apparent superior, the KGB officer Ovchinnikov, left the country when news of the government's investigation of Novosti began to become public knowledge. The agency's Geneva office remained untouched; as the center of numerous international negotiations, on neutral Swiss ground, Geneva retained its full complement of Soviet press representatives.

If there was any lesson to be learned from the Swiss experience, it was the by then standard one that Soviet intelligence and propaganda agencies do better dealing with nonparty people than with local Communist Party members. In the years since its establishment, on February 21, 1961, Novosti has experienced other charges of interference in nations' internal affairs and of espionage, and it has seen some of its representatives identified as KGB agents and expelled; the record is on par with that of other Soviet agencies operating abroad. On the whole, Novosti has succeeded remarkably in responding to the challenges posed by the competitive, deadline-haunted existence of the world's news media.

Conceived during the Khrushchev era, Novosti symbolized a Soviet effort to get away from the gray, dour image presented to the world by the Tass news service, by the image of yet another group of old men assembled atop Lenin's Tomb on Moscow's Red Square, by convoluted Marxist-Leninist verbiage, or by statistics that disguised more than they revealed. The "nongovernmental" sponsors of Novosti, at its outset, were the Union of Soviet Journalists, the Union of Soviet Writers, the Union of Soviet Societies of Friendship and Cultural Ties with Foreign Countries, and the All-Union Society for Dissemination of Political and Scientific Knowledge. Khrushchev's son-in-law, *Izvestia's* editor-in-chief Aleksei Adzhubei, was a member of Novosti's governing board at the outset. With all its promise of a new approach, the agency was born to a drumroll of standard rhetoric: "Expansion of the exchange of various types of information will contribute to establishment of a spirit of mutuality and cooperation in the struggle for peace and friendship between peoples."

The feature service frequently uses the initials *APN*, its full Russian name being *Agentsvo Pechati Novosti*. It flourished during the remaining years of Khrushchev's rule and continued to expand during the Brezhnev regime and its successors. Historical articles, contemporary reporting, interviews, travel pieces, and biographical articles have been among Novosti's extensive repertoire. At home, its material was at first to be found more frequently in provincial papers and periodicals than in major newspapers; abroad, its material was readily accepted in many Third World countries, where editorial budgets were limited and translated copy could be used without much editing.

Absorbing the Foreign Language Publishing House, a Moscow enterprise established during the heyday of the Communist International, Novosti went into the book publishing field, issuing a great number of works, some of them under the imprint of Progress Publishers. In this case, the agency quietly absorbed a competing establishment that could only benefit from a fresh approach, younger staff, and more modern production and design methods. In other areas, Novosti had to maintain itself against competent rival agencies. One of these, the State Committee for Radio and Television, threatened to absorb Novosti's television section in the fall of 1976. Personnel from various departments of the two agencies were shifted and areas of control, particularly in dealing with foreign film and television enterprises, were redefined; overlapping areas remained.

In the face of fluctuating leadership trends since the Khrushchev days, Novosti's remarkable record for continuity has been at least partly due to the agency's first chairman, Boris Burkov, who retired in September 1970 at the age of 62. He reviewed his work in the journal *Za Rubezhom* (Abroad), January 8–14, 1965. He wrote that the agency's charter specifically stated, "The Soviet state organs are not responsible for the activities, financial obligations and other actions of the Novosti Press Agency." He noted that the agency not only employed large numbers of Soviet writers on either a full- or part-time basis but also used the services of such foreign writers as Pablo Neruda of Chile and James Aldridge of Great Britain. Burkov stated that Novosti material was widely used in the East European countries, as well as in North Korea and Vietnam. As he put it, "The press in the fraternal socialist countries daily utilizes our materials: summaries and commentaries, information and photo journalism. Articles by our agency have been distributed particularly widely in the socialist countries of Europe, to approximately 10,000 publications."

Burkov added that his agency also enjoyed "extensive business contacts with western press organizations." He listed major U.S. and European newspapers and periodicals, ranging from the *Washington Post* to the weekly illustrated *Stern* in West Germany. He stated that Novosti did not "propose to abandon either its socialist character nor its primary task," which was to advance the image of the Soviet Union, worldwide. Burkov noted that *Life* had devoted an entire issue to "the life of the Soviet people, with the help of our materials" and that a British publishing house had issued a multivolume work, *Sociology in the USSR*. He specifically mentioned the agency's extensive distribution of materials in Africa, Asia, and Latin America, where "the national liberation movement in these countries has become a tremendous revolutionary force in the development of mankind."

Among the countries of South Asia mentioned by Burkov, India was listed as particularly receptive; the Soviet illustrated journal *Soviet Land* was published in 12 of the Indian regional languages, as well as in English and in Nepalese. At the time Burkov's article was published, Novosti had

1,500 "active, permanent authors," in addition to thousands who contributed to the agency's publications or services regularly.

When Burkov retired, he was succeeded as chairman of Novosti by Ivan Udaltsov, who had been minister-counselor at the Soviet embassy in Prague during the time of Russia's military intervention in Czechoslovakia in 1968. He later served as deputy director of the Communist Party's Central Committee section that deals with ruling Communist parties. One of Novosti's most demanding tasks, completed on short notice, was to publish a daily newspaper, *Tydenik Aktualit,* in Czechoslovakia that was designed to persuade Czechs of the correctness of Soviet actions and policies.

The Novosti network of enterprises is so vast that even top-level agency personnel cannot really know, at any given time, how many projects are in operation. The *Great Soviet Encyclopedia,* as of 1970, reported that the agency published 50 illustrated magazines, 7 newspapers, and more than 100 information bulletins outside the Soviet Union. The APN photo service prepared more than 120,000 photographs per year, or a total of more than 2 million prints. Between 1965 and 1967, the agency's book publishing arm produced more than 35 million books, brochures, booklets, albums, and guides in Russian and in foreign languages. It also fulfilled 250 orders from foreign publishing houses in the preparation of books about the U.S.S.R.

By 1985, APN published in 45 languages in 140 countries, had bureaus and news offices in over 70 countries, and had part-time collaborators and contributors in many more. Among the best-known English-language publications produced by Novosti was the weekly *Moscow News,* which also appears in other major languages. Its editor was Gennadi Gerasimov, a man with extensive experience in the United States, who became head of the Foreign Ministry's Information Department, and thus a major Kremlin spokesman, in 1986.

One of Novosti's most skillfully edited and produced periodicals is the magazine *Sputnik,* clearly modeled after *Reader's Digest,* which excerpts articles, anecdotes, and cartoons from Soviet publications and reproduces them in a colorful, highly readable little magazine that is geared to worldwide tastes. The magazine is well illustrated and often features attractive displays of traditional and modern art. Similarly well produced is the glossy, oversized monthly *Soviet Life,* published in the United States by reciprocal agreement with the U.S. Information Agency, which distributes its Russian-language magazine *Amerika* in the U.S.S.R. *Soviet Life* abounds in full-page color photos of exotic settings, attractive people, and upbeat feature articles.

Novosti publications are designed to meet a variety of audiences, ranging from sports fans to scholars, from students to technicians. At the same time, allowances are made for geographic, national, ethnic, and linguistic variety. Of course, in all these publications the Soviet Union and those who favor its policies are presented in unrelentingly positive terms; conversely, critics of Soviet policies are denounced in more or less strident terms.

The very success that Novosti can claim for placing its material abroad can be, and has been, analyzed as a weakness in critical judgment on the part of editors, publishers, and the non-Soviet public. The biweekly newsletter *Soviet Analyst,* published in Great Britain, in its article "Novosti: Disinformation to Order" (October 16, 1975), accused the U.S.S.R. of "exploiting détente to promote the flow of disinformation to the West." The newsletter found it "disheartening to realize how weak defenses have become." It added: "The silly effusions of some Western journalists describing their conducted tours of the USSR are bad enough, but when universally respected Western publications accept misleading contributions from Soviet organizations, the need for greater vigilance becomes clear."

What had aroused the ire of *Soviet Analyst* was the fifteenth edition of the "highly reputable" *Encyclopedia Britannica,* which contained articles on Soviet republics written by scholars provided by Novosti. In a detailed review in the *Slavic Review* (vol. 34, no. 2), Prof. Romuald Misiunas of Williams College castigated the *Britannica* for having abandoned scholarly standards and permitted the intrusion of material that ignored relevant data while playing up doubtful material. The *Slavic Review* is a quarterly journal published by the American Association for the Advancement of Slavic Studies. Prof. Misiunas concluded, "The fifteen *Britannica* articles on the republics of the USSR are not reliable sources of information." Specifically, as only three of the fourteen writers selected by Novosti were clearly drawn from the non-Russian nationalities under discussion, it could not be claimed that the Britannica editors had preferred them as native scholars, better qualified than foreign specialists. *Soviet Analyst* observed that the encyclopedia entries contributed through Novosti had been "translated—often badly—from the Russian," rather than from such languages as Azerbaijani or Lithuanian, and that names and titles appeared neither in the original languages nor in English but as transliterations from the Russian. "Even more significant, however," the newsletter said, "is that terms such as 'democracy,' 'elections,' 'independence' and 'sovereignty' are used according to Soviet practice, without any warning to the unwary reader that this has little in common with Western usage." It added further:

"The innocent reader of the present *Encyclopedia Britannica* could easily gain the impression that the Kremlin and the Communist Party do not monopolize political power in the Soviet republics, and that recent decades have been a smooth march of social and economic progress by unanimously enthusiastic Soviet peoples. Had this dubious information remained unremarked, APN could clearly have claimed a considerable victory. But equally dangerous for the West is the manner in which Soviet 'experts' are frequently able to plant misleading and inaccurate propaganda in many reputable specialist journals normally read by prominent people with little experience in reading between the lines of Soviet prose." In later editions of the *Britannica,* other authorities were used.

On a more innocent level, Novosti prepared an attractive picture book, *Soviet Almanac,* which did not pretend to be anything but a glossy primer of the Soviet Union putting its best image forward. Printed in the United States under the direction of a New York book "packaging" firm and issued by a reputable trade publishing firm (see the bibliography), the work was a tribute to the professional and artistic quality of today's Soviet photographers and film processors. It also illustrated Novosti's marketing skill in utilizing Western commercial media channels and its ability to adapt to the standards and tastes of a contemporary audience.

With its manifold contacts abroad and given the Soviet Union's propensity to utilize all available channels to enhance the country's intelligence intake, it follows that Novosti has been linked with the activities of the KGB. In a dispatch to the *New York Times* (September 11, 1970), Bernard Gwertzman reported from Moscow that "because of its close contact with foreigners, particularly newsmen and editors," Novosti had been "accused of serving as a front for the secret police, but such a link has not been substantiated." Still, the crisscrossing of personnel to and from Novosti into other Soviet party and government agencies increases the likelihood that a segment of its personnel either is directly employed by the KGB or acts as a source or conduit for information to the secret police. To the degree that Novosti plants disinformation abroad, which originates more often than not with the KGB, the news-feature agency acts as the intelligence service's transmission medium.

Aside from the role Novosti played in the Swiss "peace movement" demonstrations, some of its representatives abroad have run afoul of local investigations. As early as April 1966, Kenya expelled several Soviet officials guilty of financing opposition groups. Novosti representative Yuri Kuritsin, accused of having directed one of the agents in this plot, was among four who were asked to leave the country. A year later, on June 6, 1967, Ghana expelled Novosti representative Aleksei Kazansev, charging that he had plotted to restore the exiled former President Kwame Nkrumah to power. Ghana police searched Kazansev's home and accused him of collecting information on governmental plans and projects.

A Novosti man, Georgi Bolchakov, played an important "back channel" role during the Cuban missile crisis in October 1962 for some of the messages between the Washington administration of President John F. Kennedy and the Kremlin leadership of Nikita Khrushchev. From 1959 to

1962, he was editor of the magazine *USSR,* a Novosti publication; although the U.S. government had not yet given permission for the opening of a Novosti bureau, Bolchakov openly identified himself as a Novosti staff member—in fact, after his return to the U.S.S.R. he emerged as chief of the agency's Television Film Department. Bolchakov's selection as a messenger of high-level data and opinion suggested that he was a KGB officer functioning within the framework of the Soviet Union's diplomacy-information establishment.

Considering the fact that the KGB most certainly briefs Novosti personnel in contact with foreigners within the U.S.S.R. or when traveling abroad, it would seem inevitable that at least some of the highly trained KGB personnel should be placed in strategic Novosti positions. A one-time military intelligence officer, presumably a GRU rather than a KGB man, Evgheni Ruzhnikov, who served in Germany following World War II, has functioned as head of Novosti's American Department. Another military intelligence man, Nikolai Dziveinov, formerly stationed in Canada, was also placed in the American Department. In the 1950s, Karl Nepomnikhchi had been identified as a KGB agent stationed in Vienna. When Novosti was established, he became chief editor of its International Information Editorial Board.

According to John Barron's well-documented book *K.G.B.,* an entire division of Novosti, known as the Tenth Section, "is staffed with K.G.B. men." Barron, as well as other sources, stated that the former British intelligence executive Harold ("Kim") Philby had worked for Novosti on the KGB's behalf. Philby's former colleague and fellow Soviet spy Donald MacLean has also been reported as serving with KGB-Novosti. Considering the professional standards shown by the Soviet news-feature service and the fact that it employs a large number of foreign nationals in its translation and editing branches, the use of such experienced men as Philby and MacLean is exceedingly likely.

Among others who have been identified as intelligence officers functioning for Novosti or under Novosti cover have been Yuri N. Paporov, formerly of the KGB's Counter-Espionage Directorate, who was stationed in Cuba for Novosti. Nikolai M. Borodin, who served as deputy director of the American Department of the KGB's Counter-Espionage Directorate (later known as the Surveillance Directorate, or Seventh Directorate) in 1946 and 1947, attended a UNESCO meeting in Paris in 1962, using Novosti correspondent credentials.

Partly because of its rapid expansion and partly no doubt because of high-level demands that Novosti serve the top priorities of the Kremlin at any given time, the agency's effort to appear "unofficial" could not very well be successful. Take the case of Boris Karpovitch, at one point assigned to the United Nations and finally expelled for participating in an espionage case that involved a member of the U.S. armed forces. Karpovitch, who was a deputy chairman of Novosti in 1962, was assigned to the Soviet embassy in Washington as information officer in 1963. In this position he carried out Novosti functions and, like Bolchakov before him identified himself as a Novosti man. But when it was discovered that he was identical with the KGB man who had been involved in the earlier espionage case, Karpovitch was declared *persona non grata* in 1965 and asked to leave the United States.

In later years, such public overlapping between KGB and Novosti functions became rare, as the news-feature service could draw on newly developed talent from its own ranks and train young professionals in writing, editing, film and video techniques, publishing, translating, and the intricacies of international media negotiations.

According to an account in *Trud,* the daily paper published by the All-Union Central Council of Trade Unions, Novosti's occasional subversive functions have, in at least one instance, been reversed. The paper published a long article (July 30, 1986) which, in a somewhat convoluted ironical manner, related that a Novosti correspondent on technical affairs had undertaken black marketing and profitable influence-peddling and engaged in industrial espionage for a West German firm which, the account alleged, served as a conduit for the German intelligence service, the BND *(Bundes-Nachrichten-Dienst).*

Titled "On Guard: Subversion!" the article stated that Ilya M. Suslov, tried before the Moscow Military District's Tribunal on June 16, 1986, was found guilty of having gathered and transmitted state secrets. According to this account, Suslov began his clandestine activities by passing himself off as a man of many contacts, conning foreign businessmen into paying him large sums in order to obtain official favors and contracts. As editor of Novosti's weekly *Sovetskaya Nauka i Tekhnika* (Soviet Science and Technology), Suslov had access to industrial specialists and legitimate reason to question them on their work. The *Trud* article castigated Suslov for passing "secret" information to the German firm of Karl Schanzenbach in Frankfurt am Main and criticized those in Soviet industry who talked to him too freely.

In April 1983, Novosti advanced one of its own, Pavel Naumov, to the top post of chairman of its Council of Sponsors. His predecessor for a period of seven years, Lev Tolkunov, became editor in chief of the government paper *Izvestia.* Naumov, born in 1919, had been on the staffs of *Pravda,* the periodical *Za Rubezhom* (Abroad), and the monthly *World Marxist Review.* He also served as editor in chief of the magazine *Novoye Vremya* (New Times).

On March 10, 1986, Valentin M. Falin was named to succeed Pavel Naumov as chairman of the board of Novosti. Naumov was not moved to another position but went into retirement. Tass, in reporting Falin's appointment, mentioned that he was of Russian nationality, born in 1926, and had been a Communist Party member since 1953. He graduated from the Moscow Institute of International Relations in 1950 and worked as a journalist specializing in international relations. Early in his career he worked at the Krasny Proletary metalworking plant. After working in the Ministry of Foreign Affairs, Falin served as Soviet ambassador in West Germany from 1971 to 1978. From then until 1983, he was deputy department head in the Communist Party's Central Committee. Most recently, he wrote a world affairs commentary for the daily *Izvestia*. He was awarded the Order of the October Revolution and three orders of the Red Banner of Labor.

Falin's Novosti appointment was received with considerable attention in West Germany. He had been a prominent figure in Bonn, where political observers had regarded his efforts as largely designed to steer German policies toward a path of independence from the United States. During a return trip to Bonn on May 30 he quipped, "I don't know what we can do to satisfy the Americans—perhaps we should become the 51st state?"

PART · 3

MEN AND MEDIA

CHAPTER · 17

The Rise and Fall of Mr. Z

Nothing illustrates the changes within the Soviet propaganda apparatus as dramatically as the career of Leonid Mitrofanovich Zamyatin. In addition, he personifies the degree of interchange between propaganda and diplomacy, between the Foreign Ministry and the Communist Party's Central Committee. In appearance, Zamyatin fits the standards of a motion-picture casting director: his steely blue eyes and wavy silver hair give him an air of toughness and competence, a no-nonsense executive.

In real life, Zamyatin's ruthless bravado has been both an advantage and a handicap. In the Kremlin's chess game of bureaucratic advance and survival, he reached the zenith when he was given his own section within the Central Committee: In February 1978, during the Brezhnev era, Zamyatin became director of the newly established International Information Department, separate and outwardly equal to the large and powerful International Department. He managed to retain this post, despite various storms of opposition, through the Andropov and Chernenko administrations and well into the Gorbachev regime. But then, at last, he was given a prestigious ambassadorial position as the Soviet Union's emissary to Great Britain.

When Zamyatin established the International Information Department, he had served as director of the Tass news agency for seven years. He managed to stay on in his Central Committee position not by being a smooth-talking, plausible apologist for Russian views and actions but by being abrasive, aggressive, and even insulting. His often undiplomatic manner prompted the West German paper *Süddeutsche Zeitung* to comment (January 15, 1983) that his personality guaranteed that "Soviet propaganda

215

in the West can have only limited impact." The paper's Moscow correspondent, Eduard Neumaier, wrote: "Zamyatin has managed, without any effort, to personify the very arrogance of power for which the Soviet Union is reputed."

Over the years, a Zamyatin legend of ill manners and lack of tact grew up in Europe. It seemed likely, therefore, that the soft-spoken Andropov, who succeeded Brezhnev, would remove Zamyatin from his sensitive post. Early in 1983, when Andropov was making major personnel changes in Soviet ministries, Moscow was awash in rumor that Zamyatin was about to become ambassador to Algeria. At that time, his right-hand man, Valentin Falin, was removed from the Information Department and became world affairs commentator at the government daily, *Izvestia;* under Gorbachev, Falin was named director of Novosti. According to Moscow gossip, Andropov summoned Zamyatin to a frank discussion—without any third person present—that lasted for half an hour. Zamyatin returned from the meeting, his position and prestige intact, just as blustery as before.

Once, during a press conference in Munich, Zamyatin was interrupted by a young Russian in the audience who reminded the speaker of the bloody history of the Soviet regime and recalled that his own father and mother had been killed as alleged enemies of the state. Zamyatin, furious, turned on the young man and told him savagely that it would probably have been better if he, too, had been done away with. When a German parliamentarian reported on his visit to resistance fighters in Afghanistan, Zamyatin told a German diplomat in Moscow that it was a pity the MP had not been shot and killed during his Afghan venture.

No matter what words of conciliation other Soviet officials might utter, Zamyatin could be counted on to play the heavy, hurl epithets, and put opponents on the defense by ignoring diplomatic niceties. He did this even when he traveled with top Soviet leaders abroad, as in Vienna in 1977 when he accompanied Brezhnev to a meeting with U.S. President Jimmy Carter for a joint signature of the SALT agreement; while others emphasized common efforts at disarmament, Zamyatin used the occasion for yet another diatribe against American policies and actions. Zamyatin has been particularly ebullient in German-speaking countries, probably because he was stationed in Austria and Germany for several years and speaks German fluently. He is also a UN veteran, familiar with intimidation tactics, as used by Soviet speakers in manipulating combined East European, Afro-Asian, and Arab voting blocs.

The notion that Zamyatin has served to alienate, rather than win over, world opinion was discussed by correspondents who covered Brezhnev's visit to Germany in 1981, on his way to meet the American delegation in Geneva. The encounter lasted for two days. Dusko Doder, Moscow correspondent of the *Washington Post,* reported from Bonn (November 25,

1981) that "the propaganda battle" was "clearly dominated" by Zamyatin, whom he described as "an exceptionally intelligent man who is brutally straightforward." Doder said, "With more than 1,500 journalists covering the event, Zamyatin's rendering of Soviet positions reached all parts of Europe and beyond." Zamyatin acted as spokesman for Brezhnev, while German Chancellor Helmut Schmidt was represented by the soft-spoken Kurt Becker, who tried in vain to emphasize areas of agreement and whose every effort at conciliation was repulsed or "corrected" by Zamyatin.

As Brezhnev was in delicate health when he made his trip to Bonn (wherever he stayed, an ambulance waited outside, and he died a year later), Becker tried hard to play up Brezhnev's well-being and stamina. He said that Chancellor Schmidt had been impressed with Brezhnev's ability to carry out the very extensive program of his visit. Becker also noted that Schmidt had sought to clarify the position of the United States and to emphasize Washington's willingness to negotiate with the Soviet Union on such outstanding issues as disarmament.

Hardly had Becker finished when Zamyatin offered "two observations" that did not so much refer to Brezhnev's mission as to Becker's statement. The Soviet Union, he said, was quite capable of judging the intentions of the United States, although Becker seemed to doubt its ability to make an independent judgment. And, as far as Brezhnev's health was concerned, he had shown his well-being by spending seven hours in talks the previous day. Members of the press wondered whether the Soviet interpreter had mistranslated Becker's remarks. They assumed Zamyatin had added the hours of Brezhnev's visit with members of the German parliament, on the second day, to those he had spent with Schmidt. Relentlessly, Zamyatin countered: "Apparently, this does not agree with you, but I represent the Soviet position."

Doder, whose dispatch appeared under the heading "Brezhnev's Point Man at Bonn: Soviet Press Spokesman Wins Battle of Briefings," said that Zamyatin's "message had several themes," of which one was "to play on European fear of war" by dramatizing the specter that U.S. missiles in Europe would "bring war closer to our homes." The other was "to question the rationality" of the American position on nuclear arms. Doder concluded: "The repeated challenges appeared to throw off balance the German spokesman, a courtly former journalist."

A German correspondent, Angela Nacken, wrote in the prestigious *Frankfurter Allgemeine Zeitung* (November 25, 1981) that Becker tried to reduce the tensions Zamyatin had created, saying, "Actually, no one among us is engaged in correcting the other one as being in error; we merely present our perceptions with considerable frankness." Becker had come with 65 pages of notes, well armed to brief the press; Zamyatin appeared simply to lecture the assembled reporters. Nacken observed: "One could never tell whether he was giving his own opinions or those of the General Secretary." She noted that Zamyatin even upbraided the then deputy director of the Soviet press service Novosti, Pavel Naumov, who tried to develop a Soviet propaganda point when he addressed the spokesman in Russian and spoke of the impression Brezhnev's remarks had made in the West. Impatiently, Zamyatin interrupted, "Can you come to your question?" Western reporters, dumbfounded, shook their heads.

To what degree was Zamyatin acting the big bad bear, or is it his nature to throw his weight around? Was he simply displaying the arrogance that comes with being the spokesman of a great military power? There is an old jocular question, "Where does a 600-pound gorilla sleep?" and the answer is, "Anywhere he likes." The big bad bear image, as a propaganda tactic, may use an air of contempt for the opinions of others, beginning with foreign journalists, to create uneasiness and fear. In turn, this might facilitate campaigns of intimidation. At the time Zamyatin displayed ill manners in Bonn, the Soviet Union was trying to persuade West Germany and the other NATO powers to resist the placement of U.S. medium-range missiles in Europe, which were to counter Soviet SS-20 missiles already in place in the East.

Leonid M. Zamyatin was born March 9, 1922, at Nizhnil Devitsk, now located in the Voronezh Oblast (region). He joined the Sergo Ordzhonikidze Aviation Institute in Moscow in 1939 and graduated with a degree in engineering in 1944. He switched from aviation engineering to diplomacy, continuing his education at the Higher Diplomatic School attached to the U.S.S.R. People's Commissariat of Foreign Affairs, graduating in 1946. At this time, he became a member of the Communist Party. During World War II, Zamyatin first served as a fitter in a factory and then had a defense industry position.

His career in foreign affairs began, at the end of World War II, with service at the Soviet embassy in Berlin from 1946 to 1950. His knowledge of English and later of German was particularly useful during various assignments with the United Nations. By 1950 he was appointed first secretary and then secretary of the Ministry of Foreign Affairs; from 1952 to 1953 he was deputy chief in the Ministry's Third European Department, responsible for Germany and Austria.

Zamyatin's UN career began in 1953, when he was appointed counselor to the U.S.S.R. Permanent Representation for Disarmament Questions. In 1957 he settled in Vienna as the Soviet Union's deputy representative in the Preparatory Commission for the International Atomic Energy Commission. Two years later, he became permanent representative with the rank of envoy extraordinary and plenipotentiary, second class. United Nations personnel who recall Zamyatin and his wife during their Vienna days speak of him as aloof but well-mannered.

Zamyatin's English also stood him in good stead when, in 1960, he was transferred back to Moscow, where he became deputy chief and, later, chief of the American Countries Department in the Foreign Ministry under Foreign Minister Andrei Gromyko. The switch to propaganda came in 1962, when Zamyatin was appointed chief of the Foreign Ministry's Press Department, a post he held until 1970. He had not come up the career ladder through journalism—although he joined the board of the U.S.S.R. Union of Journalists in 1966—and this showed in his confrontational relations with the foreign press contingent in Moscow.

In a profile of Zamyatin during this period, *New York Times* correspondent James F. Clarity wrote (January 14, 1970) that he was "much more than a mouthpiece for Soviet policy," being "considered close to the men who actually make policy in the Kremlin," serving as an adviser to Gromyko, and that he was "often observed leaving meetings of the Communist Party's Central Committee." During his then rare news conferences, correspondents crowded into 9 Kalinin Prospekt, the building where the ministry held such conferences.

At that time, although serving as head of the Foreign Ministry's Press Department, Zamyatin was, in Clarity's words, "virtually inaccessible to foreign correspondents," leaving reporters to the mercies of his department's staff, "a mixture of bright young men who speak the language of reporters they deal with and crusty veterans, who, for example, say a scheduled event is 'probable,' hours after it has been officially announced elsewhere." In this tradition of denial of the obvious, it was Zamyatin who kept insisting on the benign nature of the terminal illnesses of Andropov in 1983 and Chernenko in 1985.

"Mr. Zamyatin's aides will say that he is eager to meet a particular correspondent, and hopes to do so soon, but is simply too busy at present," Clarity wrote. "Under his direction, the assistants busy themselves arranging news conferences that often produce statistics from various ministries, but rarely news. The department also arranges occasional trips out of Moscow for selected groups of correspondents. Although there is no censorship of dispatches, Mr. Zamyatin's department has, and uses, means of retaliation against correspondents whose copy is considered objectionable."

Correspondents who aroused Zamyatin's ire were not invited on out-of-town trips; all travel of individual correspondents guilty of "distortions" was hampered. On occasion, Zamyatin warned correspondents who, for example, had written about dissidents, that they had displeased the Soviet authorities. He had the power to expel foreign reporters who questioned the Soviets' self-image.

During a press conference called by Zamyatin (January 13, 1970), a correspondent of the New China News Agency, Wang Chung-chieh, chal-

lenged the Kremlin spokesman on the issue of "freedom of the press."
This was during a time of severe tension between Moscow and Peking;
Chairman Mao Zedong was alive and his policies were unrelentingly aggressive. Correspondent Wang, wearing a Mao button, stood up and asked
Zamyatin rhetorically, in Russian, "Yes, freedom of the press, but what
does your press write? You are the head of the press department." Zamyatin, unruffled, merely said, "I know what the Chinese press writes."
At that time, Chinese newspapers were continuing a campaign that labeled
the Kremlin leaders as "Russia's new czars."

That same year, 1970, Zamyatin was made director general of the Tass
news agency. He held the post for seven years, a period devoted to further
modernization of the agency (see the chapters on Tass). The Tass appointment laid to rest such rumors as the possible appointment of Zamyatin to
be Soviet ambassador in Washington and the even more daring speculation
that he might replace Gromyko as foreign minister.

During his Tass years, Leonid Zamyatin served in other capacities as
well. He became a deputy in the Council of Nationalities in the Supreme
Soviet and a member of its Foreign Affairs Commission. From 1971 to
1976 he belonged to the Communist Party's Central Auditing Commission,
an overview body. In 1971 he became chairman of the Soviet–Federal
German Republic Section of the Parliamentary Group in the Supreme
Soviet, a position that provided Zamyatin with easy access to members of
the West German parliament. Similar contacts were facilitated when, in
1972, he became chairman of the U.S.S.R.–Federal Republic of Germany
Society, a section of the cultural propaganda network represented by the
Union of Societies for Friendship and Cultural Relations with Foreign
Countries. From 1975 to 1980 he served as a member of the Organizing
Committee for the 1980 Summer Olympics in Moscow.

In his years as a diplomat-propagandist, Zamyatin gave many interviews
and delivered numerous speeches. Among his topics were the role of the
press as a servant of the Communist Party, critiques of U.S. policies, the
NATO powers, armament, and foreign policy. He coauthored a book on
Georgi V. Chicherin, commissar for foreign affairs from 1922 to 1930.
Zamyatin supervised two documentary films on the life of Brezhnev. One
of these, *The Story of a Communist,* brought him the Lenin Prize for
Science and Art in 1978. Earlier, he had received the Order of Lenin in
1971 and the Order of Friendship of Peoples in 1980.

During the Brezhnev years, Zamyatin was part of the Kremlin's inner
circle, but he avoided the taint of corruption that adhered to this clique
and which later proved the undoing of other officials and of Brezhnev
family members. But Zamyatin's services to Soviet heads of state go back
to such historic events as the visit of Premier Alexei Kosygin to the United
States in 1967, including his meeting with President Lyndon Johnson at

Glassboro, New Jersey. One leading personality under whom Zamyatin served, and who himself outlasted numerous Politburo members while he gained in status, was Foreign Minister Gromyko; allowing for differences in style and temperament, the two men implemented identical policies for several decades.

Creation of the International Information Department within the Communist Party's Central Committee could not have taken place without the active support of Gromyko, nor could Zamyatin have achieved and retained his position as head of that department without that support. Particularly during the Andropov period, Moscow rumors were rife that Boris Ponomarov, head of the International Department of the Central Committee, resented the growth and influence of Zamyatin's new unit. According to Elizabeth Teague, Soviet affairs analyst in the Research Department of Radio Liberty, Zamyatin's International Information unit was "slow to get off the ground, but by 1980 it had gathered enough momentum so that hardly a week passed without a statement, article, or public appearance by one or another of its staff. Its role has been a very visible one, presenting the Soviet Union's policy on foreign affairs to audiences both in the USSR and abroad, with particular stress on Soviet-American and Soviet–West German relations." Paul A. Smith, Jr., in "Propaganda: A Modernized Soviet Weapons System," which appeared in the *Strategic Review* (summer 1983), noted that Zamyatin's department has "the command and control responsibility for all the overt information and cultural media of the USSR abroad. This includes print media, radio and TV broadcasting, exchanges, exhibits and a variety of other activities." Smith, then editor of *Problems of Communism,* published bimonthly by the U.S. Information Agency, noted that Zamyatin also acted "personally as a kind of high-level adviser and spokesman for the Politburo and as its general secretary on international communications." Although his target was the outside world, Zamyatin was also familiar to Soviet audiences, notably the television network show *Studio 9,* a current affairs interview program.

Zamyatin's ability to add a novel touch to standard propaganda themes, while at the same time pointing up the need for the existence of his own apparatus, appeared in his article "The Washington Crusaders" in *Literaturnaya Gazeta,* the weekly paper of the Soviet Writers' Union (June 30, 1982). The article alleged that the United States had begun an "ideological war" against the Soviet Union and that this warfare ran parallel with military and economic efforts to achieve its aims. This "war," Zamyatin said, resulted from the fact that "many Western politicians were forced to acknowledge the irresistible magnetism of Soviet foreign policy" and were turning to "misinformation, distortion of facts, political demagoguery, the invention of various myths, dissemination of malevolent information and

the clouding of people's minds with fears and suspicions." Zamyatin accused Washington and NATO leaders of "trying to divorce Soviet propaganda from policy," so as to show that "propagandistic subterfuge and
political packaging, not the content of policy," were swaying opinion. He
concluded:

"Policy and propaganda! They do not exist separately. They are or-
ganically linked, so that it can be said: whatever the policy is, such is the
propaganda. A militarist policy will not be saved by any sophisticated
propaganda. No peace-loving phrases are going to disguise the aggressive
essence of the imperialist policy of militarism and war—the policy of 'cru-
sades' against the USSR and socialism whose organizers have always ended
up on the garbage heap of history."

Zamyatin's combination of analysis and emotional outburst was put
into perspective by Ernst Kux, the Soviet affairs specialist of the Swiss
daily *Neue Zürcher Zeitung* (July 18–19, 1982). Noting that the effectiveness of Zamyatin's own international propaganda apparatus "had been
questioned in the Kremlin repeatedly since April 1979," Kux saw the article
as an effort to defend the position of the International Information Department against critics at home by raising the specter of a Western "psychological attack," designed to achieve not only military superiority but
also "superior strength in the area of ideology and propaganda."

An elaboration of Zamyatin's theme was published, in booklet form,
by the Novosti Publishing House in September 1984, with the title *The
Ideological Struggle and Questions of Peace.* It was extensively reviewed
in *Literaturnaya Gazeta* (November 21, 1984), which stated that it had
been written "passionately, vividly, convincingly and sharply." The Soviet
army paper *Krasnaya Zvezda* (Red Star) said on September 27, 1984, that
the booklet "will arm propagandists and agitators with new arguments."
Radio stations broadcast summaries and excerpts from the pamphlet. Zamyatin was getting his message across, as usual, including the theme that his
International Information Department was needed more than ever.

When Gorbachev's administration replaced numerous officials from the
Brezhnev-Chernenko eras, rumors again circulated that the abrasive Zamyatin was about to yield his post to a more conciliatory spokesman. But,
at first, instead of being jettisoned, Zamyatin accompanied Gorbachev on
his meetings with President Mitterrand of France and was at center stage
during the major Soviet public relations efforts at the Reagan-Gorbachev
summit meeting in Geneva. A new, relatively soft-spoken, and apparently
unsinkable Zamyatin had emerged.

Even before the visits to Paris and Geneva, Zamyatin appeared as a
central coordinator in a wide-ranging publicity offensive. He conducted an
elaborate press conference, held in the auditorium of Moscow's Foreign
Ministry Press Center, on October 22, 1985. Zamyatin was joined by Mar-

shal Sergei F. Akhromeyev, chief of the Soviet General Staff, and Georgi M. Korniyenko, a first deputy minister of foreign affairs.

While the press conference followed the general pattern of White House or Pentagon press conferences, Zamyatin was able both to control the nature of questions and, if necessary, to eliminate undesirable queries. Reporters submitted written questions which were divided among the three officials for reply. Later, correspondents had an opportunity to address questions directly to the officials.

Zamyatin began with a statement outlining the Soviet Union's "new proposals" on "nuclear and space armaments." He cited Gorbachev's Paris statements and said the U.S.S.R. was aiming at "preventing the development and deployment of strike space weapons and radically cutting the nuclear armaments of the USSR and the United States, which reach their respective territories." He said the United States would "never have a monopoly on space weapons." Subsequent questions, addressed to either Akhromeyev or Korniyenko, came from Soviet and Eastern European correspondents, as well as from Western reporters. Among the questioners were representatives of Japanese, West German, Belgian, Czechoslovak, and Bulgarian media.

Under Zamyatin's guidance, the press conference moved along smoothly, and the participants showed themselves adept at reinterpreting or avoiding embarrassing questions. When Korniyenko was asked to evaluate the personalities of Reagan and Gorbachev, he replied, with a tight smile, "I have not had time for psychological studies." Zamyatin, asked about the status of Marshal Nikolai V. Ogarkov, prominent after the shooting down of Korean airliner 007, said he had "not disappeared" but occupied "a high position in the Defense Ministry."

Philip Taubman, writing in the *New York Times* (October 30, 1985) compared the press conference with its counterparts in Washington and said that, in transplanting the format to Moscow, "the Kremlin has made some adjustments to assure that these sessions do not get out of hand, as they sometimes do in Washington." He added: "Providing the Government with a chance to restate the positions in a way that would produce international coverage, particularly on television, seemed to be the main purpose of the briefing, a motivation not unknown in Washington." Taubman observed that many auditorium seats were "occupied by men in dark suits who sat through the conference without jotting a note or showing the slightest interest. The men, representatives of various Soviet newspapers, turn out at most news conferences, apparently to fill the hall, so that television viewers will have the impression that such sessions attract an S.R.O. [standing room only] audience." Zamyatin thus created a pattern that was later utilized by other Foreign Ministry spokesmen, such as Vladimir Lomeiko and Gennadi Gerasimov.

The Moscow press conference set the scene for Gorbachev's visits to Paris and Geneva; in both instances, Zamyatin played an important role. Prior to his trip to France, Gorbachev gave a Kremlin interview to four French television reporters; Zamyatin was credited with arranging this crucial and unprecedented exposure of the increasingly publicized Soviet leader. On October 29, Zamyatin gave the key address at a Kiev meeting of Agitprop workers from the Russian and Ukrainian republics, devoted to "ideo-educational work in labor collectives."

At the Geneva summit, Zamyatin frequently appeared seated to the right of Gorbachev, with only Foreign Minister Shevardnadze and Ambassador Anatoli Dobrynin in between. The meeting enabled the Zamyatin team—with Georgi Arbatov and Lomeiko participating—to organize several press briefings before the summit began. The presence of some 3,000 media representatives provided a ready-made audience at the city's huge International Conference Center.

Zamyatin's newfound suavity was tested during one press briefing when Irina Grivnina, cofounder of the Committee to Investigate Psychiatric Abuses, spoke in defense of Soviet citizens sentenced for "anti-Soviet agitation." Representing the Dutch magazine *Elseviers,* she addressed Zamyatin: "Can we talk about the prisoners who have been tortured in the Soviet psychiatric hospitals?" Red-faced and angry, Zamyatin called her remarks "provocative," threatened to stop the press conference, and said: "Within the Soviet Union, political prisoners do not exist."

Zamyatin cooperated, at one point, with his American counterpart, White House spokesman Larry Speakes. When they agreed to withhold reports on the substance of the Reagan-Gorbachev talks, Zamyatin checked with Gorbachev while he was posing for photographers. A White House official noted that "Zamyatin said to him in Russian what the proposal was" and that Gorbachev, who never looked at the propaganda director, said immediately, "We'll do it."

The general air of goodwill that had been achieved by Reagan and Gorbachev did not affect the long-range war of words emanating from Moscow and directed at U.S. policies. Upon his return to Moscow, Zamyatin immediately helped to reorchestrate the propaganda line. Just so there would be no misunderstanding of the Geneva outcome, a meeting of Eastern European officials took place at Bucharest, Romania, in late December. Billed as a conference on "international and ideological questions," secretaries of the Communist Party Central Committee were brought together for a detailed briefing. Zamyatin shared the limelight with Ponomarev.

On January 18, 1986, the team of Korniyenko, Akhromeyev, and Zamyatin again appeared at a Moscow press conference; it was devoted to General Secretary Gorbachev's proposal on nuclear arms control, made three days earlier. The press conference was notable for a large-scale diagram behind the speakers' rostrum, with the heading "USSR Proposal of a Program for the Complete Elimination of Nuclear Weapons in the Whole World by the Year 2000." Moscow Television broadcast a 30-minute excerpt from the conference.

Soon afterward, rumors that Zamyatin would have to give up his post and that the whole International Information Department would be dismantled could be heard in Moscow journalistic circles. But Zamyatin remained active in various directions. On January 8 he gave an interview to the Kuwaiti paper *Al-Qabas,* commenting on Near Eastern affairs and saying, among other things, "The United States and some of its NATO allies are using the Iran-Iraq conflict as a pretext for escalating their military presence in this vast region." On February 11, the Beirut paper *Al-Safir* published a lengthy interview with Zamyatin, containing a denial of reports that the Soviet Union was planning normalization of diplomatic relations with Israel, as well as increased Jewish emigration. He said, "Rumors of this kind are intended to upset Soviet-Arab relations and to give rise to doubts about Soviet policy." A few days earlier, on February 7, Zamyatin had visited Finland and addressed a meeting of the Peace Supporters of Finland, again echoing the Gorbachev proposals. He was also prominent during the party's 27th Congress.

On April 25, Tass finally reported that the Presidium of the Supreme Soviet had appointed Zamyatin ambassador to Great Britain, relieving the retiring Viktor Popov. The diplomatic correspondent of the *Guardian,* London (April 29), noted: "Even if the Kremlin has promoted Britain as a target for Soviet diplomacy, it is widely assumed that Mr. Zamyatin himself has suffered a demotion and is being sent away from Moscow as part of Mr. Gorbachev's efforts to replace many of the key figures of the Brezhnev era with officials more attuned to his policies." While details remained clouded for months, the new arrangement amounted to a merger of Zamyatin's international information setup with the Central Committee's traditional Agitation and Propaganda section, combining domestic and foreign propaganda under the committee's newly appointed secretary, Alexander Yakovlev, the former ambassador to Canada.

As Zamyatin was presenting his credentials in London, news of the Chernobyl disaster reached Great Britain, and television cameras greeted him as he left No. 10 Downing Street, the residence of the prime minister. Zamyatin sought to reassure reporters that Western reports had greatly exaggerated the extent of the nuclear accident. On June 3, he gave a press conference in which he denounced U.S. policies on nuclear weapons and said that Great Britain and the Soviet Union had "a very good experience of cooperation." He added subtly: "We think that Great Britain has its own point of view on many international issues and problems." Clearly, Ambassador Zamyatin had no difficulty in combining diplomacy and propaganda.

CHAPTER · 18

Scholar or Propagandist?

The man and his title are imposing: Academician Georgi Arbatov, director of the United States of America and Canada Institute, U.S.S.R. Academy of Sciences. True to these credentials, Arbatov travels in the highest academic and opinion-making circles throughout the world. He can be cordial, on occasion, but his manner is usually authoritative, at times condescending, and he gives every impression that he does not suffer fools gladly.

Georgi Arbatov is the prime example of that new Soviet breed, a crossbreed actually: the scholar-propagandist. He is very much in command of his material, which is the United States of America with all its lights and shadows—mostly shadows—and he has facts and opinions quickly at his fingertips and on his tongue.

Arbatov, a heavyset man with prominent jowls, is balding, bluff, and tough. He can play his own mind, vocal cords, and vocabulary like an instrument that is fine-tuned to the themes and variations of Soviet power politics. He operates from the vantage point of specialization: He knows the strengths and weaknesses of American parliamentary democracy in minute detail, and he ramrods the force of Soviet propaganda against it. At the same time, Arbatov has shown himself capable of his own brand of sweet reasonableness, particularly when seeking to ally himself with the opposition to Washington policies, be they those of Democratic President Jimmy Carter or those of Republican President Ronald Reagan.

During the Carter years, Arbatov forcefully attacked the U.S. position on Soviet human rights violations and plans for development of the B1 bomber; during the Reagan administration, his main thrust was directed against U.S. efforts in the field of military preparedness. His positions were packaged by a Dutch journalist, Willem Oltmans, who compiled a book out of Arbatov's answers to 150 questions Oltmans asked during visits to Moscow from 1979 to 1981. Subsequently, in an English translation, the book appeared in the United States under the title *The Soviet Viewpoint.* Former U.S. Ambassador to the Soviet Union Malcolm Toon, writing in the *Washington Post* (May 8, 1983) commented that it was the kind of book that gave him "an acute case of dyspepsia," because it provided "the sort of effective propaganda platform for our Soviet adversary in this country that is consistently denied us in the Soviet Union." He added:

"Most of us who have dealt professionally with the Soviet Union have long envied the access to American media and academe freely accorded to Arbatov and other Soviet spokesmen who masquerade as 'independent' but who, in fact, are fierce protagonists and apologists for official Soviet policies and behavior. I personally would give my eyeteeth for an opportunity to respond to questions from a friendly interlocutor, have them recorded in book form in the Russian language, and then have the book freely and widely distributed throughout the Soviet Union with ringing endorsements by, say, Supreme Soviet deputy Boris Ponomarev and Georgi Arbatov himself as required reading for every thinking Russian."

Toon noted that "such a format would be roughly parallel" with the opportunity given Arbatov, whose book appeared with an introduction by Senator J. William Fulbright. Another reviewer, Joseph Sobran, commented in *National Review* (March 18, 1983) on Arbatov's "sophistication about American liberalism." Sobran noted that "he speaks its idiom with near-perfect nuance," avoiding old-fashioned, hackneyed words such as "running dogs" or "Wall Street lackeys," while using agreeable terms such as need for "reciprocity," search for "mutually acceptable solutions," and avoiding "confrontations." The reviewer noted that "despite the bland language," Arbatov showed himself as "plenty aggressive, consistently denigrating the United States, just as consistently justifying the Soviet Union."

People wanting to be fair, wanting to "give the other side a hearing," might well listen with attention to the way in which Arbatov put his case concerning American self-centeredness: "I've observed many times how difficult it is for Americans to put themselves in other people's shoes, or even to imagine the consequences of American actions for others. Sometimes I think that it is not only the dubious intentions and vested interests of some Americans that cause some of the problems that are of foremost importance today, but also their inability to look at life through the eyes of the other side. We have already discussed, for instance, how the United States, in evaluating Soviet military power, ignores the real threats faced by the Soviet Union and then shouts about the 'Soviet threat.' I don't think the United States fully understands its allies either." Arbatov added, "American ignorance about the Third World is even greater."

Large audiences, notably at colleges throughout the United States, might well nod their heads when hearing such comments and even applaud vigorously—not out of political masochism or for reasons of opposition to Washington policies, but because of a feeling that the speaker was at least half-right. And half-right he might well be on these and other points, but there was surely another side to the story: the Soviet leadership's own tunnel vision and its inability to see the world through eyes other than its own.

Toon said he respected Arbatov as "an astute, albeit subjective, observer of the American scene and an accurate purveyor of the official Soviet line, but," he continued, "I have never ceased to be amazed at the man's consummate arrogance and gall; and I have long been disturbed by his one-sided assessment of the world scene and the impact of this on Soviet leaders, with many of whom Arbatov is well-connected." Toon was referring to Arbatov's position as Moscow's leading Americanologist and his potential influence on top Soviet policies.

Ideally, a scholarly institution of American studies in the U.S.S.R. would be totally objective, staffed by political scientists, sociologists, psychologists, and others who were dedicated to the detached monitoring of U.S. events and personalities. The dual function of the institute, however, as a catch basin for U.S. data and as a manufacturer of propagandistic ammunition can lead to risky distortions.

The dual aims of the institute are well reflected in its monthly journal, *SShA: Ekonomika, Politika, Ideologiya,* whose title initials stand for the Russian words *Soyedinennye Shtaty Ameriki,* or "United States of America." In issue after issue of the journal, which began publication in February 1970, articles and reviews deal with American topics and events, historical as well as contemporary, but rarely are these without an obvious ideological-propagandistic slant. Visitors to the institute are impressed by the competence and courtesy of staff members, but the aim of the institute is clearly not the purely academic collection of data, topped off by cautious analyses.

The institute grew out of the traditional Marxist practice of "criticism and self-criticism," which in 1967 prompted the Central Committee of the Communist Party to question the quality of social science studies in the U.S.S.R. Sociology and psychology had struggled through crisis after crisis during successive Kremlin policy periods, but "research for research's sake" had never emerged as a commanding slogan. Yet pure research is the baseline of science, and knowledge of the United States—if accurate even to a degree—might certainly be valuable to the Soviet leadership.

Thus when the United States of America and Canada Institute was established within the U.S.S.R. Academy of Sciences in 1968, it was viewed as unique. No other country had been singled out for such concentrated study; the addition of Canada to the institute's scope was seen by staffers and visitors as designed to diffuse its U.S. orientation by giving it a "North American" label.

For Georgi Arbatov, establishment of the institute and his own prominent, many-sided position as its director were the high points of a lively career. He was born on May 19, 1923, in Kherson, the Ukraine. According to official biographies, he served in the Soviet army from 1941 to 1944 and graduated from the Foreign Ministry's Institute on International Relations in 1949. He began his study of English early and worked as an editor-translator in the Foreign Language Publishing House in Moscow. During the 1950s, Arbatov functioned as an editor or contributor for a number of prominent periodicals. Among these were the leading ideological quarterly *Questions of Philosophy,* the Communist Party's central monthly, *Kommunist,* and the magazine *New Times,* published in several languages for an international audience.

Moscow's influence on the international Communist movement has, since Lenin's day, been through leading journals: During the existence of the Third, or Communist, International (Comintern), parties and followers throughout the world were guided by *Communist International* and *Inprecorr* (International Press Correspondence); when the Comintern was replaced, the new Information Bureau of Communist and Workers' Parties (Cominform) issued a weekly paper with the awkward name *For a Lasting Peace, For a Peoples' Democracy!* When the Cominform, in turn, was disbanded, the International Department of the Soviet Communist Party initiated a monthly magazine, *Problems of Peace and Socialism,* published in Prague in 26 languages (its English-language edition is called *World Marxist Review*). It was on this journal that, from 1960 to 1962, Arbatov served as editorial adviser or, as official biographies termed it, "political observer." He then worked, for two years, in a related capacity as head of the Ideological Section of the Institute of World Economics and International Relations.

In these activities, Arbatov appears to have been closely associated with the International Department of the Communist Party's Central Committee and its long-time director, Boris Ponomarev. In a number of propaganda campaigns, Leonid Zamyatin's International Information Department has dealt mainly with Western European target nations, while Arbatov concentrated on the United States and Ponomarev's department specialized in liaison with Communist parties abroad, as well as with fraternal "liberation movements." Yet overlapping between the responsibilities of these three men and their offices has been unavoidable.

One specialist who has worked closely with Arbatov said about his position: He "is too smart to endanger his own prominent and rather enviable position by getting into power struggles with someone as senior and well-entrenched as Ponomarev. I think that people abroad, and particularly Americans, tend to exaggerate his influence. All this talk of how the Politburo listens to Arbatov's analyses of the American scene is exaggerated. In order to give him an entree in U.S. governmental and academic circles, people in Moscow tolerate Arbatov's self-advertisements and his sly hints that he has been a close adviser to everyone on top, beginning with Brezhnev, then Andropov and finally Gorbachev. In essence, Arbatov is a skillful propagandist who is shrewd enough to wear the mantle of a high-level, behind-the-scenes policy-maker."

If Arbatov is, in fact, more a traveling salesman of Soviet policies than a scholar who has the ears of Kremlin leaders, his staff, nevertheless, is well equipped to compile both scholarly data and propaganda material. From a nucleus of about fifty hand-picked younger specialists, gathered from other government and party bodies, as well as from institutes of higher education, the institute has grown into a staff of several hundred English-speaking specialists.

When the institute was first set up, it met with misgivings among the Moscow bureaucracy, partly because it did not seem to apply serious academic standards, partly because it was suspected of being yet another KGB operation, and partly for reasons of routine bureaucratic rivalry. As in every Soviet operation of some significance, KGB involvement can be assumed; but the institute appears to use largely overt information, gathered from the ample supply of American publications and from interviews with U.S. personalities, either in the United States or during their visits to the U.S.S.R. That copies of certain reports and analyses are forwarded to the KGB, just as they are to the Foreign Ministry, to various departments of the Central Committee, and to the Institute of International Relations, should be regarded as a matter of routine.

The United States of America and Canada Institute occupies a building on Khlebny Lane, a quiet street in one of Moscow's older sections, known as Arbat. Inside, the mixture between scholarship and up-to-date propaganda techniques can be seen and felt. The institute's well-stocked library ranges from historical volumes to contemporary U.S. best-sellers. It subscribes to a wide selection of scholarly as well as popular periodicals and newspapers, its filing cabinets contain folders on topics ranging from textile mills in the south to voting patterns in Oregon. The institute maintains a computerized data bank of information on U.S. personalities and events. The clatter of a teletype machine and the presence of current U.S. newspapers, ranging from the *New York Times* to the San Francisco *Chronicle,* on researchers' desks give the place an air of immediacy.

During Arbatov's frequent absences, operations are in the hands of three deputy chiefs. The institute has one department that deals with U.S. policies at home and abroad; a second department is exclusively concerned with current and future economic development; a third is known as the Ideological Section. According to Galina Orionova, who was on the institute's staff from 1969 to 1979 as a specialist on U.S.-Japanese relations, the head of the Ideological Section is a KGB general, Radomir Bogdanov. This section originally contained a unit dealing with U.S. military affairs, headed by General Mikhail Milshteyn, a retired GRU, or military intelligence, officer. As Orionova recalls it, rivalry between Bogdanov and Milshteyn became so disruptive that the military unit was transferred to the policy section. General Milshteyn's face is familiar to American television audiences, as he occasionally appears as one of the English-speaking Soviet specialists on network talk shows and news programs, usually simply identified by his title and without any reference to the institute, and most certainly without any mention of his GRU background. He is said to have been on the staff of Marshal Georgi K. Zhukov during World War II and later taught methods of intelligence gathering and evaluation at a military academy. Bogdanov frequently appears on English-language broadcasts.

The special public role of Arbatov emerges because it broke the tradition that Soviet officials were either unapproachable or taciturn. The late Mikhail Suslov, the tall, lean, Spartan ideologist whose commanding position ranged from the Stalin years through the Brezhnev period—and who was largely responsible for Khrushchev's fall and Andropov's rise—never talked to outsiders. Even as widely traveled a diplomat as Gromyko largely avoided interviewers. But Arbatov is everywhere.

If the Italian daily *La Stampa* of Turin quotes a high Soviet official as saying that many European governments "are beginning to reflect" and are listening to the Soviet view of nuclear disarmament, the official is Arbatov (January 23, 1984). If the Finnish Communist newspaper *Kansan Uutiset* quotes "a senior Soviet adviser on North American affairs" as saying that "it is high time for initiatives and concrete steps from Europeans," that adviser is Arbatov (March 16, 1984). If the French Institute of International Relations hears a "Soviet scholar" say that American policies of "anti-Sovietism and anti-Communism have consisted solely of setbacks and have sustained a complete political and moral defeat," that scholar is Arbatov (March 23, 1984).

And so on, apparently quite fresh and spontaneous, while carefully remaining within the framework of current Kremlin policies, Arbatov's words can be read throughout the world in interviews ranging from the *Washington Post* to Moscow's political TV program *Studio 9*, from CBS-TV to the Bulgarian paper *Rabotnichesko Delo*.

The conditions under which he gives interviews illustrate the ease with which Arbatov absorbs fluctuations in Soviet policy; partly, this can be attributed to the fact that much of what he says is repetition, but it also testifies to self-assurance, an excellent memory, and his acknowledged position as a skilled spokesman. One reporter, Jonathan Power, who interviewed Arbatov for the *International Herald-Tribune,* the newspaper published in Paris jointly by the *New York Times* and the *Washington Post,* wrote (November 11–12, 1978) that their talks began "over lunch in a Moscow restaurant and continued in Mr. Arbatov's office" at the institute until 7:30 in the evening. He added: "An hour was spent the following day tying together loose ends. Altogether, I recorded five hours of conversations. It was on the record, done without notes on Mr. Arbatov's part, and without notice of questions. He answered every question I put to him. I mention this, because the number of occasions on which high Soviet officials have been interviewed in this way, at this length, is exceedingly rare."

While rare in the case of other officials, it was fairly routine for Arbatov. Power noted that the institute's position has prompted various interpretations, ranging from categorizing him as a high-level adviser to labeling him as "a source of 'disinformation'—the Soviet Union's sophisticated propaganda voice who briefs Western journalists and parliamentarians in gentle tones that belie the true nature of the harsh self-interest of Soviet power."

Arbatov is equally familiar with live audiences, be it an appearance before representatives of his election district, at Shemakhinski, where he appeared as "candidate deputy" for the U.S.S.R. Supreme Soviet of Nationalities (February 24, 1979) or at the Massachusetts Institute of Technology (MIT), where he spoke of U.S. human rights policies as a return to the "cold war" (April 13, 1977). Even in his talk to the electorate, where he ran—of course—unopposed on the single-party ticket, Arbatov spoke on world affairs and ranged from Soviet-U.S. relations to Russian difficulties with China.

Arbatov's appearance at MIT was only one of many talks to college and university audiences. For the most part, Washington officialdom watched his wide swath of lectures, press interviews, and television talk show appearances with studied detachment. In spring 1981, however, the U.S. State Department decided that "reciprocity" should no longer be ignored. The occasion was Arbatov's visit to the United States, which began on March 25, with a visa that expired on April 5. He made a number of appearances, but when he requested that his visa be extended so he could appear on PBS's *Bill Moyer's Journal,* the State Department refused:

"Soviet officials, including Dr. Arbatov, have made frequent appearances on American television in recent weeks. Americans have no access to Soviet television or other Soviet media. Our Embassy in Moscow has repeatedly asked that our Chargé d'affaires, Jack F. Matlock, Jr., be allowed to appear on Soviet television, but so far without success. Given the lack of reciprocity, we consider it inappropriate to grant the visa extension to Dr. Arbatov solely for the sake of another television appearance."

Later in the month, the State Department asked Arbatov not to speak to reporters during his appearance in Des Moines, where he was giving two talks at Grinnell College, followed by appearances at an arms control conference in Denver and addresses to business leaders at Des Moines and at the University of Iowa in Iowa City. Arbatov was also a guest at a symposium on U.S.-Soviet affairs, the Dartmouth Conference. In all, he spoke to gatherings of more than a thousand people, addressed breakfast and luncheon meetings, and gave local interviews to the Des Moines *Register* and an Iowa PBS station.

Writing in the *Washington Post* (May 2, 1983), Philip Geyelin noted that prominent Americans listened to Arbatov, "not so much because they believe what he has to say, but because what he has to say is generally taken to be what the Soviet would have us believe is their official line at any given time." He commented that Arbatov served "as a sort of rough barometer, well worth checking for significant changes in attitude or atmosphere." Reporting on a dinner arranged by the Carnegie Endowment for International Peace in Washington, Geyelin wrote, "There was, therefore, a large turnout of distinguished figures from the State Department, Congressional committee staffs, academia, leading local think tanks, television and the writing press when Arbatov did his familiar number."

Geyelin expressed the view that the State Department's restrictions on interviews with Arbatov were "petty and pointless." He questioned the wisdom of denying press contacts as being "contrary to the purposes for which his visa had been issued." To ask for "reciprocity," he added, amounted to a demand that "the Soviets have a free press—which is to say, an open society. And that in turn, is to say that the Soviets should stop being Communists."

Another columnist, Ernest Conine, in the Los Angeles *Times* (April 6, 1981), acknowledged that Soviet spokesmen had free access to American media, no matter what the State Department ruled. He added: "The U.S. Government does have a right and a responsibility, however, to do what little it can to nudge the Soviet Union into making such exchanges a two-way street." He wrote: "It would be a mistake to think that American demands for reciprocity have had no effect. For example, the Cultural Exchange Program, though loaded a bit in the Soviet favor, also has contained elements of value to this country, thanks to U.S. demands for balance. The United States has demanded, and got, acceptance of the principle that American news media are entitled to the same number of correspondents in Moscow that the Soviet Union maintains in Washington. U.S. military attachés in Moscow would not be able to rove beyond the city limits if the Soviets did not know that equal restrictions would then be imposed on their attachés in this country." Conine concluded, "Arbatov's high position and prestige guarantee that the Administration's message will be heard, if not immediately heeded, in Moscow."

Aside from his position as director of the United States of America and Canada Institute, Arbatov holds party and government posts. In 1971 he obtained a seat on the Central Auditing Commission of the Soviet Communist Party; the commission oversees the qualifications and performances of party members, and it is responsible for promotions and demotions. Arbatov became a full member of the U.S.S.R. Academy of Sciences, somewhat belatedly, in 1974. He belongs to the Permanent Commission on Foreign Affairs of the Council of Nationalities of the U.S.S.R. Supreme Soviet. In 1976 he became a candidate member of the Communist Party's Central Committee.

Georgi Arbatov's busiest period began shortly after Gorbachev came into power. The new general secretary's own flair in using public relations techniques for diplomatic ends gave new impetus to the Soviet propaganda campaign. During Gorbachev's interview with the editors of *Time*, for example, Arbatov sat directly to Gorbachev's left. Just before Reagan and Gorbachev arrived at the Geneva summit in November 1985, Arbatov was part of an overworked Soviet public relations team. On November 15 he participated in a mass briefing of the press. Stopping on his way to a lecture at a Geneva institute, he explained to Pierre Salinger of ABC and Marvin Kalb of NBC, "But I already gave my word to CBS. They were first!"

Before, during, and after the Geneva meeting, Arbatov sat through interview after interview, gave lecture after lecture, and boarded and exited planes. Having spent some of his student years in Hamburg, he could talk to editors of the German weekly *Spiegel* and the Swiss journal *Weltwoche* in German. In between, and ending on October 25, Arbatov spent two weeks on an "academic visit" in China, meeting scholars in Peking and Shanghai, and stopping briefly in Shenzhen, Communist China's special zone of economic modernization. In between came appearances on Moscow TV's *Studio 9*—even an interview by the equally versatile Vladimir Posner on Radio Moscow's English-language transmission to North America, recorded before Arbatov left for Geneva.

The unique occasion presented by the Posner-Arbatov encounter, with one propagandist interviewing another, can be gauged by the questions Posner asked, every one perfectly designed to permit Arbatov to reiterate major points of Soviet policy at well-timed length. Posner asked, to start with, "Dr. Arbatov, what would you single out as the salient features of the forthcoming summit in Geneva?" Next, Posner asked, "How would you characterize, in essence, the approach to the summit of the Soviet Union and on the part of the United States?" Not surprisingly, Arbatov answered, "I would characterize it as a very different one, even opposing," and continued for another three minutes to embellish this point. Posner then put this question: "Dr. Arbatov, speaking of extremists in the [Washington] administration, there seems to be a view that the Soviet Union will have to limit its arms, limit arms, and cut back on arms because of the situation in the economy and that, therefore, arms limitations and arms reduction are only in the interest of the Soviet Union. What is your opinion about that view?" Arbatov allowed that this viewpoint was "wrong and very primitive" and explained why. Posner concluded: "A final question, which people are talking about most nowadays: What do you expect from the summit? Would you care to predict its outcome?" Arbatov anticipated that the Geneva meeting would offer a "moment of truth."

After his return from Geneva, Arbatov in numerous appearances and interviews summarized the summit results, mixing optimism with caution, calling upon the "Geneva spirit" to be translated into deeds—and co-hosting a three-day meeting of the American Council of Learned Societies' and the Soviet Academy of Sciences' Joint Commission on the Humanities and Social Sciences in Moscow (December 3 to 6, 1985).

On December 18, at a Moscow news conference, Arbatov said that President Reagan had "an almost religious dream" that an antimissile shield could prevent a future nuclear war. Continuing to speak of Reagan, Arbatov said, "I have no reason to doubt his sincerity." On February 10, readers of the *New York Times* found an article by Arbatov, "Moscow's View on Nuclear Testing," on the paper's Op-Ed page.

Once again, he seemed to be everywhere: India, Hungary, Bulgaria, Czechoslovakia, the U.S.S.R., and Spain. In New Delhi, Arbatov appeared as a member of the Independent Commission on Disarmament and Security, where he addressed a press conference on January 21. The Budapest Radio broadcast an interview with him on February 10. The Hungarian reporter noted that the Arbatov office was in the former palaces of Princess Volkonski, and the atmosphere reminded him of Tolstoy's novel *War and Peace.* He picked up the lastest propaganda label and asked, "Georgi Arkadyevich, what is new in the New Globalism?" Arbatov told him: "Its unprecedented utopianism and adventurist character."

Next came an interview for the Sofia daily *Rabotnichesko Delo* (February 24), and another for the Czechoslovak radio station in Bratislava, in the Slovak language (February 26). During the 27th Communist Party Congress, Arbatov took note of the assassination of Swedish Premier Olof Palme. He recalled that they had last met in New Delhi. "He and I argued a lot," Arbatov said, "but we agreed on many issues. But whether we argued or agreed, I always deeply respected him." This was followed by an interview given to the Madrid daily *El Pais* (March 2). When the Spanish reporter said, "But the United States cannot be blamed entirely for the

Cold War. Has the U.S.S.R. not made mistakes too?" Arbatov acknowledged that "nobody is perfect" but added quickly that the United States
had "deliberately strayed from the path of détente, of honorable agreements."

On March 3, Arbatov spoke at a Moscow press conference. On March
11, the newspaper *Trud* in Sofia, Bulgaria, printed his analysis of the Soviet
Communist Party Congress, "Strategic Course toward Universal Security."
The same day, *Komsomolskaya Pravda*, Moscow, published an Arbatov
interview under the headline "It Is Not Too Late: The World Is Too Fragile
for Wars." That day, too, the board of the United Nations Association of
the U.S.S.R. elected Arbatov as its chairman. On April 8, Arbatov was
in Washington, representing the Soviet UN Association in a meeting with
its U.S. counterpart.

A month later, on May 5, Japanese audiences could see Arbatov on
their television screens in an English-language interview on the NHK television network. Part of the broadcast recorded Arbatov in the task of
downplaying reports on radioactive fallout from the Chernobyl nuclear
accident. Three days later, his face appeared on Polish television. One
question was, "You often appear on U.S. television. Do you get any
feedback from it?" Arbatov replied: "I do. It is said that if Arbatov appears
there, Americans should appear before us. They complain of inequality.
But for every one of my words about the Soviet Union there are a thousand
American words. But I don't complain; it is their television, after all."

Arbatov survived the major personnel changes in the Soviet propaganda
apparatus throughout 1986, and continued to combine his academic and
propagandistic abilities with maximum exposure.

CHAPTER · 19

Chameleon on a Tightrope

Viktor Louis looks around his sumptuous villa, furnished lavishly and with innumerable expensive gadgets, and says defiantly, "I work harder than other Russians. That's why I have all these things." The "things" include a swimming pool, a tennis court, and a Swedish-made sauna. His villa is located in Peredelkino, a short train ride east of Moscow, best known as a writers' colony and home of the late poet-novelist Boris Pasternak, author of *Dr. Zhivago.* Louis's sumptuous *dacha* was formerly the residence of Marshal Pavel S. Rybalco, a tank force commander who died in 1948.

Louis did, by all appearances, come by his luxurious lifestyle the old-fashioned way: he earned it. And he earned it by a mixture of enterprises unique not only in the Soviet Union but just about all over the world. Conspicuously, Louis acts as a highly informal channel for information—or disinformation—which, in one way or another, advances Soviet aims.

Louis denies all this. He wants to be regarded as just another "professional journalist," and he cultivates his relations with the Moscow foreign press corps and with writers abroad. According to the autobiographical fragments he dispenses to visitors, he was born in Moscow on February 5, 1928, and his full Russian name is Vitali Yevgenevich Lui; he says that his great-grandfather was a Frenchman and that this accounts for the "Louis," a Western version of his name.

Young Louis served as a messenger for several foreign embassies after the end of World War II. His longest employment was for the embassy of Brazil, but he also worked for the New Zealand embassy. He may also have been employed by the British, and Louis has told visitors he was arrested outside the British embassy "for political reasons" and sentenced to 25 years of forced labor. Three years after Joseph Stalin's death, in 1956, Louis was released from the labor camp and took up the study of law at Moscow University. A chance meeting at the university led to Louis's acquaintance with Jennifer Stratham, then a governess with the family of the British naval attaché.

Today the couple make a smooth-working team. What special charms do Viktor and Jennifer Louis have that no one else in Moscow possesses? They get away with an awful lot that would land other people in prison, and that includes trading in works of art. Harrison Salisbury, veteran *New York Times* specialist on Soviet affairs, recalled in his autobiography, *A Journey for Our Time,* that he first met Louis in 1959 at his apartment in the then new Cherymukha quarters on Moscow's outskirts. Louis ostensibly sought Salisbury's advice on a motor travel guide he was then compiling. He and Jennifer had toured the country by car the previous summer; he told the American correspondent, solemnly, "You can imagine how many times we were arrested by local police."

Once they had finished discussing the guide, Viktor Louis tried to sell Salisbury one thing after another. First, it was a transcript of the Writers' Union session that had expelled Pasternak; but Salisbury knew that Louis had already sold the same text to a *Time* magazine correspondent, and he "wasn't going to buy a secondhand pup." Next, Louis tried to sell him works of art. Salisbury recalled:

"It was a moment when dissident artists had just appeared on the scene. I knew that Viktor had introduced Western buyers to the artists (who were then often called in by the police). I didn't show much interest, so he brought out a portfolio of gouaches by an artist named Rabin, who was much in vogue among the diplomatic colony. When I didn't want to buy a Rabin, Louis was stunned. 'You must have a Rabin,' he said. 'Everyone has one. I'll give you one.' Hurriedly he shuffled out a half-dozen dreary-looking gouaches. 'Here, take your choice.' I selected one of the least obnoxious. Louis beamed. 'That's a fine one,' he said, examining it. Then he hastily pulled it back. 'My God!' he said. 'He forgot to sign it. You can't have an unsigned Rabin.' He took out a pencil stub, wet it with his tongue and put a neat initial 'R' into the corner."

Every foreign correspondent in Moscow has a Viktor Louis story, and the man himself seems to wallow in his notoriety and conspicuous consumption. At last count, he had a Porsche, a Mercedes, and a Land Rover in his garage. Louis shows off these possessions exuberantly. During a visit to New York he was intrigued by a $2,500 popcorn machine, and asserted that his main attraction in the city was the Hammacher-Schlemmer specialty shop, a garden of gimmickry.

Within the Soviet Agitprop machinery, Louis's role is chameleonlike. In conversation he can switch from ingratiating bonhomie to solemn defense of Soviet policies. And while his personal propaganda technique mixes suavity with good-fellowship ("As you can see, we're not such monsters, after all, right?"), his duties as a propagandist have included major political targets. Through his typewriter and his telexes to London and Paris, Louis has been able to convey dire Kremlin warnings, launch trial balloons, and make the incredible sound plausible.

Louis's usefulness to his Soviet superiors comes from the fact that his articles appear in a number of Western publications, some of them major; in turn, Western editors are impressed by Louis's Moscow contacts, whoever they are, which permit him to come up with exclusives and provocative analyses. His major outlet in the West was, for many years, the London tabloid *Evening News*. This paper was absorbed by *The London Standard,* another lively Fleet Street evening daily. Why did *The Standard* retain Louis, despite his notoriety?

According to Charles A. Garside, news editor of *The Standard,* "The situation is that Viktor Louis still files for us on the same freelance basis that operated when he was correspondent on the *Evening News.* Several executives on the *News,* including myself, came to this paper after the *News* closed, so contacts with correspondents such as Mr. Louis were maintained." What does the paper get out of its Louis connection? Garside says that he has "benefited" the paper "in many ways—not least giving us the world exclusive on the Soviets' decision to pull out of the Olympic Games" in Los Angeles in 1984.

In his book *KGB,* British author Brian Freemantle wrote: "When it had the largest circulation of any evening newspaper in the world, the now defunct London *Evening News* was the natural outlet and Louis wrote for it, with the Russians actually content for the West to know he was an official source! Frequently—satisfied his stories would be recognized and accepted as official—policy was planted and acted upon. A story in the *Evening News*—picked up and repeated in Australia, where the Communist Party has links as strong with Peking as it has with Moscow—that the Russians did not wish to exacerbate a confrontation with the Chinese at their border at the Ussari River, was sufficient for a relieved China to de-escalate their apparent belligerence."

Louis's Agitprop role in the ups and downs of Moscow-Peking relations has at times been startling, beginning in 1968 and continuing for more than a decade. Estrangement between the two giant Communist-governed nations began during the reign of Stalin, continued during the governments of Khrushchev and Brezhnev, and settled down to uneasy mutual tolerance after Mao died.

Louis became active in the war of nerves Moscow waged against Mao's government when he visited Taiwan, the seat of Nationalist China (Republic of China) in October 1968. He called on the son of President Chiang

Kai-shek, Defense Minister Chiang Ching-kuo, who succeeded his father upon his death. Louis also had talks with senior intelligence, psychological warfare, and economic officials. He later wrote an article, published in the *Washington Post,* that suggested better economic and diplomatic relations between Moscow and Taiwan. Richard Hughes, writing in the *Sunday Times*, London (May 11, 1969), noted that Louis had been granted "the first visa for a Soviet citizen" to visit Taiwan "in the role of correspondent for the London *Evening News.*" What he discussed with Chiang remained a secret, and "Louis—strangely for a journalist—never reported the interview for his paper."

Later that year, Louis caused worldwide consternation with an article in the *Evening News* (September 18, 1969) that raised the possibility of a Soviet military attack on its Chinese neighbor: "Whether or not the Soviet Union will dare to attack Lop Nor, China's nuclear center, is a question of strategy and so the world would learn about it afterwards." Noting that the Soviet Union had, only a year earlier, sent its tanks into Czechoslovakia under the so-called Brezhnev doctrine that would give the U.S.S.R. the right to act in such a manner whenever and wherever a "fraternal" regime was in danger, Louis wrote: "The fact that China is many times larger than Czechoslovakia and might offer active resistance is, according to these Marxist theoreticians, no reason for not applying the doctrine."

The Soviet affairs analyst of the *Guardian*, London, Victor Zorza, whose articles also appeared in the *Washington Post* and other papers, wrote (October 1, 1969) that Louis had been selected to engage in this particular skirmish of psychological warfare "because, if the Kremlin were to say it directly, in *Pravda* or in a diplomatic communication to China, it would lay itself open to the charge of warmongering, and that it was using the threat of aggression as an instrument of policy." The Louis article was summarized by Western news agencies and published in hundreds of newspapers in all parts of the world.

In several dispatches in October 1978, Louis kept nudging Mao's successors to fall in line with Soviet policies. On October 29, he wrote in the *Evening News* that there were clues at the Soviet-Chinese border indicating a softened Chinese attitude. In a report datelined from the border town of Blagovechensk on the Amur River, Louis stated that anti-Soviet slogans had been removed from walls of the Chinese town of Ai-Hui, across the river. As a further sign that "Russia and China will once again be friends," he noted that passengers on riverboats of both nations were waving to each other and that Chinese officials had visited a border railroad station and had accepted a drink of vodka. He commented that, while these might seem to be slight indications of a thaw, it was notable that U.S. Secretary of State Henry Kissinger regarded a rapprochement between China and the Soviet Union as not in American interest.

But by 1979, the carrot Louis had been waving transformed back into a stick. China was engaged in an armed border conflict with Vietnam, the Soviet Union's leading surrogate regime in Asia. This time Louis used another Western vehicle for his foray in psychological warfare, the West German *Bild*, a sensational daily of large national circulation. On March 2, the paper published this dispatch:

"The following is being discussed in the West: Will the Soviet Union intervene militarily in Indochina to help its ally Vietnam against the Chinese? In my opinion there is hardly any doubt that the Soviet Government will not let the matter rest with sharp words and threats unless China ends the war as quickly as possible. The Soviet Union has always stood loyally by its allies.

"Another question also has been raised in the West: Can the Chinese win the war? I do not think so. Their obsolete arms (some of them more than 20 years old) from Soviet arms production are totally inferior to those of the Vietnamese. Vietnam has highly modern war material from captured U.S. Army stocks, and the Vietnamese are continuously supplied with the most modern Soviet arms. Sooner or later the question will come up as to who is teaching whom a punitive lesson.

"Many Chinese units are surrounded on Vietnamese territory. The Vietnamese are using tactics developed by the Russians during the last war: cutting their supply lines. I am sure that the Chinese, at the end of this war, will have suffered a bloody loss, and, for a long time to come, will not have the strength to mount another military attack."

Characteristically, Louis's analysis asserted that he was answering questions being asked in the West rather than actually reflecting Soviet intentions. In his answers he appeared to give merely a personal opinion, saying "I do not think so" and "I am sure . . ." His dispatch, clearly designed to intimidate the Chinese, was part of a concerted propaganda attack. Kevin Klose, reporting from Moscow to the *Washington Post* (February 19, 1979), stated:

"The Soviet Union stepped up its propaganda campaign against the Chinese invasion of Vietnam today amid an unconfirmed report here that the Red Army has been placed on a national alert, with leaves cancelled and soldiers recalled to their units. The intensified media campaign includes battlefield accounts in the newspapers and on television, angry letters, and wide publication of statements of outrage over the invasion by many world capitals."

Klose explained that reports of a high alert for the Red Army had circulated as the result of a dispatch by Louis to the *Evening News* but that Louis had told Western correspondents there was no official basis for this news—his university student son, presumably Nikolai, had been told of leave cancellations by a friend and he had picked up "village gossip" in Moscow. Klose commented: "Nevertheless, an actual Army alert—or even a spurious report that takes on a life of its own—could do much to achieve the Kremlin's apparent aim to look tough, talk tough, but avoid acting tough and getting into a military action with the Chinese."

The pinnacle of Louis's role in Moscow's anti-Chinese campaign came later the same year, in a book with the title *The Coming Decline of the Chinese Empire*. By that time, tension between Peking and Moscow had reached a crisis point. Soviet leaders may have expected the successors of Mao Zedong, who died in 1976, to accommodate the U.S.S.R., based on common Marxist-Leninist ideology. However, historic political and geographic factors continued to feed Chinese fears that Russia sought to encircle China, to isolate and weaken it. In particular, Peking regarded the stationing of formidable Soviet forces at its northern borders, the Russian campaign in Afghanistan, and its encouragement of Vietnamese control over Laos and Cambodia as proofs of such an encirclement policy.

Louis's 1969 dispatch, implying the threat of Soviet attack on Chinese nuclear installations at Lop Nor, may have been a factor in bringing together Chinese Premier Chou En-lai and Soviet Premier Aleksei Kosygin in Peking in September of that year. But ten years later, China felt that Vietnam was acting too aggressively as Moscow's pawn in Southeast Asia and decided to "teach them a lesson." This resulted in undeclared border warfare between Vietnam and China. Soon Russia was trying to threaten Peking into pulling back but refrained from any kind of warfare, even the type of border incident that had previously occurred at the Ussuri River.

Louis's book, an unprecedented prognosis of how the "Chinese Empire" could disintegrate or be dismantled, closed with the anticipation that "future developments will show how soon the national aspirations of the Manchu, Mongols, Uighurs, Tibetans, and other non-Chinese peoples who today are incorporated territorially in China can become reality." The book presented a highly selective survey of Chinese history and of the minorities within China's borders. It alleged that their cultural and ethnic identities were being suppressed by the Han Chinese, expressed sympathy with their fate, and suggested that the Soviet Union might encourage the creation of ethnic "buffer" states between its own borders and those of a presumably much truncated "imperialist" China.

Louis's book aroused a great deal of interest. It differed from the many publications within the Soviet Union, some in foreign languages, that dealt with China in similar terms, as it was written in English and published by Times Books, then the book publishing division of the *New York Times*. The publishers, aware of the author's notoriety, decided to issue his book, as it were, with a built-in antidote, a "dissenting introduction" by Harrison Salisbury.

This introduction was, in itself, remarkable in that it represented an angry denunciation of the text it accompanied, calling it "a book of spurious content, dubious logic, flagrant untruth." Salisbury labeled the work "a political perversity seldom seen," from the pen of a KGB man who presents "a rationale intended to justify a Soviet 'war of liberation'—God help us—against the People's Republic of China." He noted that Louis's writings were "particularly relevant in light of China's recent incursion into Vietnam" and that he had, "obviously, been under special orders to engage in propaganda directed against" China. He added: "This, in itself, is of interest because it reveals the seriousness with which the KGB regards the China question and the importance it sees in assigning a top agent to that field." Salisbury, who ten years earlier had written *War between Russia and China*, in which he warned that the dangers of such a conflict were "demonstrably great," viewed the Louis work in the context of Moscow's annual output of "twenty to thirty separate works" on China, "some a mixture of scholarship and propaganda, and some genuine scholarship." He defined the Louis book as "something quite different and, in a sense much more important, for he has not bothered with minor falsifications. Instead, he has attempted to construct the Big Lie."

Essentially, Louis's thesis was that China's minorities occupy 60 percent of its territories, but he ignored the fact that they make up only 5 percent of the population—while, in the Soviet Union, non-Russians represent more than half the total population. If anything, the disequilibrium Louis projected on China applies much more accurately to the U.S.S.R. Salisbury concluded that Louis had provided "a pseudohistorical, pseudopolitical framework to justify whatever aggression the Kremlin decides upon."

Louis himself put it this way: "The granting of independence to the people of Manchuria, Mongolia, Eastern Turkestan, and Tibet, apart from bringing about a just solution of the nationalities question, would largely remove the threat of Chinese expansion toward the adjacent territories." Apparently, the pattern he envisaged was that presented by Outer Mongolia (Mongolian Peoples' Republic), a technically independent nation whose status nevertheless differs little from that of the various "republics" of the Soviet Union, ranging from Latvia to Azerbaijan. Louis recalled that the concept of "setting up a system of buffer states around China was advanced by Lenin." Lenin, he said, had received a delegation of the People's Revolutionary Party of Mongolia and "especially emphasized" Mongolia's role "as a kind of buffer." Louis added:

"Lenin's idea has by no means lost its significance even today. What is more, in the present-day international situation this concept could relate not only to Mongolia but also to an entire chain of independent state entities which could arise out of China's outlying territories. A token of the realization of those peoples' desires for independence is provided by the centuries-old tradition of statehood which all those peoples have, as well as their unending struggle against Sinification and for their national self-determination and independence."

Early in 1985, when Vietnamese troops launched yet another major attack in Cambodia (Kampuchea), fighting once again erupted on the China-Vietnam border. The Soviet Union denounced Peking in strong terms. As long as such tensions exist, the threat of Soviet action against China's military installations, or its encouragement of ethnic independence movements, remains current. Louis's propagandistic ammunition continues to provide a ready stockpile for future use.

Louis's function as a propaganda missile against Peking represents only one major aspect of his activity. And while he misses his targets just about as often as he scores hits, some of his scoops have been impressive. It was Louis who first reported in 1964 that Premier Khrushchev had lost the struggle for power in the Kremlin and would be forced to retire. Subsequently, Louis was instrumental in enabling NBC to present the television documentary *Khrushchev in Exile: His Opinions and Revelations*. The camera showed Nikita Khrushchev inside and outside his suburban residence; it accompanied him on a walk and showed him practicing his hobby, photography. NBC's documentary, in the summer of 1967, coincided with an article in *Parade* magazine (July 9, 1967) that contained material similar to that of the television program. The article's author, Jess Gorkin, wrote that "occasionally an old friend will make an appointment to chat" with Khrushchev at his *dacha*, "but his many ex-colleagues, even though they live nearby, stay away from this political leper."

One "old friend" who apparently made several visits appears to have been Viktor Louis, who also played a key role in the preparation and sale of a book published under the title *Khrushchev Remembers*. Just how this was done remains a mystery, even many years later. One translator-editor of the Khrushchev memoirs, Strobe Talbott, later diplomatic correspondent of *Time* magazine, stated in 1984: "Certain constraints under which we were operating with regard to the origin of the memoirs were lifted when Nikita Sergeyevich [Khrushchev] died [in 1971] and we brought out the second volume." Asked about Louis's role in the Khrushchev memoirs, Talbott added: "Certain constraints remain. These include a restriction against discussing with anyone how—and through whose intermediation—the book found its way to us."

The late Stewart Alsop wrote in *Newsweek* (January 4, 1971) that the Khrushchev memoirs had been permitted to be published in order to weaken the political position of then premier Leonid Brezhnev. This, he explained, had been made possible by the intervention of a mysterious "Mr. X," powerful enough to attack Brezhnev by letting Khrushchev's reminiscences

concerning Stalin, to whom Brezhnev had fallen heir, be aired. Alsop
outlined this scenario:

"Initially, the key role was played by Khrushchev's daughter, Rada,
and by her journalist husband, Aleksei Adzhubei, editor of *Izvestia* until
Khrushchev's downfall. Rada and Aleksei recorded the old man's rambling,
often inaccurate, frequently farcical and utterly fascinating memories of
the past. At some point, probably in 1969, the omniscient Soviet secret
service, the KGB, learned what the Adzhubeis were up to, and thereafter
a remarkable figure, Viktor Louis, entered the picture. There is no doubt
at all that Louis is an agent of the KGB, but he is not at all an ordinary
agent."

After describing Louis's lifestyle and propagandistic escapades, Alsop
reported that Louis negotiated an agreement with Time-Life for the sale
of the Khrushchev reminiscences, for about $600,000. He wrote that the
deal "was signed and sealed at a meeting between Louis and *Life* executive
Murray Gart in a Copenhagen hotel room." Other sources specified the
Hotel d'Angleterre. The deal "included a provision for the deposit of a
large sum of money in a Swiss bank in the name of the Khrushchev family."
Alsop called the book "a specific attack on policies with which Brezhnev
is closely identified" and noted that it therefore had to enjoy the protection
of "a Mr. X strong enough to defy Brezhnev."

Historically seen, the only man who could have held such a position
was Yuri Andropov, then the KGB's chairman or director. During the
behind-the-scenes power struggle that preceded Brezhnev's death, Andropov engaged in a number of maneuvers designed to weaken the position
of Brezhnev, his family, and close supporters by revelations of corruption
among acquaintances of Brezhnev's daughter, Galina Churbanova, and
her husband, General Yuri Churbanov, deputy minister of internal affairs.
If this assumption is correct, Louis functioned under the protection and
direction of the sophisticated and ambitious Andropov when he marketed
the Khrushchev memoirs, and presumably in other instances as well.

This does not mean that Andropov was Louis's direct superior, or even
that he was, in the strict meaning of the term, a KGB agent or staff member;
but it does suggest that Louis was regarded as a useful conduit by men in
high places and that he has been skillful and lucky in choosing his masters
or being chosen by them.

Another far more controversial—and a good deal less successful—
manuscript export project was undertaken by Louis after Svetlana Alliluyeva, Stalin's daughter, defected to the West in 1967. She was about to
publish her book *Twenty Letters to a Friend* when Louis appeared on the
international publishing scene, bearing a second copy of Alliluyeva's manuscript, a collection of Stalin family photographs, and some supplementary
interviews and analytical articles. While Louis maintained, with a straight

face, that this material had been given to him by Alliluyeva's family, it seemed perfectly clear that it must have been removed from her Moscow apartment with the help of KGB agents who seized and searched it as soon as Alliluyeva's defection to the U.S. in New Delhi became known. The KGB-Louis effort was apparently designed to undercut the public impact of Alliluyeva's writings, on the eve of the fiftieth anniversary of the Bolshevik Revolution, and to reduce the public standing of Stalin's daughter.

David Binder of the *New York Times* interviewed Louis (August 9, 1967) in Hamburg, where he was negotiating with the illustrated weekly *Stern*, a magazine which gained international notoriety years later when it began publishing the forged "Hitler diaries." Louis had started his sales trip in London, where the *Evening News* proved to be a limited market for his Alliluyeva material. He wrote about her brother, Vasily Stalin, and her son, Joseph. He sold photographs to the *Daily Express,* left the book manuscript behind, and went to Hamburg.

Louis said he had obtained some 50 photos from the "Stalin family" and denied he was acting as a representative of the Soviet government: "Why don't people believe me? Why should I be the scapegoat? Everyone expects that I should be a Soviet agent. Why can't they believe I am a professional journalist? Why couldn't I ask the family for the material? It is ridiculous to say I couldn't get it from friends." While the Alliluyeva manuscript and family pictures were more or less authentic, the same could not be said for an interview that Louis said he had with Alliluyeva's aunt, Anna Redens; she had died several years before the purported interview.

Stalin's daughter, in her second book, *Only One Year,* recalled that her defection from the Soviet Union had created consternation in Moscow and that the Soviet government had hoped that Louis might scoop Alliluyeva on her own memoirs. She wrote that his version developed "the chief points of Moscow's propaganda" by calling her "a crazy nymphomaniac and her father's closest assistant." Alliluyeva wrote that her "innocent flirtation" with a film scenario writer, Aleksei Kapler, when she was about 17 years old, was blown up into a "passionate affair with orgies." Louis also published interviews with Alliluyeva's ex-husbands, although she gathered from the content that he had never met them.

More serious perhaps was an interview that Louis alleged to have had with Alexander Solzhenitsyn before this noted Russian writer was deported from the Soviet Union and ultimately settled in the United States, establishing his family in Vermont. Louis denied trying to sell Solzhenitsyn's novel *Cancer Ward* in the West without the author's permission. His "interview" appeared in the *Washington Post* and in the *International Herald-Tribune* (March 12, 1969) with an editorial caution that it "should by no means be considered an interview authorized by Solzhenitsyn," but as shedding light on his position at the time and on "the ambivalent attitude toward him on the part of the Soviet official circles to whose moods Louis has been uniquely sensitive.''

The interview, published under the title "A Conversation with Russia's Most Controversial Writer," centered on whether Louis had smuggled the *Cancer Ward* manuscript to the Russian-language publishing firm of Grani in Frankfurt, West Germany. Solzhenitsyn was quoted as protesting his ignorance of how his writings had been smuggled abroad, as many of them had been by that time. Louis wrote that the author "can probably boast more admirers, friends and enemies than any other writer in the Soviet Union." Louis commented that Solzhenitsyn was "singularly obsessed" with the topic of life in Soviet prison camps and that this was "probably" one reason why "his works do not appear in Russian magazines."

Among Louis's odd assignments was that of companion to the Russian underground writer Valeri Tarsis, who had been declared insane by Soviet psychiatrists and permitted to emigrate to the West. Louis accompanied Tarsis to London, where he described himself as "a sort of public relations officer for Mr. Tarsis," whom he later categorized as merely a "third-rate writer." Herbert Gold, the author, who had met Louis in Moscow and later was his host in San Francisco, wrote in the *New York Times Magazine* (January 31, 1971) that the Tarsis affair was a "counterploy" developed by Louis to defuse international anger over the persecution and imprisonment of other Soviet writers. According to Gold, Tarsis had been "shipped to the West as a proof that, look, we're happy to get rid of these malcontents. 'See? We don't keep these people. They want out? See, he's out!' Who rode nanny alongside Tarsis when he arrived in London? Busy Viktor Louis, smiling and explaining. You see, he wants to go—good! Goodbye!"

In the late summer of 1984, when Western observers of the Soviet scene were becoming increasingly alarmed about the health and whereabouts of Soviet dissident physicist Andrei Sakharov, Louis intervened in his tried-and-true fashion: He provided pictures and even a videotape, designed to show Sakharov alive and well. Operating, this time, out of a hotel room in Zurich, Louis traded photographs once again to the West German paper, *Bild*; the videotape was sold for $67,500 to ABC television, which had outbid CBS.

The film, which ran for 20 minutes, gave strong indications of having been spliced together from earlier pictures, with a contemporary narration and up-to-date touches. *Newsweek* (September 3, 1984) referred to the tape as "a KGB home movie," which Louis had first sold to *Bild* and which the German paper, in turn, sold to ABC-TV. The magazine, which spoke of the film as a "tawdry little documentary," noted that it nearly always showed Sakharov and his wife apart and that all natural sound had been replaced by tendentious narrative. Shortly afterward, Louis wrote in *Bild* that Sakharov had been released from a hospital, had joined his wife at their Gorki apartment, and was "healthy again." On October 16, 1984, *Bild* carried the following text: "Kremlin confidant Viktor Louis has denied reports that civil rights advocate Sakharov (63) is once again performing nuclear research for the Soviets and in this job is exposed to dangerous radiation. Louis told *Bild*: 'Academician Sakharov is doing scientific work of his own, dating back to earlier times. As before, he is not allowed to leave the town of Gorky, nor is his wife, Yelena Bonner. Both are still living together in the same apartment.' " For months, then, Louis had been the only Soviet source of information on the dissident Soviet physicist. At a time when Sakharov's family, his colleagues abroad, and much of Western public opinion were concerned that the physical and emotional strains of his exile, together with a hunger strike, had seriously endangered his health, Louis acted as a profit-making purveyor of the Soviet version of the physicist's condition.

The *New York Times,* in an editorial (August 27, 1984), noted that the Sakharov tapes had been made available through Louis, "the Soviet operative who often serves as unofficial press broker for the KGB." The very creation of this "suspect Soviet response," the paper added, showed that Western alertness had caused concern in Moscow, which proved that there should be no letup in the "agitation over the Sakharovs or the thousands of dissenters wasting in jails and mental hospitals for the crime of free thought."

Western attention to the Sakharovs, and the ambiance created by the Reagan-Gorbachev meeting at Geneva in 1985, apparently prompted Soviet authorities to permit Sakharov's wife, Yelena, to visit the West for medical treatment. She remained abroad from December 1985 to May 1986, receiving treatment for vision problems and coronary bypass surgery. Her passport was granted on the condition that she would refrain from giving interviews. She did, however, gradually make public statements that confirmed Western information on her husband's confinement, treatment, and conditions. Specifically, she accused Soviet authorities of "disinformation" and singled out Viktor Louis as the main conduit of such reports.

Apparently in an effort to counteract Yelena Bonner's statements, another crop of alleged Sakharov quotes and pictures made its way to the West while his wife was abroad. At a time when Soviet propaganda techniques were growing increasingly sophisticated and major personnel changes took place within the Kremlin's information apparatus, the largely discredited Louis-type methods continued to be used. After the 1986 nuclear accident at Chernobyl, a film clip showing Sakharov answering questions on nuclear safety was shown on British television on May 29. He referred to destruction of the U.S. space shuttle *Challenger* and said: "The West has exaggerated Chernobyl. Out of Chernobyl and Challenger, these were both tragedies. That's life." He also seemed to say that nuclear accidents in Britain and the United States had not received sufficient attention.

On her return trip from the United States, during a stopover in Rome, Yelena Bonner told a press conference (May 30) that such films were part of the KGB's disinformation campaign. She said about her husband that "in recent years the world has only received false information about him." She called Louis the "acme" of disinformation. The day before Louis had given an interview to Reuters, the British news agency, in which he called the physicist a "normal patriot," whose wife was endangering his chances of returning from exile, as she had become "a politically outspoken figure, helping forces hostile to the Soviet Union."

Louis said that "it's not his behavior, it's hers" that was creating difficulties. "He wants a quiet life," he added, "but she would start calling press conferences." While Yelena Bonner was abroad, Louis said, Sakharov's attitude had "pleased everybody." He noted that although General Secretary Gorbachev had ruled out Sakharov's emigrating to the West, because of his knowledge of secret Soviet research, a return from Gorki to Moscow was not ruled out.

Gorbachev himself acted to resolve the abrasive public relations problem created by the Sakharov case when he telephoned the exiled physicist on December 16, 1986. Gorbachev told Sakharov that he would be permitted to return to Moscow, "to work for the public good," and that his wife, who had been convicted of "anti-Soviet activities" in 1984, would be pardoned. Sakharov planned to resume research at the Physics Institute of the Soviet Academy of Sciences.

Louis had represented his own role consistently as that of an aggressive, professional journalist. Always sensitive to criticism, he once upbraided the editors of *Problems of Communism*, a journal issued by the U.S. Information Agency, for publishing biographical data which, he said (November–December 1969), presented him in "the most unsympathetic light."

Abraham Brumberg, then the journal's editor, answered Louis's protests item by item, and then wrote: "To begin with, I am struck—as have been many others before me—by Mr. Louis' pained incredulity at the thought that anyone would question his claim to being just an ordinary 'professional journalist.' There are many professional Soviet journalists in Moscow, but none of them was eager to see me after I had been denounced in *Pravda* (August 6, 1969) as a 'key intelligence agent' (on the fanciful ground that I had gathered intelligence information while lunching with Czechoslovak writers in Prague in the summer of 1968.) Mr. Louis, however, seemed to have no qualms about getting together with me, even insisting that I visit him at his dacha in an environ of Moscow which foreigners are forbidden to enter. And surely no professional Soviet journalist would think of offering—as Mr. Louis did in his personal conversations with me—to *write* for a magazine repeatedly described by the Soviet press (most recently in the August 16 issue of *Izvestia*) as 'one of the key instruments for subversive activity against the Soviet Union and other socialist states.' "

Brumberg then reviewed Louis's lifestyle and resources, including his bank accounts in hard currencies in the United States and Western Europe and activities that could hardly have been undertaken by a mere "professional journalist." He also cited Article 153 of the Criminal Code of the Russian Republic whereby "activity as a commercial middleman carried on by private persons as a form of business for the purpose of enrichment" is punished by "deprivation of freedom for a term not exceeding three years with confiscation of property."

Brumberg emphasized that it was not, of course, his intention to portray Louis as an actual "criminal," particularly as "most of his entrepreneurial activities would strike a person living in a non-Communist country as perfectly sound and normal," nor did he question his luxurious lifestyle. In fact, like others, he found Louis "personally quite charming." Still, as long as Louis was doing things that were "patently denied to his fellow citizens," Brumberg concluded, "and so long as he refrains from explaining his seemingly privileged status in Soviet society, his claim to being 'only a professional journalist' will continue to be a puzzle to all concerned."

Viktor Louis is many things, and some of his activities are certainly journalistic. Visitors have found, behind his extroverted bonhomie, moments of wariness and caution. In any event, as top Soviet personnel shift, Louis must be forever on guard to monitor and anticipate the tastes and policies of his superiors. He is a chameleon on a tightrope.

CHAPTER · 20

The Smoothest of Them All

It is Sunday morning, and all over the United States, postbreakfast television viewers are tuned to talk shows from the nation's capital. Against a familiar landscape that includes the White House, the Lincoln Memorial, and the Capitol Building, the craggy face of David Brinkley arrives in living rooms from New York to San Francisco. With him is the tried-and-true team of ABC television reporters-commentators, and in the Washington studio is a former Soviet UN diplomat, Arkadi N. Shevchenko. Another participant in the discussion of U.S.-Soviet relations is a major grain-trade executive, Dwayne Andreas, chairman of the Archer Daniels Midland Corporation. Joining the show from Moscow via satellite is Vladimir Posner, the English-language commentator of Radio Moscow.

The Muscovite face, against a cityscape of the Soviet capital, could easily be that of any U.S. TV commentator. Posner has qualities that make him a match, or more than a match, for his American counterparts. On this particular show, Brinkley is his usual polite, urbane self, while White House reporter Sam Donaldson and commentator George Will live up to their public personae as unrelenting questioners.

To begin with, they ask, isn't Posner, as compared to American reporters, "a journalist of a special sort"? By this his interrogators mean that he is a paid propagandist, a government spokesman, or even, as Posner himself observes, at times regarded as a "Kremlin mouthpiece"? He acknowledges in his fluent, colloquial English that, like everyone in the Soviet Union, he is, of course, a government employee or in the employ of an "organization." His delivery remains calm, relaxed, professional. In appearance and demeanor, this man is a far cry from the traditional Soviet spokesmen—even the veteran Americanist Georgi Arbatov—who usually are heavyset, speak with marked accents, dress drably, and have either abrasively aggressive or defensive manners.

In the ongoing history of Leninist agitation and propaganda, Posner represents the *nouveau agitateur*, providing the lighter touch, just as *nouvelle cuisine* replaced the all-too-rich cooking of yesteryear. Oh, yes, Posner would be the first to admit that the Soviet Union still needs to do more to improve its production of consumer goods. No, he says, he would not care to speculate on the likely succession within the Politburo, as history will answer all current questions. There are, to be sure, problems in agricultural output in the U.S.S.R., and there needs to be better distribution—but then, he adds matter-of-factly, there are no homeless in the streets of Soviet cities and no lines outside soup kitchens. He does not linger on these little stabs at U.S. problems; the knife goes in smoothly and is extracted momentarily. As for the health of men in the Kremlin— why, there simply is no attention paid to the private lives of politicians, or even to those of other public figures, such as entertainers, and the Soviet press respects their privacy. Not said, and only quietly implied, is that such squalid matters are left to the sensation-mongering media of the Western bourgeoisie. And no mention, of course, is made of the fact that news of top-government deaths and appointments is sprung on the Soviet public overnight, leaving the country to sort out a succession of rumors. Posner is a pro among pros. The viewer, as likely as not, comes away feeling that the Americans were rather harsh and that the Russian, more polite than they, acquitted himself well, even deserves their sympathy, and certainly their tolerance.

Posner is a veteran of U.S. television. When a children's film festival in Moscow linked up with a children's show at the University of San Diego, Posner was the master of ceremonies, microphone in hand, guiding the two live audiences through the intricacies of a coordinated program by satellite. He has often provided the Soviet side of discussions on ABC programs, including *Nightline*, hosted by Ted Koppel, where the ambiance is that of colleagues who know one another and call each other by first names. During an interview for *New York* magazine (August 13, 1984), Nancy Collins told Koppel that ABC's use of Posner had come in for criticism. She said:

"One of the criticisms of 'Nightline,' especially from conservatives such as William F. Buckley jr., is that such guests as Vladimir Posner and Joe Adamov of Radio Moscow—you give the Soviet propaganda machine far too much public airing." To which Koppel replied: "So what? If we are a different nation—and it's my firm conviction we are—then it's only because we believe a nation is strengthened by a free exchange of ideas. One of the things that make America great is that we are willing to run the risk of letting our population listen to ideas that are alien to us. As for Vladimir Posner, do we really think our society can be undermined by some guy with a silver tongue who looks nice . . . that he'll be able to undo America? If you believe, as I do, that we need to know what our adversaries are thinking and what their rationale is, then how are you going to find out? What are we afraid of . . . that their ideas might be better than ours, their spokesmen more eloquent? No, I'm not worried."

When *People* magazine, which specializes in breezy personality profiles, ran an article (August 31, 1983) titled "Ex-New Yorker Vladimir Posner Is Moscow's Mouthpiece," it started off this way: "Like any good PR man, Vladimir Posner is a master of the firm handshake, the friendly smile and the practiced patter. To be sure, he needs these attributes more than most promoters, since his product is a tough sell—the Soviet Union." His emergence as Russia's face on American television resulted from a career that provided excellent opportunities to sharpen Posner's skills as a plausible propagandist.

Vladimir Posner was born in Paris on April 1, 1934, the son of a French mother and a Russian father. When France surrendered to Nazi Germany, the family fled to the United States and settled in New York, where Posner attended Stuyvesant High School. When his father "got an offer in the Soviet zone of Berlin," with the East German motion-picture industry, the family settled there in 1949. Three years later, the Posners moved to Moscow. Posner became a Soviet citizen and, ultimately, a member of the Communist Party.

Posner recalled that he did not suffer any "culture shock" when he came face to face with the realities of Soviet society at the age of 18. He obviously had not only mastered French and English but received a good grounding in Russian from his father; very likely, he had been tutored in Russian history, language, and culture throughout his youth, particularly during the three years in Communist-governed East Germany. Posner told *People*: "Almost any one emigrating to a new country remains a foreigner until he dies. I was lucky. I adapted to a different culture perfectly well."

Posner attended Moscow University and majored in biology. His original plan, an academic career as a biologist, was abandoned as his linguistic and literary skills became evident. When he made a better-than-average translation of sixteenth- and seventeenth-century English verse, Soviet poet Samuel Marshak asked him to become his literary assistant in 1961.

Posner's initial training as a literary propagandist began shortly afterward, when he joined the Novosti news and publishing agency. At one point he served as managing editor of the agency's English-language edition of *Sputnik* magazine. Among the many channels used by Novosti, its periodicals (*Sputnik* in particular) are clearly designed to put Russia's best foot forward and to use the methods and style of Western publications. It was a logical move, therefore, when, in 1970, Posner joined the English-language service of Radio Moscow.

When, in 1979, Radio Moscow's English-language World Service began to be broadcast domestically as well as to audiences abroad, Posner used one of his commentaries to point up what he described as the difference between Soviet broadcast policies and those of the Western governments. In his usual soft-spoken way, sounding as if he were talking to listeners more in sorrow than in anger, he noted that most people are unaware of the "very basic difference between information intended for domestic consumption and information geared for abroad, and yet the difference is important." He then went into detail:

"Take radio. The 'Voice of America' does not broadcast inside the United States on FM or AM. Mind you, I am speaking of VOA broadcasts in English. Let us not even discuss broadcasts in any foreign language, although there certainly exist enough people in the United States with the knowledge of such a language to create a potential audience. The same reasoning applies to the BBC in English. Its World Service in English is not for domestic ears, and that is doubly so in what relates to foreign language broadcasts.

"Now when one asks, how come?, the answer varies, but usually comes down to two things. The standard argument is that it would not be fair to allow government-owned and run sources to compete with private stations. But, in fact, the difference in the approach to handling information for abroad and for local consumption is often so great as to make it impossible to the abroad-oriented source at home. Now, frankly, I don't see this as any great sin. I mean, taking it on a very personal level, most people don't dress or conduct themselves the same way at home as when they have been invited out. The difference is legitimate to my mind.

"But one nagging suspicion must remain. Could it possibly be that when describing their country and life these stations stray so far from the truth as to be totally unacceptable to a home audience? Hence their not being on the local air? After all, that thought, too, is legitimate and it applies to Radio Moscow no less than to the VOA or the BBC. Well, I am happy to inform you that as of the 11th June, Radio Moscow World Service will be carried daily from 7 a.m. to 1 a.m. for Moscow and the Moscow region.

"I think that furnishes room for at least two conclusions. First, Radio Moscow World Service speaks the same factual language to both foreign and home audiences, meaning it does not serve out different dishes to the two. Second, we could reflect on what must be a truly fantastic amount of Moscovites who know English well enough to follow a radio broadcast. Clearly, if that audience did not exist in fact, the broadcast would not be worthwhile. And finally, this means that English-speaking foreigners in Moscow will always be able to get the last-minute news by switching on their hotel room radio. Not a major consideration, but a pleasant feature to look forward to."

As usual, Posner sounded plausible. However, Americans can easily listen to the Voice of America in English and other languages, if they have shortwave receiver or turn to the shortwave bands available on some radios. In Britain, too, anyone can easily tune in on the BBC World Service, as it is also transmitted over medium wave, the conventional radio channel, and many of the BBC foreign broadcasts are pickups from its home services. British newspapers list the programs of the BBC World Service.

For the most part, Americans are so satiated with news from competing television and radio stations that they have trouble rationing their intake of news. And, certainly, the U.S. government does not try to jam Radio Moscow's English-language transmissions to North America, while the Soviet Union has for years put up jamming barriers against broadcasts aimed at its population from Western stations. The Western radio listener, inundated with news, has much less motivation to listen to foreign stations—except for their exotic nature—than does the Soviet citizen, who is limited to a carefully preselected and slanted budget of items. Radio Moscow uses the same basic news diet as do Soviet domestic radio and TV transmissions and, for that matter, *Pravda* and the rest of the press, filtered through the editorial sieve of the Tass news agency.

Still, the casual listener was likely to come away from the Posner commentary with the impetus to nod agreement. Such conciliatory phrases as "I don't see this as any great sin" or "not a major consideration" added to a general air of taking the listener into the confidence of a man of goodwill, simply sharing his thoughts.

During a visit to London, where he appeared on the BBC 1 *Platform One* program, Posner gave an interview to Jonathan Steele of the *Guardian,* a daily paper. Steele observed (April 6, 1981) that Posner was "perhaps the most sophisticated propagandist for the Soviet cause that anyone could find." He saw Posner as "a skilful speaker who knows when to give a little ground, if only to move back into the attack more strongly" and as someone who "is prepared to make mild criticisms of his own system, though generally of a vague, general nature and with the plea: 'Give us time. Socialism was not built in a day. We are learning.' "

After noting Western misconceptions of the Soviet Union, Posner was asked to give some examples of Soviet misconceptions of the West. Steele wrote: "Posner hesitates and then provides two. One is that Russians tend to accept American election rhetoric as reality. They find it hard to understand how American policy works. The other is they believe that if an American President signs something like the second agreement on strategic arms control (SALT II) this means that it is certain to be ratified. Interesting examples of misunderstanding, because when you look at them, Posner is not being self-critical but only finding an oblique way of criticising the Americans again."

Michael Manning, in "The New Soviet Media Man," published in *The Nation* (February 4, 1984), noted that Posner's effectiveness "rests on more than his command of English and his skill at oratory." He added: "He understands how Americans think. He avoids Marxist buzzwords like 'imperialism,' 'neocolonialism' and 'fraternalism,' and stresses the similarities between the superpowers. He is tough without becoming combative, knowing when to hold his ground and when to take cover. He is funny, at times ironic, and he can appear indignant when it helps make his point. Above all, Posner is so personable that he challenges many of the misconceptions others have about his country."

Of course, Posner is not the average Soviet citizen; he is tailor-made for the American media market, and he carefully keeps himself in style for his highly specialized job. Just writing his five-minute commentaries for Radio Moscow, "Vladimir Posner's Daily Talk," calls for familiarity with the American scene, day in and day out. That goes beyond reading weekly newsmagazines and the copy that comes off the Associated Press and United Press International teletypes in the Radio Moscow offices; it means keeping up with the ever-changing American vernacular by monitoring U.S. broadcasts and viewing tapes of television shows. Posner keeps in touch with visiting Americans, and he visits the U.S. embassy in Moscow to catch up on Hollywood productions. Videocassettes help fill the culture gap, and Posner naturally listens to the competition: the Voice of America, the BBC, and other Western radio transmissions.

But it is Posner's basic personality that serves his role as *nouveau agitateur* better than anything else. Manning contrasted Posner's handling of delicate questions with the approach of another Radio Moscow man, the English-language announcer Joe Adamov, a veteran of the shortwave radio combat. Even in appearance, Adamov comes across as a rambling old-timer, with his unruly white hair, loud tie, and too-tight shirt. On one *Nightline* show, George Will challenged Russia's Afghanistan role, and Adamov came back, slugging:

"You have bands, armed, trained, financed by the United States, sent in from Pakistan on the conveyor-belt system into Afghanistan, and I don't think Mr. Reagan denies this. He finances them, he even receives the heads of these bands in the White House. And that is why the Soviet forces are in Afghanistan. We've said time and again, had there . . . not been this American-financed and -trained and -organized aggression from the territory of Pakistan into Afghanistan, the Soviet troops would not have been in Afghanistan. And we said the moment that aggression from outside stops, the Soviet troops will leave Afghanistan."

Manning noted that Adamov went on to denounce American "geno-cide" in El Salvador and its support for other "right-wing, extreme dictatorial" regimes, going back to the government of Fulgencio Batista of Cuba. "Posner," Manning commented, "is too savvy to engage in such diatribes." He would know that Americans remember the Soviet Union's troop airlift, on December 24, 1979, into Afghanistan's capital, Kabul, followed by 60,000 men, and an eventual buildup to over 100,000—all, in fact, because a pro-Moscow regime in Kabul had shown itself potentially too independent. Manning wrote that Posner's "value to Moscow" in conveying its message as a "peace-loving nation that cherished cooperation and coexistence" might seem "obvious," but "for the traditionally reclusive Russians, his appearances signify a change of great significance."

Posner's adaptability may have its roots in his father's remarkable skill in walking an undulating Marxist line throughout much of his life. That his father chose 1952 to return to the Soviet Union appears to be, in retrospect, either a foolhardy act or the act of a man who was very sure of a friendly welcome. The year before Stalin's death in 1953 was a period of stresses and fears and of purges of top Communist leaders in the East European countries, including East Germany, where the Posners had made their interim home. After Stalin's death, and through successive administrations, the skills of Vladimir Posner became increasingly useful and appreciated. After Gorbachev came to power, Posner grew busier than ever, not only in propaganda activities abroad, but also at home. He even met with visiting delegations.

When rock singers from all over the world joined, on July 14, 1985, in the huge "Live Aid" concert to combat starvation in Africa, the London-Philadelphia television hookup was linked to the U.S.S.R., where the Soviet rock group Autograph added its voices to the global chorus; it was Posner who introduced the group and managed to observe that "Hi-Tech is being used here for peaceful purposes."

Posner's schedule became even more crowded when, in the fall of 1985, he began to host a weekly talk show, *Top Priority,* on the North American Service of Radio Moscow. Two officials of the United States of America and Canada Institute, Radomir Bogdanov and Serge Plekhanov, were Posner's regular guests. The show began in October, before the Geneva summit, and it naturally dealt with the differing positions of the United States and the U.S.S.R. Although apparently recorded, the show has a certain spontaneity.

In December 1985, Posner visited Great Britain for a little over a week, and he was interviewed on Radio Moscow's broadcast to the United Kingdom and Ireland (November 26, 1985). Finding himself on the opposite side of the microphone, Posner answered questions from Nikolai Groshkov, who asked about British media coverage of the Geneva meeting of Reagan and Gorbachev. Posner said that Britain did not receive "a fair account" of the Soviet policy position and that there was "a bit of contradiction in the judgment and in the analysis" of British and U.S. viewpoints.

Posner became the center of a controversy in the United States when, on February 26, 1986, ABC television permitted him to comment for eight minutes on a 23-minute speech by President Reagan. In his commentary, from Moscow, Posner used sharply critical terms, which prompted White House communications director Patrick J. Buchanan to send a letter of protest to ABC. Buchanan wrote that the White House was "astonished" that the network had provided such extensive "rebuttal time to a trained propagandist for the Soviet Union," thus giving him "a standing he does not merit, a legitimacy he does not deserve."

Replying, Richard C. Wald, senior vice president of ABC News, agreed "reluctantly" that Posner "was allowed too much scope on our program last night." He added: "There is nothing wrong with asking a Soviet spokesman for his views of a Presidential speech concerning American posture in relations to the Russians. It is part of what we do. Our production error was in letting him push on at too great a length without any opposing voice to point out the errors and the inconsistencies of what he said."

Posner gave his own version of the incident when he appeared on the *Phil Donahue Show*, two months later. "I was not supposed to go on unopposed," he said. "I was in Moscow doing this via satellite, and Peter Jennings was supposed to be with me. Peter Jennings got sick. He was too ill to come. Pierre Salinger, as I understand it, was also in Moscow, didn't wake up in time, so I was out there all alone, at 4 o'clock in the morning, my time, and it wasn't ABC's idea to put me on that way." Jennings was the anchorman of ABC's evening news report, *The World Tonight*, Salinger its chief European correspondent.

The *Donahue* program featured Posner, without any other guests, on two successive days. The controversy over the President's speech had heightened his celebrity status. As a result, his month-long visit to the United States in May and June was not limited to consultations with Donahue and his syndication service, Multimedia Entertainment, Inc., but included a number of public appearances. Following a Donahue-Posner "Citizens Summit" between audiences in Leningrad and Seattle, aired earlier, a second such show, linking audiences in Boston and Leningrad, was arranged on June 22. Posner was also interviewed by talk show host Larry King, appeared on ABC's *Nightline* and met with correspondents and media critics at a Washington symposium sponsored by the American Enterprise Institute, a conservative research body.

An ABC show on which Posner appeared, *Viewpoint*, hosted by Ted

Koppel, featured a number of media and government personalities to discuss, as Koppel put it, whether American media were "being used as a platform for propaganda." Koppel said at the outset, "I don't regard Vladimir as a journalist in the American pattern. He clearly is not; he is a propagandist." Later in the broadcast, Roone Arledge, president of ABC News, said: "We have found that having Soviet spokesmen on our programs adds a dimension, adds their point of view, whether we agree with it or not. The fact of the matter is we have to live with these people. They do have a different perspective on things than we do. We have a different perspective from them. And to have Vladimir Posner or Georgi Arbatov or whomever else we have had on from the Soviet Union, I think is an educational process and a good one, and I think on the occasions that they say things that our other guests take issue with, it's immediately pointed out."

Speaking from the audience, Reed Irvine, chairman of the board of Accuracy in Media, said: "But they should be introduced, Roone, not as people who are giving their viewpoint, but as paid liars. Then it would be accurate." Koppel interceded: "I'll tell you what. I suspect if we introduced even Vladimir Posner, who seems like a very congenial fellow, if we introduced him every time as a congenital liar, I suspect he might not come on after the second or third time. There is one larger point that I think needs to be made, and that is by and large when we do live television, whether we are interviewing Vladimir Posner or whether we are interviewing someone who represents the government of Chile or Nicaragua, or for that matter the government of the United States, it would take a greater knowledge on the part of most anchormen and anchorwomen than I'm afraid any one of us has, to be able to catch every misstatement and every untruth at the time." Koppel added that a "continuum" existed whereby, "over a period of days or weeks what is covered in the media eventually comes close to approaching the truth."

Posner, whose visit to the United States was his first in 38 years, used the opportunity to make a number of personal points to his various audiences. He emphasized that he was an employee of the U.S.S.R. State Committee for Radio and Television (*Gostelradio*), but added: "I have never been briefed by anybody, and therefore that is why I say consistently that I am not an agent of the government." He told his Washington audience, "I would agree with you that if my government did not want Vladimir Posner to go on, he would not." He said that, on returning to the Soviet Union, he would be "debriefed" by government officials and would speak on radio and television about his trip.

On the *Donahue* program, Posner reported that he had visited his former high school, as well as his former grade school, in New York. He said that the grade school in particular, "was a very, very moving emotional experience," as "the people there knew I was coming and they brought some of the kids I went to school with, my classmates, and I wasn't expecting that. So that really hit me right, I mean, in the heart." Donahue asked, "Did they wonder why you had become a Commie?" Posner laughed at this and said, "Phil, as a matter of fact, they knew I had become a Commie when I was still there. Okay? But these are kids who used to come over to my house every day, a group of about five of us. We were just real chums, kind of, and it was wonderful. When we saw each other, we just jumped on each other and hugged. I mean, Commie or not."

Adding to this theme, which clearly served to establish a positive resonance with his audience, Posner said that he had never regretted his family's decision to settle in the U.S.S.R., as he preferred the Soviet system, but he added,"There was a point when I was very homesick." He explained: "I was very homesick, not for political things, but for baseball. I mean, you know, for Franks, for New York City, because there is no other city like this one. Either you love it or you hate it. Right? I happen to love it. But I made a decision that I wanted to live in the Soviet Union."

Posner made a point of expressing disagreement with certain Soviet practices. He said in Washington that he regarded the jamming of Western broadcasts as "counterproductive." He made "the very personal assessment" that "it attracts interest to something that is really not all that interesting." At the same time, he denounced the broadcasts of Radio Liberty and Radio Free Europe as being "subversive, openly." Pressed to comment on Soviet restrictions on Jewish emigration, Posner said, "My feeling is, if you want to leave the country, bye, bye. I don't make all the decisions. Do you, in your country?" Asked why there was no access to Soviet television appearances by U.S. citizens, equivalent to the presence of Soviet spokesmen on the American networks, Posner mentioned that he had interviewed *New York Times* correspondent Serge Schmemann on Soviet TV, but added, "I would like to see more Russian-speaking American journalists on Soviet television." Donahue asked, "Have you told them that in the Soviet Union?" Posner answered, "Of course I have, and I'm telling it now, and I repeat that there must be Soviet citizens at the U.N., at the Embassy and elsewhere, watching this show. So I'm saying it again. Right?"

For all his show of independent opinion, Posner was firm and harsh in commenting on such major points as the shooting down of the Korean airliner. He justified the Soviet action by asserting as a fact that the plane had been on a spying mission and that "the CIA actually risked those lives." On the treatment of dissidents he said: "In my opinion, if you're going to fight the system, any system in the world, the system is going to fight back, and the more it sees you as dangerous, the harder it's going to fight. And if you're an individual, you will usually lose, because the system is stronger. It has always been that way. If you want to take on the system, you're going to be in trouble, any system."

Later on, he recovered his bonhomie. A member of the audience asked, "You said that the Soviet government controls the press. Aren't you also being controlled here? Is Gorbachev watching you?" Posner answered with a smile, "I'm being controlled by Mr. Donahue." With this quip, the show ended on a note of good-fellowship.

CHAPTER · 21

Reporting from Moscow

The most highly publicized link between Washington and Moscow is the so-called hot line between the White House and the Kremlin. The corporation that was instrumental in making this direct telephone setup possible is ITT World Communications, a multinational corporation that prides itself on its role in worldwide information services. It was natural, therefore, that ITT should underwrite part of a unique television program put together by the Maryland Center for Public Broadcasting, at Owings Mills, Maryland. The center originates such well-known telecasts as *Washington Week in Review* and *Wall Street Week,* which are transmitted by public service TV stations nationwide. The program in question was "Dateline USSR/USA," presented as "a special report comparing the images Soviets and Americans have of one another."

The program was presented originally on October 15, 1985, on the eve of the Geneva meeting between President Reagan and General Secretary Gorbachev. The basic concept of the telecast was an exchange of views between U.S. correspondents in Moscow and Soviet correspondents in Washington, with Howard K. Smith acting as the host in the U.S. capital and Vladimir Posner doing the same thing in Moscow. As the program was set up, three Soviet correspondents were to have a dialogue with three American counterparts. This sort of pattern had previously worked well enough in U.S. talk shows, but a total of eight faces and voices crisscrossing the world by satellite turned out to be more of a cacophony than a symphony.

In its very air of frustration, suppressed anger, and transcontinental chaos, the show managed to dramatize the cleavage that exists between the perceptions that U.S. and Soviet correspondents have of their jobs, the difficulties they encounter, and the diversity of views they represent. In Moscow, Posner hosted Celestine Bohlen of the *Washington Post,* Stuart Loory of Cable News Network (CNN), and Antero Pietila of the *Baltimore Sun.* In Washington, Smith was host for Aleksandr Palladin of *Izvestia*, Vladimir Dunaev of Soviet Television, and Aleksandr Shalnev, Tass's White House correspondent.

What with announcements and switching back and forth between Moscow and Washington, viewers came away with the blurred image of an exasperated Howard Smith, a smooth-as-ever Vladimir Posner, and various degrees of exasperation expressed by both the Russians and the Americans. If any major theme emerged from the exchange, it was that the Russians accused their U.S. counterparts of picking only negative things to report about the Soviet Union, while the Americans saw the Russians as being even more one-sided in their selection of topics and in the slant of their commentaries. Excerpts from various reports, enlivened by brief video or film clips, shortened the time available to each of the speakers.

John Grassie, who produced "Dateline USSR/USA," succeeded in putting a provocative show on the air, but he had underestimated the complexity of the subject, the combative mood of the participants, and the resulting perplexity of viewers—who might be hard put even to remember the identity of the participants, much less the cultural and technical problems behind their all-too-animated performances. Future such efforts, with fewer faces and less electronic complexity, might profit from this pioneer experiment by the Maryland Center.

By pitting four Americans against four Russians, appearing to be fair and evenhanded, the show gave the impression that a parity of task and responsibility exists between U.S. reporters in Moscow and their Soviet counterparts in Washington. Yet, as Howard Smith tried to demonstrate early in the show, Soviet correspondents have a distinctly propagandistic task: They are supposed to convey an image of the United States that is ideologically proper and that implements Soviet policy; the Americans, who have no such proscribed task, aim at reports that have "news value" in the competitive media marketplace at home.

Generally and quite superficially speaking, both sides tend to report negative news; and each side accuses the other of misrepresenting and downgrading the society from which it reports. At the outset of "Dateline USSR/USA," Smith quoted these *Pravda* instructions to Soviet journalists: "It is the most important duty of our press to wage an offensive struggle against bourgeois ideology. A journalist is an active fighter in the cause of the Communist Party." To which Palladin, the *Izvestia* correspondent at the White House, replied, "Of course, but I don't see anything negative about that." Trained in the Soviet ideological tradition, not only do Russian reporters take their own inbred attitude for granted but they assume a mirror-image position on the part of U.S. correspondents in the U.S.S.R.

Cultural conditioning and news value standards may prompt American reporters in Moscow to seek out nonofficial news, to zero in on the *outré*, the exotic, or the "negative"; they are nevertheless limited by a carefully constructed Soviet framework from digressing too far from the line set down daily by *Pravda* and Tass. One former Moscow correspondent, David Satter, believes that Western reporters in Moscow essentially "serve the interests of the Soviet authorities." Satter, who was Moscow correspondent of the *Financial Times* (London) from 1976 to 1981, told a Paris conference on the status of Soviet dissident Andrei Sakharov (April 1985) that he was at first puzzled that Soviet authorities tolerated the presence of foreign correspondents at all. "I could not understand," he said, "why they did not force them to paraphrase Tass releases from offices in Helsinki." He later concluded that resident correspondents were "actually necessary" to the Russians, and added:

"The Soviet authorities do not want the Soviet Union to be like China during the Cultural Revolution. They understand that the world distrusts a country about which there is no information. They want the West to have information about the Soviet Union but they want it to be the type of information which will lead Western leaders and Western public opinion to draw consistently erroneous conclusions. And for this, they are heavily dependent on the unprofessionalism, inexperience and, occasionally, the corruption of Western correspondents."

Satter charged, in essence, that Western correspondents in Moscow, particularly those who do not speak Russian and who lack sufficient background knowledge of the Soviet state, are incapable or unwilling to resist the constant internal and external propaganda barrage, get caught up in it, and ultimately echo it. He noted that Soviet authorities "make an enormous effort" to "disinform" the West and manage to succeed through the repetition of such words as "peace," "democracy," and "imperialism," emptying these terms of their original content and substituting their own. Soviet propaganda, according to Satter, repeats its themes "in every newspaper, every radio broadcast and every television news program, as well as in every official statement or speech by a Soviet leader and every private 'chat' that a Soviet official may hold with a Western journalist."

Newly assigned Moscow correspondents, Satter said, arrive in the Soviet capital eager to be productive and soon "begin energetically to regurgitate Soviet disinformation." They rely on KGB-supplied interpreters, translators, and secretaries, and are quickly trapped in a net of disinformation. Most of the inadequacies of Western reporting, according to this view, "are the result of error, not bad intentions, but there are a number of personal factors which contribute to what is a deplorable situation." Among

these, Satter said, was the ability of Soviet authorities to manipulate reporters: "the most cooperative of them" may obtain routine information
slightly in advance of others or may be given "access" to Soviet leaders.
That such an exclusive interview amounts to no more than yet another
paraphrasing of the official propaganda line does not reduce its prestige
or news value. Satter also said:

"With about ninety Western correspondents (including those from Japan)
to cover a country which is larger than the United States, almost every
Western correspondent is expected to report on every government statement. The phenomenal duplication of effort is reflected in the high per-
centage of the total journalistic output which consists of nothing but
paraphrases of the articles in *Pravda* and Tass. Under these circumstances,
a fierce struggle develops to see who can find 'high level' Soviet sources
whose inane and unattributable remarks are attributed to 'Soviet officials'
and used by Western correspondents in an attempt to make a given Soviet
position more 'life-like,' in the process, making Soviet official lies more
plausible to the outside world."

Satter's views were strongly supported by a former colleague, Andrew
Nagorski, who served as *Newsweek* correspondent in Moscow from March
1981 until his expulsion in August 1982 for using "impermissible methods
of journalistic activities." Nagorski, who sought to practice a modified form
of investigative journalism, took several trips outside of Moscow to study
conditions. He wrote in *Reluctant Farewell* that most foreign correspondents went along with official Soviet rules and policies and that their attitude
was "shared by the headquarters of major news organizations that not only
sent correspondents without proper preparation to Moscow but accepted
and even welcomed the most predictable coverage of Soviet affairs."

One correspondent who faced harassment, but not expulsion, was Gary
Thatcher of the *Christian Science Monitor*. On August 5, 1985, returning
by car on a Soviet ferry from Stockholm to Leningrad, he was detained
for three hours. Customs and KGB officials seized 125 pages of documents
and two tape recordings, as well as magazines (*Time* and *Newsweek*) and
books. All of these were labeled potentially "anti-Soviet" by the officials
and, therefore, were not excluded from seizure by the Helsinki Final Act,
signed by Brezhnev in 1975. *Komsomolskaya Pravda* (January 23, 1986)
ran a long and blistering article on Thatcher, accusing him of violating
Soviet hospitality and displaying "ill will."

The status of U.S. correspondents in Moscow was made more insecure
when Nicholas Daniloff, who had served for more than five years in the
Soviet capital, representing the news weekly *U.S. News & World Report*,
was arrested on August 30, 1986, and charged with spying. Gennadi Gerasimov said at a Foreign Ministry briefing (September 2) that Daniloff
"was caught, unfortunately for the journalistic community, red-handed

with a sealed envelope which contained secret documents." The reporter had met an old acquaintance in the Lenin Hills park area, where they exchanged good-bye gifts; Daniloff had planned to return to the United States the following month. He was handed a sealed package which he assumed contained clippings. Instead, when he was seized by KGB agents, the package was found to contain a map and photographs, marked or at least regarded "secret."

Daniloff was arrested, imprisoned, and interrogated. The case, certainly the most critical in well over a decade, caused bitterness in Washington and shock among Moscow's foreign press corps. It was widely assumed that Daniloff had been seized to force the release, in the United States, of a Soviet employee of the United Nations, physicist Gennadi F. Zakharov, who had earlier been arrested by the FBI as he received classified documents from a young man he had employed as an agent and whom he handed $1,000 in payment. Twenty-nine American journalists, stationed in Moscow and representing 17 news organizations, sent a letter to General Secretary Gorbachev (September 5), expressing their "dismay" over the Daniloff arrest and testifying to his "reputation for honesty and integrity." They regarded the action as "an attempt to intimidate every member of the media community in Moscow," in contrast to the "greater openness in Soviet society and on the part of Soviet leadership." Washington-Moscow negotiations led to a return of Zakharov to the U.S.S.R. and of Daniloff to the United States; this was not categorized as an exchange, so that Daniloff avoided a "spy" label.

There is a flip side to Satter's critique, and that is the supposed adherence of Moscow correspondents to the orders of their "capitalist" bosses at home. Progress Publishers, the book publishing arm of Novosti, in 1981 issued *Are Our Moscow Reporters Giving Us the Facts about the USSR?* written by Philip Bonoski, since 1978 the Moscow correspondent of the *Daily World* (successor to the *Daily Worker* Communist newspaper published in New York). The book's cover was a montage of the mastheads of the *New York Times,* the *Washington Post,* the *Los Angeles Times,* the *International Herald-Tribune* (Paris), and *U.S. News.* Its content dealt largely with the output of the Moscow correspondents of these publications.

Bonoski, in essence, criticized American correspondents for not reporting on the Soviet Union in an upbeat manner, for failing to show progress, improvements, and cultural activity. In the Soviet Union, he wrote, "The direction is always onward and upward—today is good, tomorrow will be better." In the course of his book, Bonoski stated that for *New York Times* correspondent David K. Shipler, "the glass is always half-empty," never half-full. Of another *Times* reporter, Hedrick Smith, who wrote a book that won the Pulitzer Prize, he noted: "I am even told that the State Department advises tourists to read it first to prepare themselves for entry into the fearsome realm behind the Iron Curtain." Bonoski provided this analysis of the shortcomings of Moscow correspondents:

"Journalists who come to the U.S.S.R. are not—to give them their due—usually trained or prepared to report the scene they find. The rules are different. The scene is utterly different. Here news is not someone killing somebody, or someone jumping out of a building. No minister calls a press conference to denounce another minister. No shady politician declares before the press that he won't lie to the people (Carter) or that he is not a crook (Nixon). The news is different—and, from the point of view of the Western journalist—boring. It has to do with planning—how much has industry produced this year, what is the harvest like, how the peace struggle is doing, what are the vacation plans for children this year, how about schools, how many more of them have been built, and prices, no changes in basics, in rent or utilities—all, all boring stuff. Where are the scandals? Where is that story about a man killing people on orders from a dog? You won't find it: don't look. There are no 'leaked' stories, no inside stuff, no planted tales to defame or decry, to instigate or provoke."

Bonoski accused Kevin Klose, at one time the *Washington Post* correspondent in Moscow, of having developed his journalistic tastes as a police reporter in Washington and described his approach as, "Finding nothing decent in Moscow to write about! So make it up! Who's to stop you?" Bonoski appeared to agree with Satter on the supposed lack of journalistic skill on the part of U.S. correspondents, although their viewpoints otherwise diverged greatly. Bonoski said: "Though all American bourgeois reporters distort or misrepresent Soviet reality, some out of sheer incompetence—though, such being the law of anti-Sovietism, incompetence merges with malice and looks like any other piece of writing—nobody does it with greater venom and skill (though they slip up once in a while) than the reporters from *The New York Times*." The main target of Bonoski's ire was Shipler. At one point, he wrote of the *Times* correspondent: "Just a bit more and we're finished with Shipler—hopefully forever."

As to the side of Soviet society that U.S. correspondents fail to report, Bonoski cited an incident he witnessed in the Moscow subway, in which a man was reading a book and a girl sat down beside him. Bonoski continued: "Without even looking at her, he brings the book over to her. 'Look,' he says. 'Read that.' He's a complete stranger to her, but she takes the book obediently. It's poetry. 'Isn't it wonderful?' he urges her. 'Yes, it is. This is my stop.' She gets off. Strangers." Bonoski commented, "Why in all their snoopings" did not the American reporters, "all of them—never hear anything like that. They have ears as I do. Some of them have a better Russian than I do. But their ears are attuned only to slander and slander is all they 'hear.' "

Clearly, the Moscow correspondent who wants to expand his horizon beyond the drab pages of *Pravda* and the monotonous ticking of the Tass teletype faces a difficult and controversial task. Joseph Finder, in his article "Reporting from Russia," in the *Washington Journalism Review* (June 1985), interviewed three out of twenty-four U.S. correspondents in Moscow: Dusko Doder of the *Washington Post*, who was later replaced by Celestine Bohlen, Bob Zelnick of ABC television, and Serge Schmemann of the *New York Times*. Finder started on his rounds by questioning Seymour Topping, the *New York Times* managing editor and a former Moscow correspondent. Topping said that a Moscow dateline provides "authority" and directness, the same information picked up in Washington is likely to have "gone through the spectrum of information" of a U.S. government official.

Doder's office was located in a building that also contained the offices of the Associated Press, United Press International, *Newsweek,* and the *Chicago Tribune*. It formed part of a "foreigners' ghetto," a complex of buildings that both isolates its residents and gives them certain privileges. Doder recalled that his paper, the *Washington Post,* had developed a reputation for investigative, muckraking journalism ever since it broke the Watergate story that brought down the administration of President Richard Nixon. "A lot of us are used to being hard-nosed and adversarial," Doder told Finder. "Here, however, one runs the risk of taking the negative attitude too far. If you're looking for something to complain about, you'll find it in abundance." Finder asked whether there was value to a Moscow report beyond what could be taken from a Tass teletype in Washington. Doder replied: "There is nothing to report here. We analyze. Everything we do is analysis, everything else is worthless."

Zelnick, the television correspondent, does not speak Russian, so he was assisted by Maria Casby, who does speak the language. The ABC office was in a building which Finder described as "another dreary" enclave set aside for foreigners. On the day of his meeting with Finder, Zelnick was interviewing Radomir Bogdanov, whom he described as "a big shot" at the United States of America and Canada Institute. Bogdanov, generally regarded as Georgi Arbatov's number two man, is an English-speaking scholar-propagandist who appears often on Soviet media and occasionally on U.S. television. Zelnick was looking for "good sound-bite" material, a strong and provocative phrase that would be sufficiently aggressive to compete with other television news or feature items. When Zelnick asked Bogdanov what he thought of President Reagan's foreign policy, his first reply was, "I would like to leave that answer to the American people." This was not sharp enough for Zelnick, but eventually he managed to get Bogdanov to utter sufficiently apocalyptic sentences, such as, "The smell of nuclear war is very, very strong in the air." The interview gave the TV correspondent more or less what he wanted.

To Finder, the resulting ABC segment did "little more than verbalize the Tass or *Pravda* line," but Zelnick presumably had only been looking for something visual to dramatize the Kremlin line of the moment. Zelnick said that for "color" material, such as travel pictures from Armenia, Georgia, and Siberia, "you can't beat television," but he added that on other aspects of the Soviet state "there are stories that just don't come across on television." Zelnick later became ABC's reporter in Israel.

Next, Finder interviewed Serge Schmemann, one of the two *New York Times* correspondents at the paper's office. Schmemann, the son of a prominent Russian Orthodox theologian in the United States, could judge the Russian scene with an education and linguistic ability that gave particular depth to politico-cultural dispatches. Schmemann mentioned the paucity of hard news in Moscow and the relative abundance of rumors that could not be confirmed. He summarized the problems and challenges of reporting from Moscow as follows:

"Functioning in a police state is not very easy. But, oddly, life here is *intensified* by the system. Every reporter who leaves here misses the place tremendously. Nowhere else do you have these all-night discussions in the kitchen on What Is Truth. Still, the obstacles can drive you crazy. There are Soviet officials I talked to all the time when they were at the United Nations and I was covering the U.N., who have been transferred here, and now won't see me. When we get outside of Moscow we usually have somewhat better access. Then again, you can get stonewalled so royally you sit there steaming. When I was in Siberia I met the first secretary of the Party in a small town. I said to her, 'Name one major problem you have,' and she replied, after thinking a bit, 'Maybe our only problem is that we *try too hard.*' Nevertheless, I think travel is a critical aspect of covering the Soviet Union. Your juices start flowing again. I get so used to life in Moscow that I won't even notice the propaganda slogans across the street. Moscow is the center of a major empire. It's got its own tempo. It's different from the rest of the country. You begin to forget the place is atypical."

David Shipler and Serge Schmemann joined in an insightful collaboration for the *New York Times Magazine* (November 10, 1985), an article titled "How We See Each Other." Shipler provided "The View from America," in which he reflected on perceptions of the Soviet Union that he found among students at Chatham High School in Chatham, New Jersey, where he grew up. What were the images of Russia the boys and girls at the school had? They came, Shipler said, in a flood: flight 007, Communists, vodka, not real, stubborn, nuclear war, cold, Siberia, gulag, trapped, nervous, programmed, strict, Olympic boycott, Berlin, Iron Curtain, KGB, enemy, roulette, oppression, workers, regimented, hammer and sickle, chess, sports, defectors, strong-willed, wheat, propaganda, Socialist, Kremlin, long lines, absenteeism, Lenin, Cuba, Hitler, grain embargo, Marxism, Poland, terrorism.

Shipler found a "dramatic misimpression" of Russian working habits. The students imagined Soviet workers as subject to severe discipline, whereas, Shipler noted, barring occasional exceptions, the Soviet Union is "one of the world's greatest goof-off societies." This attitude is, of course, precisely the target of Mikhail Gorbachev's intense drive toward higher productivity in the country's industry and agriculture. Shipler also found that the students, together with much of the U.S. public in general, saw Russians as coldly aggressive and competitive. He added: "You have to know Russians personally, and preferably in the cloistered privacy of their own apartments, to know the warmer side of them."

Still, Shipler quoted one girl as saying, "On the street they're just being careful. This facade of being so cold and hard is just a facade." The correspondent felt that this was "precisely right" and commented that it was "a shame that Soviet authorities don't realize how much good they could do for American perceptions by opening up a little. Officialdom's suspicion of infectious foreign influence makes most Russians wary of inviting Americans home, so even tourists who travel briefly to Moscow often come away with an image of Russians in their public posture—cold, unfeeling and rude."

Serge Schmemann, providing "The View from Russia," summarized the images of opposites the Soviet population harbors about the United States: "There are greedy millionaires and the penniless homeless. There are the whites who have cars, personal computers and suburban homes, and there are the oppressed blacks. There are the militaristic and callous ruling circles led by President Reagan and the 'monopolies,' and there are the good, industrious American people. America is a land of plenty and a land of violence, and land of extreme wealth and abject poverty." Schmemann quoted one young Muscovite as commenting: "Soviet youth cannot assess the merits of the American democratic political system—our propaganda is silent on this, and for an ordinary Soviet person to get a tourist or official trip to the U.S.A. is an unachievable dream. The flaws and misdoing of the American system, on the other hand, are immediately served up by Soviet propaganda. And, though Soviet young people often treat these propaganda tricks skeptically, their effect is nonetheless great."

Schmemann noted that a Russian's view of the American way of life is "shaped from childhood by official ideology, propaganda and double talk." He emphasized that terms like "democracy, rights and freedoms are so freely applied by the Kremlin to its own political system that the words become hollow" and "the denigration of the American system is relentlessly pursued in the press and on television." Despite some Russian skepticism toward their own regime's propaganda, and despite the cynicism and the jokes, "the steady flow of half-truths and lies, backed by rigorous control of all other sources of information, does take a toll." Schmemann added: "The images of poverty and racial oppression take hold, while the dimly perceived concepts of rights and freedoms blend with their own country's often distorted use of those terms." And while individual Americans are usually received with a good deal of cordiality by Russians, their feelings "do have their dark side in the fears and suspicions nurtured by propaganda, by the nuclear threat and more deeply by the inherent Russian distrust of foreigners."

Shipler noted that Americans still tend to view the Soviet Union very much in terms of the Stalin era, with all the ruthlessness and terror it implied. In the U.S.S.R. itself, much of the Stalin heritage has been overcome and, indeed, forgotten. Yet, with the Gorbachev generation at the helm, intellectual modernization has been slow, and a lessening of cultural controls is more a matter of hope than reality. This was dramatized in a speech delivered by Yevgeni Yevtuchenko, held at a congress of Russian writers and published, with deletions, by the weekly *Literaturnaya Gazeta* (December 18, 1985).

A Yevtuchenko reference to Lenin's "unchosen successor," which clearly meant Stalin, was deleted in the published version of his speech, as were other remarks that referred to Stalinist oppression. Again, where the poet was pointedly specific, the paper deleted his comments, such as this passage: "This intellectual stagnation stopped short the economic prosperity deserved by our people, and reached such limits that in our rich and beautiful land, forty years after the war, there still exist in a number of cities the rationing of butter and meat, and this is morally impermissible." Schmemann commented that the talk had been "more than an attack by an aging rebel, emboldened by the winds of change," and that it posed a question troubling Moscow's creative intelligentsia: "Does Mr. Gorbachev's declared goal of modernizing and energizing Soviet society mean more freedom will be permitted in the arts?"

Like other writers who are Moscow residents, the U.S. correspondents were eagerly awaiting high-level answers.

CHAPTER · 22

Radio Moscow World Service

In the broadcasting studio of Radio Moscow, the clock is moving toward 11 p.m., July 1, 1985. The romantic melody "Midnight in Moscow" is floating through the giant antennas at relay stations from the Baltic to the Pacific. The station's musical signature ends in a percussion crescendo. Next, the chimes from the Kremlin's Spasski tower, reverberating with awesome immediacy, reach English-speaking listeners all over the globe. And then a cultivated, detached-sounding, British-accented voice comes on:

"This is Radio Moscow World Service. The news, read by Edward Dyatlov. First, the headlines:

"In Moscow, there has been a regular, full-scale session of the Soviet Communist Party Central Committee. The Congress of the International Physicians for the Prevention of Nuclear War has closed in Budapest. It issued a call for prevention of the arms race being extended into outer space. And the Ethiopian government has set up over 300 relief aid centers for famine victims.

"Those are the headlines. And now the news in full:

"The Central Committee of the Soviet Communist Party held a full-scale meeting in Moscow on Monday. It discussed questions pertaining to the session of the Soviet national parliament, which opens on Tuesday. A speech on those questions was made by the General Secretary of the Soviet Communist Party's Central Committee, Mikhail Gorbachev. The full-scale meeting stressed the need to consistently improve the work of the Soviet of People's Deputies, that is, the local government bodies. Each section

272

of the political system of the Soviet society is called upon to function accurately and well. The meeting further called upon the Party that it should exercise its influence on all sections of the state, economic, social, and cultural development. The full-scale meeting of the Central Committee of the Soviet Communist Party also considered organizational questions. The request of Grigori Romanov has been satisfied to release him from his duties as member of the Political Bureau and as secretary of the Central Committee of the Party. He is retiring on pension on account of his health. Eduard Shevardnadze, who was an Alternate Member of the Political Bureau, has been made Member, and Boris Yeltsin and Lev Zaikov have been elected secretaries of the Central Committee of the Soviet Communist Party.

"In Moscow there has been a regular meeting of the Presidium of the Supreme Soviet of the U.S.S.R. on Monday the first. It examined issues connected with the session of the Supreme Soviet of the U.S.S.R., the highest body of state authority, opening on Tuesday. Suggestions on the agenda of the session have been discussed and approved.

"The Congress of the International Physicians for the Prevention of Nuclear War has ended in Budapest on Monday. The International Physicians unite over 140,000 medical workers in all continents. The delegates asked speedy measures to stop the extension of the arms race into outer space and criticized the United States' declaration for Star Wars. One of the movement's founders, American cardiologist Bernard Lown, called on physicians to pool their efforts to prevent the improvements of science from being used for war preparations, which threaten to destroy civilization. The Budapest Congress also called for stopping all nuclear weapons tests. [The International Congress of Physicians, later in the year, was awarded the Nobel Peace Prize, a decision that caused worldwide controversy.]

"In Greece, the mass annual movement, the Acropolis Appeal for Peace, Life, and Culture, has announced a peace campaign will be held in the country from the 1st to the 10th of August. It held a news conference in Athens, where an appeal was made denouncing the continuing deployment of American Pershing II's and cruise missiles in Western Europe and also Washington's military plans to start an arms buildup in outer space.

"The American Vice President, Mr. George Bush, in the course of his West European tour, has resumed talks with French cabinet ministers in Paris. They are focusing on the problem of international terrorism and the Star Wars program. As Mr. Bush said, the United States would like to have French support for joint efforts by the United States and Western Europe against terrorists and countries that shelter them. What Washington has in mind is military action against a number of sovereign nations and national liberation movements. As for the plans of the United States, no West European country has responded to Mr. Bush's call to take a share in them.

"The Nicaraguan President, Daniel Ortega, has said the United States will be unable to reverse the revolutionary process in his country. In an interview granted to the Puerto Rican radio, he said the Nicaraguans, in the face of an increasing threat of American aggression, were getting ready to defend their gains. Mr. Ortega said the economic blockade of his country was an indispensable part of the White House's policy of sponsoring terrorists. He pointed out, the people of Latin America were with the Nicaraguans, as opposed to the terrorist course of the Reagan administration.

"This news comes to you from Moscow.

"The Organization of African Unity has decided to hold a conference devoted to security, disarmament, and development in Africa. The conference will be attended by the foreign ministers of African countries and representatives of a number of other nations. It will take place in the capital of Mali, from the 11th to the 15th of August. Its agenda will include the prevention of space from being used for military purposes, work against the arms race, and problems of mutual security.

"The government in Ethiopia has set up over 300 relief aid centers for famine victims. The commission in charge of aid and restoration made the announcement in the capital, Addis Ababa. Over half a million people have as yet been resettled in more fertile areas. The commission thanked the world community helping the country to conquer the effects of the disaster. As is known, the Soviet Union has helped heavily the famine victims in Ethiopia and more aid from it is forthcoming. Beside foodstuffs, the Soviet Union has sent transport vehicles and mobile hospitals to Ethiopia.

"In Bhopal, India, there have been more deaths resulting from poisoning caused by a toxic gas leak from the local plant of the American Union Carbide Company in December last year. The newspaper *Hindustan Times* says over two-and-a-half-thousand people were killed and scores of thousands of others seriously affected in December by the leak, which occurred through the company's fault.

"The Polish newspaper *Tribuna Ludu* says there has been an upsurge of provocative activity lately by revenge-seeking associations in Federal Germany. Another get-together by a group of Silesian Germans in Hannover has confirmed that there are influential forces in Federal Germany, rallying around revengeful organizations which call for annexation of Polish territory and the territories of other socialist countries.

"The member countries of the Council for Mutual Economic Assistance have experienced a rapid increase in mutual trade. The Council's secretariat in Moscow has announced that total trade among them has grown by 50 percent since 1980. Ten socialist countries in Europe, Asia, and Latin America are affiliated with the Council. Last year, their trade reached 185,000 million rubles, over 211,000 million dollars. These are record-high levels in the 36-year-old history of the organization.

"The Soviet cosmonauts Vladimir Dzhanibekov and Viktor Savinykh have made visual observations of vast areas of the Soviet Union during the more than three weeks of their flight on the Soyut T-13. They have collected valuable information on the condition of the crop in Kazakhstan and vast forest areas of Siberia. The information collected by the crew is utilized by a variety of economic organizations in the country.

"Film workers from many countries have been sending messages of greetings to the current Fourteenth Moscow International Film Festival. Italian actress Stefania Sandrelli and America's director Francis Coppola have said that the Moscow Festival unites film workers of many countries. Mr. Coppola, who has shown his works at one of the previous festivals, said it had been a great pleasure to him to meet with outstanding and emotional Moscow audiences. The current festival has had exhibitors from more than 100 countries. Among them films from Romania, North Korea, and New Zealand have been shown.

"And now, to end the news, the main points again . . ."

The announcer then repeated the news headlines, roughly as given at the beginning of the newscast, concluding, "And that is the end of the news." A female announcer then said, "The World Service of Radio Moscow presents 'The Way We See It,' a look at the Soviet Union and the world." A short musical bridge, and then, "In this issue, a short course on the arms race; the American and the Soviet position; and who organized, in 1961, the killing of the Congolese independence fighter, Patrice Lumumba." The two commentaries that followed were presented by alternating female and male voices. The first contrasted U.S missile deployment with Soviet efforts, quoting details from the Soviet magazine *New Times*. The feature emphasized space weapons, notably the use of lasers, and stated that the Soviet Union offered an "alternative to such a policy." Quoting *Izvestia*, the commentary summarized the U.S.S.R.'s position which viewed "nuclear and space armaments as interrelated." As proof of the Soviet Union's sincerity, the feature mentioned the U.S.S.R.'s moratorium on deployment of intermediate missiles in Europe. It cited *Moscow News* as saying that the Soviet Union regards the prevention of nuclear war as its major task.

The second commentary recalled that the Congolese leader Patrice Lumumba was born on July 2, 1925, 60 years ago, and said, "He was killed in a plot in 1961." It said Lumumba had personified the "raising of the national consciousness of Africa" and became the prime minister of the Congo, after Belgium's colonial rule. The commentary stated that when he opposed "foreign big business, Lumumba was declared a red agent by reactionary forces in the West." Belgium landed paratroops in the Congo "allegedly to protect Belgian nationals." The commentary quoted a book on "CIA plots," published in Paris in 1976, that cited a cable sent by the then CIA director, Allen Dulles, which said that "removing the man is top priority." It added: "Lumumba was captured in the long run and killed on January the 6th, 1961. No accurate details on how Patrice Lumumba was slain are available. Imperialists feel they have done everything to obliterate the memory of Patrice Lumumba in history. There is even no grave for the African patriot. But the entire progressive humanity still remembers the name of Patrice Lumumba." [A United Nations commission reported that Lumumba died January 17.] The commentary concluded: "History is an excellent teacher. A close look at the second chapter, in which Grenada's Prime Minister, Maurice Bishop, was killed, shows that they were similar to those in which the Congo's Premier, Patrice Lumumba, was assassinated. The motives and the methods were the same. This should be borne in mind. That ends this issue of 'The Way We See It.' "

After a musical interlude, a male announcer stated: "This is the World Service of Radio Moscow." There followed a commentary on the use of science and technology in Soviet agriculture. The program emphasized that it was "a mistaken notion that the U.S.S.R. is a large industrial power in which agriculture plays a minor part." Again, male and female voices alternated, providing variety, while offering statistics on farm output. The report noted that prices of cereals had remained the same for 30 years, that the vitamin content of the Soviet diet was satisfactory, but that the "structure" of food intake needed improving, as "in winter and spring there is as yet a shortage of vegetables and fruit." It credited the "sizable increase in the take-home earnings of the public" with causing such shortages: "With prices being stable there is an increase in the consumption of mostly high-quality food." The commentary mentioned that the Soviet Food Program, launched in 1982, was designed to create a substantial improvement in the structure of the food intake by 1990. The introduction of automated systems in farming was outlined, particularly in the allocation of resources and farm equipment.

Once again, a male announcer presented "The News in Brief." A half hour had passed. Following a musical bridge, a male voice said, "Radio Moscow World Service presents: *The Soviet Way of Life!*" The next musical bridge, more lively than those preceding, introduced a feature that explained the powers of the Supreme Soviet, as the female announcer put it, "as we call our national parliament"; an interview with a 45-year-old industrial worker; and "the opinions of foreign trade union activists about the rights and life of the Soviet people." The feature on the Supreme Soviet gave an overview of the institution's technical position under the country's constitution and sought to convey the impression of describing a legislative body, "elected by secret ballot." The worker, whose Russian words were overlaid by an English translation, said he regarded employment, shelter, and nourishment as the true basis for "human rights."

The feature *Kaleidoscope* followed, offering brief items, interspersed with short pieces of electronic music. Items ranged from plans for new hotels in the Crimea to the introduction of computer use in industry and agriculture, from the export of rose oil to French perfume manufacturers to the availability of fringe benefits to workers in high-output enterprises.

Next, a commentator answered letters from listeners. A British listener wrote that he and his wife, in addition to the news, enjoyed three features: *In the News Today*, *Moscow Mailbag*, and *Concert Requests*. Another listener praised broadcasts of choirs, "particularly Russian choirs," and still another thanked the station for playing his request, Ravel's *Pictures at an Exhibition*. He wrote, "What a fine orchestra the Moscow Philharmonic is. I was happy to hear, once more, my favorite piece of classical music." Another praised Tchaikovsky presentations, notably *The Queen of Spades* and *Eugene Onegin*. He wrote, "It is always a delight, late in the evening, to relax and listen to such music." One listener requested that the station broadcast the local weather and was told if he listened to Radio Moscow's *British Hour*, he would "know all about the weather in Moscow." A female announcer closed by thanking eight listeners by name for having sent in reception reports and concluded, "With that, I say bye-bye to all of you, until next week!"

A light music bridge followed, after which a male announcer said: "Thank you, Nina Pavlova. That was Nina Pavlova, with *Goodbye to Moscow*. And now, background information and comments on the topics of the day." A solemn musical bridge, changing to electronic rhythmic sounds, preceded the male announcer's voice: "In the news today: Ceremony of Hiroshima victims. Transport and General Workers Union puts forward a peace package. And a report on the U.S.S.R. Supreme Soviet." There were more electronic sounds. The first item was that "a delegation of the Japanese Federation of Organizations of Victims of the American Atom-Bombing is currently visiting Moscow and delegates were quoted as thanking the Soviet people "for their tremendous efforts to ease world tensions." The second item dealt with the British labor union's meeting at Bournemouth and its denunciation of "the Reagan administration's negative attitude toward the Geneva negotiations to affect arms control." The commentator said the meeting illustrated British working-class opposition to "the American Star Wars program" and "new American nuclear missiles in Western Europe," as well as "the Tory Cabinet's position as America's lackeys." The commentary accused "the British media" of being "absolutely silent about this conference." The feature on the Supreme Soviet, which duplicated somewhat the item during the first half of the broadcast, was a translation of a report given by an Azerbaijani woman delegate. Electronic music followed, and the final announcer's message: "That is all for today, and I wish you good listening, and now bye-bye." There was a musical closing, an electronic arrangement on an American jazz theme.

Before the end of the hour, the male announcer reminded listeners that Radio Moscow's program *Music and Musicians* could be heard each Friday, Saturday, and Sunday. The female announcer gave a final program note, saying that Radio Moscow also broadcasts on medium-wave frequencies, which can be heard in geographically close areas, rather than overseas.

Following the program notes, there was another musical interlude, sufficient to fill airtime until the next full hour. After a brief pause, "Midnight in Moscow" came on once more, followed by the Kremlin chimes. Another newscast was about to begin.

The propaganda themes included within the English-language newscast seem easily apparent. It also needs saying, however, that major world news on this day included the return of 39 American hostages, passengers on TWA Flight 847, which had left Athens for Rome on June 14. The plane was hijacked by Islamic extremists, shuttled between Beirut and Algiers, and one passenger was killed. Radio Moscow limited itself to stating that U.S. Vice President Bush had sought to line up support for "military actions" against "sovereign nations and national liberation movements." The second major item of the day was the removal from the Politburo of Grigori Romanov, who had been regarded as Gorbachev's major rival. This was a top news item, which Radio Moscow submerged and packaged as Romanov's "request" which had been "satisfied," adding that he was "retiring on pension on account of his health." The anniversary items of Patrice Lumumba and Hiroshima were characteristic of the propagandistic device of using commemorative dates to reiterate specific themes. By citing an Indian newspaper, the broadcast revived the Bhopal industrial disaster, and by identifying the company concerned as "American" and stating that the deaths were "the company's fault," the tragedy was targeted unmistakably. (On the following day, Andrei Gromyko, the Soviet Union's longtime foreign minister, was named chairman of the Presidium of the Supreme Soviet and Eduard A. Shevardnadze was appointed foreign minister. Gorbachev nominated Gromyko to the chairmanship, which was categorized in Radio Moscow newscasts as the position of "president," although technically such a title does not exist. Newscasts downplayed these major personnel changes, following the general policy of projecting Soviet leadership as collective.)

The newscasts and features reviewed here may be regarded as fairly typical. Press reviews, regional news, and such features as *Newsreel* serve to divide the full broadcast hour into segments that do not test the listener's attention span unduly. The whole concept of Radio Moscow's English-language World Service is a relatively new one. It was introduced on October 3, 1978, at 7 a.m., Moscow time, when announcer Karl Yegorov said, for the first time, "This is Radio Moscow World Service. Here is the news." The next day, a feature on the very same service stated, "On that day and at that time, a new radio show was born." The report added:

"It appeared as the result of your requests. Radio Moscow has always had a wide following of listeners all over the world, listeners that any radio station could be proud of, listeners that we do not talk at or even talk to, but that we converse with. Yes, it has been a dialogue, for Radio Moscow broadcasts have always been answered by hundreds of thousands of letters every year. These letters have, especially in recent times, demanded a broadening of our operations. They asked for more news from and about the Soviet Union, more information about the Soviet way of life and how people here see things, from major events to the problems of everyday life.

"Radio Moscow's World Service in English was conceived as the response to those demands. It has been tailored to fit your requests. This service will be furnishing you with the latest news, both domestic and international. It will take you into the homes of Soviet people, it will lead you into city streets, and help you strike up conversations with the man in the street. In reporting back to you, Radio Moscow World Service will not be addressing every particular country or even continent; it will be speaking to all people, and every individual person, on things that are important to all human beings, regardless of where they live and who they are; and in all cases it will be telling you about the U.S.S.R. and what makes us tick as a nation and as individuals."

The report then gave transmission times and frequencies, and concluded: "This is, in the word's most basic sense, your service: Radio Moscow World Service in English."

It was clear, from the start, that the new service closely followed the long-standing pattern of the hourly transmissions of the BBC. For decades, these have opened, on the hour, with a characteristic time signal and the opening, "This is London! BBC World Service. The news, read by Pamela Creighton," or whoever the announcer happened to be. The sounds of Big Ben have also been a standard feature. Radio Moscow had long used the chimes of the Kremlin tower but, in its early days, opened with the traditional Marxist battle hymn, the "Internationale." (When this author visited a veteran of the Communist International, Lenin's handpicked Far Eastern specialist Mahendra Nath Roy, in his home at Dehra Dun, India, at the foothills of the Himalayas, Roy confessed that his final emotional defection from Moscow came when its radio transmissions stopped using the rousing rhythms of the "Internationale.")

The strains of a popular melody, such as "Midnight in Moscow," reflect an almost coy effort to put the listener at ease, to provide something like musical anesthesia before the barbs of newscasts, commentaries, and features go out over the airwaves. Music, in fact, quickly became one of the new service's most characteristic features. The service has sought to appeal to listeners favoring classical music, folk tunes, songs, and Soviet rock bands. Western music is used regularly, and in line with the often quite colloquial delivery of the English-speaking announcers (who can be exaggeratedly "American," pronouncing "twenty" as "twenny"), there is a consistent effort to be neighborly and even folksy in texts and program structure.

The *Moscow Mailbag*, read by announcers as if they were giving answers to letters quite personally and without scripts, is closest to the service's effort to converse with listeners. Even pointed questions are answered with seemingly casual candor. When one listener wanted to know how the Soviet Union felt about Stalin, the *Mailbag* announcer said Stalin had been "both good and bad," had achieved much progress, and had been an important leader during the Great Patriotic War, but his "cult of the personality" had alienated the Soviet public. Another listener asked about the KGB. He was told the initials stood for "Committee for State Security" and, as the name suggested, it was "in charge of the national security."

If Radio Moscow World Service is the mainstream of the transmissions, there are also many tributaries. First of all, Radio Moscow has retained special regional services in English to North America, Africa, South and Southeast Asia, and Great Britain and Ireland. These overlap and total about 40 hours per day. The World Service was initiated when Leonid Zamyatin was appointed director of the International Information Department of the Soviet Communist Party's Central Committee, and some observers have credited Zamyatin with backing its streamlined, BBC-type program pattern. *The Economist*, London (November 30, 1979), commented that the new service was "much more relaxed" and "better packaged than anything the Russians have done before." *Newsweek* (April 21, 1980) noted that the service had "escalated the battle of the airwaves" and that it might prompt listeners to mistake it "for a Western broadcast—at least until the news comes on."

For all its "bourgeois" accoutrements, Radio Moscow World Service has remained characteristically Soviet and Russian. To shortwave listeners, there is a typical fruity timbre to its male and female voices. The magazine *Popular Communications* (February 1985) described these characteristics, "something not easily put into words," as having a "certain quality" that is easy to recognize. The announcers speak English of an international type, be it with a British or American intonation. One common characteristic is an air of tutorial certainty, despite the effort not to "talk at or even talk to" the listeners.

Radio Moscow's editor-in-chief, Gheli Shakov, a broadcaster for more than a quarter century, is said to have advocated such a modernized radio program since 1954. In an interview with Douglas Stangling of UPI, broadcast and TV personality Vladimir Posner said (October 5, 1979) that Radio Moscow was perhaps becoming "more sophisticated." Such words as "capitalism" and "imperialism," he said, would no longer be used, as they have "come to acquire a certain kind of color that is more political, and more propagandistic, if you wish, than merely economic." He added: "So we have discarded them, because people tend to recognize them in another way, to be antagonistic, which is not the purpose of the broadcast." Still, Radio Moscow just cannot avoid picking up the term "imperialist," which Soviet media use constantly as a code word to categorize the United States and other countries. Other antiquated Marxist terms are being used less and less in broadcasts and literature; they have also been sidetracked by top leaders, beginning with Andropov and continuing with Gorbachev.

An example of the lightheartedness the service seeks to maintain was provided by two announcers, Eduard Dyatlov and Marina Dimova: Dyatlov said, "Yes, we'll have to do it more frequently. The thing is that there have been reports in Western mass media that we are taking listeners away from the BBC World Service, and specifically in the [London] *Daily Telegraph*. Last month there was an article by its Moscow correspondent that—um, let me see; I have a clipping here somewhere; oh yes, here it is—the news service and the correspondent mean Radio Moscow World Service is a flattering copy of the BBC's English-language broadcasts, and it's possible to switch on and listen for quite a time before realizing the program is not coming from London."

Dimova replied: "Well, I think I've got your point. Of course, it's quite a flattering comparison, I should say, but it's not true. Though we have some outward resemblance with the BBC, the similarities end there. And then, every ten minutes or so, we announce that we are Radio Moscow World Service." Dyatlov added: "So, let's do it more often, so that our colleagues in the BBC World Service don't bear us a grudge."

Like antagonists at a tennis game, this sounds as if they are ready to meet at the net once the game is finished. The conversational style, including the apparent fumbling for a newspaper clipping in front of the microphone, provides the sort of touch that makes the bitter medicine of one or another news item go down more easily. The master of Radio Moscow's informal touch is "Joe" Adamov, the heavyset Armenian-born announcer who speaks with a studied all-American accent. Adamov is a radio veteran who recalls the World War II ambiance at the Moscow studios, when correspondents of the U.S. radio networks worked closely with Russian colleagues. Adamov, given to loud ties and generally relaxed garb, occasionally appears on U.S. radio and TV interview shows. He may be seen, talking to a television interviewer, sitting on a park bench and admitting with apparent casualness that there is, indeed, "some corruption" on the Soviet economic scene—one of the negative facets of Russian society that is, in fact, regularly admitted, from Kremlin speeches to scathing cartoons in *Krokodil*, the satirical weekly. Adamov has the ability of giving even a stilted official announcement an air of blustery candor.

Adamov had the task (October 13, 1985) of answering the question, "What is your attitude to terrorism?" presumably submitted by a U.S. woman. He gave the following reply:

"What is our attitude? Even before the Revolution, the founder of our nation and our party, Vladimir Lenin, said that terrorism is not the path that we will follow, and we have been true to his behest, because terrorism does not achieve any goals. We are for revolution, yes. We support the national liberation movements, yes. But on the other hand, don't forget that your country, too, was born of revolution.

"I personally believe that the world community should take very stringent measures against kidnappings, against bombings, hijacking of planes, oh yes, and of cruise ships—what will they think of next? But, of course, since we're on the subject, it is wrong to call people who fight for their home, for their lives, for the lives of their families, for a way of life which they have chosen, such as the Sandinistas, for instance, to call these people terrorists, and to call the real terrorists, the Contras, to call them freedom fighters.

"No, let's not get the terminology mixed up. Hijackers are hijackers, irrespective of the aims or the goals by which they may be guided. Let me give you an example. Two hijackers, the Brazinkas, father and son, hijacked a plane in the Soviet Union, wounded two of the crew, and killed a young girl, a flight attendant. They ended up in the United States, but were never returned to the country where the crime was committed and were never tried in the United States. Now, such an attitude to criminals breeds more actions of a similar kind."

This type of calculated informality is rarely pierced by the actual intrusion of a personal note. Over the years, only one startling exception has occurred, when on May 23, 1983, World Service announcer Vladimir Danchev departed from a script on Afghanistan, turning the official version, which spoke of infiltration from Pakistan, into a reference to "Soviet invaders." Successive newscasts, read by Danchev, began with a routinely worded item at 10 a.m. UTC: "The population of Afghanistan plays an increasing role in defending the country's territory against bands infiltrating from Pakistan. Reports from Kabul say that tribes living in the eastern

provinces Nangarhar and Paktia have joined the struggle against the counterrevolutionaries." So far, so good; this was standard Soviet propaganda
fare. But an hour later, the announcer read the second sentence so that it
said the population in the eastern provinces had "joined the struggle against
the Soviet invaders" and added the following: "A decision to give an armed
rebuff to the bandits was taken at the tribes' meeting. The participants
underlined that the activity carried out from Soviet territory endangers the
security of the population of Afghanistan."

If no one in the Moscow studios, or elsewhere in the Soviet radio control
apparatus, had noticed Danchev's deviation from the official text, listeners
at the BBC monitoring service at Caversham Park, Reading, were more
than a little puzzled. Their routine recording of the newscast clearly showed
that the item had, in fact, been revised into a version critical of the Soviet
military invasion of Afghanistan. And when the news came on the air,
once again, at noon, Danchev read the item in the identical revised version.

At 1 p.m., Danchev read a still more detailed version of the news item,
as follows:

"The population of Afghanistan plays an increasing role in defending
the country's territory against bands infiltrated from the Soviet Union.
Reports in Kabul say that tribes living in the eastern provinces Nangarhar
and Paktia have joined the struggle against the Soviet invaders. A decision
to give an armed rebuff to the bandits was taken at the tribes' meetings.
The participants underlined that antigovernment activity carried out from
the Soviet territory endangers the security of the population of Afghanistan."

When Danchev read the news headlines, at the end of the newscast,
he used the following version: "According to reports in Kabul, the population of Afghan regions bordering on Pakistan takes an increasingly
active part in action against the Soviet forces." However, when the 2 p.m.
newscast came along, Danchev had been replaced by another announcer,
Vladimir Obraztsov, who read the item in its original 10 a.m. version.

International monitors were able to add yet another oddity to Danchev's
revision of the Afghanistan item. In a broadcast on May 15, 1983, the same
announcer had delivered an item in such a manner as to accuse the Soviet
Union of failing to cooperate fairly in arms negotiations with the United
States. He read one news item that said: "The Soviet Union has said once
again that it is not prepared to work to secure constructive decisions on
limiting nuclear arms in Europe" and added that "the Soviet Union wishes
to have more missiles and warheads . . . than NATO has."

It came as no surprise when Moscow correspondents were told, on May
28, that Danchev had been ordered to leave Moscow and return to his
hometown, Tashkent, capital of Uzbekistan. Radio Moscow played down
the incident, and a spokesman said Danchev had made a "personal mis-

take" in the broadcast. Danchev, identified as the son of a senior Communist Party official, was later reported as having been sent to a psychiatric
clinic. According to the newsletter *Soviet Analyst* (November 9, 1983),
Danchev admitted during an investigation that he had "started to include
critical statements" in his broadcasts "as early as February 1983, but it was
not until the Western press wrote about his reports that the administration
realized that he had deviated from the approved texts." Either temporarily
or permanently, subsequent newscasts were prerecorded. Radio Moscow
updates news from hour to hour, and newscasts can be recorded while
commentaries and features are being broadcast, so little immediacy is lost.

On December 14, a Radio Moscow spokesman told the Reuters news
agency that Danchev had been reinstated. "He was ill," the spokesman
said, "but now he has been cured." The dispatch quoted informed sources
as saying that Danchev had been given an editorial position at Radio
Moscow but was "not permitted near a microphone." The report added:
"His mild treatment contrasted sharply with the usual Soviet attitude toward dissidents, who are rarely allowed to occupy senior positions once
they have denounced state policy."

Still, Danchev could very well have remained in Tashkent, where there
is a large broadcasting setup. Radio Tashkent transmits English-language
programs to the Far East, as well as in Hindi to India, Urdu to Pakistan,
Farsi to Iran, Uzbek to ethnic groups in western China, and Arabic to the
Middle East. The content of these programs offers regional variations, but
the main themes are identical with those of Soviet media generally. Thus,
in 1985, when the media featured the fortieth anniversary of the "victory
of the Soviet people over Fascist Germany," there was a competition,
called "Tashkent-85," that offered prizes for answers to the following questions:

"1.   Why is the war against the Fascist invaders called the Great Pa-
      triotic War of the Soviet people? When did it start and when did
      it end?

"2.   Who played the decisive role in the routing of German fascism
      and Japanese militarism?

"3.   What contribution did Soviet Uzbekistan make in the victory over
      Fascist Germany?

"4.   What impact did the victory of the Soviet people in the Great
      Patriotic War have on the rise of the national liberation movement
      in countries of Asia, Africa, and Latin America, including your
      country?

"5.   What are the lessons of World War II? What do you think about the need to fight for peace and oppose the threat of a third world war?"

The Radio Tashkent Foreign Service offered a series of awards, with the first prize an "all-expenses-paid seven-day tour of Uzbekistan." Other prizes were souvenirs, keepsakes, pictorial albums, and sets of picture cards. Such competitions encourage listener mail, which *Mailbag* and *Concert Requests* also generate. When Radio Moscow held a special contest, on the occasion of its fiftieth anniversary in 1979, it received more than 30,000 entries. Annually, the station gets some 300,000 letters from 150 countries. The Correspondence Department keeps a card index that lists the names, addresses, and areas of special interest of each letter writer and, if possible, the writer's age as well.

A German correspondent, Pierre Simonitsch of the *Frankfurter Rundschau*, visited the Moscow studios and reported (October 19, 1981) that they occupy a ten-story brick building, formerly the offices of a scientific institute, and employ 3,000 people. The reporter was told in Moscow by Vladimir Ostrogorski, resident "radio theoretician," that statistics show listeners eager to obtain a more direct picture of Soviet life and views.

Listeners complain that Radio Moscow never reports negative news from within the Soviet Union, not even major accidents or natural disasters, whereas the Voice of America and the BBC routinely report such events, as well as opposition comments and other self-criticisms. Occasionally, Radio Moscow will refer to certain shortages, but immediately overwhelms such an item with reams of positive statistics. Ostrogorski said, "We are not going to falsify the government's position, in order to please our listeners." In several countries, including Germany, Radio Moscow has rented post office boxes, but most listeners prefer to write to Moscow directly.

The vast Soviet radio networks, domestic and overseas, have long been under the supervision of Serge G. Lapin, chairman of the State Committee for Television and Radio Broadcasting (Gostelradio). Lapin took the TV-radio position in 1970, after three years as director-general of Tass. He had been ambassador to China from 1965 to 1967. Born in 1912, Lapin had a long career in press and radio before entering the diplomatic service. After journalistic work in the Leningrad area, he attended the Communist Party High School attached to the party's Central Committee, graduating in 1942. After two years on the Central Committee's staff, Lapin joined the Committee of Radio Installations and Broadcasting of the U.S.S.R. Council of Ministers. He first served as chief editor of political broadcasting and from April 1945 to 1953 as the committee's deputy chairman. Lapin advanced during the Brezhnev era. He took over at Tass after Nikita Khrushchev had been deposed and remained as head of the State Committee for Radio and Television well into the Gorbachev regime.

On December 16, 1985, Lapin retired, at the age of 73, and was replaced by Alexander Aksyonov, then 61 years old. Before this appointment, Aksyonov had been Soviet ambassador to Poland. In contrast to Lapin, Aksyonov's background did not include specific experience in communication and propaganda, but in state security. Earlier in his career, he had been prime minister of the Byelorussian Republic, and he also spent six years with the KGB and the Ministry of Interior.

Radio Moscow's vast apparatus is a major segment of the Soviet propaganda establishment. Although television has become paramount in the domestic information-and-education program of the Soviet Communist Party, radio, a favorite since Lenin's day, has remained a major force in international propaganda. Lenin, who regarded radio as "a spoken newspaper," recognized its Agitprop potential from the very beginning.

The Soviet Union's international broadcasts began in 1929. The first transmission was directed at Germany, and the words "Hier ist Radio Moskau!" could be heard on shortwave and medium-wave receivers. On the European continent, Moscow has transmitters that broadcast on the AM, or medium-wave, band, the standard broadcast band on most receivers. Radio Moscow's English-language transmissions also reach the southern United States from an AM relay station in Cuba. Havana also functions as a relay for shortwave transmissions at various times of the day. At its most aggressive, Radio Moscow has offered tapes of its shows to radio stations in the United States and Canada. *Broadcasting* magazine reported (December 18, 1978) that Moscow was offering English-language programs to U.S. stations to provide "first-hand information for people interested in the Soviet Union." The magazine stated:

"Letters have gone out to U.S. radio stations from Gheli A. Shakhov, editor-in-chief of Radio Moscow's English Service, offering them twelve different programs—ranging from *Moscow Mailbag*, a 15-minute program featuring Joe Adamov answering questions sent in by listeners, to *Science and Technology in the USSR*. According to Yuri Solton, Washington correspondent for Moscow Radio and Television, the offer has been made to 'about 1,000' stations in the U.S. He said the Service was being made primarily to university-supported stations." Radio Moscow was making the tapes available free of charge. This is a pattern the station has used in Third World countries and wherever a station might be financially limited but has airtime to fill. In the 1970s, one Canadian station was on the verge of collapse when news came that Radio Moscow was ready to prop it up, with free taped material.

Beginning February 24, 1980, the Cuban relay of Radio Moscow's North American Service came booming into southern Florida. Broadcast from a transmitter that was three times as powerful as permitted locally, or 150,000 kilowatts in strength, the relay came in at 600 kilohertz, around 60 on the

AM dial. Christopher Perzanowski, writing in the *Miami Herald* (March 1, 1981), commented that the station offered Floridians "a radical alternative" to our "bad-news-obsessed" media, being committed to the "good news" concept of information, at least where Soviet events were concerned. The Moscow relay was coming in over Cuba's Radio Rebelde, a medium-wave station that used to broadcast in Spanish to the United States but ultimately devoted all its airtime to the Moscow relay. These transmissions were separate from Radio Havana Cuba, which also transmits in English and has carried features that clearly originated with Radio Moscow, such as cultural items. (The Voice of America's Radio Martí, directed at Cuba's home audience, began broadcasting in 1985. Until then, VOA had broadcast on medium-wave to Cuba, as part of its Spanish-language transmissions to Latin America, from a transmitter in Marathon, Florida.)

Gerry L. Dexter, in his article "Soviet Broadcasting: An Inside Look," in *Popular Communications* (February 1985), noted that Radio Moscow has extensive Spanish and Portuguese transmissions to Latin America; these are supplemented by Radio Havana and, to a lesser extent, by Radio Managua, Nicaragua. Dexter wrote that Moscow's broadcasts are beamed at target areas in East and West Europe, the Middle and Near East, Africa, Southeast Asia, the Far East, and South and Central America in a variety of languages "that runs from Amharic to Zulu." The French service is called Radio Moscow International.

Moscow operates a special Spanish-language Radio Magellenes, beamed to Chile. It is not clear where this broadcast is relayed, but it may also be channeled through Cuba. Radio Mayak, directed at Russians overseas and at remote points within the Soviet Union, relays major segments of the domestic radio service. This is a 24-hour service that can be heard clearly in the Western hemisphere and, therefore, suggests a Cuban relay. A service for Soviet sailors, Radiostansiya Atlantika, is beamed at ships in and around the Atlantic Ocean. In the Pacific area, Russian sailors can listen to Radio Tikhy Okean (Radio Pacific Ocean). Dexter noted that the program was operating from a transmitter in the Soviet Far East, from studios at Vladivostok, with programs directed at the Pacific, North America, Asia, and the Middle East. He also wrote:

"Most of the various Soviet republics have shortwave facilities of one form or another, many of which carry some sort of foreign service. Here again there are problems in knowing what you're listening to, since some of these foreign services, while being produced in the capital of the republic involved, may not be coming from transmitters within that republic but from Radio Moscow facilities instead. Or, it may be a combination of both!"

Radio Kiev, for example, features an English-language service to North America, presumably aimed at second- or third-generation Ukrainians in the United States and Canada; there are often programs dealing with Ukrainian youth. These transmissions turn up on Radio Moscow frequencies. Radio Erivan, Armenia, has similar services in English to the Western hemisphere, but it also broadcasts in Armenian, French, Arabic, Turkish, and other languages. Radio Baku, Azerbaijan, transmits in Arabic, Farsi, and other languages. Radio Tallinn, Estonia, broadcasts in Finnish, Swedish, and Estonian. Radio Riga, Latvia, transmits in Swedish, Latvian, and Russian. Radio Vilnius, Lithuania, has an English service to North America, in addition to Lithuanian. An organization identified as the Soviet Committee for Cultural Relations with Compatriots Abroad, presumably civilians on diplomatic and commercial missions, operates Radiostansiya Rodina, the Voice of the Soviet Homeland.

All told, then, the Soviet radio propaganda effort is varied, complex, and massive.

CHAPTER · 23

Clandestine and "Unofficial"

In addition to Radio Moscow, Soviet propaganda uses broadcasts that are "unofficial" or clandestine. These channels do not adhere to the restrictions, such as they are, that control the tenor and content of Radio Moscow. The Soviet Union's major "unofficial" broadcast tool is Radio Peace and Progress. Like Novosti, the radio station claims that it is not a government outlet; but it is less accommodating than Novosti, often blunt to the point of crudeness, and not above the use of disinformation. In addition, radio stations that seek to give the impression that they represent non-Soviet groups and are located outside the U.S.S.R. have come and gone as changing propaganda policies dictated.

While other such radio programs have disappeared, the National Voice of Iran has continued its black propaganda activities for decades. The station pretends to be located on Iranian soil, but monitors have traced it to Baku, capital of Soviet Azerbaijan. Radio Baku's powerful transmitters broadcast in Arabic, Farsi, Azeri, Kurdish, and other Near and Far Eastern languages. By using the label "National Voice of Iran," Soviet propaganda, dispensing with any niceties of international discourse, can unleash its commentators. Still and all, even a clandestine Soviet-controlled station has to reflect the zigs and zags of Moscow's policies.

The station's role came into focus in 1979, when the U.S. embassy in Teheran was invaded by "students" and its personnel taken hostage. While Soviet policymakers clearly enjoyed the prolonged dilemma of the U.S. government, they fell short of endorsing the possible execution of the American diplomats—thinking, perhaps, that this would set an undesirable precedent. On November 4, the National Voice of Iran hailed "the strug-

289

gling young people" who had taken over the embassy as a "decisive response to the overt and covert conspiracies of U.S. imperialism and the
U.S. government's hostile act of settling the deposed Shah in the United
States." The next day, the station said that the United States had not
ceased the "hatching of plots against Iran," but assured listeners that the
"young people of our homeland" possessed "sufficient political and revolutionary awareness not to resort to certain measures against the employees of the U.S. Embassy."

While the Soviet government maintained the official position that events
in Iran contravened international agreements concerning diplomatic immunity, some of its media expressed a certain glee over the U.S. dilemma.
When Washington protested in Moscow in mid-November, both the clandestine station and Radio Moscow's Persian-language service became more
cautious. On November 20, the clandestine station noted that several U.S.
hostages had been freed and commented that it was "imperative" that the
rest should also be released.

The National Voice of Iran began broadcasting in 1959, but Moscow's
involvement in the area predates the Bolshevik Revolution. Czarist governments rivaled British economic and political influence in Persia (Iran);
Lenin, however, renounced all imperial aspirations in a treaty dated January 16, 1921, pledging nonintervention in Persian affairs. During World
War II, to forestall German influence, both Russian and British troops
occupied the country. On January 29, 1942, Iran, Britain, and the U.S.S.R.
signed an alliance that pledged foreign troop withdrawal within six months
of the war's end. U.S. troops were also stationed on Persian soil.

When the war ended, Britain and the U.S. withdrew their troops. Russia
did not. Moscow installed a Comintern veteran, Jaafar Pishevari, as president of an autonomous Azerbaijani government in northern Iran; under
the name of Sultan Zade, he had directed the Iranian Section of the Communist International in Moscow. Noting this Soviet move toward indirect
annexation, U.S. President Harry S. Truman was prompted to establish
the "Truman Doctrine" in 1947, providing economic and military aid to
Greece and Turkey.

I viewed these developments in my book *World Communism Today*
(1948) as follows:

"The importance of the Iranian events in early 1945 can hardly be
exaggerated. Here was a clear case of Soviet intervention in favor of a
government led by a veteran of the Communist International. Here also
was a clear violation of international contracts. When the foreign ministers
of the major powers met in Moscow in December 1945, the Soviet government refused to discuss the question of Iran. It is a matter of historical
record that both Premier Stalin and Foreign Minister Molotov told United
States Secretary of State [James F.] Byrnes and British Foreign Minister

[Ernest] Bevin that there was no need to settle the Iranian matter, because both Britain and Russia were pledged by their 1941 agreement to evacuate Iran on or before March 2, 1946. Stalin and Molotov were indignant that the pledge of the Soviet government should be doubted.

"But while the foreign ministers met in Moscow, Pishevari officially took control over the Azerbaijan province. And when March 2, 1946, came around, Soviet occupation troops did not withdraw from Azerbaijan. On the contrary, two Soviet armored corps of fifty heavy tanks were moved all the way from Lake Balaton in Hungary to northern Iran, to strengthen the hold of the Pishevari regime. The case was discussed before the United Nations Security Council, over the spirited objection of Soviet delegate Andrei Gromyko. On one occasion, Gromyko walked out of the Council chamber in a gesture of protest."

In the late spring of 1946, responding to increasing U.S.-British pressure, Russian troops were finally withdrawn from northern Iran. The Pishevari government folded its tents and returned to Soviet territory. But the Agitprop campaign inside Iran, with emphasis on Azerbaijani and Kurdish minorities, continued. Agents can move relatively freely from Soviet Azerbaijan, with its 4 million inhabitants, to northern Iran, with its 2 million Azerbaijanis. The region is ethnically represented in the Politburo by the Andropov-Gorbachev protegé, Geidar A. Aliyev, a former first secretary of the Communist Party of Azerbaijan and first deputy chairman of the U.S.S.R. Council of Ministers.

The function of a clandestine radio such as the National Voice of Iran takes on major significance if it is analyzed in terms of geopolitical conditions. Ethnically, Soviet Azerbaijan and Iranian Azerbaijan form a unit. The emergence of an Azerbaijani "liberation movement," directed against "oppression" within Iran, could take place, figuratively speaking, at the switch of a button in Moscow's Central Committee. If Afghanistan's resistance were subdued, and Soviet bases there consolidated, Iran would certainly find itself in a precarious position; a hostile Iraq to the west, with many weapons supplied from the Soviet Union, would complete the encirclement. The death or incapacitation of the Ayatollah Khomeini is certain to create a vacuum that opens Iran to agitation and propaganda offensives. Controlling influence could be established without military force, influencing the flow of Iran's oil, and that of neighboring countries.

The Baku Agitprop operation seeks to steer various ethnic populations of Iran, fiercely antagonistic toward each other, into Moscow's preferred channels. Radio Baku's transmissions appeal to nationalist sentiments, emphasize ethnic variety within the U.S.S.R., lash out against "imperialism," and project the image of the Soviet Union as a benevolent big brother. The station operates from a building situated in northern Baku. According to Dan Fisher, a former *Los Angeles Times* Moscow corre-

spondent (*International Herald-Tribune*, September 2, 1979), Radio Baku
sits "in the middle of a giant stone wall, topped with barbed wire, surrounding an area the size of a city block." Three transmitting towers clearly
identify this complex. Fisher also wrote:

"Moscow has apparently used the Voice to put across its views, while
generally maintaining a hands-off policy in its official press, which has
permitted it to pursue closer relations with the Shah and the Ayatollah
alike. The Voice was well out in front of the official Soviet press in calling
for the Shah's overthrow. The official press did not even identify the Shah
as the focus of the revolution until last December [1978], and made no
personal attack on him until after he left Iran." Actually, just before the
Shah's final days in Teheran, he was still being feted in the Communist
world, with a state visit to East Germany.

The National Voice of Iran is only one in a long line of clandestine
Soviet-controlled radio stations which, at one time or another, have been
directed at targets of opportunity. These did not always define their audiences directly. Even while the Stalin-Hitler Pact was in force, German-
language programs could be heard throughout Germany, introduced with
the disclaimer that they were serving inhabitants of the Volga-German
region of the U.S.S.R. This German-speaking population, originally imported by Catherine the Great, was deported by Stalin during World War
II, as were other minorities, to Soviet Central Asia. When the Comintern
was at its most active, its Moscow staff included experienced writers and
speakers in a variety of languages. During the war, all sides engaged in
the use of clandestine radios.

Nazi Germany operated what it called "East Transmitter Five," identified as the Radio of Lenin's Old Guard, which sought to arouse Old
Bolsheviks against Stalin's rule. Before it invaded various Soviet territories,
Germany also operated stations in Ukrainian, Byelorussian, and other
regional languages. Berlin ran several so-called Concordia transmitters. Of
these, "Concordia N" was identified as the New British Broadcasting Station, which was both nationalist and pacifist and "Concordia S," or the
Workers' Challenge, which appealed to revolutionary labor sentiment and
attacked British class distinctions. The Indian nationalist Subhas Chandra
Bose directed the Voice of Free India. Still another clandestine station
billed itself as the Voice of the Free Arabs.

Americans remember the seductive "Tokyo Rose" broadcasts from
Japan, directed at U.S. armed forces in the Pacific. Berlin's broadcast by
a British subject, known in England as "Lord Haw-Haw," gained wide
publicity. Among clandestine German broadcasts directed at U.S. troops
and home audiences were transmissions that sought to imitate domestic
broadcasts in all details, even including commercials for Kellogg's Rice

Krispies from Battle Creek, Michigan. British broadcasts that pretended to originate with disillusioned German army officers, notably "Gustav Siegfried Eins" and "Soldatensender Calais," showed great ingenuity in using information gained from captured German troops. In addition, underground agents received coded information through radio transmissions, such as those broadcast over Nazi Germany's "Secret Transmitter Z" station.

At all times, the use of clandestine radio stations has been timed and calibrated to fit specific situations. Until the death of General Francisco Franco and subsequent changes in the Spanish government, a transmitter calling itself Radio España Independente, staffed by members of the Spanish Communist Party, was operating from Prague. In fact, the capital of Czechoslovakia has, at one time or another, been the base for a number of clandestine radio stations. A controversial Italian-language transmission, Oggi in Italia (Today in Italy), was shut down after the Italian government sent a protest to Prague; monitors believed that the Czechoslovak embassy in Rome at times acted as a clandestine relay station. At various times, particularly during the Greek Civil War, 1947–1949, a Radio Free Greece operated either from Bucharest or Prague. The Czechs have been credited with building the high-powered transmitters of Radio Havana; the Chinese are said to have constructed the powerful station of Radio Tirana, Albania.

Useful as such intermittent operations may be, the International Department of the Soviet Communist Party's Central Committee apparently felt, after Khrushchev's departure, that a permanent but flexible "unofficial" radio operation was needed. Transmissions began on November 1, 1964, with two half-hour programs in Spanish broadcast to Latin America each day. The station, described as an organ of Soviet "public opinion," said that its sponsors were the Union of Journalists of the U.S.S.R., the Novosti news agency, the Union of Societies of Friendship and Cultural Relations with Foreign Countries, the Union of Composers of the U.S.S.R., the Soviet Znaniye (Knowledge) Society, the Soviet Committee for the Defense of Peace, and the Committee of the U.S.S.R. Youth Organizations. The broadcasts were said to be aimed at "cooperating in the development and strengthening of mutual understanding, trust and friendship" and at advancing the "sincere respect and cordial friendship that the Soviet people feel towards the countries of Latin America."

Six months later, the station added a Portuguese-language program, beamed to Brazil. By the end of 1966, it was also broadcasting in French to the Caribbean, targeting Haiti, Martinique, and other French-speaking islands. French and English transmissions, to Asia and Africa, were added, as well as a Portuguese transmission to Africa, aimed at Angola and Mozambique. The following year, Radio Peace and Progress—as the station

was now known—began a Mandarin broadcast to China, which soon became a three-hour program. Broadcasting to Israel, the station first introduced a Yiddish-language program, and then a Hebrew one as well.

As Radio Peace and Progress began to broaden its target areas in Asia
and Africa, it added further English transmissions. In time, the station
began to develop a propagandistic personality that was distinctly aggressive,
divisive, and often seriously irresponsible; the term "hate-mongering" would
be no exaggeration in describing some of its commentaries. The fiction of
the station as "unofficial" enabled Soviet diplomats to maintain that their
government had no control over these broadcasts, that they were "independent," and that the government should not be held responsible for their
content. The government of India, using monitors in the northern hill
station of Simla, pinpointed broadcasts as being relayed by Soviet transmitters near Tashkent. On July 10, 1967, Indian Foreign Minister M. C.
Chagla acknowledged in parliament that Radio Peace and Progress had
criticized individual Congress Party leaders and thus intruded into the
country's internal affairs. Chagla said India's ambassador to Moscow, Kewal
Singh, had been "instructed to raise the matter with Soviet authorities."

If the station was "unofficial," in a country where virtually every major
establishment is government-owned, how did it pay for itself? This question
was once directed, oddly enough, at Radio Moscow's *Mail Bag*. Announcer
Joe Adamov answered (November 19, 1972) by listing the organizations
that were the stations' "sponsors," and he added: "The income of Radio
Station Peace and Progress is composed of subsidies and grants from these
public organizations and also from advertising, from material that is sent
to foreign radio stations and news agencies." He did not specify what kind
of advertising the station sells; its programs do not contain any advertisements. In December 1981, the station switched from calling itself the "voice
of Soviet public opinion" to identifying itself as the "voice of Soviet public
organizations," thus further emphasizing its unique status.

Radio Peace and Progress has, at times, devoted much energy and
airtime to broadcasts directed at China. Once, on the occasion of the
U.S.S.R.'s annual "Radio Day," May 7, the station told its Mandarin-
language listeners that "Soviet state organs are not responsible for its
activities," as it is a station of "Soviet mass organizations" and "operates
on funds allocated by the above-mentioned organizations." A question
about the station's backing also came from a British listener to Radio
Moscow's *DX Club*, designed for shortwave listeners. Two speakers discussed the matter in a question-and-answer format. One voice listed the
various organizations that support the station's council, and a second voice
replied, "Goodness gracious, that certainly is representative. And how
often is this elected?" The answer was: "The new council is elected every
four years. It also controls the activities of the station. The actual broad-

casting, though, is under the direction of the chief editor, who is also the first deputy chairman of the Council of Sponsors. The staff is chosen by the Council." No names were given.

Radio Peace and Progress slips bits of disinformation into its news and commentaries. Broadcasting in Spanish to Latin America (August 10, 1981), it blamed the death of General Omar Torrijos on the U.S. Central Intelligence Agency. The commentary said: "Everything that is known, up to the present time, indicates that the Yankee CIA, corporation of murderers, is implicated in the death of Torrijos. The CIA began this hunt approximately ten years ago. His bold and consistent interventions regarding Panama's sovereignty and its undeniable right to the Panama Canal Zone led to Torrijos and many other Latin American progressive personalities being placed on the list of persons that the CIA had planned to retire from the political scene at any cost."

The broadcasts also implement the Soviet propaganda line that the United States seeks the "Balkanization" of India. Consequently, an English-language broadcast to Asia (May 22, 1982), asserted that "the people of India" were expressing "serious concern and anxiety over the mounting intrigues of the Central Intelligence Agency against their country." The commentary quoted unnamed "sources of the Ministry of Internal Affairs of India" as stating that the CIA was "financing the separatist movement in the State of Punjab" through "secret channels by way of Pakistan."

The CIA was also the target in a broadcast concerning the crisis in the Philippines, early in 1986, when President Ferdinand Marcos faced the challenge of an opposition coalition headed by Corazon Aquino. Moscow, at the time, was virtually alone in accepting Marcos's claim that he had won the election, which was widely regarded as fraud-ridden. Radio Peace and Progress, in a Mandarin-language broadcast (January 5, 1986), alleged that Marcos had "recently accused the CIA of bugging telephone lines in the presidential office in Manila." The broadcast cited this allegation as "one of the many incidents in which Washington has interfered in the internal affairs of the Philippines." At a time when media, worldwide, reported on the vast international holdings of the Marcos family and its associates, the broadcast blamed "the CIA's dirty tricks in spreading rumors about the financial activities of the Filipino leaders." The station's commentator added: "Generally speaking, such dirty tricks are the special characteristics of the policies of the imperialist countries toward the developing countries. They combine economic pressure with political schemes in an attempt to pressure the developing countries to serve imperialist purposes." Implementing several propaganda themes within a single commentary, the broadcast continued:

"The imperialist countries are now employing threatening words of armed provocations and terrorist activities in their talks with India, one of the largest developing nations and one of the acknowledged leaders of the Non-Aligned Movement. The Sikh extremists who have vowed to undermine India's national integrity and political stability, have found shelter and protection in the United States, Canada and Britain. More often than not, the imperialists organize well-planned sabotage activities against the liberated nations. In fact, such activities are undeclared wars against these countries. The United States is taking precisely such actions to aid counter-revolutionary bandits and scum in Afghanistan and Kampuchea [Cambodia]. Washington will resort to using its armed forces against the developing countries in the event that its secret agents and armed rebels fail. The invasion of Grenada, several years ago, is a case in point. Now, Washington is preparing similar action against Nicaragua."

Although much of the output of Radio Peace and Progress is directed toward the Third World, it also emphasizes the stresses in other regions. After terrorist actions at the Vienna and Rome airports, the United States sought to muster international economic pressure on Libya as the nation that had consistently backed such terrorism. Broadcasting in German to West Germany, the station said (January 7, 1986) that U.S. Middle East policy had "an anti-European thrust." It added that the United States was asking its NATO partners to "implement" actions that were directed against their own interests. The broadcast said that U.S. and Western European interests in the Middle East were "by no means identical," although the United States sought to "exert pressure on the policy of countries which are dependent on Middle Eastern oil."

Also on the issue of Libya, Radio Peace and Progress said in an Arabic broadcast (January 2, 1986) that the United States, "the largest imperialist country," was expressing its "secret criminal desire against an Arab country." It added: "The subversive actions against Libya have not ceased since the present U.S. administration assumed power, while Libya asserts its anti-imperialist, independent course and its active struggle for ensuring security in the Mediterranean, a just settlement of the Middle East issue, and acknowledgment of the Palestinian Arab people's national legitimate rights, as against any capitulationist deals."

Broadcasts by Radio Magellanes, directed at Chile and apparently relayed over Cuban transmitters, have sought to picture the Communist Party of Chile as a vigorous segment of a broad coalition, aiming at the overthrow of the government of General Augusto Pinochet. Broadcasts note the party's support of the People's Democratic Movement (PDC), in opposition to the National Accord for the Transition to Full Democracy, led by Chile's Christian Democratic Party—characterized by Radio Magellanes (December 14, 1985) as a center-right coalition, "supported by the church," and "part of the maneuvering by the United States and the Vatican." The station carried an interview with Simon Arce, Chilean Communist Party leader, who stated that the United States and the Vatican "sought to implement a changeover formula based on isolating the Communists, in order to safeguard the great power of foreign capital in Chile." The broadcast quoted Arce as saying that the Communist Party of Chile, "although it has been outlawed, openly acts amid the masses, thus appearing as a *de facto* legal party." He concluded: "We want everybody to become aware that it is necessary to stop the Yankee intervention in Chile and to prevent the Yankees from sponsoring the intervention of other Latin American forces, something they are already doing."

Moscow's various auxiliary radio transmissions are designed, on the whole, to reach specific audiences in a manner that creates a sense of emotional identity between regional and ethnic fears and aspirations, on the one hand, and Moscow's aims and policies, on the other hand. To do this, the clandestine radio programs—Radio Peace and Progress and the "National Voice of Iran"—as well as special transmissions to China, Chile, and Turkey, seek to deepen grievances and channel them into anti-U.S. and pro-Soviet attitudes and actions. Tactical changes in propaganda themes are frequent, but long-range strategies remain consistent and quite unmistakable.

CHAPTER · 24

Television's One-Way Street

Gennadi Gerasimov, director of the Soviet Foreign Ministry's Information Administration since mid-1986 and former editor-in-chief of *Moscow News*, is a skilled and experienced propagandist. Once, facing a U.S. television panel, he was asked why Soviet media do not give American spokesmen the same broadcast time that Russians receive on U.S. television. With a touch of contempt, Gerasimov replied, "We play by your rules!" And the rules of U.S. media, television above all, are to accept the one-way signs that Soviet policies have erected. The American rules are fair play and free speech; the Soviet rules are, admittedly, "Block the imperialist information media, even if it means jamming their radio broadcasts." Among rare exceptions, proving the rule, are brief statements made by U.S. ambassadors in Moscow on the Fourth of July; an interview President Reagan gave four Soviet correspondents, which appeared in *Izvestia* and was quickly drowned out by critical commentaries; and a conciliatory exchange of New Year's messages by Gorbachev and Reagan, on U.S. and U.S.S.R. TV, which followed the 1985 summit meeting.

The "rules" governing U.S. television are unwritten; they follow procedures developed for interviews with domestic politicians, consumer advocates, representatives of industry, labor, and agriculture—a wide range of opinions that clash easily and make for lively controversy. American TV is used to pigeonholing people in a few words. But when it comes to putting a Kremlin spokesman on the screen, it would surely look odd to have him identified briefly and clearly as "Soviet propagandist." Soviet spokesmen on U.S. television are provided with labels that present them as authoritative and acceptable commentators, analysts, or academicians.

298

Given the brevity of most U.S. television interviews, and the compulsion to elicit provocative comments, it is instructive to examine an interview on the CBS Sunday morning show *Face the Nation* (June 9, 1985), which featured Lesley Stahl as moderator, three U.S. participants, and Georgi Arbatov, identified as "member, Soviet Central Committee." Stahl asked Arbatov to comment on President Reagan's charge that the U.S.S.R. had violated the SALT II treaty on arms limitations. Clearly, Arbatov, or anyone else in his spot, would have to defend the Soviet position. Yet, from a TV viewpoint, defense would not be enough; some sort of aggressive, combative remark would be required. Arbatov began by saying that the United States was set on "undermining the whole arms control process," seeking to eliminate it "piece by piece." Apparently to make it easier for Arbatov, Stahl asked him to comment on "the vagueness" of the U.S. charge of "your violation." Arbatov agreed that "it's just what you ask," adding that the United States was, indeed, unable to prove its accusation.

Looking for a still more volatile reaction to the U.S. charge, Stahl asked what the effect of President Reagan's views would be on the scheduled Geneva talks and on the future of arms control in general. When Arbatov replied merely that they would have "a negative effect," Stahl pressed for something more specific, and the Soviet spokesman added that Reagan's accusation was "another step which erodes mutual trust" and lessened expectations that the U.S. government "will become serious on arms control."

Stahl then asked about the possibility of a summit meeting between Gorbachev and Reagan. Considering that Arbatov had gained the reputation of being a knowledgeable Kremlin insider, his answer was strikingly unprophetic. He charged that Americans had been "inventing" that Gorbachev "will come and then getting doubts whether he will come." As a result, he said, talk about such a summit was "not a dialogue" but "a monologue in which a lot of doubts are there." Asked about Andrei Sakharov, "his health and his whereabouts," Arbatov pointed out that he, like Sakharov, was a member of the U.S.S.R. Academy of Sciences; he added, "As a member of the Academy, I know that nothing bad happened with him." Why, among the thousands of academy members, news of the well-being of one member should be disseminated did not seem clear.

Stahl asked, "Could you describe, in your mind, what the state of U.S.-Soviet relations are right now, as the President is about to announce his decision on SALT II?" Arbatov complied by saying that "it is very bad" and "at one of the lowest points in many years." Stahl felt, "frankly," that Arbatov had not reacted "all that negatively" to the issue under discussion. "You don't seem to be saying," she argued, "that the door is closed or that the future is all that bleak. You seem to be saying maybe, maybe we can get back on the track with this. Is that a, is that a fair read of what you're saying?" That, at last, evoked an appropriately gloomy comment from Arbatov: "I don't think that life will stop after this declaration. I don't think even that war will start with this declaration. But I think this is a step, and all this story, I mean all this fanning-up of bad feelings toward Soviet Union, all this talk, giving bad ideas to everybody, that you can cancel the, the treaties, et cetera. It makes all of it more shaky."

Under the moderator's goading, Arbatov had finally used some emotion-inducing terms, such as "war," although he managed to stay firmly within the framework of Soviet policies at that point. Stahl's use of the phrase "in your mind" implied that viewers were receiving Arbatov's personal evaluation, rather than yet another paraphrase of Moscow's official policies. Arbatov, Posner, Adamov, and other Soviet spokesmen make it a habit, on U.S. television, to intersperse their remarks with such personalized remarks as "It seems to me" and "As I see it," which perpetuate the fiction of their individual views.

There are established talk show rituals on television. Participants, in effect, play assigned roles. The producers of such shows are not deliberately misleading the public when they ask Gostelradio to let them have yet another spokesman—with a good command of English, plus the imprimatur of ideological purity, against a backdrop of the Kremlin towers—to provide four minutes of opinion from "the other side," as editorial "balance."

The dilemma faced by U.S. television was well illustrated by the National Broadcasting Company (NBC) in September 1984. The network had made elaborate arrangements with the Soviet State Radio and Television Committee, gaining live coverage from a third-floor studio at the Hotel Rossiya in Moscow, together with taped interviews and commentaries from New York. The two main outlets for these transmissions were NBC's *Today* show and *NBC Nightly News*. Clearly, the network had made the most of its contacts with the Soviet embassy in Washington and with its counterparts in Moscow, even employing Soviet TV crews to make the arrangements workable.

Inevitably, such veteran propagandists as Georgi Arbatov and Vladimir Posner made appearances on these transmissions. However, NBC News, aware that its efforts might turn into a Soviet Agitprop blitz, took pains to avoid one-sided coverage. At one point, the network's interviewer Marvin Kalb even asked U.S. Secretary of State George Shultz, "Do you think we're being used by the Russians?" It was a loaded question, to be sure, and the secretary of state politely responded, "Oh, I don't think so."

To counterbalance the material emanating from Moscow and, for the most part, supplied in one way or another by the Soviet information apparatus, NBC's John Chancellor used his evening commentaries to point out obvious contradictions, one-sided presentations, gaps, or distortions. But the major problem was not the obvious Soviet bias toward supplying glossy personalities, such as a prosperous family in a well-furnished apartment, but the fragmented nature of the network shows themselves.

On the one hand, NBC News undertook the task of bringing serious material into American living rooms during prime time; on the other hand, viewers were getting snippets of information, thin slices of interviews or quick glances of Russian sites, scattered among competing news and feature material. On the *Today* show, Bryant Gumbel in Moscow and Jane Pauley in New York were doing what was expected of them, including homey chitchat. Viewers had to stitch together impressions of Soviet spokesmen, dancers, and athletes—and, over and over, the Kremlin's Cathedral of St. Basil—while absorbing news of Hurricane Diana, the Pope's visit to Montreal, the charms of comedian-director Carl Reiner, and, of course, the standard avalanche of commercials.

The series showed that Moscow propagandists were receptive to live television's need for on-the-spot coverage. This involved certain risks, notably answers to provocative questions from the TV interviewers. The Soviet spokesmen, for the most part, acquitted themselves ably, often avoiding direct answers to a question and by neatly paraphrasing routine Soviet policy positions. Not everything was truly authoritative. When Gumbel interviewed Soviet Deputy Foreign Minister Georgi Korniyenko (September 11, 1984), the diplomat reiterated that arms negotiations could not be resumed unless the United States removed its intermediate missiles from European soil; yet a few months later, negotiations did resume. Together with the newly appointed Soviet chief of staff, Sergei Akhromeyev, the deputy foreign minister stonewalled questions about the health of Konstantin Chernenko, who died a few months later, insisting that Chernenko was "working." When Gumbel said to Korniyenko that Soviet spokesmen had enjoyed "the opportunity here to talk directly to U.S. citizens," and asked whether the U.S.S.R. would "consider extending the same opportunity to our leaders to speak with [Soviet] citizens," the official replied, "Well, you made an initiative. You wanted very persistently to speak; but that doesn't mean, automatically, having an opportunity for U.S. representatives . . . is not logical."

The interviews with Korniyenko and Akhromeyev, spontaneous and live, were a distinct novelty. NBC's rivals among the print media took notice of the breakthrough. *Time* (September 24, 1984) observed that NBC reporters "noted meticulously whom and what they had been refused permission to film and when supervision had been imposed." Gumbel, the magazine observed, said when visiting a Moscow apartment that it seemed "more idyllic than typical." NBC News President Lawrence Grossman said: "Even questions the Soviets wouldn't answer were revealing, and we were surprised by how much access we had."

John Corry observed in the *New York Times* (September 13, 1984) that the TV news team, "simply by showing up in force in Moscow," had become "participant as much as reporter." Its journalistic hardheadedness, he added, was occasionally in conflict with emphasis on charm and folksiness, so that coverage at times seemed "unsure of itself." Corry concluded: "NBC, in fact, is making a wholly commendable effort to show us the Soviet Union. It is also showing us both the strength and the weakness of television news. The strength is in the immediacy of the news; the weakness is that sometimes the news has no meaning."

In contrast to the cozy atmosphere created by the *Today* staff, coverage on *NBC Nightly News* emphasized the factual. Garrick Utley, who had visited parts of the Soviet Union with a TV crew, reported on such trends as the country's rapidly increasing Moslem population. He said (September 11, 1984), "The Moscow TV tower dominates the city, a symbol of the importance Soviet leaders attach to televised propaganda." Utley also said: "It includes a barrage of news and images about American life. It is always presented in a way to make life in the United States look bad, compared with life in the Soviet Union. The emphasis is on violence, unemployment, human misery." Viewers were then shown the picture of a derelict on a U.S. street, as presented on Soviet television, with a translation of the commentary that accompanied the image: "He has no home, no place to lay his head. Should we approach him, talk to him? That would be impossible in America. In a society where the only criterion of a human life is success, success at any price, to admit you are a failure means to disown yourself. We were forced to resort to a hidden camera." Utley added the following commentary:

"Soviet journalists insist they are objective, but their job is not to show things the way they are, but, rather, as they are supposed to be, according to Communist ideology and the dictates of the Communist Party. That can be seen each night at nine o'clock, when every television station in the country carries the news, the same newscast. On this night, the lead story was a message of congratulations to Romania on its national holiday, followed by a report on this year's harvest from the Central Statistical Administration, followed by a new record set by coal miners. The impression an American gets, watching the Soviet Evening News, is not just that it gives a distorted picture of the United States as well as the Soviet Union, but also that it is excruciatingly dull. You'd think no one would want to watch it, or, if they did, they wouldn't believe what they see. But it is a captive audience out there. The system works."

This was followed by capsule interviews with a cross section of Moscow people, giving their impressions of the United States, as based on news and pictures presented by Soviet media. One man, interviewed on Red Square, said: "The people don't have power in your country. What you have is crime, sadism, unemployment, drug addiction. I don't think your young people do anything but harm to their country." One woman said: "The Americans are preparing for war. We don't want war. We are preparing for self-defense. America tries to supply other countries with more and more armaments. What do they need all those weapons for?" A student commented: "There are so many problems about you, about unemployment. It's terrible, because people have no future." Another man, interviewed on Red Square, said: "Ordinary people in America are living in poverty. If they have work, they are lucky; but if they don't, they live in poverty. Our television can always be trusted. I would never trust American T.V. All those channels and different programs."

Another effort to counter the implicit Soviet propaganda relayed by the NBC series—which, incidentally, bore the title "The New Cold War"—was Chancellor's commentaries. One night (September 10, 1984) he commented on the secretive way in which Soviet Chief of Staff Marshal Nikolai Ogarkov had been removed from his post, without any details and without explanation. Chancellor noted that "secrecy implies intrigue" and "intrigue implies instability." He wondered how the Soviet Union could demand the world's respect when their government "replaces its second-most important military leader and won't say a word about why he has been replaced." He added:

"Is the Kremlin that insecure? Is secrecy that important? The Russian Revolution took place almost seventy years ago. But sometimes the Kremlin acts as though the counter-revolutionaries were gathering outside the walls. And when a government acts that way, it will always have trouble getting the respect of its neighbors in the world."

On the last day of the series, Gumbel interviewed Vitali Kolysh on the *Today* show, identifying him as "a major figure in the International Information Department of the Communist Party Central Committee" and adding, "His group accesses the official press points of the Kremlin and also oversees the way in which the United States is portrayed to the Soviet people." Gumbel asked his guest whether he regarded himself as "one engaged in ideological warfare with the United States." Kolysh replied, "I wouldn't say that," and called his position merely an "information job." Kolysh's presence suggested that the International Information Department had been instrumental in organizing NBC's television series. Gordon Manning, vice president of NBC News, acknowledged that the network's efforts had involved "many confidential talks, and some tough negotiations, with various Soviet officials." And while he said, "There was no real secrecy involved in my efforts," he was reluctant to reveal the steps NBC had taken to complete the arrangements. He said: "It all turned out well, I believe, but the give-and-take of our long-range negotiations, and intricacies of various discussions, conducted both in Washington and Moscow, must be regarded, I believe, as private." U.S. television networks are in a highly competitive business, and Manning's decision to keep "our contact and experience" confidential was clearly designed to protect the network's "future planning and future programming."

A less ambitious effort on the part of Metromedia, also aired in the fall of 1984, illustrated the limitations faced by routine coverage of the Soviet scene. According to John Parsons, news director of WNEW, New York City, the network had set out to "go to nightclubs and farms and see the people at work and play." The coverage included an interview with dissidents in a Moscow apartment, a singer in a Riga (Latvia) nightclub, and a park bench interview with that Old Moscow radio hand, Joe Adamov—fluent in English, burly, and smoothly aggressive.

NBC and ABC were involved in controversial projects early in 1986. In early February, NBC aired a miniseries, *Peter the Great*, a costume docudrama that had been partly filmed at Moscow's Gorki Studio and in Suzdal, a twelfth-century town, 150 miles from Moscow, which had been restored to a museumlike ambiance. The ambitious series, with a total budget of $26 million, had paid $5.3 million for the use of Soviet facilities, personnel, and services.

The arrangement with Soviet authorities did not, according to the producers, give them script control or veto power. While the Soviet press, initially, warmly welcomed the project, the press eventually became rather disenchanted—possibly because the resulting eight-hour film (presented on four successive evenings by NBC) contained passages that were somewhat unflattering to Russian historical figures. Actually, the result was a well-photographed, although inevitably simplified and vulgarized, version of history, notable for its elaborate sets and incongruously luxurious costumes.

ABC got into hot water because it had scheduled a futuristic series, entitled *Amerika*, for production in 1986 and presentation in 1987. The series, budgeted at between $30 and $35 million, was to offer an image of what the United States might be like ten years after a successful, bloodless KGB coup. The project was temporarily shelved after Soviet Foreign Ministry officials expressed their displeasure to ABC's Moscow correspondent, Walter Rodgers, with the implication that the network might endanger its news operations in the U.S.S.R.

The *New York Times*, in its editorial "Amerikan Broadcasting" (January 14, 1986), took a dim view of the project itself and of ABC's intention of putting it "on the shelf for at least three years." The paper said: "Even by the lax standards of prime-time television, the premise of 'Amerika,' a

16-hour mini-series planned by ABC Entertainment, seemed conspicuously feeble. The tale would depict life in the United States a decade after its bloodless capture by Soviet agents. Having now got cold feet about spending $40 million on such nonsense, the network has put off the project, but in ways that imply a bloodless surrender to Soviet pressure. That is dumbness squared."

Eventually, ABC decided to go ahead with the *Amerika* project. If Soviet pressures were to be continued, or renewed prior to presentation of the series, Moscow's objections would certainly help the network to obtain additional publicity. Tass (January 23) carried a dispatch from New York, denouncing ABC's project as a "piece of television hack work that is a routine murky variation on the theme of the 'Soviet military threat.' " The news agency commented that ABC's final decision resulted from "unconcealed annoyance in the White House" and revealed "with great clarity who is orchestrating the large-scale anti-Soviet campaign which has been unleashed by the U.S. film industry in recent years."

The commentary grouped the *Amerika* series with two motion pictures, *Red Dawn* and *Rambo: First Blood II*, adding, "Now, the baton of anti-Sovietism, judging by everything, is being passed to ABC." Later in the year, the Soviet motion-picture industry produced its own answer to *Rambo*, a film entitled *Solo Voyage*, that showed a rugged, triumphant Soviet hero, in a violence-filled feature, overcoming a bevy of "imperialist" villains.

Despite its contretemps with Moscow, ABC was able to cover the 27th Congress of the Soviet Communist Party, in February 1986, with a large staff and through the use of extensive Soviet facilities. The network added a carefully edited background series to its coverage, presenting a variety of features under the title "Inside the Other Side." With Richard Threlkeld in Moscow as ABC's chief correspondent, the following topics were covered: Soviet family life, working conditions in a Siberian town, Leningrad as compared to Minneapolis (both being northern cities), medical services, the special status of the port of Murmansk, "what a Soviet citizen reads and sees," automation in industry, education, Americans married to Soviet citizens, and a pianist banned from performing in public. With supplementary commentaries, the series reached a high degree of the balance it set out to achieve.

Another delicate effort at balancing out material filmed in cooperation with the U.S.S.R. State Committee for Television and Radio was *Comrades*, a 12-segment series aired in the United States through the *Frontline* program of the Public Broadcasting Service (PBS) in late summer of 1986. Filmed by the BBC over a 21-month period, the series included features on the lives of people ranging from a prosperous, self-assured Moscow eye surgeon to a father and son who hunted fur-bearing animals in Siberia. Other segments dealt with an Estonian fashion designer, a woman party official in the Far East, an army recruit, the trial of a hospital orderly who had stolen equipment while drunk, a family on a collective farm, and a student at Moscow's State Pedagogical Institute. One segment, which showed a young rock musician, was filmed "unofficially" by the BBC crew. Both in England and the United States, the question of whether *Comrades* was, after all, little more than a vehicle for Soviet propaganda was countered by the producers. In the United States, each segment was followed by a studio discussion that sought to place the visual material into perspective.

Two authorities have cautioned U.S. television networks on their dealings with Soviet sources. Dr. Zbigniew Brzezinski, national security adviser to President Jimmy Carter, told an interviewer for the *Washington Journalism Review* (January 1986) that he had "made it a policy not to appear on U.S. television with Soviet propagandists," because "we are denied reciprocity in the Soviet Union." He said, "We should insist that if former or current American policy makers appear on television, they be matched by their Soviet counterparts and not by paid Soviet flacks." Brzezinski emphasized that such conditions were not to be set "by government fiat" but that the mass media should "informally agree" to guidelines which "would over time generate some pressure on the Soviets to grant this reciprocity."

Arkadi N. Shevchenko, the Soviet diplomat who served as undersecretary general of the United Nations and defected to the United States, wrote in *TV Guide* (August 9, 1986) that Soviet spokesmen appeared on U.S. television networks 130 times in 1985 as official "workers on the ideological front." He, too, noted that there was "no reciprocity" and "no American Posners and Arbatovs on Soviet television." Shevchenko added: "I am not suggesting that we should never invite Soviets to participate in our TV programs. But I do think we should at least insist on equal time on Soviet television. I do not believe for a minute that the Soviets would agree to any such thing, but the demand should be made and repeatedly publicized when equal time is not given."

Gostelradio, the U.S.S.R. State Committee for Television and Radio Broadcasting, has learned how to play the competing U.S. television networks off against each other. An aggressive newcomer to the field, the Turner Broadcasting System, signed an agreement with Gostelradio in June 1985 that called for exchanges of entertainment and sports programs between the Soviet Union and WTBS, Atlanta. Following two visits to Moscow by the company's owner, Ted Turner, his Cable News Network (CNN) agreed to exchange news programs with Intervision, the East European television network that links the Communist-governed countries. In addition, CNN would sell programs around the world, including Japan, Australia, Canada, the Caribbean, and Mexico.

The Atlanta-Moscow deal reflected Turner's maverick approach to public affairs. He had earlier talked at length with Fidel Castro and concluded that U.S.-Cuban relations might benefit from a "breakthrough" by way of baseball competitions, a form of "baseball diplomacy," following the pattern of "ping-pong diplomacy" that initiated improved Washington-Peking relations. The Turner agreement with Gostelradio met different needs on both sides. It gave Turner an end run around the major networks' ability to bid on such events as the Olympic Games; it enabled Moscow to build up its Goodwill Games as an alternative to the Olympics, while being paid in U.S. dollars.

The Goodwill Games opened on July 5, 1986, and the Soviet television service transmitted the opening ceremonies for two-and-a-half hours from Moscow's Lenin Stadium. Most of the government and Communist Party leadership was present. General Secretary Gorbachev welcomed the "representatives of nearly seventy countries" and said the games symbolized a hoped-for "improvement of the international atmosphere." He added that Soviet "peace initiatives" seek to reverse "the dangerous race toward the abyss and turn it in the opposite direction, toward disarmament." Gorbachev urged "those in responsibility" to "listen, at long last, to protests against the arms race, resounding ever louder on all continents."

The games, with 3,000 athletes participating, were divided into 20 major events, ranging from track and field competitions to boxing and swimming. Many of the facilities used had been erected to accommodate the 1980 Olympics. Soviet TV and the Turner Broadcasting System (TBS) broadcast between 120 and 150 hours of the proceedings, which concluded on July 20. Two days earlier, Turner was received by Gorbachev. Radio Moscow's newscasts listed Turner ahead of former U.S. President Richard Nixon and President Moussa Traore of the Republic of Mali, who also met with General Secretary Gorbachev that day.

The games did not attract wide attention among U.S. viewers, nor did TBS succeed in gaining substantial advertising for its coverage. More surprising was the relative indifference of the Moscow public. Even though the TV cameras sought to concentrate on those present at the 103,000-seat Lenin Stadium, the Sports Palace, the Friendship Gym, and other facilities, it was clear that attendance was sparse. Turner shrugged this off, saying, "Moscow just ain't a good sports town—just like Atlanta."

As to his financial stake in the Goodwill Games, Turner noted, "It is not unusual to lose money in a capitalist society." Reporting its second-quarter financial results for 1986, TBS recorded a loss of more than $85 million of which $26 million had been set aside to cover losses from the Moscow games. Turner's newly found views were reflected in his organization of a Better World Society, which counted Arbatov and U.S. ex-President Carter among its board members. The society produced an antinuclear documentary, *Dark Circle,* broadcast twice over the Turner network in December 1986. Corry, in the *New York Times* (December 7), wrote that the show "plays like propaganda" and questioned whether Turner "has bothered to think this through."

The problems faced by U.S. television in programming goodwill shows in cooperation with their Soviet counterparts were further illustrated by "A Citizens' Summit," broadcast early in 1986. The show brought 175 Soviet men and women into a Leningrad studio, with Vladimir Posner acting as a local master of ceremonies; linked by satellite, a similar group gathered in a Seattle studio with U.S. talk show host Phil Donahue. The show, produced by the Documentary Guild, was syndicated to private and public TV stations throughout the United States.

The actual interchange took more than two hours. An effort was made to make the two groups "representative," including men and women, older and younger people, and members of ethnic minorities. The basic concept was to create a better understanding between Americans and Soviet citizens through a people-to-people exchange of views and information.

Donahue, experienced at the lively give-and-take of his own nationwide show, which brings controversial topics to a largely female viewing audience, began with a surprisingly heavy-footed caution to the Leningrad group. He said: "Not a few Americans believe that you are not really able to speak from your soul, for fear of reprisal from Soviet government authority. There are even some people in this country who feel that you will all serve as mouthpieces for the official party line, because to do otherwise might earn you a visit to a psychiatric hospital or perhaps a prison. That is not to say that all Americans believe this."

Predictably, this opening line provoked nervous laughter in Leningrad. Considering that advisers to the show included at least one knowledgeable Soviet specialist, Prof. Stephen Cohen of Princeton University, Donahue's opening gambit was astonishingly naive and uninformed. Few Soviet citizens are aware that dissidents are actually taken to psychiatric wards and subjected to "mind-changing" drug treatment; and, for the average man or woman in the U.S.S.R., imprisonment for remarks that do not follow the official policy line must seem remote.

The mixed Leningrad audience appeared to include several men and women who, because of Communist Party membership or their professions, such as teaching, were quick to echo the party line. Yet an innocent spontaneity also permeated much of the group. One young woman, asked about her hopes for the future, said she was looking forward to a career, to marriage, and to children—and she was quick to add that all this would be possible only if there were peace! The implication, within this framework, was that her happiness was only in doubt because of the threat of war emanating from the United States. But she projected a wide-eyed sincerity that comes with the certainty of being right, saying the right thing, and therefore speaking with total conviction.

At no time did the Soviet replies go beyond the party line. They did not even echo the kind of criticism that appears in the letter column of *Pravda*. Although complaints about Soviet husbands' unwillingness to help with household chores are numerous, the problem of the overburdened wife-mother-worker was glibly turned aside: The Americans were told that Soviet women have all the necessary facilities available, including day care for their children, to manage the burdens of a three-cornered life. The U.S. group included one woman who spoke angrily of antiminority discrimination in the United States, including Seattle itself. This quickly prompted remarks by a Leningrad woman with Asian features who said she belonged to a minority but enjoyed all rights, being free to vote and even to be elected to office. Good television manners presumably forebade Donahue from raising the question of "elections" under a one-party system. Nor could a young Asian woman in Leningrad, possibly a student, be expected to reflect the resentment of Russification that might be found, let's say, in Uzbekistan.

When the question of Andrei Sakharov's exile to Gorki was raised, one of the "heavies" in the Leningrad audience quickly echoed the official viewpoint: "He is a traitor." A key Soviet sentence at the citizens' summit was: "We express our views from the heart. We support our Government because it is right." For the most part, the nimble Posner had no need to intervene; but when the shooting down of Korean airliner 007 was mentioned, he quickly provided a paraphrase of the official version: The plane had been on a spy mission, it was brought down because it had violated Soviet airspace, and the United States would do the same thing if the situation were reversed. Donahue was quick to answer that there had, in fact, been several Soviet violations of U.S. airspace, which had merely resulted in the Soviet planes' being led back to their appropriate course.

In their closing remarks, Posner and Donahue mixed optimism and pessimism. Posner expressed himself "discouraged" and "disappointed" by American ignorance about the Soviet Union, but voiced the hope that future exchanges might be fruitful. Donahue mentioned that the crushing of the Solidarity labor movement in Poland, and other Soviet-inspired actions, had alienated Americans; but he, too, said "A Citizens' Summit" might serve as an encouraging beginning.

Posner, writing in *Moscow News* (December 22, 1985), noted that such "telebridge" transmissions, utilizing satellites and large screens, began in September 1982 with Soviet Central TV studies linked to an audience in San Bernardino, California. The Seattle-Leningrad show was part of a series. One of these, devoted to the anniversary of physicist Niels Bohr's birth, had linked Copenhagen, Moscow, and Washington. Posner stated that each program had enabled "up to 100 million Soviet people to watch contacts between audiences from two or even three countries," while "none of these telebridges have been shown on national TV networks in the United States, and only a few Americans heard about them, to say nothing about watching them."

"A Citizens' Summit," for all of Posner's and Donahue's skills, suffered from multiple, and probably inevitable, restraints that reduced its mass appeal. Despite its spontaneity, the Seattle-Leningrad show had a staged quality and an air of polite distrust. The faces, on both sides, were varied and, in many cases, attractive. One Leningrader, an artist, said he would like to paint one of the Americans, an Alaska fisherman. One U.S. serviceman, a Vietnam veteran in uniform, spoke of his disillusionment with war, and concluded that he would like to join forces with two uniformed Russians in the Leningrad audience, implying that the Afghanistan and Vietnam wars should both be denounced; this segment was cut when the show was telecast on Soviet television on February 19, 1986, although other controversial segments were retained.

A second program organized by Donahue and Posner, linking Leningrad with Boston, was recorded in the summer of 1986. In this instance, the two groups were exclusively made up of women. At the outset, women's pension rights, child care facilities, and family matters were the topics of questions and answers. The Boston audience then asked about the Chernobyl accident and the Soviet role in Afghanistan. Leningrad's beauty was praised from both sides. Abortion was discussed. The demographic imbalance between men and women in the U.S.S.R. was linked to wartime losses, and one Leningrad woman said, "If we continue to have peace, however, I do not think we will have this problem in the future." Her statement was strongly applauded.

When one Boston woman asked whether the Soviet government was involved in selecting the Leningrad audience, Donahue said, "Let us accept that neither in our audience nor in theirs are there people placed there by an official organization." He acknowledged, however, that the Boston audience had "a greater inclination to speak about our problems, be they family problems, or problems in social or political life," while to the Leningrad women he said, "You will scarcely criticize anything, whether it is your government or about your husbands."

Toward the end of the show, women in both cities noted that there had been tension during their interchange. A member of the Leningrad audience said that many of the Boston questions had reflected "a note of mistrust." Nevertheless, there was an exchange of names and addresses between the two audiences. Posner concluded, "You talk in your way, and we in ours. That is the difficulty. But today we have seen that we can talk." Both audiences applauded.

Shows of the telebridge kind can bypass the networks and provide exotic programming at little cost to regional or cable services. At the same time, their edited versions provide excellent material for domestic Soviet propaganda. Increasingly sophisticated exploitation of the complex U.S. television scene began in the early 1980s. A. O. Sulzberger reported in the *New York Times* from Washington (March 13, 1981) that the Soviet Union had "embarked on a blitz of the American media, worthy of a well-run Madison Avenue public relations operation." He added: "Soviet officials who once steered well away from the glare of American journalism have been appearing, attired in three-piece suits, on such television interview programs as 'Face the Nation' and 'Issues and Answers.' " The report noted that Soviet officials were appearing "not only on the network interview shows but on nightly news broadcasts as well," on the lecture circuit, at colleges, and before various organizations.

Even in 1981, Sulzberger credited Leonid Zamyatin with having "dramatically increased the speed with which the Russians respond to news events around the world." Zamyatin, four years later, was presumably instrumental in arranging the exchange of New Year's greetings between Reagan and Gorbachev, videotaped in Washington and Moscow and shown in both the U.S. and the U.S.S.R. The very act of such an exchange could have the propagandistic effect of projecting the image of a more modern, conciliatory Soviet leadership. President Reagan's message, aired on the *Vremya* program on January 1, 1986, concluded with two phrases in Russian; he said: "On behalf of the American people, I wish you all a happy and healthy New Year. Let's work together to make it a year of peace. There is no better goal for 1986, or for any year. Let us look forward to a future of *cheestoye nebo* [clear sky] for all mankind. Thank you. *Spaseeba* [thank you]." General Secretary Gorbachev concluded with these words: "For the Soviet people, the year 1986 marks the beginning of a new stage in carrying out our constructive plans. These are peaceful plans. We have made them known to the whole world. I wish you a Happy New Year. To every American family I wish good health, peace and happiness."

For about five minutes, that New Year's Day, Soviet-U.S. television became a two-way street.

A year later, Moscow changed signals. When the White House suggested that Reagan and Gorbachev exchange New Year's messages on the two nation's television networks on January 1, 1987, the Soviet Union refused. Foreign Ministry spokesman Gerasimov said that such an exchange would "instill in people illusions that everything is in order," while his government saw "no reason for an optimistic tone."

CHAPTER · 25

Disinformation, Worldwide

Two terms in the Soviet propaganda vocabulary convey a mixture of conspiracy and camouflage; they are *aktivnyye meropriatia* (active measures) and *dezinformatsia* (disinformation). "Active measures" cover a wide range of overt and covert manipulative activities, which include "disinformation," a catchall term for fraudulent information. Definitions and applications of these terms vary among practitioners and analysts. Misleading or misdirecting an antagonist is as old as trapping animals, hiding Greek warriors inside a wooden "Trojan Horse," or building Potemkin villages. The history of forgeries, designed to divert attention or blacken reputations, is long and colorful. What is new, and what gives it a special place within the Soviet propaganda machine, is the peacetime planning and centrally directed execution of active measures, including a variety of disinformation techniques. Here are a few examples.

- Just before the British elections in 1983, a tape reached journalists in Holland that appeared to be the transcript of a telephone conversation between U.S. President Reagan and British Prime Minister Margaret Thatcher, in which Reagan was heard to say, "If there is a conflict, we shall fire missiles at our allies, to see to it that the Soviet Union stays within its borders." Thatcher's voice asked, "You mean Germany?" and Reagan replied, "Mrs. Thatcher, if any country endangers our position, we can decide to bomb the problem area and so remove the instability." The tape also had Thatcher admitting that Britain sank the Argentine cruiser *Belgrano*, in order to forestall any agreement with Argentina over the Falkland Islands.

312

To which the Reagan voice replied, "Oh, God!" Dutch journalists were suspicious of this too-bad-to-be-true recording and did EBON publish it. Analyses showed that the voices were authentic, but had been spliced and rearranged from public speeches. If the tape had been authentic, it would have had a particularly damaging effect in Germany.

- On February 7, 1983, the Madrid news weekly *Tiempo* published excerpts from an alleged U.S. National Security Council memorandum, dated March 13, 1978, signed by the council's director, Zbigniew Brzezinski, and addressed to President Jimmy Carter. The forged memorandum identified Poland as "the weakest link in the chain of Soviet domination of eastern Europe" and advocated a U.S. policy of internal Polish destabilization, including "politicians, diplomats, labor unions, the mass media and covert activity." Three months later, the magazine published a letter from Brzezinski, stating that he never wrote such a memorandum. Apparently, an authentic memo blank had been used and a forged text superimposed on it.

- A White House letterhead was used, in 1981, incorporating a facsimile of the signature of President Reagan and allegedly addressed to King Juan Carlos of Spain. The letter, circulated in Madrid, urged the king to destroy internal opposition to Spain's membership in NATO. The forged text also contained slighting references to France and to several North African states. As it also suggested that the United States was ready to back Spain's claim to Gibraltar, against Great Britain, the forgery had the potential of arousing serious anti-American resentment in the United Kingdom. The Madrid news weekly *Cambio 16* unmasked the forgery.

- On April 13, 1983, newspapers in Nigeria accused U.S. Ambassador Thomas Pickering of having ordered the assassination of two of the opposition Unity Party. The papers cited a memorandum, allegedly circulated within the embassy, which stated that one leader, Chief Abiola, had "outlived his usefulness to our services." The memo continued: "His flirtation with the opposition led by Obafemi Awolowo exemplifies the need to go ahead with operation Heartburn and Headache to solve the problem of these two." The forged memo also emphasized that the State Department "must be well briefed on these wet affairs. In view of these 'catastrophes' a premise will be created to install a friendly military government in Nigeria, after a random purge of the present corrupt federal administration." Actually, the term "wet affairs," a direct translation from the Russian, is a Soviet secret service synonym for killings, going back to the

Stalin era. Although this linguistic point and other discrepancies were pointed out to Nigerian officials and the Lagos press, publication of the fraudulent memorandum created an atmosphere of distrust. Press association reports, based on the Lagos account, were published in other African nations. The paper's "revelations" were also printed in the Soviet Union and Eastern Europe.

The foregoing examples are recent selections from a disinformation campaign that began shortly after World War II. There has been an ebb and flow of such forgeries and distortions, originating in the U.S.S.R. and in such Eastern European countries as the German Democratic Republic (East Germany) and Czechoslovakia. Western officials, notably in the United States and West Germany, have differed on tactics in dealing with disinformation items. The U.S. Department of State established, as of January 1, 1987, an Office of Disinformation Analysis and Response, in compliance with a congressional directive.

The U.S. Central Intelligence Agency, itself often a target of disinformation items, has provided congressional committees with data on this topic. Since 1981, the Department of State has reported on disinformation, from time to time, and has published analyses of active measures. There has been disagreement as to whether or not U.S. media have permitted themselves to be taken in by Soviet disinformation. A former CIA official, Harry Rositzke, writing in the *New York Times* (July 20 and 22, 1981), concluded: "The Soviet disinformation program was designed for the Third World. It will not sell in the American market." His appraisal was disputed by several authorities, notably Arnaud de Borchgrave, then a senior associate at the Center for Strategic and International Studies in Washington and subsequently editor of the *Washington Times*. Writing in the *New York Times* (August 12, 1981), de Borchgrave commented, "We are being asked to believe that, while the Soviet Union does spend billions on propaganda and disinformation, American news operations remain untainted by these efforts." He wrote that this assumes "the American public and American journalists are not gullible in the world of international intrigue" and "can spot forgeries—or more subtle forms of disinformation—the minute they come clattering over the wires." De Borchgrave added: "Well, anyone who believes that must be suffering from terminal naiveté."

American newspaper and magazine readers, and TV watchers, had an opportunity to judge disinformation techniques in November 1985 when Elena Bonner, wife of Soviet dissident physicist Andrei Sakharov, visited Italy and the United States for medical treatment. Although Bonner herself was banned by the KGB from giving interviews, members of her family revealed that Sakharov had been on a hunger strike at a time when Western media—through news stories, still photographs, and TV films—pictured him walking in the street and eating. Video segments showing Sakharov eagerly consuming food had been broadcast repeatedly on U.S. and other Western television programs. They were thus retroactively revealed as disinformation supplied by the well-connected Viktor Louis.

The magazine *TV Guide* (June 7, 1982) noted that KGB disinformation material was increasingly aimed at television audiences. The magazine quoted former Soviet diplomat Arkadi Shevchenko as saying, "To get on American television—that is one of the highest priorities on the KGB agenda." *TV Guide* quoted former CIA director William Colby on successive stages of a disinformation campaign: "They plant a story—totally fictitious—in a leftist paper in, say, Bombay. Then it gets picked up by a Communist journal in Rio. Then in Rome. Then Tass, the Soviet news agency, lifts it from the Rome paper and runs it as a 'sources say' news item, and soon the non-Communist press starts to pick up on it, using such terms as 'it is alleged that . . . ' And thus an absolute lie gets into general circulation."

Quite often, in recent years, disinformation items have superimposed slanted interpretations on news events, notably those with strong emotional content. Thus Soviet sources have stated, implied, or suggested by juxtaposition that the CIA was responsible for the killing of former Italian Premier Aldo Moro by terrorists and that the United States was responsible for the takeover of the Grand Mosque in Mecca, actually the work of pro-Iranian extremists.

Disinformation has been the subject of a controversy involving members of the U.S. intelligence community and academic observers of Soviet affairs. The dispute emerged from the publication of a joint study by Richard H. Shultz and Roy Godson, entitled *Dezinformatsia: Active Measures in Soviet Strategy*. Published in 1984, the book seemed to be exactly what its authors claimed, a compilation which concluded: "Propaganda and political influence techniques do in fact constitute significant instruments of Soviet foreign policy and strategy." Such a conclusion would, at first glance, be no more startling than the observation that the sun consistently rises in the East. And yet, the Shultz-Godson study ran into fierce criticism, of all places, in a scholarly quarterly, *Studies in Intelligence*, published by the Central Intelligence Agency, with circulation restricted to members of the U.S. intelligence community. The critique, written by Avis Boutell, identified as an analyst with the CIA-operated Foreign Broadcast Information Service, was published in the journal's winter 1984 issue under the title "On Shultz and Godson on Disinformation." The text of the book review, somehow "leaked," appeared in a bimonthly newsletter, *Foreign Intelligence Literary Scene* (August 1985).

Boutell's major objection to the Shultz-Godson book appeared to be that the authors' "detailed examination of Soviet overt propaganda misrepresents reality to prove the simplistic point that the Soviets are hostile to the United States." She accused Shultz and Godson of employing methodology that reflected "at best, a superficial understanding of current history and the Soviet Union." Boutell specifically objected to their statistical analyses of *New Times*, the Soviet foreign affairs weekly, and of the *Pravda* column "International Affairs." Their evaluation, she wrote, suffers from exclusion of such periods as "the entire first half of the 1970s, when détente was in its heyday." She added that, contrary to Shultz and Godson's view, "It is clear that the defining motivation for Soviet propaganda is not irrational hostility but rather, as with all states, perceived national interests." Boutell emphasized, "To understand Soviet interests and priorities, a scholar or analyst cannot dismiss changes in the relative degree of hostility toward the West in Soviet propaganda." Finally, she wrote, such "naive assumptions and erroneous history" serve "neither scholarship nor the national interest."

A careful rereading of the Shultz-Godson book fails to give the impression that they viewed Soviet hostility as "irrational" or that they ignored tactical changes or fluctuations in the manner in which the Soviet Union plays the keyboard of its propaganda. Shultz-Godson utilized, in their chapters on disinformation, material presented by the CIA to congressional committees. Their book actually implemented, at least indirectly, official efforts to increase public alertness to Soviet disinformation activities. The CIA's deputy director, John McMahon, told the Permanent Select Committee on Intelligence of the House of Representatives on July 13, 1982: "There is a tendency sometimes in the West to underestimate the significance of foreign propaganda and to cast doubt on the effectiveness of active measures as an instrument of foreign policy. Soviet leaders, however, do not share such beliefs. They regard propaganda and active measures as important supplemental instruments in the conduct of their foreign policy by conventional diplomatic, military and economic means. Indeed, the Soviet leadership marshals all the relevant resources, conventional and unconventional." McMahon noted that "for a brief period, in the mid-1970s, the Soviets had reduced and then curtailed altogether their production of anti-U.S. forgeries" but that they had resumed them in 1976 as "an integral part of their active measures program."

J. P. Morgan, the legendary U.S. financier, when asked his views about the future performance of the stock exchange, said sagely, "The market will fluctuate." Much the same can be said about the intensity and specific nature of Soviet propaganda, scholarly or nonscholarly disputes notwithstanding. Still, a certain amount of further clarification may be necessary, as the term "disinformation" is quite amorphous. Shultz and Godson defined it as "a non-attributed or falsely attributed communication, written or oral, containing intentionally false, incomplete, or misleading information (frequently combined with true information), which seeks to deceive, misinform and/or mislead the target." They added, "Either foreign governmental or non-governmental elites, or a foreign mass audience, may comprise the target." Herbert Romerstein, an officer of the U.S. Information Agency, in a paper presented to the conference on disinformation in Paris, 1984, cited a Soviet definition from the Russian military magazine *Zarubezhnoye Voyennoye Obozreniye* (January 1983). While the journal claimed disinformation was being used against the Soviet Union, he noted that it actually "described their own methods." The magazine defined disinformation as "nothing but the dissemination of reports aimed at deliberately deluding people, at imposing on people a distorted and outright false idea about realities."

Inasmuch as independent observers cannot possibly monitor the world's media, the CIA and the State Department have been the main sources of material on Soviet disinformation. Some of the cases they have listed lack detail, clear identification of the media concerned, extended quotations, or essential background. Among the more fully documented cases is that of Pierre-Charles Pathé, son of the French motion-picture pioneer who produced one of the world's leading newsreels, *Pathé News*, featuring the popular logo of a crowing rooster. According to a congressional report, *Soviet Active Measures*, issued in 1982, Pathé came to the attention of Russian recruiters when he published an article highly favorable to the U.S.S.R.'s position. According to this account, he was recruited as an "agent of influence" in 1959 and guided by KGB officers who "worked under the cover either of the Soviet delegation to UNESCO or the Soviet Embassy in Paris." At first, the agents and Pathé met openly at receptions and in restaurants, but after 1962 their contacts became clandestine. He began to publish a series of articles with either a subtly or a strongly pro-Soviet bias. At times Pathé used the pseudonym "Charles Monard." His writings, skillful and professional, appeared in such liberal periodicals as *Libération* and the glossy monthly *Réalités*.

At the suggestion, and presumably with the financial support, of his KGB "handlers," Pathé issued a confidential journal in 1961, identifying his enterprise as the Center for Scientific, Economic and Political Information. The congressional report stated that Pathé did not receive a regular agent salary but "was paid for individual analyses of French and international political developments he provided for the Soviets." In 1976, Pathé started a biweekly newsletter, *Synthesis*, which developed an elite following among opinion makers, including parliamentarians, ambassadors, and journalists.

Shultz and Godson wrote that Pathé did not receive complete articles from his Soviet contacts but "was provided with general instructions and thematic guidelines on which to base his articles." They commented, "this sort of arrangement is not unusual," and added: "The relationship between a Soviet case officer and an agent of influence apparently is flexible and based on shared interests, especially when the agent is a prominent individual. Particularly in the latter case, the KGB provides general instructions rather than specific orders." Pathé enjoyed prestige because of family connections and social-professional contacts. According to Godson and Shultz, he knew people across the political spectrum, from General Charles de Gaulle to Socialist leader and later President François Mitterrand. The weekly magazine *Paris Match* (July 11, 1980) said that Pathé had a good reputation as a political analyst and was widely appreciated for his initiative and writing talent. Because of his relatively prominent position, Pathé was well placed to put his KGB contacts in touch with others who might be either sources of information or potential agents of influence.

The discovery of Pathé's KGB connections came indirectly. In 1978, a Soviet official, Igor Kuznetsov, tried to recruit a French parliamentarian, who reported these advances to the French secret police. Kuznetsov was shadowed and led the security police to Pathé; both men were arrested as they exchanged money and documents. At a subsequent trial, Pathé admitted his activities and, in 1980, was sentenced to five years in prison. His conviction came during a period when French opinion makers, including a new generation of writers and artists, emerged from several decades of near-reflexive endorsement of "left" ideas and identification with Soviet aims; such incidents as the Pathé conviction prompted a more critical attitude toward Soviet policies and propaganda.

One characteristic of Soviet disinformation is the repeated use of a specific item over a relatively long period of time, bouncing it around the world with the deftness of a basketball team. Among major tools of disinformation has been the so-called *U.S. Army Field Manual FM 30-31B*. This is one of the best forgeries to have come to Western attention. Allegedly designed to instruct U.S. Army intelligence officers, the manual implies U.S. readiness to interfere in the internal affairs of friendly countries, even to the point of encouraging left-wing extremism to stiffen government policies.

In its use of U.S. military language, in its typefaces and format, the bogus manual is identical with legitimate documents. It carries a facsimile of the signature of U.S. General William Westmoreland. Only in its classification, "Top Secret," does the forgery become evident; field manuals of this type are never that highly classified. Genuine field manuals numbered FM 30-31 and 30-31A were, in fact, issued by the U.S. Army, but a genuine FM 30-31B is nonexistent.

The bogus manual appeared first in Bangkok, Thailand, at the Philippines embassy; it was addressed to President Ferdinand E. Marcos, care of the Philippines ambassador. An accompanying letter, directed to President Marcos in Manila, was dated September 14, 1976, and read as follows:

"Dear Mr. President:

"In 1974 I sent to Mr. Kukrit Pramoj, who is well-known to you and whom I deeply respect, some secret American documents revealing the dangers for the countries concerned of having U.S. troops and U.S. advisers on their territories. Recent developments in Thailand suggest that these documents were both timely and to the point for Mr. Kukrit Pramoj.

"Now I am sending these documents to you in the hope that they will also be of use to your Government. I am doing this as one of an American group opposed to excessive U.S. military involvement in matters beyond the scope of reasonable American interest."

The letter, marked "Personal/Confidential," was unsigned but implied that the writer was a U.S. citizen, possibly a member of the military, who had access to classified information, opposed "excessive U.S. military involvement," and wished to alert friendly governments to U.S. interference. The enclosed manual was divided into four parts, including introduction, background, and sections headed "U.S. Army Intelligence Tasks" and "Intelligence Guidance."

To assure the unsuspecting reader of its legitimate character, the manual was identified as a supplement to a genuine document numbered FM 30-31, which "provided guidance on doctrine, tactics and techniques for intelligence support of U.S. Army stability operations in the internal defense environment." The document, referring to a "host country" as an "HC," stated that FM 30-31B, "on the other hand, considers HC agencies themselves as targets for U.S. Army intelligence."

The manual stated that "operations in this special field are to be regarded as strictly clandestine, since the acknowledged involvement of the U.S. Army in HC affairs is restricted to the area of cooperation against insurgency or threats of insurgency." The document added: "The fact that the U.S. Army involvement goes deeper can in no circumstances be acknowledged." The forged manual also stated that "intelligence efforts be directed towards the HC army and related organizations for internal defense operations."

In circumspect language, the document suggested enlisting the members of the officer corps of a host country and discouraging cordial relations between host country armies and insurgents, warned "against the possibility of HC army personnel reinsuring their own future by developing active or passive contacts with the insurgency," and advocated "the promotion of HC officers known to be loyal to the United States."

Clearly, such a patronizing and manipulative approach on the part of U.S. Army personnel would raise the hackles of any self-respecting foreign official. The forgery was intended to sharpen existing resentments and suspicions and to heighten the kind of friction that the presence of U.S.

Army units in any country, no matter how friendly, is likely to create.

The forgery contained specific instructions—under the heading "Recruitment for Intelligence Purposes"—which targeted "officers from families with longstanding economic and cultural associations with the United States and its allies," officers who "received favorable impressions of U.S. military training programs, especially those who have been trained in the United States itself," as well as "officers mentioned for assignment to posts within the HC intelligence structure." With appropriate bureaucratic caution, the forged manual added that such officers "require special though not exclusive attention."

The manual's instructions dealing ostensibly with the subject "Penetration of the Insurgent Movement" contained its most explosive suggestions. This section began with a cross-reference to the genuine FM 30-31 manual, which had drawn attention to "the importance of HC agencies penetrating the insurgent movement by agent means with a view to successful counteraction." The forged document added that, should the host country fail to take effective action, U.S. Army intelligence should infiltrate insurgent movements and organize provocative actions. It stated:

"There may be times when HC government show passivity or indecision in face of Communist or Communist-inspired subversion, and react with inadequate vigor to intelligence estimates transmitted by U.S. agencies. Such situations are particularly likely to arise when the insurgency seeks to achieve tactical advantage by temporarily refraining from violence, thus lulling HC authorities into a state of false security. In such cases, U.S. Army intelligence must have the means of launching special operations which will convince the HC government and public opinion of the reality of the insurgent danger and of the necessity of counteraction.

"To this end, U.S. Army intelligence should seek to penetrate the insurgency by means of agents on special assignment, with the task of forming special action groups among the more radical elements of the insurgency. When the kind of situation envisaged above arises, these groups, acting under U.S. Army intelligence control, should be used to launch violent or non-violent actions, according to the nature of the case."

The forgery added: "In cases where the infiltration of such agents into the insurgent leadership has not been effectively implemented, it may help towards the achievement of the above ends to utilize ultra-leftist organizations."

The usefulness of this exceedingly well-prepared forgery lies in its timelessness and the fact that it can be potentially and repeatedly disruptive within a great number of nations—from the Philippines, where President Marcos, in fact, faced a growing Communist-led insurgency, to El Salvador, where guerrilla warfare, kidnapping, and other terrorist actions have run side by side. The bogus manual was utilized in Spain by Fernando Gonzalez, a Communist writer with links to Soviet and Cuban intelligence officers. Gonzalez published the forged document in the daily *El Pais* (September 18, 1978), with a commentary; both were reprinted in the pro-Communist periodical *El Triunfo* (September 23). The following December, the Prague monthly *Problems of Peace and Socialism* (World Marxist Review), which serves as the theoretical journal of the world communism movement, wrote:

"Let us note what another Italian journal suggested. 'There arises the suspicion that the "Red Brigades" (or those who manipulate them in Italy) are pro-fascist organizations skillfully camouflaged as "reds." . . .' The abduction and subsequent murder of Aldo Moro could, in the logic of things, have been the results of the CIA's realization that the policy pursued by that statement was dangerous. A few months later this was confirmed by a secret document which appeared in the journal *L'Europeo*. It bore the signature of U.S. General Westmoreland and said that U.S. special services should use 'leftist' outfits in 'friendly countries' to promote the interests of the United States."

The "secret document" published in *Europeo*, a mass-circulation illustrated magazine, was, of course, none other than the bogus FM 30-31B. The abduction and killing of a respected statesman, such as Moro, was ready-made for the disinformational use of the forged manual. That it referred to U.S. Army intelligence, while the Prague journal intimated that the CIA was involved, was obscured in this propagandistic sleight of hand.

Few known items of disinformation have such universal application. For the most part, they are tailored to local conditions and seek to exploit national fears and stresses. The alert action of an Austrian official prevented a forged letter, supposedly sent by the U.S. ambassador to the country's defense minister, from creating an uproar or, at least, a misunderstanding. Early in 1984, while Austria's minister of defense, Friedhelm Frischenschlager, was on vacation, a letter addressed to him by U.S. Ambassador Helene A. von Damm, arrived at the Defense Ministry. At the same time, copies of the letter were sent anonymously to several Austrian newspapers.

In the absence of the defense minister, the letter could have awaited his arrival, while one or another enterprising newspaper might have decided to publish it. The journalistic temptation to do so was obvious, as the letter suggested a number of diplomatic-military steps that would have violated Austria's much-valued East-West neutrality. The country had emerged from World War II under joint occupation by Russia and the Western Allies. Not until ten years after the war, in 1955, did the Soviet Union agree to withdraw the last of its occupation troops, and then only in return for a declaration of neutrality, which Austria pledged and, subsequently, carefully maintained.

The forged letter, written in German, asked the defense minister "in the name of the United States Government" to secretly compromise Austria's neutrality in a number of ways, such as engaging in radar monitoring in case of a Soviet nuclear attack on the West. Instead of waiting for the minister to return from his vacation, a staff member called the U.S. embassy to confirm the genuineness of the letter. Something about it, including German terminology that von Damm, born in Austria, would not be likely to use, had puzzled him. Von Damm wrote Defense Minister Frischenschlager that the letter, "purportedly written by me," in form, content, and "matter of delivery" appeared to "fit a general pattern with which my government is quite familiar." The ambassador enclosed a State Department file on Soviet active measures.

The Vienna tabloid *Kurier* published both the forgery and the denial (February 17, 1984). The public reacted to the half-ridiculous, operetta-like forged-letter episode with a good deal of amusement. Officials brushed it off. Foreign Minister Erwin Lanc told the press, "Of course it's a fake." The Vienna daily *Die Presse* (May 25, 1984) referred to "active measures" as a "power tool of the eastern superpower . . . designed to fill the gap between official propaganda and the activity of its agents." While such techniques were not entirely new, the paper wrote, "the intensity with which this kind of thing is being done, is certainly novel."

CHAPTER · 26

Feeding Fear and Suspicion

Over and over again, Soviet propaganda and disinformation campaigns have been designed to create European distrust of the United States, to picture Moscow as peace-loving and Washington as war-minded, and to foster European fear of war. Among the "don't trust America" themes has been the message that, in case of war, the United States would sacrifice its European allies in order to protect itself. For several years, a skillfully assembled pseudo-U.S. Department of Defense document has been used to dramatize this point. Presented as a collection of authentic papers, this pamphlet bears the title *Top Secret Documents on US Forces Headquarters in Europe: Holocaust Again For Europe;* these words are superimposed on the seal of the U.S. Department of Defense.

The propagandistic impact of this collection is heightened by the fact that the collection intermingles genuine and forged documents. These are indistinguishable to the average reader, whether he or she might be a government official, parliamentarian, opinion maker, or journalist. A persuasive air of authenticity is created through the use of documents stolen in the 1960s by U.S. Army Sergeant Robert Lee Johnson, a courier stationed in Paris, who was convicted as a Soviet agent and sentenced to 25 years in prison. Cover pages from genuine Department of Defense papers, accurate terminology, and actual Department of Defense typography make the collection remarkably authentic looking.

The collection originally appeared in 1967 in the Norwegian magazine *Orienteering*. Later, some or all of the papers in the collection were mailed to newspapers and periodicals throughout Western Europe. The whole collection, published as a single pamphlet, purports to originate in England.

Presented as a compilation of U.S. war plans, it is particularly disturbing to European readers as it conveys the impression that military contingencies include the use of nuclear weapons against the territories of its NATO allies.

By continuing to circulate this collection, the distributors perpetuate uneasiness and distrust. In December 1982, for example, questions prompted by the pamphlet were raised in the City Council of Graz, Austria. The anonymous introduction to the papers meets the forgery charge head-on; it says "any hopes that they might be a brilliant fake no longer exist," a denial which, of itself, is a disarming bit of propaganda.

As forgeries of the disinformation type have improved in quality, the term "brilliant fake" might, indeed, be applied to some of them. One letter from U.S. General Alexander M. Haig, then NATO commander, addressed to NATO Secretary General Luns, could be spotted as a forgery only because it referred to Luns as "Dear Joseph" rather than, in Haig's usual way, "Dear Joe." Using correct letterhead, typewriter print, and details such as indentations, the forgery was designed to play on fears of a nuclear war limited to Europe. Dated June 26, 1979, and supposedly written on the eve of General Haig's departure for the United States, it was addressed to "His Excellency Joseph M. A. H. Luns," Secretary General of NATO, and signed by Haig as "General, United States Army: Supreme Allied Commander." The signature, "Al," was a reasonable facsimile of Haig's handwriting.

The letter, covering two pages and divided into seven paragraphs, was composed to convey a sense of threatening urgency. It sought to imply a conspiratorial relationship between Haig and Luns, designed to undermine the secretary general's position at home in the Netherlands. The Haig letter stated, in its second paragraph: "On leaving the post of Supreme Allied Commander in Europe, I feel it my duty to stress once again certain aspects of allied strategy which demand our further attention and efforts." The letter continued, "As you know, one of our presuppositions in nuclear planning is that, under certain circumstances likely to develop in Europe, we may be forced to make first use of nuclear weapons." The letter referred to a "crisis inside the Alliance over neutron weapons deployment," denounced "the faint-hearted in Europe," and referred darkly to "appropriate and effective action of a sensitive nature which we have frequently discussed." The letter concluded on a menacing note: "The courses of action which we have in mind may become the only sure means of securing the interests of the West."

The forged letter, stamped "NATO SECRET," first appeared in the Belgian weekly De Nieuwe in April 1982. It was declared a forgery by NATO, but published in a Luxembourg Communist paper the following month. The immediate tactical aim of the forgers was to hint at behind-the-scenes maneuvering by Haig and Luns, particularly with regard to NATO's modernization of intermediate-range missiles. It could encourage suspicion among other NATO members of the secretary general, following Haig's departure.

An earlier effort to embarrass Luns by means of a forged letter took place in 1978. In June, several Belgian newspapers received photocopies of a letter allegedly written by Luns, stating that the names of journalists opposed to the neutron bomb had been turned over to the Belgian Defense Ministry. The implication was that the ministry would blacklist these journalists or circumscribe their activity. Such a threat to freedom of the press was, of course, unacceptable to Belgian newspapers and reporters. NATO immediately denounced the letter as a forgery, but it was nevertheless published by *De Nieuwe* (July 28).

Another NATO-related forgery was the letter allegedly sent by President Reagan to King Juan Carlos of Spain, mentioned briefly in the preceding chapter. This letter, written on White House stationery, was dated October 23, 1981, and addressed simply to "His Majesty the King of Spain, Madrid, Spain." Phrased in informal terms, it was full of diplomatic booby traps. Basically, its supposed aim was to pressure King Juan Carlos into hastening Spain's entry into the NATO alliance, but it also sought to create anti-U.S. antagonisms among the king's advisers, among Spanish domestic groups, and on the part of France, Great Britain, and unnamed North African states, presumably including Algeria and Morocco. The forgery implied that the U.S. President had spies among the king's inner circle, a suggestion likely to displease Juan Carlos.

At the outset, the letter referred to "a delicate and confidential matter" and to "private talks" between President Reagan and the king of Spain. The letter stated that Reagan had "learned that several persons close to you [Juan Carlos] oppose Spain's entry into the North Atlantic Treaty Organization." It added that, according to "highly secret information," these opponents came from the armed forces, political parties, the government, and "even the Catholic Church." The letter was supplemented by a memorandum in Spanish, equally forged, supposedly drawn up by the opposition group.

In effect, the Reagan letter asked the king to crush "the group influenced by the OPUS DEI pacifists." Opus Dei, a Roman Catholic social action group in Spain, represents a variety of viewpoints. The letter stated that Spain's position in NATO ought to be a reliable one, as "we cannot permit another objectionable posture, like the attitude of the French." This phrasing implied that NATO should operate according to U.S. policies and wishes, a viewpoint naturally repelling to any sovereign NATO partner. The fake Reagan letter continued, "My advisers inform me there are good grounds for destroying the left-wing opposition" in Spain, which would "improve" U.S.-Spanish relations and facilitate Spain's entry into NATO.

Rather crudely, the letter suggested that, as a trade-off, the United States would "consider the final solution to Gibraltar in favor of Spain," against Great Britain's policy of leaving Gibraltar's status to the decision of its population. In addition, the letter referred slightingly to "the over-sensitive North African states" and implied support "with reference to Spanish territories in Africa and the Canary Islands."

The U.S. congressional report *Soviet Active Measures* contained a CIA commentary on this letter which noted that copies of the forgery were mailed in early November 1981 to Spanish journalists and to all delegations of the Conference on Security and Cooperation in Europe (the "Helsinki Accord"), shortly before its meeting in Madrid. The forged document was delivered by mail, postmarked Madrid. The commentary noted that the letter "was clearly intended to complicate U.S.-Spanish relations by making it appear that the U.S. was interfering in Spain's internal affairs, to fuel opposition to Spain's entry into NATO, and to damage the king's domestic position," while designed to "damage U.S. interests" elsewhere. The commentary concluded: "The forgery had no noticeable impact in Spain or on U.S. relations with Spain. Press commentary in Spain noted that the documents were bogus, and several journalists speculated that this forgery operation was Soviet-instigated. It is not certain who perpetrated the forgery, but the operation followed standard Soviet modus operandi and, in effect, supported Soviet opposition to Spain's entry into NATO. Moreover, this type of forgery operation is not characteristic of the methods used by legitimate domestic opponents of Spain's entry into NATO. We therefore conclude that it was a Soviet operation."

Along similar lines, Spanish journalists in Belgium received a supposed draft of a NATO publicity leaflet that took Spain's membership for granted, although the Spanish parliament had not yet voted on the matter. The forgery, mailed October 19, 1982, bore the label "NATO unclassified," a category that does not exist; an unclassified document bears no category notice at all. The draft, supposedly designed to provide data released by the NATO Information Service, stated specifically, "We call your attention to Spain mentioned as a member country and that minor alterations are made on the lay-out in consequence of it." The forged document, identified as such, was the basis of news reports in two Spanish newspapers, *El Pais* (October 21) and *Diario* (October 23); both papers linked the forgery to Soviet opposition to Spain's NATO membership.

Stress points in U.S.-European relations can be found on many levels, including the military-strategic, the economic, and the cultural. A vast number of historical and ethical elements are involved, and attitudes change not only within national boundaries but also with shifts from generation to generation. Many factors were involved, for example, when European countries defied U.S. pressures to refrain from supporting a Soviet oil pipeline. Nations were split, internally and among each other, as to whether to support a U.S. boycott of the Olympic Games in Moscow in 1984. Reaction to the Soviet invasion of Afghanistan in 1979 was mixed, as was the attitude toward economic sanctions against Poland, because of its Soviet-backed suppression of the Solidarity movement and the imposition of martial law.

Stresses exist within the European Economic Community (EEC), as well as on a global basis. To alleviate such stresses, periodic international consultations are arranged. One of these, an economic summit of heads of states, including U.S. President Reagan, took place in the early summer of 1982. On the eve of this meeting, an alleged memorandum from U.S. Secretary of Commerce Malcolm Baldrige was circulated among foreign correspondents in Brussels. The three-page document, dated February 18, 1982, appeared on memoranda letterheads bearing the seal of the U.S. Department of Commerce and marked "Secret."

Except for its rather central error of misspelling the Commerce secretary's name as "Baldridge" (a more common spelling of the name), the forgery followed the pattern and style of U.S. internal government communications with remarkable accuracy. The tenor of the memorandum was one of U.S. economic bullying of its European partners, clearly designed to deepen and widen existing rifts. The bogus document outlined various economic pressures the United States could exert in order to force European nations to cancel their pipeline agreements with the Soviet Union. The memorandum pretended to be the product of a group called the "Special Presidential Working Group on Strategic Economic Policy." It listed prominent officials of four government agencies as members of the group, representing the Departments of Commerce, State, and Treasury, as well as the CIA.

The memorandum proposed "actions whose objectives would be the definite severance of the pipeline contract between the Soviet Union and some of our Western European partners." It suggested that pressures on European nations include use of "anti-dumping" rulings to reduce European steel shipments to the United States to "surmount our own steel crises" and "deepen the crises within the exporter states." This tactic, the forged memo explained, could lead to cabinet crises which the United States might use to "influence" governments "in a desirable direction, for example, blocking anti-nuclear and other campaigns not advantageous to our interests in Europe."

The memorandum, which bore the forged signature of the secretary of commerce, concluded: "We are convinced, that we can additionally supplement our arguments in that our plan serves first of all the political, military and economic interests of the West as a whole and eliminating the dependence of NATO states on oil, gas and coal from the Soviet bloc." The misspelling of the secretary's name, the use of the plural "crises" when the singular "crisis" was correct, as well as minor typographical errors could, in fact, have been typist's mistakes. Although distribution of the forgery, on the eve of the economic summit, made it newsworthy, it did not receive media publicity. It is, however, quite possible—in this as in other cases—that an elaborate piece of disinformation was primarily aimed at government officials, rather than at the press.

As Edward Jay Epstein has pointed out in his article "Disinformation" in *Commentary* (July 1982), "Disinformation, which aims at extending state policy, is a very different concept in Soviet doctrine from propaganda." He added: "Whereas disinformation aims at misleading an enemy government into making a disadvantageous decision, propaganda aims at misleading public opinion so that it resists the advantageous decisions of its government." Epstein considered the audience for disinformation as "government decision-makers, and the prime channel for reaching this audience is through the intelligence service upon which they rely for their secret information." He made the point that the KGB uses disinformation, through such channels as double agents, to introduce misleading information into the intelligence networks of its antagonists.

On occasion, however, governmental decisions have been made on the basis of disinformation funneled into public media. On March 31, 1983, a press conference at Accra, capital of Ghana, heard Kojo Tsikata, special adviser to the Provisional Defense Council, accuse the U.S. embassy of trying to overthrow the government of Flight Lieutenant Jerry J. Rawlings. He referred to an alleged West German embassy report, which quoted U.S. Ambassador Thomas Smith as dissatisfied with the performance of the local CIA staff. The alleged German document quoted Smith as stating that CIA personnel "will only prove themselves if they achieve basic changes in the country and succeed in overthrowing Rawlings." The government-owned paper, *People's Daily Graphic* (April 1, 1983), published the report under the headline "West Germany Tells About CIA" and printed the German-language text. The following day, the West German government stated that the report was a fabrication, and the U.S. government protested to the government of Ghana on the matter. The *State Department Bulletin* (October 1983) commented: "Although Ghana eventually accepted the fact that the report was a forgery, the incident had an immediate, damaging impact on U.S.-Ghanaian relations by creating the false impression that the United States was supporting Rawlings' opponents."

Typical of such disinformation cases, the incident deepened existing sensitivities and suspicions. Meanwhile, President Rawlings's cousin Michael A. Soussoudis befriended a CIA employee stationed in Ghana, Sharon M. Scranage. Scranage gave her lover information on local CIA operations, including names of U.S. agents. On November 25, 1985, Scranage was sentenced by a Washington judge to five years in prison and 1,000 hours of community service; she also received two years of probation. At the same time, Soussoudis was released by the U.S. Justice Department, after having been found guilty of violating the espionage act. In what appeared to be an exchange for Soussoudis's freedom, the Rawlings government released eight Ghanaians accused of spying for the CIA or "friendly" to U.S. interests, permitting them to go abroad.

In countries prone to coups and countercoups, the United States is easily viewed as favoring one side over another and as providing behind-the-scenes support to rival groups. U.S. relations with the Republic of South Africa add to stresses in relations between Washington and African nations; these, in turn, encourage disinformation ploys. Glenn Frankel, reporting from Harare, Zimbabwe, in the *Washington Post* (December 3, 1983) noted that disinformation "appears to have been most effective in Africa, where suspicions about U.S. policies already are high, especially when it comes to the issue of American support for white-ruled South Africa."

According to Robert V. Keeley, U.S. ambassador to Zimbabwe, "The fact is that many people assume we're working hand-in-glove with South Africa, so if someone comes up with a story it often gets printed without anyone bothering to check with us to see if it's true." Ambassador Keeley's comments had been prompted by a report in the country's semiofficial newspaper, the *Herald*, stating the United States was planning to test and deploy cruise missiles in South Africa. Keeley countered the report by stating that the paper was "lending itself wittingly to being used as a tool by the world-wide disinformation effort by the Soviet Union to discredit the United States."

The *Herald* story, citing as its source Soviet Lieutenant-Colonel Yuri Gavrilov, had earlier been exposed in two Zimbabwean publications, the weekly *Financial Gazette* of Harare and *The Chronicle* of Bulawayo; both had printed an article by the British journalist Colin Legum, an Africa specialist, saying that the missile story was fraudulent. A year earlier, the same report had appeared in a Mozambique paper without attribution. Then, in classical disinformation pattern, it was reprinted in the U.S.S.R., East Germany, and Bulgaria. Next, like a ball bouncing out of control, it was published in Ethiopia, Mali, Zambia, the Seychelles, and Angola.

The Harare *Herald* had published an earlier forgery (June 5, 1982), which suggested clandestine military arrangements between South Africa and the United States. The letter, dated April 6, 1982, was written on a letterhead of Aviation Personnel International, a New Orleans corporation, and signed "Michelle Lang, Assistant Registrar." It purported to be addressed to Lt. Gen. A. M. Muller of the South African air force in Pretoria. The three-paragraph letter read, in full:

"Based on our agreement dated 12 December 1981 in which you request a continual supply of incoming pilots who are capable of working inside the SASCAF, we now forward the personal data of pilots who—according to our evaluation—meet standards stipulated by you. Said pilots are qualified to operate Type YAH-64 helicopters and are well trained in jungle warfare.

"We repeatedly wish to direct your attention to the fact that we only recruit and recommend the pilots and the engagement procedures are the responsibility of your representatives. On instructions received from the competent bodies of the U.S. Government and because of political factors, this go between activity of our organization calls for top secrecy from your side in full accordance with earlier guarantees. This is especially justified by circumstances that emerged as a result of the Seychelles action. We do not desire to undertake a similar risk that stems from the lack of careful judgement of given circumstances.

"We believe you will understand our motives and can be mutually satisfied with how our business relations are shaping-up. We completely understand your position so we shall continue to seek out comrades-in-arms who are trustworthy in every respect."

The forgery gave the impression that Aviation Personnel International was either a front for the U.S. government, presumably the Air Force, or a recruiter of mercenaries from the United States for the South African air force, with the knowledge and support of the U.S. government. The emphasis on "top secrecy" made the forgery particularly intriguing, and news stories based on this item of disinformation also appeared in Tanzania and Zambia; Tass gave it worldwide distribution. The New Orleans company provided an affidavit stating that it had no dealings with South Africa. The forged text had been inserted in a form letter the company routinely mailed to prospective job seekers.

Another piece of disinformation was accomplished by simply typing in the name and address of the commander of South Africa's air force. Northrop Aviation, a U.S. aircraft manufacturer, simultaneously sent sales letters, signed by its vice president for marketing, to several countries. The mailing did not include South Africa, because of the U.S. embargo of military sales to that country. However, a Northrop letter addressed to South Africa was printed in the newsweekly *Jeune Afrique* (November 17, 1982), published in Paris and widely read in French-speaking African countries. Northrop Aviation denounced the letter as a fake, but the magazine maintained (January 19, 1983) that it was authentic. Indeed, the body of the letter was authentic, Northrop observed, but the company had never addressed it to South Africa; so whoever promoted this particular piece of disinformation had only to switch addresses.

The querulous reference to "the Seychelles action," in the forged letter, recalled a failed coup attempt on the Seychelles Islands on November 25, 1981. A group of mercenaries had landed on the Seychelles by air from South Africa with the intent of overthrowing the government of President France Albert René. Soviet news reports, citing unidentified "African radio commentaries," implied that the CIA had been involved in the coup attempt. Although President René said (December 2, 1983) that his government had no indication that any foreign government, other than South Africa, had been involved in the operation, Soviet media continued to accuse the United States of complicity with the mercenaries. The *Nairobi Times* of Kenya and the *Lagos Daily Times* of Nigeria repeated the Soviet charges; this enabled Tass and Radio Moscow to subsequently cite these two papers as sources for the Soviet version.

Shortly after Olof Palme, prime minister of Sweden, was assassinated in Stockholm in February 1986, Soviet media began a campaign that implied the U.S. Central Intelligence Agency was responsible for his death. Georgi Arbatov, writing in *Izvestia* (March 2), stated in general terms that Palme had been hated by people in Sweden and the U.S. for his advocacy of "cooperation between Social Democrats and Communists for peace, disarmament and international security." Tass commentator Anatoli Kraskov wrote (March 2) that the CIA had kept Palme "under surveillance" during the Vietnam War, just as, he asserted, the FBI had kept Samantha Smith "under surveillance after her 1983 visit to the USSR." (Other Soviet media had implied earlier that Samantha's death had somehow been engineered to sabotage her peace mission.) Mikhail Ozerov wrote in *Sovetskaya Rossiya* (March 13) that Palme's death was part of international terrorism; he referred to a U.S. training school for mercenaries in the state of Georgia and stated: "Washington has finally elevated terror to the rank of state policy." Leonid Levchenko, speaking on Radio Moscow World Service in English (March 3), mentioned the "vicious murder" of Palme and said that the United States was "using its mercenaries to conduct terrorism against whole nations." Chingiz Aytmatov, interviewed in the Stockholm daily *Dagens Nyheter* (March 17), insisted that a commentary he had written for *Pravda* did not specifically accuse the CIA. He said: "The people who murdered Olof Palme do not need to have come from the United States or the CIA—even though it does seem to be a case of reactionary forces."

The charge was renewed, however, when Tass (June 25) reported from Moscow: "The Swedish newspaper *Norskensflamman*, analyzing the circumstances of the assassination of Prime Minister Olof Palme, has drawn the conclusion that the CIA was behind the crime." What Tass failed to mention was that the paper happened to be the organ of the Swedish Communist Party. Tass also quoted the Stockholm newspaper as alleging that "the CIA had been hatching a plan for the physical annihilation of the Prime Minister" three weeks before his death and that "the assassin's weapon had been smuggled from the U.S.A."

A former Tass reporter and KGB operative, Ilya Dzhirkvelov, told a Washington press conference (February 10, 1986): "It is not easy to prepare disinformation. If you want to be primitive and crude, sure. I heard someone say that it is possible to find disinformation in American and English newspapers all the time. This is a big exaggeration." Dzhirkvelov, who defected in 1980 and settled in Great Britain, recalled that he was stationed as a Tass correspondent in Tanzania in the 1960s, but traveled to Uganda when the Soviet Union decided to identify the U.S. Peace Corps as a CIA operation, in order to discredit it in Third World countries. He bribed a Ugandan journalist to write such a story under his byline. The report gained some credence, Dzhirkvelov said, partly because the KGB had discovered that one Peace Corps representative was a retired intelligence officer.

Dzhirkvelov, editor of the monthly newsletter *Active Measures and Disinformation*, said he had participated in a disinformation campaign to discredit the conservative West German leader, Franz Josef Strauss. The prominent, ebullient Bavarian politician was regarded in the 1960s as a possible successor to Chancellor Konrad Adenauer, and Moscow policymakers could very well have regarded this prospect as detrimental to their interests. According to Dzhirkvelov, the thinking among Soviet disinformation operatives then ran as follows:

"We have a very big problem in West Germany. It's very possible that, after Adenauer, the Chancellor of Germany could be Strauss. We have to do everything necessary to compromise him. Who can compromise Strauss? Of course: journalists."

As the former Tass-KGB man recalled, it was decided to use intermediaries to plant an article with the widely read news weekly *Der Spiegel*. The magazine, which practices investigative journalism aggressively, subsequently published material that was considered damaging to Strauss. The British news magazine *Now*, which later ceased publication, printed a speech by its publisher, the international financier Sir James Goldsmith, which charged the German magazine with spreading Soviet disinformation. *Der Spiegel* took Sir James to court, but the case was settled without a trial in 1984. The periodical agreed to drop the case, and the two parties agreed that the German magazine had not been "conscious" of any manipulation. This permitted continued speculation that *Der Spiegel* had fallen into a disinformation trap, although unaware that the material had been played into its hands by the KGB (or another Soviet source) through a third party.

Reminiscent of Soviet innuendo that the CIA had been responsible for the death of prominent personalities—from Olof Palme to Samantha Smith—was the implication that the U.S. intelligence service was responsible for AIDS, the virus that destroys human immunity to disease and is therefore fatal. U.S. Ambassador Arthur Hartman, in Moscow, addressed letters to *Literaturnaya Gazeta* and *Sovetskaya Rossiya* on June 25, 1986, protesting their assertion that the CIA and the Pentagon had genetically engineered the AIDS virus as part of a biological warfare program. Ambassador Hartman categorized these allegations as being "as reprehensible as they are false." He cited Soviet immunologists who had suggested that the virus had originated in Africa. He added:

"I can only conclude . . . that they represent nothing more than a blatant and repugnant attempt to sow hatred and fear of Americans among the Soviet population and to abuse a medical tragedy affecting people all over the world, including the Soviet Union, for base propaganda purposes."

Soviet bloc defectors, notably Stanislav Levchenko, who had been a KGB agent operating as a *New Times* magazine correspondent in Tokyo, have testified to the increasing use of active measures, including disinformation. In addition to the CIA and the State Department, a NATO special committee and West Germany's Ministry of the Interior have collected and published data on Soviet and East bloc activities in these fields. There is general agreement that covert propaganda is the special province of Service A of the KGB's First Chief Directorate. Estimates as to the personnel and budget of such an operation, which is highly flexible and overlaps with other agencies, are, by their very nature, imprecise. At the core of the operation, some 200 persons may be involved; the extended disinformation apparatus may employ several thousand full-time and part-time specialists. Liaison with Cuba and such East bloc nations as East Germany and Czechoslovakia is at least partly in the hands of the International Department of the Soviet Communist Party's Central Committee. The Agitprop network also links the KGB's disinformation functions with the Soviet Foreign Ministry and such overt communications services as Tass and Novosti.

It should be taken for granted that a good part of disinformation work goes undetected and unrecognized. Running parallel with forgeries in print appears to be a KGB-operated rumor factory, dispensing half-facts and backroom gossip, that has the same tactical and strategic aims as overt propaganda and the circulation of forged documents: to advance the aims of the Soviet state, encourage dissension and distrust in the West, and heighten Third World resentment of the industrialized nations. High government officials, all over the world, are as likely to become the all-too-willing victims of a disinformation campaign as is the general public. Aware of the role that emotion-tainted judgment plays in public affairs, the disinformation specialists follow an old maxim: "Tell them what they want to hear!"

PART · 4

TACTICS IN TRANSITION

CHAPTER · 27

Where Is the "New Soviet Man"?

Generation after generation, the people of the Soviet Union have been the target of a propaganda campaign designed to create a "new Soviet man." According to the original blueprint, this man or woman would be devout in adhering to Marxism-Leninism, unquestioning in obedience to shifts in Communist Party policies, diligent at work, devoted to collective activities, and fiercely opposed to temptations of "bourgeois" and "imperialist" origins.

The image of this personage appeared in innumerable sculptures and paintings: a man and a woman, side by side, moving onward and upward, clear of vision, handsome of face and body, unsmiling, determined to overcome whatever hurdles might block the path toward higher production figures and ever-greater ideological purity. Generation after generation, this "Soviet man" eluded the professionals who formulate Soviet propaganda. Human traits created an elusive mixture of good and bad, with special elements characteristic of Russian society and other ethnic components that form the U.S.S.R. from Estonia to Uzbekistan. On January 17, 1986, the first secretary of the Turkmen Communist Party, S. A. Niyavo, said at the 23d Regional Party Congress in Ashkabad that Soviet society was intent on "further developing socialist social relations and the New Man." While this ultimate ideal has proved elusive, the continuous Agitprop barrage made a lasting impact on every level of Soviet society.

The temptation to overestimate or underestimate the influence of Soviet propaganda at home is all too great. Soviet society is far from monolithic, despite the impressions of a uniformity some outsiders report. Other visitors are impressed, naively and superficially, by likable human qualities

337

they encounter in major cities, from Leningrad to Kiev—just as others, on the basis of personal encounters, tend to generalize unduly from incidents of boorishness or incompetence.

Soviet society, like societies all over the world, is changing rapidly. Much of the time, Kremlin propagandists attempt, frantically, to insulate the people from the push and pull of the rest of mankind. They cannot succeed totally, but they try hard, and they do succeed in part. Soviet sociologists and psychologists have made surveys that could, at least, give the country's leadership a fairly accurate picture of what people think, like, resent, desire, and plan. These efforts at opinion research encounter severe handicaps, notably an ingrained tendency to tell an interviewer what the interviewee thinks is the proper, and safe thing to say. After all, anyone who asks questions embodies state authority and, therefore, represents that threatening figure, the interrogator.

At times people are fearless, even foolishly so. At other times they get carried away, in the course of a conversation, and reveal more than they originally meant to say. At still other times, as in all societies, people are unable to acknowledge their real thoughts and, instead, project an idealized image of themselves. By the time such surveys are reported, recorded, analyzed, and published, they have gone through a series of sieves that further distort results. More spontaneous comments, spoken on trains or in vacation spots, and even letters to Soviet newspapers provide the raisins, nuts, and fruit in this otherwise uniform pie of public opinion.

For the outsider, the central image that needs erasing is that of a Soviet society in restless ferment, eager to rid itself of the Communist Party and its leaders, dissatisfied with Kremlin policies at home and abroad, and deeply desirous of adopting the substance and veneer of parliamentary democracy and economic-cultural diversity. Soviet leadership detests "pluralism," be it in multiparty systems or free competition in the marketplace; and so, it appears, does the majority of the citizenry. First, of course, because they do not truly know any alternative system; and second, because freedom of choice can be bewildering to the point of panic.

The strongest underlying element here is fear of anarchy, of loss of the existing structure, where everyone has a place and there is, theoretically, a place for everyone. Fear of anarchy has historical roots of which the average Soviet citizen is unaware. But like so many other underlying anxieties and prejudices, these are elements which Soviet propaganda continually reawakens and reinforces. Overall, Soviet society is projected, in the public media, as solid, stolid and law abiding. Other societies, notably the United States, are pictured in near-chaos, overrun with crime and racial conflict and swamped by cultural decadence.

As it happens, the editorial selection process of Western news media, with their emphasis on conflict and the bizarre, favors the images that

Soviet propaganda wishes to create at home. Internal propaganda is continually involved in damming up negative domestic news and encouraging the flow of negative news from abroad. After decades of practice, damming has become so habitual that day-to-day distillation functions automatically: letting one type of news flow, while at least delaying another type; sprinkling selected bits and pieces of news, here and there, or letting dammed-up information cascade forward.

The more sophisticated Soviet newspaper reader, radio listener, or television watcher knows that he is not getting the full picture. But as residue after residue of images settles in public memory, shaping unconscious thoughts and reflexes, even the judgment of world-conscious Soviet citizens is warped. The influence of such Western media as the Voice of America, Radio Liberty, the British Broadcasting Corporation (BBC), and West Germany's Deutsche Welle, broadcasting in Russian and other languages of the U.S.S.R. has increased; but only a minority of Soviet citizens have access to these broadcasts, and a good number of listeners receive them with the same mental reservations they maintain toward domestic news and comment.

Ultimately, it isn't the damming up or cascading of propaganda that forms Soviet minds, but the steady and unceasing drizzle that descends on everyone from Riga to Vladivostok, from the Caucasus to Outer Mongolia. It is so inescapable, so unrelenting and total, that the propagandists themselves are subject to its impact and, most serious of all, top officials tend to become prisoners of ideas with which they grew up, have echoed, and now propagate themselves. Arkadi Shevchenko, former undersecretary of the United Nations, said in his book *Breaking with Moscow* that Foreign Minister Andrei Gromyko, sitting in New York and spooning honey into his tea, remarked, "American bees were turning out a distinctly poor product." What he did not know was that the Soviet mission was serving the cheapest available honey. When he understood this, Gromyko asked Shevchenko and Soviet Ambassador Anatoli Dobrynin about other items and their cost. He had simply never visited American stores and barely knew anything about the U.S. standard of living.

Self-isolation is a danger that high officials face everywhere. It is the bane of U.S. presidents. They, however, are subjected to questions at press conferences and exposed to pressures from "pluralist" politicians, so the risk of isolation is lessened. A man like Gromyko, who for decades shouldered the major responsibility for Soviet foreign policy, certainly ought to have known details of the American economy, as well as of the rough-and-ready nature of daily life in other parts of the world. Yet Shevchenko quoted Gromyko's daughter Emilia as saying, "My father lives in the skies. For 25 years he has not set foot on the streets of Moscow. All he sees is the view from his car window."

True, Soviet officials receive the special Tass versions of world news, a far wider selection than what reaches the average reader, but a selection nevertheless. Even the personnel at Soviet embassies and at such privileged establishments as Moscow's United States of America and Canada Institute is likely to scan publications and texts with a biased, if practiced, eye, looking for items and comments that will help either to boost the U.S.S.R. or to downgrade the United States. Soviet officials, at whatever level, have gone through a process of ideological training that inevitably slants their judgment. They must submerge themselves in this manner, if only to remain and advance within the machinery of government and party.

Lifelong conditioning affects the thought processes, and even more the unconscious mental reflexes, of Soviet citizens. The steady drizzle of daily propaganda virtually begins at the cradle and hardly ever stops short of the grave. The images picked up by a toddler in a nursery school, the lessons learned in early school grades, the training of boys and girls in the Young Pioneers and of older children in *Komsomol* groups, and the unending ideological sessions at universities, in plants, on collective farms, and in neighborhood "actives" are all part of the total structure of Soviet agitation and propaganda.

Aside from these institutionalized Agitprop activities, the Soviet citizen floats in an ocean of propaganda, as matter-of-fact as a fish in water, hardly aware that the ever-present element surrounds him, much of the time oblivious to slogans on the wall, voices from the loudspeaker, characters in a novel or play, films, photographs, paintings, sculptures, poems, and, increasingly, television programs. Until just a few years ago, the big gun of Soviet information was *Pravda*, the official daily newspaper of the Communist Party, with a circulation of some 11 million copies; it was the uncontested prime Soviet information medium. Today, the nightly *Vremya* newscast, originating in Moscow and carried on nationwide networks, is tops in popularity. While the newscast is as carefully controlled and edited as *Pravda* or Tass, it nevertheless provides a visual dimension that is missing in the print media. Because Soviet society discourages star worship, even in sports and entertainment, nothing like the popular TV personalities that have emerged in the United States and Western Europe has developed in the U.S.S.R. Nevertheless, in terms of quality and technology, Soviet television standards are high, and there is clearly an effort to create a pattern of dramatic immediacy on *Vremya* and other TV programs. When the U.S. space shuttle *Challenger* exploded on January 28, 1986, the fiery image was shown on Soviet news that night.

For all its popularity, television is just another arm of the Soviet propaganda machinery, subject to guidances that affect all media and ultimately controlled by the Communist Party's Central Committee and the U.S.S.R. Council of Ministers. Vassili A. Shamshin, who was appointed minister of communications on October 24, 1980, said in a Tass interview (August 18, 1984) that the country was setting up "thousands of small television transmitters," not only "in densely populated regions" but also in territories with only tens or hundreds of thousands. Most of these are relay stations that bring programs to outlying districts, as part of a massive investment in this highly effective medium of education, agitation, and propaganda. Shamshin told Tass the Politburo had endorsed the development of a "material and technical basis for television transmission during the 1984–1990 period," providing "new opportunities for the development of multiprogram color television."

Generally, Soviet viewers are served by the two major national channels, frequently supplemented by a regional channel. The first channel covered not only the European part of the country, Shamshin said, but also Siberia, the Far East, Sakhalin, and Chukotka. He added: "While attention was previously focused on expanding the reception area for the first All-Union channel, the problem we now face is that of expanding the transmission area for the second Central Television channel." Main emphasis was placed on satellite communication receiving stations that provide local relays. Shamshin said that TV screens were "lighting up at reindeer herdsmen's camps, mountain hamlets, meteorological stations, and geologists' field bases."

The communications minister said that the per-person investment in these facilities amounted to "thousands, sometimes tens of thousands of rubles per viewer." Clearly, this investment was considered justified in terms of the programs' propaganda value. As Shamshin put it, "Television plays a large part in our people's spiritual life and in the formation of public opinion" and makes a major contribution to "the working people's ideological and cultural education."

The overall direction of Soviet agitation and propaganda was, for many years, in the hands of Mikhail Suslov, the veteran Politburo member and chief ideologue who died in 1982. Day-to-day administration of domestic information was conducted by the Central Committee's Department of Propaganda and Agitation. The post of department director was taken over, in June 1965, by Vladimir I. Stepakov, former editor of *Izvestia* (a post in which he succeeded Khrushchev's son-in-law, Aleksei Adzhubei). Stepakov replaced Leonid F. Ilyichev, an appointee of the Khrushchev administration, and Pyotr N. Demichev, a temporary department director.

In the party's theoretical organ, *Kommunist* (November 1965), Stepakov acknowledged that the "new Soviet man" had not been achieved. He stated, "The process of education of a new person cannot be completed during socialism, for socialist society, which grew out of capitalism, still bears within itself the birthmarks of an exploiting regime." Propaganda policies, he explained, should be directed against "survivals of the past in the consciousness and attitude of the people." These "survivals" he defined as "religious conceptions, nationalistic prejudices, robbery, hooliganism, a psychology of petty personal ownership (by which I mean an attitude of getting as much as possible, while giving as little as possible), bureaucratism, careerism and others." Twenty years later, Mikhail Gorbachev listed very similar shortcomings as holding back the country's economic progress. His predecessors, Andropov and Chernenko, had made the same points.

Is domestic propaganda, perhaps, directed not so much against survivals from a pre-Soviet era as at basic human characteristics that are sharpened under centralized control of the nation's political, economic, and cultural life? Stepakov dealt with this question as candidly as possible. "To our great regret," he said, "we have not accomplished as yet a deep and well-reasoned study which investigates the causes for the survival of capitalism in the consciousness and behavior of the people." Such candor, apparently, was not sufficient to ensure Stepakov's position during the Brezhnev years. He was removed from his post early in 1970 for obscure reasons of ideological incompatibility. When China refused to accept him as ambassador to Peking, Stepakov was named ambassador to Yugoslavia, a position he obtained in February 1971.

Once again, the Central Committee's Agitprop Department was placed under Pyotr Demichev, one of the committee's secretaries. Next, Demichev was given the post of minister of culture in 1974; it was he who negotiated the details of U.S.-Soviet cultural exchanges with Charles Z. Wick, director of the U.S. Information Agency, in Moscow, during a ten-day visit in January 1986. Demichev was relieved of this post, after 12 years, in June of that year. On August 16, Vasili G. Zakharov took his place. The Agitprop Department was placed, in 1971, under the supervision of Mikhail V. Zimyanin, a committee secretary who emerged as a leading spokesman on issues of propaganda, agitation, information, and education. Technically, the post of director for domestic propaganda remained vacant for seven years. Finally, on May 27, 1977, Yevgeni M. Tyazhelnikov was moved from a post as first secretary of Komsomol to that of propaganda director.

Tyazhelnikov was in charge when, in 1979, the Kremlin leadership launched a massive effort at strengthening and enlivening the propaganda field. Brezhnev had laid the groundwork for this campaign in a speech to the Central Committee in November 1978. He reported that the Politburo had formed a special commission on "ideological and mass-political work." On May 6, 1979, *Pravda* published a Central Committee decree, "On The Further Improvement of Ideological, Political and Educational Work," that accused propagandists of a tendency to "smooth over and avoid unresolved problems and acute questions, to hush up shortcomings and difficulties existing in real life." The document called for a "systematic, purposeful and uncompromising struggle," using "all means of propaganda and education." Once again, the text emphasized the need to "eradicate ugly vestiges of the past" and called for the "use of both verbal persuasion and the harsh force of law in the struggle against these phenomena."

To this decision from the Communist Party, government initiative was added when the U.S.S.R. Supreme Soviet adopted a resolution, "On the Tasks of the Soviets of People's Deputies Arising from the CPSU Central Committee Resolution 'On Further Improving Ideological and Political Education Work.' " The Supreme Soviet, the country's pseudo parliament, instructed local soviets "to elaborate and implement measures aimed at further improving educational work" in "residences and in hostels, small collectives and remote settlements," as well as through "mass cultural and sports work in houses of culture, clubs, movie theaters, libraries, museums, stadiums and other sports facilities."

As quoted in *Pravda* (June 3, 1979), the resolution urged propaganda and agitation to heighten "civic awareness and industriousness, patriotism and internationalism," and demanded "the eradication of ugly phenomena still present in our lives, such as money-grubbing and bribe-taking, thrift-lessness and extravagance, hooliganism, parasitism, and violations of labor discipline and public order." These were restatements of earlier Agitprop targets centering on the commanding role of the Communist Party, but their reiteration had the ring of urgency.

What happened between 1979 and 1986? The Communist Party's 27th Congress adopted a program, outlining progress toward the end of the century, which once more demanded that "public opinion and the force of law" be directed against continued "manifestations of alien ideology and morals and all negative phenomena." The program stated: "The Party attaches paramount significance to doing away steadily and consistently with violations of labor discipline, pilferage and bribe-taking, drunkenness and hooliganism, private-owner psychology and money-grubbing, toadyism and fawning." Except for the addition of drunkenness, reflecting an anti-alcoholism campaign which Gorbachev had launched, the party program was only a strong echo of the past.

Calls for more effective ideo-propagandistic work sounded, in fact, like echoes of echoes. More than three decades earlier, on October 5, 1952, at the start of the party's 19th Congress, Georgi Malenkov had also demanded an end to the "harmful underestimation of ideological work." Malenkov, who succeeded Stalin upon his death the following March, exhorted party members as follows: "It is necessary to develop and perfect socialist culture, science, literature and art, to mobilize all means of ideological and political education, our propaganda, agitation, and the press, for improving the ideological training of Communists, for raising the political vigilance and the political consciousness of the workers, peasants and the intelligentsia."

Quite correctly, then, more than 33 years later, Gorbachev said that "the Central Committee has often discussed the task of the Party's politico-educational and ideological work," allowing only that "some progress has been made there." But, he added, more needs to be done to "couple ideological work most closely with life." What, exactly, did he mean by that? Even Gorbachev, who sought to avoid a convoluted and abstract vernacular, could only say, "Formalism and mentorism continued to be a hindrance." Formalism? Mentorism? He probably meant that there was a huge gap between Soviet talk and Soviet reality. He said next: "Quite often the loss comes from talk, from the inability to speak with people in the language of truth. And it sometimes happens that a person hears one thing, but sees quite a different thing in real life. This is a serious question, and not only an educational but a political one."

To close this gap, Soviet media could actually begin to report the news, including earthquakes, accidents, high-level personnel changes, perhaps even crimes, judicial proceedings, and specific economic conditions. This would bring the reality of daily life into the unreality of media coverage. Soviet reporters might even factually cover all that pilferage and bribe taking, hooliganism, and money grabbing, including corruption among party and government officials—stopping short, for the sake of their lives and liberty, below the level of the Central Committee and the Politburo.

The *Vremya* newscast was quick to transmit pictures of a severe earthquake in Mexico City, in mid-1985, but similar events in Soviet Central Asia—which could not really be blamed on the local officials—were treated as nonevents or relegated to short items on the newspapers' inside pages. Soviet journalism, with all its training in ideology and technology, does not consistently deal with questions of Who, When, and Where as it reports events. Reporters and commentators are all too aware that they are supposed to write and rewrite their findings in order to make an ideo-propagandistic point. Ironically, the very speeches, documents, commentaries, and editorials urging improved, lively, gripping reporting have uniformly been written in nonspecific, elusive, haughtily sermonizing terms.

Still, the Gorbachev era brought—although not exactly break-throughs—hints of possible changes. These could be traced back to Andropov, who actually, in one speech (November 22, 1982), was specific to the point of saying, "One can't call it a normal situation when the question of buttons, shoe polish and other such items is virtually decided in the State Planning Commission of the USSR." This was the very height of finger pointing, of citing actual overcentralization within the Soviet economy!

Still, later on, some items were startlingly specific. For example, the Moscow City Council announced, and Radio Moscow reported (January 1, 1986), that the city's population had reached 8.71 million. And, according to *Sotsialisticheskaya Industriya* (October 1985), in the northern port city of Murmansk the "road and municipal services were unprepared" when a heavy "fierce snow storm collided with a hurricane." More than a year later, Tass actually reported (December 18, 1986) anti-Russian rioting in Alma Ata, capital of Kazakhstan. Tass blamed Kazakh "nationalistic elements" for apparent protests against the removal of the regional party leader, Dinmukhamed A. Kunayev, and his replacement by an ethnic Russian, Gennadi V. Kolbin.

Implementing the Gorbachev team's drive against rigid bureaucracy, alcoholism, and inefficient management, newspapers increased their coverage of these topics and published an increasing number of reader's letters on related themes. The town of Voloshilovgrad came in for a good deal of nasty publicity when students and Komsomol members, mainly sons of local party and industry officials, engaged in a series of drunken orgies, robbing people, undressing and tatooing girls, and otherwise imitating outrages they had seen in war films. The Communist Youth League's own paper, *Komsomolskaya Pravda*, published details of these scandals.

Coverage of the Soviet army's activities in Afghanistan, practically non-existent after the invasion of 1979, became increasingly detailed during the Gorbachev period. The army's daily paper, *Krasnaya Zvezda* (Red Star) strengthened its coverage—always, of course, implementing such themes as the "peace-making mission" of Soviet troops and the destructive resistance of the "Dushmans," the official epithet for the Afghan guerrillas.

Soviet television began sporadic coverage in July 1985, with shots of Soviet soldiers in action. On December 25, TV reports included a one-hour documentary, "Afghanistan: The Revolution Cannot Be Killed," narrated by Mikhail Leshinski. The viewer was given the impression that the Afghan War had been started by outsiders, showing routes leading from Pakistan and Iran into Afghanistan and using film clips from German, French, and British TV documentaries to suggest that guerrillas were acting as "mercenaries." One captured "bandit" was identified as a Turkish national, "arrested in northern Afghanistan, where he was sent to carry out a mission for the CIA."

The show closed with shots of women protesting outside the White House in Washington, pro-Soviet Afghan troops hailed by a crowd, the official flag on top of a hill, and a song about the Afghan homeland adding a folkloric upbeat mood in the background. All major propaganda themes were implemented by this video presentation, which indicated long and careful preparation, intensive research, and skillful professional camera work and editing.

With some 100,000 Soviet troops in Afghanistan and 10,000 casualties per year, the Afghan War represented a minute segment of the Soviet Union's economic-military effort. Still, dead and wounded did return to the homeland, troops were rotated, and reports of young men seeking to avoid military duty increased in frequency. After virtually ignoring the war at first, more and more detailed reports began to appear. *Pravda*, for instance, published a two-part dispatch, "A Very Long Night: From an Afghan Notebook," in its issues of January 17 and 19, 1986. The dispatch mentioned Soviet army units in east Afghanistan receiving reports on "Dushmans" in the area "robbing columns and attacking villages," with "shelling and attacks coinciding with penetration into the province by special groups from Pakistan." The dispatch described a successful "reconnaissance" by the "Moskva" company, ignoring any lessons suffered by it but reporting on its return with "Dushman trophies," including "personal documents" of those killed.

Soviet propaganda made no major effort to popularize or even publicize such versions of the Afghan War abroad. United Nations resolutions, with the backing of most Third World and Islamic countries, uniformly denounced the Soviet invasion and its continued efforts to crush Afghan resistance. Soviet actions in Afghanistan were a major hurdle for Moscow's efforts to strengthen relations with Peking. Nicholas Daniloff, reporting from Moscow to *U.S. News* (December 18, 1985), noted a "propaganda offensive," designed to "stiffen national resolve." He wrote that Gorbachev had permitted "state-controlled media to dramatically broaden coverage of the war, an about-face that has startled millions of Soviets." He added: "The onslaught on Soviet public opinion is in obvious response to increasing war weariness as the costs of the conflict are driven home," although "the propaganda campaign at home gives strong indications that Moscow has no intention of pulling out its troops until it has turned the Moslem nation into a docile buffer state willing to bow to the Kremlin's every demand."

Soviet propaganda faced the tactical difficulty of compartmentalizing public response to (1) encouraging a patriotically aggressive spirit in backing the Afghan War, while (2) continuing its various peace and disarmament campaigns, (3) reviving memories of World War II, as during its elaborate fortieth anniversary celebrations in mid-1985, and (4) denouncing such U.S. actions as the atom-bombing of Hiroshima to hasten the end of the war in 1945. The anniversary of the end of World War II was celebrated on May 9 by a gigantic parade in Moscow's Red Square, with Gorbachev and other Politburo members standing atop the Lenin Mausoleum.

Integrating the sometimes contradictory aspects of Soviet policies in agitation and propaganda is one of the tasks of the *Znanie* (Knowledge) Society. Its lecturers delivered some 25 million talks in 1983 to a total audience of more than 1.1 billion people. In "Propagating Communist Values in Russia," which appeared in *Problems of Communism*, the U.S. Information Agency bimonthly (November–December 1985), Stephen White of the University of Glasgow emphasized the impact of this lecture program. On balance, the impact of the Znanie lectures—and of ideological talks in clubs, factories, etc., generally—fell far below that of the mass media. Sociological evaluation of Soviet ideological work began in the mid-1960s, White wrote, "at about the same time sociology was establishing itself in the USSR as a legitimate academic discipline."

According to White, a study at an industrial enterprise in the Moscow region found that television was the most widely used source of information, reaching 81.7 percent of the people who were polled; next came newspapers, reaching 78.9 percent; then radio, 24 percent; political information sessions, 24 percent; propagandists and lecturers, 21.5 percent; and, finally, "agitators," with only 3.6 percent. White noted: "Fewer than a quarter of those polled in another survey could remember the subject of the last political information session they had attended and the name of the lecturer, and more than a third were unable to name the agitator attached to their local work group, with whom they were supposedly in constant touch."

The crucial role of domestic propaganda control was, as noted earlier, placed in the hands of Tyazhelnikov, the former Komsomol head, in 1977. Still, the Brezhnev period was not really suited to any basic modernization. Long-winded, cliché-ridden speeches, turgid commentaries, and convoluted lectures dominated the Agitprop scene. All this changed quickly when Andropov succeeded Brezhnev—beginning with the general secretary's own speeches and interviews. He sent Tyazhelnikov to Romania and replaced him with Boris I. Stukalin.

Born in 1923, Stukalin worked for local newspapers in the city of Voronezh from 1948 to 1960. Once in Moscow, he directed the Russian republic's State Press Committee from 1963 to 1966, then became Zimyanin's deputy as *Pravda* editor. Beginning in 1970, Stukalin was chairman of the U.S.S.R. Committee for Press and Publishing, later renamed the State Committee for Publishing Houses, Printing, and the Book Trade; it was in this capacity that he directed Soviet-supported publishing ventures in Greece, including the controversial launching of the daily newspaper *Ethnos* (see Chapter 31).

When Andropov came to power in November 1982, he unseated a substantial number of Brezhnev appointees. According to Elizabeth Teague, Soviet affairs analyst of Radio Liberty in Munich, Andropov sought to "revamp outmoded techniques of political indoctrination, which was widely recognized as having lost credibility among growing sections of the Soviet's population, young people in particular." Within a month after

taking power, Andropov had installed Stukalin. Since Gorbachev, in many
ways, has continued and strengthened Andropov's policies, it came as a
surprise that, on July 21, 1985, Stukalin was moved from his propaganda
post and made ambassador to Hungary.

Stukalin's successor as the Central Committee's propaganda director
was Alexander N. Yakovlev. Like his predecessor, Yakovlev was born in
1923—on December 2, to be exact. The British newspaper the *Guardian*
(July 24, 1985) described him as "a short, plump intellectual," with "man-
icured nails, bright eyes, and an air of relaxed competence and self-assurance common to top civil servants and executives in any political system."
Yakovlev, who came to his propaganda post from the directorship of Moscow's prestigious Institute of World Economy and International Relations,
had served in the 1940s and 1950s in the Communist Party organization of
Yaroslavl. As the city had been Andropov's starting point, he may have
come to Moscow with the former KGB chief's backing. Yakovlev was in
the army from 1941 to 1943. He graduated from the Yaroslavl Pedagogical
Institute. Following seven years in local party organizations, he was transferred to the Central Committee in Moscow. After working as deputy
director of the committee's Department of Science and Culture, he attended the party Academy of Social Sciences.

Yakovlev's specific orientation toward propaganda began with the Central Committee's Agitprop Department in 1962. For two years, he served
as a departmental instructor. During 1963 and 1964, Yakovlev directed
the section which controlled radio and television. He became the department's first deputy director in 1965. The following year, the department's
name was shortened and "westernized" when the term "Agitation" was
dropped and it became simply the Department of Propaganda. Beginning
in 1967, when the department's director, Stepakov, was relieved of his
duties, Yakovlev was the office's acting head.

Ann Sheehy, a Radio Liberty researcher, has noted that Yakovlev's
career revealed "academic interests in the field of American foreign policy." She reported: "In 1959, at the age of thirty-five, he spent some time
at Columbia University in New York as an exchange student, and later
earned the title of Candidate (1965) and Doctor of Historical Sciences. In
the course of the 1960s, Yakovlev published four monographs on U.S.
foreign policy, as well as a 'Znanie' pamphlet on 'bourgeois democracy'
in the United States. In addition, he edited another book on the United
States, published in 1969, and in 1971 he was one of those who prepared
for publication a volume on the so-called Pentagon Papers [documents
concerning the Vietnam War, prepared by the U.S. Department of Defense
and publicized by U.S. newspapers]. Finally, Yakovlev headed a collective
of authors who produced a 352-page textbook, entitled *Bases of Political
Knowledge*, for the Party education system, that was published in 1972

with a printing of 250,000. A second edition of the book was published in printings of 200,000 each in 1973 and 1974, and the book has since appeared in a variety of Soviet and foreign languages."

Yakovlev's career in the propaganda establishment was temporarily diverted in 1972. He lost out in a policy-and-personnel dispute that centered on the role of Russian nationalism, or "Russophilism," on the cultural-political level. His detailed attack on Russophilism was published in *Literaturnaya Gazeta* (November 15, 1972) and took up two pages in the weekly paper's issue. In the article, "Against Anti-Historicism," Yakovlev criticized several authors by name and lashed out at a "cult" of "patriarchal peasantry" and its anti-intellectual undertones. The article provoked wide discussion and controversy at the time, and Sheehy noted: "Some said that Yakovlev was trying to nullify the glorious Russian past, while others argued that, if Russian nationalism was not kept in check, the flood gates would be opened to potential excesses on the part of other nationalities."

Yakovlev was made ambassador to Canada, and this gave him the opportunity of arranging Gorbachev's successful cross-Canada trip in May 1983, while Chernenko was still alive but ailing. With Gorbachev increasingly influential, Yakovlev was brought back to Moscow from Ottawa the following month and appointed director of the Institute of World Economy and International Relations of the U.S.S.R. Academy of Sciences. In 1984 he was elected to the Supreme Soviet, became a corresponding member of the Academy of Sciences, and was named chairman of the Association for Promoting the United Nations in the U.S.S.R. Yakovlev was a member of the group that accompanied Gorbachev and his wife to Great Britain in December 1984. That year, he published a monograph, *From Truman to Reagan: Doctrines and Reality of the Nuclear Age.*

Yakovlev accompanied Gorbachev on other trips, and the two men appeared to share distrust of Russophilism, as well as of nationalistic trends among other ethnic groups. Certainly, the Central Committee's Propaganda Department provided a superior base for discouraging such trends and of reining in their protagonists. Moscow's appointment of such an internationally minded propaganda specialist as Yakovlev foreshadowed the dissolution of Zamyatin's International Information Department. Both men accompanied Gorbachev to his Geneva meeting with President Reagan.

Trud, the newspaper of the Soviet trade unions, published an interview with poet Yevgeni Yevtuchenko (January 26, 1986) which expanded on his talk at the earlier writers' congress. Asked about "the changes taking place in our life," Yevtuchenko answered, "Economic thinking is impossible without the development of moral awareness." He said that "moral processes" called for "the development and institution of broad publicity." He added: "This process is not all that simple, because inertia—thinking

as they are prompted—has become firmly entrenched within some bureaucratic brains." He noted that a younger generation was emerging, that
men of his own age were now party officials and government executives.
Yevtuchenko also gave an interview to the Rome paper *La Repubblica*
(January 18). He was quoted as saying that, for years, he had "condemned
the blank pages in our history, pseudo-culture, intolerable privileges." The
interviewer—reminding him that Gorbachev, in his New Year's address
to the nation, had said, "We now give things their proper names: we call
success, success; shortcomings, shortcomings; and mistakes, mistakes"—
asked Yevtuchenko, "Please, help me to understand what is going on."
Pointing to the "new generation," Yevtuchenko said it "grew up at the
same time I did, and with the literature of my time" and was "now becoming
the country's leadership class."

Letters from readers and reporters' accounts of shortcomings, coinciding with criticism and demotion of regional leaders, marked the period
preceding the 27th Communist Party Congress. Seemingly spontaneous
outpourings of complaints and "investigative reporting" were clearly part
of official drives against corruption, drunkenness, and inefficiency. While
Yakovlev's propaganda office orchestrated media participation in this campaign, together with agitation for increased production and labor discipline,
the Gorbachev drive also had a power target: the Stalin generation was
being pushed out of office and Brezhnev holdovers were losing the battle
for control and elite privileges. By calling "shortcomings" and "mistakes"
by their real names, the propaganda campaign was taking aim at thousands
of party and government bureaucrats.

Moscow vernacular used to be studded with such standard phrases as
"It is no accident that" and "As is well known." As the Gorbachev team
made its strength felt, announcements of officials' resignations multiplied,
and with them the phrases "freed of his duties in connection with retirement" and "freed of his duties in connection with transfer to other work."
Ever so topical, Alexander Misharin wrote a play that implemented the
new propaganda themes, with the provisional title *Freed of His Duties in
Connection with Other Work*. But when it reached the stage of the Moscow
Art Theater, during the 1985–1986 season, the play bore the less provocative title *The Silver Anniversary*.

Misharin's play dealt with a high official who returns to his hometown
to celebrate his silver anniversary. He is shocked to discover that two of
the men he had helped to gain public office are enmeshed in corruption.
What's more, they had framed and imprisoned a reporter who threatened
to expose their machinations. In the ensuing drama, with its clashes of
personalities, accusations, and counteraccusations, major Agitprop themes
were covered, including the drive against alcoholism. Aleg N. Yefremov,
director of the Moscow Art Theater, managed to obtain the play's approval

by Gorbachev's right-hand man, Politburo member Yegor K. Ligachev. It gave Ligachev the opportunity to translate his own exhortations, directed at writers and artists, into specific action and endorsement. Production of *The Silver Anniversary* quickly became the talk of the Moscow season, not so much for artistic excellence as for the play's political theme; it was a sellout, and it spotlighted Ligachev's decisive role.

Theatrical productions, which can be put on quickly and may even be revised from one evening to another, are able to respond rapidly to policy changes. Rivalries and personality clashes are also reflected in conflicts over content and execution. The Soviet motion-picture industry came under attack in *Literaturnaya Gazeta* in late December 1985; a veteran actor, Nikolai Kriuchkov, criticized the film monopoly as being riddled with nepotism and managing only a "very mediocre" output. The critique appeared to be directed at Philip T. Yermash, chairman of the State Commission for Cinematography (*Goskino*), who had been at his post since 1972.

The impact of outside cultural elements was most strongly reflected in the increasing popularity of imported videocassettes. When video players first made their appearance in the U.S.S.R., in the 1970s, they were rare and their existence was officially ignored. By 1985, the number of video cassette recorders (VCRs) had greatly increased, and so had legally or illegally obtained cassettes. Sale, duplication, and rental multiplied. In order to counteract the black market in smuggled and duplicated cassettes, Soviet equipment was designed to be incompatible with Japanese and Western European models; however, Soviet-made equipment could be adapted for use with foreign material.

Television, which can also respond rapidly to propaganda directives, presented a greater challenge than the theater—if only because it had a much greater impact and demanded ever-fresh material. Even pure entertainment must guard against political slips. Once, when *The Memoirs of Sherlock Holmes* was being filmed for television, rumors in Moscow artistic circles had it that the series was being canceled as ideologically harmful. Vladimir Voinovich, who left the U.S.S.R. in 1980, recalled that such a ban seemed odd, as Sir Arthur Conan Doyle's stories of the British supersleuth had long been popular in book form. Voinovich said, "The mystery was solved when the offending passage was identified." The passage follows:

Holmes: "How are you? You have been in Afghanistan, I perceive."

Watson: "How on earth did you know that?"

Holmes: "The train of reasoning ran: Here is a gentleman of a medical type, but with the air of a military man. . . . He has just come from the tropics, for his face is dark and that is not the natural tint of his skin. . . . He has undergone hardship and sickness, as his haggard face shows clearly. His left arm has been injured. . . . Where in the tropics could an English army doctor have seen much hardship and got his arm wounded? Clearly, in Afghanistan."

Eventually, the Sherlock Holmes series was rescued. The offending reference to Afghanistan was replaced with, "You have visited a country in the Orient, I perceive." Voinovich, in his article "Sidelight on Soviet Censorship," which appeared in the British quarterly journal *Survey* (Autumn 1984), wrote: "It might be thought that this change, which was based on purely political considerations, would have little or no effect on the artistic quality of the film. But it does! Because, as a literature figure, Sherlock Holmes is remarkable for his ability to pinpoint exactly where someone has been. And when he is made to say, 'in a country in the Orient,' the approximateness, the impreciseness, of his inference can hardly interest us, for without much effort we could reach the same conclusion ourselves."

Voinovich explained the function of *Glavlit*, the Soviet censorship agency responsible for preventing military and state secrets from appearing in the press, radio, TV, literature, films, and the theater. He said: "Glavlit censors have long lists of military and geographical locations, industrial objects, scientific discoveries and names of persons, references to which are either wholly prohibited in the press or require special permission from Party security organs. The lists become lengthier each passing year. They include the names of former Party leaders (from Trotsky to Khrushchev), of numerous writers and dissidents, and of scientists engaged in secret projects."

To no one's surprise, Yevtuchenko's reference to Khrushchev, in his speech to the Writers' Union, was eliminated—together with other references not among the new propaganda themes—from the version later published in *Literaturnaya Gazeta*. It was more striking to see a similar reference, contained in Gorbachev's *Time* interview, deleted from the version that simultaneously appeared in *Pravda*.

Voinovich mentioned that Glavlit is "one of many agencies" involved in censoring material before it reaches the public. "The first censor of a work," he wrote, "is its author himself." A written work is first passed through reviewers, then editors on several levels, all of whom must judge "ideological and artistic requirements." These, Voinovich maintained, "are almost without exception mutually contradictory." The demands of Gorbachev, of the Communist Party program, 1986–2000, and of all those who echoed these calls were for a critical and self-critical approach which had long been fraught with risk in Soviet society. The charge that words, actions, and behavior were "anti-Party," "anti-Soviet" or "anti-state," could always be made to embrace the most trivial of critical observation—despite the fact that party demands for "criticism and self-criticism" were among the standard clichés, going back to Lenin's day.

As Voinovich wrote, editing a manuscript always meant conformity to the "basic canons of Socialist Realism, which means that it must have a positive hero, that the (from the communist point of view) good must defeat the (from the communist point of view) evil, and that the general thrust and tone of the work must be optimistic." What would make any writer hesitant to follow Gorbachev's apparent proscription of frank criticism was the tradition, as Voinovich summarized it, "to eliminate not only any criticism of the Soviet system, but even any implication of such criticism, ensuring that Soviet life is consistently portrayed in a rosy light and life in capitalist societies in a gloomy light." He added that "the last requirement is enforced even more strictly than the first," which is why "travel articles by persons who have been abroad are, if they fail to give sufficient attention to unemployment, crime, inflation and the like, usually subjected to withering criticism."

One of the totally safe subjects for Soviet writers of fact, fiction, plays, films, and television scripts has always been Lenin. Another quite safe theme is the wickedness of the United States, and of "bourgeois society" in general; for this reason, certain books by such U.S. authors as Upton Sinclair and John Steinbeck, or plays by Arthur Miller and Lillian Hellman, could be safely offered to the Soviet public. Miller's play *Death of a Salesman*, a highly esteemed work of social criticism, was also one of the first American plays presented in Peking. Of course, while in the West such plays are part of a complex web of artistic expression, in the Soviet Union they are offered as examples of the disintegration of "capitalist" society.

U.S. baiting is often a reflex, encouraged at the regular Central Committee propaganda meetings. These briefings, which editors of newspapers, periodicals, and radio and television programs attend in rotation, point up which events should be played down and which are to be played up. At its most crude, the media are encouraged to recount airplane accidents in the United States when such an accident has occurred in the U.S.S.R.— even if the accident is being suppressed, since news of it has inevitably begun to circulate by word of mouth. Consistent with this, sparse initial reports on the Chernobyl nuclear disaster in May 1986 were immediately diluted with accounts of nuclear incidents abroad, notably in the United States. American campaigns in favor of human rights have caused Soviet propaganda to search for replies in kind. As American Indians have, in the minds of many Russians, retained a romantic image created by nineteenth-century authors, such as James Fenimore Cooper, Soviet propagandists have selected the case of Leonard Peltier, serving two consecutive life sentences for the murder of two FBI agents. On November 15, 1985, Tass reported that deputies of the U.S.S.R. Supreme Soviet had sent a message to the U.S. Senate and House of Representatives, saying: "Glaring judicial arbitrariness is being practiced against the courageous fighter for the civil rights of American Indians, Leonard Peltier, whose name has become the symbol of the suffering of the native population of the United States." *Moscow News* (September 29, 1985) stated in an editorial that the "vile and ruthless" policy of the United States had assured that "American Indians have every right to say that they are being subject to genocide."

In May 1985, when the Philadelphia headquarters of the "Move" cult was bombed, after its armed occupants refused to leave, Soviet media pictured the attack as a racist offensive against blacks, ignoring the fact that the mayor and many of the city's administrators were themselves black. Neither did Soviet media take notice of the postbombing analyses, public hearings, anti-"Move" sentiments of much of the local black community, and rebuilding and reimbursement efforts. Instead, the incident was categorized as an example of U.S. "racism" and "state terrorism."

In April 1986, Soviet television aired a documentary, "The Man from Fifth Avenue." It showed affluence and misery in Manhattan, ranging from the Plaza Hotel to shots of the unemployed and homeless. As its guide, it employed Joe Mauri, who was identified as one of the victims of the capitalist system, himself without work or home. Mauri was subsequently invited to the U.S.S.R. so that he might testify to his fate, and that of other unfortunates, in person. When he returned to the United States, investigative reporters, notably those of the New York *Daily News*, discovered that Mauri was on a list of part-time employees in the mailroom of the *New York Times* and that he could earn as much as $35,000 per year if he took advantage of available work. He lived in a residential hotel, while he and his estranged wife also rented an apartment on Columbus Avenue; they had been separated for 18 years, but Mauri said, "I go there on a regular basis. We're friends." He also said: "I'll show you a lot of homeless people living in New York City. They cut and edited the film the way they wanted to. I have no control of the film. I am a patriot. I think we can make our society better. It's not a political thing. It was a humanitarian gesture."

The bleak picture which domestic Soviet propaganda paints of conditions in the "capitalist" world, and which is also the image created in Eastern European and other Soviet-influenced nations, contrasts with the attraction that the free world seems to hold for much of the population of the Soviet Union. While much of the outside world's image, as perceived within Soviet society, is in its own way a distortion—based on motion pictures and novels, plus fragmentary other information—it troubles Moscow leaders. They attribute most of this cultural magnetism to calculated Western propaganda, and their reply to it is consequently labeled "counter-propaganda." In actual fact, this drive is traditional Agitprop activity, directed at what the Central Committee perceives as particularly vulnerable elements of Soviet society, notably youth and religious groups. Surveys have also singled out residents of border territories, sailors, and merchant seamen as among targets of "imperialist propaganda," mainly because they have access to foreign broadcasts, television, literature, and cassettes.

Cartoons in Moscow's satirical magazine, *Krokodil*, make fun of young people's fascination with exaggerated Western dress, manners, and music. KGB director Viktor Chebrikov devoted a long article in the Komsomol journal, *Molodoi Kommunist* (April 1981), to the receptive attitude of youths toward foreign ideas. He blamed poor Soviet propaganda for the impact of ideological "revisionism," "bourgeois nationalism," religion, and such subversive political ideas as "pluralism" and "consumerism." He wrote: "It must be stressed that imperialism's ideological sabotage succeeds where the dissemination of hostile ideology does not meet with the rebuff it deserves, and where young people are not provided with clear and precise answers to the questions that trouble them." Young people's newly found interest in religion, if only through the artistic appeal of icons, church music, and architecture, also troubles Soviet ideological educators. The concept that Marxism-Leninism might win out in the battle for young minds, simply because it is superior to "bourgeois" ideology, does not enter into the blueprints of "counter-propaganda."

Pravda (October 18, 1984) published an editorial titled "Atheistic Convictions for Young People," which cited sociological research as pointing to "a considerable proportion of the population that remains under the influence of religious ideology," including "young people in particular." The paper called for "more active propaganda of scientific materialist views and greater attention to atheistic education." Propaganda on this theme, the paper noted, was being neglected by "some party, Komsomol, soviet and trade union organizations, which have altogether lost sight of atheist education among adolescents." *Pravda* demanded the use of "all forms and means of disseminating scientific atheism: clubs, agitation and culture teams, question-and-answer evenings, scientific societies, readers' meetings, talks, lectures, movie lectures, visits to museums of religion and atheism, and to historical-architectural monuments (churches, cathedrals and monasteries)."

A year later, *Pravda* commented on the revised Communist Party program in its editorial "Important Tasks of the Press" (December 12, 1985), calling for "an increased role of the mass media and propaganda in our society." It cited the program as saying that "press, television and radio are called upon to convince people through political clarity and purposefulness, depth of content, efficiency, information richness, and accessibility of their articles." The editorial demanded that the press utilize "the language of truth" in order to achieve "the democratic norms of Soviet people's power and raise the authority of the press and its propagandistic, agitational and organizational role." The media, in other words, must engage in the education of the "new Soviet man" with modernized techniques and improved skills.

Still, and although Soviet ideologues may not be aware of it, the new Soviet man (and woman) apparently already exist. From Erivan to Alma Ata, and particularly among the Moscow-Leningrad elite, this elusive individual seems to have evolved. Now that the curtain of history has fallen on the Lenin-to-Stalin-to-Brezhnev type, an upwardly mobile generation of men and women is knocking on the doors of offices occupied by officials in their fifties and sixties.

Who is this new Soviet man? He does not resemble the Spartanic robot of post-Lenin design. Rather, he has the universally human characteristic of wishing to live better and happier than did his father and grandfather, even if these hopes fall into such categories as "individualism" and "consumerism." He seeks to protect and advance his family, and he knows how to paraphrase whatever ideological fad needs to be echoed to enhance his career, to achieve and maintain his privileges. This new Soviet man does not go around noisily denouncing "shortcomings" or "mistakes," nor does he devote much time to hailing the "successes" of the social system under which he lives. He simply acts on the knowledge that happiness means doing well, while managing to stay out of trouble.

CHAPTER · 28

Tears for Samantha

In the spring of 1983, ten-year-old Samantha Smith of Manchester, Maine, received a letter from Soviet leader Yuri Andropov. Like many other Americans, young and old, and people the world over, Samantha had written a letter to Andropov after he succeeded Leonid Brezhnev to the top leadership of the U.S.S.R. in November 1982. Andropov's accession to the post of general secretary of the Soviet Communist Party prompted a good deal of public optimism about a possibly more accommodating or realistic Soviet policy; the new leader himself, despite his 15 years as head of the KGB, was widely pictured as relatively liberal, or at least more pragmatic than his predecessors. Could and would Andropov, many asked, give the Soviet Union a less threatening demeanor?

Samantha Smith had written her congratulations to Andropov on his new and important position, expressed concern about strains between the Soviet Union and the United States, and asked the Russian leader what he intended to do. She wrote, "Why do you want to conquer the world or at least our country?" On April 11, *Pravda* published a selection of letters addressed to Andropov by Americans, including excerpts from Samantha's. Her original communication had remained unacknowledged, but a second letter, mailed to the Soviet embassy in Washington, appeared to have reached an official who was alert to the public relations potential of Samantha's question. As a result, a typewritten letter, three pages long, and with "Y. Andropov" typed in place of a signature, arrived at Samantha's home in Maine in late April.

Following are the major passages of General Secretary Andropov's letter, as received by Samantha Smith:

357

Dear Samantha,

I received your letter as well as many others coming to me these days from your country and from other countries around the world.

It seems to me from your letter that you are a courageous and honest girl, in some ways resembling Becky, Tom Sawyer's friend from the well-known book by your compatriot Mark Twain. All the children in our country, boys and girls alike, know and love this book.

You write that you are worried about our two countries getting into a nuclear war, and you ask whether we will do something to prevent it.

Your question is the most important of those that are close to the heart of everyone. I will respond to it in an earnest and serious manner.

Yes, Samantha, we in the Soviet Union are endeavoring to do everything possible so that there will be no war between our two countries, so that there will be no war at all on earth. This is the wish of everyone in the Soviet Union. That's what we were taught to do by Vladimir Lenin, the great founder of our state.

Soviet people know only too well how disastrous and terrible a war can be. Forty-two years ago nazi Germany, which aspired to dominate the whole world, attacked our country, burned and destroyed thousands and thousands of our cities and villages, killed millions of Soviet men, women and children.

In that war, which ended with our victory, we were allies with the United States. We fought together to liberate many nations from the nazi invaders. I hope that you know this from your history lessons at school. Today, we want very much to live in peace, to trade and cooperate with all our neighbours around the globe, no matter how close or far away they are, and, certainly, with such a great country as the United States of America.

America, like us, has a frightful weapon which can instantly annihilate millions of people. However, we do not want this weapon to be used ever, that is why the Soviet Union solemnly declared to the world that it will never, never, be the first to use nuclear weapons against any country. As a matter of fact, we propose, in general, that an end be put to the further production of these weapons and that the elimination of all nuclear stockpiles on earth be started.

I believe this is a sufficient reply to your second question, "why do you want to conquer the world or at least the United States?" We want nothing of the kind. Nobody in our vast and beautiful country—workers or peasants, writers or doctors, children or grownups, or members of the government—want war, be it big or small.

We want peace. We have a lot to do: grow grain, build, invent, write books and make space flights. We want peace for ourselves and for all people of the planet, for our own kids and for you, Samantha.

Andropov's letter invited Samantha to visit the Soviet Union. Although the public perceived it as a personal invitation from Andropov to Samantha, the members of the Smith family were technically guests of the Union of Societies of Friendships with Peoples of Foreign Countries; the union paid for the trip, including about $10,000 for first-class round-trip air tickets for Samantha and her parents, Arthur and Jane Smith. The overriding propaganda theme of Andropov's letter and Samantha's visit was the Soviet Union's devotion to peace, with the implication that this differed from the attitude of the American government, putting large parts of the U.S. population at odds with their own government's position.

At the outset, these propaganda aims were blurred by vague images of international goodwill. Samantha's parents were alert to Soviet efforts to exploit their daughter's role as an "ambassador of peace." The Moscow correspondent of *U.S. News*, Nicholas Daniloff, wrote (July 18, 1983): "No matter what her well-meant intentions, Samantha's message to Andropov is being used here to tell the Soviet people that average Americans want peace but are being pushed in the opposite direction by their government."

The Smiths arrived in Moscow on July 8 for two weeks of sightseeing and meetings, and with the anticipation that the visit's climax would be a personal meeting with Andropov. Samantha carried what she called a "secret gift" for Andropov. She looked forward to asking him, "Do you promise me the Soviet Union will never start a war?" The Smith family received VIP treatment, beginning with the appearance of a large black Chaika limousine at the airport and top-flight accommodations at Moscow's Sovietskaya Hotel.

In the Soviet capital, Samantha was taken on a tour of the Kremlin and other traditional sights, including the Lenin Mausoleum on Red Square. United Press International reported on July 10: "People waiting in line at the Lenin Mausoleum asked about the girl who was followed by all the television cameras and whispered, 'It's Samantha Smith, the one who wrote Andropov.' " The Smiths then went by plane to Yalta, on the Black Sea. From Simferopol Airport, they were driven to the International Artek Young Pioneer Camp, a vast seaside camp of boys and girls still too young to join the Komsomol, or Young Communist League.

In a time-honored ritual, Samantha was received by a Young Pioneer girl who told her in halting English, "It has become a good tradition to welcome guests with bread and salt. It is the symbol of the people's labor and friendship. Accept from us bread and salt, please." In a ceremony that was shown on worldwide television, the girl from Maine was welcomed by some 1,000 children, the girls in aquamarine skirts with white blouses, the boys in aquamarine shorts and white shirts. Samantha ate in the camp dining room and spent the night with the Young Pioneers, while her parents stayed at a hotel. The original Andropov letter had said, "I invite you, if your parents can let you go, to come visit us, best of all in summer. You will get to know our country, will meet children of your age, spend time on the seashore in a youngsters' camp called 'Artek,' where schoolchildren of our and other lands come to spend their vacations. There you will see for yourself: everybody in the Soviet Union stands for peace and friendship among nations." As part of the visit, Samantha was paraded through the Young Pioneers stadium, a spotlight following her as she was cheered by the crowd of youngsters.

An especially selected friend and escort, Natasha Kashirina, helped guide Samantha during the next stop, Leningrad. There, too, she visited the main tourist attractions, including the czars' Summer Palace. Again, of course, there were many encounters with schoolchildren. Samantha managed the crowded schedule well; only in a dressing room, behind the scenes at Leningrad's Kirov Ballet, was she nauseated by the smell of perspiration. The Leningrad night air rectified this quickly.

Souvenirs included a piece of charcoal from a bonfire at the Black Sea camp. Presents were numerous, including teddy bears in pink, white, blue, and brown, as well as a multicolored one. She arrived home on July 22, landing at Augusta State Airport, with a crowd of 350 cheering her. Homecoming included a red carpet, a dozen balloons with "Welcome Home, Samantha" written on them, as well as a bouquet of roses. A Rolls Royce took her home to Manchester, and she was guest of honor at the Manchester Festival Day, riding at the front of the parade.

Samantha Smith never did get to see Yuri Andropov. Although the Smith family and Moscow officials seemed certain that the two would meet, Andropov finally excused himself, sending word that he was too busy to meet the girl from Maine. As the world learned much later, the Soviet leader was severely ill during the summer of 1983, and this illness led to his death early the following year. Yet his invitation to Samantha had lasting propaganda effect, not only abroad but at home as well. When Samantha visited the memorial to Soviet war dead in Moscow, Tass reported that she was "pale with emotion as, together with her parents, she was laying flowers to an eternal flame." She also placed flowers at the grave of Yuri Gagarin, the world's first cosmonaut, and Tass said she read his name aloud to herself, "needing no translation."

The domestic use of Samantha's visit appeared to be targeted particularly toward youths, a segment of the Soviet population whose ideological loyalty and lifestyle are matters of continuing concern to officials. The image of an American girl paying, in effect, homage to symbols of Soviet society was apparently being used, among other things, to strengthen the devotion of Soviet youngsters to these symbols and their historic-political implications. While Samantha said repeatedly that, as a result of her visit, she no longer feared that the U.S.S.R. was bent on war, she was cautious enough—and her parents guarded against any slipup—not to be maneuvered into expressions of criticism of the United States. Nevertheless, among the roomful of letters that awaited Samantha Smith in her Manchester home were several that criticized her, and her parents, for acting as a pawn of Soviet propaganda.

Andropov had made Samantha Smith into an international celebrity. In December 1983 she participated in the Children's Twenty-first Century Symposium at Kobe, Japan, together with three youngsters representing Children's Express, a U.S. news service written by children. She presented the mayor of the city of Kobe with a jar of Maine maple syrup and urged world leaders to "send their granddaughters to nations where they have little understanding," as part of an "International Granddaughters Exchange."

At home, the Disney Channel on cable television asked Samantha to interview six of the Democratic Party's rivals for their party's presidential nomination. The TV channel aired the result in a 90-minute special, "Samantha Smith Goes to Washington—Campaign '84." She also received numerous lecture invitations and prepared a book on a trip to the U.S.S.R., complete with photographs, entitled *Journey to the Soviet Union*, which Novosti translated into Russian.

Samantha, a dog lover, had said several times that she wanted to become either a veterinarian or an actress. In 1985, she became a television actress, appearing in a series called "Lime Street." Filming of the series took place in England, where Samantha was accompanied by her father. Returning from London, father and daughter were passengers on a Beechcraft 99 plane on a flight from Boston to Manchester. On Sunday, August 25, the plane crashed in inclement weather in Auburn-Lewiston, Maine. Arthur and Samantha Smith were killed.

As the Associated Press noted, in a dispatch from Augusta (August 29) which reported on the funeral of father and daughter at St. Mary's Roman Catholic Church, "Her acting career grew out of the fame accompanying her visit to the Soviet Union two years ago at the invitation of the then Soviet leader, Yuri V. Andropov." Indirectly, then, Andropov's invitation led to Samantha's death. Nearly identical sentiments over the young girl's death were expressed in the United States and the Soviet Union, although some Soviet propagandists implied that foul play might have been involved, suggesting that Samantha's death had been arranged by those who wished to harm her peace efforts.

The U.S. State Department waived travel restrictions for Vladimir Kulagin, first secretary for cultural affairs at the Soviet embassy, so he could attend Samantha's funeral. Kulagin read a letter from Soviet leader Gorbachev, who wrote that people in the U.S.S.R. were saddened by the deaths of Samantha and her father. Gorbachev also wrote: "You should know millions of mothers and fathers and kids back in Russia share this tragic loss. The best thing would be if we continued what they started with, good will, friendship and love."

Samantha's visit to the Soviet Union had created a wave of spontaneous interest in the girl, her personality and ideas. With her death, the momentum of these sentiments was being channeled in propagandistic ways, some subtle and evidently sincere, others calculated and blatant. The memory of "Samantha, the Little Ambassador of Peace" could be molded into the image of either a fighter or a martyr for peace—possibly, both. *Komsomolskaya Pravda*, the youth daily, commented: "Frightening, scalding news has come across the ocean: Samantha is no more. A small person with a bold heart, in her twelve years she already understood what many grown Americans do not want to or cannot understand. She spoke loudly to all of America: 'The innermost wish of the Soviet people is to preserve peace.'"

The paper stated that, after her visit to the Soviet Union, Samantha had devoted "many interviews and appearances on American radio and television to bring to grownups the truth about the Soviet people, about their love of peace, their warm yearning to live in friendship with all peoples." The paper ignored Samantha Smith's budding career in television and thus conveyed the impression that her death had occurred, more or less, in the midst of an ongoing personal campaign in favor of the Soviet Union's peace-loving intentions.

Tass seemed to throw doubt on the official version of the plane crash. As *New York Times* correspondent Serge Schmemann noted (August 28), the news agency "juxtaposed its reports in a way that seemed to underline questions about the cause of the crash." Tass said that, according to one newspaper, "the type of plane which crashed in Auburn-Lewiston has a record of being one of the safest types of aircraft." Antero Pietila, Moscow correspondent of the Baltimore *Sun*, reported (September 12) that "an apparently organized whisper campaign is spreading the rumor" that Samantha "was killed by the CIA." He added: "Rumors that the Smith girl was killed by the CIA began almost as soon as the official Tass news agency reported her death in a plane crash Aug. 26. The original Tass report may have encouraged speculation about a conspiracy because it said that the plane carrying Samantha and her father 'had been diverted for an unspecified reason.' That reason was bad weather, but Tass never mentioned it. Although no direct allegations of foul play have appeared in the Soviet media, people from ordinary citizens to intellectuals seem to believe that Samantha was silenced so that she could not continue her efforts to build goodwill toward the Soviet Union."

In Lithuania, a horticulturist named a newly bred violet "Samantha," in honor of the American girl. In Yakutsk, eastern Siberia, a rare and beautiful diamond was named after her, to be safeguarded at the Kremlin diamond treasury. A Soviet poet, Julia Druninan, dedicated a poem, "Little Star," to the memory of Samantha Smith, which contained the lines: "You thought about the laws of life/About the lawlessness of the world."

On December 2, a "Children's Space Bridge" was established between a Moscow television studio and a studio in Minneapolis, Minnesota. Linked by satellite, several hundred children in both cities were interviewed on the experiences and ideas they shared. It was an occasion to honor Samantha Smith and her efforts. In her home state, a statue of Samantha was erected at Auburn Mall, in Auburn, Maine. The statue showed the girl holding a dove, with a small bear sitting at her feet. Maine Governor Joseph E. Brennan attended the unveiling ceremonies on December 18. Later that month, the Soviet Union issued a five-kopek postage stamp, featuring an artist's drawing of Samantha Smith. ABC television prepared a two-hour movie, *The Samantha Smith Story*, in cooperation with Soviet TV.

As the letters and travels of Samantha were transformed into legend, sincere sentiment and propagandistic opportunism became inextricably interwoven. As a follow-up, an 11-year-old Soviet girl, Katerina ("Katya" or "Katyusha") Lycheva, visited the United States for a two-week, five-city tour in March 1986. Sponsored by the San Francisco–based Children of the Peacemakers Foundation, the girl, accompanied by her mother, attracted wide and uniformly favorable attention. In New York, the *Daily News* headlined its report "Sov's Littlest Ambassador: In city, she lights candle for kids." Katya, who had done acting and made other public appearances in the U.S.S.R., spoke English without an interpreter's help and answered reporters' questions with emphasis on her children-to-children "peace mission."

Katya had brought a "secret" present for President Reagan, whom she did not get to meet. The present was a stuffed globe with a smiling face. The girl's basic message was: "If it were up to children, it would take us a minute or so to get together." Her trip brought her to such diverse places as the Statue of Liberty and the Broadway musical *Big River* in New York, the NASA Space Center in Houston, and the Children's Museum and Ronald McDonald in Chicago. She also visited San Francisco, met Chicago's mayor, Harold Washington, appeared on NBC's *Today* show and the *CBS Morning News*, and toured Washington, D.C.

Katya's visit, officially part of a delegation of the Soviet Peace Defense Committee, was covered extensively by Soviet press and television. Moscow TV reported (March 28) that, before her departure, she had a meeting at the International Friendship Club at the Pioneer Palace. The broadcast said: "Having chosen Katya as their ambassador, the children asked her to pass on to U.S. school children their drawings, letters, and full-length essays about the most important thing: how to strengthen friendship and preserve peace." The girl was given a reporter's card from the newspaper *Pionerskaya Pravda*, which has a circulation of 11 million among Soviet children. *Moscow News* reported the trip in a two-page spread, with 13 photographs, and noted that Katya had appeared in four feature films, including *Bambi's Childhood*.

The mobilization of children in peace campaigns continued on many levels, and through a variety of conduits and events, of which the Twelfth World Festival of Youth and Students, which took place in Moscow in July–August 1985, was the major happening. When a group of West German schoolchildren wrote to General Secretary Gorbachev, in Russian, he replied to one of them, Kerstin Vetter. Gorbachev wrote of the need to halt armaments and eliminate nuclear weapons, and he quoted the German poet Johann Wolfgang von Goethe on the role of freedom in life. Gorbachev also wrote: "It is necessary to stamp out, in the world community, the vestiges of the past, such as hostility, hatred and lack of understanding, and the rejection of the just rights of any people, whether big or small."

CHAPTER · 29

KAL 007: Propagandistic Confusion

On September 1, 1983, Radio Moscow's foreign and domestic services broadcast their usual mixture of news items designed to enhance the image of the Soviet Union and question the aims and means of the United States and its allies. Every hour on the hour, announcers repeated 11 news items that, given the standards of Radio Moscow, were unexceptional—except for one, the ninth on the schedule. It was a Tass report that also appeared in the Soviet press, and it read as follows:

"An unidentified plane entered the airspace of the Soviet Union over the Kamchatka Peninsula from the direction of the Pacific Ocean and then for the second time violated the air space of the U.S.S.R. over Sakhalin Island on the night from August 31 to September 1. The plane did not have navigation lights, did not respond to queries and did not enter into contact with the dispatcher service. Fighters of the anti-aircraft defense, which were sent aloft towards the intruder plane, tried to give it assistance in directing it to the nearest airfield. But the intruder plane did not react to the signals and warnings from the Soviet fighters and continued its flight in the direction of the Sea of Japan."

No one depending only on Soviet media for information could have known, from this report, that more than 22 hours earlier a Korean Airlines Boeing 747 (KAL Flight 007), carrying 269 passengers from New York to Seoul, South Korea, had been shot down by a Soviet jet fighter in the Sea of Japan. While news reports on this catastrophic event crisscrossed the world and statesmen at the United Nations, in Washington, Seoul, and Tokyo expressed their gravest concern over the incident, Moscow's propaganda machinery appeared to be stalled.

The Tass–Moscow Radio report spoke of an "unidentified plane," while the whole world was fully aware of its identity as a civilian Korean aircraft. Moscow sought to convey a benign image of the Soviet fighter's action by stating that it had tried to give the plane "assistance in directing it to the nearest airfield," and it totally ignored the tragic fact that an air-to-air missile had brought the unarmed plane down and drowned all its passengers and crew.

The United States, which had secured translations of the monitoring report on the Soviet fighter's messages to its ground control, presented excerpts from a Russian-language tape and translation at the United Nations. The Soviet pilot of the supersonic SU-15 had been monitored as telling his ground control, "I see it visually and on radar," apparently awaiting instructions. Later, the pilot radioed, "I am closing on the target. . . . Distance to target is eight [kilometers]." He added that the plane's missile warheads had been locked on, saying, "I have already switched it on." And finally, "I have executed the launch. . . . The target is destroyed. . . . I am breaking off attack." Contrary to the Tass report that the airliner was without lights, the pilot had observed the Korean aircraft's blinking strobe lights.

While people within the Soviet Union specifically, and within the Soviet realm generally, were advised of the incident in a peripheral and fragmentary way, the rest of the world received continuous accounts of details and heard interpretations from specialists in aircraft technology and international law. The U.S. Information Agency's Voice of America added 56 hours of broadcasting daily, including broadcasts in Russian and other languages of the Soviet Union. USIA director Charles Z. Wick said, "The Soviets are giving their own people even less than they are giving us."

Soviet leaders were, in fact, giving the impression that their major concerns in the matter were not with world opinion, but with political alignments and views at home. Major among these appeared to be the following:

1. The need to overcome an initial communications problem between the Soviet Eastern Command headquarters and military-political leadership in Moscow.

2. Efforts to project the image of a strong, fearless, even aggressive position, at a time when Soviet leader Andropov had not appeared in public for well over a month and was, in fact, deathly ill.

3. The desire to counteract any weakening of the image of the Soviet military establishment, which might be viewed as having overreacted to a violation of Soviet airspace and disregarded the human

and political consequences of the shooting down of the civilian plane.

4. Counteracting possible rumors concerning irresponsibility or human error on the part of the military personnel involved, including emotional instability and drunkenness.

5. Downplaying the incident in general, so that confidence among the general populace would remain intact and prestige of the Kremlin leadership would emerge undamaged.

After the initial coverage by the Soviet media, which was woefully fragmentary, propaganda directives—emanating most probably from the International Department and the International Information Department of the Central Committee—specified that the incident be blamed on the U.S. military intelligence agencies and on the Central Intelligence Agency. Soviet propaganda statements wavered between placing the blame for the incident on a U.S. reconnaissance plane, RC-135, and on the role of KAL 007 itself.

By September 3, Tass issued a comprehensive commentary, complete with citations from outside sources. As a document in the modern history of political propaganda, it is worth examining the full text, as follows:

"Washington is feverishly covering up traces of the provocation staged against the Soviet Union with the utilization of the South Korean plane, which has flown out of the United States and intruded into the Soviet Union's airspace.

"The White House and the Department of State are mounting a worldwide rabid anti-Soviet campaign. The tone is set by the U.S. President. In his statement permeated with frenzied hatred and malice for the Soviet State, for Socialism, using as a coverup bombastic phrases about 'humanism' and 'noble feelings,' the head of the White House is trying to convince public opinion that the USSR allegedly is guilty of loss of life. Issuing forth torrents of vicious abuses, representatives of the U.S. Administration want to avoid answering clear questions: Why did the plane happen to find itself in the airspace of the Soviet Union, deviating by 500 kilometers from the existing international route? Why did the authorities of the U.S. and Japan, whose air traffic controlling services control flights of planes on this route, knowing that the plane had remained for a long time in Soviet airspace, not take appropriate measures to put an end to this flagrant violation of the sovereignty of the Soviet Union?

"U.S. journalists also have been putting these questions to the U.S. Administration, and each time its representative has been wriggling out of answering them. However, the answer is necessary to find out the truth on who and for what purposes sent this plane into Soviet airspace.

"Let us quote a statement on this score, which was made on French television by General Gallois, a specialist of France in strategic issues: 'The Soviet armed forces have two zones which may be considered as being top secret; the area of Murmansk in the Kola Peninsula and the zone of the Sea of Okhotsk, where the Kamchatka Peninsula and the island of Sakhalin are situated.' There are, the general said, 'a considerable part of the Soviet Navy concentrated and intercontinental ballistic missile testing facilities located there.' General Gallois recalled that several years ago the Soviet Air Force in the area of the Kola Peninsula compelled what also was a 'South Korean' plane to land. Now an aircraft of the same company emerges in another strategically important area of the USSR. The scientific commentator of the French television program TF-1 summed up explicitly what had happened: 'The Boeing 747 deliberately veered off course with the purpose of performing an intelligence mission.'

"Professor Stephen Meyer from the Massachusetts Institute of Technology said that in the existing conditions the corresponding Soviet bodies had every reason to suspect that the plane was fulfilling an intelligence mission over a strategically important area.

"U.S. officials are striving to prove that all this is 'mere coincidence,' that the plane 'wandered off its flight path,' that it 'lost communication contact,' etc. What 'loss of communication contact' can it be, if the U.S. authorities admitted that they had been following the flight throughout its duration? The flimsiness of the attempts of the White House to justify the 'appearance of the South Korean plane in the airspace of the Soviet Union by some technical malfunction' is also made obvious by the statements of the former head of the Joint Chiefs of Staff of the Japanese armed forces, at present the military observer of the newspaper *Mainichi Shimbun*, G. Takeda. 'With Boeing having a computer on board, two pilots and a system of double-triple checking, the deviation of the plane of the South Korean air company looks more than strange,' he writes in this newspaper. This is also confirmed by a report published by the *New York Times*.

"Materials, which were made public by the Japanese news agency Kyodo, prove the discourse of U.S. Administration spokesmen about some 'technical troubles' on the intruder plane to be wholly untenable. Quoting sources which had been carefully monitoring that flight, the news agency reported that the South Korean liner's radio communications with the Japanese air traffic controller stations had been maintained almost until the very moment of the plane's disappearance.' Thus, the Washington version, that the plane's radio equipment got out of order and that its crew could not respond to the signals given to it, does not correspond to reality. That is confirmed also by the fact, reported by Kyodo, that more than an hour after the Soviet planes' first attempt to establish contact with the

Boeing, a telegram was sent from aboard the plane, which said, in particular, 'the plane's navigational equipment is operating normally.'

"According to Australian newspapers, the U.S. Central Intelligence Agency followed the plane's flight most closely. A BBC broadcast pointed out that U.S. and Japanese tracking services had been continuously tracking the South Korean plane over the entire length of its route but had not adopted measures to correct its path.

"The Western press reported also that the crews of the South Korean liners on this route are made up solely of air force pilots. The Australian newspaper *Sydney Morning Herald* pointed out, in its turn, that the South Korean plane could have been mistaken in the Soviet Union for a U.S. spy plane since on its radar it looked like an intelligence plane of the U.S. Air Force, and that it could also well be mistaken for a U.S. E4B bomber.

"All this corroborates the fact that the corresponding U.S. services had a direct relation to this provocation. The conclusion drawn by the New York correspondent of the Australian radio and television network, ABC, that the C.I.A.'s conduct in that whole affair appeared very suspicious, therefore, looks to have its grounds. Isn't it the involvement of the well-known terrorist center of the United States in the whole affair that caused U.S. State Department spokesman [John] Hughes to sidestep on more than one occasion at a press conference in Washington journalists' questions of why the corresponding U.S. and Japanese services had not warned the plane that it had violated the airspace of the USSR and why they had not guided it out of there?

"In this connection, it is proper to ask: what is the thoroughly hypocritical 'sorrow' demonstrated by the White House based on? Or does Mr. President believe that the very concept of national sovereignty no longer exists and one may intrude with impunity into the airspace of independent states? Or is he viewing the whole world now as a 'zone of U.S. vital interests'?

"There is one more side to this question: The U.S. President asks: How one can conduct negotiations with a state which is capable of such actions? This phrase in itself explains a great deal. Why so? Because the U.S. Administration is going out of its way to disrupt the process of the normalization of the situation in the world, to evade solving problems facing the world which are vital to the interests of nations.

"The head of the White House is shedding hypocritical tears over what has happened! More than once the world witnessed the situation when Washington officials speak of 'humaneness,' while at the same time U.S. Marines, acting in concert with Israeli aggressors, commit mass killings in Lebanon, when, under the guidance of American instructors, bandits perpetrate atrocities in sovereign Nicaragua and make short work of Salvadoran patriots. The world knows the worth of this 'sorrow' and 'concern for humaneness.' Some time ago it brought about the killing of several million people in Indochina.

"The purpose of this provocation with the plane is more than obvious. However, the Washington administration will be unable to put the Soviet Union and its people in a bad light, as it is frantically trying to do these days. Its designs are frustrated by irrefutable facts. It will be impossible to cover up the traces of dirty deeds with the help of vicious abuses."

A casual reader of this Tass commentary may be excused if, by the time he has finished reading it, he may no longer remember that it was prompted by the news that a Soviet fighter plane had shot down a civilian plane carrying 269 passengers. The commentary testifies to the thoroughness with which Tass reporters throughout the world comb newspapers and monitor radio and television commentaries in order to extract items that can be cabled to Moscow for inclusion in roundups such as this. Of course, a French general's observation that the Murmansk and Kamchatka regions are regarded as top secret by the U.S.S.R. is indisputable. And observers anywhere are free to speculate about the appearance of one type of plane or another on Soviet radar screens. As for the ability of U.S. and Japanese air controllers to guide a plane that has gone off course, that was a matter of wide-ranging discussion.

In the days following, Tass and other Soviet media elaborated on the theme of U.S. involvement in the Korean airliner incident, developing the aspect that it was on a "spy" mission and generally seeking to deflect attention from the Soviet Union's role in the matter. On September 6, *Pravda* reported on Soviet tracking of seven U.S. reconnaissance planes, RC-135s, which were on missions off the Soviet Far East coast between 3:45 P.M. and 8:49 P.M. Moscow time on the day of the incident. But even by then the Communist Party's daily could not bring itself to admit that the Korean plane had, in fact, been shot down; instead, the account merely said two "fighter groups" had scrambled to intercept the passenger plane. *Pravda* stated: "The Soviet forces showed restraint. If they had the goal of destroying the plane, as claimed by President Reagan, they could have done so many times over and in a guaranteed way, and without even scrambling fighter planes. They could have done so over Kamchatka, using heat-seeking missiles fired from the ground."

Washington provided Moscow with propaganda ammunition when it announced on September 4 that an RC-135 had been in the general area of the incident one and a half to two hours before the Soviet fighter shot down the Korean plane. Tass, which set the tone throughout the campaign, said the next day that the Korean plane and the RC-135 had been involved in the same spy mission. Soviet television commentators took up this theme, and it was elaborated upon by other media. "The Americans," Tass said, "not only closely followed the actions of the intruding plane with the help of a satellite, but also directed, into that same region, their reconnaissance plane RC-135, which flew parallel to the Korean airliner's flight path."

Colonel General Semyon F. Romanov, chief of the headquarters staff of Soviet Air Defense, told *Pravda* that, as "the aircraft was flying with its lights out, and its contours greatly resemble the RC-135 American reconnaissance plane," the Soviet flyer could not know that he was dealing with a civilian aircraft. One television commentator, Genrikh Borovikh, said, "Our anti-aircraft defenses fulfilled their duty in defending the security of our motherland," but he failed to specify either the use of an air-to-air missile or the actual shooting down of the Korean plane.

New York Times correspondent Serge Schmemann, in an analysis from Moscow (September 6, 1983), suggested that these propaganda tactics were paying off, at least inside the Soviet Union itself. He wrote: "In a country where secrecy, insecurity and suspicion of the outside world permeate all aspects of life, the explanations offered by the Kremlin about the South Korean jetliner seem certain of widespread acceptance." Schmemann noted that, at first, Russians had reacted "with incredulity and dismay on hearing that a civilian jetliner had been downed" but that official explanations, "branding the plane a hostile intruder, attributing its fate to American anti-Soviet aggression and mentioning challenges to Soviet sovereignty and prestige," had appealed to "some of the strongest instincts nurtured by the Soviet state."

The correspondent observed that official propaganda themes had "steered the public away from the United States report that a Soviet pilot had shot down a civilian jumbo jetliner carrying 269 people—facts that have yet to be explicitly acknowledged by Moscow—and to the familiar patterns of Soviet-American rivalry." Schmemann reminded his readers that, until then, Soviet officials had only volunteered that "its interceptors followed and tried to signal the jetliner, then fired warning tracer shells across its path and that the pilot could have mistaken it for an RC-135 surveillance plane."

Nevertheless, in an extraordinary show of concern over worldwide alarm, the Soviet leadership designated one of its highest officials, the chief of the general staff, Marshal Nikolai V. Ogarkov, to give a detailed presentation at a two-hour news conference in the auditorium of the Foreign Ministry Press Center on September 9. The impression that proved most memorable to reporters was Marshal Ogarkov's quiet firmness, his obvious knowledge of logistic-technical details, and the general air of professional self-assurance he displayed.

Ogarkov did not stray from the official version presented in the Soviet media, but he conveyed it with an air of quiet patience. The word used by observers most frequently was "unprecedented," and it referred both to the nature of the press conference, complete with maps and directional pointers, and to Ogarkov's manner of presentation. He told Soviet and foreign reporters that the order to shoot down the airliner was "not an accident or an error." He specified that this command to "stop the flight" had come from the district commander of the air defense forces when the commander and other local officers concluded that the plane was on a spying mission. Marshal Ogarkov said: "All our defense systems, which for two and a half hours took action to force it to land, as of the beginning of the flight, at all command posts, were completely sure that we were dealing here with a reconnaissance plane."

The spokesman stood before a wall-sized map of the Soviet Far East that showed the route the Korean plane was said to have taken and spots indicating where, Ogarkov said, American reconnaissance planes had been located at the same time. The press conference was shown repeatedly on Soviet television and later surveys indicated that it had played a considerable part in influencing domestic opinion.

At Marshal Ogarkov's side were Georgi M. Korniyenko, a first deputy foreign minister, and Leonid M. Zamyatin, head of the International Information Department of the party's Central Committee. Zamyatin became agitated when a British correspondent asked whether the Soviets would have acted the same way if the airliner had carried 2,000 people instead of 269. He said angrily that "if the Soviet Union had any anti-humanistic feelings" it could have destroyed the plane much earlier. Zamyatin said that the delay in shooting it down indicated the "human character" of the air defense forces and added: "We tried to save lives."

Toward the end of the press conference, Marshal Ogarkov was asked, "Do you think that the protection of the sacred borders of the Soviet Union was worth the lives of 269 persons aboard the jetliner?" Ogarkov answered: "Protection of the sacred, inviolable borders of our country, and of our political system, was worth to us—as you know very well— many, many millions of lives and it was exactly preservation of our borders, of our frontiers and of our system and we would not add to the list of those millions the 269 victims of those who victimized those people for reasons other than the defense of the sacred frontiers. Those other people should be asked why." These references compared the defense of Soviet soil during World War II with the shooting down of the Korean plane and, once again, although indirectly, placed the blame on the United States.

Ogarkov's responses suggested that, as a matter of principle, the Soviet Union would act with equal ruthlessness against any other airliner that might stray into its territory. Zamyatin, during the press conference, said that the United States would have acted in exactly the same manner. But such violations of U.S. airspace had actually taken place, specifically when Soviet planes passed the Eastern coastline on their flights to Cuba. In 1981, one Aeroflot aircraft departed from its normal flight pattern off the Atlantic Coast and flew over Groton, Connecticut, site of a busy naval shipyard. The matter was handled quietly, with a warning that such diversion should not be repeated.

The day after the surprising Ogarkov press conference, the pilot who actually shot down the Korean plane was interviewed on Soviet television. His name was not given; he appeared to be a man in his midforties. He was questioned by Alexander Tikhomirov of the state television network on a base on Sakhalin Island. The pilot said he had fired warning tracer shells across the jetliner's path. The pilot also said the Korean plane had stayed at the same altitude and course after the warning shots, whereas Marshal Ogarkov had claimed the plane had "tried to escape." Authenticity was provided by television pictures of a darkened air defense control room, complete with blinking lights and a radar screen. Both TV films were distributed abroad.

Michael Dobbs, writing from Moscow in the *Washington Post* (September 11, 1983), observed that "the successive reactions from Moscow of silence, evasion, grudging acknowledgement that one of its planes shot down the jumbo jet" were providing insights into "the Soviet system and the Russian obsession with security." He cited the view of Western analysts in Moscow that "the Kremlin could have succeeded in limiting most of the damage" to its prestige if it had "promptly acknowledged that an error had been made, offered to pay compensation to relatives of the victims and promised to ensure that nothing similar would ever happen again." He cited an experienced Western diplomat as saying, "It is almost impossible for a society that puts so much emphasis on collective values to admit that a mistake has been made," adding: "This is first and foremost a Russian trait rather than a specifically Communist one. It is also very difficult for individuals to oppose the values of the collective, which is why the rare ones who do, feel such a sense of liberation." Dobbs interpreted the Ogarkov press conference and the interview with the pilot as efforts "to seize the propaganda initiative away from the Reagan administration by telling the world its version of what had happened."

To the degree that Soviet propaganda technicians were actually able to plan the tactics and strategies of their campaign concerning the Korean airliner, it appeared to follow this pattern:

1. The Soviet propagandists sought to establish *maximum isolation of the Soviet population from the actual horrors of the human tragedy involved*; Soviet citizens were not to identify with the passengers and crew of the plane and their deaths. Thus the term "shooting down" was totally avoided and even Ogarkov limited himself to saying that the Soviet pilot had been ordered to "stop the flight,"

and he maintained, "We still do not know that many people were aboard that plane."

2. Further, with emphasis on its domestic target audience, the Soviet propagandists emphasized *the role of the fighter pilots in safeguarding the country's population*, providing an impenetrable wall of security against hostile intruders. At the same time, the image of the United States as the major antagonist of Soviet society was reinforced.

3. In this propaganda campaign, *world opinion appeared to be of secondary importance* to the Soviet policymakers. To the non-Communist countries, the basic themes of the domestic campaign were conveyed through the established channels; but Western analysts felt the Kremlin leadership counted on the short memory of the general public and on the world media's fickleness and constant need for a "new angle."

4. Finally, for long-range and strategic propaganda purposes, the Soviet Union sought to *establish a basis of distrust in U.S. motives* and to saddle the United States with the charge that it had caused the incident by using the plane for "spy" purposes.

Domestically, the leadership's propaganda aims appeared to be achieved by the relatively novel device of the television appearances by Ogarkov and the fighter pilot. In addition, Agitprop briefings at party groups, offices, factories, and agricultural units played a major role. This was not realized by the Western press at the time, but it emerged from a public opinion survey conducted for Radio Free Europe/Radio Liberty and compiled in April 1984. Under the title "The Korean Airline Incident: Western Radio and Soviet Perceptions," the radio services' Soviet Area Audience and Opinion Research tabulated the reactions of Soviet citizens, presumably travelers questioned abroad, and found that, of those who approved of the downing of the aircraft, most cited television as having influenced their judgment. The researchers commented:

"The effectiveness of Soviet television can be linked to the press conference given by Marshal Ogarkov on 9 September, and to the following day's edition of *Vremya* (the main television evening news program), which featured an interview with the pilot who shot down the aircraft. It is conceivable that this apparent openness on the part of the authorities influenced the attitudes of certain respondents, and led them to conclude that the government had nothing to hide."

John F. Burns, reporting from Moscow to the *New York Times* (September 11, 1983), noted: "Once the official rationales were offered, the reflex to accept authority's word, to rally to invocations about the 'sacred' borders, the honor and vigilance of the armed forces and the threat from the insidious West, was evident. After Marshal Ogarkov's news conference was repeated several times on television, there was even smugness. 'There you are,' said a middle-aged woman. 'I told you that we were in the right.' " Burns commented: "As the Russians measure things, this kind of reaction may have counted for more than all the angry headlines in the West."

Next to the impact of television, according to the public opinion researchers, radio was the most persuasive means of Soviet domestic propaganda, "with agitprop meetings in third place," while "least successful in this respect was the Soviet written press." Although the segment of the Soviet audience who did not listen to Western radio stations tended to favor the downing of the Korean plane, "among respondents who cited Western radio as a source of information on the KAL incident, the trend went the other way, with respondents showing a far greater inclination to condemn than to support the downing of the Korean aircraft."

Among those who listened to Western radio stations, 22 percent approved of the downing, 47 percent disapproved, and 31 percent said they had no opinion on the matter. Among those who did not listen to Western stations, the approval rate was 70 percent, disapproval was 11 percent, and no opinion was expressed by 11 percent. There was an overlap between 1 percent of those responding, where presumably dual opinions were expressed.

The researchers noted that the Voice of America was most frequently cited as a source of information, and added: "Since the United States was the major Western participant in the verbal hostilities precipitated by the incident, it is natural that Western radio listeners in the USSR would be eager to hear the American position from VOA." The surveyors commented that their research had generally shown that the Voice of America had "the largest audience of Western broadcasters in the USSR."

Although civilian propagandists and army leaders had closed ranks in defying criticism of the downing of KAL 007, little-publicized events suggested later that the incident had caused friction and led to personnel changes. Washington analysts observed early in October that a shake-up in the Soviet Far Eastern defense command was under way. Presumably basing their findings on intercepts of Soviet communications, these analysts suggested that the high command in Moscow had been dissatisfied with the Far Eastern services' ability to deal with intrusions. On the basis of the Korean airliner incident, the local command had revealed that its personnel was unable to differentiate between commercial and military planes, and had interpreted standing orders in a rigid, immature manner.

Romanov, chief of staff for air defense at the time of the incident, died in May 1984. His obituary revealed that he had been demoted from his central post and given a liaison post in East Germany. It was Romanov who gave one of the first accounts of the incident, on September 4, saying the pilot had confused the 747 with an RC-135, which suggested that he had mistaken the jetliner for a plane about half its size.

Military attachés at Western embassies in Moscow read the January 1984 issue of the magazine *Aviation and Cosmonautics* with interest, as it contained a lead article by Colonel General Sergei V. Golubev that could be interpreted as a criticism of the pilot who shot down the KAL 007. The article began by mentioning the violation of Soviet airspace, "as happened on the night of September 1 in the Soviet Far East," and proceeded to balance approval of the pilot's decisive action with the caution that "resourcefulness and tactical skill," application of standard rules, and cooperation with ground controllers were essential. Golubev emphasized that, in a combat situation, "the main person is the pilot, and it is his job to solve the problems that confront him in the air." He specified: "The situation in the air must be such that the pilot himself must take the final decision, for example, to force the intruder to land at the nearest airport." As various accounts had suggested that the pilot of the Sukhoi-15 fighter, photos of which accompanied the article, had fired on the Korean plane without making a definitive identification, Golubev appeared to be expressing a retroactive critique. He also upbraided ground commanders who try to avoid delicate decisions and try to "hide behind the backs of others."

By far the most startling personnel change was the removal of Ogarkov from his position of chief of staff on September 6, 1984, a year after the Korean airliner incident. He had held this post since 1977 and was replaced by his deputy, Marshal Sergei F. Akhromeyev. No official announcement of a new post was made, although military specialists heard privately that Ogarkov had been appointed to head the Voroshilov Military Academy of the Soviet General Staff, a military training college named after Marshal K. Y. Voroshilov.

The downgrading of Ogarkov was widely ascribed to his self-assertive nature, which had made such a strong impression during the televised press conference, but apparently clashed with the more low-keyed personalities of others, notably Defense Minister Dmitri F. Ustinov. However, in July 1985, as part of extensive personnel realignments under Gorbachev, Ogarkov was quietly appointed to the command of the Warsaw Pact forces and named first deputy minister of defense.

A year after the Korean aircraft had been shot down, there was a brief flurry of reappraisals, with a to-be-expected trend toward conspiracy theories and counterhypotheses. To the degree that informed summaries were possible, these pointed to errors on the part of the airliner's crew, as well as misjudgments on the part of the Soviet command and pilot. The International Civil Aviation Organization (ICAO) found that the flight team had not undertaken a "premeditated deviation from the flight plan" for intelligence purposes. Instead, the ICAO found that two theories assuming navigation errors could be entertained. The organization reported: "Each of these postulations assumed a considerable degree of lack of alertness and attentiveness on the part of the entire flight crew, but not to a degree that was unknown in international aviation."

Two articles tolerant of the Soviet position were published in the West. One, by David Pearson, a doctoral candidate in sociology, appeared in the New York weekly *The Nation* (August 18–25, 1984) under the title "K.A.L. 007: What the U.S. Knew and When We Knew It." The study arrived at 17 questions, ranging from "Why was K.A.L. 007 delayed in its departure from Anchorage?" to "Was there a cover-up by U.S. officials?" Its main thesis was that the United States had more knowledge of the flight of the plane than it acknowledged publicly and that it conceivably could have alerted the crew to the fact that the plane was off course—unless, of course, the plane was involved in a mission designed to draw Soviet interception action and permit such action to be observed and recorded. The article concluded: "We cannot control the paranoia of a Soviet society that shoots when in doubt, whether on order from above or on impulse from below. We can and should, however, take responsibility for our own contribution to this tragedy and the tensions, fears and international disorder that it has promoted."

In a letter to the *New York Times*, Henry E. Catto, Jr., a former assistant secretary of defense and a contributing editor to the *Washington Journalism Review*, criticized *Times* columnist Tom Wicker for a column, "A Damning Silence" (September 7, 1984), that had summarized the Pearson article. Catto wrote the United States did not "monitor flight-pattern accuracy for civilian planes—the thousands of flights which span the globe every day." He added: "We have here a classic example of two facets of the American psyche: love of the idea of conspiracy, no matter how flimsy the evidence, and the peculiar readiness of many to assume the worst of our people and our Government." Tass (August 10, 1984) quoted Pearson as stating that the KAL incident involved "the biggest intelligence operation in U.S. history, which had involved not only U.S. military radar in the region but also intelligence eavesdropping facilities on Shemya, one of the Aleutian Islands, in Alaska and in Japan."

In England, the June 1984 *Defence Attaché* magazine contained the article "Korean 'Spy' Plane: The New Evidence," by "P.Q. Mann," which alleged that the KAL 007 flight had been sent over Soviet territory to test defensive responses and permit them to be monitored by various means, including the U.S. space shuttle *Challenger*. NASA officials commented that the shuttle was never close enough to the region to act as a monitor. Korean Airlines took exception to the article in *Defence Attaché* and, on November 19, 1984, accepted a public apology and a "substantial" sum of money from the magazine. In March 1985, the periodical published an article by James Oberg, an engineer with the U.S. space shuttle program, which provided a point-by-point critique of the earlier article.

As the original article prompted worldwide media attention, while the Oberg rebuttle went largely unnoticed, *AIM Report*, the newsletter of Accuracy in Media, a Washington-based organization, published an extensive analysis of the postincident discussion of the case, under the title "KAL 007 Disinformation Exposed" (April 1985). The newsletter, edited by Reed Irvine, provided this appraisal:

"We cannot prove that the widespread attention given to the spy-charge article in a publication with only 3,500 circulation by an unidentified author was the work of the Soviet KGB and its Department of Disinformation. The author used a pseudonym and little is known about him. The magazine itself has not been known as anti-American or a vehicle for Soviet propaganda or disinformation. Putting aside the motivations of the author and the editor of the magazine, it can be said that the incident demonstrates the alacrity with which some media in the Free World will transmit misinformation detrimental to the United States and ignore proof that the story is false. Whether or not the story was inspired by the Soviets is less important than what this experience tells us about the vulnerability of our media to disinformation."

The *AIM Report* analysis quoted another British magazine, *Defence*, as expressing surprise that the original "Mann" article had received worldwide attention, as much of its data appeared to have been derived from *Pravda*, Tass, and Novosti, notably *Pravda* articles published on September 6 and 20 and November 5, 1983. The "Mann" article had, in fact, quoted from an article by Soviet Marshal of Aviation Pyotr Kirsanov, which was published in *Pravda* on September 20, 1983. As part of the settlement agreed upon by Korean Airlines and *Defense Attaché*, the following statement, which the magazine's legal counsel made in court, was published.

"My Lord, on behalf of the publishers and editors of *Defence Attaché*, I am instructed to state that there is no foundation for any suggestion that either Korean Air Lines or any of its staff on the aircraft concerned took part in any spy mission or that the plaintiffs thus chose to put at risk the safety of their passengers and crew. My clients stated in an editorial introduction to the article that they did not necessarily agree with the author's views and that their editorial position was that they did not believe KAL 007 had a spy mission and they are happy to reiterate that. However, if the article has given rise to any misunderstanding, or in particular has been taken to suggest that Korean Air Lines would consider putting at risk the safety of their passengers and crew, that is a matter sincerely regretted by my clients and one for which they are pleased to have this opportunity of expressing their apologies."

Still, Soviet spokesmen and media continued to maintain that the Korean airliner had, in fact, been on a spy mission and that this justified its destruction. An alternate hypothesis was offered by Seymour Hersh, an investigative reporter, in his book *The Target Is Destroyed*. Hersh, a writer often critical of official U.S. government policies and personnel, based his findings on interviews with Soviet specialists, on monitoring records, and even on transcripts made by the U.S. National Security Agency of internal Soviet communications. Ultimately, Hersh concluded that neither the Soviet pilot who shot down the plane nor the officials who authorized this action were aware at the time that they were dealing with a civilian passenger plane.

On the other hand, Hersh also found that KAL 007 "was not on an intelligence-gathering mission for the CIA or any other agency of the United States or South Korea" and that its blundering into Soviet airspace was due to "ordinary human failings" on the part of the flight crew. Hersh suggested that U.S. officials had been aware of Soviet misperceptions of the plane's identity, but persisted in blaming the shooting down on a cold-blooded official decision. It is fair to assume that historians will continue to subject this case of propagandistic confusion to further examination, analysis, and dispute.

CHAPTER · 30

Chernobyl: Multidamage Control

At 1:23 A.M., on April 26, 1986, an explosion tore through the roof of an engine room at the Number Four Reactor in the Chernobyl AES (atomic energy station), located at the town of Pripyat, Soviet Ukraine. News of this accident reached the outside world indirectly: Monitoring equipment at Sweden's Forsmark Nuclear Power Plant, north of Stockholm, recorded abnormally high levels of radiation at 9 A.M., April 28. Swedish technicians at first assumed the radiation came from their own plant. Geiger-counter readings revealed radioactive emissions at four to five times normal levels.

Wind patterns indicated that the increased radiation originated from the Soviet Union, specifically from the Ukraine. Western analysts concluded that a major nuclear accident had taken place on Soviet territory. Inquiries by the Swedish embassy in Moscow were, initially, met with Foreign Ministry replies that, as far as was known, nothing unusual had happened. However, at 9 P.M., April 28, a Moscow television announcer read a brief Tass statement; here is its full text:

"An accident has occurred at the Chernobyl nuclear power plant, as one of the reactors was damaged. Measures are being taken to eliminate the consequences of the accident. Aid is being given to those affected. A government commission has been set up."

The brevity of the announcement and its lack of detail created an information vacuum that was quickly filled by outside data, rumor, speculation, and protests. The Scandinavian countries, notably Sweden and Denmark, expressed dismay at Soviet reluctance to advise the rest of the world of the extent of radiation dangers, thereby making it difficult to warn populations and guard against contamination. Instead, Soviet media, including Tass, listed and described earlier nuclear accidents that had occurred elsewhere, notably in the United States. This propagandistic pattern, traditional in distracting Soviet domestic audiences from setbacks or accidents at home, was in sharp contrast with Gorbachev's repeated call for *glasnost*, or candor; he had told the Soviet Communist Party Congress two months earlier: "Extensive, timely and frank information is evidence of trust in the people, respect for their intelligence and feelings and their ability to understand events of one kind or another on their own."

For days and weeks, Soviet media fell back on rephrasing additional brief announcements, while accusing Western press and radio of deliberately spreading rumors detrimental to the Soviet Union. Rumors did, in fact, get into circulation, including a UPI dispatch from Moscow, quoting an anonymous female informant in Kiev, the Ukrainian capital some 70 miles from Chernobyl, alleging that as many as 2,000 people had died as a result of the nuclear accident. Visiting New York for a media conference, Vladimir Lomeiko, the Foreign Ministry spokesman at that time, picked up a copy of the New York *Post* which carried the front-page headline "Mass Graves." It featured a report, based on rumors reaching a Ukrainian periodical published in New Jersey, that spoke of clandestine burials of fallout victims. Lomeiko, in New York and later in Moscow, asserted that such reports were the outgrowth of a concerted anti-Soviet propaganda campaign.

The news blackout inside and outside the Soviet Union was only partly explained by official statements and briefings. These pointed to evaluation and communications problems at Chernobyl and Moscow, heightened by unpreparedness and administrative rigidity. These, it appeared, not only had indirectly endangered the populations of Eastern and Western Europe but had directly caused a delay in the evacuation of people from the area around Chernobyl, presumably prompting serious long-range health risks.

While attacking Western media for sensationalism, Soviet propaganda officials soon realized that at least a show of *glasnost* was essential. In Paris, the newspaper *Le Monde* (May 2) published an editorial, "The Reticence of Agitprop," which said that Gorbachev's supposed new policy was being tested by the Chernobyl accident, as it "immediately cast doubt on the whole information system behind which the leadership of totalitarian regimes protects its power and privileges."

The Soviet embassy in Washington took a novel step when it sent a junior staff member, Vitali Churkin, to testify before an energy subcommittee of the U.S. House of Representatives on May 1. Lars-Erik Nelson, chief of the New York *Daily News* Washington bureau, reported (May 2) that Churkin's "two-hour grilling" was "a deft triumph of style over substance—but style is what the Soviets have most lacked in handling the international disaster." Although the Soviet spokesman did not significantly add to the Moscow statements, he admitted that the Chernobyl disaster presented a continuing problem. He said at one point:

"Definitely, there has been an accident which has not been liquidated yet and which poses certain threats not only to people in the Soviet Union but may pose, theoretically at least, some threats to a certain extent to people outside the Soviet Union."

While this amounted to a highly qualified and hedged understatement, it was a candid admission of sorts, and Representative Michael Bilirakis (Republican, Florida) expressed his appreciation by telling Churkin, "It took a lot of courage on your part to appear here." Nelson commented, "For a Soviet diplomat to submit himself to a congressional grilling is extremely rare."

Equally novel was a hookup arranged by the BBC World Service with Georgi Arbatov in Moscow, answering questions from English-speaking listeners who telephoned the London studios. The broadcast, on May 4, was moderated by the BBC's Sue McGregor and gave Arbatov numerous opportunities to turn his answers into combative comments on the West's "psychological warfare type of propaganda." At one point Arbatov suggested that British tourists might be under greater danger from radiation while visiting Las Vegas—a slap at U.S. nuclear tests in Nevada. Arbatov also alleged that, whatever radiation might exist "in Scotland or in Wales or in northern Norway," in Kiev "it is normal."

Calls came from Holland, West Germany, France, and elsewhere. One caller, Alexander Benedictov, telephoned from Leningrad and asked Arbatov: "My question is if it is necessary for an ordinary Soviet citizen to learn to speak English first, in order to put questions to such high-ranking Soviet officials or politicians?" To which Arbatov replied, "Oh yes. Please phone me any day, even in Russian. We can have this talk in ordinary Russian. I will give my telephone number if you need it. It is now in directories."

Arbatov's allegation that radiation was normal in Kiev followed the propaganda theme then being implemented by Soviet media. The implication was that the Chernobyl accident had been relatively minor and that, it being springtime, Ukrainians generally were in high spirits. While the rest of the world saw threatening satellite photographs of fires at the Chernobyl plant, Soviet television featured smiling May Day celebrants in Kiev, including, literally, dancing in the streets.

Contradictions were also observed by seven foreign correspondents who, in May, were permitted to visit Kiev. Pierre Lesourd, of Agence France Presse (AFP) began his dispatch: "The sun is shining and flowers are blooming in this Ukrainian capital, yet the main north-west highway to the accident-hit Chernobyl nuclear plant is still closed to traffic." He added: "Fishermen, knee-deep in the Dnieper River, relax as they wait for a catch, seemingly without care in the world—despite the fact that they are standing downstream from the stricken plant."

Reporters noted that Kiev residents had been warned not to drink fresh milk, not to eat lettuce, to wash their hair daily, to rinse dust off the soles of their shoes, and to sweep dust from their homes. Children had been evacuated, and police were using Geiger counters to check cars and passersby for radiation levels. While announcements suggested that risks were then, and perhaps had been right along, minimal, figures on actual radiation levels were withheld.

During this three-week period, General Secretary Gorbachev made no public statements, and speculation about the failure of his much-publicized *glasnost* policy was widespread. The International Atomic Energy Agency (IAEA), headquartered in Vienna, sent a telex to the Soviet State Committee on the Utilization of Atomic Energy, requesting information for the use of its member nations. The Netherlands Foreign Ministry, speaking for the 12 member nations of the European Economic Community (EEC), stated that it was the "duty" of Soviet authorities to "provide full information, on short notice, about the causes and consequences" of the Chernobyl disaster. British Foreign Minister Sir Geoffrey Howe said Soviet reluctance to provide information amounted to "a serious lapse in European good-neighborliness." West German Foreign Minister Hans-Dietrich Genscher urged the Soviet Union to authorize IAEA experts to examine the Chernobyl site "to see exactly what had happened."

Soviet authorities did invite the director general of the IAEA, Dr. Hans Blix, a Swedish national, to visit the Chernobyl region and to view the accident site from a helicopter. He was accompanied by Maurice Rosen, a U.S. national, head of the agency's department of security matters. Blix told a Moscow press conference on May 9 that there had been an agreement to strengthen an international warning system designed to alert member nations in case of the escape of nuclear substances. The Moscow correspondent of the Swiss daily *Neue Zürcher Zeitung* reported (May 11) that the IAEA representatives showed "considerable restraint" in commenting on the Chernobyl situation itself, reflecting mainly the information issued by Soviet authorities.

While Soviet media made extensive use of the visit, Blix's difficult position was highlighted in an interview he gave the German weekly *Der Spiegel* (May 20). Asked what the flight over Chernobyl had shown, Blix stated: "Well, everything was deserted, as was the entire region within the off-limits zone of thirty kilometers." He commented that the sight of the destroyed reactor was "shocking," adding: "We saw the hole in the roof of the building, with a lot of debris around it. This was a sad sight. We prefer to see working and functioning reactors, and not any that are destroyed."

Blix and Rosen acknowledged they had little chance to gather direct impressions. In effect, they had been on something of a guided tour, arranged through the Soviet mission at their agency's Vienna office. Rosen noted, "We do not speak Russian, which made matters more difficult." Asked whether they had, in fact, received "a satisfactory explanation of the accident," Blix replied: "No. The answer was that they have a number of theories as to the accident's cause, but had not yet decided which was the most probable. They declined to discuss any of the theories before arriving at a final conclusion." Once a detailed analysis became available, Blix explained, it would be restricted to "nuclear experts of our organization's member states."

The *Spiegel* editors noted that Blix had said earlier that Chernobyl radiation consequences were "much more serious than those of any preceding accident." Blix affirmed this, saying, "Yes, of course." But Valentin Falin, the newly appointed director of Novosti, had told the magazine that the Chernobyl accident was not among the worst. Blix countered: "Let him speak for himself. So far, there has been no accident in any of the world's civilian power plants that involved a significant release of radioactivity."

During the *Spiegel* interview with Falin (May 12), he was asked "just when did the 'Novosti' chief hear about the reactor accident at Chernobyl?" He replied: "I knew on Sunday [April 27] that something had happened in the Ukraine. On Monday there was a Politburo meeting, at which a detailed report by the investigative commission, formed on Saturday, was discussed." Falin added that Gorbachev had been informed on Saturday, "but the question remains, to what degree." Asked why the "supergoof" at the atomic energy plant had also led to a supergoof in Soviet "information policy," Falin said that "local technicians" at the Chernobyl power station had "underestimated" the extent and potential of the accident and had "believed they were in a position to bring the situation under control."

Falin, and other Soviet officials who offered briefings during this period, said that a chemical explosion had taken place inside the reactor. Had the local technicians taken appropriate measures immediately, damage might have remained limited. As they had failed to comprehend overall risks, Falin added, "Certain steps were taken with a degree of delay. That's life, and in the end we are all smarter."

Several Communist Party organs abroad reflected domestic concern over Soviet atomic policies and the dangers of fallout. *Volksstimme* (June 14), published in Vienna, managed to respond to the interest of its readers by reprinting an interview Falin had given to the West German weekly

DVZ/Die Tat. Even the Moscow correspondent of the Italian Communist daily, *L'Unita,* engaged in relatively hard-hitting interviews with Soviet officials. On the other hand, Soviet media quoted such papers as *Humanité* (Paris) and *Rude Pravo* (Prague) as critical of Western reporting on the Chernobyl disaster, without identifying them as Communist organs—a tactic of omission that is practiced, on and off, throughout the Soviet propaganda apparatus.

A turning point on the information treatment of Chernobyl came with General Secretary Gorbachev's long-awaited comments, televised on May 14 and running just short of half an hour. Considering that, since coming to power, Gorbachev had come to be regarded, quite widely, as a master of public relations, rivaling U.S. President Reagan as a "great communicator," the speech was relatively unsophisticated—harking back to standard propaganda themes and falling short of the candor the Gorbachev administration had sought to exude.

Instead of stating what had been slowly revealed—that the Soviet government had been emotionally and administratively unprepared for a disaster of Chernobyl's dimensions—Gorbachev reiterated the claim that all that could be done had, in fact, been done: "A stern test has been passed and is being passed by all—firemen, transport and building workers, medics, special chemical protection units, helicopter crews and other detachments of the Ministry of Defense and the Ministry of Internal Affairs." He emphasized that people had "acted and are continuing to act heroically, selflessly." And while he acknowledged outside help, including that of two U.S. physicians, Gorbachev reiterated the by then standard propaganda point that "governments, political figures and the mass media in certain NATO countries, especially the U.S.A." had "launched an unrestrained anti-Soviet campaign." Referring to reports that spoke of thousands of casualties and "mass graves of the dead," Gorbachev said the U.S.S.R. had faced "a veritable mountain of lies," designed by "certain Western politicians" to "blast the possibilities for balancing international relations, to sow new seeds of mistrust and suspicion toward the socialist countries." Opinions had, in fact, been expressed which questioned whether the Soviet Union, unable to be candid about a civilian nuclear accident, could be expected to be more candid in such matters as arms control.

Rather than providing an accounting on the Chernobyl event, possibly in a detached and relatively factual manner, Gorbachev's speech sounded like little more than a not too skillful attempt to distract from the unprecedented accident and turn it into yet another vehicle for the Kremlin's ongoing "peace-and-disarmament" campaign. Gorbachev concluded: "The nuclear age forcefully demands a new approach to international relations, the pooling of efforts of states with different social systems for the sake of putting an end to the disastrous arms race and of a radical improvement of the world political climate."

Gorbachev's speech did set the tone for a change in Soviet media treatment of the Chernobyl developments. Reporting in press and on television began to emphasize individual as well as collective efforts to help the sick, the evacuees, and displaced children, to insulate the damaged facilities, to reduce radiation, and to repair the countryside. And while these reports were overwhelmingly and even relentlessly upbeat, news of failure, cowardice, and bungling also emerged. Grigori I. Revenko, Communist Party leader of Kiev Province, was quoted in the illustrated weekly *Ogonyok* as stating, "There were cases of people deserting, panicking and trying to pin the blame on others." He added: "A thorough examination of each individual is being undertaken. We had already rid ourselves of a few people, including some in leadership positions. They have lost their party cards." *Pravda* reported (June 15) that one deputy director at the Chernobyl plant, R. Solovyev, deserted his post "at the most difficult moment" and two other deputy directors, I. Tsarenko and V. Gundav, "did not fulfill their official duties with proper responsibility and did little to ease the living and working conditions of people working at the station." The paper also said that "a portion of the workers from the power station are still on the run," including "foremen of shifts and senior technicians."

On July 4, Tass reported that Boris Y. Shcherbina, the deputy prime minister who had been named director of the government's investigating commission right after the accident occurred, had been replaced. Moscow rumors suggested that Shcherbina had become seriously ill from radiation exposure. At that time, according to official accounts, 26 people had died as a result of radiation exposure. Tass gave no reason for Shcherbina's resignation. Generally, Soviet media de-emphasized dangers from low-level radiation, notably long-range risks that may not be detected for years or may never be associated with radiation and possibly diagnosed in a manner that deflected from nuclear fallout. On the whole, because radiation risks have not been publicly discussed, the population initially seemed to take a relatively lighthearted view of radiation exposure.

Television and photographs showed medical workers and Geiger-counter–equipped policemen checking individuals and items suspected of having been exposed to radiation; but the examiners themselves did not wear clothing that would have shielded them from radiation. On May 22, Moscow TV's *Vremya* newscast showed robot tractors in the Chernobyl area, turning over soil. The announcer said: "Two such bulldozers are now functioning in the direct proximity of the building of the fourth reactor of the Chernobyl Atomic Energy Station, where various electronic blocks and hydraulic control units are being finished and hooked up, and new crews are being trained." The television picture showed several men, wearing ordinary clothing, standing at a distance; one of them appeared to be working the remote control of the bulldozer. Thus while the bulldozers functioned without a driver, keeping one man from radiation, others did not seem to be shielded against possible exposure.

Soviet spokesmen, replying to Western criticism during the first few weeks, emphasized that authorities were careful to guard against panic. In fact, such Western media as Radio Liberty and Radio Free Europe, which broadcast news on the disaster and world reaction in the languages of the U.S.S.R. and Eastern Europe, were accused by such officials as Arbatov of seeking to create panic. The Soviet Union's tradition that bad news is only news when it happens abroad was only partly broken after the Chernobyl events. And, on-the-scene observers confirmed that the Soviet public largely went along with its leadership's "Trust us!" appeal. An AP reporter, interviewing a young woman at a Moscow bus stop shortly after the accident, recorded that she said, "Of course, as any Soviet citizen, I am concerned. But I'm quite sure that everything will be taken care of and the Soviet government will do all that is necessary."

A strikingly more probing position was taken by a participant in the Eighth U.S.S.R. Writers' Union Congress which ended its five-day session on June 28, 1986. During one discussion, Yekaterina Sheveleva attributed the Chernobyl disaster to the same kind of bureaucratic rigidity that had plagued Soviet authors. As quoted in *Literaturnaya Gazeta* (July 2), she told the meeting that the late poet-novelist Alexander T. Tvardovski, if speaking at a writers' congress, "would have linked the national disaster at Chernobyl to the pernicious shortcomings in literature." Sheveleva added that Tvardovski "would have asked whether those shortcomings and the terrible accident at Chernobyl had not grown from the same root system that has sprouted hack work, incompetence, money-grubbing, servility, corruption and cadre failings."

While Kremlin policy clearly sought to avoid the emergence of Chernobyl either as a symbol of the Soviet society's "shortcomings" (that much-used, seemingly safe word!) or as a deeply traumatic event, it remained a continuing challenge. The TV news show *Vremya*, at one point even subject to sharp criticism by *Pravda*, faced particularly difficult tasks. The show's editor, G. I. Shevelov, was sharply questioned by the Moscow correspondent of the Rome newspaper *La Repubblica* (June 28). The correspondent, Alberto Jacoviello, noted that Shevelov regarded Western TV coverage as reflecting "almost frantic haste." Jacoviello asked, "But don't you think that you handle things a bit too undramatically?" He mentioned that on the night U.S. planes had bombed Libya, the first *Vremya* news item had been an interview with a milkmaid. Shevelov replied that Soviet audiences were used to a tradition whereby the newscast opened with domestic items, while his program was trying to find "a proper balance between tradition and innovation."

The Italian correspondent said, "Well, I do not consider the announcement of the Chernobyl explosion, halfway through the program and in approximately only twenty words, a good example of balance between tradition and innovation." The *Vremya* editor replied, "You are being unfair, Mr. Jacoviello. You live here, so you know what happened. We have explained it several times, honestly and candidly. Initially it was not realized what had actually happened. But once a government commission was able to gather definite information, *Vremya* broadcast, in full, the press conference given by members of the commission. I should add that our correspondents in the area worked miracles, often risking contamination, to provide the most accurate possible pictures of the situation."

Jacoviello answered, "I grant you that. The fact remains, however, that when one watches *Vremya*, it is difficult to avoid the impression that, in general, given a choice between saying something and not saying it, you prefer to leave it unsaid. Or, at least, that you are afraid of saying more than those at the top would like."

Given the delicate position of a top Soviet media man, the Italian correspondent's question was, in fact, somewhat unfair. *Glasnost* or not, an experienced Soviet editor would still be tempted to make a risky decision by coming down on the side of caution. Shevelov said: "No, that is a poor way of stating the issue. You must never forget that ours is a state television service, of a socialist state, and that it is therefore normal for us to follow the indications given us by those who represent the state. This is not a constraint but a stimulus to us. Having established this, the rest is entrusted to our professionalism. It is up to us to present a particular situation effectively."

Aside from matters of actual deaths and illness and the effect of radiation on people, farm animals, and vegetation, Soviet media found it particularly trying to deal with the topic of mass evacuations of adults and children. Official statistics spoke of columns of vehicles that had taken a total of 92,000 persons from the immediate Chernobyl area. According to Shcherbina, speaking at a Foreign Ministry press conference (May 6), evacuation did not begin until some 36 hours after the initial explosion. Media emphasis was on the speed and efficiency of the evacuation and on the adaptability shown by evacuees, forced to settle in an alien environment.

Clearly, then, the darker realities of mass dislocations would not be treated by Soviet media in *glasnost* fashion. Instead, the organizing efforts of Communist Party officials and other authorities, including the militia of the Ministry of the Interior, were highlighted in press, radio, and television coverage. Typically, the Moscow paper *Selskaya Zhizn* (Agricultural Life) carried an article by the chairman of a district adjoining Chernobyl (May 25) that reported flawless cooperation between members of a local agricultural collective and emergency evacuees. The chairman, A. Prokopov, wrote, "From the very first day of the arrival of those in need of settlement, members of the kokhoz (collective) shared everything they had: housing, foodstuffs, bedding." In turn, he said, the settlers volunteered help; they "immediately offered their labor services," asking, "Which jobs need most attention today?"

The report also stated that as soon as the first contingents were evacuated from the Chernobyl-Pripyat danger zone, "joint sessions of village Soviets were held everywhere" to discuss the topic "The Soviets Tasks in Attending to the Life and Daily Needs of the Evacuated Population." Prokopov wrote that in addition to absorbing the evacuees, providing housing, and finding work for them, the district had to "dispatch some 13,000 people" from its confines. "These," he added, "were schoolchildren, mothers with young children, pregnant women—that is, all those whom it was necessary, as a precaution measure, to relocate in completely safe places," including children's camps, vacation homes, sanatoria, and clinics.

Other press reports indicated that evacuees assumed, at first, that they might be able to return to their homes within a few days or weeks. Officials even implied that Pripyat, a town of some 25,000 inhabitants, might be decontaminated and rehabilitated. Evacuees, in many cases, left with no property whatever; Y. Yavorivski, writing in *Pravda* (May 23), noted that Pripyat residents could only "take their most precious possessions—their children and their souls." After giving examples of people's behavior under stress, Yavorivski wrote, "The misfortune will not only put everyone, uncompromisingly, in his proper place, but will also, like an X-ray, reveal the soul of everybody who enters its zone." In addition to those officially evacuated, thousands of people, including residents of Kiev, left the region on their own initiative. Serge Schmemann, writing in the *New York Times* (May 26), noted, "The sudden scattering of many people, in a country where the Government is accustomed to carefully controlling the movements of its citizens, has created unusual problems for the authorities." He added:

"Among the most critical but rarely mentioned problems with the evacuees is the long-term effect of the radiation to which they were exposed. The residents of Pripyat and the six-mile zone immediately around the power station, where the most lethal fallout was concentrated, were not moved until 36 hours after the accident. The rest of the 18.6-mile danger zone was not evacuated until a week later.

"The Soviet press has made no mention of the increased risks of leukemia and other cancers associated with radiation, evidently to avoid further frightening the evacuees. The papers have repeatedly said that all evacuees were given thorough physical examinations and blood tests on leaving the zone, that the tests were followed up regularly, and that most have been found healthy."

The Chernobyl accident dramatically tested the limits of Soviet candor. News and comment on the events caused by the Chernobyl fire and explosion reflected a pattern of propaganda policies that sought to ensure multidamage control: avoidance of panic or widespread distrust at home; emphasis on nuclear accidents abroad; efforts to discredit foreign reporting and public antifallout actions abroad; and, overall, dilution of the Chernobyl accident's impact by linking it to the dangers of nuclear war.

This final theme was carried over into the report which the Soviet government submitted to the IAEA in Vienna on August 25, 1986, and which attributed the Chernobyl disaster to grave errors committed by key personnel at the nuclear power station. The report stated that the reactor's staff had been engaged in an equipment test, designed to find out how long turbine generators would run, in case of an unforeseen shutdown. Adronik M. Petrosyants, chairman of the U.S.S.R. Committee for the Peaceful Uses of Atomic Energy, said: "The accident took place as a result of a whole series of gross violations of operating regulations by the workers." The report listed six errors committed by the Chernobyl staff which bypassed safety controls, provoked two explosions that blew the roof off the reactor building, and caused 30 separate fires.

The Soviet report, which covered 2 volumes and 382 pages, provided charts and drawings that represented a blueprint of the nuclear plant. A model of the plant was also on display in Vienna. While the report contained a great amount of data and was in many ways remarkably candid, it fell short of suggesting a revision of basic Soviet design and security standards in future production of nuclear power. Instead, the by then standard theme was repeated: "The accident at the Chernobyl nuclear power plant has again demonstrated the danger of uncontrolled nuclear power and highlighted the destructive consequences to which its military use, or damage to peaceful nuclear facilities during military operations, could lead." Philip Taubman commented from Moscow to the *New York Times* (August 22) that the report sought "to make the disaster serve the nation's foreign policy" by emphasizing "the link between Chernobyl and the arms race."

Domestically, Soviet media soft-pedaled the Vienna report, notably indications that the areas affected by radiation were more extensive than assumed earlier and estimates that radiation-hastened cancer deaths ranged from 2,500 to 24,000, over a period of 70 years, though some projections were much higher. Most of these deaths were expected to occur among the 135,000 exposed persons who had been evacuated. Internally, the Soviet press noted hardships among some evacuees, and local Estonian papers even referred to unrest among reservists who had been sent to the contaminated zone and who had rebelled against overwork and contamination dangers. Ultimately, news of radiation illness and cancer deaths would undoubtedly be diffused among general health statistics. News of crop yields and livestock production, as well as normal civil and cultural activities in the Ukraine, would help to cover Chernobyl's wounds, leaving as few scars as possible.

CHAPTER · 31

The "Ethnos" Case

On June 12, 1978, five Greek visitors were approaching Moscow in a plane from Athens. Even before they landed, they knew that they were most welcome. They were part of a carefully planned Soviet propaganda coup: the publication of a Moscow-oriented daily paper. The visitors included George Bobolas, a wealthy and well-connected businessman; Yannis Yannikos, a veteran member of the Communist Party of Greece; Alexander Philipopoulos, an experienced newspaper editor; and Constantine Rondiris, a prominent corporate lawyer.

The high point of the visit was an invitation for Bobolas and Philipopoulos to meet Konstantin Chernenko, then party leader Leonid Brezhnev's right-hand man and later, following Andropov's death, his successor. Chernenko's career had given him years of propagandistic expertise. He used the occasion to emphasize Soviet-Greek cooperation and to recall his own earlier visit to Greece, including a meeting with then Prime Minister Constantine Karamanlis. Chernenko spoke of his hopes for the success of the many publishing projects the Greek visitors had been discussing during their week's visit.

What, exactly, were these projects? They were an extension of an arrangement that Yannikos had administered for several years, for which a Greek edition of the *Great Soviet Encyclopedia* was the financial and educational centerpiece. Like other export-import deals made by Soviet agencies, the publishing projects provided the government with a means of crediting funds to pro-Soviet enterprises abroad. Favorable conditions for publishing additional volumes of the encyclopedia were among the topics discussed in Moscow, including a book by Brezhnev. Publication of a series of educational and technical volumes was also agreed upon.

While Bobolas and Philipopoulos were elated by the Moscow talks, Yannikos had reason to wonder about his own future; he had been excluded from the Chernenko meeting. Such slights began to embitter Yannikos, who had devoted all his life to unstinting support of the Soviet Union. His association with the Communist Party antedated World War II. He was active in the Communist-controlled section of the partisan movement that fought the occupation armies of Nazi Germany, but which also warred against rival guerrillas and anti-Communist civilians. In 1945, Yannikos was found guilty of having taken part in the execution of 18 people who, rightly or wrongly, were accused of collaboration with the Nazis. Yannikos was condemned to death, but his sentence was commuted to imprisonment.

Released from prison in 1955, at a time when the Communist Party was illegal in Greece, Yannikos made contact with party leaders then living in the Soviet Union. One means of reactivating pro-Soviet sentiment inside Greece was through economic relations, including publishing projects. At the suggestion of Soviet propaganda officials, Yannikos founded a publishing firm that issued such works as *History of Ancient Greece,* by a Soviet author (Sergiev), *A True Man,* by Boris Polevoi, various scientific works, and even a Russian cookbook.

Yannikos's book publishing firm was financed by Soviet advances, and it may be assumed that he was not required to forward royalties to the Soviet Union. One major translation project was the *Universal Encyclopedia for Youth,* in 12 volumes, which had the dual function of introducing young people to Soviet ideas and projecting Soviet educational efforts in terms of academic respectability. Another multivolume project was a translation of the *Soviet Thematic Encyclopedia.* Although the 1960s were a period of official Greek anticommunism, works such as the *Great Soviet Encyclopedia,* classified as reference rather than propaganda, were being accepted by libraries and educators.

Yannikos was jailed in 1967 for seven months, shortly after the military dictatorship of a group of colonels came to power. Their rule collapsed in 1974, and Karamanlis returned from self-exile in France. Parliamentary democracy was reestablished, and the Communist Party was legalized. In fact, two such parties were established, of which one was frankly pro-Soviet in operations and policies, while the other followed a national line, similar to that of "Eurocommunist" movements elsewhere. However, even during the colonels' rule, the Soviet Union maintained economic contacts through export-import agencies and cooperative Greek companies.

The pro-Soviet Communist Party of Greece already had a morning paper, *Rizospastis,* that appealed mainly to the party faithful. What the

Soviet propagandists had in mind was a lively paper, in the Münzenberg tradition, that might encourage an anti-American, pro-Soviet trend among a new generation of readers (and voters), then being courted by Andreas Papandreou and his Pan-Hellenic Socialist Party (PASOK). In Bobolas, the Soviet officials felt they had a suitable front man, but they made the error of dumping their veteran follower Yannikos too unceremoniously; if they had enabled him to save face, as well as a slice of the financial pie, their whole scheme might have succeeded unnoticed.

To advance the plans for the expanded book publishing program, which would help to underwrite the projected newspaper project, Soviet officials made several trips to Athens. On September 16, 1978, following the Moscow contract signing, two specialists visited the Greek capital for consultations. Other such consultations also took place, but Yannikos did not participate in them. Meanwhile, Bobolas expanded his commercial activities, and even the conservative government cooperated in several ventures, including an exhibit of Greek trade projects in Moscow.

The publishing venture achieved a great deal of publicity when Boris Pankin arrived in Athens on March 3, 1980, to participate in the publication of the seventeenth volume of the encyclopedia. The event was a plush reception at the city's most prestigious hotel, the Grande-Bretagne. But while Bobolas and Philipopoulos received the guests at the door, Yannikos simply mingled with the crowd.

The paper that eventually resulted from all these plans was called *Ethnos* (The Nation), and it hit the streets one month before the national elections of 1981. Philipopoulos, during an international press survey, made earlier for another publisher, had examined such popular newspapers as the New York *Daily News* and the London tabloids. He concluded that only a paper featuring multicolor printing and lively news coverage, with emphasis on sports and entertainment, could hope to attract a wide audience. *Ethnos* did, in fact, revolutionize the Greek press. Despite the fact that it had to compete against 12 established Athens dailies, it reached a circulation of 180,000, although by 1987 it had settled at 81,000.

Two events gave the paper an element of publicity that it did not anticipate: Yannikos sued Bobolas for his stake in the joint publishing venture and an investigative reporter, Paul Anastasiades, published a book on the paper's Soviet connections. The events that followed prompted international attention, court battles, charges, and countercharges. Anastadiades, a correspondent for the *Daily Telegraph* (London) and part-time correspondent for the *New York Times,* gave an account of his experiences at a Paris conference on the topic "The Role of Disinformation in the Modern World" (December 5–6, 1984), sponsored by Resistance International. The speaker, whose dispatches appear under the name Paul Anastasi, used a promotional slogan of *Ethnos* as the title of his book, which translates as *Hold the Nation in Your Hand.*

Anastasi's investigations were greatly helped by Yannikos's disillusionment. He said that when the Russians "abandoned their loyal communist ally in favor of Mr. Bobolas, who was well connected with the economic and political establishment, and therefore much more useful than a well-known Communist Party member, Yannikos began a legal battle to get back his rights." Anastasi called the publishing project a creation of the KGB's First Chief Directorate, responsible for operations abroad, "designed to covertly influence Greek public opinion and the government to support Soviet foreign policy objectives through a purportedly independent newspaper." Anastasi viewed the establishment of *Ethnos* as "the first-ever experiment of its kind in a Western country and a member state of both NATO and the European Economic Community."

Anastasi's book angered Bobolas. He began court proceedings against the author, charging him with libel. Anastasi said in Paris, "I went through about twelve court hearings that ultimately resulted in my conviction and the banning of the book. I was strongly attacked both by *Ethnos* and by the government press spokesman, and was repeatedly pressured to make a public statement of apology in order to have the legal action against me dropped."

One of the blows Anastasi suffered was the last-minute refusal of Yannikos to testify. As it was, one of the two defense lawyers yielded to behind-the-scenes pressure and abandoned his client. And, on the eve of the first court date, Bobolas settled Yannikos's claim with a payment equivalent to $50,000, prompting him to withdraw his support of Anastasi, who recalled, "I was, however, given strength by at least one very positive development. On the basis of a dramatic and, I would say, very humane decision, Yannikos' son, Christos, turned up at the trial and testified in my favor at the time his father kept away. He confirmed all the details of the Soviet involvement, including the fact that his father had sent a feasibility study for such a newspaper to the Russians."

While the court found Anastasi guilty of libel and defamation for using the term "agents of influence," it accepted his charge that the newspaper was "evidently pro-Soviet" and, indeed, used "raw Soviet propaganda." Concerning *Ethnos*'s anti-U.S. stance, editor Philipopoulos said the paper's line was "strictly anti-imperialist," while another editor, Michael Naskos, stated: "For us there is no Soviet imperialism. Only American." Asked why the paper had totally ignored the Pope's historic visit to Poland in 1983, Philipopoulos said: "Events in Poland are an American attempt to set fire to Europe, and we are not going to help in this effort." Questioned further as to how any paper, regardless of political coloration, could over-

look such a major news event, the chief editor said that, as Greek Orthodox Christians, the staff was not interested in a Roman Catholic Pope's
activities.

During the successive hearings and trials, the *Ethnos* staff and lawyers
were asked repeatedly to produce at least one article critical of the Soviet
Union, of one of the East bloc countries, or of a Soviet ally or a single
article favorable to a Western point of view. None could be presented.
Yet Philipopoulos claimed the paper was "profoundly anti-imperialist, profoundly democratic, free and truly objective within the measure of our
ability." The editors thus appeared to have adopted the Soviet mind-set,
together with its terminology. According to Anastasi's analysis of *Ethnos*'s
handling of news and comment, the paper supported the Soviet position
on all major international issues.

Needless to say, *Ethnos*'s coverage of the United States, the NATO
countries, and Japan emphasized the darker sides of these societies. Its
editorials used the theme of Greek independence and patriotism to urge
the dismantling of U.S. bases in Greece and an end to links with NATO
and the European Economic Community. The paper's one-sided reporting
from the United States and Great Britain was ensured by the men the
paper had selected as correspondents. The position of "American commentator" was filled by Carl Marzani, who served a prison term after World
War II, having hidden his Communist Party membership while a State
Department staff member. In England, *Ethnos* chose as its correspondent
Stanley Harrison, previously chief subeditor of the London *Morning Star,*
the Communist Party organ.

While Soviet officials had sought to settle the conflict between Yannikos
and Bobolas, in order to halt undesirable publicity, they either did not
stop or actually facilitated another explosive undertaking: wiretapping. In
October 1984, the Athens public prosecutor charged Bobolas and Philipopoulos with wiretapping telephone conversations between Anastasi and
Panayotis Zotos, a lawyer-friend, and with publishing excerpts in *Ethnos.*
The newspaper presented the telephone conversations as having taken
place between two CIA agents and as concerning plans to destabilize Greek
democratic institutions, arrange for the murder of *Ethnos* personnel, and
extend these activities to other European countries. However, nothing in
the published excerpts supported these sensational claims.

By that time, the court cases concerning Anastasi and *Ethnos* were
running side by side. On November 23, 1984, the Greek Supreme Court
overturned the earlier libel sentence against Anastasi, criticized the appeals
court for not following the prosecutor's request that sentence be suspended,
and ordered another appeals hearing. The action, in effect, indefinitely
postponed the case; at the end of the year, its statute of limitations ran
out, although the sentence remained on Anastasi's legal record.

When the wiretap case came before the Athens court on April 25, 1985, Bobolas did not appear, claiming ill health. He was sentenced in absentia, as was Philipopoulos, who was present, to five months in prison, or to a fine equivalent to $500 each. The court rejected the defense claim that publication of the wiretap had been "a national and social duty," designed to expose a "conspiracy." Anastasi told the court that publication had been "a vulgar and crude attempt by *Ethnos* to discredit me personally, as well as my revelations on the paper's connections with the KGB." On June 30, 1986, Anastasi was cleared by a three-member council of district attorneys of the *Ethnos* charges that he had threatened to destroy the paper's offices and to kill staff members. But the paper still faced two trials, as Anastasi had charged its publisher and staff members with defamation of character, perjury, filing false charges, and insulting authorities.

In the history of Soviet propaganda ventures, the *Ethnos* enterprise had been well thought-out and daring. In theory, as seen from Moscow, it combined elements of modern journalism and publishing technology with the nondogmatic traditions of Willi Münzenberg. Abandoning a veteran Communist like Yannikos was a logical step, judging by the ruthless logic applied by the Soviet Communist Party at home, where even top leaders are erased from history books. But the KGB–Central Committee officials had not counted on Yannikos's sense of *philotimo,* his eminently Greek feeling of personal pride and integrity, nor on his son's and family's standards of fairness.

By putting all their chips on George Bobolas, Soviet officials had bet on a capitalist's selfish interests but overlooked his inability to understand that certain things, such as Anastasi's book, were best ignored. Instead, the trials served to publicize the book's charges, and the wiretapping stunt forced the hands of a government that might otherwise endorse *Ethnos*'s editorial policies. Still, public memory is notoriously short, and *Ethnos* is living up to the Münzenberg tradition, mixing ideology with massive doses of tabloid journalism.

CHAPTER · 32

To the Year 2000

Soviet propaganda is engaged in a war of words but in war nevertheless. Whether it speaks of it as a "struggle against imperialism" or as "class warfare," Moscow's intense and continuous propaganda campaign is only one aspect of its struggle for ever-increasing worldwide influence. The original Communist vocabulary, with its emphasis on "world revolution," has been retired, as one scraps outdated weaponry. Even the epithet "capitalism" occasionally gives way to such terms as "consumerism" or "market economy." Successive Soviet rulers, in particular Andropov and Gorbachev, eliminated much of the archaic terminology that used to permeate Soviet speeches and writings.

The outdated phrases of Marx and Engels, with their nineteenth-century connotations, have virtually disappeared from Soviet propaganda and agitation. Today's Agitprop specialists often appear to use Lenin's words as occasional decoration, to add a traditional touch, rather than as an element of persuasion. Propagandistic strategies and tactics come covered by ever-more conciliatory camouflage, polished to a blinding gloss. Still, key documents remain harshly revealing.

When the Communist Party of the Soviet Union met for its 27th Congress in February 1986, it passed on a program of "ideological and educational work" which provided guidelines for the "struggle against bourgeois ideology," to be valid toward the year 2000. The program said:

"The most acute struggle between the two world outlooks on the international scene reflects the opposition of the two world systems—socialism and capitalism. The CPSU sees its task in carrying to the peoples the truth about real socialism and about the home and foreign policy of the Soviet Union, in actively advocating the Soviet way of life and in exposing vigorously and in a well-argued manner the anti-popular, inhuman nature of imperialism and its exploiter substance."

The program noted that "the mass media and propaganda bodies are playing a growing role in society's life" and said that the media must "analyze domestic and international affairs and economic and social phenomena in depth, extend active support to everything that is new and advanced, raise pressing issues of concern to the people and suggest ways of solving them." At home, the Communist Party urged, "The press, television and radio networks are to convince the people with a politically cogent, purposeful, profound, prompt, informative, clear and intelligible news coverage and commentary." Generally, the party committed itself to "giving the press and all other mass news and propaganda bodies ready help and support in their work."

The program outlined "the tasks of the CPSU on the international scene" in terms that managed to be both assertive and conciliatory: "The approach of the CPSU to foreign policy matters combines firm protection of the interests of the Soviet people and resolute opposition to the aggressive policy of imperialism with a readiness for dialogue and for constructive settlement of international programs through negotiations." The program called for "constant development and expansion of cooperation between the USSR and the fraternal socialist countries and all-round promotion and consolidation and progress in the world socialist system," the "development of relations of equality and friendship with newly-free countries," as well as "internationalist solidarity with Communist and revolutionary-democratic Parties, with the international working-class movement and with the national-liberation struggle of peoples." And while a call for "world revolution" could not have been more elegantly paraphrased, the party program led off with the traditional Marxist slogan, "Workers of all countries, unite!" The program itself said, at the outset, "Capitalism is the last exploiter system in the history of mankind," an "obstacle to social progress."

The language, with all its modern touches, was still that of the "class struggle," despite the fact that Soviet policy and propaganda has become an extension of the Soviet Union's national interests, whether they be seen as self-protective or as expansionist-imperialist. Moscow's terminology differentiates between its own propaganda and that undertaken by "class enemies" or "imperialists." A key work on this topic, *The Battle of Ideas in the Modern World,* by Vadim U. Kortunov, was issued by Novosti's Progress Publishers in 1979. The author charged that "bourgeois propaganda" seeks to "mix up the conceptions of 'ideological struggle' and 'psychological war.' " He wrote: "The ideological struggle has always been and will continue to be an objective phenomenon of the historical process.

It is inevitable so long as opposing classes exist. But if no one can possibly 'abolish the ideological struggle,' it is the governments and the ruling political parties who shoulder the subjective responsibility for the choice of the means and methods of conducting it. It is one thing to compare ideas, prove their advantages and spread practical experience with the view to winning over public opinion (ideological struggle) and a totally different one to misinform the public, slander other countries and carry on ideological subversion against their existing order ('psychological warfare')."

Put a bit more bluntly: The Soviet Union is engaged in "ideological struggle" (which is proper); what others, such as the United States, do is "psychological warfare" (which is subversive). Nor does Kortunov raise the hope that during any period of getting along well, Soviet propaganda will cease its efforts. No, he says, "détente does not in the least signify a decline in the ideological struggle." This is not one man's opinion, of course. The Soviet propaganda machine extends far beyond the borders of the U.S.S.R. It is particularly active in East Germany, where a leading ideologue, Albert Norden, dealt with this point in *Questions of the Struggle against Imperialism.* The book, published by the Propaganda Department of the (Communist) Socialist Unity Party, was specifically prepared "For Agitators, Propagandists and Lecturers." Norden made clear that there could be no "ideology-free" relations "in cultural, scientific and other areas." He explained: "Ideology-free regions do not exist—certainly not in the realm of relations between states of a differing social order. The development of peaceful coexistence does not, therefore, lead to any lessening or even weakening of ideological conflict. The pitiless destruction of all imperialist theories and arguments, by means of agitational, propagandistic and scientific destruction, is a virtual presupposition, if the imperialists are to be forced into respect for peaceful coexistence. Therefore: Peaceful Coexistence—Yes! Ideological Truce—Never!"

Another East German author, Günther Wirth, referred to propaganda campaigns as *The War Before the War.* In a book published in 1978, he provided the following definition: "Psychological warfare is, in content and method, part of the preparation for an imperialist war. It is a special variant of influence on opponents of the imperialist forces, before and during armed conflict. Today, it is directed against the socialist states, their governments and people, against states that have liberated themselves from colonial oppression, against national liberation movements, against progressive forces within the capitalist states, against the peoples of these states, against the international labor movement and other international associations that fight for peace. Psychological warfare actually makes war total, as it combines the effort at physical annihilation of the opponent with accompanying psychological annihilation. It is, therefore, the expression of extreme anti-human barbarism."

Wirth added that the tools of psychological warfare developed along with the multiplicity of communications media: newspaper propaganda and leaflet distribution was supplemented by posters, film, radio propaganda, and television. "At present," he wrote, "communications satellites represent a peak in the development of tools that serve psychological warfare. With the aid of this instrumentation, the most varied methods of psychological warfare have come into use: rumors, propaganda lies, vicious attacks, intimidation, slander, defamation, manipulation, diversion, corruption, espionage, sabotage. These serve as methods of psychological warfare: the insights of psychology are being utilized to influence people, so they will act against themselves, their ethical responsibilities, against a humanistic image of mankind, against reason, and against their own interests." All told, Wirth presented a rather comprehensive inventory of propagandistic techniques. One wonders, could he possibly have engaged in a not-so-subtle critique of Soviet propaganda techniques, using the reverse device of attributing them to the "class enemy"?

The time-worn use of certain Marxist terms, such as "class" this and "class" that, occurred in yet another East German collection of papers, *The Fourth Front,* edited by Herbert Kruse for the Military Publishing House of the German Democratic Republic. One contribution, by Colonel Dr. D. Langer, carried the heading "Firm Socialist Class Position—Effective Weapon against Imperialist Psychological Warfare." Langer wrote, "It is irrelevant whether the imperialist enemy faces us at the border or on the airwaves, and it doesn't matter whether he insults us, tries to ingratiate himself, smiles, pretends to be friendly. Enemy remains enemy!"

Langer undertook the task of reinforcing resistance, presumably among East German soldiers, against the temptations of Western culture, including the siren songs of Western television. East Germany has found itself unable to keep the population from tuning in soap operas, situation comedies, and newscasts, just as Hungary cannot escape transmissions from Austria, or Soviet Estonia the broadcasts from Finland. Langer specifically warned against "enemy transmissions" and "all imaginable attempts at establishing 'contacts.' " He said that "class recognition" leads to the conclusion: "One draws a clear dividing line between one-self and the enemy. His word is not to be believed; the enemy who means well does not exist; whoever dines off the enemy will die of the enemy."

Of course, West Germans are free and able to tune in all East German transmissions, and the Finns even retransmit Soviet television. Austrians, if they wish, can listen to broadcasts from Hungary and Czechoslovakia. Only the Communist-governed states would like to shut out any and all outside images and information. Within the Soviet Union itself, even the facts of censorship are censored. The existence of Glavlit, the long-established central censorship bureau, is on the long list of don't-mentions that govern the country's media.

The psychohistorical origins of Russo-Soviet sensitivity toward intrusions, be they ideas or aircraft, are elusive. One political analyst, Nathan Leites, has spoken of elements of true paranoia and of "pseudo paranoia" in Soviet governmental behavior. *Pseudo paranoia,* in this context, means the conscious effort of pretending to be sensitive to words and events to a paranoid degree, to act as if Soviet society truly believed that it is encircled and threatened by Western "imperialism," although its opinion makers actually know better. The trouble with creating such a siege mentality is, however, that it eventually infects its very creators: The propagandists come to believe their own propaganda, and thus become the victims of a pseudo-paranoid Frankenstein monster of their own making.

It is here that the ultimate danger of Soviet propaganda may very well lie. Its mechanism is aimed at various societies, using a variety of methods. Playing on legitimate fears, natural resentments, or irrational emotions, Soviet propaganda is able to persuade and mobilize sentiments, from the Near East to Central America, perpetuating and sharpening anti-U.S. feelings, deepening the resentment of (have-not) nations of the "South" against the (have) nations of the "North," and putting itself in the pose of a champion of the underdog, the "oppressed" in search of endless "liberation." This campaign, which extends from Indian villages to the well-appointed offices of UNESCO's Paris headquarters, can be countered, at least to a degree. Within Eastern European nations, cultural and political traditions provide a counterpoint. In the Soviet Union itself, the contrast between daily realities and propagandistic images makes for instinctive doubts of agitatorial claims. But within the Soviet elite, the relatively insulated and prosperous governing majority, few antipropaganda safeguards exist.

In theory, the Kremlin's decision-making elite should be immune to the propaganda which it generates; it has, after all, access to intelligence, diplomatic information, and the confidential Tass material. In actuality, the self-interests of this elite make it vulnerable to the echoes of its own voice. To stay in power, with all the privileges this entails, the Kremlin elite must continually redirect public feelings, away from its own shortcomings, from the economic failures of centralized economics, from the pervasive daily restrictions on personal freedom.

I do not, of course, wish to exaggerate the Soviet public's desire for a pluralistic democracy. For one brief moment, after the czar's fall in 1917, Russia had the opportunity to move toward a truly parliamentary system of government. But war conditions, with their political-economic chaos, made the emergence of such a system extraordinarily difficult; and Lenin quickly crushed the tender growth. In our time, if the Soviet people—by some unimaginable miracle—had the opportunity to vote freely, during the first few months of Andropov's rule or the first year of Gorbachev's governing period, they would almost certainly have chosen Andropov and Gorbachev.

Even Stalin, as a symbol of firm rule, retained a high degree of mass popularity. Andropov was seen as replacing Brezhnev's all too tolerant, nepotistic administration with a welcome turn toward great discipline. Gorbachev's emphasis on tighter controls, denunciations of nepotism, and general firmness found a wide response for his image as a new strong young leader. The Agitprop machinery, tightly in place, proceeded to implement the policies of the Gorbachev regime. From Riga to Vladivostok, from Odessa to Murmansk, domestic propaganda reiterated the party program's "Main Guidelines for the USSR's Economic and Social Development for 1986–1990 and the Period through the Year 2000." Abroad, Soviet propaganda reaffirmed, reiterated, and restated traditional slogans and formulae. Western media, forever in search of novelty, found in Gorbachev—and in his wife, Raisa—a new and hopeful image. The Swiss weekly *Weltwoche* (September 26, 1985), which hailed Gorbachev's wife under the heading "After 70 Years of Babushka, at Last a First Lady," found her "charming, beautiful and intelligent." *Time*'s editor-in-chief, Henry Anatole Grunwald, told Gorbachev on the eve of the Geneva summit meeting that the Western media had "fallen in love" with his wife. To which Gorbachev replied, with much-appreciated debonairism, that he might have to reconsider taking her to Geneva with him.

The Soviet public relations campaign moved into high gear on September 30, 1985, when Gorbachev gave an interview to a group of French reporters. Against a background of gold lamé wallpaper, in one of the Kremlin's more opulent rooms, he made a statement that emphasized cordial Soviet-French relations and replied freely to questions. He interspersed his remarks with such references as, "Once Voltaire dreamt of the triumph of reason as an indispensable condition for normal human life." He said: "We would betray the memory of the fallen in that sacred struggle [against fascism] if we forgot how the French pilots of the Normandie-Niémen regiment heroically fought against the fascists in Soviet skies, and how the Soviet partisans fought in the ranks of the Maquisards on French soils." He answered questions, some of them pointed, smoothly and forcefully.

Then followed Gorbachev's visit to France, where he met with President François Mitterrand, again gave interviews freely, and addressed the French parliament, the Chamber of Deputies. His wife was, once more, a center of media attention. She visited Notre Dame Cathedral and the Louvre, walked on the Place de la Concorde, and passed the bookstalls along the Seine. In line with her own image as a well-dressed woman and in tribute to French eminence in fashions, she visited the salons of designers Pierre Cardin and Yves Saint Laurent. A writer in the Paris magazine *Match* concluded, "The image of the Soviet Union has changed, by virtue of a woman's face." Mrs. Gorbachev accompanied her husband to India in December 1986.

Under Gorbachev, the Soviet propaganda machine sought to change the image of the Soviet Union in many different ways, particularly in seeking to reassure the Western European countries of its own goodwill and of U.S. stubborn imperialist designs on world peace. As Gorbachev had done during his Paris visit, the U.S.S.R. generally struck a "We Europeans" pose in discussing U.S. policies. A cartoon in the British weekly *The Economist* showed Soviet Foreign Minister Eduard A. Shevardnadze facing a European audience while the accompanying article bore the headline "Aren't These Americans Silly!" The magazine observed that Shevardnadze himself conveyed the impression of being more Europe-oriented, more cosmopolitan—in the accepted sense of the word—than his predecessor, the dour, unsmiling Andrei A. Gromyko. (In Soviet ideological terminology, "cosmopolitan" came to suggest someone who was unpatriotic, alien, an enemy of the Stalin regime; the word never quite recovered a normal meaning in the Russian language.) A leading European analyst of Soviet affairs, Dr. Ernst Kux, noted in the Swiss daily *Neue Zürcher Zeitung* (August 8, 1986) that in appointing Shevardnadze, Gorbachev had decided to "send a more agreeable Georgian as Foreign Minister out into the world." Kux saw no essential difference between the new and old policies, although "known demands and proposals are, at most, being served up with more aplomb and greater media impact."

The Swiss observer recalled that, even before Chernenko's death, Gorbachev had presented a hard-line policy speech to a party ideology meeting in Moscow on December 10, 1984. He viewed capitalism as facing an economic, social, and political, as well as a spiritual and moral, decline. "Not we, but capitalism is forced to maneuver and to disguise itself," Gorbachev said, "and to resort to war, terror, falsification and subversion, in order to halt the inexorable train of events." Kux noted that *Pravda,* the next day, published only one-third of Gorbachev's speech, eliminating most of his significant comments on the world situation.

In the underpublicized version of this speech, Gorbachev also dealt with the challenge presented to the U.S.S.R. by Western psychological warfare. He defined it as "a special form of aggression," used by the "ideologists of capitalism" through enormous propaganda facilities and up-to-date technology. He said that behind the "mask of defenders of human rights," efforts were under way to infect the "socialist world" with "the habits of bourgeois society," to make it receptive to "petty bourgeois ideas and shallow temptations, individualism, philistine consumerism, as well as spiritual and cultural gluttony."

Gorbachev's speech, which seemed designed to establish him as a leading party figure in the field of ideology, demanded that the "front line of the ideological struggle" cannot be restricted to "political alertness and intolerance of foreign views" but called for "corrections of our own conceptions and practice." With this, Gorbachev outlined a blueprint of propagandistic principles which, when he came to power, were quickly translated into action. He demanded that "the offensive strength of our ideology" be exercised more rapidly, that counterpropaganda needed to be intensified, and that the propagation of our historic road" must never falter.

As the revitalized Soviet propaganda machine swung into action, Gorbachev relied on experienced communications professionals and expanded the functions of other specialists. Frequently by his side was a veteran of foreign affairs and propaganda campaigns, the self-effacing Andrei M. Aleksandrov. He had been observed whispering into the ears of Soviet leaders, from Brezhnev, through Andropov and Chernenko, to Gorbachev. As a specialist in U.S. affairs and advisers to Soviet leaders, Aleksandrov was regarded by some Sovietologists as outranking Arbatov, whose role appeared to be more that of propagandist than expert adviser. Christopher Walker, reporting to the *Times* (London) on November 19, 1985, noted that Aleksandrov accompanied Gorbachev to Geneva and had generally remained as a "member of the Old Guard on whose experience Mr. Gorbachev has chosen to lean, adding to the in-built resistance inside the Kremlin structure for any dramatic switches in the substance of the Soviet line, as opposed to its new, slicker, more open presentation."

While the unobtrusive Aleksandrov was quietly retired in 1986, the new propaganda offensive began with the prominence of Vladimir B. Lomeiko, then director of the Foreign Ministry's Press Section. In contrast to his counterparts in the U.S. State Department in Washington, Lomeiko not only conducted frequent press briefings in the Little Hall or Large Hall of the ministry's press center but also gave interviews to reporters from papers as diverse as Bulgaria's *Zemedelsko Zname* and Kuwait's *Al-Anba*.

Lomeiko's briefings (for which the English word has been co-opted into Russian) began in June 1984 and reached their crescendo at the time of the Geneva summit, November 1985. *New York Times* correspondent Seth Mydans commented (October 1, 1984) that Lomeiko's unprecedented role as Foreign Ministry spokesman had "not been instituted to increase the flow of information," but "to make the Soviet propaganda apparatus competitive with those in the West and to give their policy pronouncements a human face." The face was that of a studious-looking, balding, bespectacled man in his late forties, quietly dressed, careful in his choice of words but capable of conversing in Russian, English, German, and Norwegian. As a former journalist, Lomeiko was familiar with the practices and technical needs of his interlocutors. As he grew into his job, he became more ready to answer questions on a variety of topics but was always careful not to exceed the established framework of Soviet policies.

Like Arbatov, Posner, and other propagandistic practitioners, Lomeiko provided yet another channel for the conveyance of Soviet views. He said, at the start, that "briefing" was "a new word here" and admitted that Western press conferences had provided a model for his role. "Each country has its special approach," he said, "and we study these examples to be up to date with the most interesting forms of work. There are people in the Foreign Ministry with experience in different countries, and we meet and exchange ideas about these." The briefings were expanded, on occasion, to bring in other spokesmen, particularly deputy foreign ministers who were regional specialists.

Lomeiko's briefings settled down to at least one Foreign Ministry press conference per month, but his schedule grew more crowded with the Geneva summit meeting in 1985. On the whole, Lomeiko managed to conduct the briefings in a low-keyed manner. Among exceptions was a press conference on July 19, devoted to human rights, with Vsevolod N. Sofinski, chief Soviet delegate to an earlier conference in Ottawa. Under questioning from reporters, Sofinski and Lomeiko sought to establish the Soviet positions that unemployment, homelessness, and racial discrimination represented human rights violations in the West. Mydans, reporting the briefing in the *New York Times* (July 20), wrote, "The session was marked by an unusual degree of emotion, as Mr. Lomeiko raised his voice to argue, for example, that Soviet citizens are limited in their travel overseas as a result of the nation's continuing suffering from World War II." Lomeiko also said:

"These gentlemen in Western countries who are prepared in any convenient situation to hold forth on so-called human rights violations in socialist countries are very often modern slave traders. They take part in big-capital networks of houses of prostitution, where on their free time from the business of speaking out against socialist countries, they go to amuse themselves on the weekend."

Lomeiko's odd generalizations pointed to the dangers inherent in the "echo effect," as propagandists and policymakers begin accepting the selected, isolated items as representative of an overall picture, distorting their own image of the societies they seek to influence. Lomeiko, continuing his criticism of "these gentlemen," added: "They travel to debauch young girls of developing countries, and after that put on their fancy suits and make speeches and try to teach other countries to live by their standards. That is Phariseeism, hypocrisy and unparalleled demagoguery." Mydans wrote that it "was not clear whether Mr. Lomeiko had in mind any specific instances" of what he called "the buying of little girls," although he referred to the nightclubs of pre-Castro Cuba when he said the island came to be known as "the whorehouse of America." In a more relaxed manner, Lomeiko accompanied Foreign Minister Shevardnadze to the United States, late in the month, conducting press conferences in New York and Washington, while familiarizing himself with the setting and procedures at the United Nations.

All told, the press briefings provided an additional forum for the reiteration of Soviet policies and propaganda themes. The utilization of specialists, in such areas as international law and Asian affairs, furnished the Foreign Ministry with a means of offering details in support of its positions. The briefings also illustrated cooperation between the Central Committee and the Ministry of Foreign Affairs. Lomeiko personally, except for small outbursts of impatience, established himself as a skilled and well-informed professional among the community of Moscow correspondents. Yet he was perhaps too highly strung, and therefore was replaced in June 1986 by Gennadi Gerasimov, who was named director of the Foreign Ministry's Information Department.

The use of novel terms, such as "new globalism," as epithets with either strong negative or positive connotations, illustrates the evolution of the Soviet Communist vocabulary. Just as "cosmopolitanism" was given an accusatory, traitorous meaning, the terms "internationalism" or "proletarian internationalism" were reinforced as supportive of Soviet aims. While "peace" or "peace and disarmament" were used increasingly as auxiliary terms for Soviet policies, words such as the ever-present "imperialist" and the somewhat rarer "neocolonialist" were used to label the United States, its NATO allies, and Japan.

The former U.S. ambassador to the United Nations, Dr. Jeane Kirkpatrick, in her article "The Subversive Denigration of Western Values and Beliefs," published in *Imprimis* (Autumn 1985), commented that "the Soviets have made extraordinarily great progress" in "projecting their own semantic rules upon the rest of the world." She specifically noted the distortion of the term "human rights." Kirkpatrick wrote that this concept is "enshrined as the purpose of the United Nations Charter and at the heart of the American and the Western democratic traditions" but has been "redefined in contemporary international discourse and utilized by the great human rights organizations in their new definitions." According to these definitions, she wrote, "human rights violations are failures of governments, *vis-à-vis* their citizens. Terrorist groups do not violate human rights in the current vernacular; only governments violate human rights. The government of El Salvador is continually attacked for gross violations of human rights in responding to terrorist assault." Kirkpatrick added:

"Guerrillas are not attacked for violations of human rights, although they may massacre half of the inhabitants of a hamlet, dragging them from their beds in the middle of the night. That is not a violation of human rights, by definition. That is a protest by a national liberation movement. The guerrillas, by definition, are a national liberation movement. National liberation movements do not violate human rights. They have their human rights violated. National liberation movements assault societies, and when governments respond, they (the governments) are criticized vigorously as repressive and unethical."

Just as, at a Moscow press briefing, the concept of a "new globalism" is introduced, succeeding such earlier epithets as "hegemonism" in the Communist vocabulary of denunciation, Kirkpatrick noted, "Conceptions of reality are continually manipulated as part of the process of redefinition." She observed that, along with this kind of redefinition, falsification, and utopianism (setting unreachable standards for Western democracies) goes "a simply colossal historical denial," notably of the Soviet Union's own history and practices. These, she explained, included not only the Ukrainian famine and the Katyn forest massacre but "current shipments of arms from Nicaragua to El Salvador," treated as "a nonevent" as well.

Harold Lasswell, in *World Politics and Personal Insecurity,* made this observation: "Revolutionary propaganda selects symbols which are calculated to detach the affection of the masses from the existing symbols of authority and to attach their affections to challenging symbols and to direct hostilities toward existing symbols of authority." A related analysis, presented by Stefan T. Possony to the House Committee on Un-American Activities (March 2, 1959), was published under the title *Language as a Communist Weapon.* Possony noted that the evolution of Communist terminology became particularly noticeable after the Seventh Comintern Congress in 1935. As a result, "revolution" became "liberation" and even the word "communism" was successively replaced by "anti-fascism" and "anti-imperialism." He explained that "class warfare," or the "class struggle," was seen as a continuous process and added: "Propaganda does not stop. Political warfare does not stop. Infiltration does not stop. The class war, the class struggle, or as it is styled in modern Communist semantics, the struggle between the peace-loving and the imperialist, war-mongering forces never stops." Possony defined the following six roots of Communist semantics:

"1. Every problem, however unprecedented it may be, must be handled in original or purified Marxist-Leninist terminology.

"2. Every change in doctrine or 'line' must be dressed up as a 'restatement' and its 'deviationist' character must be concealed.

"3.   Every Communist communication must convey an orthodox, that is, a revolutionarily activating message to the party and its followers.

"4.   This same communication must convey a different, i.e., soothing, pacifying and paralyzing message to the opponent of communism.

"5.   Every communication has a specific meaning within the context of the incessant intraparty struggle.

"6.   Every communication must be proof against counterpropaganda by all external and internal opponents of communism."

Possony added that "Communist semantics are more than a tool of deception and concealment," serving also as "a tool of legitimacy—the Soviet regime can assert its legitimacy only within the framework of its sacred ideology." In the light of Possony's analysis, the program presented to the 27th Congress of the Soviet Communist Party was, indeed, a restatement of earlier concepts; technically, it was merely a new edition of the party's Third Program, adopted in 1961 and reflecting some of the style and ambitions expressed by Nikita Khrushchev. The First Program was adopted by the Bolshevik Party in 1903, the Second Program followed the Bolshevik Revolution, in 1919. In presenting their redraft of the Third Program, the authors had "rethought those formulations that had not stood the test of time."

While the 1961 program had announced that the U.S.S.R. would succeed "in the main" in building a "communist society," by 1980, the new draft only stated: "The advance of humanity towards socialism and communism, though uneven, complex and controversial, is inexorable." The Khrushchev version had promised that "the entire population will be able adequately to satisfy its need in high quality and varied foodstuffs" and that life expectancy would increase (neither has occurred); the new draft cautioned that the Soviet Communist Party "does not set itself the aim of foreseeing in detail the features of full communism."

In addition to the party program, the congress received a "Comprehensive Program for the Development of Consumer Goods, 1986–2000" and "Economic and Social Guidelines" for the same period. Content analysis of the party program indicated that the Gorbachev group indirectly criticized its predecessor regimes in terms of the Kremlin's evolving semantic code. The program called for the removal of "the consequences of the personality cult," a reference to Stalin's ever-present image, and of "deviations from the Leninist norms of party and state guidance," a reference to Stalinist and secret police purges in party and government. It also took a swipe at Khrushchev's personal style, pledging to "rectify errors of a subjectivist, voluntaristic nature." Referring to the Brezhnev era, its

nepotism and corruption, the program stated: "The party takes into account the fact that, in the 1970s and the early 1980s, there were certain
unfavorable trends and difficulties."

The program retained traditional terminology when it noted that the
world of capitalism "is yet strong and dangerous, but has already passed
its peak." The program also noted: "In conditions of world socialism's
growing influence, the class struggle of working people at times compels
the capitalists to make partial concessions, to grant certain improvements
in conditions of labor and its remuneration, and social security. This is
being done to preserve the main thing—the domination of capital."

These key Communist Party documents provide a blueprint of Soviet
propaganda campaigns, up to the year 2000. Soviet party congresses in-
corporate the machinery and aims of the defunct Communist International.
The old Comintern's files and functions were clearly transferred to the
Central Committee's International Department. Its aging, longtime director, Boris Ponomarev, continued to maintain direct contacts with Communist parties and "liberation movements" abroad. While Ponomarev
traveled frequently and spoke with key individuals in movements abroad,
much of the ideological guidance emanating from the International Department came from Vadim A. Zagladin, its first deputy director. Early
in 1987, Ponomarev was replaced by Anatoli Dobrynin, the long-time
Soviet ambassador to Washington. Dobrynin soon became extraordinarily
active and influential.

Zagladin contributed a long historical article, "Time, Events, Assessment," to *Problems of Peace and Socialism* (September 1984), the central
theoretical organ of world communism. Geared to the 120th anniversary
of the First International, the International Workingmen's Association,
Zagladin's article featured an array of Marx, Engels, and Lenin quotations.
It concluded, however, with a very contemporary call to pacifists and other
evenhanded peace movement participants, designed to enlist them on the
side of the U.S.S.R. and against "imperialism." Zagladin wrote: "It is
known that many of those people who actively oppose war are far from
being consistent on imperialism, while a not inconsiderable proportion of
them even represent the interests of certain imperialist circles which are
not inclined to adventurings." He called for a basis "upon which all other
members of the anti-imperialist, anti-war struggle actually do unite (irrespective of whether or not they are aware of this)." What is needed, he
wrote, "is a new internationalism which embraces all fighters for peace
and against imperialism."

Early in 1986, Zagladin published an article linking the new Soviet
Communist Party program to action abroad. As published in the Slovak-
language *Pravda,* issued in Bratislava, Czechoslovakia (January 16), his
article was titled "A High International Mission: The New Edition of the

CPSU Program on the World Communist Movement." He noted that the Soviet party had "always considered itself one of the detachments of the world revolutionary workers movement" and would continue to do so. Far from being in decline, he wrote, the worldwide Communist movement was "operating in almost 100 countries in the world" and had "about ninety million people in its ranks," or twice as many members as 25 years earlier. He emphasized that allegiance to Soviet interest, "the principle of proletarian internationalism," remains "of extraordinary significance, as one of the main principles of Marxism-Leninism."

While in some countries, such as the United States, the Communist Party, as such, has lost influence, it has occasionally achieved electoral successes that placed it into coalitions with Socialist parties, such as in France and Greece. In Italy, Spain, and Portugal, the party's strength has fluctuated, but its role as a pro-Soviet pressure group remained potent. In West Germany, left-wing socialists and the Green Party have shown themselves vulnerable to Soviet propaganda, and similar trends could be observed in the Netherlands and in the Scandinavian countries. In Finland, an internal split has weakened the local Communist Party, much to the displeasure of its Soviet mentors.

The strongest Communist parties, therefore, are those in countries under Communist rule, in Eastern Europe or in countries such as Cuba and Ethiopia. As propaganda channels in non-Communist countries, the parties occupy a relatively minor role. They do, of course, furnish the hardcore operatives of front organizations, whether rallies or peace marches are to be organized, resolutions drafted, or conferences held.

For the most part, the Soviet propaganda machine seeks to utilize (1) the mass media, appealing directly to readers, listeners, and viewers, and (2) special target audiences ranging from academic and scientific specialists to professionals, writers, artists, and international civil servants. For each of these audiences and segments of the public there are special tactics, channels, and terminologies.

In the reorganization of the Soviet propaganda apparatus that followed Gorbachev's emergence in top leadership, Yegor K. Ligachev surfaced as the likely number two man in the Politburo. Ligachev came to hold a key position as secretary of the CPSU Central Committee, apparently in charge of overall ideological guidance, second only to Gorbachev himself, as well as chairman of the Foreign Affairs Commission of the Soviet of the Union and the Soviet of Nationalities of the U.S.S.R. Supreme Soviet. In a role that seemed to categorize him as Gorbachev's understudy, Ligachev traveled to industrial centers, exhorting workers to stricter work habits and greater discipline.

In contrast to Gorbachev's seeming efforts to create an image of modernity and moderation, at least abroad, Ligachev spoke in unrelentingly tough terms. He upbraided propagandists as much as Baku oil field workers, writers as harshly as bureaucrats, television and broadcasting executives as firmly as party officials. Among the strongmen in the Politburo, side by side with Geidar A. Aliyev, Ligachev emerged as one of the Kremlin's leading movers and shakers. People like Gerasimov and Arbatov had the function of implementing policies; Ligachev was in a position to develop and establish such policies, including those governing propaganda tactics. Born on November 29, 1920, he began his studies in aircraft construction and graduated as a technical engineer. He worked as an engineer in Novosibirsk during World War II, and as a party worker he became director of the Novosibirsk Culture Department. After other party activities, Ligachev served as deputy chief in the Agitprop Department of the Russian Bureau within the Central Committee from 1961 to 1965. From that time on and until he came to Moscow in 1983, Ligachev was first secretary in Tomsk, as well as a member of the Military Council of the Siberian Military District.

Ligachev's strongest role was in the field of transportation and communication, areas of weaknesses the Gorbachev team has sought to correct. In 1983, Ligachev was made director of the Department for Party Organizational Work in the Central Committee and, later that year, was made Central Committee secretary in charge of cadres, which gave him authority in personnel placement. Together with Gorbachev, he supervised election campaigns to local party committees and the Supreme Soviet in 1983 and 1984. Meanwhile, he emerged as the Kremlin's top ideo-propagandist.

In November 1985, Ligachev addressed the staff of the State Committee for Television and Radio Broadcasting. As quoted in *Pravda* (November 21), he told his audience that it was their "honorable and responsible mission to propagandize the great tasks set by the party and socialism's achievements and advantages, and to recreate, from program to program, the image of the modern Soviet person, the active builder of communism." He told them that in the field of foreign policy, propaganda "should vividly and convincingly display socialism's advantages and true values, and reveal the exploitative essence of capitalism, with its unemployment and inflation, with its large illiterate and homeless population, and with its preaching of racism and chauvinism."

There was, clearly, going to be no respite for the class warriors of propaganda and agitation.

APPENDICES

APPENDIX · A

Forty-Four Slogans

Continuous campaigns of agitation and propaganda in the U.S.S.R. call for the repetition and implementation of a series of slogans. Each year, on the anniversary of the October Revolution, these slogans are publicized anew, updated, and revised. On the occasion of the revolution's sixty-eighth anniversary in 1985, 44 such slogans were announced by the Central Committee of the Communist Party of the Soviet Union. Some of the slogans were purely ritualistic, others were traditional, and still others showed emphasis on policies that were either newly emphasized or freshly introduced.

Certain slogans were addressed to specific segments of the population. Some called for propagandistic efforts, such as "Communist ideological commitment"; others implemented contemporary efforts, calling for thrift, improved food and consumer goods production, high-quality output, and the strengthening of discipline and order. On the international scene, slogans denounced "the imperialist policy of aggression and violence" and cited specific world-policy goals. Thus, in the simplest of terms, goals and tactics were publicized, to be reiterated in diplomacy and propaganda on all levels of Soviet society, at home and abroad. As published in Pravda *(October 13, 1985), these are the slogans:*

1. Long live the 68th anniversary of the Great October Socialist Revolution!
2. Glory to Great October, which opened a new epoch in the history of mankind—the epoch of the transition from capitalism to socialism and communism!
3. Long live Marxism-Leninism—the eternally living revolutionary international teaching!

4. Long live the Communist Party of the Soviet Union—the leading and directing force of Soviet society!

5. Glory to the great Soviet people, the builders of Communism and staunch and consistent fighters for peace!

6. Long live the unbreakable alliance of the working class, the kolkhoz peasantry, and the people's intelligentsia!

7. Long live the indissoluble international unity and fraternal friendship of the peoples of the USSR!

8. Glory to Leninist Bolsheviks, veterans of the party, Heroes of October, all fighters for victory of socialism!

9. May the unparalleled feat of the Soviet people, who won the victory in the Great Patriotic War, live on through the ages! Eternal glory to the heroes who fell in the fighting for our motherland's freedom and independence!

10. Working people of the Soviet Union! Let us greet the 27th CPSU Congress with new labor achievements and with high achievements in nationwide socialist competition! Let us work in a shock, Stakhanovite fashion!

11. Working people of the Soviet Union! Let us fulfill the 1985 plan and successfully complete the 11th 5-Year Plan!

12. Communists! Be in the vanguard of the nationwide movement to accelerate the country's socioeconomic development!

13. Workers and kolkhoz members, specialists in the national economy! Persistently introduce into production advanced experience and the achievements of science and technology! Seek the intensification of the economy in every possible way and enhance labor productivity!

14. Engineers and technicians, inventors and rationalizers! Augment your contribution to accelerating scientific and technical progress!

15. Soviet scientists! You are in the front line of the struggle to accelerate scientific and technical progress! The country awaits highly effective new scientific and technical developments from you!

16. Machine builders! You have the decisive say in the retooling of the national economy! More rapidly create highly productive machines and equipment!

17. Working people in the fuel and energy complex! Increase extraction of oil, gas, and coal and production of electricity and heat! Struggle actively to fulfill the energy program!

18. Construction and installation workers! Increase the effectiveness of construction! Build economically and to a high standard, on the basis of modern technology! Hand over projects for commissioning with high quality and on time!

19. Working people in transport and communications! Strive for uninterrupted shipments of freight and a high standard of service to the population!

20. Working people in the countryside and in the entire agro-industrial complex! Persistently fulfill the food program and increase production of crop farming and livestock products!

21. Working people in all sectors of the national economy! Participate actively in implementing the comprehensive program for developing the production of consumer goods and the services sphere!

22. Working people of the Soviet Union! Strengthen discipline and order and enhance organization in production!

23. Citizens of the Land of the Soviets! The policy of thrift is a law of socialist economic management! Be economical and thrifty!

24. Working people in all sectors of the national economy! Produce high-quality output and struggle for the honor of the Soviet trademark!

25. Citizens of the Soviet Union! Struggle actively to affirm a socialist way of life and communist morality!

26. People's deputies! Persistently resolve questions of state, economic, and sociocultural building and seek to implement the voters' instructions! Long live the Soviets of people's deputies—truly democratic organs of power!

27. Soviet trade unions! Develop the labor activeness, initiative, and technical creativity of the masses and seek the further improvement of their working, daily living, and leisure conditions! Long live the Soviet trade unions—the school of administration, the school of economic management, the school of Communism!

28. Komsomol members and young people! Tirelessly master knowledge, culture, and professional skill! Multiply the revolutionary, combat and labor traditions of the party and the people! Long live the Leninist Komsomol—the militant assistant and reliable reserve of the Communist Party!

29. Women of the Land of the Soviets! Participate actively in production and social life! Glory to mothers! Peace and happiness to the children of the whole world!

30. Glorious veterans! Pass on your knowledge and rich life experience to the younger generation! Educate young men and women as ardent patriots of our motherland and selfless fighters for the cause of Lenin and for Communism!

31. Working people in public education! Improve the teaching and the communist education of the rising generation! Persistently implement the reform of general and vocational education!

32. Literary figures, artists, and working people in culture! Bear aloft the banner of communist ideological commitment, party-mindedness, and popular spirit! Create works which affirm the truth of life and the lofty communist ideals!

33. Soviet servicemen! Guard vigilantly and reliably the peaceful labor of our people and the historic gains of socialism! Glory to the valiant Armed Forces of the USSR!

34. Long live the Leninist foreign policy of the Soviet Union—a policy of consolidating peace and the security of the peoples and of broad international cooperation!

35. Fraternal greetings to Communist and workers' parties! May the unity and cohesion of the Communists of the whole world grow stronger!

36. Proletarians of all countries, unite! Long live proletarian, socialist internationalism!

37. Fraternal greetings to the peoples of the socialist countries! Long live the unity, cooperation, and cohesion of the countries of the socialist community and their unshakable resolve to strengthen and defend the gains of socialism and peace on earth!

38. May the alliance of world socialism, the international proletariat, and the national liberation movement grow stronger!

39. Peoples of the world! Struggle resolutely against the imperialist policy of aggression and violence! Demand an end to the aggressive actions of the United States against Nicaragua! Strive for the withdrawal of Israeli troops from all the seized Arab lands and for an end to the imperialist interference in the affairs of the Arab countries! Demand an end to aggressive actions with respect to independent African states and the elimination of the shameful system of apartheid in South Africa! Freedom to the people of Namibia!

40. Peoples of all countries! Intensify the struggle to remove the threat of nuclear war, to prevent an arms race in space, and to end it on earth! Seek the total elimination of nuclear weapons!

41. Peoples of Europe! Struggle for lasting peace and cooperation in Europe and for the return of détente! Seek the elimination of chemical weapons on the continent!

42. The safeguarding of peace and security in Asia is a matter for all Asian peoples! Through joint efforts let us turn Asia and the Pacific region into a zone of peace, good-neighborliness, and cooperation!

43. Long live the Union of Soviet Socialist Republics—the motherland of Great October!

44. Under the banner of Lenin and under the leadership of the Communist Party, forward to new victories in communist creation!

APPENDIX · B

Propaganda Tasks

A detailed outline of Soviet propaganda aims and tactics was presented by the Central Committee of the Communist Party of the Soviet Union in 1979, when it adopted the resolution "On the Further Improvement of Ideological and Political Education Work." After noting that "rich experience of propaganda and agitation work has been accumulated," the resolution found that the Soviet Union enjoyed "a powerful information and propaganda apparatus, provided with modern equipment, including a highly developed press, television and radio." The resolution referred to the "clear political line" that had been defined by the party's 25th Congress, but cautioned that there were "still many weaknesses and shortcomings, and very substantial ones at that, in the organization of information and ideological education."

In a lengthy commentary on the party resolution, Pravda *(May 6, 1979) noted that the Communist Party "cannot tolerate the fact that educational work is frequently relaxed" and presented the following "urgent tasks" to the public:*

Constant concern for steadily enhancing the awareness and activeness of the people's masses, V.I. Lenin taught, remains as always the basis and the important content of party work. The improvement of ideological education work is a paramount task for all party organizations. Every communist, wherever he works, must act as the propagandist and purveyor of the ideas of Lenin's party. He must give all his knowledge and spiritual strength to this exceptionally important matter.

It is essential to focus the attention of the party organizations and ideological institutions and of the propaganda cadres and *aktivs* on the following urgent tasks of political education work:

Insuring a High Scientific Standard in Propaganda and Agitation. Showing clearly the greatness of communist ideals, the all-conquering force of Marxism-Leninism, the CPSU's fruitful, tireless activity in consolidating the might of the Soviet motherland and improving the people's well-being, and socialism's historical advantages and its true democracy and humanism. Revealing convincingly, on the basis of specific facts, the essence of the Soviet way of life, the achievements of the developed socialist society, and the paths of its gradual development into a communist society. In theoretical and all ideological activity it is essential to consider the features of social development linked with the influence of the scientific and technical revolution. To explain what is being done and what has to be done for the successful solution of the next tasks of socioeconomic and cultural building and for the further development of Soviet democracy and the consolidation of socialist statehood. Forming in all Soviet people a sense of pride in the socialist fatherland, indestructible fraternal friendship of the USSR's peoples, respect for national culture, and implacability toward any manifestation of nationalism. Promoting the further consolidation of the unity and cohesion of the great Soviet people;

Intensifying the Efficiency and Specificity of Propaganda and Agitation and Its Link with Life and the Solution of Economic and Political Tasks. Explaining the CPSU's socioeconomic policy aimed at improving the people's material well-being and culture and developing by every means socialist competition and the movement for a communist attitude to labor. Actively promoting the successful solution of the historical tasks of uniting the advantages of socialism with the achievements of the scientific and technical revolution, and generalizing and widely publicizing advanced experience and the successes of Soviet science and technology. Struggling persistently for the consolidation of labor and state discipline, the enhancement of responsibility for the matter in hand, and the saving and careful handling of socialist property and against extravagance, departmentalism and localistic tendencies. The Soviet person must be clearly aware of the social significance of his personal participation in the fulfillment of national economic plans and the acceleration of scientific and technical progress as a decisive condition for the further consolidation of the might of the motherland and the victory of communism;

Developing the Offensive Nature of Propaganda and Agitation. Supporting by every means everything new, progressive and promising and struggling resolutely against that which hinders our advance. Proceeding from the premise that the innovators' record indicators are not an end in themselves but a very important means of mobilizing the masses' labor energy toward raising labor productivity and a powerful reserve for improving production efficiency and work quality. Enterprising, creative participation in labor and social life is an indicator of a person's ideological and civic maturity.

Consolidating the positions of world socialism and all progressive forces creates favorable conditions for communist building and for the development of an ideological offensive against imperialism and hegemonism, militarism and reaction. It is necessary to continue to tirelessly publicize the CPSU's Leninist foreign policy course and the successes of real socialism, to strengthen solidarity with the peoples of the socialist community countries and the international working class and national liberation movement, and to expand and intensify ideological cooperation with the fraternal parties. One of the constant tasks of the Soviet mass information media is to elucidate regularly the life of the socialist countries in all their diversity, drawing special attention to the specific positive experience of the fraternal parties' solution of topical social problems, political, ideological and economic cooperation between the fraternal states, and the equal and mutually advantageous nature of their relations. Regularly elucidating the selfless struggle of the fraternal communist and workers parties against imperialism and the danger of a new war and for the ideals of communism and the fundamental interests of the working class and all working people and for social progress.

It is essential to expose most resolutely the imperialist preachers of cold war and the aggravation of international tension and the arms race which threatens to place the world on the brink of nuclear disaster. Revealing the antipopular, inhuman essence of present-day capitalism, the predatory nature of the neocolonialism policy and the true complexion of the hypocritical defenders of "rights" and "freedoms." Exposing the hegemonist, great-power course of the Beijing rulers and their aggressive aspirations and closing of ranks with the forces of imperialism, reaction and war. Dealing a fitting rebuff in good time to acts of ideological subversion by imperialism and its henchmen. Waging a consistent struggle against any forms of opportunism and revisionism.

Our duty is to pit unshakable cohesion, the powerful ideological unity of our ranks and the deep conviction and political vigilance of every Soviet person and his readiness to defend the motherland and the revolutionary gains of socialism against the subversive political and ideological activity of the class enemy and his malicious slandering of socialism.

The core of ideological and political education work has been and remains the formation in Soviet people of a scientific world outlook, selfless devotion to the cause of the party and communist ideals, love for the socialist fatherland, and proletarian internationalism. In the system of party study, economic education, Komsomol political enlightenment and mass forms of propaganda, it is necessary to insure in-depth study of the works

of K. Marx, F. Engels and V.I. Lenin, the history of the CPSU, the
documents of the 23d, 24th and 25th party congresses, and the works of
Comrade L.I. Brezhnev and other party leaders, stressing here the CPSU's
loyalty to the principles of Marxism-Leninism, the party's tireless collective
activity on the creative development of the theory and practice of scientific
communism. Knowledge of revolutionary theory and the party's policy
must be transformed in Soviet people into conviction and into the active
life stance of the staunch fighter for communism and against any manifestations of alien ideology, into a guide to action for the solution of the
urgent problems of developed socialism.

The success of political and economic training depends wholly on the
theoretical and methodological standard of the propaganda worker cadres.
It is the duty of all party committees to select, teach and educate propaganda workers skillfully and to surround them with daily concern and
attention. A sense of high responsibility for the content and results of
educational work and the creative quest for new forms and methods of
work with people must be inherent in propaganda and ideological workers.

The resolution provides for a number of measures to improve the system
of the communists' Marxist-Leninist study and the improvement of the
propaganda cadres' theoretical and methodological standards.

APPENDIX · C

Top Priority

In summer 1985, Radio Moscow's English-language service began a program, seemingly modeled after popular U.S. talk shows, with the title Top Priority. *The program, which soon became a weekly feature, was moderated by Vladimir Posner, who frequently appears on U.S. television and radio shows. His regular guests are two high-level staff members of the United States of America and Canada Institute, the Soviet Union's prime think tank on North American affairs. The two participants, Dr. Radomir Bogdanov and Dr. Serge Plekhanov, are deputies to the institute's well-known director, Dr. Georgi Arbatov.*

Following are excerpts from a program broadcast on July 27, 1986, shortly after Posner had returned from a visit to the United States. The exchange is indicative of the careful scrutiny to which U.S. events and trends are subjected by some Soviet observers and of the manner in which their analyses reflect the official viewpoint.

Posner: Not long ago, on June 22, a month ago now, I was in Leningrad to host my end of a space bridge with Phil Donahue. It was called Citizens Summit II and it involved 200 women in Leningrad and 200 women in Boston. And during the exchange, at one point, we got to the issue of SALT II and the fact that the U.S. Administration wanted to break out of it, and we also spoke about the nuclear test ban and the Soviet moratorium, unilateral moratorium, and I asked my audience if they would kindly raise their hands if they were against all testing, all production of nuclear weapons and for disarmament. And my entire audience voted yes, that they were against that, and they didn't want testing and they did want disarmament. And they then asked me to ask Phil Donahue to do the same thing with his audience, and he did it. And the entire Boston audience was in total solidarity with the Leningrad audience.

Now, to me the Leningrad audience reflected the mood, the desire of the Soviet nation; and I do not know whether the Boston audience has unanimously reflected the mood of the American nation, but I think it's fair to say that it certainly reflected the majority opinion, that most Americans would like to see a test ban, most Americans would like to see a stop in the arms race and would like to see disarmament. The reason I bring this up is because of a series of articles that have appeared recently in different American newspapers, in particular the *New York Times,* which reflect what they seem to call the differences of opinions in the U.S. Administration on this issue: that, for instance, we have Mr. [Caspar] Weinberger who takes pride, at least he says that, in not even looking at Soviet proposals, repudiating them without even reading them, and other people seem to be somewhat more compromising and who would like, perhaps, to get some kind of agreement with the Soviet Union. And all of this is seen, at least by some in the United States, as a reflection of American democracy; that is, that there are different opinions and that there is discussion and debate. Now I would like to have this discussion with you on this issue of if it's indeed democratic and what is democracy in this case and what about majority opinion? Dr. Bogdanov would you care to begin?

Bogdanov: Let me tell you one thing. I would like to remind to our American listeners the famous Secretary of State [Henry] Kissinger memoirs and some very interesting, you know, instances of American democracy in that sense, how it was used, deliberately used by American politicians. You know, they were always creating an impression that there are bad guys and good guys in the American democracy.

Bad guys, just like Secretary Weinberger, they won't even look at the Soviet proposals and there are good guys like, for instance, Secretary Shultz or somebody else, they are for trying to find a compromise, you know. And for instance, while in Moscow Kissinger was always telling our people, please hurry up with the conclusion of this treaty or agreement until [Helmut] Sonnenfeldt comes from Helsinki, because he's a bad guy, you know, if he comes he will spoil everything. Let's hurry up. And I should tell that for some time our people were hooked on that and they really hurry up until Sonnenfeldt comes to Moscow.

Then they came to realize it was just a trick, you know, just a kind of pressure, very sophisticated pressure on us, just to get more concessions from us, just trying to frighten us by Sonnenfeldt. And, I'm sorry, but I came to know that only many, many years after that one of the participants in that play told me that story, you know. So, Vladimir, I'm sorry I don't know how you or my friend Serge, I don't believe in that fairy tale any longer, it's a fairy tale for me: Good guys, bad guys in the American administration. But at the same time, of course, I recognize that they may have different opinions.

Posner: You seem to have touched on an interesting idea and I'd like to explore this with you, Dr. Plekhanov. Do you think that the differences that are being aired, that I would almost say are being publicized in the United States, the differences on the issue of a test ban, of an agreement in the area of SALT II, the differences which supposedly exist between Mr. Weinberger, on one hand, and his kind of people and, let us say, Mr. Shultz on the other hand. Do you think that these are real differences? Or would you say that this is also a bit of a play? What is your feeling as an expert on that American scene?

Plekhanov: I think it's both. I think there's a lot of play in it, and they really make political capital of it, but I think that the differences are real. The question is whether they are significant. Because, you know, people can fight over bureaucratic terms, having almost the same views, but just can't really agree about sharing the—their authority in the matters of national security. Or, sometimes, if a policy is wrongheaded, there are and will be differences over minuscule detail, strong fights because there is that feeling that, you know, we are going in the wrong direction. So, therefore, there's both the element of playing and the element of reality in it. But I would like to continue on another theme: Nuclear weapons and democracy. I think the existence of governments who, by pushing a button can put an end to the whole planet as a living thing, is a challenge to any kind of democracy.

Bogdanov: Maybe it's a denial of democracy.

Plekhanov: It's an ultimate denial of democracy. . . .

Posner: If you look at this diverse opinion existing in the U.S. Administration today, which in my opinion is being played up, it's very, very visible, it's there for all to see. Do you think there's a possibility that it could be used for two purposes? One purpose would be for its own people. That is to say, show the people that there is debate going on and that, therefore, their aspiration, their desire for a test ban, for disarmament is not hopeless. . . .

Plekhanov: It's being taken care of.

Posner: Because there is debate.

Plekhanov: Yeah, there is.

Posner: That's on the one hand. On the other hand, it might, like, be a signal for the Soviet Union to say also: Oh well, they're debating it, so perhaps we should hold off for another period, because there is hope that they will come to a positive decision. Do you think that kind of situation could be used?

Bogdanov: That's really excellent assessment of the situation you have given to us, Vladimir, and I wouldn't like to flatter you. I really believe in it. You know America, we call sometimes American political system an establishment and that's exactly what the establishment is doing. What is the American establishment? It's different branches of power. One of them is mass media. Mass media is taking very active part in all these games, in all these plays, you know. They are interconnected you know. I don't insist that all that is done deliberately, there is a grand conspiracy or something like that. No, I don't say that. I say that's what, how the establishment works. It works in different directions, to give food for its own people, to give something, you know, to the outside world and to get satisfied themselves; how great democrats they are, how discussions are great within this great American establishment. But if you come down to the essence of the problem, you will see that discussions are discussions, but the policy is the policy. It's a very different thing. When the administration says that no stopping of testing is in the interest of American national security whatever Congress says, whatever petitions, whatever demonstrations resolutions you have, that's the policy which is the real one.

Posner: Right, yes. Please, Dr. Plekhanov.

Plekhanov: I would like to get back to this question of democracy and nuclear weapons. I recently read a story in the *International Herald Tribune* about a project underway in Arizona to build a huge bunker which would allow people to survive nuclear war and to live in total isolation from the outside world for years, maybe decades. . . . The idea is to prepare the best, the cream of the crop in America for the eventuality of a nuclear war. . . .

Posner: I wanted to get back to another thing, here, we were talking about. As you remember, a group of—an international group of scientists was recently in the Soviet Union and among them American scientists who went down to—close to Semipalatinsk, which is where the Soviet nuclear tests are conducted, to install seismographic equipment to monitor on—you know, and all of that, we talked about this. But these scientists later met with General Secretary Gorbachev and asked if the United States does not join with the nuclear test ban before 6 August, which is the day when your unilateral moratorium ends, would you please consider prolonging it. And there is talk about, you know, well, keep prolonging it because after all, America will ultimately some day join in this because, after all, time will show, and so on and so forth. I have the view that part of this so-called diverse opinion upstairs might quite be— might be quite insidious in, you know, kind of playing on the Soviets for them to prolong, prolong, and prolong and prolong the test ban while the United States just keeps on progressing in whatever areas it wants to progress. Do you feel worried about that?

Bogdanov: I do feel worried about that, because, you know, Vladimir, within one year they have tested already 15, 15 nuclear devices. All of them are new, not only new but improvement of the existing nuclear charges but also many of them are new. Fifteen. From our side, none. So I feel a little bit worried about that and I agree with you, you know, sometimes it comes to my mind that it might be that people trying to convince us that we should not resume our testing, that we should stick to that policy, they just do not figure out with whom we have to deal at the other end, with what kind of people, you know. They will be very happy that we don't do that, you know. Just they will [continue] increasing, increasing, increasing their capabilities, you know, enhancing their nuclear might, you know, and we will be sitting idle.

You know, that worries me, and I'm sure that not only me, it might worry you, might worry Serge and the other Soviet citizens too. So, your question is very, very important, a very substantial one.

Posner: Well, time is running out on us, and I'd like to finish or wind up with what we started out from, and that is if we're agreed that democracy means majority rule basically, it means reflecting the desires of the majority rule basically, it means reflecting the desires of the majority in the decisions that are taken by the people elected to office by that majority. Would you not say that on this issue that we are looking at, of disarmament, of testing, the Soviet government unequivocally reflects the desires of the absolute majority of the Soviet people, whereas judging from the polls that we get from the United States today, the Reagan administration is reflecting a minority opinion. Would you agree with that?

Bogdanov, Plekhanov (simultaneously):   Yes.

Plekhanov: I think that's an accurate description, and one would like to see a little more democracy in the United States for the sake of the whole humanity.

Posner: Well, on that note and . . . it's not really a pessimistic note, because I think we all share the view that ultimately the desire of the majority will triumph, we end this edition of "Top Priority." We welcome your suggestions and your views, please write us, and we'll be back a week from today at the same time.

APPENDIX · D

Internal Army Propaganda

During the early years of the Soviet state, the ideological guidance of army and navy personnel was in the hands of political commissars attached to units on all levels. Today, this task lies with the Soviet Army and Navy Main Political Directorate. The Soviet army newspaper Krasnaya Zvezda *(Red Star) carried a report on June 27, 1986, that noted the role of the armed forces' Propaganda and Agitation Section in "political education work." Reporting on a high-level conference, the paper entitled its coverage, "At the Soviet Army and Navy Main Political Directorate: Ensuring Highly Efficient Ideological Work."*

The army newspaper referred to "substantial shortcomings in this activity" and said that "not enough effort is being made to gear ideological education work to strengthening military discipline and carrying out tasks connected with troops' combat readiness and combat training." Reflecting overall concern about ideological waywardness among Soviet youths, the account stressed that "special attention must be paid to young troops." The text of the report follows.

A conference of ideological personnel of branches of the Armed Forces and categories of troops has been held at the Soviet Army and Navy Main Political Directorate to discuss the question of progress in the study and implementation of 27th CPSU Congress decisions. Its participants listened to reports by Colonel N. Yermolayev, chief of the Propaganda and Agitation Section and deputy chief of the Central Group of Forces Political Directorate, and Major General V. Khrobostov, chief of the Propaganda and Agitation Section and deputy chief of the Soviet Army and Navy Main

Political Directorate. The conference was addressed by Colonel General D. Volkogonov, deputy chief of the Soviet Army and Navy Main Political Directorate.

It was noted at the conference that considerable work has been done to familiarize all categories of personnel, workers and employees, and members of servicemen's families with the documents of the 27th CPSU Congress. The activity of political directorates, commanders, political bodies, and party and Komsomol organizations in the study, propaganda, and fulfillment of congress decisions is planned on a long-term basis. The forces have been supplied with recommendations and methodological aids and materials to assist political officers and the party and Komsomol *aktiv*. Study of the congress documents has been organized in the political training and party education system. Political bodies have conducted a number of instructional and methodological classes with the party and ideological *aktiv*. This has had a positive effect in terms of intensifying political education work. It is noticeable that it is moving more and more into the actual subunit. Leading political command personnel are becoming more actively involved in political education work.

At the same time, there are substantial shortcomings in this activity. The main forms of political training are still overly didactic. The standard of ideological, theoretical, and methodological training of some members of the ideological *aktiv,* especially political training group leaders, is manifestly inadequate. Not enough effort is being made to gear ideological education work to strengthening military discipline and carrying out tasks connected with troops' combat readiness and combat training.

The main reason for this situation is the defective style of activity of a number of political bodies in directing political education work and organizing it in units and subunits. There is still considerable dedication to the bureaucratic, formal approach. Not all ideological formations and members of the ideological *aktiv* are properly involved in explaining and propagandizing the congress materials. Insufficient use is being made of the mass media and the potential of cultural enlightenment establishments and the military press to this end. The discrepancy between words and actions, between propaganda of the 27th CPSU Congress decisions and the thorough mastery and practical implementation of its guidelines by all categories of personnel has not been completely overcome.

In light of the CPSU Central Committee June (1986) Plenum guidelines and in view of the first lessons of the implementation of the 27th party congress decisions, the attention of the conference participants, ideological personnel, and the ideological *aktiv* of the Army and Navy was drawn to the fact that study and implementation of the congress decisions are a task of long-term, strategic significance which must be tackled more persistently, systematically, and efficiently. It is necessary to organize in-depth study of the congress materials, ensure the firm mastery of its ideas and guidelines by all categories of personnel, and make them a guide to action for all servicemen, workers, and employees.

In this connection it is important not to yield to the illusion of quantity in mass measures. Efforts should be directed toward the specific individual soldier, toward improving his political competence, ideological tempering, and social and service activity. Special attention must be paid to young troops. The main emphasis must be placed on improving the organization and the ideological and theoretical standard of all forms of political training and on intensifying individual educational work. Wider use must be made of active methods of conducting classes: seminars, discussions, talks and so forth.

Political bodies and party organizations are recommended to fundamentally improve the ideological, theoretical, and methodological training of people in charge of the main forms of political training and the entire ideological aktiv. Special attention should be paid to the *aktiv* membership at grassroots level, who should be given better guidance in the main ideas and provisions elaborated by the 27th party congress and CPSU Central Committee June Plenum. All ideological efforts must be focused on resolving the chief questions of the forces' life—raising the level of combat readiness and strengthening military discipline. It is important always to remember that the main criterion today is what has been done to fulfill the congress decisions since the congress, in the spirit of its guidelines and demands.

BIBLIOGRAPHY

Throughout this book, wherever appropriate, quotations have been directly attributed to sources; in most cases, it mattered not only what was said but by whom, when, and where. The listing below should serve to supplement the sources cited in the text. Given the extensive literature relevant to the topic of Soviet propaganda, only a selection can be provided here.

The reader who wishes to engage in further study will find certain bodies of work of particular significance. Among authors who deserve special attention, Bertram D. Wolfe and Sidney Hook, history makers in their own right, stand out in breadth and style. Students might further note, especially, the works of Frederick C. Barghoorn, James H. Billington, William L. O'Neil, Donald R. Shanor, Nina Tumarkin, and James L. Tyson; these are of contemporary as well as historical significance.

Periodicals cited in the text should also be included in any reading or study program.

Abshire, David M. *International Broadcasting*. Beverly Hills, Calif.: Sage Publications, 1976.

Alliluyeva, Svetlana. *Only One Year*. New York: Harper, 1969.

Anisimov, Oleg. *The Ultimate Weapon*. Chicago: Regnery, 1953.

Bailey, George. *Armageddon in Prime Time*. New York: Avon, 1985.

Barghoorn, Frederick C. *Soviet Foreign Propaganda*. Princeton, N.J.: Princeton University Press, 1964.

————. *The Soviet Image of the United States: A Study in Distortion*. New York: Harcourt, Brace, 1950.

Barrett, William. *The Truants*. New York: Anchor Press, 1982.

Barron, John. *KGB: The Secret Work of Secret Agents*. New York: Readers Digest Press, 1974.

Bauer, Raymond Augustine. *The New Man in Soviet Psychology*. Cambridge, Mass.: Harvard University Press, 1952.

Billington, James H. *The Icon and the Axe*. New York: Knopf, 1966.

Binyon, Michael. *Life in Russia*. London: Hamish Hamilton, 1983.

Board for International Broadcasting. *Annual Report, 1985*. Operations of Radio Free Europe/Radio Liberty, October 1, 1983, through September 30, 1984. Washington, D.C., 1985.

Bonosky, Philip. *Are Our Moscow Reporters Giving Us the Facts about the USSR?* Moscow: Progress Publishers, 1981.

Bookbinder, Alan, Olivia Lichtenstein, and Richard Denton. *Comrades: Portraits of Soviet Life*. New York: New American Library, 1986.

Borkenau, Franz. *World Communism*. New York: W.W. Norton, 1939.

Brown, Anthony C., and Charles B. MacDonald. *On a Field of Red*. New York: Putnam, 1981.

Butson, Thomas G. *Gorbachev: A Biography*. New York: Stein & Day, 1985.

Buzek, Antony. *How the Communist Press Works*. New York: Praeger, 1964.

Carr, E. H. *Twilight of the Comintern, 1930–1935*. New York: Pantheon, 1982.

Caute, David. *The Fellow-Travellers*. New York: Macmillan, 1973.

Choldin, Marianna Tax. *Censorship in the Slavic World*. New York: New York Public Library, 1984.

Clarkson, Jesse D. *A History of Russia*. New York: Random House, 1961/1969.

Clews, John C. *Communist Propaganda Techniques*. London: Methuen, 1964.

Crankshaw, Edward. *Russia and the Russians*. New York: Viking, 1948.

———. *The Shadow of the Winter Palace*. New York: Viking Press, 1976.

Crossman, R. H., Ed. *The God That Failed*. New York: Harper, 1950.

Dash, Barbara L. *A Defector Reports: The Institute of the USA and Canada*. Washington, D.C.: Delphic Association, 1982.

Deriabin, Peter, and Frank Gibney. *The Secret World*. Garden City, N.Y.: Doubleday, 1959.

Doob, Leonard. *Public Opinion and Propaganda*. Hamden, Conn.: Arden Books, 1966.

Draper, Theodore. *The Roots of American Communism*. New York: Viking Press, 1957.

Dreiser, Theodore. *Dreiser Looks at Russia*. New York: Liveright, 1928.

Dunham, Donald. *Kremlin Target: USA*. New York: Washburn, 1961.

Ebon, Martin. *World Communism Today*. New York: McGraw-Hill, 1948.

Elul, Jacques. *Propaganda: The Formation of Men's Attitudes.* New York: Knopf, 1965.

Evans, F. Bowen. *Worldwide Communist Propaganda Activities.* New York: Macmillan, 1955.

Fast, Howard. *The Naked God.* New York: Praeger, 1958.

Field, Frederick Vanderbilt. *From Right to Left.* Westport, Conn.: Lawrence Hill, 1984.

Finder, Joseph. *Red Carpet: The Connection between the Kremlin and America's Most Powerful Businessmen.* New York: Holt, 1983.

Fischer, Ruth. *Stalin and the German Communists.* Cambridge, Mass.: Harvard University Press, 1948.

Gide, André. *Retouche à mon Retour de l'U.R.S.S.* Paris: Gallimard, 1937.

———. *Retour de l'U.R.S.S.* Paris: Gallimard, 1936.

Gross, Babette. *Willi Münzenberg.* Stuttgart: Deutsche Verlags-Anstalt, 1967.

Hazan, Baruch. *Soviet Impregnational Propaganda.* Ann Arbor, Mich.: Ardis, 1982.

Hersh, Seymour. *The Target Is Destroyed.* New York: Random House, 1986.

Hicks, Granville. *John Reed: The Making of a Revolutionary.* New York: Macmillan, 1936.

Hollander, Paul. *Political Pilgrims.* London: Oxford University Press, 1981.

Hook, Sidney. *Heresy—Yes, Conspiracy—No!* New York: John Day, 1953.

Kaiser, Robert. *Russia.* New York: Atheneum, 1976.

Khrushchev, Nikita. *Khrushchev Remembers.* Strobe Talbott, editor. Boston: Little, Brown, 1974.

Kirkpatrick, Evron M., Ed. *Target: The World; Communist Propaganda Activities in 1955.* New York: Macmillan, 1956.

Klehr, Harvey. *The Heyday of American Communism.* New York: Basic Books, 1984.

Koestler, Arthur. *Darkness at Noon.* New York: Modern Library, 1941.

Kortunov, Vadim V. *The Battle of Ideas.* Moscow: Progress Publishers, 1979.

Kruglak, Theodore E. *The Two Faces of Tass.* Minneapolis: University of Minnesota Press, 1962.

Labin, Suzanne. *The Technique of Soviet Propaganda.* A Study Presented to the Subcommittee to Investigate the Administration of the Internal Security Act and Other Internal Security Laws of the Committee on the Judiciary, U.S. Senate, Eighty-sixth Congress, Second Session. Washington, D.C.: Government Printing Office, 1960.

Lee, Andrea. *Russian Journal.* New York: Random House, 1981.

Leites, Nathan. *A Study of Bolshevism.* Glencoe, Ill.: Free Press, 1953.

Lendvai, Paul. *The Bureaucracy of Truth.* Boulder, Colo.: Westview Press, 1981.

Lindahl, Rutger. *Broadcasting across Borders: A Study on the Role of Propaganda in External Broadcasts*. Gothenburg, Sweden: Liberlaromedel, 1978.

Lottman, Herbert R. *The Left Bank*. Boston: Houghton Mifflin, 1982.

Louis, Victor. *The Coming Decline of the Chinese Empire*. New York: Times Books, 1979.

Lyons, Eugene. *Assignment in Utopia*. New York: Harcourt, 1937.

Macnaghten, Lindley. *Propaganda*. London: Oxford University Press, 1957.

Mayenburg, Ruth von. *Hotel Lux*. Munich: C. Bertelsman Verlag, 1978.

McGregor, James P. *Soviet Cultural and Information Activities, 1982*. Washington, D.C.: U.S. Information Agency, 1983.

Medvedev, Roy A. *Let History Judge*. New York: Knopf, 1971.

Monas, Sidney. *The Third Section: Police and Society in Russia under Nicholas I*. Cambridge, Mass.: Harvard University Press, 1961.

Münzenberg, Willi. *Propaganda als Waffe*. Frankfurt a.M.: März Verlag, 1972.

O'Neil, William L. *A Better World*. New York: Simon & Schuster, 1982.

Pipes, Richard. *Survival Is Not Enough*. New York: Simon & Schuster, 1984.

Pond, Elizabeth. *From the Yaroslavsky Station: Russia Perceived*. New York: Universe Books, 1984.

Possony, Stefan D. *Language as a Communist Weapon*. Presentation to the Committee on Un-American Activities, House of Representatives, Eighty-sixth Congress, First Session, March 2, 1959. Washington, D.C.: Government Printing Office, 1959.

Revel, Jean-Francois. *How Democracies Perish*. New York: Doubleday, 1984.

Le Role de la Désinformation dans le Monde Moderne. Proceedings of Conference, December 5 and 6, 1984. Paris: European Institute for Security, 1984.

Salisbury, Harrison L. *A Journey for Our Time*. New York: Harper & Row, 1983.

———. *Black Night, White Snow: Russia's Revolutions, 1905–1917*. New York: Doubleday, 1978.

Sartre, Jean-Paul. *The Communists and Peace*. New York: Braziller, 1968.

Schwartz, Morton. *Soviet Perceptions of the United States*. Berkeley and Los Angeles: University of California Press, 1978.

Serge, Victor. *Memoirs of a Revolutionary, 1901–41*. London: Oxford University Press, 1963.

Shanor, Donald R. *Behind the Lines*. New York: St. Martin's Press, 1985.

Shipler, David K. *Russia: Broken Idols, Solemn Dreams*. New York: Times Books, 1983.

Shultz, Richard H., and Roy Godson. *Dezinformatsia: Active Measures in Soviet Strategy*. McLean, Va.: Pergamon-Brasseys, 1984.

Signoret, Simone. *La nostalgie n'est plus ce qu'elle était*. Paris: Seuil, 1976.

Smith, Hedrick. *The Russians*. New York: Times Books, 1976.

Strong, Anna Louise. *The Stalin Era*. New York: Mainstream Publ., 1956.

Strong, Tracy B., and Helene Keyssar. *Right in Her Soul: The Life of Anna Louise Strong*. New York: Random House, 1983.

Szamuely, Tibor. *The Russian Tradition*. London: Secker & Warburg, 1974.

Tucker, Robert C. *The Soviet Political Mind*. New York: W. W. Norton, 1971.

Tumarkin, Nina. *Lenin Lives!* Cambridge, Mass.: Harvard University Press, 1983.

Tyson, James L. *Target America: The Influence of Communist Propaganda on U.S. Media*. Chicago: Regnery Gateway, 1981.

Wilson, Edmund. *To the Finland Station*. New York: Farrar Straus, 1940/1972.

Wolfe, Bertram D. *Three Who Made a Revolution*. New York: Stein & Day, 1964/1984.

U.S. Advisory Commission on Public Diplomacy. *1985 Report*. Washington, D.C., 1985.

U.S. Congress. House of Representatives. *Soviet Active Measures*. Hearings before the Permanent Select Committee on Intelligence, House of Representatives, Ninety-seventh Congress, Second Session July 13–14, 1982. Washington, D.C.: Government Printing Office, 1982.

————. *Soviet Covert Action (The Forgery Offensive)*. Ninety-sixth Congress, Second Session, February 6 and 19, 1980. Washington, D.C., 1980.

————. *CIA Report on Soviet Propaganda Operations*. Hearings before the Subcommittee on Oversight of the Permanent Select Committee on Intelligence, Ninety-fifth Congress (excerpt of April 20, 1978, hearing, "The CIA and the Media"). Washington, D.C.: Government Printing Office, 1978.

Index

Gorbachev, Mikhail (*cont.*):
  statement on American imperialism,
    3
  talks with Reagan (*see* Geneva)
  Time and television interviews, 5,
    109, 352
Gorbachova, Raisa, 403–404
Göring, Hermann, 71
Gorki, Maxim, 33, 34–35, 40, 63, 84,
    85, 113, 114
Gorkin, Jess, 244
Goryunov, Dmitri F., 173, 180
Gosbank, 91
Gostelradio (*see* State Committee for
    Television and Radio Broadcast-
    ing)
Gottwald, Kurt, 45
GPU, 72
Grachov, Andrei, 147–148
Graham, Billy, 94–95, 96
Granada Television (British), 18–19
Grassie, John, 263
Great Patriotic War (*see* World War
    II)
Great Soviet Encyclopedia, 19, 38, 43–
    45, 48, 170, 171–172, 207
  Greek edition, 392–393, 394
Grechant, Alexander, 123
Green Party (Germany), 411
Grenada, 276, 296
Grigoryev, Alexei, 190
Grishchenko, Boris, 202
Grivnina, Irina, 224
Gromyko, Andrei A., 219, 220, 221,
    231, 278, 291, 339, 404
Gromyko, Emilia, 339
Groshkov, Nikolai, 257–258
Gross, Babette, 51, 52, 53, 56, 59, 63,
    69, 70, 72, 75, 76
Grossman, Lawrence, 302
GRU, 194, 195, 210, 231
Grunwald, Henry Anatole, 403
Guardian (London), 167, 225, 240,
    255, 348

Gubkin, I. M., 44
Guéhenno, Jean, 115
Gumbel, Bryant, 301–302, 303
Gundav, V., 386
Gwertzman, Bernard, 209

Haig, Alexander M., 199, 324, 325
Hamer, Erna, 162
Hamilton, Iain, 70
Hammett, Dashiell, 122, 123
Harries, Owen, 145
Harriman Institute for Advanced
    Study of the Soviet Union, 109
Harriman, W. Averell, 119
Harrison, Stanley, 396
Hartman, Arthur, 333
Hartman, David, 19
Hays, Arthur Garfield, 71
Helbig, Georg Adolf Wilhelm von, 6–
    7
Hellman, Lillian, 121–125, 127, 353
  Little Foxes, The, 122, 123
  Scoundrel Time, 122, 123–124
  Unfinished Woman, An, 122
Helsinki Accord, 326
Helsinki Final Act, 265
Herald, The (Zimbabwe), 329–330
"Hero Cities," 188–189
Hersh, Seymour, 379
Hesslich, Lutz, 192
Higgins, Marguerite, 166
"High International Mission, A"
    (Zagladin), 410–411
Hillman, Sidney, 57
Hindustan Times, 274
Hingley, Ronald, 6
History of Russia, A (Clarkson), 43
Hitler, Adolf, 11, 44, 51, 58, 67, 68,
    69, 73, 76, 85, 109, 118, 124, 125,
    193, 246
Ho Chi Minh, 104, 164
Hoggart, Richard, 139, 140, 141
Hold the Nation in Your Hand (Anas-
    tasi), 395

About the Author

Following service with the U.S. Office of War Information in World War II, Martin Ebon published the encyclopedic reference work *World Communism Today* (1948). He was subsequently on the staff of the Foreign Policy Association and, during the Korean War, was with the U.S. Information Agency. Ebon has lectured on world affairs, generally, and Communist tactics, in particular, at New York University and at the New School for Social Research. He is the author or editor of more than sixty books, including *Malenkov: Stalin's Successor* (1953), *Svetlana: The Story of Stalin's Daughter* (1967), *Che: The Making of a Legend* (1969), and *Lin Piao* (1970). His two most recent books are *The Andropov File* and *Psychic Warfare: Threat or Illusion?* both published in 1983.

Mr. Ebon's articles and reviews have appeared in a wide variety of newspapers and periodicals, including the *New York Times, Psychology Today,* the *Review of Politics, Problems of Communism,* the *U.S. Naval Institute Proceedings,* and the *Far Eastern Economic Review.*

Mr. Ebon divides his research and writing activities between New York City and Athens, Greece.